Dictionary of
Media and Communication Studies

Dictionary of

Media and Communication Studies

8th edition

James Watson and Anne Hill

BLOOMSBURY ACADEMIC

Eighth edition published in 2012 by:

Bloomsbury Academic

An imprint of Bloomsbury Publishing Plc
50 Bedford Square, London WC1B 3DP, UK
and
175 Fifth Avenue, New York, NY 10010, USA

Copyright © James Watson and Anne Hill 2012

First edition published in Great Britain in 1984
Second edition 1989
Third edition 1993
Fourth edition 1997
Fifth edition 2000
Sixth edition 2003
Seventh edition published by Hodder Education in 2006.

CIP records for this book are available from the British
Library and the Library of Congress.

ISBN 978-1-84966-528-5 (paperback)
ISBN 978-1-84966-562-9 (ebook)

This book is produced using paper that is made from wood grown
in managed, sustainable forests. It is natural, renewable and
recyclable. The logging and manufacturing processes conform to
the environmental regulations of the country of origin.

Printed and bound in Great Britain by the MPG Books Group, Bodmin, Cornwall.

Cover images: Shutterstock

www.bloomsburyacademic.com

Preface to the 8th edition

If there is one word which defines the evolution of media since the 7th edition of this *Dictionary of Media and Communication Studies* in 2006 it is *participation*: the audience is king; and this has largely come about as a result of the opportunities for feedback and interactivity made possible by new and improved technology. Once upon a time there were TV sets. The whole family sat in front of them and the choice was either, or.

Today young people see less of their parents. They retire to their rooms, click a button and a universe of information, entertainment, games opens up to them. They can contact their hundreds if not thousands of 'friends' on Facebook, watch a score of five-minute videos a night on YouTube – and may appear to have less need to interact with real people in the real world.

Ironically, for this same generation many educational experiences will be shared with others, in the traditional manner, in seminars and lectures. True cyberspace will be available on electronic whiteboards, but what happens on a daily basis is little different from the educational experiences of their parents and or indeed their grandparents. We ask, has the bounty of the Internet, the access our SMARTPHONES have made possible, changed culture that much? Are people meeting each other less frequently, reading less, watching conventional TV less; is the newspaper on the verge of extinction?

Also, taking into account the fashionable political mantra, the 'big society', in which we all rise up and take command of the heights of decision-making, opening our own schools, choosing where we'll have our babies or our heart surgery, are we experiencing the beginning of a world turned upside down, of power rising from the depths to assert itself over former privilege, of the power of SMART MOBS?

Whether the answer is a qualified yes or no, what is important is who is asking and attempting to answer the question. For example, has power of a sort shifted to social networks (see NETWORKING: SOCIAL NETWORKING), where petitions and protests can be organized swiftly and on a large scale? Faced with public opinion expressed online, do the power elites (see ELITE) adjust their position, promise more public consultation in future, reverse their decisions – or do they wait till online interactivity returns to the more normal, 'I hate Monday mornings'/ 'So do I' discourse?

Interactive culture

Technological innovation is not the only source of change confronting the twenty-first-century citizen. To use Eric M. Eisenberg's phrase, the sociocultural 'surround' in which much everyday social interaction takes place has also changed for many of us. Most Western societies have seen a growth in cultural diversity. The challenges this presents for successful interaction has been the focus of much contemporary research within the field of INTERPERSONAL COMMUNICATION and the entries for this field of study have been revised to reflect such developments.

Arguably the forces of GLOBALIZATION usher-in social fragmentation and uncertainties – not least uncertainties about self-identity. So, research focused on the contemporary odyssey of the search for SELF-IDENTITY, which Anthony Giddens terms the PROJECT OF SELF, is considered. The potential of everyday communication to contribute to the forging of a sense of self-identity informs numerous entries, such as those for DRESS, GENDER, the JOHARI WINDOW, PERFORMATIVITY, ROLE MODEL and SELF-DISCLOSURE.

Much of modern life is mediated and thus the interplay between interpersonal and mass communication also needs to be considered. ADVERTISING and other aspects of media culture contain many messages that may impact on the development of a sense of identity; the entry on self-identity thus embraces discussion of second-life identities. The arrival of FACEBOOK and other social networking sites also opens up the debate about what it is to have a 'sense of self'.

The Internet has not so much taken over and transformed traditional media as appropriated the way we think about the broad spectrum of communication. Change has been in the air, but how fundamentally has hegemony been shaken, how seriously has it been stirred?

A key issue concerning claims to 'democratization' and popular involvement in the exercise of power is whether the 'usual suspects' – the corporations, the financial organisations, the mass media – have at any time of late lost or surrendered their powers. It could be that we are so busy talking among ourselves, networking, vanishing into the magic whirlpools of our iPods, iPlayers and iPads that we fail to notice something: the power elites have not gone away; nor have they undergone any Pauline conversion except to embrace the opportunities, for commerce and control, that the Network Society offers the alert entrepreneur.

Paging Mr Murdoch

This is not to say that predictability rules. Until the summer of 2011 the global media empire ruled by Rupert Murdoch was widely seen as an unstoppable force, a threat to the plurality of media and a malign influence on governments, obtaining from them concessions in return for a generally supportive press: 'Touch Your Forelocks to Mr Murdoch' was embossed on the dance-card of every politician ambitious to achieve power or hold on to it (see BRITISH SKY BROADCASTING, BSkyB).

The phone-hacking scandal (see JOURNALISM: PHONE-HACKING) involving News International's *News of the World*, and the dramatic closure of the 168-year-old paper in July 2011, may well have brought about a sea-change, not only for the MURDOCH EFFECT specifically but for the media generally in its relation to politics and policing.

Some would say it is 'not before time' that politicians and public in the UK paid attention to the systemic practice of prying electronically (and illegally) into the lives of citizens high and low. Public outrage and a united parliament forced Murdoch to retreat, at least temporarily, from his ambition to own the whole of BSkyB; something Culture Secretary Jeremy Hunt had, until revelations turned from a trickle to a tsunami, been 'mindful' of accepting.

It is fitting to celebrate the true purpose of journalism in action, holding power – that of government, corporations, institutions, the police and the media themselves – to account. Varyingly called 'the best political thriller of our times' and likened to the 'crumbling of the Berlin Wall', the hacking scandal – fearlessly revealed by the *Guardian*, initially alone in the UK and battling against denial and indifference – raised wider issues concerning media ownership and its connection with politicans and police.

Not least among public concerns was the way the Murdoch empire did everything in its power to hush up the scandal. The *Daily Mirror* editorial of 15 July declared that 'News International has mishandled the crisis engulfing it with the finesse of an elephant trying to tap-dance on an oil-smeared floor'. History was truly made when Rupert Murdoch, his son James, Chairman of News International, and (just resigned) Chief Executive Rebekah Brooks were summoned to appear before House of Commons special committees for questioning; this in the same week as the Commissioner of the London Metropolitan police, Sir Paul Stephenson, and his Assistant Commissioner, John Yates, resigned following evidence of their connections with the under-scrutiny organization.

For the present, we leave it to media watchers to monitor the after-shock of such seismic events; to track how far remonstration, indignant headlines, mass petitions, committees of inquiry actually impact, in the long run, on the status quo; and whether a new dawn will produce a less exploitative, more balanced media more answerable to public interest, to the law and to media ethics.

Meanwhile, back on the ground

Less sensational than the hacking saga, but of equal interest and sometimes of concern in the study of media trends, is what Graeme Turner calls 'the demotic turn'. In *Ordinary People and the Media: The Demotic Turn* (Sage, 2010) Turner writes: 'For a start we can say that the institutional model of the media has given way to a more thoroughly commercial and industrial model; that, in many instances, the idea of a national media is giving way to a more conjectural blend of national, transnational and sometimes even local formations; and that the media audience is mutating from a model of receptiveness we might identify with broadcasting, towards a range of more active and more demotic modes of participation that vary from the personalized menu model of the YouTube user to the content creation activities of the citizen journalist or the blogger.'

As for whether increased public (demotic) participation is, as some commentators believe, also empowering (see DIGITAL OPTIMISM), whether the new media are a force for democratization, Turner remains sceptical, believing that outcomes 'are still more likely to be those which support the commercial survival of the major media corporations rather than those which support the individual or the community interests of the ordinary citizen'.

The demotic turn is a shift 'towards entertainment' and this 'may prove to have constituted an impoverishment of the social, political and cultural function of the media; the replacement of something that was primarily information – as in, say, current affairs radio – with something that is primarily entertainment – as in, say, talk radio – is more realistically seen as generating a democratic deficit than a democratic benefit'.

This edition of the *Dictionary* recognizes the options and the possibilities with regard to technology and cultural change, but also acknowledges that the pace of change of one is more rapid than the other. It is undoubtedly true that the Internet has opened portals to individual and group participation and interactivity that permit a diversity of viewpoint and expression rarely, if ever, experienced in the past.

Cyberspace is a constellation of bloggers, a territory of streams emerging from and flowing into and across contemporary life, and on a global scale. Salem 9, blogging from Iraq, fed an information-hungry Western society glimpses of life in an invaded and occupied country that traditional news reporting could not match. During the so-termed African Spring of 2010–11, blogger Slim Amamou's invitation to join the interim government of Tunisia was described by Jo Glanville in her *Index on Censorship* (No. 1, 2011) editorial, 'Playing the long game', as 'one of the most remarkable acknowledgments of the role of digital activists in civil society, not to mention the symbolism of his appointment in a country that has stifled free speech for decades'.

Yet for every optimist such as Glanville there is a pessimist such as Evgeny Morozov, whose *The Net Delusion: How Not to Liberate the World* (Allan Lane, 2011) puts the case that the 'twitter revolution' might do more harm than good to the cause of democratization.

The jury is out, as it is on the efficacy of what has come to be termed *citizen journalism* (see JOURNALISM: CITIZEN JOURNALISM). This raises lively issues concerning the relationship between amateurs and professionals, particularly in the light of the cost-cutting in news services by traditional media organizations intent on putting profit before public service; the result, Graeme Turner's 'impoverishment of the social, political and cultural function of the media'.

Equally we note the concerns of Tim Wu, inventor of the term NET NEUTRALITY (and author of *The Master Switch: The Rise and Fall of Information Empires*, Knopf/Atlantic Books, 2011), when he posits the theory that traditional media moved from the freedoms of the open prairie to corporate enclosure and that this process may be being repeated in the Network Society. Already, he writes in his introduction, 'there are signs that the good old days of a completely open network are ending'. Acquisition, alliances, expansion, synergies are pursued with missionary zeal by the new leviathans. Industries become empires. Jostling for attention becomes jostling for control, not unlike that exercised by governments rarely hesitant about legislating against freedom of expression.

Looking on the bright side, it could be said that the difference is that new technology has greatly loosened up patterns of hierarchy and may even have made inroads on hegemony. Students of communication would do well to carefully scrutinize competing visions of the future of the 'networking society', in particular the role of information and knowledge in a context driven by economics and 'must have it now' public attitudes.

Above all, the case must be made and remade that in the information age the communications industry is, in Tim Wu's words, 'fundamental to democracy', needing to be resistant to wholesale appropriation and to the controlling ambitions of governments.

———————

The 8th edition of the *Dictionary of Media and Communication Studies* has over 100 new entries. The main labour has been the revision and updating of existing entries, a task that affirms just how much has changed on the media and communication scene since 2006. For example, in the light of the growth of the Internet, entries such as AGENDA-SETTING, GATEKEEPING, EFFECTS OF THE MASS MEDIA and NEWS VALUES have not only had to be updated but also reinterpreted; and it has been worth asking whether they might have undergone such shifts in practice that they need to be placed within inverted commas or deemed anachronisms.

The *Dictionary* opens its columns to new kids on the block – assertive, expansionary; Davids intent on becoming Goliaths (if they are not these already), risk-taking and fleet of foot. In come entries on FACEBOOK, GOOGLE, MySPACE, TWITTER, YAHOO! and YOUTUBE (and belatedly APPLE MACINTOSH, AMAZON and MICROSOFT WINDOWS). Social networking commands its own substantial entry and its impact permeates many other new and revised entries.

What has not changed in this edition is the alphabetic format, a detailed Topic Guide (useful for linking subject-related topics; handy for essay-writing, we feel), ample cross-referencing and plenty of end-of-entry suggestions for further reading. In book references, partly to make space, we have dropped the inclusion of country of origin.

A note on the terms *text*, *texts* and *texting*. Except when referring to texting specifically, we write of text and texts in the broadest sense, using the terms to describe all forms of communicative content from a poem to a newspaper report, painting, poster or film (see TEXT). Equally, every message we text on our mobiles is a text, even if it is reduced to a smiley (no entry).

As writers committed to the principle of open source, we express a *soupçon* of disappointment at the charges publishers make for models/diagrams which have been as familiar as road signs to students of communication, sometimes for generations. Where an actual model does not appear with its analysis, the reason is either that we consider an accompanying diagram not strictly necessary, or that we baulk at the publisher's fee. Authors who feel as we do about open source and who wish their work to be given the public attention it deserves should contact their editors.

Our Appendix: Chronology of Media Events aims to provide readers with a time-line of discoveries, inventions and developments from 105 AD when paper from pulp was introduced to the world in China. A quiz of media history we once gave to new undergraduates during Freshers' week had a rather depressing number of them opting for the eighteenth century as being the period when moveable type was introduced in Europe.

Old John of Gutenberg (1450) can, at least for readers of this book, cease to turn in his grave, though whether he would have been among the first to mail a birthday card to Rupert Murdoch (80 in March 2011) or a note of commiseration to the *News of the World* (deceased 12 July 2011) is anybody's guess.

James Watson and Anne Hill

A checklist for use

Words in SMALL CAPITALS mean that there is a separate entry.

Use is made of an arrow (▸) at the end of some entries: here books of special interest or value for further reading on the topic are recommended.

Source references are included in the text of the relevant entry rather than presented in an end-of-dictionary bibliography.

to, including resistance to, social subordination. See CULTURE; HIGHBROW; TASTE CULTURES; YOUTH CULTURE.
▸ Pierre Bourdieu, *Distinction* (Routledge, 1984) and *The Field of Cultural Production* (Polity Press, 1993).
Cultural Indicators research project See MAINSTREAMING.
Cultural industry See FRANKFURT SCHOOL OF THEORISTS.
Cultural memory That which the community recalls, re-encodes in a process of making sense of the present. Cultural memory contrasts with what has been termed *instrumental* or *electronic* memory – that which can be numerically encoded and recorded, as on a computer. In *Communication, Culture and Hegemony: From the Media to Mediation* (Sage, 1993), Jesus Martin-Barbero writes, 'In contrast to instrumental memory "cultural memory" does not work with pure information or as a process of linear accumulation'; rather, it is 'articulated

Communication models are for the most part listed using the name of the person(s) who conceived them (e.g. SHANNON AND WEAVER'S MODEL OF COMMUNICATION, 1949), and commissions/committees on the media are referred to by the name of the chairperson(s) (e.g. PILKINGTON COMMISSION REPORT ON BROADCASTING (UK), 1962).

A star symbol (★) is used to denote that an illustration of that communication model is included.

Acknowledgments

The authors and publishers are grateful to the following for permission to reproduce copyright material:

AEJMC for 'White's gatekeeper model, 1950', from *Journalism Quarterly* 27 (1950); 'Wesley and MacLean's model of communication, 1957', from *Journalism Quarterly* 34 (1957); 'McNelly's model of intermediary communicators in news flow, 1959', from *Journalism Quarterly* 36 (1959); and 'Bass's "double action" model of internal news flow, 1969', from *Journalism Quarterly* 46 (1969).

American Psychological Association for 'Newcomb's ABX model of communication, 1953', from 'An approach to the study of communicative acts' in *Psychological Review* 60 (1953).

Cengage Learning for 'Berlo's SMCR model of communication, 1960', from *The Process of Communication: An Introduction to Theory and Practice*, by David K. Berlo, Holt, Rinehart & Winston (1960); and 'Andersch, Staats and Bostrom's model of communication, 1969', from *Communication in Everyday Use* (Holt, Rinehart & Winston, 1969).

Hans-Bredow-Institut for 'Maletzke's model of the mass communication process, 1963', from *The Psychology of Mass Communications*, Verlag Hans-Bredow-Institut (1963).

HarperCollins Publishers for 'Barnlund's transactional models of communication, 1970', from *Foundations of Communication Theory* edited by K.K. Sereno and C.D. Mortensen, Harper and Row (1970).

International Communication Association for 'Eisenberg's model of communication and identity, 2001', from *Building a mystery: toward a new theory of communication and identity* by Eric A. Eisenberg, published in the *Journal of Communication*, September 2001.

Mary Schramm Coberly for 'Schramm's models of communication, 1954' from W. Schramm (ed.) *The Process and Effects of Mass Communication* (University of Illinois Press, 1954).

National Press Books for 'The Johari window', from Joseph Luft and Harrington Ingram Luft's *Of Human Interaction* (National Press Books, 1969).

Palgrave Macmillan Ltd. for 'The news revolution model' from *News Revolution* by Mark D. Alleyne (1997). [Reproduced with permission of Palgrave Macmillan]

Ronald Yaros for 'PICK model 2009' from *Journalism and Citizenship: New Agendas in Communication* (Sage, 2009, ed. Zizi Papacharissi).

SAGE Publications Ltd. for 'Rogers and Dearing's agenda-setting model, 1987', from *Communication Yearbook* 11; 'Westerståhl and Johansson's model of news factors in foreign news, 1994', from *European Journal of Communication*, March 1994; 'McLeod and Chaffee's "kite" model, 1973', from 'Interpersonal approaches to communication research' in *American Behavioural Scientist* 16 (1973); and 'Models of audience fragmentation' from *Audience Analysis* by Denis McQuail, 1997.

Sam Becker for 'Becker's mosaic model of communication, 1968', from the University of Minnesota's Spring Symposium in Speech Communication (1968).

Springer for 'Gerbner's model of communication, 1956', from 'Towards a general model of communication' in *Audio Visual Communication Review* 4.

University of Chicago Press for 'Bales's interaction process analysis' from R.F. Bales's *Interaction Process Analysis: A Method for the Study of Small Groups* (1950).

Every effort has been made to trace all copyright holders, but if any have been inadvertently overlooked, the publishers would be pleased to make the necessary arrangements at the first opportunity.

Abbreviations: a selection

AA	Advertising Association
AAP	Association of American Publishers
ABA	Australian Broadcasting Authority
AFDC	Australian Film Development Corporation
AFP	Agence France-Presse
AI	Amnesty International
AIJ	Association of Investigative Journalists
ALCS	Author's Lending & Copyright Society
AOL	America On Line
AP	Associated Press
AR	Audience Research
ASA	Advertising Standards Authority
BAFTA	British Association of Film & TV Arts
BARB	Broadcasters Audience Research Board
BBC	British Broadcasting Corporation
BFI	British Film Institute
bit	binary digit
BMIG	British Media Industry Group
BSkyB	British Sky Broadcasting
BT	British Telecom
CCTV	Closed-circuit Television
CD	Compact Disc
CDN	Content Delivery Network
CIR	Copyright Infringement Report
CMC	Computer Mediated Communication
CMCS	Computer Mediated Communication Systems
CPBF	Campaign for Press & Broadcasting Freedom
CPJ	Campaign to Protect Journalists
CPSR	Computer Professionals for Social Responsibility
CPU	Central Processing Unit
CSCW	Computer-supported Cooperative Work
CSS	Content Scrambling System
CTR	Click Through Rate
DAB	Digital Audio Broadcasting
DBS	Direct Broadcasting Satellite
DIT	Digital Imaging Technology
DMB	Digital Multimedia Broadcasting
DoS	Denial of Service
DP	Data Processing
DVB-S	Digital Video Broadcasting-Satellite
DVB-T	Digital Video Broadcasting-Terrestrial
DVD	Digital Video Disc
EBU	European Broadcasting Union

ECHR	European Convention on Human Rights
EDP	Electronic Data Processing
EFF	Electronic Frontier Foundation
ENG	Electronic News Gathering
FAIR	Fairness & Accuracy in Reporting (US)
fax	facsimile
FCC	Federal Communications Commission (US)
FM	Frequency Modulation
FOIA	Freedom of Information Act
GCHQ	Government Communications Headquarters
GFA	Global Framework Agreement
GPS	Global Positioning System
GUI	Graphical User Interface
HBO	Home Box Office (US)
HDTV	High-Definition Television
HDVS	High-Definition Video System
HF	High Frequency
HTML	Hypertext Markup Language
HTTPS	Hypertext Transfer Protocol Secure
IAD	Internet Addiction Disorder
IAMCR	International Association for Media & Communication Research
IC	Integrated Circuit
ICA	International Communication Association
IFJ	International Federation of Journalists
IMC	Independent Media Centre
Intelsat	International Telecommunications Satellite (Consortium)
IPA	Institute of Practitioners in Advertising
IPC	Interpersonal Communication
IPR	Intellectual Property Right
ISBN	International Standard Book Number
ISA	Ideological State Apparatus
ISP	Internet Service Provider
IT	Information Technology
ITU	International Telecommunications Union
ITV	Independent Television
IWMF	International Women's Media Foundation
JICNAR	Joint Industrial Council for Newspaper Audience Research
JICTAR	Joint Independent Committee for TV Advertising Research
LAN	Local Area Network
laser	light amplification by stimulating emission radiation
LED	Light Emitting Diode
LSI	Large-scale Integration
MEF	Media Education Foundation
MO	Mass Observation
modem	modulator-demodulator
MPAA	Motion Picture Association of America
MR	Motivation Research
NBC	National Broadcasting Company (US)
NFT	National Film Theatre
NGO	Non-Governmental Agency
NN	Net Neutrality
NPA	Newspaper Publishers Association (UK)
NSM	New Social Movement

NT	National Theatre
NUJ	National Union of Journalists (UK)
NWIO	New World Information Order
OB	Outside Broadcast
OCR	Optical Character Recognition
Ofcom	Office of Communications (UK)
OVP	Online Video Platform
PA	Press Association (UK)
PC	Politically Correct; Personal Computer
PCC	Press Complaints Commission (UK)
PDF	Portable Document Format
PEN	Poets/Playwrights/Editors/Essayists/Novelists: Pen International
PII	Public Interest Immunity
PKC	Public Key Cryptography
PLR	Public Lending Rights
PR	Public Relations
PSB	Public Service Broadcasting
PSI	Parasocial Interaction
PSN	Public Switched Network
P2P	Peer-to-Peer
RAJAR	Radio Joint Audience Research (UK)
RI	Reaction Index
RIPA	Regulation of Investigatory Powers Act (UK)
RP	Received Pronunciation
rpm	revolutions per minute
RSA	Repressive State Apparatus
RSF	Reporters Sans Frontières (Reporters Without Borders)
RSI	Repetitive Strain Injury
RSS	Rich Site Summary; Really Simple Syndication
SEO	Search Engine Optimization
SIGINT	Signals Intelligence
SMS	Short Message Service
SXSW	South by South West
SYNCOM	Synchronous Communication Satellite
TAM	Television Audience Measurement
TBDF	Trans-Border Data Flow
TNC	Transnational Corporation
TTL	Through The Lens
UDC	Universal Decimal Classification
UDHR	Universal Declaration of Human Rights
UHR	Ultra High Frequency
UNESCO	United Nations Educational Cultural & Scientific Organization
UNI	Union Network International
URL	Uniform Resource Locator
VDU	Visual Display Unit
VHF	Very High Frequency
VHS	Video Home System
VR	Virtual Reality
WELL	Whole Earth Lectronic Link (US)
WPFC	World Press Freedom Committee
WSET	Writers & Scholars International Trust
www	World Wide Web

Topic guide

Entries are summarized under the following topic headings:

ADVERTISING/MARKETING
AUDIENCES: CONSUMPTION & RECEPTION OF MEDIA
BROADCASTING
COMMISSIONS, COMMITTEES, LEGISLATION
COMMUNICATION MODELS
COMMUNICATION THEORY
GENDER MATTERS
GLOBAL PERSPECTIVES
INTERPERSONAL COMMUNICATION
LANGUAGE/DISCOURSE/NARRATIVE
MEDIA ETHICS
MEDIA: FREEDOM, CENSORSHIP
MEDIA HISTORY
MEDIA INSTITUTIONS
MEDIA ISSUES & DEBATES
MEDIA: OWNERSHIP & CONTROL
MEDIA: POLITICS & ECONOMICS
MEDIA: POWER, EFFECTS, INFLUENCE
MEDIA: PROCESSES & PRODUCTION
MEDIA: TECHNOLOGIES
MEDIA: VALUES & IDEOLOGY
NETWORK SOCIETY
NEWS MEDIA
REPRESENTATION
RESEARCH METHODS
TEXTUAL ANALYSIS

The Topic Guides include basic references rather than attempting to incorporate every relevant entry, though all the models referred to in the *Dictionary* are named under COMMUNICATION MODELS.

ADVERTISING/MARKETING

Advertising; Advertising Standards Authority (ASA); Attention model of mass communication; Audience: active audience; Audience: fragmentation of; Audience differentiation; Audience measurement; Brand; Campaign; Cognitive Consistency theories; Consumerization; Consumer sovereignty; Consumption behaviour; Content analysis; Culture: consumer culture; Custom audience research; Demographic analysis; Effects of the mass media; Epistle; Ethnographic (approach to audience measurement); Focus groups; Gantt chart; Glocalization; Hidden needs; Hot buttons; Identification; Idents; Image; Image: rhetoric of; Infomercials; JICNARS scale; Johnson and Scholes: stakeholder mapping; Marketing; Market research; Maslow's hierarchy of needs; Motivation; Motivation research (MR); News: public relations news (PR); Niche audience; Nielsen ratings; Opinion leader; PIE chart; Psychological Reactance theory; Product placement; Public Affairs; Public Relations (PR); Reception studies; Sampling; Sponsorship; Sponsorship of broadcast programmes (UK); Stakeholders; Subliminal; Role model; Tactics and strategies; Ten commandments for media consumers; Uses and Gratifications theory; VALS typology.

AUDIENCES: CONSUMPTION & RECEPTION OF MEDIA

Accessed voices; Attention model of mass communication; Audience; Audience: active audience; Audience: fragmentation of; Audience differentiation; Audience measurement; Boomerang response; Brand; Button apathy; Catharsis; Cognitive Consistency theories; Commercial laissez-faire model of (media) communication; Compassion fatigue; Complicity of users; Consensus; Consistency; Constituency; Consumerization; Consumer sovereignty; Consumption behaviour; Cultural capital; Culture: consumer culture; Culture: globalization of; Demotic turn; Dependency theory; Disempowerment; Desensitization; Displacement effect; Dissonance; Dominant, subordinate, radical; Effects of the mass media; Emancipatory uses of the media; Empowerment; Epistle; Ethnographic (approach to audience measurement); Expectations, horizons of; Focus groups; Frankfurt school of theorists; Gossip networks; Glocalization; Hegemony; Hot buttons; Hyperdermic needle model of communication; Identification; Information blizzards; Information gaps; Intervening variables (IVs); J-Curve; JICNARS scale; Kuuki; Latitudes of acceptance and rejection; Misinformed society; Mobilization; Motivation research (MR); Networking: social networking; Network neutrality; Niche audience; News: audience evaluation, six dimensions of; Ofcom: Office of Communications (UK); One-step, two-step, multi-step flow model of communication; Open source; Opinion leader; Panopticon gaze; Parasocial interaction; Passivity; Pay wall; Psychological Reactance theory; Public opinion; Publics; Reception studies; Reflexivity; Reinforcement; Resistive reading; Role model; Self-fulfilling prophecy; Self-identity; Semiotic power; Socialization; Surveillance society; Ten commandments for media consumers; Uses and Gratifications theory; VALS typology.

BROADCASTING

Annan Commission Report on Broadcasting (UK), 1977; Balanced programming; BARB; BBC digital; BBC, origins; Beveridge Committee Report on Broadcasting (UK), 1950; British Sky Broadcasting (BSkyB); Broadband; Broadcasting legislation; Cable television; Campaign for Press & Broadcasting Freedom; CCTV: closed-circuit television; Channel Four; 'Clean-up TV' movement; Commercial radio: origins; Commercial radio (UK); Communications Act (UK), 2003; Community radio; Cross-media ownership; Digitization; Duopoly; Hankey Committee Report on Television (UK), 1943; High-definition TV; Hunt Committee Report on Cable Expansion and Broadcasting Policy (UK), 1982; Hutton Report (UK), 2004; Independent Television (UK); Interactive television; Internet: wireless Internet; News Corp; Ofcom: Office of Communications (UK); Pilkington Committee Report on Broadcasting (UK), 1962; Pirate radio; Podcast; Podcasting; Public service broadcasting (PSB); Radio broadcasting; RAJAR; Reality TV; Reithian; Satellite transmission; Scheduling; Selsdon Committee Report on Television (UK), 1935; Sitcom; Soap opera; Soundbite; Sponsorship of broadcast programmes (UK); Teletext; Television: Television broadcasting; Television drama; Television news; Ullswater Committee Report on Broadcasting (UK), 1936; Video; Web or online drama; Web 2.0; Westminster view; YouTube.

COMMISSIONS, COMMITTEES, LEGISLATION

Annan Committee Report on Broadcasting, 1977; Broadcasting Act, 1980; Broadcasting Act, 1990; Broadcasting Act, 1996; Broadcasting legislation; Butler Report (UK), 2004; Commissions/committees on the media; Communications Act (UK), 2003; Cross-media ownership; Communications Decency Act (US); DA (Defence Advisory) Notices; Defamation; Digital Economy Act UK (2010); Fairness Doctrine (USA); Franchises for Independent Television (UK); Franchises from 1993; Freedom of Information Act (UK), 2005; Human Rights Act (UK), 2000; Hunt Committee Report on Cable Expansion and Broadcasting Policy (UK), 1982; Hutton Report (UK), 2004; Libel; Phillis Review of Government Communications (UK), 2004; Prior restraint; Regulation of Investigatory Powers Act (RIPA) UK, 2000; SLAPPS; Sponsorship; Sponsorship of broadcast programmes (UK); Terrorism: Terrorism, Crime and Security Act (UK), 2001; Video Recording Act (UK), 1984; Wireless Telegraphy Act, 1904; World Trade Organization (WTO) Telecommunications Agreement, 1997.

COMMUNICATION MODELS

Alleyne's news revolution model, 1997; Andersch, Staats and Bostrom's model of communication, 1969; Attention model of mass communication; Ball-Rokeach and DeFleur's dependency model of mass communication effects, 1976; Barnlund's transactional models of communication, 1970; Bass's double action model of internal news flow, 1969; Becker's mosaic model of communication, 1968; Bernstein's wheel, 1984; Commercial laissez-faire model of (media) communication; Dance's helical model of communication, 1967; Eisenberg's model of communication and identity, 2001; Galtung and Ruge's model of selective gatekeeping, 1965; Gerbner's model of communication, 1956; Grunig and Hunt: four models of public relations practice, 1984; Herman and Chomsky's propaganda model (see CONSENT, MANUFACTURE OF); Hypodermic needle model of communication; Jakobson's model of communication, 1958; Kepplinger and Habermeier's model of media events, 1995 (see EVENT); Lasswell's model of communication, 1948; Maletzke's model of the mass communication process, 1963; McCombs and Shaw's agenda-setting model of media effects, 1976; McLeod and Chaffey's 'kite' model, 1973; McNelly's model of news flow, 1959; McQuail's accountability of media model, 1997; McQuail's four stages of audience fragmentation (see AUDIENCE: FRAGMENTATION OF); Newcomb's ABX model of communication, 1953; Noelle-Neumann's spiral of silence model of public opinion, 1974; One-step, two-step, multi-step flow models of communication; Riley and Riley's model of mass communication, 1959; Schramm's models of communication, 1954; Rogers and Dearing's agenda-setting model, 1987; Self-to-Self model of interpersonal communication, 2007; Shannon and Weaver's model of communication, 1949; S-IV-R model of communication; Tripolar model of competing agendas (see ROGERS AND DEARING'S AGENDA-SETTING MODEL, 1987); Wesley and MacLean's model of communication, 1957; Westerståhl and Johansson's model of news factors in foreign news, 1994; White's gatekeeper model, 1950; Yaros' 'PICK' model for multimedia news, 2009.

COMMUNICATION THEORY

Attribution theory; Audience; Codes; Codes of narrative; Communication; Communication: intercultural communication; Communication models; Communication, Non-verbal (NVC); Congruence theory; Convergence; Culture; Cybernetics; Decode; Deconstruction; Dependency theory; Discourse; Eisenberg's model of communication and identity, 2001; Encode; Frankfurt school of theorists; Functionalist (mode of media analysis); Hegemony; Identification; Ideology; Interpersonal communication; Johari Window; Linguistics; Marxist (mode of media analysis); Mass communication/mass self-communication; Meaning; Media theory: purpose and uses; Medium; Message; Metamessage; Narrative; Narrative paradigm; Noise; Normative theories of mass media; Panopticon gaze; Paradigm (paradigmatic); Paradigms of media; Play theory of mass communication; Postmodernism; Postulates of communication; Primacy, the law of; Proxemics; Queer theory; Roles; Sapir-Whorf linguistic relativity hypothesis; Scripts; Self-concept; Self-fulfilling prophecy; Self-identity; Semiology/Semiotics; Sign; Social action (mode of media analysis); Supervening social necessity; Symbolic convergence theory; Symbolic interactionalism; Technique: Ellul's theory of technique; Technological determinism; Texts; Transactional analysis; Uses and Gratifications theory.

GENDER MATTERS

Empowerment; Expectations; Feminism; Gender; Gender and media monitoring; Gendered genre; Genderlects; He/man language; Ideology of romance; Intimization; Male-as norm; News:

the 'maleness' of news; Patriarchy; Pleasure: active and reactive; Profane language; Queer theory; Report-talk, rapport-talk; Representation; Semiotic power; Stereotype.

GLOBAL PERSPECTIVES

al-Jazeera; Blogging; Blogosphere; Communication: intercultural communication; Consumerization; Convergence; Core nations, peripheral nations; Culture: globalization of; Cyberspace; Ethnocentrism; Europe: cross-border TV channels; Globalization (and the media); Globalization: three engines of; Global media system: the main players; Glocalization; Hybridization; Internet; Localization and transnational TV; M-time, p-time; MacBride Commission; McDonaldization; McWorld Vs Jihad; Media imperialism; Media Studies: the internationalization of Media Studies; Media moguls: four sources of concern; Mediapolis; Murdoch effect; Network neutrality; News: globalization of; Organization cultures; Post-Colonial Studies; Postmodernism; Press barons; Publics; Transculturation; Yamousoukrou declaration; Workers in Communication and Media; World Trade Organization (WTO) Telecommunications Agreement, 1997.

INTERNET See MEDIA: TECHNOLOGIES; NETWORK SOCIETY.

INTERPERSONAL COMMUNICATION

Accent; Apache silence; Assertiveness training; Attitudes; Attribution theory; Bad language; British Black English; Civil inattention; Closure; Cognitive Consistency theories; Communication; Communication: intercultural communication; Communication, Non-verbal (NVC); Congruence theory; Confirmation/disconfirmation; Conversational styles; Defensive communication; Dress; Eisenberg's model of communication and identity, 2001; Elaborated and restricted codes; Empathy; Eye contact; Facebook; Facework; Facial expression; First impressions; Framing; Ethnophaulisms; Interpersonal; Gender; Gesture; Gossip; Groups; Groupthink; Halo effect; Id, Ego, Super-Ego; Identification; Impression management; Indicators; Influence; Insult signals; Integration; Interpersonal communication; Intervening variables (IVs); Johari Window; Kineme; Kinesics; Latitudes of acceptance and rejection; Leadership; Life positions; Listening; Mother tongue; Metamessage; Metasignals; M-time, p-time; Multicultural London English; Networking: social networking; Newcomb's ABX model of communication, 1953; Non-verbal behaviour: repertoire; Orientation; Other; Overhearing; Perception; Personal idiom; Personal space; Postural echo; Posture; Projection; Proxemics; Pragmatics; Psychological Reactance theory; Roles; Role model; Scripts; Self-concept; Self-disclosure; Self-fulfilling prophecy; Self-identity; Self-monitoring; Self-presentation; Self-to-Self model of interpersonal communication, 2007; Silence; Spatial behaviour; Strategy; Stigma; Territoriality; Tie-signs; Touch; Transactional analysis; Twitter; Values.

LANGUAGE/DISCOURSE/NARRATIVE

Arbitrariness; Bad language; British Black English; Codes; Codes of narrative; Cognitive (and affective); Communication: intercultural; Cultural memory; Cultural modes; Culture; Deep structure; Determiner deletion; Diachronic linguistics; Dialect; Discourse; Disqualifying communication; Dominant discourse; Eisenberg's model of communication and identity, 2001; Elaborated and restricted codes; Emotive language; Ethnophaulisms; Gendered genre; Gossip; Ideational functions of language; Idiolect; Journalese; Kineme; LAD (Language Acquisition Device); Language pollution; *Langue* and *parole*; Lexis; Linguistic determinism; Linguistics; Metaphor; Metonomy; Modality; Morphology; Mother tongue; Multicultural London English; Narrative paradigm; Object language; Onomatopoeia; Open, closed texts; Paradigm; Performatives; Personal idiom; Phatic language; Phoneme; Phonetics; Phonology; Pragmatics; Profane language; Projection; Propp's people; Proxemics; Reading; Realism; Received Pronunciation (RP); Redundancy; Reflexivity; Register; Report-talk, rapport-talk; Rhetoric; Sapir-Whorf linguistic relativity hypothesis; Semantics; Semiology/semiotics; Sentence meaning, utterance meaning; Sign; Slang; Soaps; Style; Traditional transmission; Verbal devices in speech-making.

MEDIA ETHICS

Advertising: pester power; Alter-EU; Butler Report (UK), 2004; Commercial confidentiality; Communications Decency Act (US); Data protection; Democracy and the media; Human Rights Act (UK), 2000; Human Rights Watch; Index; Internet: monitoring of content; Journalism; Journalism: phone-hacking; McQuail's accountability of media model, 1997; Media activism; Mediapolis; Media theory: purpose and uses; Normative theories of mass media; People's Communication Charter; Privacy; Reithian; Supervening social necessity; Taste; Television: Ten commandments for media consumers; Universality.

MEDIA: FREEDOM, CENSORSHIP

'Areopagitica'; Article 19; Butler Report (UK), 2004; Clipper chip; Commercial confidentiality; Communications Decency Act (US); Conspiracy of silence; DA (Defence Advisory) Notices; Data protection; Democracy and the media; Defamation; Digital Economy Act (UK), 2010; Echelon; First Amendment (US, 1791); Freedom of Information Act (UK), 2005; Gagging order; Hays Office; H-certificate; Historical allusion; HUAC: Hutton Report (UK), 2004; House Un-American Activities Committee; Human Rights Act (UK), 2000; Human Rights Watch; Icelandic Modern Media Initiative (IMMI); Internet: monitoring of content; 'Libel tourism'; Journalism: phone-hacking; Lord Chamberlain; Milton's paradox; Network neutrality; News management in times of war; Official Secrets Act (UK); Open source; Oz Trial; Panopticon gaze; Paperwork Reduction Act (US), 1980; Phillis Review of Government Communications (UK), 2004; Prior restraint; Privacy; Psyops; Regulation of Investigatory Powers Act (RIPA) (UK), 2000; Re-regulation; SLAPPS; Spycatcher case; Stamp Duty; Street View (Google Maps); Super-injunction; Supervening social necessity; Surveillance society; Taste; Tactics and strategies; Terrorism: anti-terrorism legislation (UK); USA – Patriot Act, 2001; Video nasties; WikiLeaks; World Press Freedom Committee; World Trade Organization (WTO) Telecommunications Agreement, 1997; Zinoviev letter, 1924; Zircon affair.

MEDIA HISTORY

Agit-prop; Agora; Alexandra Palace; BBC, origins; Beveridge Committee Report on Broadcasting, 1950; British Board of Film Censors; British Film Institute (BFI); Calotype; Camera; Cigarette cards; Cine-clubs; Cinema legislation; Cinematography, origins; Cinéma Vérité; 'Clean up TV' movement; Comics; Commercial radio: origins; Communications Act (UK), 2003; Computer; Cylinder or rotary press; Daguerreotype; Digitization; Fourteen-Day Rule (UK); Fourth estate; Franchises for Independent Television; Franchises for 1993; Gramophone; Hays Office; H-certificate; HUAC: House Un-American Activities Committee; Kinetoscope; Linotype printing; Lithography; Lord Chamberlain; *March of Time*; Mass Observation; McGregor Commission Report on the Press (UK), 1977; Minority Report of Mr Selwyn Lloyd; Miracle of Fleet Street; Monotype printing; Newspapers, origins; Newsreel; Nickelodeon; Northcliffe revolution; Persistence of vision; Photography, origins; Photogravure; Photo-journalism; Picture postcards; Pilkington Committee Report on Broadcasting (UK), 1962; Pirate radio (UK); *Poor Man's Guardian*; Posters; Press barons; Printing; Privacy; Public service broadcasting (PSB); Radio broadcasting; Radio drama; Reithian; Roll film; Satellite transmission; Selsdon Committee Report on Television (UK), 1935; Shawcross Commission Report on the Press (UK), 1962; Sound Broadcasting Act (UK), 1972; Stamp Duty; Stereoscopy; Synchronous sound; Telegraphy; Telephone; Telerecording; Television broadcasting; Thaumatrope; Typewriter; Ullswater Committee Report on Broadcasting (UK), 1936; V-discs; Victim funds; Video; Vitaphone; *War of the Worlds*; Watergate; Wireless telegraphy; Yellow Kid; Zinoviev letter, 1924; Zoopraxography.

MEDIA INSTITUTIONS

Advertising Standards Authority (ASA); BBC, origins; Amazon.com; Apple Macintosh; British Board of Film Censors; British Film Institute (BFI); British Sky Broadcasting (BSkyB); Casualization; Commanders of the Social Order; Commercial radio; Communications Act (UK), 2003;

Conglomerates; Core nations, peripheral nations; Deregulation; Deregulation: five myths of; Diversification; Europe: cross-border TV channels; Facebook; Globalization (and the media); Google; Guard dog metaphor; Independent producers; Independent Television (UK); Institution; Media Imperialism; Microsoft Windows; Network; Network neutrality; News agencies; News Corp; News: globalization of; News management in times of war; Newspapers, origins; Normative theories of mass media; Ofcom: Office of Communications (UK); Organization cultures; Power; Press; Press barons; Press Complaints Commission; Public service broadcasting (PSB); Radio Broadcasting; Regulatory favours; Underground press; World Trade Organization (WTO) Telecommunications Agreement, 1997; Yahoo!.

MEDIA ISSUES & DEBATES

Audience: active audience; Censorship; Churnalism; Consumerization; Core nations, peripheral nations; Culture: globalization of; Data protection; Dependency theory; Deregulation; Deregulation: five myths of; Disempowerment; Effects of the mass media; Empowerment; Ethnocentrism; Feminism; Freedom of Information Act (UK), 2005; Gatekeeping; Globalization (and the media); Hegemony; Hyperreality; Ideological state apparatuses; Ideology; Impartiality; Information gaps; Information surplus; Journalism; Journalism: citizen journalism; Journalism: phone-hacking; 'Libel tourism'; Liberal Press theory; McDonaldization; McQuail's accountability of media model, 1997; McWorld Vs Jihad; Media activism; Mediapolis; Media Studies: the internationalization of Media Studies; Media theory: purpose and uses; Mobilization; Murdoch effect; Network neutrality; News management in times of war; News: the 'maleness' of news; Objectivity; Open source; Other; Polysemy; Pornography; Power; Predatory pricing; Privacy; Privatization; Professionalization (of political communication); Public opinion; Public service broadcasting (PSB); Public sphere; Queer theory; Racism; Right of Reply; Showbusiness, age of; Sponsorship; Surveillance society; Tabloid, tabloidese, tabloidization; Text, integrity of the text; Virtual reality; Wedom, Theydom.

MEDIA: POWER, EFFECTS, INFLUENCE

Accessed voices; Agenda-setting; Attribution theory; Ball-Rokeach and Defleur's dependency model of communication effects, 1976; Bigotry; Catalyst effect; Colonization; Compassion fatigue; Consensus; Consent, manufacture of; Conspiracy theory; Consumerization; Contagion effect; 'Coups and earthquakes' syndrome; Crisis (definition); Cultivation; Demotic turn; Deviance amplification; Digital optimism; Disempowerment; Displacement effect; Effects of the mass media; Frankfurt school of theorists; Hypodermic needle model of communication; Ideological state apparatuses; Ideology; Information blizzards; Inheritance factor; Intervening variables (IVs); Journalism; Kuleshov effect; Kuuki; Labelling process (and the media); Legitimation/delegitimation; Mainstreaming; McCombs and Shaw's agenda-setting model of media effects, 1976; Media imperialism; Media moguls: four sources of concern; Mobilization; Moral panics and the media; Narcotizing dysfunction; Network neutrality; News management in times of war; Noelle-Neumann's spiral of silence model of public opinion, 1974; Pornography; Power; Power law phenomenon; Primacy, law of; Public opinion; Self-fulfilling prophecy; Showbusiness, age of; Significant spiral; Sleeper effect; Slow-drip; Smart mobs; Stigma; Survivors and the media; Twitter; VALS typology; Virtuous circle; Visions of order.

MEDIA: OWNERSHIP & CONTROL

Berlusconi phenomenon; British Sky Broadcasting (BSkyB); Casualization; Churnalism; Citizen Kane of the Global Village; Class; Commercial confidentiality; Communications Act (UK), 2003; Cross-media ownership; Conglomerates; Consumerization; Convergence; Cultural apparatus; Culture: copyrighting of culture; Culture: globalization of; Deregulation; Diversification; Elite; Europe: cross-border TV channels; Frankfurt school of theorists; Functionalist (mode of media analysis); Globalization (and the media); Globalization: the engines of; Hegemony; Ideological state apparatuses; Ideology; Leadership; Marxist (mode of media analysis); Mass communication/

mass self-communication; McGregor Commission Report on the Press (UK), 1977; McLeod and Chaffee's 'kite' model, 1973; Media control; Murdoch effect; Network neutrality; News Corp; News: globalization of; News management in times of war; Northcliffe revolution; Ofcom: Office of Communications (UK); Power elite; Press barons; Privatization; Public service broadcasting (PSB); Publics; Public sphere; Regulatory favours; Social action (mode of media analysis); Sponsorship of broadcast programmes (UK); Synergy; Technology: the consumerization of technology; World Trade Organization (WTO) Telecommunications Agreement, 1997.

MEDIA: POLITICS & ECONOMICS

Accessed voices; Alleyne's news revolution model, 1977; Berlusconi phenomenon; Butler Report (UK), 2004; Consent, manufacture of; Conspiracy of silence; Core nations, peripheral nations; Cultural apparatus; Cultural, or citizen's rights and the media; Culture: globalization of; Democracy and the media; Deregulation, five myths of; Elite; Empowerment; Frankfurt school of theorists; Functionalist (mode of media analysis); Freedom of Information Act (UK), 2005; Gagging order; Guard dog metaphor; Glocalization; Hegemony; Human Rights Act (UK), 2000; Hutton Report (UK), 2004; Ideological state apparatus; Ideology; Intervention; Leaks; Lobby practice; Legitimation/delegitimation; Machinery of representation; Market liberalism; Marxist (mode of media analysis); Media imperialism; Media moguls: four sources of concern; McWorld Vs Jihad; Misinformed society; News Corp; Orientalism; Politics of accommodation; Post-Colonial Studies, Power; Press barons; Privatization; Professionalization (of political communication); Public opinion; Public service broadcasting (PSB); Public sphere; Synergy; Technology: the consumerization of technology; USA – Patriot Act, 2001; Zinoviev letter, 1924.

MEDIA: PROCESSES & PRODUCTION

Agenda-setting; Anchorage; Blogging; Churnalism; Computer; Convergence; 'Coups and earthquakes' syndrome; Culture globalization of; Demonization; Diffusion; Digitization; Fly on the wall; Framing: media; Gatekeeping; Hammocking effect; Historical allusion; Immediacy; Impartiality; Intensity; Journalism; Journalism: citizen journalism; Journalism: data journalism; Journalism: investigative journalism; Label libel; Labelling process (and the media); Legitimation/delegitimation; Mainstreaming; Mediation; Mediatization; Mobilization; News; One-step, two-step, multistep models of communication; Open source; Packaging; Personalization; Podcast; Programme flow; Representation; Scheduling; Socialization; Streaming; Tabloid, tabloidese, tabloidization; Three-dimensional (3D); Vox popping.

MEDIA: TECHNOLOGIES

Apple Macintosh; BBC digital; Biometrics; Blogosphere; Bookmark (electronic); Broadband; CCTV: closed-circuit television; Computer; Cyberspace; Cylinder or rotary press; Daguerrotype; Data footprint; Digitization; Digital retouching; Digital video disc (DVD); Downloading; e-book; Fibre-optic technology; Gramophone; Google; High-speed photography; Holography; Internet; Kinetoscope; Kuleshov effect; Linotype printing; Lithography; Microsoft Windows; Mobilization; Omnimax; Open source; Photography, origins; Photomontage; Phototypesetting; Podcasting; Printing; Projection of pictures; Satellite transmission; Speech-recognition technology; Stereoscopy; Streaming; Technique: Ellul's theory of technique; Technological determinism; Technology: the consumerization of technology; Telegraphy; Telematics; Telephone; Telerecording; Television broadcasting; Three-dimensional (3D); Tor; Typewriter; Video; Vitaphone; Web: World Wide Web (www); Web 2.0; Wireless telegraphy; Xerography; Zoetrope; Zoopraxography.

MEDIA: VALUES & IDEOLOGY

Accessed voices; Agenda-setting; Agenda-setting research; Audience; Balanced programming; Bias; Bigotry; Censorship; Chapultepec, Declaration of, 1994; 'Clean up TV' movement; Communications Decency Act (US); Consensus; Consent, manufacture of; Conspiracy of silence; Conspiracy theory;

Cultivation; Cultural apparatus; Culture: copyrighting culture; Culture: globalization of; Culture of deference; Culture: popular culture; Defamation; Democracy and the media; Demonization; Deregulation, five myths of; Deviance; Discourse analysis; Disempowerment; Emancipatory use of the media; Emotive language; Empowerment; Ethnocentrism; Feminism; Fiction values; Freedom of Information Act (UK), 2005; Globalization (and the media); Global scrutiny; Hegemony; Glocalization; HUAC: House Un-American Activities Committee; Human Rights Act (UK), 2000; Ideological presumption; Ideological state apparatuses; Ideology; Impartiality; Information gaps; International Federation of Journalists (IFJ); Issues; Jingoism; Journalism: phone-hacking; Kuuki; Labelling process (and the media); Legitimation/delegitimation; Mainstreaming; McCombs and Shaw's agenda-setting model of media effects, 1976; McQuail's accountability of media model, 1997; Media activism; Media imperialism; Mediapolis; Moral entrepreneurs; Moral panics and the media; News: the 'maleness' of news; News values; New World Information Order; Normative theories of the mass media; Objectivity; Open source; Other; People's Communication Charter; Pornography; Post-Colonial theory; Preferred reading; Prejudice; Privacy; Propaganda; Public Affairs; Public opinion; Public service broadcasting (PSB); Public sphere; Racism; Reithian; Representation; Rogers and Dearing's agenda-setting model, 1987; Sexism; Status quo; Surveillance society; Teledemocracy; Underground press; Values; Violence and the media; Visions of order; Watchdogs; Watergate; Wedom, Theydom; Whistleblowing.

NETWORK SOCIETY

Amazon.com; Apple Macintosh; Blogging; Blogosphere; Computer; Computing: cloud computing; Convergence; Cybernetics; Data footprint; Digital Economy Act (UK), 2010; Digital optimism; Downloading; e-book; Facebook; Digital natives, digital immigrants; Google; Green Dam; Hacker, hacktivist; Hyperreality; Information surplus; Internet; Internet: monitoring of content; Internet: wireless Internet; Journalism: citizen journalism; Mass communication/mass self-communication; Microsoft Windows; Mobilization; MySpace; Networking: social networking; Network neutrality; N-Gen; New media; Online campaigning; Open source; Paywall; Plasticity: neuroplasticity and the Internet; Podcast; Podcasting; Power law phenomenon; Regulation of Investigatory Powers Act (RIPA) (UK), 2000; Signature files; Smart mobs; Streaming; Technology: the consumerization of technology; Teledemocracy; Text: integrity of the text; Television: Catch-up TV; Tor; Transculturation; Twitter; USA – Patriot Act, 2001; Virtual reality; Web or online drama; Web: World Wide Web (www); Web 2.0; Wiki, Wikipedia; WikiLeaks; Yahoo!; Yaros' 'PICK' model for multimedia news, 2009; YouTube.

NEWS MEDIA

Agenda-setting; Agenda-setting research; Alleyne's news revolution model, 1997; al-Jazeera; Anchorage; Bass's 'double action' model of international news flow, 1969; Churnalism; 'Coups and earthquakes' syndrome; Critical news analysis; Embedded reporters; Event; Fiction values; Framing: media; Frequency; Gagging order; Galtung and Ruge's model of selective gatekeeping, 1965; Horse-race story; Immediacy; Impartiality; Indymedia; Intensity; J-curve; Journalism; Journalism: celebrity journalism; Journalism: citizen journalism; Journalism: data journalism; Journalism: investigative journalism; Journalism: phone-hacking; Journalism: 'postmodern journalism'; Knowns, unknowns; Kuuki; McLeod and Chaffee's 'kite' model, 1973; McNelly's model of news flow, 1959; News; News agencies; News: audience evaluation, six dimensions of; News elements: breaking, explanatory, deep background; News Corp; News: globalization of; News management in times of war; News: public relations news (PR); News: the 'maleness' of news; News values; News waves; One-step, two-step, multi-step flow models of communication; Paywall; Personalization; Photojournalism; Pool system; Representation; Rogers and Dearing's agenda-setting model, 1987; Significant spiral; Spot news; Television news: inherent limitations; Visions of order; War: four stages of war reporting; Westerståhl and Johansson's model of news factors in foreign news, 1994; White's gatekeeper model, 1950; WikiLeaks; Yaros' 'PICK' model for multimedia news, 2009; YouTube.

REPRESENTATION

Caricature; Chronology; Colonization; 'Coups and earthquakes' syndrome; Demotic turn; Deviance; Deviance amplification; Dominant, subordinate, radical; Ethnocentrism; Folk devils; Gender; Gender and media monitoring; Hegemony; Invisibility: Label libel; Labelling process (and the media); Machinery of representation; Mediapolis; Narrative; News: the 'maleness' of news; Orientalism; Other; Paraproxemics; Pornography; Primary, secondary definers; Propaganda; Public opinion; Publics; Queer theory; Racism; Realism; Reality TV; Representation; Self-fulfilling prophecy; Self-identity; Sign; Soap operas; Stereotype; Stigma; Style; Visions of order.

RESEARCH METHODS

Agenda-setting research; Analysis: modes of media analysis; Audience measurement; Consumption behaviour; Content analysis; Control group; Critical news analysis; Custom audience research; Demographic analysis; Discourse analysis; Ethnographic (approach to audience measurement); Experimental group; First impressions; Focus groups; Functionalist (mode of media analysis); Glasgow University Media Group; Groups; HICT Project; Interviews; JICNARS scale; Marxist (mode of media analysis); Mass observation; Media theory: purpose and uses; Motivation research (MR); Narrative paradigm; Nielson ratings; One-step, two-step, multi-step flow models of communication; Paradigms of media; Participant observation; People meter; Pleasure: active and reactive; Proxemics; Public opinion; Reception studies; Research centres (into the media); Sampling; Segmentation; Semantic differential; Sleeper effect; Social action (mode of media analysis); Sociometrics (and media analysis); Viewers: light, medium and heavy; Vox popping.

TEXTUAL ANALYSIS

Aberrant decoding; Anchorage; Bad language; Berlo's SMCR model of communication, 1960; Bowdlerize; Bricolage; Codes; Codes of narrative; Connotation; Content analysis; Conventions; Cultural metaphor; Culture: consumer culture; Culture: copyrighting culture; Culture: popular culture; Decode; Deconstruction; Deep structure; Discourse; Discourse analysis; Dominant discourse; Dominant, subordinate, radical; Encode; Encrypt; Establishing shot; Exnomination; Expectation, horizons of; Film noir; Framing: media; Gendered genre; Genre; He/man language; Hybridization; Hypertext; Iconic; Ideology; Interpretant; Intertextuality; Journalese; Kineme; Kinesics; Kuleshov effect; Lexis; Linguistics; Machinery of representation; Male-as-norm; Meaning; Mediation; Medium; Message; Metamessage; Metaphor; Metasignals; Metonymy; Mimetic/semiosic planes; Montage; Morphing; Multi-actuality; Narrative paradigm; Naturalistic illusion (of television); Open, closed texts; Phoneme; Polysemy; Pragmatics; Preferred reading; Propp's people; Reaction shot; Referent; Representation; Resistive reading; Reterritorialization; Rhetoric; Semantic differential; Semantics; Semiology/semiotics; Shot; Sign; Signal; Signification; Signification spiral; Sound-bite; Special effects; Stereotype; Storyboard; Storyness; Symbol; Syntactics; Syntagm; Syntax; Tabloid, tabloidese, tabloidization; Tag questions; Text; Text: integrity of the text.

A

AA-certificate, A-certificate See CERTIFICA-
TION OF FILMS.

Aberrant decoding See DECODE.

Abstraction, ladder of See NARRATIVE: LADDER
OF ABSTRACTION.

ABX model of communication See
NEWCOMB'S ABX MODEL.

Accent The entire pattern of pronunciation typical of a particular region or social group. Accent
is a feature of DIALECT and can be classed as an
aspect of NON-VERBAL COMMUNICATION. The
use of most languages is marked by differing
dialects and their accompanying accents. In
Britain a range of regional accents still survive
and are important signs of regional identity
and affiliation. Simon Elmes commenting on
contemporary uses of accent found in the BBC
Voices survey in his book entitled *Talking for
Britain: A Journey through the Nation's Dialects*
(Penguin Books, 2005) notes that, 'A striking
feature of many of the ... interviews has been
the way in which specific accents and words
are identified as belonging very narrowly to a
particular village or town.'

Regional accents also appear to have the potential to influence social evaluations; evaluations
that can affect perceptions of both the sender
and content of the message. In an article entitled,
'It's not what you say, it's the way that you say it',
in the UK *Independent* (15 October 1997), Emma
Haughton identifies Received Pronunciation
(RP), Refined Scots, Welsh and Irish, Yorkshire
and Estuary English as being favourably received
but Brummie, Belfast, Glaswegian and West
Country accents as being viewed unfavourably.
Judgments will vary, though; an individual with a
Brummie accent may not share the general view.
Peter Trudgill in *Sociolinguistics: An Introduction to Language and Society* (Penguin, 2000)
argues that evaluations of the use of accent and
dialect tend to be social rather than linguistic, for
'there is nothing at all inherent in non-standard
varieties which makes them inferior'. Reactions
to regional accents are also subject to change.

Differences in accents will often reflect differences in the social structure of a society, and in
particular its patterns of social stratification.
Peter Trudgill notes a pattern as regards this
relationship in Britain. Typically those from the
higher social classes are more likely to use standard dialect and an accent close to RP, the prestige accent, whilst those from the lower classes
are more likely to use non-standard dialect and
a localized, regional accent. However, as several
researchers have noted, individuals can and do
adjust their use of accent and dialect to fit in
with the social context.

Trudgill also points out that among certain
groups within society a 'covert prestige' can
be attached to accents generally viewed as not
prestigious, especially when they are part of
'non-standard' speech. Such accents and 'non-
standard' speech may also be used to convey an
image of toughness and masculinity in certain
situations, irrespective of the actual social status
of the speaker.

Accessed voices Within any society, these are
the people who have a ready and privileged
access to the channels of mass communication:
politicians, civil servants, industrialists, experts
of various kinds, pundits, royals and celebrities;
and it is their views and styles that are given
voice in preference to the views of others in
society. Roger Fowler in his *Language of News:
Discourses and Ideology of the Press* (Routledge,
1991) writes of this selectivity, 'The political
effect of this division between the accessed and
unaccessed hardly needs stating: an imbalance
between the representation of the already privileged, on the one hand, and the already unprivi-
leged, on the other, with the views of the official,
the powerful and the rich being constantly
invoked to legitimate the status quo.'

With the advances in communicative exchange
brought about by the INTERNET the public has
more choice in terms of who and what they
access. However, though there is less reliance on
traditional channels of mass communication, the
'usual suspects' as listed by Fowler still dominate
the press and national broadcasting.

Accommodation, politics of See POLITICS OF
ACCOMMODATION (IN THE MEDIA).

Accountability of media See MCQUAIL'S
ACCOUNTABILITY OF MEDIA MODEL, 1997.

Acculturation, deculturation The process by
which a society or an individual adapts to the
need for cultural change. The conditions for
such change occur, for example, when encounters with other cultures continue on a prolonged
basis such as in colonization, emigration and
immigration. In analysing the process by which
individuals adapt to life in a new country, Young
Yun Kim in 'Adapting to a new culture' in Larry
Samovar and Richard Porter, *Intercultural
Communication: a reader* (Wadsworth, 1997)
comments, 'They are challenged to learn at least
some new ways of thinking, feeling, and acting
– an activity commonly called acculturation ...
At the same time, they go through the process
of deculturation ... of unlearning some of their

1

previously acquired cultural habits at least to the extent that new responses are adopted in situations that previously would have evoked old ones.'

Such a process produces stress and anxiety and necessarily affects the communicative performance of those undergoing it. However, communication with those in the new culture is essential to adaptation. Interestingly Kim argues that the mass media can be a useful source of information for those trying to acclimatize to a new culture, as the messages they carry 'explicitly or implicitly convey the world views, myths, beliefs, values, mores and norms of the culture'. See COMMUNICATION: INTERCULTURAL COMMUNICATION.

▶ Young Yun Kim, *Becoming Intercultural: An Integrative Theory of Communication and Cross-cultural Adaptation* (Sage, 2001).

Accusatory studies Jib Fowles in *The Case for Television Violence* (Sage, 1999) uses this term to describe the research studies that have focused on the effects of screen violence. The studies are 'accusatory' in the sense that they purport to prove the connection between screen and real violence, the one likely to instigate the other, or to desensitize audiences in their response to real violence. Such studies, in Fowles's view, 'amplify the derogatory discourse' concerning violence in the cinema and on TV. See VIOLENCE ON TV: THE DEFENCE.

Action code See CODES OF NARRATIVE.

Active-audience thesis See AUDIENCE: ACTIVE AUDIENCE.

Active participation Occurs in situations where media interest in a news story becomes involvement, and the story takes on a media-induced direction. An appetite for stories of scandal and sensation, and the cut-throat competition for circulation, can lead newspapers into playing the role of *agent provocateur*, as handy with the chequebook as the reporter's notebook.

Activism See MEDIA ACTIVISM.

Actuality Material from real life – the presentation in a broadcast programme of real events and people to illustrate some current theme or practice. RADIO, in parallel with film documentary, pioneered actuality in the 1930s. Producers such as Olive Shapley and Harry Harding were early innovators in this field. The radio programme *Time to Spare*, made in 1934, documented unemployment, broadcasting the voices of the unemployed and their families and creating an impact that was both moving and disturbing.

Actualization See MASLOW'S HIERARCHY OF NEEDS.

Adaptors See NON-VERBAL BEHAVIOUR: REPERTOIRE.

Advertising The extent of the *reliance* of all forms of mass media upon advertising can be gauged by glancing at any monthly edition of BRAD, which comprises some 400–500 pages of information on where advertisements can be placed and how much they will cost. Everything is there – the national and local PRESS, TV and RADIO, CINEMA, POSTERS, bus shelters, parking meters, litter bins and transport advertising. Powerfully occupying the driving seat is INTERNET advertising (see ADVERTISING: INTERNET ADVERTISING).

If advertising merely sold products, it would cause less critical concern than it does. But it also sells images, dreams, ideal ways of life, ideal images of self; it sells, then reinforces time and again, values – those of consumerism; and it trades in stereotypes. In *The Shocking History of Advertising* (Penguin, revised edition, 1965), E.S. Turner states that 'advertising is the whip which hustles humanity up the road to the Better Mousetrap'.

For some analysts, advertising is a kind of magic. Raymond Williams in *Problems in Materialism and Culture* (Verso, 1980) argues that it has the ability to 'associate consumption with human desires to which it has no real reference. The magic obscures the real sources of general satisfaction because their discovery would involve radical change in the whole common way of life'. Judith Williamson in *Decoding Advertisements* (Marion Boyars, 1978, 1998) shares a similar concern: 'Advertisements obscure and avoid the real issues of society, those relating to work, to jobs and wages and who works for whom. The basic issues in the present state of society which do concern money and how it is earned, are sublimated into "meanings", "images", "lifestyles", to be bought with products not money.'

Further, the magic of advertising may mean that we believe commodities can convey messages about ourselves; this leads to us being 'alienated from ourselves, since we have allowed objects to "'speak" for us and have become identified with them'. Such alienation may well lead to feelings of fragmentation and discomfort within the self; feelings which could fuel a desire to seek solace in further consumption.

A number of critics point to the danger that advertising messages and the consumption they partly fuel may undermine and distort self-development. Anthony Giddens writes in *Modernity and Self-Identity* (Polity Press, 1991) that 'the consumption of ever-novel goods becomes a substitute for the genuine develop-ment of self: appearance replaces essence'. Self-actualization is 'packaged and distributed according to market criteria. Mediated experi-ence is centrally involved here. The mass media routinely present modes of life to which, it is implied, everyone should aspire'. For Don Slater in *Consumer Culture and Modernity* (Polity Press, 1997), 'Consumer culture "technicizes" the project of self by treating all problems as solvable through various commodities.'

Not all would agree with such criticisms. Those subscribing to the doctrines of nineteenth-century Liberalism, for example, would argue that consumer culture, of which advertising is an integral element, liberates rather than oppresses, in providing the individual with many opportu-nities to rationally pursue his/her self-interest. The range of choices offered by consumer culture and post-traditional society is to be celebrated rather than seen as a cause for concern – to be able to choose being seen as the essence of being human. It should also be borne in mind that the messages of advertising have to compete with a range of other influences on behaviour in their battle for hearts, minds and identities.

Tony Yeshin in *Advertising* (Thomson Learning, 2006) reminds us of the important economic role played by advertising. 'Although it is widely criticised, it can be argued that adver-tising, particularly within a capitalist society, provides the means for encouraging competi-tion. By making information about competing products and services widely available, it ensures that no single product can, ordinarily, dominate a market.' Arguably, advertising has speeded the introduction of useful inventions to a wide as distinct from a select circle of consumers; it has spread markets, reduced the price of goods, accelerated turnover and kept people in employ-ment. It also funds a diverse range of media.

The many modes of advertising may be categorized as follows: (1) *Commercial consumer* advertising, with its target the mass audience and its channel the mass media. Latterly, of course, the Internet has become the new fron-tier for commercial advertising. (2) *Trade and technical* advertising, such as ads in specialist magazines. (3) *Prestige* advertising, particularly that of big business and large institutions, gener-ally selling image and good name rather than specific products (see PR: PUBLIC RELATIONS). (4) *Small ads*, directly informational, which are the bedrock support of local periodicals and the basis of the many giveaway papers which have been published in recent years. (5) *Government*

advertising – health warnings, for example. (6) *Charity* advertising, seeking donations for worthwhile causes at home and abroad. (7) Advertising through *sponsorship*, mainly of sports, leisure and the arts. This indirect form of advertising has been a major development; the risk is that recipients of sponsorship come to rely more and more heavily on commercial support. Sponsors want quick publicity and prestige for their money and their loyalties to recipients are very often short-term.

The effect of advertising upon newspaper and broadcasting editorial and programme content is rarely overt; rather it is a process of media people 'internalizing' advertisers' demands. Ad-related newspaper features have grown enormously in the post-Second World War period, especially in the 'quality press', such as, in the UK, *The Times*, *Guardian*, *Independent* and *Daily Telegraph*, which derive over half their revenue from adver-tising. In press advertising, numbers count for less than the estimated purchasing power of the target readership. This explains why two major UK newspapers with big circulations – the *Daily Herald* (see MIRACLE OF FLEET STREET) and the *News Chronicle* – were closed down in the 1960s. They simply did not appeal to the advertisers.

Advertising has suffused our culture and our language, helping to form a consumer culture (see CULTURE: CONSUMER CULTURE). Its influence has been felt in modern art move-ments such as pop art; its snappy techniques as developed for TV have been widely adopted in the cinema. It has drawn into its service actors, celebrities, artists, photographers, writers, designers and film makers. It is often said that on TV the adverts are better than the programmes; there is a grain of truth here, as there is in the claim that it is because of the adverts, and the goals of those who commission and make them, that the programmes are not better, more original or more challenging. See ADVERTISING STANDARDS AUTHORITY (UK); ADVERTIS-ING: TARGETED ADVERTISING; AIDA MODEL; COMMERCIAL RADIO (UK); BRAND: GRAPHIC REVOLUTION; HARMONIOUS INTERACTION; PRODUCT PLACEMENT; SPONSORSHIP; SPON-SORSHIP OF BROADCAST PROGRAMMES (UK); SUBLIMINAL.

▸ Anne M. Cronin, *Advertising and Consumer Citizenship: Gender, Images and Rights* (Routledge, 2000); John Tullock, *Watching Television Audiences: Cultural Theories and Methods* (Arnold, 2000); Peter N. Stearns, *Consumerism in World History: The Global Transformation of Desire* (Routledge, 2001); Sean Brierley, *The Advertising Handbook*

(Routledge, 2002); John O'Shaughnessy and Nicholas Jackson O'Shaughnessy, *Persuasion in Advertising* (Routledge, 2004); Ken Burtenshaw, Nik Mahon and Caroline Barfoot, *The Fundamentals of Creative Advertising* (AVA Publishing, 2006); David Ogilvy, *Ogilvy on Advertising* (Prion, 2007); Vance Packard, *The Hidden Persuaders* (Ig Publishing, 2007 edn with introduction by Mark Crispin Miller); Mark Tungate, *Adland: a global history of advertising* (Kogan Page, 2007).

Advertising: ambient advertising Advertisements that feature in contexts other than the printed page, on film or in broadcasting, which we encounter in everyday life situations and are designed to surround and confront the prospective customer – in the street, on bus shelters, in underground stations and trains, in airports, public lavatories and latterly in places of education; indeed wherever there is space for the advertiser to press home image and message.

An alternative term is *captive audience* advertising. David Bollier of the Annenburg School of Communications, in an article entitled 'The grotesque, smirking gargoyle: The commercialization of America's consciousness' published on the tom.paine.com website (8 August 2002), writes of advertising 'ambushing people as they use public restrooms, gas pumps, elevators ... By ones and twos, such actions generally are inconsequential. In aggregate, however, the sheer pervasiveness of commercialism in public spaces and contemporary life has the malodorous whiff of a Corporate Big Brother'. Bollier believes that the 'sheer ubiquity of marketing in hundreds of nooks and crannies of daily life has become a defining framework of cultural values'.

Advertising boycotts The reliance of the press and of commercial television upon advertising for revenue indicates the important influence advertisers and their clients can wield over the media. Where a newspaper may be deemed to be publishing material or expressing views which might be detrimental to consumerist interest, companies pull out their expensive advertisement – or threaten to do so, and thus exercise censorship. The financial consequences of such boycotts can be devastating.

Advertising: Internet advertising There is consensus that the INTERNET has had the effect of redrawing the landscape of advertising. Essentially, advertisers know more about us as consumers because, as we use the Net, operate our Internet-accessible mobile phones, we reveal more information about who we are, what our tastes are and how we exchange information about ourselves with others. On FACEBOOK, Bebo and MYSPACE, in TWEETS and in social networking generally (see NETWORKING: SOCIAL NETWORKING) we make ourselves easy targets for advertisers. Our sharing is an advertiser's opportunity, hence the growth of *behavioural targeting*.

Not only do advertisers track our activities, our patterns of behaviour, and then match them with appropriately directed commercials, they encourage us – in the spirit of the Internet – to participate in our own marketization: we purchase a romantic novel online and a galaxy of other romances are presented for our delectation. For ad purposes, we have been typecast; we have become consumer-engaged.

Ads appear on personal and group blogs (see BLOGGING), in many cases allowing bloggers to recoup their costs. Marketers have quickly come to recognize that 'in-your-face' advertising meets resistance online, while a key strategy is to make ads seem more informational, and more personal and more discreet.

Online ad-dramas such as Bebo's *Kate Modern* (2008) have integrated advertising into the narrative, usually with a degree of finesse that avoids detracting from the story. 'Integrations', as the ad business refers to them, are the Net's version of PRODUCT PLACEMENT in films and TV, only with Net ad-drama the viewers themselves can be integrated into the story by, for example, inviting them to be film extras.

Production costs have remained problematic: sponsors want their products integrated, thus the number of sponsors has to be limited to the number of products or services that can be reasonably absorbed in the drama. Bebo pulled out of funding ad-drama in 2009 despite the success, albeit temporary, of a number of online productions such as *Kirill*, *The Gap Year*, *Gotham Girls* and *Zombie Bashers*. See ADVERTISING: TARGETED ADVERTISING; WEB OR ONLINE DRAMA.

Advertising Standards Authority (ASA) Independent body set up by the advertising industry to police rules incorporated in advertising codes. On 1 November 2004 the ASA became the regulatory authority for broadcasting advertising following the COMMUNICATIONS ACT, 2003 and the creation of the Office of Communications (Ofcom). The Authority's mission is to 'apply the advertising codes and uphold standards in all media on behalf of consumers, business and society'. It offers a 'one-stop' approach to customer complaints, a 'single point of reference for consumers, advertisers and broadcasters, while respecting the different obligations inherent in broadcast and non-broadcast media – the one licensed, the other not'.

The Committee of Advertising Practice (CAP) revises and enforces the CAP Code, which is 'primarily concerned with the content of market communications'. The ASA endorses and administers the Code, ensuring that the self-regulatory system works in the public interest. There are codes for non-broadcast media, radio and TV and text services. The Non-Broadcasting Code covers topics such as Decency, Honesty, Truthfulness, Matters of Opinion, Fear and Distress, and Safety.

For example, Section 11, on *Violence and Anti-Social Behaviour*, states that 'marketing communications should contain nothing that condones or is likely to provoke violence or anti-social behaviour', while Section 13, *Protection of Privacy*, urges marketers 'to obtain written permission before referring to or portraying members of the public or their identifiable possessions'; however, 'the use of crowd scenes or general public locations may be acceptable without permission'.

The Broadcasting Committee of Advertising Practice (BCAP) is under contract from Ofcom to supervise advertising on radio and TV. Section 9 of the Radio Code deals with *Good Taste, Decency and Offences to Public Feeling*: 'Each station is expected to ... take into account the sensitivities of all sections of its audience when deciding on the acceptability or scheduling of advertisements.'

Under Section 11, *Children and Younger Listeners*, the code states that 'prices of products advertised to younger listeners must not be minimized by words such as "only" and "just"'; nor should ads 'lead children to believe that unless they have or use the product advertised they will be inferior in some way to other children or liable to be held in contempt or ridicule'. Inviting children to ask Mum to ask Dad to buy an advertised product also breaks the rules. Section 13 of the Radio Code, *Racial Discrimination*, declares that advertising 'must not include any material which might reasonably be construed by ethnic minorities to be hurtful or tasteless'.

The TV Code covers similar ground to the other codes. Section 4, *Political and Controversial Issues*, states that no advertisement '(a) may be inserted by or on behalf of any body whose objects are wholly or mainly of a political nature (b) may be directed towards any political end (c) may have any relation to any industrial dispute (with limited exceptions)'. Section 10 on *Religion, Faith, Systems of Belief* forbids '(a) advertising by or on behalf of, any organization or individual whose objectives are or appear to be wholly or mainly concerned with religion, faith or other philosophies or beliefs (b) any other advertising which appears to have a doctrinal objective (c) advertising for commercial products or services which reflect doctrine'.

While the TV Code seeks to 'prevent causing offence to viewers generally or to particular groups in society (for example by causing significant distress, disgust or insult, by offending against widespread public feeling)', it recognizes legitimate differences of opinion on certain matters: 'The ASA and BCAP will not act ... where advertising is simply criticized for not being in "good taste" unless the material also offends against generally accepted moral, social or cultural standards. Apart from freedom of speech considerations, there are often large and sometimes contradictory differences in views about what constitutes "bad taste" or what should be deplored.'

On matters of redress, the ASA states: 'The vast majority of advertisers, promoters and direct marketers comply [with the codes]. Those that do not may be subject to sanctions. Adverse publicity may result from the rulings published by the ASA weekly on its website. The media, contractors and service providers may withhold their services or deny access to space. Trading privileges (including direct mail discounts) and recognition may be revoked, withdrawn or temporarily withheld. Pre-vetting may be imposed and, in some cases, non-complying parties can be referred to the Office of Fair Trading for action, where appropriate, under the Control of Misleading Advertisements Regulations.'

The ASA publishes regular news and reports on its adjudications of high-profile ad campaigns, and it carries on its website (www.a.s.a.org.uk) instructions on how the public can make complaints, including a complaint form with space for 1,500 words of explanation. See SPONSORSHIP: BROADCAST PROGRAMMES (UK).

Advertising: targeted advertising Each consumer leaves a 'purchasing trail' registered either at the checkout of a shop or store or by ordering goods and services online. This trail constitutes a personal story in which the consumer's tastes and patterns of consumption can be measured. Prior knowledge allows companies to more accurately predict purchasing behaviour. See SURVEILLANCE.

Aesthetic Code See CODES.

Affect displays See NON-VERBAL BEHAVIOUR; REPERTOIRE.

Affective See COGNITIVE (AND AFFECTIVE).

Agenda-setting Term used to describe the way the media set the order of importance of current issues, especially in the reportage of news. Closely linked with the process of GATEKEEPING, agenda-setting defines the context of transmission, establishes the terms of reference and determines the limits of debate. In BROADCASTING the agenda is more assertive than in newspapers where the reader can ignore the order of priorities set by the paper's editorial team and turn straight to the small ads or the sports pages. Broadcasting is linear – one item following after another – and its agenda unavoidable (except by switching off). Interviewers in broadcasting are in control of pre-set agendas. They initiate and formulate the questions to be asked, and have the chairperson's power of excluding areas of discussion. Very rarely does an interviewee break free from this form of control and succeed in widening the context of debate beyond what is 'on the agenda'.

G. Ray Funkhouser and Eugene F. Shaw in an article entitled 'How synthetic experience shapes social reality' in *Journal of Communication*, Spring 1990, subdivide agenda-setting into *micro-agenda-setting* and *macro-agenda-setting*. The first describes the way the mass media are able, through emphasis on content, to influence public perceptions of the relative importance of specific issues. The second they define as follows: 'The potential of electronic media to colour, distort, and perhaps even degrade an entire cultural world view, by presenting images of the world suited to the agenda of the media (in the US case, commercial interests), we might term "macro-agenda-setting"'.

In recent years agenda-setting has been viewed as working from two levels, that of *subject* and that of *attribute*; and the theory is that the media's attention to the attributes of a subject is met with a corresponding image in the mind of the public. Level 1 of agenda-setting concerns the central theme or object of a public issue/ news story; Level 2, the salient characteristics of the theme or object as emphasized by the media.

In an article, 'Agenda-setting in the 1996 Spanish General Election', published in the *Journal of Communication*, Spring 2000, Maxwell McCombs, Esteban Lopez Escobar and Juan Pablo Llamas refer to 'agendas of attributes, those characteristics and traits that fill out the picture of each object'. Some attributes are emphasized, given prominence, others de-emphasized, 'while many are ignored'. McCombs and his colleagues explain: 'Just as objects vary in salience, so do

the attributes of each object. Just as there is an agenda of public issues, political candidates, or some other set of objects, there is also an agenda of attributes for each object. Both the selection by journalists of objects for attention and the selection of attributes for detailing the pictures of these objects are powerful agenda-setting roles.'

The authors point out that 'although object and attribute salience are conceptually distinct, they are integral and simultaneously present aspects of the agenda-setting process'. In their research into public attitudes to candidates at the 1996 election in Spain, the following attributes of the major contenders were measured: the ideology/ issues position of rival candidates, biographical details, perceived qualifications and integrity.

The function of MASS MEDIA as agenda-setters has, to a degree, been diluted by INTERNET rivals, in particular the advent of the BLOGO-SPHERE. Zizi Papacharissi in her chapter, 'The citizen is the message: alternative modes of civic engagement' in the book she edited, *Journalism and Citizenship: New Agendas in Communication* (Routledge, 2009), writes: 'For monitorial citizens, blogs present the space where what is defined as public, can be challenged, and where hierarchies of issues determined by power elites can be revised, and agendas re-aligned ... A post on a blog, a video log in YouTube, even the practice of following a blog represents public expressions of private dissent, albeit mild, with a mainstream media agenda determined by elite power constellations.' See DEMOTIC TURN; FACEBOOK; JOURNALISM: CITIZEN JOURNALISM; McCOMBS AND SHAW'S AGENDA-SETTING MODEL OF MEDIA EFFECTS, 1976; PROTOTYPING CONCEPT; ROGERS AND DEARING'S AGENDA-SETTING MODEL, 1987; TWITTER; YOUTUBE.

Agenda-setting research A key area of research into the relationship between mass communication and audience consumption of media, agenda-setting research generally takes two forms. James W. Dearing and Everett M. Rogers in *Agenda-Setting* (Sage, 1996) explain that research has traditionally taken a *hierarchical* form; this they describe as 'one-point-in-time correlation comparisons of media content with aggregated responses by the public to survey questions about issue salience', that is, their perceived importance. More recently the research approach has been through *longitudinal* studies. Such investigations 'include over-time participant observation in media organizations' as well as the analysis of quantitative variables such as REAL WORLD INDICATORS.

Longitudinal studies can detect trends and directions of influence; tease out whether media coverage prompts public awareness and interest or whether the media perch on the 'bandwagon' of public opinion. The over-time study can identify variants of events and issues and thus, as Dearing and Rogers put it, 'illuminate the nature of media effects with special clarity ...'

A further focus of research into agenda-setting involves what Dearing and Rogers term 'trigger events'. These act as a 'cue-to-action that occurs at a point in time', each trigger event serving 'to crystallize attention and action'. A trigger event essentially 'simplifies the nature of a complex issue into a form that the public can more easily understand'.

Agitprop The Department of Agitation and Propaganda was created in 1920 as part of the Central Committee Secretariat of the Communist Party of the Soviet Union. Its responsibility was to use all available media – especially film – to disseminate information and ideas to the population of the world's first Communist state. The term 'agitprop' has come to be used to describe any unashamedly political propagandizing.

Agora In the city states of ancient Greece the agora was the place of assembly where the free citizens debated matters of public concern; where public *opinion* was formulated and asserted. Public spaces have long been surrendered to enclosure or to shopping malls, but the concept remains; its practice continues at second remove – the media speak for the people, purporting to articulate and defend public interest in their role as WATCHDOGS, guarding the public from the abuses of state. PUBLIC SERVICE BROADCASTING (PSB) is perceived as an extension of the agora; hence the concern often expressed about the privatization of broadcast media, that it is turning the agora into a marketplace of commodities rather than a marketplace of ideas and debate. However, it could be claimed that a modern, and expanding, form of the agora is the INTERNET. See BLOGOSPHERE; INFORMATION COMMONS; MEDIASPHERE; PUBLIC OPINION; SALON DISCOURSE.

AIDA model Guide to the principal stages of advertising a product or service: A – create Awareness; I – create Interest; D – promote Desire; A – stimulate Action or response.

Alexandra Palace Birthplace of television in the United Kingdom. The first TV broadcasting took place from London's 'Ally Pally' on 2 November 1936. Initially the service reached only a few hundred privileged viewers in and around the capital. Some 400 TV sets, each costing around £100 – the price of a small car – were in use. With the coming of the Second World War, TV broadcasts came to an abrupt end on 1 September 1939, by which time there were an estimated 20,000 TV sets in operation. The Alexandra Palace studios opened for business again on 7 June 1946 but had to briefly shut down transmission once more in early 1947 because of the acute fuel crisis. The Alexandra Palace studios remained in service until 1955. See BROADCASTING; TELEVISION.

Alienation As a concept, derives largely from the work of Karl Marx (1818–83), who argued that the organization of industrial production robbed people of opportunities for meaningful and creative work, performed in cooperation with others and over which they had some control. Researchers have posed the question whether the mass character of the modern communications industry produces a sense of alienation in its own workers. Lewis Coser in *Men of Ideas* (Free Press, 1965) believes that the industrial mode of production within media organizations hamstrings the individual producer by denying his or her creativity in the quest for a mass culture, and that this results in alienation.

The term has a wider application. Alienation is seen as a socio-psychological condition which affects certain individuals. William Kornhauser in *The Politics of Mass Society* (Free Press, 1959) argues that the breakdown and decline of community groups and the extended family in modern society produces feelings of isolation and increases the possibility that people will be influenced by the appeals of extremist political groups. Some theorists view alienation as a potentially significant variable in determining an individual's receptivity to mass communication. There are echoes of the notion of the alienated and isolated individual in the mass society theory of the media, for example. See ANOMIE; INTERVENING VARIABLES (IVS).

▶ Denis McQuail, *Mass Communication Theory* (Sage, 2010).

Alignment See FRAMING.

al-Jazeera Arab satellite TV network, sharing news and current affairs in high-definition. Started up in 1996, al-Jazeera grabbed world headlines with its exclusive news footage from Taliban-held areas during the war in Afghanistan, 2002 and the US pursuit of Osama bin Laden, thought to have masterminded the events of 11 September 2001. Translated as 'Peninsula', al-Jazeera scooped rival Western channels with bin Laden's pre-recorded video messages. The channel's coverage of world affairs, including the Israeli-Palestinian conflict and the second Gulf War (2003) and the occupation of Iraq, has offered alternative perspectives and analysis, braving CENSORSHIP whenever it is threatened.

Often referred to as the Arab world's BBC, al-Jazeera is based in Qatar, and is substantially funded by its liberalizing emir. It was through al-Jazeera that viewers were able to witness the destruction by the Taliban of the giant Bamiyan Buddhas. Noureddine Miladi in 'Mapping the Al-Jazeera Phenomenon' in *War and the Media: Reporting Conflict 24/7* (Sage, 2003), edited by Daya Kishan Thussu and Des Freedman, says that with a regular audience of 35 million and available to most of the world's 310 million Arabs, al-Jazeera 'has redefined Arab broadcasting': 'The weekly talk shows and discussion programmes often tackle crucial yet taboo subjects, like human rights, democracy and political corruption, women's freedom, banned political groups, polygamy, torture and rival interpretations of Islamic teachings', which other Arab channels 'would not even consider screening … The animated political discussions that were confined to private spaces in Arab countries have been brought into the open after decades of stagnation and state censorship, to be debated at a transnational level …'

Unmediated by Western media influences, al-Jazeera has incurred the wrath both of the West – the US in particular – and of Arab governments. In a UK *Guardian* article entitled 'Reality Television' (21 April 2004), writing of his time as London correspondent for the website al-jazeera.net, Arthur Nelsen refers to al-Jazeera's 'track record of honest and accurate reporting', commending its 'principled pluralism in face of brutal and authoritarian regimes within the region, and increasingly from those without'. This, in Nelsen's view, 'is why it has been vilified, criminalized and bombed. It is also why it should be defended by those who genuinely believe that successful societies depend upon an independent media'.

A significant advance occurred with the introduction of al-Jazeera English (AJE) in November 2006; and global interest in the organization's news service accelerated as it reported the massed rallies of popular protest against North African and Arab regimes in 2010 and 2011 (see MOBILIZATION).

al-Jazeera English is available in over a hundred countries and broadcasts from Doha, Kuala Lumpur, London and Washington DC. The reluctance in the US to strike distribution deals limited TV access to America, but AJE's services were readily available online and prominently carried on YouTube.

▶ Mohammed El-Nawawy and Adel Iskander, *Al-Jazeera: The Story of the Network That Is Rattling Governments and Redefining Modern Journalism* (Westview, 2003); Mohamed Zayani, ed., *The Al-Jazeera Phenomenon: Critical Perspectives on New Arab Media* (Pluto, 2005); Hugh Miles, *Al-Jazeera: How Arab TV News Challenged the World* (Abacus, 2005).

★**Alleyne's news revolution model, 1997** In *News Revolution: Political and Economic Decisions about Global Information* (Macmillan, 1997), Mark D. Alleyne offers a model which 'is both a description of the international news system's political economy and a theory of the international relations of that system'. The Global News System comprises 'the system of companies, organizations and people that produce the world's news'. It works according to two necessities, Economic and Democratic, the latter describing 'the body of reasons used to justify the existence of the news media' – the political justifications; and these Alleyne classifies as (1) watchdogs on government; (2) 'conduits for the two-way flow of information between people and their government'; and (3) 'as a source of information in the so-called marketplace of ideas'.

Along with political justification there is economic necessity: 'The press system and the economic system interact at a basic level whenever the media carry advertising. At a more sophisticated level, the media perform the information functions needed for trade, currency, equities, and bond markets to perform'. Not least of the factors relating to economics is the capacity of the media to attract or deter capital: 'News of political instability scares away investors. More positive news attracts them'.

The Global News System operates in relation to three structures of power/authority: the political structure (states, international organizations, etc.); the production structure (international trade in goods and services); and financial structures (markets in currency, financial services, etc.). The model identifies a dynamic of interacting and sometimes conflicting claims, which often operate in a process of exchange – what Alleyne terms a 'trade in claims'; what the media want from the power structures and what those structures want from the media with regard to the nature of information and its flow.

Says Alleyne, 'Like the news media, these actors [states, companies, international orga-

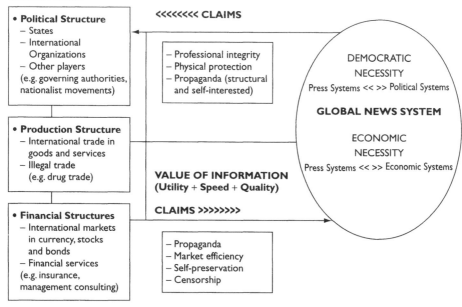

POWER/AUTHORITY STRUCTURES:

• **Political Structure**
 − States
 − International Organizations
 − Other players (e.g. governing authorities, nationalist movements)

<<<<<<<< CLAIMS

− Professional integrity
− Physical protection
− Propaganda (structural and self-interested)

DEMOCRATIC NECESSITY

Press Systems << >> Political Systems

GLOBAL NEWS SYSTEM

ECONOMIC NECESSITY

Press Systems << >> Economic Systems

• **Production Structure**
 − International trade in goods and services
 − Illegal trade (e.g. drug trade)

VALUE OF INFORMATION (Utility + Speed + Quality)

CLAIMS >>>>>>>

• **Financial Structures**
 − International markets in currency, stocks and bonds
 − Financial services (e.g. insurance, management consulting)

− Propaganda
− Market efficiency
− Self-preservation
− Censorship

Alleyne's news revolution model, 1997

nizations] like to manage what information the news media disseminate about them. They do this through censorship and propaganda. Like the news media, these actors seek self-preservation, and the actors operating in the market place are particularly concerned with getting information that will help them make efficient decisions.' Alleyne's own claim for his model is that it 'takes us from the stage of merely describing the wonders of new technologies and assuming positive political consequences from the so-called information revolution to a clear explanation and understanding of how the news media function in international relations'.

Allness attitude Gail and Michelle Myers in *The Dynamics of Human Communication* (McGraw-Hill, 1985) refer to what Alfred Korzybski termed 'allness', that is the attitude that you can know or say all there is about a person, group, issue and so on. As Myers and Myers point out, the allness attitude can constitute a considerable barrier in communication. It may mean that you communicate with certain people on the basis that you know all there is to know about them or the topic under discussion, and few people take kindly to such assumptions.

The attitude may also affect how you receive messages. For example, you may believe you already know all that you are being told, or you

may reject a message which contradicts what you think you know. As Myers and Myers conclude, 'The allness attitude may do much to prevent you from developing satisfying relationships with others and from communicating effectively with them.'

Allusion See HISTORICAL ALLUSION.

Alternative computing See HACKER, HACK-TIVIST.

Alternative (radical) media See MEDIA ACTIV-ISM.

Amazon.com US Seattle-based electronic superstore selling everything from books to computers, from cameras to furniture, from gourmet food to health products, clothing and groceries worldwide. Named after the earth's longest river and with ambitions to be the first and biggest online shopping mall, Amazon was founded in 1995 by Jeff Bezos, beginning life with books only and achieving profitability by 2001. The company soon began to run the retail websites of major corporations, at the same time acquiring network-related enterprises such as Bookpages (UK), Telebook (Germany) and the Internet Movie Database that would drive forward Amazon business. The company moved into online music retailing in 1998, launching the Amazon MP3 in 2007 and the e-book reader, Kindle, in the same year.

As with all the online traders, diversification has been key to survival and prosperity; the company partnered 20th Century Fox in a film production, *The Stolen Child* in 2008. Amazon also ensured that it was in the vanguard of enterprises supporting the increase of independent, print-on-demand (POD) publishing, creating in 2010 Amazon Encore (republishing works of quality that had gone out of print, suffered neglect, or both) and Amazon Crossing (translating and issuing French works into English, the first of these being *The King of Kahel*, 2010).

Like other online operators Amazon has been involved in controversies concerning anti-competitiveness, price discrimination, CENSORSHIP and acting outside international copyright laws. It took flak in 2010 for putting a bar on WIKILEAKS' business, justifying its decision on the grounds that the WHISTLEBLOWER had broken Amazon's rules for usage.

Amplitude See NEWS VALUES.

Analysis: modes of media analysis See DISCOURSE ANALYSIS; ETHNOGRAPHIC (APPROACH TO AUDIENCE MEASUREMENT); FUNCTIONALIST; MARXIST; SOCIAL ACTION (MODES OF MEDIA ANALYSIS).

Anarchist cinema Epitomized in the work of French film-maker Jean Vigo (1905–34) who was twelve when his anarchist father, known as Miguel Almereyda, was found strangled in a French police cell in 1917. In *A propos de Nice* (1930), Vigo expressed the anarchist's views on inequality, contrasting the luxurious, suntanned life of wealthy holidaymakers with the underfed, deformed bodies of slum children. In his comic masterpiece *Zero de Conduite* (*Nought for Conduct*) produced in 1932, Vigo used anarchist friends as actors. His theme was the rebellion of schoolchildren against the rigidity of the school authorities. It was immediately banned by the French authorities. Vigo was a direct inspiration for the 'anarchistic' film of a modern, public school rebellion in Lindsay Anderson's *If*, made in 1968. (*Anarchy*: complete absence of law or government.)

Anchorage The part that captions play in helping to frame, or anchor, the meaning of photographic images, as reproduced in newspapers and magazines. French philosopher Roland Barthes used this term to describe the way captions help 'fix' or narrow down the choice of meanings of the published image. He defines the caption as a 'parasitic message designed to connote the image'.

★Andersch, Staats and Bostrom's model of communication, 1969 Environmental or contextual factors are at the centre of the communication model devised by Elizabeth G. Andersch, Lorin C. Staats and Robert N. Bostrom and presented in *Communication in Everyday Use* (Holt, Rinehart & Winston). Like BARNLAND'S TRANSACTIONAL MODEL, this one stresses the transactional nature of the communication process, in which messages and their meanings are structured and evaluated by the Sender and subjected to reconstruction and evaluation on the part of the Receiver, all the while interacting with factors (or stimuli) in the environment. See TOPIC GUIDE under COMMUNICATION MODELS.

Anecdote A short narrative, usually of a personal nature, used to illustrate a general issue. Anecdotes are often used in media coverage to heighten the emotional aspect of an issue. Colin Seymour-Ure in *The Political Impact of the Mass Media* (Constable, 1974) recounts the use made of one such anecdote by the politician Enoch Powell in his efforts to bring the immigration issue to public attention during 1967 and 1968. Powell claimed to have received a letter from a correspondent in Northumberland expressing concern about an elderly widow in Wolverhampton who feared harassment by newly arrived immigrants in the area. This anecdote was widely reported by the press, yet, despite strenuous efforts, no trace of the elderly widow could be found. The story did, however, do much to fuel the emotive manner in which the immigration issue was discussed in the popular press. See LOONY LEFTISM.

Animatic Sequence of drawings representing the story of a television advertisement, prior to filming. Another term for STORYBOARD.

Animation The process of filming still drawings, puppets, etc. in sequence to give the illusion of movement; also the actual direct drawing and painting on to positive or negative stock or on to clear celluloid itself. Long before CINEMATOGRAPHY was invented, devices were in use which gave drawings the illusion of movement. By 1882 Emile Reynauld had combined his Praxinoscope with a projector and a decade later opened the Théâtre Optique in the Musée Grevin in Paris.

Live-action cinema became all-important once the Lumière brothers had shown its possibilities in 1895, but animation soon captured interest, from 1908 onwards, with the work of J. Stuart Blackton in the US and Emile Cohl in France. New York Herald cartoonist Winsor McCay made *Gertie the Dinosaur* in 1909, and in 1919 the first animated feature, *The Sinking of the Lusitania*.

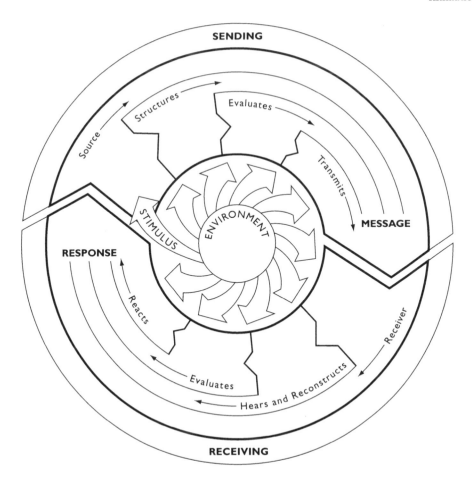

SENDING

Structures

Source

Evaluates

Transmits

MESSAGE

STIMULUS

ENVIRONMENT

RESPONSE

Reacts

Receiver

Evaluates

Hears and Reconstructs

RECEIVING

Andersch, Staats and Bostrom's model of communication, 1969

In November 1928 Walt Disney (1901–66) presented Mortimer, later Mickey Mouse, to the world using synchronous sound, in *Steamboat Willie*, along with his *Skeleton Dance* (1929), one of the true classics of animation film. The laboriousness of producing thousands of drawings for filming was dramatically altered in the 1980s by the introduction to animated film-making of computer graphics.

Cel (handdrawn) animation was generally displaced by computer-generated (CG) animation, increasingly in the film industry in 3D (see THREE-DIMENSIONAL (3D). Live action using actors is integrated by CG imaging, blending the real with the synthetic. What has been termed *motion capture* (extensively used in video games) records actor movement to activate digital character models. When facial expression and finger movement are included, the process becomes *performance capture*.

Among the most celebrated movie examples using performance capture are Andy Serkis's Gollum in Peter Jackson's *Lord of the Rings: The Fellowship of the Ring* (2001), and James Cameron's *Avatar* (2009), the highest grossing film of all time. Here, the Na'vi, inhabitants of Pandora, are seven-foot CG fantasies yet capturing human motion and emotion with an amazingly heightened sense of reality.

At one time during the making of *Avatar* the New Zealand visual effects company Weta Digital employed 900 people, an indicator of the prodigious scale and expense of Cameron's innovative enterprise.

Motion capture animation has also become familiar in projects for TV, an example in the UK being *Headcases* (2008), a satirical current affairs show created by Henry Naylor for ITV, using 3D animation in the style of *Spitting Image* (ITV, 1984–96).

▶ Paul Wells, *Understanding Animation* (Routledge, 1998); Wikipedia.

Annan Commission Report on Broadcasting, 1977 Historian Lord Annan chaired the Royal Commission on the Future of Broadcasting, whose main task was to decide what should happen to the BROADCASTING industry once the right to broadcast of the RADIO and TELEVISION companies lapsed at the end of July 1979. The Annan Commission was also asked to make recommendations on a fourth television channel.

What Annan wanted above all was a shift from duopoly to a more diverse system of broadcasting in Britain: 'We want the broadcasting industry to grow. But we do not want more of the same ... What is needed now are programmes for the different minorities which add up to make the majority.' Annan also declared that there was 'a widely shared feeling that British broadcasting is run like a highly restricted club –managed exclusively by broadcasters according to their own criteria of what counts as good television and radio.'

The then Labour Government published a white paper, *Broadcasting* (July 1978), in response to Annan, but before there was time for legislation, the Conservatives came to power in May 1979. The Queen's Speech promised the fourth channel to commercial television and the Annan proposal for an Open Broadcasting Authority was rejected. See CHANNEL FOUR. See also TOPIC GUIDE under COMMISSIONS, COMMITTEES, LEGISLATION.

Anomie It was Emile Durkheim (1858–1917), a French sociologist, who first used this term to describe a state of 'normlessness' in which the individual feels that there are no effective social rules governing behaviour, or that those rules and VALUES to which he/she is exposed are conflicting and therefore confusing. The anomic state is most likely to occur when contact with others is limited. Durkheim linked anomie with the disturbance caused by social change and upheaval, and saw it as a temporary social phenomenon. Several contemporary observers consider it a more permanent feature of modern industrial society.

MASS SOCIETY theorists have tended to view those suffering from anomie as being particularly vulnerable to over-influence by mass communication. Observers have also found that some behaviour that was considered anomic was in fact sub-cultural. Another feature of anomie is that the individual may react to it by becoming ceaselessly ambitious, and this in some cases can lead to severe agitation and discontent.

Dissatisfied ambition is a target for much advertising and is often seen as a desirable trait in modern capitalist societies – a perspective reinforced by some of the outpourings from the mass media. A question of concern, then, is the contribution of the mass media and in particular advertising to the condition of anomie. Anomie can lead to extensive personal as well as social breakdown, to suicide and mental illness as well as to crime, delinquency, drug addiction and alcoholism.

Anticipatory compliance Phrase used by Bruce Dover in his book *Rupert's Adventure in China* (Tuttle Publishing, 2008) to describe how editors working for the Murdoch media empire know by nature, rather than directive, what they can or cannot publish or broadcast. Dover, a former vice-president of Murdoch in China, writes 'Murdoch very rarely issued directives or instructions to his senior executives or editors'. What was expected was 'a sort of "anticipatory compliance". One didn't need to be instructed about what to do, one simply knew what was in one's long-term interests'.

Anti-language According to Martin Montgomery in *An Introduction to Language and Society* (Routledge, 1995), anti-languages 'may be understood as extreme versions of social dialects'. Typically, anti-languages are developed by subcultures and groups that take an antagonistic stance towards mainstream society. This stance may be general or relate to a specific area of social activity. Further, the core activities of the group – those around which the anti-language often develops – may well be illegal. The anti-language serves both to establish a boundary and a degree of separateness between the group and society, and to make its activities more difficult for outsiders to detect and follow.

By their nature anti-languages are difficult to study, but Montgomery discusses several types including those developed in Polish prisons and those used by the Calcutta underworld. Another example could be that of Polari, described by Ian Lucas in 'The colour of eyes: Polari and the Sisters of Perpetual Indulgence' in Anna Livia and Kira Hall, eds, *Queerly Phrased: Language Gender and Sexuality* (Oxford University Press, 1997) as a kind of 'British gay slang'. Polari was popular among the homosexual community in Britain during the 1950s and 1960s, before crossing over into the mainstream. It has sometimes been employed in the comic portrayal of camp characters. There is thought to be limited contemporary use of Polari by the homosexual community.

Anti-languages are created by a process of *relexicalization* – that is, the substitution of new vocabulary for old, usually those words which refer to the activities which mark the group off from the wider community. The grammar of the parent language is often preserved. Making up new words happens frequently in anti-languages, thus making them even more difficult to penetrate. *Overlexicalization* is often also a feature of anti-languages. Here a variety of new words may refer to an activity and may be used interchangeably in order to mislead or confuse 'outsiders'.

Anti-Terrorism, Crime and Security Act (UK), 2001 See TERRORISM: ANTI-TERRORISM, CRIME AND SECURITY ACT.

Apache silence The complex meanings of silence, as observed by the North American Apache tribes, have been tabulated by K.H. Basso in 'To give up words: silence in Western Apache culture' in P. Giglioli, ed., *Language and Social Context* (Penguin, 1972). Basso describes Apache silence as 'a response to uncertainty and unpredictability in social relations'. Often baffling to the outsider, Apache silence was an important element in the courtship process; when meeting strangers; even when greeting children back from a long journey; and in the presence of other people's grief. See COMMUNI-CATION, NON-VERBAL.

▶ Adam Jaworski, *The Power of Silence: Social and Pragmatic Perspectives* (Sage, 1993).

Apocryphal stories Those of doubtful origin, false or spurious. See DEMONIZATION; FOLK DEVILS; LOONY LEFTISM; MYTH; RUMOUR.

Apple Macintosh Name derives from an apple cultivar, the McIntosh (called 'the Mac'), popular in New England and fixed on by the founders of Apple Computers, Steve Wozniak and Steve Jobs, 1 April 1976, though the names of other pioneers of the personal computer (PC) – Jef Raskin, Burrell Smith and Bill Atkinson – should be equally celebrated. From its inception Apple has been synonymous with innovative excellence and good design.

A David in the PC world compared with the Goliath of MICROSOFT, Apple (commanding 4 per cent of the computer market globally) nevertheless is a chart-stopper in terms of admiration for its computer hardware and software and for its enterprise in the field of digital telephony.

Both in terms of innovation and business success Apple languished in the 1990s, this in part because the dynamic Jobs fell out with the company's Chief Executive Officer and took his energies elsewhere. However, with the return of Jobs to the company the Mac revolution picked up apace. Innovations such as the HyperCard, the MultiFinder, the Powerbook, the iMac – advanced and stylish – and the iBook (Apple's first laptop computer) did good business and established the company as a world leader.

In 2005 came the MacMini, a relatively inexpensive version of the Mac, proving immensely popular and profitable. Jobs has been quoted as saying, 'I get asked a lot why Apple's customers are so loyal. It's not because they belong to the church of Mac! It's because of the best service and the quality of Apple's products'.

Apple is associated with 'the next big thing' in computing, creating landmarks such as the iPhone, the iPod and sensationally in 2010, the iPad tablet which in three days in June registered sales of a quarter of a million and within six months was approaching sales of ten million. The iPod, a portable media player, was introduced in 2001, taking 90 per cent of the US market and selling a hundred million by 2007. *PC World Magazine* judged that the iPod had 'altered the landscape for portable audio players'. It has proved as useful for business as for entertainment. The music software iTunes Store, opened for business in 2003, soon offered movies and computer games. In 2007 iTunes Wi-Fi Music Store followed, and the celebrated iPhone in the same year.

In 2011 Apple introduced its iCloud service, allowing people to listen to music purchased online for any Apple device with Internet connection, this in competition with similar offerings available from rivals AMAZON and GOOGLE.

Like other global operators such as Google and MICROSOFT, Apple Inc. has been involved in controversy and litigation. In June 2006 the UK *Mail on Sunday* reported on the suicides of several workers at a factory run by Taiwan-based electronics firm, Foxconn, manufacturer of components for Apple (and Dell, HP and Nokia). Evidence of guards at the Shenzhen factory beating workers was captured on video – a situation the Apple management rushed to remedy.

Similar problems arose in China in August 2009 when it was revealed that another Apple supplier at the Wintek factory in Suzhou, Jiangsee Province, incurred a strike following illness breaking out among workers as a result of the illegal use of n-hexane instead of (the more expensive) alcohol to clean screens of mobile phones.

Apple has taken legal action to protect its apple trademark. In April 2000 the Beijing

Number One Intermediate People's Court ruled in favour of the Guangdong Apples Industry Company, manufacturers of leather goods, keeping its (winged) apple trademark. However, in 2008 the Shenyang Municipal Intermediate People's Court found against the New Apple Digital Technology Company, judging that a trademark infringement had taken place and was a case of unfair competition, although the claimed damages were reduced.

Though Apple's triumph with the multi-functional iPad boosted the company's profits and reputation for innovation, the death of Jobs in October 2011 cast a shadow of uncertainty over Apple's future.

Arbitrariness One of the characteristic features of human LANGUAGE is that between an object described and the word that describes it there is a connection which is purely arbitrary – that is, the speech sound does not reflect features of the object denoted. For example, the word 'chair' describes the object, chair, because the English have arbitrarily decided to name it thus as a matter of convention. In contrast, *onomatopoeic* expressions are representative rather than arbitrary in that they reflect properties of the nonlinguistic world (for example, clatter, buzz, flap – and snap, crackle and pop).

'Areopagitica' Title of a tract or pamphlet by the English poet John Milton (1608–74) in defence of the freedom of the press, published in 1644. Milton spoke out, with eloquence and courage, following the revival of censorship by parliamentary ordinance in 1643 (traditional press censorship had broken down with the Long Parliament's abolition of the Star Chamber in 1641). The title was taken from the Greek, *Areopagus* – the hill of Ares or Mars in Athens, where the highest judicial court held its sittings; a 'behind closed doors' court.

Milton celebrated the power and influence of the printed word: books 'do preserve, as in a vial, the purest efficacy and extraction of that living intellect that bred them. I know they are as lively, and as vigorously productive, as those fabulous dragon's teeth; and being sown up and down, may chance to spring up armed men. And yet, on the other hand, unless wariness be used, as good almost kill a man as kill a good book: who kills a man kills a reasonable creature, God's image; but he who destroys a good book, kills reason itself, kills the image of God, as it were, in the eye'. See MILTON'S PARADOX.

Article 19 This clause in the European Convention for the Protection of Human Rights and Fundamental Freedom states: '(1) Everyone has the right to freedom of expression. This right shall include freedom to hold opinions and to receive and impart information and ideas without interference by public authority and regardless of frontiers. (2) The exercise of these freedoms, since it carries with it duties and responsibilities, may be subject to such formalities, conditions, restrictions or penalties as are prescribed by law and are necessary in a democratic society, in the interests of national security, territorial integrity or public safety ... for preventing the disclosure of information received in confidence, or for maintaining the authority and impartiality of the judiciary.'

The upholding of the Convention is the task of the European Court of Human Rights, based in Strasbourg. The article gave birth to a pressure group, Article 19, centred in London, using electronic media to monitor state censorship around the world. See CENSORSHIP and *TOPIC GUIDE* under MEDIA: FREEDOM, CENSORSHIP.

Arqiva Commercial Radio Awards See COMMERCIAL RADIO (UK).

Assertiveness To be assertive is to be able to communicate one's thoughts, feelings, beliefs, ATTITUDES, positions and so on in a clear, confident, honest and direct manner; it is in short to be able to stand up for oneself whilst also taking into consideration the needs and rights of other people. Anne Dickson in *Women at Work* (Kogan Page, 2000) argues that, 'Being assertive ... springs from a fulcrum of equality. It springs from a balance between self and others ...'

Being assertive differs from being aggressive in that aggressiveness involves standing up for one's own rights and needs at the expense of others. In recent years there has been much interest in assertiveness training – that is, in enabling people to develop techniques and strategies, verbal and non-verbal, for INTERPERSONAL COMMUNICATION which will encourage them to assert themselves in social situations. The ability to be assertive is linked to self-esteem and self-confidence and thus to a positive SELF-CONCEPT. Such training provides the opportunity for considerable exploration of the relationship between the self-concept and interpersonal behaviour.

Whilst assertiveness in communication may be encouraged in some individualistic cultures, such as those of the US or UK, collectivistic cultures, like those of Japan or China, tend to stress the importance of respect for others, tact, politeness and the maintenance of interpersonal harmony. Thus in such cultures assertiveness may be perceived as rudeness. Larry A. Samovar,

Richard E. Porter and Edwin R. McDaniel note in *Intercultural Communication: A Reader* (Thomson Wadsworth, 2006) the degree to which concern for the face of others may be taken in Japanese culture: 'So strong is that concern for the feelings of others that the Japanese are notorious for avoiding the word "no," which they find harsh.'

These different perspectives on assertiveness can be found within a culturally diverse society. Larry Samovar and Richard Porter in *Communication Between Cultures* (Wadsworth/ Thomson Learning, 2001) provide the following example from the US: 'In yet another experiment Caucasian mothers tended to interpret as positive those aspects of their children's speech and behaviour that reflected assertiveness, excitement and interest.

'Navajo mothers who observed the same behaviour in their children reported them as being mischievous and lacking discipline. To the Navajo mothers, assertive speech and behaviour reflected discourtesy, restlessness, self-centredness, and lack of discipline …' It would seem that assertiveness in communication is a potential barrier to successful intercultural communication. See COMMUNICATION: FACEWORK; INTERCULTURAL COMMUNICATION; HIGH AND LOW CONTEXT COMMUNICATION.

▶ Sue Bishop, *Develop Your Assertiveness (Creating Success)* (Sunday Times/Kogan Page, 2010).

Attention model of mass communication Denis McQuail in *Mass Communication Theory: An Introduction* (Sage, 1987; 6th edition, 2010) writes that 'the essence of any market is to bring goods and services to the attention of potential customers and keep their interest'. Thus, in mass media terms, the attention model is about stimulus to buy: communication is considered to have succeeded as soon as AUDIENCE attention has been won, regardless of how this was brought about. This paradigm contrasts with the TRANSMISSION MODEL OF MASS COMMUNICATION which essentially relates to notions of PUBLIC SERVICE BROADCASTING; that is, the function of communication is to deliver *messages*; to transmit information, knowledge, education and enlightenment as well as to entertain. Hence public *service*. See *audience-as-public* and *audience-as-market* in the entry on AUDIENCE.

Attitudes We all hold a range of attitudes on a variety of topics and issues. An attitude, according to Milton Rokeach in 'The nature of attitudes', *Encyclopaedia of the Social Sciences* (Collier-Macmillan, 1965), is '… a relatively enduring organization of beliefs around an object or situation predisposing one to respond in some preferential manner'.

Attitudes are learned from direct experience or through socialization and are capable of being changed. Attitudes may vary in their direction (that is they may be positive, negative or neutral), their intensity and in the degree of importance attached to them. It is possible to discern three component elements of an attitude: the *cognitive* component, that is the knowledge one has, true or false, about a particular subject which may have been gathered from a wide range of sources; the *affective* component, that is one's emotional response or feelings towards a particular subject which will be linked to one's beliefs and VALUES; and the *behaviour* component, that is how one reacts with respect to a certain subject.

Attitudes cannot be seen. Their existence can only be inferred from what people say or do. It is for this reason that accurate attitude measurement is considered to be highly problematic: people may not be willing to communicate what they really think or feel. It is basically through communicating with others that one develops attitudes. Attitudes, once developed, influence the way in which we perceive other people and thus how we behave towards them. The mass media may shape, reinforce or challenge attitudes. For example, in conveying STEREOTYPES, mass media messages may shape people's attitudes towards GROUPS with which they have had little, if any, contact. CAMPAIGNS, such as ADVERTISING campaigns, may be designed to change people's attitudes towards a certain product.

Attribute dimensions of agenda-setting See AGENDA-SETTING.

Attribution theory Concerned with the psychological processes by which individuals attribute causes to behaviour. Such attribution can be *dispositional* – behaviour attributed to such factors as personality and attitude; or *situational* – behaviour attributed to factors in the situation. We may, for example, blame a person's failure to gain employment on his/her laziness (dispositional attribution) or on the state of the economy (situational attribution). Richard Gross in *Psychology: The Science of Mind and Behaviour* (Hodder Arnold, 2005) explains that such attributions are subject to the *fundamental attribution error*, that is 'to the general tendency to overestimate the importance of personal/ dispositional factors relative to situational/ environmental factors as a cause of behaviour'. We seem particularly prone to this error when making judgments about other people's behaviour, but are more likely to recognise the influence of situational factors on our own behaviour.

Carole Wade and Carol Tavris in *Psychology* (HarperCollins, 1993) note that 'when it comes to explaining their own behaviour, most Westerners tend to choose attributes that are favourable to them ... This self-serving bias means that people like to take credit for their good actions and let the situation account for their bad ones'. Dispositional attribution can be difficult to change as evidence suggests that we are unwilling to discard dispositional attributions even when they are discredited. This may help explain the persistence of STEREOTYPES and PREJUDICE.

Several studies have, however, noted cross-cultural differences in the attribution process. For example, J.G. Miller conducted a study comparing subjects from the US with Hindus in India as regards the use of dispositional and situational attribution. In 'Culture and the development of everyday social explanation' in the *Journal of Personality and Social Psychology* (1984, issue 46) Miller reported his discovery that the subjects in the US were more likely than the Hindu subjects in India to employ dispositional rather than situational explanations for behaviour.

▶ William Gudykunst and Young Yun Kim, *Communicating with Strangers: An Approach to Intercultural Communication* (McGraw-Hill, 1997).

Audience Students of media communication recognize the term *audience* as overarching all the reception processes of message sending. Thus there is the audience for theatre, TELEVISION and cinema; there is the RADIO listener. There is the audience for a pop concert or at a public meeting. Communicators shape their messages to fit the perceived needs of their audience: they calculate the level of receptiveness, the degree of readiness to accept the message and the mode of delivery.

Audience is readership too, and the success in meeting audience/readership needs relies extensively on FEEDBACK; also, perhaps more significantly of late, identification of what audience actually is. Does it in any meaningful sense actually exist, bearing in mind the inevitable fragmentation of the traditional audience for media as a result of the diversification of the modes and channels of mass communication on the one hand, and the accelerating growth of network communication on the other?

Denis McQuail in *Audience Analysis* (Sage, 1997) writes of the 'audience problem', acknowledging that 'there is much room for differences of meaning, misunderstandings, and theoretical conflicts'. He goes on, 'The problems surrounding the concept [of audience] stem mainly from the fact that a single and simple word is being applied to an increasingly diverse and complex reality.'

McQuail's book addresses these problems in an interesting and illuminating manner. We know that audiences exist; the trouble is that without rigorous and sustained monitoring through research in one form or another, they are liable to 'escape', that is from agencies of control, whether these are governments, institutions, advertisers or organizations that exist to place audiences under surveillance and produce the data on which decision-making is based.

McQuail does not go as far as agreeing with some commentators that the audience for mass media is verging on the extinct. In his chapter on 'The future of the audience concept' there is a subhead, 'The audience lives on', suggesting that the determination of communicators to hold on to mass audiences along with that of those who measure and monitor responses, has been sufficiently successful to rescue audience from escape.

In other words, fragmentation has been checked if not halted. Audiences for mass media have been slower to switch allegiance – from public-service broadcasting services, for example – than some have predicted; and a look at the popularity of many programmes offered in the UK by the BBC and independent television would give substance to that argument. We may still, in the words of the title of Ian Ang's 1991 publication, be *Desperately Seeking the Audience* (Routledge & Kegan Paul), but research indicates, as McQuail points out, that the 'dispersion of [audience] attention among channels has been marked by moderation and gradualness'.

Current definitions and evaluations of audience, however, take in the enormous expansion of INTERNET communication which, with the advance of easy-to-use digital technology, allows audiences also to be creators of media texts in all their forms. In an online post to *Press Think* (2006), Jay Rosen writes of 'people formerly known as the audience'. That 'humble device' the blog 'has given the press to us', while PODCASTING 'gives radio to us'. Rosen celebrates the fact that now 'the horizontal flow, citizen to citizen, is as real and consequential as the vertical one'. In other words, people are fast turning the 'one-to-many' media experience to a 'many to many' one.

Graeme Turner in *Ordinary People and the Media: The Demotic Turn* (Sage, 2010) writes, 'In a context within which media outlets and platforms are multiplying and audiences are fragmenting, for many elements of the media the search for a mass audience is fast losing its rationality as the basis for doing business.'

See BLOGOSPHERE; DEMOTIC TURN; DIGITAL OPTIMISM; JOURNALISM: CITIZEN JOURNALISM; MOBILIZATION; NETWORKING: SOCIAL NETWORKING; WEB 2.0. See also *TOPIC GUIDE* under AUDIENCES/CONSUMPTION AND RECEPTION OF MEDIA.

▶ Pertti Alasuutari, ed., *Rethinking the Media Audience: The New Agenda* (Sage, 1999); Andy Ruddock, *Investigating Audiences* (Sage, 2007); Michael Higgins, *The Media and Their Publics* (Open University, 2007); Dan Hind, *The Return of the Public* (Verso, 2010); Philip M. Napoli, *Audience Evolution: New Technologies and the Transformation of Media Audiences* (Columbia University Press, 2011).

Audience: active audience An age-old media debate centres on the nature of audience reaction to traditional mass-media messages. The notion of the active audience considers audiences to be proactive and independent rather than docile and accepting. The active audience is seen to use the media rather than be used by it (see USES AND GRATIFICATIONS THEORY). This perception has come about substantially through findings of research which has observed members of audiences consuming media in their own homes (see ETHNOGRAPHIC APPROACH TO AUDIENCE MEASUREMENT).

Writing in the 1980s, American media analyst Herbert Schiller took issue with the optimistic view of the active or resistive audience. In *Culture Inc.: The Corporate Takeover of Public Expression* (Oxford University Press, 1989) Schiller argues that transnational corporations have colonized culture and cultural expression, in the US and globally. He writes of 'corporate pillaging of the national information supply' and the 'proprietary control of information'. Such manifest power, he believes, calls into question the active-audience paradigm: 'A great emphasis is given to the "resistance", "subversion", and "empowerment" of the viewer. Where this resistance and subversion of the audience lead and what effects they have on the existing structure of power remain a mystery.'

In turn Schiller has been criticized for underestimating the potential resistance of audience to 'corporatization'. John B. Thompson in *The Media and Modernity: A Social Theory of Media* (Polity, 1995) says that 'even if one sympathizes with Schiller's broad theoretical view and his critical perspectives, there are many respects in which the argument is deeply unsatisfactory'. In particular, Thompson counters Schiller's view that American cultural imperialism has wreaked havoc with indigenous cultures throughout the world, and that it is a seemingly unstoppable force. Thompson is of the opinion that 'Schiller ... presents too uniform a view of American media culture ... and of its global dominance'.

The landscape of media-use has been substantially altered with the advent of network communication (see NETWORKING: SOCIAL NETWORKING). Mass media has lost some of its centrality in relation to audience; and audiences have become much more proactive not only in receiving messages, but also in becoming producers of messages. They are able as never before to pick and choose their online sources, to feedback more readily, to become practised communicators through blogs and enrolling on various platforms of social interaction. See AUDIENCE: FRAGMENTATION OF; BLOGOSPHERE; FACEBOOK; MYSPACE; TWITTER; SELF-IDENTITY; SEMIOTIC POWER; YOUTUBE.

★**Audience: fragmentation of** In *Audience Analysis* (Sage, 1997) Denis McQuail publishes the following models, with acknowledgment to Jan van Cuilenburg, illustrating in four succeeding stages how audiences for mass media have become fragmented since the early years of TV. The Unitary Model 'implies a single audience that is more or less coextensive with the general public'. The texts of media – BROADCASTING in particular – were shared by all, and homogenous.

With the expansion of provision and the increase in the number of channels, diversity is shown in the Pluralist Model, representing a 'pattern of limited internal diversification'. The Core-Periphery Model 'is one in which the multiplication of channels makes possible additional and competing alternatives outside this framework'.

At this stage, says McQuail, 'it becomes possible to enjoy a television diet that differs significantly from the majority or mainstream'. The Breakup Model is characterized by 'extensive fragmentation and the disintegration of the central core. The audience is distributed over many different channels in no fixed pattern, and there is only sporadically shared audience experiences'.

McQuail says that for the most part the 'core' still dominates audience use of TV: 'The reasons lie primarily in the near-universal appeal of mainstream content and the advantages to media organizations of continuing with mass provision, plus the continuing habits and patterns of social life.' The author believes that 'media change is

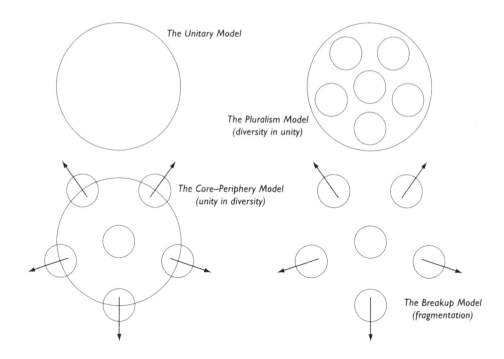

The Unitary Model

The Pluralism Model
(diversity in unity)

The Core–Periphery Model
(unity in diversity)

The Breakup Model
(fragmentation)

Models of audience fragmentation

not enough on its own to disrupt established patterns of shared culture'. The Breakup stage 'is certainly becoming more possible', but it is 'still a hypothetical pattern and has not been realized'. See TOPIC GUIDE under NETWORK SOCIETY.

Audience differentiation Like the 'mass', audiences – for RADIO, TELEVISION, cinema or readers of the PRESS – are often simplistically regarded as a homogeneous lump. It is easier to make generalizations that way, but misleading. Audience differentiation works from the premise that analysis of audience response to media messages can only be purposeful if it recognizes that the mass is a complex of individuals, differentiated by gender, age, social class, profession, education and CULTURE. See ANALYSIS: MODES OF MEDIA ANALYSIS.

Audience measurement Investigation of the size and constitution of mass media audiences evolved into one of the world's major service industries. Initially, audience measurement, or audience research (AR) is about number-crunching: how many readers? How many listeners or viewers? This data is then broken down along lines of class, gender, spending-power, age, occupation, etc. There are two categories of measurement – quantitative and qualitative – with pressure always to translate the one into the other.

In the UK, audience measurement of one kind or another has operated since the beginning of BROADCASTING. Once the monopoly of the airwaves held by the BBC gave way to competition with the advent of commercial television, audience preferences became increasingly significant and audience measurement was quickly regarded as a duty and a lifeline for survival.

Two key terms are *ratings* and *shares*. A rating is defined as the estimated percentage, in the case of television, of all the 'TV households' or of all the people within a demographic group who view a specific programme or station. A share refers to the percentage of the overall viewing figures which a particular programme commands.

As long ago as the 1980s, in *Inside Prime Time* (Pantheon, 1983) Todd Gitlin dubbed the obsession of the TV networks with ratings 'the fetish of immediate numerical gratification'. This fetish now extends to ways of measuring audience response using sensory devices that register viewing habits, but the trickiest problem concerning audience measurement is fragmentation of use, through cable, video, DVD, satellite, network communication and the multiple functions of hand-held device, not to mention the difficulties facing measurement with the

zapping and zipping that goes on, facilitated by the remote control pad. See ETHNOGRAPHIC APPROACH TO AUDIENCE MEASUREMENT.
▸ Shaun Moores, *Interpreting Audiences: The Ethnography of Media Consumption* (Sage, 1993); James S. Ettema and D. Charles Whitney, eds, *Audiencemaking: How Media Create the Audience* (Sage, 1994); Raymond Kent, ed., *Measuring Media* Audiences (Routledge, 1994); Denis McQuail, *Audience Analysis* (Sage, 1997); Marie Gillespie, ed., *Media Audiences* (Open University, 2005); Michael Higgins, *The Media and Their Publics* (Open University, 2007).

Audience needs See USES AND GRATIFICATIONS THEORY; MASLOW'S HIERARCHY OF NEEDS. See also *TOPIC GUIDE* under AUDIENCES/CONSUMPTION & RECEPTION OF MEDIA; MEDIA: POWER, EFFECTS, INFLUENCE.

Autocue Or teleprompt. A device which uses angled mirrors to project the words of a script on to a screen just below the lens of the TV camera. This enables a presenter to 'read' a script without looking down.

Avaaz See ONLINE CAMPAIGNING.

Avant-garde The innovative, advance guard in any art form; usually assaulting tradition and boundaries of acceptability. The phrase was used as early as 1845 by Gabriel-Desire Laverdant, and the anarchist Michael Bakunin named a periodical *L'Avant-garde* in 1878.

B

Bad language Lars Gunnar Andersson and Peter Trudgill in *Bad Language* (Penguin, 1990), whilst acknowledging that the term 'bad language' is far from clear and unambiguous, refer to it as 'all those things (sounds, words and phrases) that may be dangerous to use. Language contains explosive totems that should be handled with care'. The authors state that bad language can be usefully analysed by explaining the possible explosions which may be caused by certain words, pronunciations or use of grammar. They also argue that '"Badness" is not found in the language itself but in people's views of the language', indicating the importance of examining the values, attitudes and ideologies within societies that underpin the evaluation of some language as 'bad'.

When ordinary people are asked, Andersson and Trudgill argue, 'What do you think of when you hear the phrase, bad language?', most of them will certainly say 'swearing'. However, Andersson and Trudgill point out that the term is also used to refer to the use of slang and jargon, the incorrect or misuse of words, certain accents and dialects and the use of 'non-standard' English. Several studies have shown that the evaluation of language as 'bad' in a particular instance will depend on a number of variables, which include the degree to which taboo words or words relating to taboo behaviour are used, the social context and the social roles, age and gender of the interactors.

So bad language can be difficult to pin down. Edwin L. Battistella in *Bad Language: Are Some Words Better Than Others?* (Oxford University Press Inc., 2005) argues that '... good and bad language cannot be defined in absolute terms. The standard language of one era, generation, medium, or region might well differ from the standard of another'.

The media also has to be mindful of the limits of acceptability as regards bad language, or complaints will ensue. The Broadcasting Standards Council, for example, undertook a study in the early 1990s to explore perceptions of and attitudes towards bad language in response to the number of complaints received about its use, particularly on television. The results were published in a report edited by A. Millwood Hargrave entitled *A Matter of Manners? – The Limits of Broadcasting Language* (Broadcasting Standards Council, Research Monograph Series: 3, John Libbey, 1991).

The time of viewing and social context in which the programme was likely to be viewed, particularly the likelihood of children being around, were key variables affecting judgments regarding the acceptability of language used. Generally speaking, the study found that the possibility that a word might offend others to be an important factor in judging the acceptability of its use.

Bad or offensive language in UK broadcasting is dealt with in Section 1 of the Broadcasting Code of OFCOM, Protecting the Under-Eighteens.

Back region, front region See IMPRESSION MANAGEMENT.

Balanced programming The PILKINGTON REPORT, 1962, put forward three criteria for the creation of balance in TV programmes. Balance would be achieved, Pilkington stated, if channels provided the widest possible range of subject-matter; if the fullest treatment was given to each subject within the range; and if scheduling did not create imbalances by concentrating certain types of popular programmes at peak viewing times while relegating others, deemed less accessible, to inconvenient times.

Balance has a more controversial, political connotation, when it is seen as a device to counter and control bias. More than any other medium, public broadcasting aspires to *equilibrium*. Being fair to all sides can have paradoxical results: if one programme, for example, condemns the destruction of Amazon rainforests, must the balance be sustained by allowing a programme which defends that destruction? It is questionable whether fairness is actually achieved by giving air-time to ideas which flout the very principle of fairness.

Balance might ultimately mean always sitting on the fence; it may indicate a position which considers all standpoints to be tenable. Yet the balanced position – the fulcrum, as it were – from which other viewpoints are presented, has to be decided by *someone* whose IMPARTIALITY in turn might be questioned by others.

Ball-Rokeach and DeFleur's dependency model of mass communication effects, 1976 (See also, DEPENDENCY THEORY.) Sandra Ball-Rokeach and Melvyn DeFleur's model poses the question, to what extent is contemporary society dependent, for information and for viewpoints, on the all-pervasive mass communication industry; and, arising from this question, how far are we dependent on the media for our orientation towards the world beyond our immediate experience? In 'A dependency model of mass media effects' in *Communication Research*, 3 (1976), the authors argue that the nature and degree of dependency relate closely first to the extent to which society is subject to change, conflict or instability and second to the functions of information provision and attitude-shaping of the mass media within those social structures.

The model emphasizes the essentially interactive nature of the processes of media effect. There are societal and media systems, and these interact with audience, producing cognitive, affective and behavioural effects, inducing varying degrees of dependency; in turn audience-response feeds back and influences society and media.

The cognitive effect is that which relates to matters of the intellect and the affective to matters of emotion. In the cognitive area, the following areas of effect or influence are identified: creation and resolution of ambiguity; attitude formation; agenda-setting; expansion of people's belief systems; value clarification. Under the affective heading, the media may be perceived as creating fear or anxiety; increasing or decreasing morale and establishing a sense of alienation.

In terms of the third category, behaviour,

the effects may be to activate or de-activate; to formulate issues and influence their resolution. They may stimulate a range of behaviours, from political demonstrations to altruistic acts such as donating money to good causes. The authors cite the model as avoiding 'a seemingly untenable all-or-nothing position of saying either that the media have no significant impact on people or society, or that the media have an unbounded capacity to manipulate people and society'.

Where the model is open to most serious criticism is in its assumption that the societal structure and the media structure are independent of one another, and that these are in some sort of equilibrium with audience. In many cases the media are so interlinked with power structures that a free interaction is more likely in theory than in practice. See COGNITIVE (AND AFFECTIVE); CULTURAL APPARATUS; HEGEMONY; MEDIATION; POWER ELITE.

Band-wagon effect See NOELLE-NEUMANN'S SPIRAL OF SILENCE MODEL OF PUBLIC OPINION, 1974.

Bandwidth Range of frequencies available for carrying data and expressed in hertz (cycles per second). The amount of traffic a communication channel can carry is roughly proportional to its bandwidth. See BROADBAND.

BARB Broadcasters' Audience Research Board; organization responsible for collecting and collating TV viewing figures in the UK. The data is gathered from over 5,000 homes of independent TV-owning households representative of the whole of the UK. Viewing habits are electronically monitored, requiring householders to register their presence in the room where a TV is located and switched on, and to deregister when they switch off or leave the room. See AUDIENCE MEASUREMENT.

★Barnlund's transactional models of communication, 1970 In 'A transactional model of communication' in K.K. Sereno and C.D. Mortensen, eds, *Foundations of Communication Theory* (Harper & Row, 1970), Dean C. Barnlund attempts to address the 'complexities of human communication' which present 'an unbelievably difficult challenge to the student of human affairs'. His models pay due respect to this complexity. For Barnlund, communication both describes the evolution of meaning and aims at the reduction of uncertainty. He stresses that meaning is something 'invented', 'assigned', 'given' rather than something 'received': 'Meanings may be generated while a man stands alone on a mountain trail or sits in the privacy of his study speculating about internal doubt.'

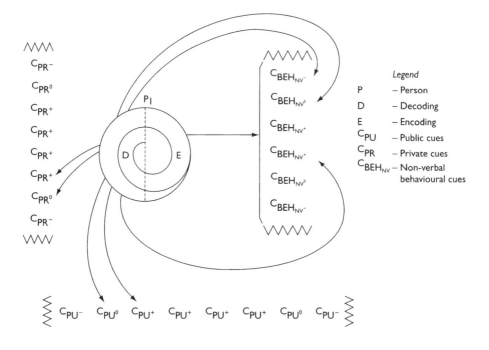

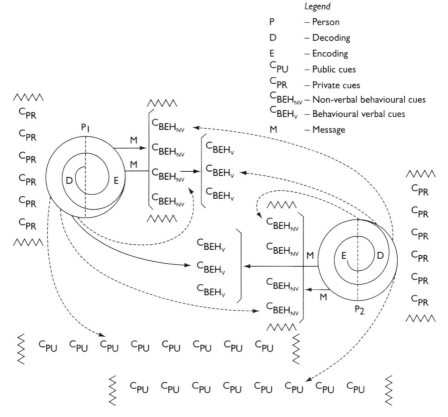

Barnlund's transactional models of communication, 1970

Within and around the communicant are *cues* of unlimited number, though some carrying more weight – or valence – than others at any given time. Barnlund's model indicates three sets of cues, each interacting upon one another. These are *public* cues, *private* cues and *behavioural* cues. DECODING and ENCODING are visualized as part of the same spiralling process – continuous, unrepeatable and irreversible.

Public cues Barnlund divides into *natural* – those supplied by the physical world without the intervention of people, such as atmospheric conditions, natural occurrences – and *artificial*, those resulting from people's modification and manipulation of their environment. For example, Barnlund places his communicant, Mr A, in a doctor's waiting room which contains many public artificial cues – a pile of magazines, a smell of antiseptic, a picture by Joan Miro on the wall.

Private cues emanate from sources not automatically available to any other person who enters a communicative field: 'Public and private cues may be verbal or non-verbal in form, but the critical quality is that they were brought into existence and remain beyond the control of the communicants.' The third set of cues – behavioural – are those initiated or controlled by the communicant him/herself and in response to public and private cues, coloured by the communicant's 'sensory-motor successes and failures in the past, combined with his current appetites and needs', which will establish 'his set towards the environment'.

In the second diagram, INTRAPERSONAL COMMUNICATION becomes INTERPERSONAL COMMUNICATION, with the multiplication of cues and the introduction of the message (M). Barnlund emphasizes the *transferability* of cues. Public cues can be transformed into private ones, private cues may be converted into public ones, while environmental and behavioural cues may merge. In short, the whole process is one of *transaction*, and few models have explored so impressively the inner dynamics of this process as Barnlund's, which also has useful application to the dynamics of mass communication. See *TOPIC GUIDE* under COMMUNICATION MODELS.

Barrier signals Used as personal defence mechanisms in communication situations, gestures such as the placing of hands and arms across the body, or folding the arms across the chest. According to Allan and Barbara Pease in *The Definitive Book of Body Language* (Orion Books, 2005) the 'Crossed-Arms-on-Chest' posture 'is universal and is decoded with the same defensive or negative meaning almost everywhere'.

Barriers can be formed with physical objects as well as the body. For example, as Samovar and Porter note in *Communication Between Cultures* (Wadsworth/Thomson Learning, 2004) furniture can be used as a barrier to social encounters. In the business world, the classic defensive barrier is the desk. On its role in the relationship between the executive and this modern version of the old moated castle and drawbridge, much has been written – about the size and dominance of the desk, its angle to the office door, the distance between the desk and the chair placed for those who approach the boss's territory.

Basic needs See MASLOW'S HIERARCHY OF NEEDS.

★Bass's 'double action' model of internal news flow, 1969 A development of two earlier classic models addressing the processes of media news production – WHITE'S GATEKEEPER MODEL, 1950 and MCNELLY'S MODEL OF NEWS FLOW, 1959. In his article, 'Refining the gatekeeper concept' in *Journalism Quarterly*, 46 (1969), A.Z. Bass argues that the most important 'gates' in the exercise of GATEKEEPING are located within the news organization. Bass divides the operation into a news-gathering stage and a news-processing stage.

Writers, reporters and local editors are closer to the 'raw' news, the event, than those involved

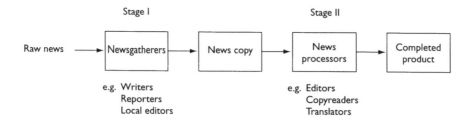

Bass's 'double action' model of internal news flow, 1969

in Stage II of the gatekeeping process, while those involved at Stage II are closer to the power centre of the organization and therefore more subject to the organization's norms and VALUES and to pressures from competing stories. See MALETZKE'S MODEL OF THE MASS COMMUNICATION PROCESS, 1963.

Baton signal Chiefly manual gestures with which we beat time to the rhythm of spoken expression and which give emphasis and urgency. They are the stock-in-trade of declamatory communication, especially that of politicians. It is not only the hands which are employed in baton signals; the head, shoulders and feet are involved too. See NON-VERBAL BEHAVIOUR: REPERTOIRE.

BBC (British Broadcasting Corporation): origins The BBC began life as the British Broadcasting Company, incorporated on 15 December 1922 and receiving its licence to broadcast on 18 January 1923. It was a private company made up chiefly of manufacturers of broadcasting equipment. The company was incorporated with 100,000 shares of stock worth £1 each. Any British wireless manufacturer could join by purchasing one or more shares, making a £50 deposit and agreeing to the terms that had been drawn up by the negotiating manufacturers and the Postmaster General.

The six largest manufacturers, in return for guaranteeing the continuing operation and financial solvency of the company, were given control. Although other manufacturers could buy stock and be admitted to membership, the principals could choose six of the company's nine directors and these in turn had the power to select its chairman. Each wireless-set owner had to pay a 10 shilling (50p) licence fee to the Post Office annually, and the government agreed to issue licences only to people using receivers made by members of the company. Thus the manufacturers were guaranteed protection against competition.

The company was to establish eight broadcasting stations in different parts of the British Isles. Only news originating from four established NEWS AGENCIES (such as the Press Association and Reuters) could be used in broadcasting and there was to be no advertising. By April 1923 the Postmaster General had appointed a seven-man investigating committee to review the status of the British Broadcasting Company, headed by Sir Frederick Sykes, with a mandate to consider 'broadcasting in all its aspects'.

The Sykes Committee faced questions on widespread evasions of the equipment monopoly and condemnation by Beaverbrook newspapers

of the control of 'the Six'. After thirty-four meetings, the Committee recommended – and the government accepted – a single receiver licence of 10 shillings to cover all types of radios, and the ban was raised on foreign receivers. Most importantly Sykes forecast the eventual replacement of private by public operation: '... We consider that the control of such a potential power [of broadcasting] over public opinion and the life of the nation ought to remain with the State, and that the operation of so important a national service ought not to be allowed to become an unrestricted commercial monopoly.'

A new committee under the chairmanship of the Earl of Crawford and Balcarres, set up in 1925, led to the Charter and Licence which created the British Broadcasting Corporation and authorized it to broadcast for ten years from 1 January 1927. It was established on three principles which were to apply to British broadcasting until the coming of commercial television: broadcasting became a monopoly, financed by licence fees and administered by an independent public corporation.

▶ Asa Briggs, *The History of Broadcasting in the United Kingdom* (Oxford University Press, vol. 1, 1961; vol. 2, 1965; vol. 3, 1970; vol. 4, 1979); Andrew Crisell, *An Introductory History of British Broadcasting* (Routledge, 1997).

BBC See BBC DIGITAL; BBC WORLDWIDE; BROADCASTING; BROADCASTING LEGISLATION; PUBLIC SERVICE BROADCASTING (PSB); RADIO BROADCASTING; REITHIAN; SELSDON COMMITTEE REPORT ON TELEVISION, 1935; TELEVISION BROADCASTING; ULLSWATER COMMITTEE REPORT ON BROADCASTING, 1936. See also *TOPIC GUIDE* under BROADCASTING.

BBC digital The UK BBC anticipated, in 2001, the eventual shift from analogue to digital transmission of TV and RADIO, with a digital supplement to BBC One, giving viewers equipped with digital sets, or set-top conversion boxes, access to a broader range of programmes, including an interactive facility, than those available to viewers with analogue sets. The same extra provision became available to viewers of BBC Two. On air shortly afterwards were the following new services: CBBC, a channel for children aged between six and thirteen; Cbeebies, for children under six; BBC Four, an in-depth culture channel; BBC News 24; and BBC Choice, aimed at a young adult audience, eventually to be retitled BBC Three (soon retreating from its youth remit) and given the go-ahead by government in September 2002.

With the collapse in 2002 of ITV Digital, a pay

service, the BBC was permitted by government to take up the shortfall in digital services, making these an impressive – and *free* – alternative to existing commercial digital channels. Switch-over for all TV channels in the UK is scheued for 2012.

Access to digital radio via the BBC has been available since 1995 on BBC Radio 1, 2, 3, 4 and Five Live. From 2002 a number of new services came on stream – BBC Five Live Sports Extra; 6Music, this being rescued from closure in 2010 by public demand; and Radio 7, initially special-izing in drama and children's programmes, and later limiting its content to the archives of Radio 4 and renamed 4 Extra. The BBC Asian Network was closed down in 2010. The longstanding BBC World Service became available in the UK digi-tally in 2002. The BBC estimated that its digital radio services would be available to 90 per cent of the UK population by 2011.

BBC: Government White Paper, 1994 The future of the BBC was guaranteed for another ten years by the White Paper, *The Future of the BBC: Serving the Nation, Competing Worldwide.* In renewing the Corporation's charter, the White Paper confirmed that the BBC would continue as the main provider of PUBLIC SERVICE BROADCASTING (PSB). It should contribute to the growth of cable and satellite services; further develop commercial TV services worldwide; continue to provide a broad spectrum of TV and radio programmes; guarantee special support for news, current affairs and educational programmes; and cover cultural and sporting activities which 'bring the nation together'. As well as recommending that more attention be given to the views of audience on matters of taste and decency, the White Paper proposed the merger of the Broadcasting Standards Council with the Broadcasting Complaints Commission, the function of the new council being to monitor standards and provide guidance. See COMMUNI-CATIONS ACT (UK), 2003.

BBC iPlayer Launched in December 2007, this is the BBC's CATCH-UP TV service. It offers both a STREAMING and a downloading of the last seven days' worth of TV programmes for INTERNET consumption.

BBC Worldwide Commercial arm of the BBC, responsible for marketing the corporation's programmes and media products worldwide; also involved in joint ventures with major opera-tors in the private sector.

BBC Written Archives In the words of Paddy Scannell, in *A Social History of British Broad-casting, Vol. 1 1922–1939: Serving the Nation* (Blackwell, 1991) by Scannell and David Cardiff, the Archives 'must surely be one of the most important historical depositories in Britain' on all aspects of British life. They are located in the grounds of the BBC Monitoring Service at Caversham Park, Reading, and contain at least 200,000 files on all aspects of broadcasting from the early 1920s to the early 1960s.

Beamwidth The angular width of a radio or radar beam.

★**Becker's mosaic model of communication, 1968** Messages are rarely single, coming along one line, so the concept of a mosaic as a model of the communication process is a useful variant on the linear theme. Samuel L. Becker in 'What rhetoric (communication theory) is relevant for contemporary speech communication?', a paper presented at the University of Minnesota Spring Symposium in Speech Communication, 1968, posed the theory of a 'communication mosaic' indicating that most communicative acts link message elements from more than the immedi-ate social situation – from early impressions, from previous conversations, from the media, from half-forgotten comments: a mosaic of source influences.

The layers of Becker's mosaic cube correspond to layers of information. Some elements of the mosaic assert themselves, others are blocked out. The model illustrates the complexity of the many layers of the communication process and the interaction between its 'cubes' or 'tesserae' of information, showing the internal as well as the external world of communication; that which is isolated or unique, that which is recurring in a dense and ever-changing pattern. See TOPIC GUIDE under COMMUNICATION MODELS.

Behavioural cues See BARNLUND'S TRANSAC-TIONAL MODELS OF COMMUNICATION, 1970.

Behavioural targeting See ADVERTISING.

Behaviourism A school of psychological thought which maintains that a scientific understanding of human behaviour can only be attained from objective, observable action. Consciousness, feeling and other subjective aspects of human behaviour are not regarded as suitable bases for investigations.

★**Berlo's SMCR model of communica-tion, 1960** David K. Berlo, who studied with Wilbur Schramm (see SCHRAMM'S MODELS OF COMMUNICATION) at the University of Illinois, produced the model opposite in his *The Process of Communication: An Introduc-tion to Theory and Practice* (Holt, Rinehart & Winston, 1960). It is a development in a sociological direction of the SHANNON AND

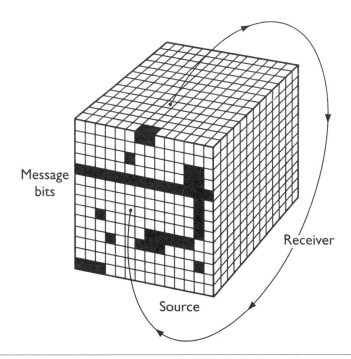

Message
bits

Receiver

Source

Becker's mosaic model of communication, 1968

WEAVER'S MODEL OF COMMUNICATION, 1949. Features of the process have been made explicit, due acknowledgment being made of the significance to both Source and Receiver of the CULTURE and the social system in which the act of communication takes place. Berlo's model does not record the *flow* of communication, though the assumption must be that it is conceived as linear – in a line from Source to Receiver. Both FEEDBACK and the interaction of elements are implied rather than made explicit.

In a successful act of communication, Berlo's model suggests, the skills of Source and Receiver must, to a considerable extent, match each other. The same may be said for attitudes or values; and knowledge must be *acknowledged*. The model rewards analysis and testing out, especially its elegant portrayal of the message. See *TOPIC GUIDE* under COMMUNICATION MODELS.

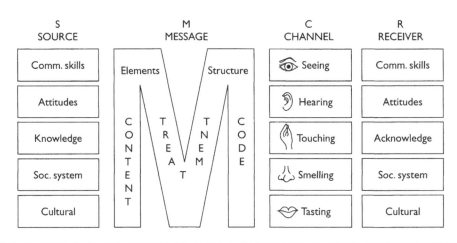

Berlo's SMCR model of communication, 1960

Berlusconi phenomenon Term used by Gianpietro Mazzoleni in 'Towards a "Videocracy"? Italian political communication at a turning point' in the *European Journal of Communication*, September 1995, to describe the remarkable entry into politics, and election to Prime Minister of Italy in March 1994, of the media mogul Silvio Berlusconi. Mazzoleni identifies a number of interconnected factors that led to Berlusconi's success in forming a political party, Forza Italia, and in less than fifty days of electioneering, displacing the traditional duopoly of political power in Italy (the Christian Democrats and the Communists).

Forza was essentially the party of commercialization and it won popularity because Berlusconi, the media man, calculated the needs of the nation's electorate-as-audience. Because of his dominant control of commercial TV in Italy, Berlusconi has been able to provide himself with the kind of 'tame press' every politician dreams of.

However, Mazzoleni is of the opinion that to attribute Berlusconi's electoral success solely to his media power is a short-sighted reading of the complexity of the Berlusconi phenomenon. Rather his message, greatly aided by the power to communicate it across the nation, 'was successful because it found several ears ready to listen to it'. Further, Berlusconi understood perhaps more clearly than any other media mogul that today's elections are not only fought out on the television screen, but are also about grabbing popular attention by combining the emotive with the entertaining.

Though Berlusconi's first premiership was short-lived – he resigned office within months – it set agendas for the future of political communication; and to prove that his electoral success was not a flash in the pan, Berlusconi was returned to office in the Italian elections of 2001, narrowly defeated in 2006 but restored to power in the election of April, 2008. His position as Prime Minister has allowed him indirect control over state broadcasting.

Berlusconi's reputation for womanizing and controversial statements seemed to do his popularity with the Italian public no harm – until Italy's Eurozone financial crisis in the autumn of 2011 forced his resignation. See TOPIC GUIDE under MEDIA: OWNERSHIP & CONTROL.

Bernstein's wheel, 1984 Refers to a model designed by David Bernstein to aid the planning of an organization's communication activities, for example public relations and associated activities. At the hub of the wheel is the organization. This in turn is located in the context of its industrial or commercial sector and its country of origin. Each of these contextual factors will, of course, have an impact on the nature of the communication activities.

The inner circle of the wheel represents the options available as regards channels of communication that may be used to reach the designated *publics*: advertising, correspondence, point of sale, public relations, personal presentation, impersonal presentation, product, literature, and placement media.

At the outer circle of the wheel are the various publics to be reached: the trade, the media, government, financial, customers, general public, internal, local, and influential groups. A message may of course be designed to reach several publics, and it may be appropriate to divide them into primary and secondary publics or audiences.

The wheel can be spun such that the inner circle can turn within the outer circle to match channels to publics. Thus the wheel can be used when planning which types of publics need to be reached and by what means. Several channels may be used to reach any one public. In *Company Image and Reality* (Holt, Rinehart and Winston, 1984) David Bernstein argues that the wheel is designed to 'stimulate some fresh thoughts and encourage the thinker to regard corporate communications as a totality rather than a series of discrete messages to discrete audiences'. He continues, 'A company needs to take a holistic view of communication because it is communicating all the time (even if it doesn't want to or doesn't realize it), to all of those nine publics.'

Beveridge Committee Report on Broadcasting, 1950 Both from a theoretical and a practical point of view, the Committee chaired by Lord Beveridge conducted the most thorough examination of broadcasting in Britain since its inception. Beveridge went to considerable lengths to identify and discuss the dangers of monopoly, as then held by the BBC. Nevertheless proposals for competitive broadcasting were rejected on the grounds that programmes would deteriorate in quality if there were rival corporations. Beveridge was equally firm in believing that broadcasting should be independent of government control, and declared against suggestions that the power of the BBC should be curbed through closer parliamentary supervision.

To prevent broadcasting becoming an uncontrolled bureaucracy, Beveridge recommended more active surveillance of output by the BBC's Board of Governors and a 'Public Representation

Service' to bridge the gap between the BBC and the general public. Additionally, the Committee proposed regional and functional devolution of some of the Corporation's activities, more comprehensive reports by the BBC on its work, and five-year reviews by small independent committees. A major recommendation which made no headway was that the monopoly of broadcasting be extended to local authorities and universities, allowing them to operate FM radio stations.

Commercial broadcasting in the US style was not approved of: 'Sponsoring ... puts the control of broadcasting ultimately in the hands of people whose interest is not broadcasting but the selling of some other goods or services or the propagation of particular ideas.' Interestingly, four of the eleven committee members (including Lord Beveridge) dissented from the majority verdict against any form of commercial advertising. See *TOPIC GUIDE* under COMMISSIONS, COMMITTEES, LEGISLATION.

Bias, biased From the French, *biais*, slant; a one-sided inclination of the mind. The student of communication approaches this term with extreme caution, for bias generally belongs to the realm of PERCEPTION, and other people's perceptions at that: like beauty, bias lies in the eye of the beholder whose vision is coloured by VALUES and previous experience. The accusation of bias tends to be predicated on the assumption that there is an opposite – OBJECTIVITY; that there is an attainable ideal called IMPARTIALITY; that freedom from bias is not only possible but desirable.

To speak, publish or broadcast without bias would imply the use of LANGUAGE which is value-free. Yet however careful we might be in what we say, we disclose something of ourselves: what shaped and formed us; what counts with us; what we value. When other people appear to call that value into question, we may be tempted to classify them as biased.

▶ Barrie Gunter, *Measuring Bias on Television* (University of Luton Press, 1997).

Bigotry An inability and/or unwillingness to consider views, beliefs, values and opinions other than the ones you already hold. The term refers to the rigid way in which an individual may hold his/her views, beliefs and so on. Bigotry is often allied with PREJUDICE. Clearly bigotry is a cause of NOISE within INTERPERSONAL COMMUNICATION. As regards the process of mass communication, one area of debate is whether or not television programmes designed to ridicule bigotry, particularly racial bigotry,

succeed in doing this among all sections of the viewing audience or have a tendency to reinforce bigotry. See RACISM.

Binary opposition See POLARIZATION; SEMANTIC DIFFERENTIAL; WEDOM, THEYDOM.

Black English See COMMUNICATION: INTERCULTURAL COMMUNICATION.

Blacklisting See HUAC: HOUSE UNAMERICAN ACTIVITIES COMMITTEE.

Biometrics The analysis of human body characteristics chiefly by technological means. Biometrics scrutinises and banks information drawn from DNA, fingerprints, earlobes, the retinas and irises of the eyes, voice patterns and signatures, the prime aim being to identify a person's unique characateristics for a range of purposes centring around verification. It is used in all aspects of security, crime prevention and general social, political, commercial and employment surveillance. See CCTV: CLOSED-CIRCUIT TELEVISION; SURVEILLANCE SOCIETY.

Blogging Derives from *weblogging*, the practice by thousands worldwide of 'diary writing' for consumption on the Internet. Fascination with other people's lives, their intimate thoughts and reflections, is only one factor explaining what draws visitors to blogging. For example, Salam Pax, recording his experiences from the heart of Baghdad during the second Iraq War (2003), provided a unique insight into the situation of an ordinary Iraqi subject to the awesome firepower of the Coalition forces of the US and UK. A woman's take on the military occupation of Iraq, *Bagdad Burning: Girl Blog from Iraq*, written under the pseudonym Riverhead, was published in 2005 in the US by the University of New York Press and in the UK by Marion Boyars. The book was a prize-winner in the LETTRE ULYSSES AWARDS for the art of reportage, 2005.

In 'Disruptive technology: Iraq and the Internet' published in *Tell Me Lies: Propaganda and Media Distortion in the Attack on Iraq* (Sage, 2004), edited by David Miller, Alistair Alexander cites blogging as a significant contributor, along with message boards and mailing lists, to the dissemination of alternative narratives to those provided by traditional mass media – such narratives serving as 'a tool for mobilizing a global protest movement on an unprecedented scale'.

'Weblogs,' says Alexander, 'provide an open-source platform for engaged individuals to challenge professional journalism on their own terms.' Indeed professional journalists are themselves writing their own weblogs, 'further blurring the lines between the traditional news

culture and the "blogosphere'" (see BLOGO-
SPHERE).

Inevitably blogging has excited the attention
of authorities anxious to curtail, if not censor
altogether, bloggers' freedom of expression. In
China, for example, the information industry
ministry ordered that by the end of June 2005 all
owners of blogs or bulletin boards would have
to be registered or shut down. Pursuit of bloggers by those in authority remains a hazardous
undertaking, considering that some 80,000
new weblogs are created every day worldwide,
though many of these are shortlived.

In her introduction to *Blogging* (Polity Press,
2010), Jill Walker Rettberg refers to blogs as
'part of the history of communication and
literacy' and deems them 'emblematic of a shift
from uni-directional mass media to participatory media, where viewers and readers become
creators of media'. See AGENDA-SETTING; ECHO
CHAMBER EFFECT; JOURNALISM: CITIZEN JOUR-
NALISM; NETWORKING: SOCIAL NETWORKING;
NETWORK NEUTRALITY; POWER LAW PHENOM-
ENON; PROJECT OF SELF; PUBLIC SPHERE;
YAROS' 'PICK' MODEL FOR MULTIMEDIA NEWS,
2009.

Blogosphere Term reflecting the exponential
growth in INTERNET blogging in the twenty-first
century. New technology has made it possible
for any computer user to set up his or her own
blog and broadcast it to either a few readers or
subscribers, a hundred of them, or a million or
more. The blogosphere resembles a firmament of
countless stars, being created, surviving a while,
then becoming eclipsed by lack of time, energy
or commitment.

In March 2007 Technorati, a search engine
tracking the blogosphere, reported over 70
million weblogs – 120,000 new ones a day – and
daily postings of 1.4 million. Blogs make incursions on the PUBLIC SPHERE, long the communicative monopoly of traditional mass media,
by news feeds, comment, analysis, protest and
propaganda, often political or cultural in orenta-
tion though more characteristically focusing on
the personal and the interactive.

The blogosphere in recent years has acquired
galactic structures as a result of the growth of
networking providers such as FACEBOOK, MYSPACE,
TWITTER and YOUTUBE, all facilitating contribution and exchange; between them commanding
the attention of the public which previously was
the preserve of newspapers, radio and TV. See
AGENDA-SETTING; DEMOTIC TURN; JOURNAL-
ISM: CITIZEN JOURNALISM; NET NEUTRALITY;
NETWORKING: SOCIAL NETWORKING.

▶ Matthew Hindman, *The Myth of Digital Democracy*
(Princeton University Press, 2009); Graeme Turner,
Ordinary People and the Media: The Demotic Turn
(Sage, 2010).

Body language See COMMUNICATION,
NON-VERBAL; GESTURE; INTERPERSONAL
COMMUNICATION; NON-VERBAL BEHAVIOUR:
REPERTOIRE; PROXEMICS; TOUCH. See also
TOPIC GUIDE under INTERPERSONAL COMMU-
NICATION.

**Body of European Regulators in Electronic
Communications (BEREC)** Association of
twenty-seven regulators of the European Union,
formed in 2009; held its inaugural meeting in
January 2010. The body succeeds the European
Regulators Group (ERG), its aim to coordinate
regulation between EU member states and
improve consistency of implementation of the
Unions' regulatory framework. See OFCOM.

Boomerang effect Term used by Gail and
Michele Myers in *The Dynamics of Human
Communication* (McGraw-Hill, 1985) to describe
a situation in which a message falls within your
latitude of rejection, that is the known views on
any given issue which you do not accept. It has
the effect of then shrinking or narrowing your
latitude of acceptance: positions on that issue
which might have been acceptable or tolerated
before will now be rejected. The authors argue
that messages which threaten your attitudes and
views may produce this effect. See LATITUDES
OF ACCEPTANCE AND REJECTION.

Boomerang response Effect of a mass media
message which, in terms of audience reaction,
proves to be the opposite of that which was
intended.

B-Picture In the 1940s and 1950s it was
cinema practice to put on two films, the main
feature – the A-Picture – and a cheaply and
quickly made supporting film – the B-Picture.
The equivalent of the 'flip-side' of a popular
record, the B-Picture, or B-movie, was
invariably Budget and almost invariably Bad.
Time, however, lends enchantment and film
enthusiasts often have a soft spot for a 'genre'
the like of which just is not made any more.
Examples are Joseph H. Lewis's *Gun Crazy*
(1949), Nathan Juran's *Attack of the 50 Foot
Woman* (1958) and Roger Corman's *Little Shop
of Horrors* (1960), which the director claimed
to have made in two days.

Brand A brand enables a company to differentiate
its products from those of its competitors – even
though there is often, arguably, little actual difference between them. Tony Yeshin in *Advertising*
(Thomson Learning, 2006) comments that 'a

brand is defined as a name, term, design, symbol or any other feature that identifies one seller's good or service as distinct from those of other sellers. A brand name may identify one item, a family of items or all items of that seller.' Brand attributes are both tangible and intangible and they have both a functional and a psychological purpose. To be successful a brand needs to have a strong, distinctive identity and personality that resonates with consumers and generates brand loyalty. Thus the process of branding a product requires a well-considered communication strategy, particularly with regard to ADVERTISING. As Yeshin argues, 'advertising exists to communicate information about and promote brands'. Examples of well-known brands include Nike, Coca Cola, McDonald's, APPLE MACINTOSH and Virgin.

▶ Celia Lury, *Brands: The Logos of the Global Economy* (Routledge, 2004); Peter Cheverton, *Understanding Brands* (Kogan Page, 2006); Laura Hill, ed., *Superbrands Annual 2011: An Insight into Some of Britain's Strongest Brands* (Superbrands, 2011).

Breakup model of audience fragmentation See AUDIENCE: FRAGMENTATION OF.

Bricolage Term derived from anthropology, referring to the construction of meaning through an improvised combination of communicative elements originating prior to their current creative use. According to John Clarke in 'Style', published in *Resistance Through Rituals: Youth Subcultures in Post-War Britain* (Hutchinson, 1976), edited by Stuart Hall and Tom Jefferson, bricolage is a 'reordering and recontextualization of objects to communicate fresh meanings'.

Perhaps the most famous 'bricoleurs' were the Surrealists, who took familiar images and objects out of their traditional contexts and rearranged them in juxtapositions that startled and initiated new discourses. As Dick Hebdige states in *Subculture: the Meaning of Style* (Methuen, 1979; reissue, Routledge, 2002), 'the teddy boy's theft and transformation of the Edwardian style revived in the early 1950s by Savile Row for wealthy young men about town can be construed as an act of bricolage'. With the advent of NEW MEDIA the term has been used to describe the nature of message-assembly, of the *recombination* of communicative elements characteristic of digital-age online interactivity. See MEDIATION.

▶ Mark Deuze, 'Participation, remediation, bricolage: Considering principal components of digital culture', *The Information Society*, 22 (2), 2006.

British Black English See COMMUNICATION: INTERCULTURAL COMMUNICATION; ETHNIC.

British Board of Film Censors (BBFC) Set up in 1912 to approve films for public showing. The right of local authorities to ban films had been granted in the Cinematography Act of 1909, and resulted in a chaos of contradictory judgments. The Cinematograph Exhibitors Association and the main production companies set up their own vetting office – the BBFC. The Board consists of a president and a secretary, both appointed by the film industry.

Like most censorship bodies, the Board lagged behind public tastes for decades and was susceptible to influence by government. Under the more liberal regime of John Trevelyan (1958–71) it acquired a new image, casting off its earlier reputation for over-cautiousness. Since then the general trend of the Board's activity has been towards greater toleration while at the same time maintaining a protective attitude towards children.

British Broadcasting Company/British Broadcasting Corporation See BBC (BRITISH BROADCASTING CORPORATION): ORIGINS.

British Film Institute (BFI) An outcome of the Report of the Commission on Educational and Cultural Films, financed chiefly by the Carnegie trustees (1929–32), the BFI was set up in 1933 to foster the use of film for educational purposes to preserve the cultural heritage of commercial film in the vaults of the National Film Library. Today the BFI's services to film in the UK are considerable. They include: the national film archive; the National Film Theatre on London's South Bank; the financing of films by British directors; widening commitments to film education; and the publication of works on cinema.

British Sky Broadcasting (BSkyB) Part of the media empire of Rupert Murdoch (see NEWS CORP), BSkyB was launched in 1990 having merged with a rival, British Satellite Broadcasting (BSB). It supplies by satellite-transmission, programmes of sporting events, films and entertainment to over ten million susbscribers in Britain and Ireland.

The organization has proved a formidable contender in the competitive market of non-PSB television provision. Its key policy features have been growth and dominance of the market. In November 2006 BSkyB bought a stake in ITV plc, heading off a bid by NTL for an ITV-NTL merger. This led to a complaint by NTL to the UK Office of Fair Trading, which took no action.

An HD (High Definition) TV service was on offer by May 2006 and 3D television broadcasting in 2010, shortly followed by the acquisition of Virgin Media Television (MVtv), renamed Living TV Group, the public hi-fi network The Cloud (in anticipation of SkyAnywhere, 2011), and – for an estimated £125m – Amstrad, manufacturer of satellite boxes. In February 2011, teaming up with HBO of America, Sky launched the Sky Atlantic channel, while pressing ahead with its ambition to convert Murdoch's 39 per cent holding of Sky into 100 per cent ownership and control. Objections to what has been widely viewed as a threat to media plurality were raised by other media and the public alike, the issue being presented first to Ofcom (see OFCOM: OFFICE OF COMMUNICATIONS, UK), which recommended that the matter be referred to the Competition Commission. Culture Secretary Jeremy Hunt declined to do this and was 'of a mind' to give Murdoch what he wanted, conditional upon safeguards. Murdoch proposed to partly offload Sky TV news under an independent chairman for a period of ten years.

A YouGov survey commissioned in March 2011 by the campaign network Avaaz found that over 60 per cent of the British public felt that Murdoch was already too powerful to be permitted total control of BSkyB. Alice Jay, Campaign Director of Avaaz, was of the opinion that 'the deal gives one man the keys to the media kingdom', adding that 'Rupert Murdoch's so-called "safeguards" of BSkyB's independence are about as reliable as a British airport in a blizzard'. It has been estimated that BSkyB's income would be twice that of the BBC by 2015.

Such a deal, which the coalition government of the UK was willing to accept, met with a widespread and hostile reception. It was described by Sly Bailey, Chief Executive of Trinity Mirror, as a 'whitewash', while according to a London *Evening Standard* editorial (3 March 2011) it did 'not smell right'. A leader headline in the *Daily Telegraph* declared it a 'body blow to the notion of a vibrant, diverse press'.

However, the Murdoch empire was shortly afterwards engulfed in a sensational phone-hacking scandal. This resulted in the dramatic closure of the chief offender, the 168-year-old *News of the World* (see JOURNALISM: PHONE-HACKING), the resignation of the Chief Executive of News International, Rebekah Brooks, and the appearance before a House of Commons Committee of Brooks, Rupert Murdoch and his son James. Temporarily at least, Murdoch's ambition to acquire BSkyB in its entirety was put on hold. See CONGLOMERATES; MURDOCH EFFECT; PLURALISM; REGULATORY FAVOURS.

Broadband High-speed electronic facility that allows for multiple informational and entertainment use – of films, computer games, music, etc. – transmitted over airwaves, copper or fibre wires to a personal computer, telephone, television or electrical appliance. Some of the most substantial advances in the use of broadband are occurring in 3G (third generation) mobile handsets. A 2005 report by Ofcom, the UK broadcasting regulator, predicted that over 99 per cent of British homes would have access to a broadband connection by the end of that year. See DIGITIZATION.

Broadcast and narrowcast codes See CODES.

Broadcasting See *TOPIC GUIDE* under BROADCASTING.

Broadcasting Act (UK), 1980 Receiving its Royal Assent on 13 November 1980, the Act extended the life of the Independent Broadcasting Authority (IBA) until the end of 1996 (see next entry); defined the Authority's responsibility for the new CHANNEL FOUR; set out special measures for the Fourth Channel in Wales, Saniel Pedwar Cymru (S4C); and contained a number of other important provisions relating to the future of broadcasting, including the establishment of a BROADCASTING COMPLAINTS COMMISSION.

Broadcasting Act (UK), 1990 Ushered-in far-reaching and controversial changes to BROADCASTING in Britain. The Act constituted a further and substantial assault on the part of government upon the traditional duopoly (BBC/IBA) of broadcasting control that had prevailed since the birth of commercial television in the UK in 1956. The Conservative government's White Paper, *Broadcasting in the '90s: Competition, Choice and Quality* was published in 1988. The *Observer* (13 November 1988) called it 'the biggest bomb put under British TV in half-a-century'.

The White Paper proposed a fifth TV channel, an expansion of Direct Satellite Broadcasting (DSB), more local TV stations, three new national radio networks and a growth in localized radio. The Act of 1990 wound up the Independent Broadcasting Authority (IBA) and replaced it with a 'light-touch' Independent Television Commission (ITC), whose most important first task was to select companies for the new commercial TV franchises to operate from 1 January 1993 (see FRANCHISES FROM 1993).

Controversy raged over the manner in which the franchises were to be allocated – through secret auction. Would-be future franchise-holders were invited to put their case for selection and make a money bid, without any idea of what a reasonable bid might be. The result was regarded in many quarters as farcical: some companies bid vast amounts; others very little.

The highest monetary bidder was not automatically selected, for there was an extra qualifier, a so-called 'Quality Threshold', though at no time were the criteria for quality ever spelt out.

Prior to the announcement of the franchises by the ITC (on 16 October 1991), existing franchise-holders had tightened their financial belts – cutting back on programme investment, laying off staff – in order to have enough cash to place a winning bid. Decisions on the future of the BBC were not dealt with in the Act.

A study by the Third World and Environmental Broadcasting Project was to report that, following the 1990 Act, significant reductions occurred in DOCUMENTARY and current affairs programmes on all terrestrial TV services in the UK. On commercial channels there was a drop of 80 per cent in documentary programmes dealing with international issues. See DEREGULATION; PUBLIC SERVICE BROADCASTING (PSB); OFCOM: OFFICE OF COMMUNICATIONS (UK); PRIVATIZATION.

Broadcasting Act (UK), 1996 A key piece of deregulatory legislation in the UK, the Act removed regulations preventing independent TV companies from owning more than two licences, opening up the field for a new round of takeovers. However, no company would be permitted to own in excess of 15 per cent of total TV output.

Newspaper companies were permitted for the first time to control TV companies, though newspapers with more than 20 per cent of national circulation were barred from owning ITV licences – a ruling directly affecting Rupert Murdoch's News International and the Mirror Group.

A central focus of the Act was the future of digital television. Proposals for the DIGITIZATION of the airways offered the prospect of many more TV channels, with the BBC being awarded its own digital TV multiplex. See BBC DIGITAL.

Broadcasting Code (UK) See OFCOM: OFFICE OF COMMUNICATIONS (UK).

Broadcasting legislation (UK) The first act of its kind in the world was the Wireless Telegraphy Act of 1904, in which the British government commanded substantial powers over the regulation of wireless telegraphy. The Act gave the Postmaster General the duty to license all wireless telegraphy apparatus. The British Broadcasting Company received its licence from the Post Office in 1923.

The TELEVISION ACT, 1954 created commercial television in the UK with the formation of the Independent Television Authority (later the Independent Broadcasting Authority). ADVERTISING was to be kept separate from programming. Requirements were laid down to govern programming content.

The Copyright Act, 1956 initiated copyright protection of broadcast material. In 1972 the Sound Broadcasting Act inaugurated commercial radio and the ITA became the IBA. The Independent Broadcasting Authority Act, 1979 empowered the IBA to create CHANNEL FOUR, while the Broadcasting Act (1980), among other regulations, created the Broadcasting Complaints Commission, later to be merged with the Broadcasting Standards Council, which in turn was absorbed into the Office of Communications – Ofcom, the 'super regulator' borne of the COMMUNICATIONS ACT (UK), 2003. In 1984 came the Video Recording Act requiring the certification of all new video releases. The Cable and Broadcasting Act of the same year set up the Cable Authority, whose task was to select operators for particular areas and to oversee organizational and programming stipulations.

Broadcasting research See AUDIENCE MEASUREMENT.

Broadsheet Traditionally most newspapers were broadsheets, the term generally referring to the large size of the page as contrasted with the tabloid. The implication is also that broadsheets are 'serious' (sometimes 'heavy') in comparison with the tabloid paper. In the UK *The Times*, the *Guardian* and the *Independent* remain 'broadsheets', even though they have become tabloid in size, because they are seen as 'quality' papers for 'discerning' readers. Only the *Daily Telegraph* has persisted with the broadsheet size. Tabloid dailies such as the *Sun*, *Daily Mirror* and *Daily Star* are also referred to as the Red Tops. See TABLOID, TABLOIDESE, TABLOIDIZATION.

BSkyB See British Sky Broadcasting (BSkyB).

Butler Report (UK), 2004 Lord Butler was appointed to scrutinize, and report on, the intelligence made available to the British government concerning Iraq's alleged weapons of mass destruction (WMDs), the threat of which was deemed justification for military invasion of the country by the US and UK in 2003, and the overthrow of the incumbent president of Iraq, Saddam Hussein.

Reporting in the knowledge that Iraq's WMDs were never found, Butler judged that the government's September 2002 key dossier 'did not make clear that the intelligence underlying these conclusions was very thin ... How grave a fault that was in the context of the lead up to war is,' Butler believed, 'a matter on which people will and should reach their own conclusions. But we regard it as a serious weakness, a weakness which subsequently came home to roost as the conclusion about deployable stocks of chemical and biological weapons have turned out to be wrong'.

In other words, Britain went to war on inadequate and unreliable information against a threat that did not exist. The Report is scathing about a 'high proportion' of unreliable sources of information; the inadequate way in which MI6 verified its sources; reliance on third-hand reporting; and the 'seriously flawed' information provided by external agencies.

However, Lord Butler drew back from apportioning blame; indeed he seemed to be saying that nobody was culpable, a judgment that prompted amazement in many quarters, though as one commentator put it, the public was served up a 'typical English compromise': things were badly wrong, but not by deliberate intention. The conclusion was taken by New Labour government as exoneration.

Shortly after the publication of the Butler Report, John Scarlett, the head of Joint Intelligence Services which had been so robustly criticized, was appointed by Prime Minister Tony Blair to become the new head of the Secret Intelligence Service. See CONSENT, MANUFACTURE OF; DISINFORMATION; FREEDOM OF INFORMATION ACT (UK), 2005; HUTTON REPORT (UK), 2004; PHILLIS REVIEW OF GOVERNMENT COMMUNICATIONS (UK), 2004.

By-line Use of the journalist's/author's name on a report or article. These are very common now in the PRESS, but at one time the granting of by-lines was a rare honour, to distinguish top writers or as a reward for outstanding reportage.

C

Cable and Broadcasting Act (UK), 1984 Drawn up by the Conservative government with the intention of facilitating the 'cabled society', the Act followed most of the recommendations of the HUNT COMMITTEE REPORT ON CABLE EXPANSION AND BROADCASTING POLICY (UK), 1982, which proposed a cable network for Britain with the minimum of rules and regulations. The Act set up a Cable Authority to select cable operators for particular areas and to maintain an overview on general matters of organization and programming.

Cable television Below-ground cable networks were established in the 1930s in the UK to relay radio broadcasts. These were later adapted to transmit TV to areas which received poor 'off-air' signals. Reception problems were also the reason for the US 'cabling up' in the 1950s. Until the election of the Conservative government in 1979, the commercial potential of cable in developing information technology had stimulated only modest interest. In March 1982 the Tory Cabinet's Information Technology Advisory Panel (ITAP), appointed in July 1981, recommended a rapid and substantial expansion of cable networks, to be established and operated by private companies.

The Hunt Report (see HUNT COMMITTEE REPORT ON CABLE EXPANSION AND BROADCASTING POLICY (UK), 1982) also urged the 'wiring up' of the nation, with a minimum of rules and regulations. Today cable networks compete in broadcasting and INTERNET services with satellite transmission, often carrying the same TV programmes. In the UK, examples of cable TV providers are Challenge, Dave and G.O.L.D., the dominant provider being Virgin Media. In the US the best-known cable services are ESPN, HBO, USA Network and Nickelodeon. See FIBRE-OPTIC TECHNOLOGY.

Cahiers du Cinéma French film magazine founded by Andre Bazin in 1951; associated with, and very often written by, the Nouvelle Vague, or New Wave directors such as Claude Chabrol and François Truffaut. The young critics of *Cahiers* reacted against the current ideological conservatism in the film world – against its reluctance to face up to or to express the facts of contemporary life.

Calcutt Committee Reports on Privacy and Related Matters, 1990 and 1993 Lawyer and Master of Magdalene College, Cambridge, David Calcutt was the government-appointed chairman in 1990 of a committee set up to examine British PRESS intrusions into personal privacy, after complaints from many quarters. Calcutt's chief recommendation was the creation of a non-statutory PRESS COMPLAINTS COMMISSION. The tenor of Calcutt's first report was a warning to the newspaper industry – either set your own house in order, or it will be done for you by government legislation.

Subsequent high-profile press 'intrusions' into the 'private' lives of the Royal family and of government ministers – stories that incidentally proved very popular with the newspaper-buying public – decided Calcutt that the voluntary route to better press behaviour had not worked. Calcutt's 1993 report, a solo effort, was greeted by Lord McGregor, Chairman of the Press Complaints Commission, child of Calcutt Mk

1, as potentially 'a disaster for democracy' and 'direct censorship for the first time in 300 years'.

Calcutt recommended: (1) A statutory code of practice for journalists and other press practitioners; (2) A press complaints tribunal comprising a judge and two lay assessors appointed by the Lord Chancellor; (3) New criminal offences to cover invasion of privacy, including bugging and the use of telephoto lenses. His report was was highly critical of the performance of the Press Complaints Council, which had not been constituted, or evolved, in line with his 1990 recommendations. He dismissed the PCC as an ineffective regulator, too much in the hands of the newspaper owners.

The first government response to Calcutt Mk 2 was cool towards statutory enforcement through recommendations (1) and (2), but more persuaded concerning Calcutt's third recommendation – although not sufficiently persuaded to take any legislative action. Two decades later, the situation remained as it was when Calcutt made his reports. See DEFAMATION; JOURNALISM: PHONE-HACKING. See also *TOPIC GUIDE* under COMMISSIONS, COMMITTEES, LEGISLATION.

Camera The first photographic camera on sale to the public was produced by London optician Francis West, for 'Photogenic Drawing' (1839). In the same year Baron Saguier introduced a lightweight bellows camera with three 'firsts' in equipment – a darkroom tent, a photographic tripod and a ball-and-socket head. Binocular-type cameras were introduced as early as 1853, by John Benjamin Dancer of Manchester. In 1858 Thomas Skaife introduced his 'Pistolgraph': a spring shutter worked by rubber bands was released by a trigger. He once aimed his Pistolgraph at Queen Victoria and was nearly arrested for an attempt on her life. 1880 saw the first twin-reflex camera, a quarter plate with a roller-blind shutter attached to the taking lens, made by R. & J. Beck of London.

George Eastman produced the first camera incorporating roll-film, calling it the Kodak (1888). The simplicity of this camera ('Pull the string – turn the key – press the button') made mass photography possible, especially as Eastman recommended the return of the camera to the factory for development and printing. Miniature cameras, as scientific precision instruments, were produced from 1924 (the Ermanox made by the Ernemann Works of Dresden).

In 1912 George P. Smith of Missouri produced a 35mm camera taking one by one-and-a-half inch pictures on cine-film which was being mass-produced at the time. The prototype of the Leica was constructed by Oskar Barnack in 1914; Rolleiflex was put on the market by Franke and Heidecke Braunschweig in 1947, and Voigt-lander's zoom lens was introduced in 1959.

In the 1960s and 1970s the application of electronics revolutionized camera and lens design. The silicon chip allowed amazing feats of miniaturization. In 1963 Eastman Kodak introduced the 126 'instant loading' cartridge, a modernization of an old idea going back to the Expo Watch camera of 1905. In 1972 they produced the pocket 110, an ultraminiature cartridge-load camera. Polaroid, in the same year, launched the SX-70 instant photo system, which abandoned the method whereby a protective covering had to be peeled off the print; with SX-70, the photo image develops automatically in the light, protected by a plastic coating.

1976 saw Canon introduce its famous AE-1, a fully automatic SLR camera incorporating very advanced digital electronic technology, produced by automated methods. In the early 1980s Kodak launched its disc-camera. Three-dimensional (3D) cameras also came on to the market at this time. An offshoot of the 35mm camera is the Advanced Photo System (APS) offering smaller, lighter cameras in which 35mm film is inserted into the camera in cassette form.

DIGITIZATION – for popular rather than professional use – made film redundant. Picture storage and transmission online soon became commonplace, as was still picture-making and video combined in the same camera. Mobile phones quickly became cameras, their pictures capable of being sent as swiftly as voice messages and text. Current developments focus on improving high-speed image resolution for scientific and popular use.

The availability of digital cameras at moderate cost has made possible the arrival of citizen journalism (see JOURNALISM: CITIZEN JOURNALISM), where members of the public record events, often in advance of the professionals, and swiftly transmit news pictures to the media. See HIGH-SPEED PHOTOGRAPHY; PHOTOGRAPHY, ORIGINS.

Camera obscura Latin for 'dark chamber'; an early means of projecting an image – a box or room with a lens at one end and at the other a reflector which throws an external image upon a screen or table. Antonio Canaletto (1697–1768) used the camera obscura to considerable effect in his paintings of Venice, though the device was referred to as early as Aristotle (384–322 BC).

It was French army officer Joseph Nicéphore

Nièpce (1765–1833) in 1826 who first exposed a metal plate coated with a layer of bitumen to the image in a camera obscura. The light hardened the bitumen, which was washed away to reveal the fixed image. Photography, or as Nièpce termed it, 'Heliography' – sun drawing – was born.

Where the camera obscura possessed a reflector, the camera lucida had a prism. When placed in front of an artist's eye the prism projects image onto paper, thus allowing accurate copying.

Campaign This term is most often used in the media-studies context to refer to a conscious, structured and coordinated attempt at persuasion. The goals of such persuasion are varied. ADVERTISING campaigns for example aim to change people's choice of product or to persuade them to buy new products.

Election campaigns aim to reinforce or change people's voting behaviour. PRESSURE GROUPS use campaigns to alert the public to a particular issue, to influence the public's opinion on that issue, and to mobilize support and pressurize those in power to take some desired action. Access to the mass media is often crucial for a pressure group's successful campaign. Media personnel may also initiate campaigns to raise their audience's awareness of certain issues – child abuse, for example. Indeed such campaigns can be seen as part of the mass media's AGENDA-SETTING role. One focus for media research has been the measurement of how effective campaigns are.

Campaign for Press and Broadcasting Freedom UK organization founded by John Jennings in 1979 as a broad-based non-political party pressure group dedicated to making Britain's media more open, diverse and accountable. It is a stalwart supporter of PUBLIC SERVICE BROADCASTING (PSB). The Campaign publishes a bi-monhly bulletin, *Free Press*.

Campaigning See ONLINE CAMPAIGNING.

Captive audience advertising See ADVERTISING: AMBIENT ADVERTISING.

Cards See CIGARETTE CARDS; PICTURE POSTCARDS.

Caricature A distorted REPRESENTATION of a person, type or action. Though we generally associate caricature with humorous cartoons, the process of distortion has played an important role in art. Known to the Egyptians and Greeks, caricature was revived by Italian artists of the Renaissance and developed throughout Europe in the eighteenth century. In England artists such as Rowlandson (1756–1827) combined high-quality draughtsmanship with trenchant social and political satire. Though the best known, *Punch* was only one among many magazines carrying cartoons in the nineteenth century. In England, *Vanity Fair* (founded 1868) proved a rival. In the US, *Puck* (1876), in France, *Le Rire* (1894) and in Germany, *Simplicissimus* (1896) made the cartoon the most impactful form of printed illustration prior to the regular use of photography. Best known of all US magazines carrying cartoons, the *New Yorker*, was founded in 1925.

Cartoons In fine art, a cartoon is the final preparatory drawing for a large-scale painting, tapestry or mosaic. The Leonardo cartoon in the National Gallery, London, is a notable example – ready for final working, but never completed by the artist. In modern terms, the cartoon is a humorous illustration or strip of illustrations. In 1841 a series of fine-art cartoons was designed for paintings in the new Houses of Parliament in London. The satirical magazine *Punch*, founded in that year, poked fun at the drawings, with sketches entitled 'Punch's Cartoons'.

According to Alan Coren in his foreword to W. Hewison's *The Cartoon Connection* (Elm Tree Books, 1977), cartoons were born 'in the far Aurignacian days of 20,000 BC', when 'a squat, hirsute, browless man one morning dipped his stick in a dark rooty liquid, bent straight again, and, on the cave-wall of Lascaux, drew a joke about men running after buffalo'.

Hewison calls the cartoon 'drawn humour' and lists the following cartoon categories: (1) Recognition humour (where the viewer recognizes the workings of human nature); (2) Social comment (very often Recognition humour with a message); (3) Visual puns; (4) Zany (or screw-ball); (5) Black humour (or sick, or in bad taste); (6) Geometric (where, for example, lines are made to fall in love with dots); (7) Faux Naïf (pretended naïvety) – 'When an ideas man can draw but cannot develop a satisfactory comic style of cartoon drawing, he quite often throws in the towel and adopts a deliberately childlike style'; and (8) the Strip cartoon, the originator of which was Wilhelm Busch (1832–1904).

On the screen, Walt Disney has dominated the field of the *animated cartoon* but there have been many others: Paul Terry's *Terrytoons*, Pat Sullivan's *Felix the Cat*, Tex Avery's *Chilly Willy*, the endlessly warring Tom and Jerry created by William Hanna, Joe Barbera and Fred Quimby, along with countless others such as *Top Cat*, *Scooby Doo* and the *Flintstones*, Walter Lantz's *Woody Woodpecker* and Terry Gilliam's *Monty Python's Flying Circus*.

Among those artists who have attempted to push the cartoon on film in an innovative direction are the Hungarian John Halas and his wife Joy Batchelor, Richard Williams and Bob Godfrey. In recent years Matt Groening's *The Simpsons* has become arguably the world's most watched TV cartoon. Today's TV and movie cartoons have vastly benefited from advances in computer-generated imaging.

Catch-up TV See TELEVISION: CATCH-UP TV.

Catalyst effect Where a book, newspaper, film, TV or RADIO programme has the effect of modifying a situation, or taking a mediating role. The actual presence of TV cameras may, it is believed, influence the course of events. The debate continues as to whether such effects are substantial or marginal, for reliable proof is hard to come by. See MEDIATION.

Catharsis From the Greek, 'purging', catharsis is the effect upon an audience of tragedy in drama or the novel. The Greek philosopher Aristotle perceived the function of great tragedy to be the release of pent-up emotions in the audience. As a consequence, the mind is cleansed and purified. The so-termed *catharsis hypothesis* suggests that violence and aggression on films and TV has a therapeutic effect. Exponents of this idea argue that the involvement in fantasy aggression may serve as a form of displacement, providing a harmless 'release' from hostile impulses which might otherwise be acted out. See EFFECTS OF THE MASS MEDIA.

CCTV: Closed-circuit television One of the key means of public and private surveillance (see SURVEILLANCE SOCIETY). Used in public locations in the UK as early as the coronation of Queen Elizabeth II, in 1953, and as a permanent fixture in London from the 1960s. By 2006 it was estimated that there were in excess of four million CCTV cameras operative in Britain, one for every fourteen citizens. That figure has increased substantially, to the point where the British people are considered not only the most 'watched' people in Europe, but, differences in population being taken in to account, camera surveillance outstrips that in the US. In urban areas a person can expect to be captured on camera some 300 times a day. See BIOMETRICS; ECHELON; REGULATION OF INVESTIGATORY POWERS ACT (RIPA)(UK), 2000.

Ceefax Trade name of the teletext service offered by the BBC since September 1974, giving viewers access to information on a wide range of services. The commercial television equivalent is Oracle.

Celebrity See CULTURE: POPULAR CULTURE; DEMOTIC TURN; JOURNALISM: CELEBRITY JOURNALISM; REALITY TV; REINFORCEMENT.

Cellular radio Comprises RADIO frequencies divided up into 'cells' of air waves facilitating, in particular, personal communications systems. For example, anyone operating a car telephone will be switched automatically from one radio frequency to another as the operator passes through the air-wave cells. See MEDIA TECHNOLOGY.

Censorship Pre-emptive censorship is censorship before the event; punitive, after the event. They often work in tandem: one punishment serves as a warning to others. Censorship involves the curtailment, usually by or on behalf of those in authority, of the major freedoms – of belief, expression, movement, assembly and access to information. The most common form of censorship is that applied by the self: a thing is not expressed because of the risk of external censorship – from the law, from organizations and institutions, from PRESSURE GROUPS. Thus we have censorship by omission or evasion.

Few if any communities tolerate completely free expression. In the UK, for example, laws of DEFAMATION exist to protect persons against acts of communication which may offend or injure them, or their reputation in the community. Equally protective are restrictions upon material transmitted to children (see CERTIFICATION OF FILMS). Such forms of censorship meet with general approval, but they represent only the tip of a large legal iceberg.

The UK's Official Secrets Act is one of the most far-reaching weapons of legal censorship ever devised. The Act (or Acts, 1911–91) makes it an offence for anyone to obtain and communicate documents and information that could be harmful to the safety and interest of the State.

In addition, the State protects a commonality of interests with a wide range of laws. The UK's Public Order Act of 1936 restricted the way we behave, or what we say, in public. If an individual uses threatening or insulting words, likely to cause a breach of the peace, this is a punishable offence. The common-law offence of Sedition, of long standing, protects the sovereign, the government and its institutions from individuals or groups causing intentional discontent and hatred, while the Incitement to Disaffection Act of 1934 made it an offence to try to persuade a member of the armed forces to an act of disloyalty. Equally, the Police Act of 1964 made it an offence to promote unfaithfulness by a police officer towards his duties.

It remains an offence to issue a Blasphemy

– this is, to speak or communicate in writing, etc. matters which may cause hatred, contempt, insult or ridicule against the Church. It is a rarely used law, but a law's potency lies in its existence – in the knowledge that it can always be used when free speech appears to be getting out of hand. One of the first pieces of legislation brought in by the New Labour government after its re-election in 2005 was the Incitement to Religious Hatred Act, outlawing comments made in public or in the media as well as written material likely to incite religious hatred. Critics expressed grave concern that the new legislation would stifle free comment and debate.

Obscenity too has occupied the minds of lawmakers. Since the seventeenth century, certain types of indecent expression or behaviour have been subject to punishment by the law. Material considered likely to 'deprave and corrupt' has often been subject to punitive legal censorship (see OZ TRIAL). Defining what is obscene and what is liable to deprave and corrupt has proved immensely difficult.

The targets of censorship tend to be those actions or expressions which appear to endanger, by subversion, ridicule, defiance or just plain disrespect, the VALUES and value systems of the dominant hierarchy of society – its establishment. In the UK, 'sacred cows' have been the Monarchy, the Church, Nationality, the Family, Defence, each a symbol in some way or other of law and order; of control. Censorship is a weapon to counter the ever-present threat – real or imagined – of social, and therefore political, destabilization.

The INTERNET has become the most significant and controversial domain attracting censorship. In its early days perceived as free of controls by those in authority, the Net has, in many countries, been reined in by legislation designed to facilitate surveillance (see SURVEILLANCE SOCIETY).

Even so, exercising Net censorship presents immense challenges simply because of the ease and speed with which information can be transmitted, between a few users, thousands or millions. Recently the chief driving force of government censorship has been the so-termed 'war on terror' following the events in the US of 9/11 (the terrorist destruction of New York's Twin Towers and the attack on the Pentagon) and the terrorist bombings in London in July 2005, both prompting legislation aimed at increasing national security, but with serious implications for free speech (see USA – PATRIOT ACT, 2001; RACIAL AND RELIGIOUS HATRED LEGISLATION,

UK). Multicultural societies such as Britain are having to learn how to cope with religious 'certitudes', whether Christian, Moslem or Sikh; and writers, artists, film-makers and broadcasters are having to steer a course between freedom to express (and thus criticize) and the rights of others to protect what they deem sacred. See ANTICIPATORY COMPLIANCE; BLOGGING; CCTV: CLOSED-CIRCUIT TELEVISION; COMMERCIAL CONFIDENTIALITY; DEFAMATION; DIGITAL ECONOMY ACT UK (2010); GENRE; 'LIBEL TOURISM'; JOURNALISM: PHONE-HACKING; PRIVACY; REGULATION OF INVESTIGATORY POWERS ACT (RIPA) (UK), 2000; TERRORISM: ANTI-TERRORISM, CRIME AND SECURITY ACT (UK), 2001. See also TOPIC GUIDE under MEDIA: FREEDOM, CENSORSHIP.

▶ Julian Petley, *Censorship: A Beginner's Guide* (One World, 2010); Mickey Huff, Peter Phillips and Project Censored, *Censored 2011: Top Stories 2009–10* (Seven Stories Press, 2010); Brian Winston, *A Right to Offend: Free Expression in the Twenty-first Century* (Bloomsbury Academic, 2011); *Index on Censorship* (published quarterly).

★**Centrality** Within the communication structure of any social group, some members will derive certain advantages or disadvantages resulting from their position in that structure; in particular, from the FREQUENCY with which they communicate with other members of the group. By using a sociogram such as that illustrated opposite, the *centrality* of a person within the communication structure can be measured: the sociogram indicates that D's centrality index is highest; it is arrived at by taking the total number of communication links between group members and then dividing that by the total number of such links between one member and the other members of the group. In the diagram, D's centrality may arise because of his/her status, role, articulacy, personality, etc.

The concept of a centrality index enables observers to estimate quantitatively the degree of influence members of the group may have by virtue of their position in the group. The more central a member is in a communication network, the sooner he/she will be in possession of all the information at the disposal of the group. Influence is closely related to possession of information, because the possessor has the power to choose what information to pass on, and to whom. Communication networks differ in the degree of centrality and the number of levels of centrality possible within them.

However, more information would be needed other than that provided by a sociogram alone

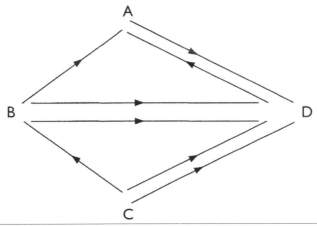

C

Example of a sociogram

in order to ascertain the precise role that D is playing in the sociogram illustrated; in particular, information would be needed about the content of the communication and of the pattern of interaction over time. It may be that D is not normally that central to the group's communication, and that when this sociogram was drawn he/she was playing a 'blocking' role in the group and receiving criticism. See INTERACTION PROCESS ANALYSIS.

Centres for research into the media See RESEARCH CENTRES (INTO THE MEDIA).

Certification of films (UK) For several years until December 1982, the BRITISH BOARD OF FILM CENSORS had the following system of certification: X, denoting films with high sex and violence content or other disturbing subject-matter which those under 18 were not permitted to see in cinemas; AA films, from which children under 14 were barred; A films, to which children were admitted if accompanied by an adult; and U-certificate films admitting all.

These were replaced in 1982 with: 18 (permitting admission for those aged 18 and over); 15 (replacing AA, and raising the admission age from 14 to 15); PG (Parental Guidance, a symbol used in the US, and intended to show that a film contains some scenes which individual parents may feel unsuitable for children); and U as before. A 12 certificate was introduced in 1989, mainly to target the first film in the *Batman* series.

In August 2002 the British Board of Film Classification, under pressure from a number of sources, including that of parents and children, made an adjustment to the 12 certification by adding a 12A rating, meaning that children could

see formerly restricted films – such as *Spider-Man* – as long as they were accompanied by an adult over 18.

The 12A certificate marked the arrival of former civil servant Sir Quentin Thomas as chief censor. It brought Britain into line with other countries, including the US, Canada, Japan, Ireland, New Zealand and Spain. The first film to carry a UK 12A certificate was *The Bourne Identity* starring Matt Damon. 12A certification requires that posters advertising such films should carry warnings about scenes involving violence, sex and bad language. The 12 rating remains for film videos. See H-CERTIFICATE.

Chamberlain, Lord See LORD CHAMBERLAIN.

Channel Each MESSAGE-carrying signal requires a route along which it is transmitted from the sender to the receiver and along which FEEDBACK may be obtained. Channels may be physical (our voices or bodies), technical (the telephone) or social (our schools, media, etc.). In business organizations or institutions they may be vertical, hierarchical, formal and predominantly one-way – from the boss downwards; or horizontal, democratic, informal and two-way as between workmates and groups with common tasks, interests and sympathies. Like country paths, channels need to be kept open and frequented – and sometimes repaired – if they are to continue to be recognized as viable. See COSMOPOLITE AND LOCALITE CHANNELS; JAKOBSON'S MODEL OF COMMUNICATION, 1958; PHATIC (LANGUAGE); SHANNON AND WEAVER'S MODEL OF COMMUNICATION, 1949.

Channel capacity C.E. Shannon and W.E. Weaver use this term to describe the upper limit of information that any communication system can handle at a given time. To discover this limit, it is first essential to know how much uncertainty – or *entropy* – a given signal will eliminate. See REDUNDANCY.

Channel 4 (UK) Under the direction of Jeremy Isaacs, in 1982, C4 became the UK's fourth TV channel; the 'quality' arm of commercial television. Jean Seaton argued in James Curran and Jean Seaton's *Power without Responsibility* (Routledge, 1997) that Channel 4 was '... an important (and perhaps the last) reinterpretation of the public service role of broadcasting. In this version, the freedom of creative individuals to risk making the programmes they want to make is seen as the guarantor of public good.'

Seaton identifies a number of reasons for the establishment of Channel 4: the need for television fare to better reflect Britain's growing cultural diversity; the need to widen the terms of political debate on television; the need to foster greater creativity in programme-making; and the need to address the requirements of niche or minority audiences. In addition there was also the desire of the then Conservative government to subject the DUOPOLY to the influence of market forces. The adoption by Channel 4 of the publisher–contractor model for programme-making, and the subsequent boost to the independent production sector, was one of the ways it was hoped that these needs would be met.

The new organization quickly became a major sponsor of independently made movies, drama series and documentaries. From the start the channel set out to challenge established ways and attitudes. Much of its programming was international in theme, whether the subject was poverty in the Third World or American football. The new channel proved the argument for *broad*casting – mixing popular viewing with minority-interest programmes and showing that the entertaining could be combined with the serious without sacrificing standards.

C4 became the first channel to provide a full hour of news daily. It was to create a high reputation for the funding of feature films, some of which, like *Four Weddings and a Funeral* (1994), proved worldwide cinema successes. The BROADCASTING ACT, 1990 cleared the way for C4 to negotiate directly its own advertising revenue. The Welsh fourth channel is called Saniel Pedwar Cymru (S4C). See COMMUNICATIONS ACT (UK), 2003; OFCOM: OFFICE OF COMMUNICATIONS (UK).

Channel 5 (UK) The Independent Television Commission of the UK awarded Britain's fifth national terrestrial TV channel to Channel 5

Broadcasting in October 1995. It began broadcasting in January 1997.

Chapultepec, Declaration of, 1994 Adopted on 11 March in Mexico City by the Hemisphere Conference on Free Speech, organized by the Inter American Press Association (IAPA), the Declaration states that 'A free press enables societies to resolve their conflicts, promote their well-being and protect their liberty.' The defence of the freedom of the press is absolute and unqualified: 'No law or act of government may limit freedom of expression or of the press, whatever the medium.' Chapultepec rejects prior CENSORSHIP (Clause 5), the imposition of licences for the importation of paper, newsgathering equipment and the assigning of RADIO frequencies (Clause 7), and asserts that no news medium or journalist may be punished for publishing the truth or for criticizing or denouncing government (Clause 10). See TALLOIRES DECLARATION.

Characteristics of mass communications See MASS COMMUNICATION: SEVEN CHARACTERISTICS.

Chequebook journalism A euphemism for bribery – newspapers paying someone for exclusive rights on his or her story. The police pay their 'snouts' or 'grasses' for the common good; the press pay their informants for tomorrow's headline, to serve the public's 'right to know' and to boost sales in the war for circulation. While the UK Bribery Act (2010) which came into force in July 2011 is primarily targeted at the worlds of business, commerce and industry, it applies equally to the media, covering both individual and organizational behaviour.

Chronology News narratives on TV are often compared to those of fictional stories (see STORYNESS) but there are obvious differences, an important one being divergence over chronology. 'In news,' writes Allan Bell in *The Language of News Media* (Blackwell, 1991), 'order is everything but chronology is nothing.' Indeed, in the news narrative the climax is reported first, whereas in a story this usually comes at the end. Chronology has a low priority in the construction of news stories to the point where AUDIENCE has to be highly news-literate to follow what is going on. Bell says, 'The time structure of news stories can make the shape of a difficult film or novel look straightforward in comparison.' See AGENDA-SETTING.

Churnalism When JOURNALISM is subjected to demands for more and faster news content in an era of 24-hour media provision and demand, it is in danger of 'churning' out copy, text and pictures; then it becomes *churnalism*. Pressures of competition and commercialization result in corner-cutting, facts not checked-out thoroughly, dependence on single rather than a variety of sources and over-readiness to opt for sensation over verifiable truth.

In *Flat Earth News: An Award-winning Reporter Exposes Falsehood, Distortion and Propaganda in the Global Media* (Vintage Books, 2009), Nick Davies writes that pressures on modern journalists are such that 'only 12% of their stories turn out to be their own work; and only 12% of their key facts are effectively checked'.

Davies believes that the 'problems of churnalism have become even worse with the arrival of news websites involving reportage whose prime principle is speed imposed on reporters for the press and TV alike', the majority activity being recycling second-hand stories. He writes of 'the tendency for the media to recycle ignorance', producing what he terms 'flat earth' stories – news stoked up by conjecture and headline-seeking but with questionable, or no, substance.

The author cites as a flat earth story the wild predictions concerning the Millennium Bug which, according to media predictions, would cause catastrophic mayhem as computers adjusted from 1999 to 2000. As it turned out, nothing could have been smoother; a transition without fuss. Blame is laid at 'the behaviour of the new corporate owners of the media who have cut editorial staffing while increasing editorial output, slashing the old supply lines which used to feed up raw information from the ground; and, with the advent of news websites, added the new imperative of speed'. See the Media Standards Trust website churnalism.com, created to track and publicize cases of churnalism and to expose PLAGIARISM.

Cigarette cards: cultural indicators A US company, Allen Ginter, produced the forerunner of the first British cigarette card when they packed with their Richmond Gem brand a pair of oval cards held together by a stud, one section of which was a calendar for 1884, with UK parcel postage rates on the back. By the 1890s the larger British tobacco companies were issuing cards, beginning with advertisements then progressing to series on particular themes such as soldiers, ships, royalty, sport and famous beauties.

The first company to issue photographic cigarette cards on a large scale was Ogdens who, in 1894, began their Guinea Gold and Tabs cards covering, in the next thirteen years, practically every facet of life of that period. In the early 1900s there were around fifty companies issuing cards in the UK and Ireland. Reflecting the dominance of the British Empire, the cards represented many military issues, along with major inventions of the time – the motor car and the aeroplane. Exploration and discovery, and the Edwardian craze for collecting things – birds' eggs, butterflies, porcelain – were prominently reflected in the choice of subject-matter, as were the music hall and the scouting movement.

Early in the First World War (1914–18) the Wills company actually issued cards as miniature recruiting posters, while Gallahers put out several series of Victoria Cross Heroes in 1915 and 1916. Carreras issued Women on War Work and Raemaekers' War Cartoons portraying the Germans as barbarians.

Later examples of these cultural ephemera were Gallahers' *Boy Scouts*, *Fables and Their Morals*; Wills's *Cinema Stars* and *Radio Celebrities*. Ogdens produced a series on *Broadcasting*. With the approach of the Second World War (1939–45) Carreras produced *Britain's Defences* (1938); Players issued *Aircraft of the RAF* in the same year, and in 1939, *Modern Naval Craft*. The most ambitious cigarette-card enterprise of the period was the Imperial Tobacco Company's *Air Raid Precautions*, made available in a variety of cigarette brands.

Cigarette-card production remained popular in the post-war era, though the 1960s saw a marked decline. In the 1970s came the much sought-after series from Player, *The Golden Age of Motoring*, packed in Doncella cigars. The Golden Age continued with *Steam* (1976), *Flying* (1977) and *Sail* (1978). See PICTURE POSTCARDS.

Cine-clubs These played an important role in the development of cinema in many countries. Where, in the commercial film theatres, popular entertainment monopolized programmes, the cine-clubs showed new experimental and often non-fictional work. John Grierson (1898–1972) organized the first British showing of Sergei Eisenstein's *Battleship Potemkin* at the London Film Society (formed in 1925) in 1929, along with his own seminal documentary *Drifters*. Minister of Propaganda in Nazi Germany, Goebbels, outlawed all cine-clubs because of their 'subversive' nature and a similar fate befell the cine-club movement in pre-Second World War Japan.

The Depression and the failure of the media to meet its causes head-on helped give belated birth to the US cine-club movement. The Workers' Film and Photo League, soon renamed the National Film and Photo League, was formed in New York in 1930. Members of the League made films as well as watched them, concentrating on filming the hunger marches and other mass protests of the time. Among their creations was a Workers' Newsreel, which the League persuaded some commercial cinemas to screen.

Cinema See CINEMATOGRAPHY, ORIGINS; FILM.

Cinema legislation The first legislation in the UK relating to cinema use was the Cinematograph Act of 1909. It concerned the licensing of exhibition premises and the safety of audiences. In 1922, the Celluloid and Cinematograph Film Act drew up safety rules for premises where raw celluloid or cinematograph film was stored and used. The Cinematograph Film Production (Special Loans) Act, 1949 established the National Film Finance Corporation and in the same year came the British Film Institute Act.

The Cinematograph Films Act, 1957 provided a statutory levy on exhibitors and exhibitions to be collected by Customs and Excise and paid to the British Film Fund Agency, which would use the monies to support film production in the UK and the work of the Children's Film Foundation. This made the formerly voluntary levy, the British Film Production Fund, compulsory. The Cinematograph (Amendment) Acts of 1982 extended provision of the 1909 Act to include 'all exhibitions of moving pictures for private gain', bringing under regulation pornographic cinema and video 'clubs'. The Acts exclude from regulation bona fide film societies.

The Films Act, 1985 abolished the Cinematograph Films Council and the Eady Levy, and dissolved the National Film Finance Corporation, replacing it with the British Screen Finance Consortium. The government provided a 'starter' of £1.5m for five years to the loan fund of the BSFC, whose function would be to raise funds independently of state support. See BROADCASTING LEGISLATION.

CinemaScope Wide-screen process copyrighted by 20th Century Fox in 1953 but invented much earlier by Henri Chrétien.

Cinématographie Word first used by G. Bouly in 1892 in a French patent specification for a movie camera.

Cinematography, origins Among the earliest moving-picture inventions was the *Thaumatropical Amusement* of Englishman Henry Fitton (1826). Exploiting the phenomenon of PERSISTENCE OF VISION the Thaumatrope consisted of a round box inside of which were a number of discs, each with a design on it. When the discs were twirled round, the images merged and gave the impression of a single movement.

Joseph Plateau's *Phenakistoscope* (1833), a circular design opposite a mirror, worked the same little miracle. The ZOETROPE or 'wheel of life', invented by Englishman W.G. Horner (1834), offered a revolving drum with strip sequences inside, enabling figures to jump, gallop or even do cartwheels. Emile Renauld's *Praxinoscope* of 1877 improved on the Zoetrope by removing the slots of the drum and using mirrors to reflect the images, thus avoiding the dizziness to viewers caused by the Zoetrope; and the wonder of this device was extended with the *Projecting Praxinoscope* using a revolving disc-blade shutter to project animated images on to a screen.

The main impetus in the development of cinematography came, however, from another direction. Working in the US, English photographer Eadweard Muybridge (1830–1904) in the 1870s took multiple photographs of animals, birds and humans in movement. His most famous experiment was one in which a line of cameras, using exposures of less than one-thousandth of a second, 'filmed' a galloping horse. The horse triggered each camera as it passed – and proved, incidentally, that there are moments in a horse's movement when all its hooves are clear of the ground.

The next step was the projection of these in-sequence pictures. In 1890 William Friese-Green (1855–1921) revealed the potential of moving film when he set up a small slide projector in which the usual slide carrier had been replaced by a glass disc bearing a ring of pictures. Friese-Green's revolving disc was later demonstrated, to eager crowds, in the window of his studio in Piccadilly.

In France meanwhile Étienne-Jules Marey (1830–1904) had invented a photographic 'gun' (1882) to take pictures of birds in flight; he soon followed this with a camera capable of snapping sixty pictures a second on a paper-based film. In the US, Thomas Alva Edison (1847–1931) produced his *Kinetograph* to take moving pictures and his *Kinetoscope* to show them. The viewer looked through a peephole in the foot-high box. The 50 feet of film ran for about 13 seconds. 'Kinetoscope parlours' were set up in which people could view films by putting a coin in the slot.

The most important year in the development of cinematography was 1895, with the invention of projectors in the US by Thomas Armat and Woodville Latham, in France by the Lumière brothers – Auguste (1862–1954) and Louis (1864–1948) – and in the UK by Robert Paul. With the arrival of the Lumières on the scene, the cinema was truly born.

Their vision and entrepreneurialism turned experiment into performance, private screenings into public, commercial profit. 'What did I do?' Louis Lumière is reported to have said. 'It was in the air.' Auguste Lumière was less modest than Louis: 'My brother,' he said, 'invented the cinema in one night.' On 28 December 1895, the Lumières, already highly successful in the photographic business, opened in the Salon Indien, in the Grand Café on the Boulevard des Capucines.

Seats were priced at one franc. Within weeks they were a worldwide success. Immediately the Lumières trained a brigade of cameramen-cum-projectionists and sent them abroad to several foreign countries; in quick time, some 1,200 single-shot films were produced, including the Diamond Jubilee procession in London.

Cinéma vérité Or *Catalyst* cinema. In a 1961 DOCUMENTARY, *Chronique d'un Été* (*Chronicle of a Summer*), Jean Rouch, instead of simply recording the daily routines of Parisians, challenged them to face the camera and answer the question, 'Tell us, are you happy?' Rouch and co-producer Edgar Morin were suddenly on-camera participants. Their subjects, having been filmed, were invited to see the film rushes. Their discussion of these was filmed and recorded and used as part of the end-product.

The style was named *cinéma vérité* in homage to the Russian movie pioneer Dziga Vertov (see SPINNING TOP), and translated from the term used by Vertov and his associates, *kino pravda*, film truth. Erik Barnouw in *Documentary* (Oxford University Press, 1974) writes, 'The direct cinema documentarist took his camera to a situation of tension and waited hopefully for a crisis; the Rouch version of cinéma vérité tried to precipitate one. The direct cinema artist aspired to invisibility; the Rouch cinéma vérité was often an avowed participant.'

Cinerama Extra-wide screen system invented by Fred Waller and first demonstrated in *This is Cinerama* (1952). Three projectors, electronically synchronized, created a three-section picture on the screen, giving a disturbing visual wobble at the joins. The first film story using the process was *How the West Was Won* (1962). Shortly afterwards the three-camera system was abandoned in favour of 'single-lens Cinerama', practically identical to CINEMASCOPE, though with higher definition.

Circumvention tools Alternative term to describe online anti-censorship tools. See TOR.

Citizen journalism See JOURNALISM: CITIZEN JOURNALISM.

Civil inattention Phenomenon of INTERPER-SONAL COMMUNICATION observed by Erving Goffman in *Behavior in Public Places* (Free Press, 1963), where, after initial EYE CONTACT, a person quickly withdraws visual attention from another to avoid any further recognition or need for further contact. As Goffman says, 'In performing this courtesy the eyes of the looker may pass over the eyes of the other, but no "recognition" is typically allowed.' The ritual of civil inattention, Goffman explains, is one that 'constantly regulates the social intercourse of persons in our society'. See INDICATORS.

Clash of Civilizations See McWORLD VS JIHAD.

Clapper board See SHOT.

Claptrap See VERBAL DEVICES OF SPEECH-MAKING.

Class A factor of vital importance in the analysis of interpersonal and mass communication is the concept of class; and the most significant impact on the development of that concept was made by the German philosopher Karl Marx (1818–83). For him, class denoted a relationship to the *means of production* in any given society. Marx identified two main classes: the owners of the means of production (land, factories), whom he called the *bourgeoisie*, and those who were obliged to sell their labour to the owners to make a living – the *proletariat*. Although aware of other classes, he considered them of minor importance.

Marx argued that as a result of their position in the economic order, members of each class shared common experiences, lifestyles and certain political and economic interests. He believed that there was and would remain, in a capitalist society, an inevitable conflict between the interests of the bourgeoisie and the proletariat. He further argued that GROUP identity, class-consciousness and collective political and economic action would develop in the course of economic and political conflict. Proletarian class-consciousness was particularly likely to emerge as its members were thrown into serious difficulties and close daily associations at work.

The dominant class – the bourgeoisie – would, according to Marx, seek to impose its culture upon the rest of society. Its culture would become the *dominant* culture, its IDEOLOGY the dominant ideology. Consequently the communication systems of society would reflect the dominant culture of the bourgeoisie and also the conflict between the two classes. From a Marxist viewpoint, control of many facets of the mass media by the ownership of capital gives that class the opportunity to disseminate its own culture and ideology. Such control, in Marxist terms, plays a vital role in the maintenance of HEGEMONY.

The term is also commonly used when what is meant is *social* class. Social class membership is based, primarily, upon occupation rather than ownership or non-ownership of the means of production. For the ADVERTISING industry and media management, social class is a significant factor in the profile of an audience. Market researchers are primarily interested in income and spending power. For those media organizations that are dependent on advertising revenue, the social class composition of its AUDIENCE is of obvious importance. The interrelationships between the social class structure and the communication processes of society are complex, and research in this area is wideranging; of particular concern is whether the narrowness of social class backgrounds of those who control and work in the media is reflected in its output. See *TOPIC GUIDE* under MEDIA: VALUES & IDEOLOGIES.

Classic FM Commercial radio station broadcasting nationwide in the UK since the autumn of 1992. Its menu of popular classics presented in a lively and unpatronizing way, together with a policy of winning audience loyalty through competitions and sponsored musical events, has proved a notable success.

'Clean up TV' movement Established in Birmingham in 1963 by Mary Whitehouse and others; later called itself the National Viewers' and Listeners' Association (NVLA). Over the years the movement has succeeded in gaining access to practically every forum in which the issues of broadcasting are discussed; additionally, the NVLA has been active as a 'morality watchdog' in other arts, especially the theatre and publishing. NVLA thinking is based on traditional Christian ethics; the belief that the VALUES of chastity and the family underpin all that's best in Western society, and that such values are constantly under threat and have to be protected. Of equal concern to the NVLA is the increase in the display, in film, on TV and in the theatre, of scenes of violence. See BROADCASTING STANDARDS COUNCIL; CENSORSHIP; MORAL ENTREPRENEURS.

Climate of compliance See KUUKI.

Climax order In the process of persuading others, the order in which arguments and evidence are placed is of considerable importance. Research has been conducted into the climax order and anti-climax order, that is when the best point of an argument is reserved till last (climax) or used at the outset (anti-climax). The two orders have varying advantages depending on the particular conditions under which the communication is presented, including the audience's predisposition and the type of matter being transmitted. Similar concepts are the *law of primacy* (see PRIMACY, LAW OF) and the *law of recency.*

Clipper chip A microchip, called the spy in the computer, the 'sleeping policeman on the superhighway of information'. It was feared in the mid-1990s that this would become a compulsory element in US-made computers, allowing government agencies, by means of an electronic back door, to snoop on data into and out of computers. Such was the determination of users of the INTERNET and their campaign against the clipper chip that the Clinton government temporarily retreated from its plans.

However, in February 1996 Clinton signed a Telecommunications Bill requiring that from 1998 all TV sets with a screen size of 13 inches or more should be fitted with a 'V' (for violence)-chip. In the same month the European parliament voted in favour of a similar measure – the insertion of V-chips into every new TV set sold in Europe under the Television Without Frontiers directive. See ENCRIPT; PRIVACY.

Clique A close-knit group of people within a social system whose communication is largely with each other. *Clique analysis* is used to determine communication groupings within a social system, and its main tool is SOCIOMETRICS.

Closed text See OPEN, CLOSED TEXTS.

Closure Occurs in a communication situation when one participant, usually the receiver of information, closes down attention, and thus deflects the message or the messenger, or terminates an encounter. The reasons for closure may relate to the unacceptability of the MESSAGE: it may conflict with the attitudes, beliefs or VALUES of the receiver; it may be an 'uncomfortable truth' which causes in the receiver a feeling of DISSONANCE. Alternatively it may have something to do with the messenger rather than the message – personal dislike of the sender on the part of the receiver, or a simple unwillingness to receive this kind of message from this messenger; or it may simply reflect a wish to terminate the encounter and move on.

The means of closure will involve NVC (Non-verbal Communication) as well as verbal strategies. The term is also used in relation to NARRATIVE, in the sense of *narrative closure.* This does not mean bringing the narrative to a close, but employing narrative devices to close down alternative readings or interpretations. See OPEN, CLOSED TEXTS; PREFERRED READING.

Cloud computing See COMPUTING: CLOUD COMPUTING.

Cocktail party problem In *On Human Communication* (MIT Press, 1966) Colin Cherry writes, 'One of our most important faculties is the ability to listen to, and follow, one speaker in the presence of others. This is such a common experience that we may take it for granted; we may call it "the cocktail party problem". That is, how do we filter out a barrage of communication messages, selecting one to concentrate upon?' Cherry experimented with two different taped readings being played at once, with the instruction to the subject to concentrate on one and ignore the other.

Though the tapes produced a 'complete babel', and though wide-ranging texts were used, considerable success in deciphering the message was demonstrated, illustrating the importance of 'our ingrained speech habits at the acoustic, syllabic, or syntactic levels'. Cherry and his colleagues also experimented to see what happened when a subject was asked to read a text out loud while simultaneously listening to another one. This process – of testing the subject's ability to select from competing message channels, they called 'shadowing'.

Code of broadcasting (UK) See OFCOM: OFFICE OF COMMUNICATIONS.

Codes of advertising practice See ADVERTISING STANDARDS AUTHORITY (ASA); OFCOM: OFFICE OF COMMUNICATIONS.

Code of semes See CODES OF NARRATIVE.

Codes A code is generally defined as a system into which signs are organized, governed by consent. The study of codes – other than those *arbitrary* or *fixed codes* such as mathematics, chemical symbols, Morse Code, etc. – emphasizes the social dimension of communication. We have codes of conduct, ethical, aesthetic and LANGUAGE codes (see ELABORATED AND RESTRICTED CODES).

Non-verbal communication is carried on through what have been classified as *presentational codes*: gesture, movement of the eyes, expression of the face, tone of voice. A *representation code* can be speech, writing, music, art, architecture, etc. Speech itself has non-verbal characteristics: *prosodic codes* affect the MEANING of the words used, through expression or pitch of voice.

The media are often referred to as employing *broadcast* and *narrowcast codes* in gearing content, level and style to expected audiences. *Aesthetic codes* are crucially affected by their cultural context, some of it highly conventional, some AVANT-GARDE, subject to textual rather than commonly recognized cues to meaning. Much modern art, for example, has been encoded in visual languages accessible only to a small number of people. However, over time, innovative aesthetic encoding becomes conventionalized. The obscure code has become familiar. A case in point is Surrealism, whose intention was to shock cultural convention, yet whose dream symbols and often disturbing juxtapositions of objects have become a commonplace of mass advertising. What began as a code specific to itself has been transformed to one given its meaning by cultural convention. See CODES OF NARRATIVE; DECODE; DOMINANT, SUBORDINATE, RADICAL; ELITE; HIGHBROW; SEMIOLOGY/SEMIOTICS.

Codes of narrative Roland Barthes in *S/Z* (Blackwell, 1990; translated from the French by Richard Miller) applies a number of narrative codes in a book-length analysis, or deconstruction, of a twenty-three-page short story, *Sarrasine*, written by Honoré de Balzac in 1830. Barthes describes 'five major codes under which all the textual signifiers can be grouped' in a narrative. The *Proiaretic* or *Action* code (the Voice of Empirics) tells us of events – of what happens, and thus is instrumental in the sequence of the story.

The code of the *seme* or sign ('semantically the unit of the signifier') refers to character and is categorized by Richard Howard in the Preface to *S/Z* as the *Semantic* code (though Barthes does not actually use this term in the text). Barthes speaks of this as the Voice of the Person. Under the *Hermeneutic* or *Enigma* code (the Voice of Truth) 'we list the various (formal) terms by which an enigma can be distinguished, suggested, formulated, held in suspense and finally disclosed'. *Cultural* or *Referential* codes 'are references to a science or a body of knowledge' – 'physical, physiological, medical, psychological, literary, historical, etc.'. These are the Voice of Science. Finally there is the *Symbolic* code, the Voice of Symbol.

Barthes writes of the codes that they 'create a kind of network, a *topos* [Greek: a place, location] through which the entire text passes (or rather, in passing, becomes text)'. This taxonomy of codes is widely used in the analysis of texts of all kinds. Nowhere, however, does Barthes suggest that such coding is prescriptive or exact. He writes, 'The code is a perspective of quotations, a mirage of structures; we know only its departures and returns.'

Barthes talks of a 'galaxy of signifiers, not a

structure of signifieds'. For him the text 'is not unitary, architectonic, finite' and the approach to it is characterized by 'blanks and looseness of analysis'. The meaning of the 'readerly' as contrasted with the 'writerly' text is ultimately elusive.

Cognitive (and affective) That area or domain of human behaviour which can be described as intellectual – knowing, understanding and reasoning – is often referred to as the *cognitive*. A substantial amount of media communication is aimed at producing cognitive responses in the receiver. That area which is involved with attitudes, emotions, VALUES and feelings is termed the *affective*. Obviously the two overlap and intertwine.

Whether the content of a MESSAGE is cognitive or affective in its orientations will greatly influence the mode chosen for its communication. If the content of a message is judged to be of cognitive intent, then LANGUAGE will generally be couched in neutral terms; presentation will strive after objectivity and balance. An affective message will be more likely to be framed in emotive language, its imagery directed towards emotional responses.

However, recent media research has been directed towards a more critical analysis of the allegedly objective modes of cognitive messages. There is concern as to whether the dissemination of apparently neutral information – especially if that dissemination is of some FREQUENCY and CONSISTENCY of treatment – influences an audience's perception of national and world events. From the mass of available information, the media select and reject. They give emphasis – and legitimacy – to some issues rather than others, and they set the order of priorities (see AGENDA-SETTING) as well as seeking to establish links between occurrences and their causes in the minds of the audience. See EFFECTS OF THE MASS MEDIA; GLASGOW UNIVERSITY MEDIA GROUP.

Cognitive capture See IMPARTIALITY.

Cognitive Consistency theories The basic premise of cognitive consistency theories is that people prefer consistency among the various elements of their cognitive system, for example between attitudes and beliefs. Heider (1958) investigated reactions to balance or imbalance in dyads and, particularly, triads of elements. The triads are known as POX triads. P represents the person 'you'; O represents the other person and X represents a stimulus, for example an object or event. The relationship between any two elements can be positive or negative and their combination can produce balanced or imbal-

anced triads. An example of a balanced triad would be when you and the other person like each other and you both like Coldplay. However, if you and the other person disliked each other but both liked Coldplay, an imbalanced triad would be formed. Heider argued that people prefer balance and seek to establish or restore balance but can tolerate imbalance.

Osgood and Tannenbaum (1955) sought to investigate the effect of differences in the degree of like or dislike between the elements on the process of dealing with imbalance. The principle of congruity as advanced by Charles Osgood and Percy Tannenbaum in 'The principle of congruity in the prediction of attitude change', *Psychological Review* 62 (1955) holds that when change in evaluation or attitude occurs, it always occurs in the direction of increased congruity with the prevailing frame of reference. That is, it will be the weaker attitude or belief that will give way.

The opposite of cognitive balance is *cognitive dissonance*, a notion analysed by Leon Festinger in *A Theory of Cognitive Dissonance* (Row Peterson, 1957). Cognitive dissonance results from a lack of consistency between two cognitions – attitudes, values, beliefs, ideas and so on. Festinger argued that cognitive dissonance motivates the individual to try to resolve the resulting lack of harmony, and he identified strategies by which individuals try to achieve this. Three such strategies are: to change the less important cognition; to deny evidence that the cognitions are in conflict; or to change the importance of the cognitions. Take for example the dissonance that might be felt by a heavy drinker who values their health. To reduce the dissonance they could cut down on their alcohol consumption, or they could deny the validity of the evidence that suggests that heavy drinking is bad for one's health, or they could decide that it is much more important to continue heavy drinking and enjoy life than to live for longer.

The theory predicts that people will seek out information that confirms existing attitudes and views of the world or reinforces other aspects of behaviour. Similarly it predicts that people will avoid information which is likely to increase DISSONANCE. If you dislike a person, and you dislike his/her views, what he/she says is unlikely to cause cognitive dissonance, for there is a congruence here. Dissonance is acute when a liked person says something seemingly 'out of character' or fails to accord with expectations or the image held of him/her. Clearly, cognitive dissonance theory can shed much light on why acts of communication may be resisted and rejected.

Psychological Reactance theory, developed by Brehm (1966), can also be classed as a consistency theory. Psychological reactance occurs when we are restricted from doing something that we were previously free to do and we perceive that restriction to be illegitimate or unjustified. Psychological reactance motivates us to restore the threatened freedom of action. The degree of reactance we experience will depend upon the extent of the restriction placed upon behaviour, how important that behaviour is to us, and whether there are similar alternative choices open to us. There are also some individual differences in our response to restrictions on our behaviour. Take for example the imposition of CENSORSHIP. Robert Cialdini notes in *Influence: Science and Practice* (Pearson Education, Inc., 2009) that 'almost invariably, our response to banned information is to want to receive that information to a greater extent and to become more favourable toward it than we were before the ban'.

Theodore Newcomb (1953) developed a version of balance theory – the ABX model of communication (see NEWCOMB'S ABX MODEL) – that focuses upon equilibrium within interpersonal communication. Our preference for cognitive consistency can leave us prey to its use in persuasive communication. As Robert Cialdini comments in *Influence: Science and Practice* (Pearson Education, Inc., 2009), 'The drive to be (and look) consistent constitutes a highly potent weapon of social influence, often causing us to act in ways that are clearly contrary to our own best interest'. See COGNITIVE (AND AFFECTIVE); DEFENSIVE COMMUNICATION; EFFECTS OF THE MASS MEDIA; GROUPTHINK; RESONANCE; SYMMETRY, STRAIN TOWARDS. See also *TOPIC GUIDE* under COMMUNICATION THEORY.

Cognitive dissonance See COGNITIVE CONSISTENCY THEORIES; CONGRUENCE THEORY; DISSONANCE.

Cold media, hot media See HOT MEDIA, COLD MEDIA.

Collocation The tendency of words to occur in regular association; words set together through customary usage such as 'fair' and 'play', 'auspicious' and 'occasion'.

Collodion or wet-plate process See PHOTOGRAPHY, ORIGINS.

Colloquialism An expression used in common, informal speech, but not as far removed from acceptable modes as SLANG. If your comments 'cut no ice' with somebody, that is a colloquialism; if you are told to 'keep yer 'air on', that is slang. It is a modest distinction, for as Ronald

Ridout and Clifford Witting say in *The Facts of English* (Pan Reference Books, 1973), 'the slang of yesterday becomes the colloquialism of today'. See DIALECT; JARGON; REGISTER.

Colonization Term used to describe the process by which various cultural material is acquired from a variety of contexts and then reassembled to construct particular messages. In this process the MEANING of the original signs is often changed, if not subverted; their use may appear to celebrate differences between people, but the goal to which they are put may have as its purpose the REINFORCEMENT of the DOMINANT CULTURE, and the denial of differences and the conflict which they bring.

Advertising messages contain many examples of colonization. For example, the signs and symbols widely associated with certain YOUTH CULTURES are often employed to sell goods and services to various audiences – whether young people themselves, or older consumers who are presumed to identify with a particular youth culture. Ironically, whilst youth cultures are often a site of resistance and challenge to the dominant culture, their signs and symbols are in this way used to draw them further into the dominant culture, for instance through encouraging certain patterns of consumption.

Comic impetus See SITCOM.

Comics The first newspaper comic-strip is generally considered to be that which appeared on 16 February 1896 in the *New York Sunday World*. It was a three-quarter-page feature in colour called 'The Great Dog Show in M'Googan's Avenue'. Kids in the city's slum backyards were organizing their own dog show; the hero, dressed in a bright yellow nightgown, soon became the 'Yellow Kid' and 'Hogan's Alley' achieved immediate popularity as a long-running comic strip (see YELLOW KID).

The idea was not new. English cartoonist Thomas Rowlandson (1757–1827) created a comic character, Dr Syntax, who was popular with the public, and considerably earlier William Hogarth (1697–1764) included speech 'balloons' in his engravings satirizing London life. George Orwell took comics seriously enough to write about them.

In 'Boys' Weeklies' (1939), published in *Selected Essays* (Penguin, 1957), Orwell analysed the social and political connotations of early publications in the genre. What seemed to characterize comics in Orwell's day was their social changelessness – deep down, if not in the surface detail. Orwell did find differences between the older and the new generation of weeklies, however: in the new, 'better technique, more scientific interest, more bloodshed, more leaderworship'; in 'social outlook there is hardly any advance'.

As life appears to have become more complex, and society more complicated, the STEREOTYPE of the hero has had a sustaining appeal. Picture-strip heroes such as Clark Kent, alias Superman, who first made his appearance in *Action Comics* (1938) in the US, have not only led popular (and charmed) lives on the printed paper but have also translated into immensely popular film heroes. The debate concerning comics, and comic books, centres around the extent to which they seem to legitimize dominant social values.

A comic which has reversed this tendency is *Viz*, started up in Newcastle-upon-Tyne in 1979 by brothers Chris and Simon Donald and Jim Brownlow with a first issue of 150 copies. In a UK *Guardian* article 'All in the worst possible taste' (18 November 2004), William Cook described *Viz* as 'a brilliant hybrid of punk fanzine and kids' comic'; the comic proved immensely popular and circulation temporarily rose to a million copies.

Viz mercilessly (and hilariously) satirizes the UK tabloids, public figures and politicians, issuing spoof news stories and adverts. Among its many comic characters have been the Fat Slags (Sandra and Tracey), Spoilt Bastard, and Roger Mellie the Man on Telly.

Among the *Viz* annuals have been the Five Knuckle Shuffle, the Full Toss, the Pork Chopper and the Dogs' Bollocks. In Cook's opinion, *Viz* 'changed the sense of humour of the nation'. In 2009 an exhibition of the original artwork of *Viz* was held at London's Cartoon Museum.

▶ William Cook, *The Silver Plated Jubilee – 25 Years of Viz* (Boxtree, 2004).

Commanders of the social order Term used by Herbert I. Schiller in *Culture, Inc.: The Corporate Takeover of Public Expression* (Oxford University Press, 1989), referring to the vast transnational corporations which, he argues, have come to dominate and shape CULTURE; establish prevailing discourses; set political, economic and cultural agendas; and call the tune of mass media. Schiller talks of the PRIVATIZATION of public space: in a literal sense (public areas being transformed into privately owned and controlled shopping malls and pleasure domes); and in an intellectual sense, through the 'corporatization' of arts, literature and media. He cites the extent to which the entire world of information (libraries, museums, universities, mass communication), of expression (architecture, music,

art) and of public spectacle (sport) have been colonized by corporations – particularly in the US, but increasingly in the rest of the world. See AUDIENCE: ACTIVE AUDIENCE; BERLUSCONI PHENOMENON; CONSENSUS; ELITE; HEGEMONY; MANUFACTURE OF CONSENT; POWER ELITE; PRESS BARONS; PUBLIC SPHERE. See also *TOPIC GUIDE* under MEDIA: OWNERSHIP & CONTROL.

Commercial confidentiality A CENSORSHIP device employed to prevent the media transmitting, or the general public receiving, information on the grounds that such information might be commercially damaging (regardless of whether that information might be in the public interest). One particularly sensitive area of commerce which is shrouded in mystery is the arms trade.

For example, Britain is among the world's top arms-trading nations. Its government maintains an arms marketing and advisory service, the Defence Exports Services Organization, yet this organization is notoriously secretive whenever journalists seek to find out about its work, invariably answering that information cannot be supplied for reasons of 'commercial confidentiality'. Louis Blom-Cooper, Chairman of the Press Council in 1990, expressed the view that 'traditional English law places a higher value on commercial interests than on the public's right to know'. See FREEDOM OF INFORMATION ACT (UK), 2005.

Commercial Laissez Faire model See LIBERAL PRESS THEORY.

Commercial radio: origins Although PIRATE RADIO attempted to buck the broadcasting monopoly of the BBC during the 1960s, legitimate commercial broadcasting in the UK was not in operation till the 1970s, following the Conservative government's Sound Broadcasting Act of 1972. The Independent Broadcasting Authority (IBA) had, by 1983, thirty-seven commercial RADIO stations operating under licence throughout the UK and plans for over sixty more.

In the US the first commercial radio station was KDKA of Pittsburg, which went on the air on 2 November 1920. In 1921 there were eight commercial radio stations; by 1922, 564. Development of radio in the US was spectacular and chaotic. In 1927 (the year that the BBC, by Royal Charter, was given a monopoly of radio broadcasting in the UK) Congress passed a Radio Act setting up the Federal Communications Commission to allocate wavelengths to broadcasters.

Four radio networks were created as a hedge against monopoly – National Broadcasting

Commission (NBC), Columbia Broadcasting Service (CBS), Mutual Broadcasting System (MBS) and the American Broadcasting Company (ABC), while the FCC worked towards the growth of projects of educational interest.

Despite the BBC's monopoly in the UK, commercial broadcasts in English were transmitted from abroad as early as 1925. Radio Paris, broadcasting from the Eiffel Tower, presented a fashion talk in English, sponsored by Selfridges. Only three listeners wrote to the station to say they had heard the broadcast, but the commercial lobby was undaunted.

In the 1930s Captain L.F. Flugge, who had arranged the fashion talk, formed and ran the International Broadcasting Company. The IBC's Radio Normandy transmitted 15-minute shows for several hours a day from 1931; by the following year twenty-one British firms were paying sponsorship money for commercial broadcasting, and the UK was being beamed at commercially from The Netherlands, Spain and Luxembourg.

The IBC actually set up offices in Portland Place, London, and had its own outside broadcasting vehicles, each painted black with 'Radio Normandy 274 metres' on the side. An important part of the company's operation was the International Broadcasting Club, formed in 1932, with free membership. By 1939, the IBC had 320,000 members.

Radio Luxembourg began broadcasting on 1191 metres long wave in 1933, its first two sponsors being Zam Buk and Bile Beans. Though the UK Post Office conducted a sustained campaign to close down these commercial stations, it was Adolf Hitler and the Second World War that did the trick: many transmitters were either destroyed by the Nazis or taken over. Radio Luxembourg became Hitler's major PROPAGANDA weapon against the British.

Of the commercial stations, Luxembourg was the only one to start up again after the war (finally closing down in 1992). The first accredited commercial radio station on British soil was Manx Radio, which began broadcasting in 1964. With the election of the Conservatives in 1970, the Minister of Posts and Telecommunications produced a White Paper, *An Alternative Service of Broadcasting*, proposing a network of about sixty commercial stations under the Independent Television Authority (to be renamed the Independent Broadcasting Authority).

From the beginning, in 1972, local independent radio was to broadcast on stereo VHF as well as medium wave. The first FRANCHISES were awarded in 1973, to bring into existence the all-news London Broadcasting Company (LBC) and Capital Radio for London, with regional stations following soon afterwards. Additional franchises were granted by the IBA in 1981. By 1988 there were forty independent local radio stations (compared to twenty-seven BBC local stations).

The BROADCASTING ACT, 1990 separated out the statutory overseeing of radio and television, creating for TV (in place of the IBA) the Independent Television Commission (ITC) and for radio, the Radio Authority. These bodies were empowered to assign frequencies, appoint licensees and regulate programming and advertising. They were also required to draw up and periodically review codes of practice concerning programmes, advertising standards and other matters. Both the Radio Authority and the ITC ceased to exist with the inaguration of the Office of Communications (OFCOM), born out of the COMMUNICATIONS ACT (UK), 2003. See TELEVISION BROADCASTING.

Commercial radio (UK) Licensing of UK commercial radio stations is the responsibility of OFCOM: THE OFFICE OF COMMUNICATIONS. By the end of 2009 there were over 370 local radio stations, more than 200 providing for DAB (Digital Audio Broadcasting) reception and in excess of 350 streaming their services for online reception. There are three national stations, Absolute Radio, Classic FM and TalkSPORT, and eighteen regional stations such as Magic (London), Galaxy (North East, Central Scotland and Yorkshire), Real Radio (London, East Midlands, West Midlands, North East and North West) and the Coast (Solent).

The commercial radio landscape is subject to flux as individual stations change hands; ownership is rarely if ever local, more generally constituting part of the portfolio of large media companies. Global owns (at the time of writing) Capital Radio (London), Galaxy, Heart (London, East Midlands and West Midlands) and two other London stations, LBC 97.3 and XFM, while Bauer Media own Kerrang! (West Midlands), Kiss (London, East of England and the Severn Estuary) and Wave 105 (Solent). National Radio Wales is part of the Town and Country holding.

The UK has the biggest DAB network in the world, with 103 transmitters and fifty-one digital stations available in London alone. The switchover date to DAB is 2015. By 2009, 35 per cent of the UK population had DAB, though the figure for adults with mobile-phone access to radio transmission was 89 per cent.

While for most commercial radio stations

music is the chief fare, news broadcasting is a requirement. Ofcom guidelines stress 'localness', that is content and approach of specific local relevance 'which offers a distinctive alternative to UK-wide or nations' service'. All stations 'should broadcast local news at least hourly throughout peaktime' both on weekdays and weekends.

RadioCentre, the trade body of commercial radio companies, estimated that in 2009 commercial radio had an audience of over 30 million. Standards are not only monitored by Ofcom, but celebrated by the Arqiva Commercial Radio Awards, Bauer Radio winning five of these in 2010. See WI-FI.

Commissions/committees on the media See *TOPIC GUIDE* under COMMISSIONS, COMMITTEES, LEGISLATION.

Common sense In the study of media communication and its links with culture and politics, the term 'common sense' connotes an over-readiness to believe in the apparently obvious. The Italian philosopher Antonio Gramsci (1891–1937) defined common sense as being a composite of the attitudes, beliefs and assumptions of the mass of the people, and operating within a hierarchical social order.

Common sense tends towards conformism to the IDEOLOGY of the dominant social order, and in part is the product of that ideology. It accepts 'the way things are' – the *status quo* – as 'the way things should be'. Indeed such structures and circumstances are so obvious (so commonsensical) that they do not warrant being questioned.

Gramsci believed that what he termed the 'chaotic aggregate of disparate conceptions' comprising common sense should be challenged by intellectuals, and the complacency of common sense explained and exposed. Many commentators have focused on the role the media play in nurturing and reinforcing rather than unpacking commonsensical visions of society. See EXNOMINATION; HEGEMONY.

Commons knowledge See GENRE.

Communication While the definitions of communication vary according to the theoretical frames of reference employed and the stress placed upon certain aspects of the total process, they all include five fundamental factors: an initiator; a recipient; a mode or vehicle; a message; and an effect. Simply expressed, the communication process begins when a MESSAGE is conceived by a *sender*. It is then ENCODED – translated into a signal or sequence of signals – and *transmitted* via a particular MEDIUM or CHANNEL to a *receiver*, who then decodes it

and interprets the message, returning a signal in some way that the message has or has not been understood – that is, provides FEEDBACK. The models of Shannon and Weaver (1949) and Osgood and Schramm (1956) were early representations of this process.

Osgood and Schramm's model also highlighted the importance of the process of encoding and decoding in the exchange of meaning. Communication requires CODES and codes require signs. Thus SEMIOLOGY/SEMIOTICS and the ideas of theorists such as Charles Pierce or Ferdinand de Saussure are integral to a study of communication (see SIGN; SIGNIFICATION).

Shannon and Weaver's model highlighted what has been termed NOISE, or interference, that may impede the message. The concept of noise points to the potential barriers to effective communication: technical, semantic or psychological. Noise may be internal (resistance to the message or to the sender, for example, on the part of the receiver) or external (actual noise, distraction, language level, etc.). During the communication process, sender, message and receiver are subject to a multitude of cues which influence the message, such as a person's appearance, his/her known status or the expression on his/her own face as the message is communicated or responded to (see BARNLUND'S TRANSACTIONAL MODELS).

Schramm's model, for example, identifies the importance of common 'fields of experience' on the part of sender and receiver for successful communication, whilst Berlo's model (1960) further provides a useful indicator of the complex range of factors to be found in the communication process; these include psychological and cultural variables. Lack of shared attitudes, values, knowledge, experiences or cultural expectations can be a significant source of noise (see SCHRAMM'S MODELS OF COMMUNICATION, 1954; BERLO'S SMCR MODEL OF COMMUNICATION, 1960).

While INTERPERSONAL COMMUNICATION is that which occurs between two or more people, INTRAPERSONAL COMMUNICATION is what you say within and to yourself. Inner thoughts, impressions, memories interact with external stimuli to create a silent discourse, continuously changing and renewing itself and influencing your perceptions of self and the world.

It is important to hold in mind, as Raymond Williams points out in *Keywords* (Fontana, 1976), the 'unresolved range of the original noun of action, represented at its extremes by "transmit", a one-way process, and "share" ...

a common or mutual process'. This polarity of meaning – of the one-way process as against aspects of communion, of cultural *exchange* – is fundamental to the analysis of communication, hence the attempt to generalize the distinction in such phrases as *manipulative* communication and *participative* communication.

Frank Dance in 'Toward a theory of human communication' in the book he edited, *Human Communication Theory: Original Essays* (Holt, Rinehart & Winston, 1967), observes that communication is something that changes even while one is in the act of examining it; it is therefore an interaction and a *transaction*. Dance and C. Larson in *The Functions of Human Communication: A Theoretical Approach* (Holt, Rinehart & Winston, 1976) detail their examination of 126 definitions of communication. They specify notable differences but also common agreement that communication is a *process*. The authors conclude with a definition of their own: 'the production of symbolic content by an individual, according to a code, with anticipated consumption by other(s) according to the same code'. Or, as Colin Cherry succinctly puts it in *On Human Communication* (MIT Press, 1957), communication is 'essentially a social affair'.

As early as 1933, Edward Sapir differentiated between *explicit* and *implicit* modes of communication, while T.R. Nilson in 'On defining communication' in *Speech Trainer* (1957) – and reprinted in K.K. Sereno and C.D. Mortensen, eds, *Foundations of Communication Theory* (Harper & Row, 1970) – distinguishes between communication which is *instrumental*, that is intended to stimulate a response, and *situational*, in which there need not be any intention of evoking a response in the transmission of stimuli.

Most recently, Eisenberg's model (2001) focuses on the role of communication in the search for identity in an uncertain world. Eisenberg argues that communication is the means by which we search for, define and establish personal identity. In late modernity this quest takes place within a dynamic and fluid 'surround'; thus in a changing world a key challenge will be that of 'developing a robust but dynamic conception of identity that continually adapts to a turbulent environment'. The forces within the 'surround' influence both how we see ourselves and how we activate ourselves towards others, and thus how we communicate with them. These forces include spiritual, biological, cultural, economic and interpersonal factors. At the centre of the surround is a dynamically inter-active trio of forces: communication, mood and personal narrative. (See EISENBERG'S MODEL OF COMMUNICATION AND IDENTITY, 2001.)

A precept that few commentators would challenge is that it is *impossible not to communicate*. By saying nothing, by remaining blank-faced, by keeping our hands stiffly to our sides, we are still communicating, however negatively. We are still part of an interaction, whether we like it or not. For Jurgen Ruesch, communication is 'all those processes by which people influence one another' (in 'Values, communication and culture', J. Ruesch and G. Bateson, eds, *The Social Matrix of Psychiatry* (W.W. Norton, 1951)). At first we may resist the claim that whatever we do, we are exerting an influence. Yet by trying not to influence, we are arguably still affecting the patterns of communicative action, interaction and transaction. In our absence from the scene – from our family or work group, for example – as well as in our presence, we may still exert influence, however little, however unintended. See COMMUNICATION: INTERCULTURAL COMMUNICATION; COMMUNICATION, NON-VERBAL (NVC); SEMIOLOGY/SEMIOTICS.

Communication: intercultural communication Larry A. Samovar, Richard E. Porter and Edwin R. McDaniel in *Communication between Cultures* (Wadsworth, 2010) note that '... intercultural communication involves interaction between people whose cultural perceptions and symbol systems are distinct enough to alter the communication event'. Such distinct differences do not only occur across societies but also between the various co-cultures found within one society, especially those with a wide mix of people from diverse cultural backgrounds such as the US or Britain. Intercultural communication, then, can take place both within and across societies.

William B. Gudykunst and Young Yun Kim in *Communicating With Strangers: An Approach to Intercultural Communication* (McGraw-Hill, 1997) note that 'the underlying process of communication between people from different cultures or sub-cultures is the same as the underlying process of communication between people from the same culture or sub-cultures'. We should not, therefore, overestimate the differences and underestimate the similarities. To explore the dynamics of intercultural communication they propose a model that focuses on the potential influence of four types of perceptual filter: *cultural*, *sociocultural*, *psychocultural* and *environmental*. Each of these filters influences the exchange of messages and meaning in the process of intercultural communication.

LANGUAGE and NON-VERBAL COMMUNICA-TION clearly vary across cultures, but the impact of culture may go further than causing the obvious problems of translation. The SAPIR-WHORF LINGUISTIC RELATIVITY HYPOTHESIS proposes that language determines thought and thus different languages may carry with them different perceptions of the world. This hypothesis remains controversial, but a number of researchers would argue that whilst language may not determine thought, it does influence it. Richard Hudson, for example, in *Sociolinguistics* (Cambridge University Press, 1996) comments, 'In short, language does affect thought in ways that go beyond the rather obvious effects of the specific lexical items. On the other hand, language is not the only kind of experience which does affect thought.'

A number of theorists have sought to explore key cultural variables and clearly these have the potential to impact on the process of intercultural communication. In *Culture's Consequences: Comparing Values, Behaviours, Institutions and Organisations across Nations* (Sage, 2001) Geert Hofstede identifies five dimensions along which cultures can be compared: Power Distance; Uncertainty Avoidance; Masculinity-Femininity; Long versus Short-term Orientation; and Individualism versus Collectivism.

Another widely used profile of key cross-cultural variables is that developed by Fons Trompenaars and Charles Hampton-Turner. In *Managing People Across Cultures* (John Wiley & Sons, 2004) they identify seven key variables: Universalism versus Particularism; Individualism versus Communitarianism (similar to Individualism versus Collectivism); Specific versus Diffuse; Neutral versus Affective; Achievement versus Ascription; Sequential versus Synchronic Time; and Internal versus External Control.

A key variable is, arguably, that of Individualism versus Collectivism, and it is one that appears to impact considerably on communication. A culture may be predominantly, though not exclusively, collectivistic or individualistic. Cultures in which collectivistic tendencies predominate stress the importance of the ties and obligations attached to membership. These will exercise considerable and general influence over members (for example, the family, faith-groups). The interests of the in-group are seen as more important than those of individuals, whose duty is to abide by the norms and values of the in-group. There are often marked differences between the manner in which in-group members

communicate with each other compared to their communication with members of out-groups.

In contrast, cultures in which individualistic tendencies predominate stress the importance of the individual and the individual's aims, interests, achievements and self-development. Individuals are expected to be self-reliant and take responsibility for themselves and their close family. Individuals may be members of a number of in-groups – most of which will have relatively limited and specific influence over their members. Individuals are encouraged to be competitive, to speak out and to stand out. There are likely to be fewer marked differences between the ways in which people communicate with in-group and out-group members.

It should be borne in mind, however, that people in any culture may have both collectivistic or individualistic orientations, even though one will tend to be stronger. Further, not all people will necessarily identify strongly with the predominant tendency of the culture in which they live.

There are many cross-cultural contexts in which the variable of Individualism versus Collectivism affects communicative behaviour. One is the approach taken to conflict management. Stella Ting-Toomey in *Communicating Across Cultures* (Guildford Press, 1999) notes that those from individualistic cultures tend to focus on outcomes and the achievement of goals in contrast to those from collectivistic cultures, who focus on the process and on behaving appropriately.

Marieke De Mooij in *Global Marketing and Advertising: Understanding Cultural Paradoxes* (Sage, 1998) discusses the impact of the Individualism versus Collectivism variable in the encoding and decoding of advertisements. One example here is that of a lone figure featuring in an advertisement. This image is likely to be interpreted in a negative light in collectivistic cultures, as it runs the risk of suggesting that the person has 'no friends, no identity' – not a connotation that advertisers normally wish to have associated with their products. So in collectivistic cultures people are often shown in groups enjoying the product, whereas in individualistic cultures it is not unusual to see just one person and individualistic appeals in advertisements.

An important influence of the same variable on communication lies in its relationship to the use of what Edward Hall in *Beyond Culture* (Doubleday, 1977/81) terms *high-context* and *low-context* communication. High-context communication relies heavily on the aspects of the context, for example the status differences between the communicators, to provide MEANING, and considerable use is made of non-verbal signs.

Hall writes, 'When talking about something that they have on their minds, a high context individual will expect his interlocutor to know what's bothering him, so he doesn't have to be specific. The result is that he will talk around and around the point, in effect putting all the pieces in place except the crucial one. Placing it properly – this keystone – is the role of the interlocutor. To do this for him is an insult and a violation of his individuality.'

As Gudykunst and Kim argue, 'High-context communication can be characterized as being indirect, ambiguous and understated with speakers being reserved and sensitive to listeners.' High-context communication is favoured by collectivistic cultures, such as that of Japan, in which the centrality of in-group membership ensures the degree of shared knowledge and understanding of contextual factors, essential for its effective use.

Individualistic cultures, such as that of European Americans, on the other hand, favour low-context communication. Here, such a degree of shared knowledge and understanding of contextual factors cannot be taken for granted, so meaning is made obvious and less use is made of non-verbal signs – especially silence. As Gudykunst and Kim comment, 'Low-context communication ... can be characterized as being direct, explicit, open, precise and consistent with one's feelings.'

Whilst the cultural variable of Individualism/ Collectivism may predispose individuals to favour one pattern over another, they may in certain circumstances employ the contrasting pattern. So whilst those in individualistic cultures may generally employ low-context communication, in certain situations, for example when talking to a longstanding friend, they may use high-context communication.

In cross-cultural encounters confusion and possible conflict can occur when high-context meets low-context. Those from collectivistic, high-context communication cultures, for example, may find the direct, open approach of those from individualistic, low-context cultures socially inept and tactless; whilst those from individualistic, low-context cultures may get frustrated with the failure of those from collectivistic, high-context communication cultures to 'get to the point'.

The influence of cultural variables interplays with other key factors – for example, social identities, those of age, GENDER, social CLASS and ethnicity. Thus, for example, the GENDERLECTS noted by Deborah Tannen in *You Just Don't Understand: Men and Women in Conversation* (Virago, 1992) could be expected to modify the degree to which, say, the cultural variable of individualism influences a person's communicative performance. Also part of the equation are psychocultural influences such as stereotyping, ETHNOCENTRISM and PREJUDICE and environmental influences such as population density and terrain.

Encounters between people of different cultures can also be reflected in language; a *Pidgin*, for example, may be generated. In trading and doing business with the English in the Far East, the Chinese and other peoples, such as the Malays, communicated in a very basic, utilitarian mode of half-English. Pidgin is a Chinese corruption of the word 'business' but the term is more widely used to to denote such basic means of communication. According to Elizabeth Closs Traugott and Mary Louise Pratt in *Linguistics* (Harcourt Brace Jovanovitch, 1980), a Pidgin may be 'roughly defined as a language that is nobody's native language'.

Pidgins are developed in situations where people with differing native languages are brought together, some often in a relatively powerless position, and have to communicate. Pidgins, though, tend to meet only the basic needs of communication and are strongly reliant on the accompanying use of NON-VERBAL COMMUNICATION for their effectiveness. Creoles are normally developed by the children of Pidgin speakers and these are more complex and more flexible languages. Over time, through the process of *decreolization*, a Creole often changes to resemble more closely the predominant or prestige language that was its base, if this language is still used in the area. This was the case with Jamaican Creole. In Britain, British Black English, derived largely from Jamaican Creole, is widely used by people with Afro-Caribbean origins as a linguistic marker of ETHNIC identity, and typically is part of a linguistic repertoire that also includes other varieties of English. See APACHE SILENCE; ASSERTIVENESS; FACEWORK; M-TIME, P-TIME.

▶ Sang-Pil Han and Sharon Shavitt, 'Persuasion and culture: advertising appeals in individualistic and collectivistic societies', *Journal of Experimental Social Psychology*, Vol. 30 (4) 1994; Fons Trompenaars and Peter Woolliams, *Marketing Across Cultures* (John Wiley & Sons, 2004); Harry C. Triandis, *Individual-*

ism-collectivism (Westview, 1995); Richard D. Lewis, *When Cultures Collide: Leading Across Cultures* (Nicholas Brealey International, 2006); Marieke De Mooij, *Global Marketing and Advertising: Understanding Cultural Paradoxes* (Sage, 2009); Marieke De Mooij, *Consumer Behaviour and Culture: Consequences for Global Marketing and Advertising* (Sage Publications Inc., 2010).

Communication, functions Many and varied listings have been made by communications analysts. The following eight functions are usually quoted as being central: *instrumental* (to achieve or obtain something); *control* (to get someone to behave in a particular way); *information* (to find out or explain something); *expression* (to express one's feelings or put oneself over in a particular way); *social contact* (participating in company); *alleviation of anxiety* (to sort out a problem, ease a worry about something); *stimulation* (response to something of interest); and *role-related* (because the situation requires it). See JAKOBSON'S MODEL OF COMMUNICATION.

Communication integration See INTEGRATION.

Communication, interpersonal See INTERPERSONAL COMMUNICATION.

Communication, intrapersonal See INTRAPERSONAL COMMUNICATION.

Communication: mobile concept of See MOBILIZATION.

Communication models See *TOPIC GUIDE* under COMMUNICATION MODELS.

Communication, non-verbal (NVC) Michael Argyle in *Bodily Communication* (Methuen, 1988) identifies the main codes of NVC: TOUCH and bodily contact; SPATIAL BEHAVIOUR (PROXEMICS and ORIENTATION); appearance; FACIAL EXPRESSION; GESTURE and HEAD NODS; POSTURE; gaze (eye movement and EYE CONTACT); and NON-VERBAL VOCALIZATIONS. Varyingly, NVC conveys much of what we wish to say, and much of what we would wish to withhold. Common functions of non-verbal communication include: the conveying of interpersonal attitudes; the display of emotional states; self-presentation; the regulation of interaction; the giving of meaning to verbal communication; the maintenance of interest in a communicative encounter; the provision of advance warning of the kind of verbal communication to follow; and, very importantly, the provision of FEEDBACK in communication.

Affiliation, sexual attraction, rejection, aggression, dominance, submission, appeasement, fear, grief, joy are often best expressed – and in some cases can only be expressed – through NVC. The amount of NVC in the repertoire of different peoples and nations varies considerably in range, emphasis, frequency and rules for use.

Some non-verbal signs appear to be universal, for example the eyebrow flash used in greeting. There are also many cultural differences in non-verbal communication, for example the rules regarding proximity, that is the amount of space or distance people should keep between them when communicating. These are different for Middle-Eastern countries when compared with our own. The use of non-verbal communication may also be influenced by aspects of an individual's personality. Extroverts, for example, are thought to be more expansive in their use of gestures. Some GENDER differences have been noted in the use of NVC. Several studies have shown that women are more likely to touch each other in conversation than men are.

Ambiguity often surrounds the interpretation of non-verbal signs, not least because quite a lot of body movement is not communicative in intent and it may be difficult for the receiver to know whether a particular sign was intended to communicate a message or not. Judy Gahagan in *Social Interaction and its Management* (Methuen, 1984) argues that the ambiguity surrounding the interpretation of non-verbal signs is essential to one of their major functions in communication – dropping hints.

People may wish such messages to be open to varied interpretation so that the hint can be retracted later, if necessary. Non-verbal signs thus provide what Gahagan calls 'diplomatic flexibility'. As she remarks, 'non-verbal communication is a language adapted for hints and innuendo'. See ACCENT; BART; NON-VERBAL BEHAVIOUR: REPERTOIRE; OBJECT LANGUAGE; SILENCE.

▶ Roger E. Axel, *Gestures: The Do's and Taboos of Body Language Around the World* (John Wiley & Sons, Inc., 1998); Stella Ting-Toomey, *Communicating Across Cultures* (Guildford Press, 1999); Desmond Morris, *People Watching* (Vintage, 2002); Allan and Barbara Pease, *The Definitive Book of Body Language* (Orion, 2004); Ted Polhemus and UZi PART B, *Hot Bodies, Cool Styles: New Techniques in Self-Adornment* (Thames and Hudson, 2004).

Communication postulates See POSTULATES OF COMMUNICATION.

Communications Act (UK), 2003 Legislation bringing far-reaching changes to the landscape of telecommunications and broadcasting in Britain; and creating a 'super regulator' in the Office of Communications (OFCOM). Telecommunications and BROADCASTING are seen in the Act to be twin parts of the same pattern of technological CONVERGENCE.

Deregulation, or at least 'light touch' regulation, was the guiding principle of the Act, the key focus the interests of broadcasting as a business rather than, as some critics have stated, the interests of audience. Rules concerning CROSS-MEDIA OWNERSHIP were largely abandoned: there is now no bar to foreign ownership of British media and thus no impediment to corporate media interests worldwide competing for swathes of British commercial broadcasting. Gillian Doyle in an article 'Changes in media ownership' in *Sociology Review* (February 2004) wrote, 'In effect these changes allow unprecedented opportunities for major commercial radio and television broadcasters to expand their share of the UK media market.'

The Act scrapped the following regulatory rules: (1) those preventing single ownership of ITV; (2) those preventing ownership of more than one national commercial radio licence; (3) those preventing joint ownership of TV and radio stations; (4) those obstructing large newspaper groups from acquiring Channel 5 TV or radio licences; and (5) those preventing non-European ownership.

OFCOM took over regulatory responsibilities from five bodies: the Broadcasting Standards Commission, the Independent Television Commission (ITC), the Office of Telecommunications (Oftel), the Radio Authority, and the Radiocommunications Agency. It has a 'statutory duty to further the interests of citizens and consumers by promoting competition and protecting consumers from harmful or offensive material'. It is empowered to conduct research, develop policies, create codes of practice, consult widely, make recommendations concerning not only independent broadcasting but also the BBC (which in terms of *control* does not come under Ofcom's remit) and deal with complaints.

Pressure from various bodies, including many MPs and a media committee chaired by Lord Puttnam, brought about government modifications to the original Bill. A 'public interest plurality' clause was inserted into the Act, allowing the Secretary of State to block any deals which might be judged to compromise plurality. See BRITISH MEDIA INDUSTRY GROUP; COMMANDERS OF THE SOCIAL ORDER; REGULATORY FAVOURS.

Communications conglomerates See CONGLOMERATES: MEDIA CONGLOMERATES.

Communications Decency Act (US) Law passed overwhelmingly by the US Congress and signed by President Bill Clinton in February 1996, designed to ban pornography on the Internet (see INTERNET: MONITORING OF CONTENT). The measure has faced a number of formidable and ongoing obstacles; first, the means of exercising censorship on the Net; second, arriving at any definition of 'decency' (as compared, for example, with 'obscenity') which can win CONSENSUS in America; third, controlling indecency across frontiers (it is easy for American citizens to 'emigrate' across the Net by transmitting under the guise of 'anonymous remailers'); and fourth, persuading other nations to introduce similar legislation. Perhaps the strongest impediment to the Communications Decency Act has been the United States Constitution, the First Amendment of which prohibits Congress from 'abridging the freedom of speech'. See REGULATION OF INVESTIGATORY POWERS ACT (RIPA) (UK), 2000.

Communication theory See *TOPIC GUIDE* under COMMUNICATION THEORY.

Communication workers See WORKERS IN COMMUNICATION AND MEDIA.

Communicative rationality Jürgen Habermas in his vast and seminal work on communication and the public sphere, *The Theory of Communicative Action, Vol. 1: Reason and Rationalization* (Beacon, 1981), and *Vol. 2: The Critique of Functionalist Reason* (Polity, 1983), poses the notion of communicative rationality as being characterized by truth, appropriateness and sincerity. The operation of these criteria in public life rests upon the existence of free, open and egalitarian DISCOURSE – an 'ideal speech situation' – which in turn makes understanding between elements of society more likely. Communicative rationality rests essentially on an equality of opportunity to participate in communication.

Communicology The study of the nature, process and meanings systems of all forms of communication in what Dean C. Barnlund has described as 'the totality of time, space, personality and circumstance' (in 'A transactional model of communication', K.K. Sereno and C.D. Mortensen, eds, *Foundations of Communication Theory*, Harper & Row, 1970).

Community radio Because RADIO BROADCASTING is the cheapest form of mass communication, it lends itself to 'grass roots' use by communities of interest – geographical, cultural, political. Its potential is to be run by and for local communities, special interests and followings. The development of local radio in the UK has made some progress towards the community ideal, but full independence in terms of appointments, policy, financing, programming, etc. remains at levels other than the local.

Though the term 'community radio' was probably first used in the UK by Rachel Powell in a pamphlet *Possibilities for Local Radio* (Centre for Contemporary Cultural Studies, University of Birmingham, December 1965), the idea goes as far back as the BEVERIDGE REPORT, 1950, which proposed the use of VHF frequencies to 'establish local radio stations with independent programmes of their own. How large a scope there would be in Britain for local stations broadcasting programmes controlled by Universities or Local Authorities or public service organizations is not known, but the experiment of setting up some local stations should be tried without delay'.

In 1962 the PILKINGTON REPORT recommended that the BBC provide 'local sound broadcasting' on the basis of 'one service in some 250 localities', stations having a typical range of 5 miles. The 1971 government White Paper launched COMMERCIAL RADIO, but radio broadcasting through the next decades was to remain under the duopoly of the BBC and the Independent Broadcasting Authority (IBA).

Pressure to produce a 'third' force in broadcasting in the UK, to consist of highly individual and genuinely local stations, grew in the 1980s. Throughout the country, groups dedicated to the furtherance of community radio multiplied, providing information, exerting pressure at national and local levels. The question that needs to be asked in identifying and characterizing community radio is whether, as well as aiming to serve the perceived interests of the community, that radio is also run *by* the community.

Though the most familiar model is generally associated with PUBLIC SERVICE BROADCASTING (PSB) initiatives, variations on community radio are to be found throughout the world, particularly in the United States. Here, in January 2000, the Federal Communications Commission (FCC) approved the use of Low Power FM (LPFM) or micro-radio services that would be used for community-orientated programming, to serve schools, civic clubs, state and local governments, churches and other non-profit-making organizations.

However, the fullscale development of this *microcasting* met with the obstacle of vested interest as represented by corporate radio. The National Association of Broadcasters (NAB), working on behalf of the commercial sector, pressurized Congress for legislation that had the effect of eliminating the majority of the new

voices, on the grounds of possible interference with high-power transmission.

As INTERNET services have expanded, so has interest in, and development of, web-radio, often referred to as 'web-casting'. Both public and private radio broadcasters already make available programmes on the Web, but the opportunities for individuals, groups and communities to offer alternative broadcasting services through the Net have burgeoned worldwide.

Web-radio draws benefit from low start-up costs and relatively cheap equipment, as illustrated by Groovera (formerly OverXposure FM) of Seattle, US, where Tim Quigley webcast programmes from his sitting room from 2003. Paris-based Deezer claims over 4m users, while Whole Wheat Radio (WWR) of Talkeetna, Alaska, offers 24-hours-a-day music run by an all-volunteer community.

Former London pirate radio Rinse FM received its broadcasting licence in June 2010, while Forge Radio (formerly Sure Radio) broadcasts in term-time at Sheffield University. Cost and increased competition prove constant hazards, as the Isle of Wight station, Wight FM, found in 2009 – starting up on 1 February and closing down in December of the same year. See DAB: DIGITAL AUDIO BROADCASTING; PODCAST; RADIO 'SHOCK JOCKS'; STREAMING; YOUTUBE.

Compassion fatigue Media reportage of world suffering risks affecting mass media audiences in unintended ways, often prompting resistance rather than EMPATHY. The news becomes too much to bear, causing what is termed *compassion fatigue*. Susan D. Moeller in *Compassion Fatigue: How the Media Sell Disease, Famine, War and Death* (Routledge, 1999) defines it as a 'defence mechanism against the knowledge of horror'. Moeller is highly critical of what she terms 'formulaic coverage' of world disasters which, in American reporting, suffers what she sees as *Americanization of events* (see EVENT: AMERICANIZATION OF).

Ultimately, Moeller argues, the fault lies in piecemeal, often haphazard, selective and potentially hysterical media coverage of foreign news: 'Compassion fatigue, and even more clearly, compassion avoidance are signals that the coverage of international affairs must change.' That, she asserts, means a need for 'great reporters, producers and editors' and a will 'to invest in such an un-sexy news beat as international affairs'. She urges that events beyond our shores should be reported 'day in day out, year in year out'; in short, 'to get back to the business of reporting all the news, all the time'. See COUPS

AND EARTHQUAKES SYNDROME.

Competence In LINGUISTICS, a term used to describe a person's knowledge of his/her own language, its system of rules; his/her competence in understanding an unlimited number of sentences, in spotting grammatical errors, etc.

Compliance See ANTICIPATORY COMPLIANCE.

Compliance, climate of See KUUKI.

Compliance, identification and internalization See INTERNALIZATION.

Complicity of users Term employed by Cees J. Hamelink to describe the reluctance of audiences to be told the truth about crises – particularly war situations, but also in cases concerning government and corporate matters. In 'Ethics for media users' published in the *European Journal of Communication*, December 1995, Hamelink cites findings that indicated nearly 8 out of 10 Americans supporting restrictions on information imposed by the Pentagon, while 6 out of 10 said they believed the military should have exercised greater censorship. 'The [1st Gulf] war demonstrated that official censorship, journalistic self-censorship and the users' refusal to be informed reinforced each other.' Hamelink goes on, 'The complicity of users was an essential component in the reduction of freedom of media performance.' See NEWS MANAGEMENT IN TIMES OF WAR.

Compression technology A key science in the Age of Information, in particular the era of DIGITIZATION: the more data becomes available, the broader the available bandwidth, the greater the requirement to compress information, to compact data for transmission. See BROADBAND.

Computer Name derives from the French, *computer*, to calculate and the Latin, *putare*, to think, determine by number. The computer is a general-purpose information processor, its origin reaching back over a thousand years to the abacus. It then progressed via the Pascaline, a numerical wheel calculator, invented by French philosopher (then a teenager), Baise Pascall (1623–62). This was improved by a German mathematician named Gottfried Willem von Leibnitz (1646–1716), who extended the machine's capacity for addition to multiplication.

By general consent, the true father of the computer was English professor and mathematician Charles Babbage (1791–1871). In 1822 he introduced the concept of a steam-powered Difference Engine, as he called it. It was – in theory, for the machine was never built – the first automated computer with a stored program; its purpose was to perform differential equations. This was followed a decade later with the Analyt-

ical Engine. Babbage was assisted by Augusta Ada King, Countess of Lovelace (1815–1842), daughter of Lord Byron, whose expertise qualified her to be called the first female computer programmer. In her honour the US Defence Department named a programming language after her – ADA – in the 1980s.

The story of the computer comprises the diversification of its uses, the speed of its operation and the progressive reduction of its size, from mainframe to desktop, to laptop to palmtop. Events boosted progress, in particular the Second World War (1939–45); the Z3 computer developed by Konrad Zuse was used to design airplanes and missiles while Colossus, Britain's code-breaking computer, was specifically designed to decipher German war communications.

Technical specifications improved performance and reduced size rapidly, vacuum tubes and resisters giving way to transistors, and once components could be fitted on to single chips – semiconductors – programming advanced dramatically. The Intel chip of 1971 proved a landmark in computer design at a period when diversification of computer functions was matched by growing public interest.

Soon the computer was central to the operation of practically every aspect of modern life, from defence to building-design, typesetting to criminal investigation, satellite communication to the automobile industry, filming to fashion, electronic voting and gaming to word processing and traffic control. A key expansion was the microprocessor making possible the introduction by the IBM company in 1981 of the first personal computer, followed three years later by a global rival, the APPLE MACINTOSH.

Networking of computers followed, using telephone lines or Local Area Networks (LAMs) and, for better or worse, the e-mail. Soon the computer was to lead us into the Digital Age – one of breathtaking new developments, many amazing, some worrying; an age, of course, touched upon throughout this dictionary.

▶ To follow the story of the computer in the late twentieth and early twenty-first centuries, see the thorough and readable account by Paul A. Friebeger and Michael R. Swaine in the online *Encyclopaedia Britannica*, or the entry 'Computers: history and development' in the *Jones Telecommunications and Multimedia Encyclopaedia*; also, for a detailed technical analysis, Wikipedia.

Computing: cloud computing INTERNET computing system in which sources are shared in similar ways to an electricity grid, with key providers such as GOOGLE, AMAZON, YAHOO! and MICROSOFT. Works by customers renting usage from a third-party provider. The system attracts in particular small and medium business enterprises (SMEs) which on their own might be unable or reluctant to invest in capital expenditure in traditional IT. Users are billed, or charged through subscription, only for what they use.

Conative function of communication See JAKOBSON'S MODEL OF COMMUNICATION, 1958.

Concurrence-seeking tendency See GROUPS, GROUPTHINK

Confederates See SLIDER.

Confirmation/disconfirmation Through communication with others we gain feedback on our SELF-CONCEPT. Several authors, among them Gail and Michele Myers in *The Dynamics of Human Communication* (McGraw-Hill, 1985), use the terms *confirmation* and *disconfirmation* to describe the kind of messages about yourself and your view of the world you may receive in feedback. Confirming responses tend to confirm or validate the view of yourself you have put forward and/or the views you have expressed in conversation. Examples of confirming responses include direct acknowledgment of your message, agreement with the content of your message and expression of positive feelings about you.

Disconfirming responses are likely to leave you feeling confused, dissatisfied, and maybe undermined. They are not clear expressions of either approval or rejection; they are ambiguous. Such responses include the *impervious response* when the receiver gives no acknowledgment of your message; the *interrupting response* when the receiver does not let you finish your message; and the *incongruous response* when the receiver's non-verbal response is clearly contrary to the verbal response he/she is making; for example, when a fixed smile accompanies words of praise.

Conglomerates: media conglomerates The increasing cost of entering the media market has, in part, fostered a concentration of ownership in the various sectors of the communications industry. Peter Golding and Graham Murdock in an article entitled 'Culture, communications and political economy' in *Mass Media and Society* (Arnold, 1996), edited by James Curran and Michael Gurevitch, write, 'The rise of communications conglomerates adds a new element to the old debate about the potential abuses of owner power. It is no longer a simple case of proprietors intervening in editorial decisions or firing key personnel who fall foul of their political philosophies. Cultural production is also strongly influenced by commercial strate-

gies built around "synergies" which exploit the overlaps between the company's different media interests.' (See also Curran, ed., *Media and Society*, 5th edition, Bloomsbury Academic, 2010).

A communications conglomerate is an amalgam of corporations such as Sony, Disney, Time Warner, Bertelsmann and News Corporation (see NEWS CORP) which operate mainly or wholly with communications or leisure interests and function globally. Significant sectors of the communications industry are part of *general* conglomerates whose main business concerns are outside the communications field.

The mass media can be seen as related to the industrial system in two ways: first, they are part of it as large-scale buyers and sellers and makers of profit; second, they are preachers of its (industry's) messages (see MEDIA IMPERIALISM).

The concentration of ownership, the increased potential for power which it facilitates, and the interrelationship between the communications industry and other industrial and commercial interests constitute important areas of current media research; in particular the focus of attention is on the role of conglomerates in the world of the INTERNET. Considering that in the UK alone Net advertising has been estimated (in 2010) to be worth in excess of £100 billion, corporate ownership and control is a hot issue of the day.

What big business is uneasy about is the Net allowing free use of online content, a worry which in 2010 decided Rupert Murdoch's News International to introduce charges for the online services of its flagship newspaper, *The Times*. See AGENDA-SETTING; BERLUSCONI PHENOMENON; BLOGOSPHERE; COMMUNICATIONS ACT (UK), 2003; GLOBALIZATION (AND THE MEDIA); GLOBAL MEDIA SYSTEM: THE MAIN PLAYERS; MOBILIZATION; MURDOCH EFFECT; NETWORK NEUTRALITY; WORLD TRADE ORGANIZATION (WTO) TELECOMMUNICATIONS AGREEMENT, 1997. See also *TOPIC GUIDE* under MEDIA: OWNERSHIP & CONTROL.
▶ Tim Wu, *The Master Switch: The Rise and Fall of Information Empires* (Knopf/Atlantic, 2010).

Connotation Roland Barthes' second order of SIGNIFICATION in the transmission of messages. The second order comprises connotation and myth. *Denotation*, the first order of signification, is simply a process of identification. The word 'green' represents a colour; but green, at a higher level, can connote the countryside, permission to go ahead, the Irish, etc. *Connotation* is the act of adding information, insight, angle, colouration, value – MEANING, in fact, to denotation.

▸ Roland Barthes, *Mythologies* (Paladin, 1973).

Consensus That which is generally agreed; an area or basis of shared agreement among the majority. Three elements crucial to the function of consensus are: common acceptance of laws, rules and norms; attachment to the institutions which promulgate these laws, rules and norms; and a widespread sense of identity or unity, of similar or identical outlook. The opposite term is *dissensus*.

The elements of consensus obviously vary independently, yet the strength of any one helps to strengthen the others. Consensus, states the *International Encyclopaedia of Social Sciences* (ed. D.L. Sills; Macmillan and Free Press, 1968), 'operates to restrict the extension of dissensus and to limit conflict ...'. Beliefs about consensus 'usually concern the rightness and the qualifications of those in authority to exercise it' and thus relate to the legitimacy of institutions, accepted standards and practices, and dominant principles.

Such beliefs tend to affirm existing patterns of the distribution of authority. Consensus, therefore, is largely defined by those who have the power and the means to disseminate their definition; and the definition is employed as a means of acknowledging and reinforcing the legitimacy of the powerful. Equally important in this context is the close affinity of outlook of the central cultural system with the central institutional system. Stuart Hood in *Hood on Television* (Pluto, 1980) says, 'It is the essence of the idea of consensus that it attempts, at a conscious and unconscious level, to impose the view that there is only one "right" reading. This assumption derives from the view that we – that is the audience and the broadcaster – are united in one nation in spite of class or political definition.' See CULTURAL APPARATUS; HEGEMONY; IMPARTIALITY; NEWCOMB'S ABX MODEL OF COMMUNICATION, 1953.

Consent, manufacture of Noam Chomsky has defined the manufacture of consent as a complex process whereby powerful interests inside democracies such as the US and the UK create in the public mind patterns of acceptance. In an article written for *Index on Censorship, 1* (1987) entitled 'No anti-Israeli vendetta', Chomsky refers to 'devices of thought control' in democratic societies 'which are more pertinent for us than the crude methods of totalitarian states'.

The devices arise from such aspects of the media process as control over resources and the locus of decision-making in the state and private economy. Where state policy on an issue such as the Arab-Israeli conflict, or with regard to Central American politics, is rigorously committed to one side or the other, alternative options which the public might be interested in considering, are declared out of bounds – through what Chomsky describes as 'suppression, falsification, and Orwellian manipulation.'

The process of consent manufacture is most comprehensively analysed in *Manufacturing Consent: The Political Economy of the Mass Media* (Pantheon, 1988; Vantage paperback, 1994) by Edward S. Herman and Chomsky. They pose a model of propaganda, and that propaganda issues from the media on behalf of the interests of the POWER ELITE in any society. Essentially this is a GATEKEEPING model in the sense that the media select and shape material that aligns with the interests and VALUES of those who exercise control; in turn, the media censor material which may run counter to those interests and values.

Because the media are largely owned, controlled and run by institutions, it follows that the media 'toe the line' with the IDEOLOGIES of those institutions and those who run them. Herman and Chomsky argue that the propaganda model describes 'the forces that cause the mass media to play a propaganda role' and assert that 'the workings of the media ... serve to mobilize support for the special interests that dominate the state and private activity'.

Leaders of the media 'claim that their news choices rest on unbiased professional and objective criteria, and they have support for the contention within the intellectual community. If, however, the powerful are able to fix the premises of discourse, to decide what the general populace is allowed, to see, hear, and think about, and to "manage" public opinion by regular propaganda campaigns, the standard view of how the system works is at serious odds with reality'.

Herman and Chomsky refer to five interconnecting *filters* in the processing of mass communication news which serve to regulate and constrain. These are: (1) 'the size, concentrated ownership, owner wealth and profit orientation of the dominant media firms; (2) advertising as the primary income source of the mass media; (3) the reliance of the media on information provided by government, business, and "experts" funded and approved by these primary sources and agents of power; (4) "flak" as a means of disciplining the media [see FLAK]; and (5) "anti-communism" as a national religion and control mechanism'. Such filters 'interact and reinforce one another'.

The authors are of the view that the media constitute an ideological apparatus for the elite (see IDEOLOGICAL APPARATUSES), but their theory has incurred both criticism and the occasional academic cold shoulder – arguably for the reason that certain truths, while being self-evident, are too uncomfortable to accept.

The manufacture of consent becomes particularly imperative in times of crisis. Following the terrorist attacks on the Pentagon and New York's Twin Towers on 11 September 2001 (9/11), public consent to the war in Afghanistan, while needing little coaxing from a shocked nation, nevertheless progressed in part as a result of the denial of opportunities for critics to suggest alternative responses.

William Blum points out in *Rogue State: A Guide to the World's Only Superpower* (Zed Books, 2002), 'Many critics of the bombing campaign, who were in vulnerable positions, suffered consequences: a number of university teachers who had spoken out against the war lost their positions or were publicly rebuked by school officials ... the only members of Congress who voted against the "Authorization for Use of Military Force" received innumerable threats and hate mail ...'

A similar scenario played out when American (and British) forces invaded Iraq in 2003. Support for the war and occupation was almost universal in the US, and critics were accused of being unpatriotic. By 2005, however, both media and public support began to slip as the deaths in Iraq and Afghanistan of American servicemen and women increased: sooner or later the manufacture of consent bends to the force of evidence. The process thus enters a new phase, usually by shifting the grounds of justification: what was to be a swift war is now to be a long-haul.

With the the multiplication of information sources brought about by the Internet, and the opportunities networking offers for audiences to express their own opinions (see BLOGOSPHERE; MOBILIZATION), some commentators have predicted a lessening of the power of mass media to cultivate consent, if only because people are so busy surfing the Net that mass media messaging is increasingly ignored. See AGENDA-SETTING; DEMOTIC TURN; DIGITAL OPTIMISM; DISCOURSE; HEGEMONY; JOURNALISM: CITIZEN JOURNALISM; NEWS MANAGEMENT IN TIMES OF WAR. See also *TOPIC GUIDE* under MEDIA: POLITICS & ECONOMICS; MEDIA: VALUES & IDEOLOGY.

Consistency See COGNITIVE CONSISTENCY THEORIES; EFFECTS OF THE MASS MEDIA; FREQUENCY; INTENSITY.

Consonance, hypothesis of See NEWS VALUES.

Conspiracy of silence The tacit agreement among those with significant information to 'keep mum' about it – say nothing. An early use of the phrase is ascribed to the head of BBC News in 1938 at the time of the Munich crisis, referring to the Corporation's failure to broadcast any close examination of Neville Chamberlain's policy of appeasement towards Nazi Germany. See CENSORSHIP; NOELLE-NEUMANN'S SPIRAL OF SILENCE MODEL OF PUBLIC OPINION, 1974.

Conspiracy theory Not so much a theory, more a hunch or suspicion. As far as the media are concerned, the 'conspiracy' relates – in the view of those who claim it exists – to the practice of manipulating messages in order to support those who own the means of communication, their social CLASS (i.e. middle and upper) and their interests. The conspiracy theorists argue that in a capitalist society where the media are owned or strongly influenced by the capitalist ESTABLISHMENT, information is shaped to underpin existing social, economic and political conditions (see CONSENT, MANUFACTURE OF).

In his introduction to the GLASGOW UNIVERSITY MEDIA GROUP publication *Bad News* (Routledge & Kegan Paul, 1976), Richard Hoggart ventures to locate two levels or forms of conspiracy theory, High and Low – the one aligning with the Marxist view of media operation; the other with the generality of people who at some time or another suspect that the media project the interests and value systems of those who own, control or run them. See HEGEMONY.

Contiguity See YAROS' 'PICK' MODEL FOR MULTIMEDIA NEWS, 2009.

Constituency Term generally applied to an electoral area which returns a parliamentary candidate, but it is also used by researchers to refer to the readership of a newspaper, and carries with it the implication that the reader's political views may be influenced by the paper's coverage of events. The notion of audience as constituency was particularly prevalent in the age of PRESS BARONS such as – in the UK – Lords Northcliffe, Rothermere and Beaverbrook, who claimed access to political decision-making on the strength of the constituency of their papers' readership.

Consumerization Describes a vision of contemporary life dominated by the marketplace and prompting fears that, with the global advance of transnational corporations, and their substantial buying-in to media and CULTURE generally, society has become one-dimensionalized – the consumer dimension.

Some commentators see consumption as being a modern substitute for religion – spending as a substitute for praying – while the cathedrals of today are shopping malls. Big business sponsors art and thereby brings it under the wing of consumer criteria – is there a market for it, and will it directly or indirectly make a profit? Big business also sponsors schools and thus is in at least a pole-position to appropriate education itself.

American writer Herbert J. Schiller, until his death in 2000, proved himself a scourge of corporate intrusions into the life of communities. In *Culture Inc.: The Corporate Takeover of Public Expression* (Oxford University Press, 1989), Schiller believed that 'the Corporate voice, not surprisingly, is the loudest in the land' and it also rings around the world. He was of the view that consumerism 'as it is propagated by the transnational corporate system and carried to the four corners of the world by new information age technologies, now seems triumphant'. He talked of 'corporate pillaging of the national information supply' and the 'proprietory control of information'.

Even the museum has 'been enlisted as a corporate instrument': history is adopted for corporate use through sponsorship. Thus eventually museums become reliant on corporate 'approval' of the past. The pressure upon them is to choose to record the kind of history that suits the corporate purpose. Corporate power in the field of communication is so great, Schiller argued, that the active-audience paradigm is called into question: 'A great emphasis is given to the "resistance", "subversion", and "empowerment" of the viewer. Where this resistance and subversion of the audience lead and what effects they have on the existing structure of power remain a mystery'.

He expressed the view that 'it is not a matter of people being dupes, informational or cultural. It is that human beings are not equipped to deal with a pervasive disinformational system – administered from the command posts of social order – that assails the senses through all cultural forms and channels'.

Schiller's theme is echoed in the work of the French philosopher Jean Baudrillard, whose *The Consumer Society: Myths and Structures* made its first appearance in English – translated by Chris Turner and published by Sage – in 1998. A question engaging twenty-first-century commentators is the extent to which the digital age of the INTERNET has seen challenges to corporate ambitions to consumerize world soci-

eties. See McDONALDIZATION; TECHNOLOGY: THE CONSUMERIZATION OF TECHNOLOGY.

▶ Jeff Hearn and Sasha Roseneil, eds, *Consuming Cultures: Power and Resistance* (Macmillan, 1999); Peter N. Stearns, *Consumerization in World History: The Global Transformation of Desire* (Routledge, 2001); Paul Ransome, *Work, Consumption and Culture* (Sage, 2005).

Consumer sovereignty A phrase used in the Peacock Report, 1985, summarizing the attitude towards BROADCASTING of the Committee on Financing the BBC. The Committee took the market-place view that the customer knows best and that consumer tastes should be the guiding principle of RADIO and TELEVISION programming. See PUBLIC SERVICE BROADCASTING (PSB).

Consumption behaviour Term used by researchers to describe the ways in which audiences respond to product marketing – attitudes towards ADVERTISING, knowledge of commercials and people's buying behaviour. At the nub of market research into consumption behaviour is *motivation*. Why do people watch a TV commercial, what makes them pay attention and heed the message?

Regularly cited are three major reasons for a positive audience response: (1) social utility – watching commercials in order to gain information about the 'social significance' of products or brands, and the association of advertising objects with social roles and lifestyles; (2) communication utility – watching in order to provide a basis for later interpersonal communication; (3) vicarious consumption – participating at second-hand in desired lifestyles as a means of indirect association with those people possessing glamour or prestige. See VALS TYPOLOGY.

▶ Martin Evans, Ahmed Jamal and Gordon Foxall, *Consumer Behaviour* (John Wiley & Sons, 2009).

Contagion effect Power of the media to create a craze or even an epidemic. Examples of this are the so-called Swastika Epidemic of 1959–60, in which an outbreak of swastika-daubing in the US was accelerated by media coverage, and the UK Mods v. Rockers seaside battles of the 1960s. Debate continues as to whether media coverage 'worsens' or prompts the street riots, often named Copycat Riots.

Stanley Cohen in 'Sensitization: the case of the Mods and Rockers' in *The Manufacture of News* (Constable, 1st edition, 1973), edited by Cohen and Jock Young, writes, 'Constant repetition of the warring gangs' image ... had the effect of giving these loose collections a structure they never possessed and a mythology with which to justify the structure', and the court scenes at which those arrested by the police were tried were 'arenas for acting out society's morality plays'.

In relation to 'loose connections' being given a 'structure', claims have been made by commentators in the aftermath of the 9/11 terrorist assault on New York's twin towers, that the directing of attention to Al-Qaeda had a similar contagion effect: even though there was very little evidence that Al-Qaeda was a worldwide organization, treating it as such has been in danger of becoming a SELF-FULFILLING PROPHECY. See EMPOWERMENT; MORAL PANICS AND THE MEDIA.

Content analysis David Deacon, Michael Pickering, Peter Golding and Graham Murdock in *Researching Communications: A Practical Guide to Methods in Media and Cultural Analysis* (Hodder Education, 2007) note that, 'The purpose of content analysis is to quantify salient and manifest features of a large number of texts, and the statistics are used to make broader inferences about the processes and politics of representation.' Content analysis thus seeks to compare material as presented in differing sources in order to identify any patterns or trends in coverage or representation. Typical sources include newspapers, magazines, websites, advertisements, and television programmes.

The media content is compared using standards or categories. For example, a researcher may seek to discover differences in the coverage given to financial matters between UK tabloid and broadsheet newspapers during the week in which the spring Budget is announced. Examples of categories that might be used are the number of column inches devoted to coverage, and the number of negative terms and positive terms employed in the coverage.

Deacon *et al* argue that as a quantitative method, content analysis is best used to capture the broad 'big picture' and manifest levels of meaning. It is not that suitable for exploring implicit or latent levels of meaning, so it is often combined with other research methods such as interviews or focus groups to provide a more rounded and in-depth analysis. So, using the above example of coverage of the budget, whilst content analysis may tell us the number of positive and negative terms used by broadsheet and tabloid newspapers, focus group discussions with samples of readers might be able to tell us how the readers interpret and react to such terms.

Content analysis serves an important function by comparing the same material as presented in different media within a nation, or between different nations; or by comparing media content with some explicit set of standards or abstract categories. On the basis of the existing body of quantitative and qualitative research, several broad generalizations may be hazarded about the content of MASS COMMUNICATION: what is communicated by the mass media is a highly selected sample of all that is available for communication; what is received and consumed by the potential AUDIENCE is a highly selected sample of all that is communicated; more of what is communicated is classifiable as entertaining rather than informative or educative, and, because the mass media are aimed at the largest possible audience, most material is simple in form and uncomplicated in content. See AUDIENCE MEASUREMENT; ETHNOGRAPHIC (APPROACH TO AUDIENCE MEASUREMENT); GLASGOW UNIVERSITY MEDIA GROUP. See also *TOPIC GUIDE* under RESEARCH METHODS.

Control group In comparative research methods, the group against which the behaviour of the experimental group is measured. The experimental group is exposed to the variable to be tested and the control group is not. So, to take an example of a possible experiment: in attempting to ascertain the influence of a celebrity on the audience's willingness to be persuaded by an argument, the experimental group might hear the argument from a well-known celebrity and the control group might hear the argument from an unidentified source. The groups could then be tested for their attitude towards the argument and these could be compared to the results of the prior testing of their positions on this argument. Efforts would be made in forming the composition of the groups to reduce the influence of any other significant variables – for example, prior knowledge of the topic under discussion. Thus, in the case of AUDIENCE MEASUREMENT, the test group is exposed to a TV programme, for example, and their responses analysed against identical monitoring of the control group who have not seen the programme.

Control of the media See MEDIA CONTROL.

Conventions Established practices within a particular CULTURE or SUB-CULTURE. Conventions are identifiable in every form of communication and behaviour – some strict, like rules of grammar; others open to wider application, such as dress. Conventions are largely culture-specific and context-specific. It is an accepted convention that a candidate dress smartly for a job interview, yet it would be deemed unconventional if he/she appeared on the beach clad in the same manner.

Media practices have established many

conventions which have become so familiar that they appear 'the natural way to do things'. TELEVISION news holds to the convention of having on-screen newsreaders; documentaries generally hold to the convention of having a voice-over narration. Innovators – for example in the arts –break with convention. The shock of the new often stirs among the conventional a sense of affronted VALUES. The chances of the new becoming conventionalized will depend on various factors, such as opinion leaders, prevalent tastes and fashions, even newsworthiness. See LEADERSHIP; REDUNDANCY.

Convergence The coming-together of communication devices and processes; a major feature of the development of media technology in the 1990s onwards. In *Of Media and People* (Sage, 1992), Everette E. Dennis writes of forms converging 'into a single electronically based, computer-driven mode that has been described as the nearly universal integration of systems that retrieve, process, and store text, data, sound, and image'; in short, multi-media. Dennis points out that convergence is far more than 'the stuff of hardware and software: it is the driving force that has spurred major change in the media industries and almost everywhere else'.

Convergence has operated at the technical and operational level and at the level of ownership and control. Just as individual items of hard and software have been centralized into one multimedia outfit, so media production has been centralized into fewer corporate hands, most of these transnational.

A further question is whether technical and operational convergence will lead to transcultural convergence and extend the reach of what some would see as the already well-established strategy of cultural and MEDIA IMPERIALISM. For those who support this thesis, GLOBALIZATION fosters homogeneity and works in the interests of Western – chiefly American – cultural dominance, whilst undermining the indigenous cultures of the less-powerful receivers of such artefacts.

However, such a view is seen by others as underestimating the degree to which those who receive such artefacts adapt them in the process of absorbing them into the host culture. The resultant blend may limit the degree of convergence. It should also be noted that artefacts destined for a wide market are often tailored to take account of differentiation within the market, and in this process characteristics of the differing host cultures may be considered in the construction of the artefact.

Moreover, the flow of cultural artefacts is arguably more complex than is suggested by the cultural or media imperialism thesis. A number of theorists point to the essential heterogeneity of culture(s) and argue consequently that it is unlikely that cultural convergence would occur. See CYBERSPACE; DIGITIZATION; MOBILIZATION; NEW MEDIA. See also *TOPIC GUIDE* under MEDIA: PROCESSES & PRODUCTION.

▶ Michael Kackman *et al, Flow TV: Television in the Age of Media Convergence* (Routledge, 2011).

Conversational styles In a study of conversation among friends at dinner, entitled *Conversational Style: Analyzing Talk Among Friends* (Ablex, 1984), Deborah Tannen identifies different conversational styles which she terms 'High Considerateness' and 'High Involvement'. Each style has different priorities. The 'High Considerateness' style places a premium on being considerate of others in conversation, of not interrupting, of listening to what someone is saying. The 'High Involvement' style on the other hand is characterized by enthusiastic involvement in a conversation, and this may be at the expense of giving sufficient space to others.

One style is not necessarily better than the other, but often reflects cultural differences; for example, in her study, the Briton was the most considerate of all. However, this categorization can help explain problems in INTERPERSONAL COMMUNICATION. To the highly considerate speaker the highly involved speaker may seem an exhibitionist, whilst the highly involved speaker may perceive the highly considerate speaker as aloof or distant.

Co-orientation approach See MCCOMBS AND SHAW'S AGENDA-SETTING MODEL OF MEDIA EFFECTS, 1976.

Copycat effect See CONTAGION EFFECT.

Copyrighting culture See CULTURE: COPYRIGHTING CULTURE.

Core nations, peripheral nations Cees Hamelink makes this differentiation with regard to the distribution of information in and between nations in 'Information imbalance: core and periphery' in *Questioning The Media: A Critical Introduction* (Sage, 1990), edited by John Downing, Ali Mohammadi and Annabelle Sreberny-Mohammadi. Hamelink argues that the transnational picture of information distribution is one of *imbalances* between core – usually industrial – nations such as the US, Canada, Western Europe, Japan and Australia and the economic periphery, predominantly rural countries such as Africa, parts of Asia and Latin America.

Peripheral countries, in comparison with core nations, possess fewer newspapers, broadcasting stations and telephones, and less computer hardware. Hamelink believes that 'information imbalance ... undermines cultural self-determination'. A number of critical questions arise from this situation. Might, for example, imbalances be resolved through greater integration – links – between core and peripheral nation systems? Should peripheral nations bargain for 'fairer schemes and terms of trade, for cheaper transfers of technology' by pooling resources and energy? Or, more radically, should the peripherals dissociate themselves – de-link – from international networks that hamper development?

Collective effort across the periphery, argues Hamelink, 'in itself requires the solving of many old and difficult conflicts among the poorer countries themselves'. In addition it requires 'a visionary leadership willing to forego the immediate benefits of links with the core'. See INFORMATION GAPS; YAMOUSOUKROU DECLARATION.
▶ Jan van Dijk, *The Deepening Divide: Inequality in the Information Society* (Sage, 2005).

Corporate speech Best defined in a US context: that speech which is employed in the public domain by corporations, most obviously in terms of ADVERTISING, but applicable to a whole host of discourses in which industry and commerce address the public. Corporate speech in the US is classified as having the same right as the speech of individuals, and is thus protected by the First Amendment of the US Constitution that guarantees freedom of speech. Thus, a tobacco company cannot be restrained from propagandizing, through public advertisement, its products. In such a case, corporate speech could be deemed life-threatening.

Even taxes on advertising have been fought against by corporations. An attempt to impose an advertising tax by the State of Florida in 1987 was repealed within six months, due to corporate pressure. According to Herbert I. Schiller in *Culture, Inc.: The Corporate Takeover of Public Expression* (Oxford University Press, 1989), corporations use the First Amendment to do two things: protect their profits, and duck social accountability.

Corporations and media See CONGLOMERATES: MEDIA CONGLOMERATES; CONSUMERIZATION; CULTURE: CONSUMER CULTURE; CULTURE: GLOBALIZATION OF; NETWORK NEUTRALITY; PRIVATIZATION. See also *TOPIC GUIDE* under MEDIA INSTITUTIONS.

Cosmopolite and localite channels The situation in which the sender and receiver of a message belong to different social systems or sub-systems is referred to as *cosmopolite*. *Localite* channels are those in which both sender and receiver belong to the same social system or sub-system.

Cosmopoliteness In most social structures there are individuals who have considerable awareness of other social situations and frequent contact with those outside their own social structure. In general the more cosmopolite an individual, the more receptive he/she is to messages containing new ideas.

Couch potato US term for a confirmed and dedicated TV viewer. *20th Century Words* (Oxford University Press, 1999), edited by John Ayto, says that the term was first used in 1979, its 'neat encapsulation of vacuous indolence' ensuring 'its success in the censorious 1980s'.

Counter-culture A type of SUB-CULTURE firmly antagonistic to the dominant or prevailing CULTURE of a community. The term is generally used to describe the collection of mainly middle-class youth cultures which developed in the 1960s, and whose central feature was the call for the adoption of alternative social structures and lifestyles. In 'Sub cultures, cultures and class', John Clarke and others in *Resistance Through Rituals* (Hutchinson, 1976), edited by Stuart Hall and Tony Jefferson, explore some of the distinguishing features of such a counter-culture as compared with other types of youth sub-cultures. Its opposition to the dominant cultures took very open political and ideological forms, and went beyond the registering of complaint and resistance to the elaborate construction of alternative institutions.

More recently, examples of counter-cultural protests that have received significant media attention are those surrounding ecological issues – protests which challenge many of the environmental assumptions and values of Western societies. 'Eco-warriors', as the more radical of the protesters are sometimes called, may adopt a radically different lifestyle based on the principles underpinning their protest.

A favoured communications device of contemporary counter-cultures is the INTERNET, its global reach aiding the international nature of protests concerning corporate and state threats to the environment. Through the Net, the likeminded can bond, plan and organize – most famously focusing on protests wherever the nations of the World Trade Organization meet – and, by their collective protests, command global media attention.

Countermodernization See CULTURE: GLOBALIZATION OF.

Coups and earthquakes syndrome Term coined by American journalist Mort Rosenblum to describe the Western attitude to news emanating from developing nations in, for example, Africa and South America. For events in such countries to be deemed of NEWS VALUE they must come under the category of 'coups and earthquakes' – the overthrow of governments by force or natural disasters. Rosenblum wrote *Coups and Earthquakes* (Harper & Row) in 1979, but current practice seems not to have improved.

Referring to the 'coups and earthquakes' syndrome, Mark D. Alleyne in *News Revolution: Political and Economic Decisions about Global Information* (Macmillan, 1997) writes, 'It sometimes seems that there is a malicious attempt to stereotype these countries, and this attitude might be propelled by various factors, including racism, political idealogy and ethnocentrism.' Alleyne believes that 'in this way, international news can be seen as a weapon of those with power in the international system, a tool to maintain the status quo, at least in regard to the inferior status of some peoples and nation-states'.

The key problem lies with prevailing news values, for the definition of news 'controls the way in which journalists decide what is important'. At the same time 'journalists often use vague, shorthand terms to describe complex issues and regions'. See COMPASSION FATIGUE.

Creole See COMMUNICATION: INTERCULTURAL COMMUNICATION.

Crime: types of crime on screen A number of types of on-screen crime are identified by Jessica Allen, Sonia Livingstone and Robert Reiner in an article entitled 'True lies: changing images of crime in British postwar cinema' in the *European Journal of Communication*, March 1998. The authors surveyed 1,461 crime-related films released between 1945 and 1991, and popular with the public, reporting that 'contrary to general beliefs about increased crime content of the media … our data shows a constant rate of representation, at least in the cinema over 50 years'.

The authors discuss *primary, consequential, collateral* and *contextual* crimes. To the first – that which animates the NARRATIVE – they ascribe the term McGUFFIN, borrowed from film director Alfred Hitchcock, 'to refer to the object whose pursuit provides the driving force of the narrative'. Consequential crimes are those which are committed in the course of, or in order to cover up, the McGuffin, while collateral crimes are not directly related to the McGuffin though

they may be committed by the central criminals. Contextual crimes may also be unrelated to the McGuffin, the primary crime, 'but portray aspects of the wider society'.

Chief among McGuffins, say Allen, Livingstone and Reiner, is homicide, 48 per cent of their sample films having a homicide McGuffin – contrasting substantially with crime figures in the real world, where 90 per cent of recorded offences are property crimes. The authors note an increase in contextual crimes during the 1960s: 'This is significant because it is contextual crime perhaps even more than the McGuffin which creates a sense of society as a whole being threatened by crime.'

This trend is linked to the 'increasing predominance of police heroes rather than amateur "sleuths"'; 'towards an increasingly graphic representation of violence in the portrayal of crime'; the degree to which crime traumatizes the victim; and the perception that crime has social origins. In their analysis, the authors emphasize the complexity of the representation of crime in contexts of the 'collapse of moral certainties' in society, the dominance of Hollywood, the retreat from strict forms of CENSORSHIP and the demographic nature of AUDIENCE – largely made up of young people.

Crimes of self-publicity See TERRORISM AS COMMUNICATION.

Crisis definition How do we know when a crisis is a crisis? One answer is – when the media tell us it is a crisis. Their capacity for AGENDA-SETTING, of selecting the front-page headlines or the lead stories, can not only crystallize the notion of crisis in the public mind but also in some cases help precipitate one, at least in the sense that people in authority – such as governments – can be forced into a crisis response to a crisis stimulus.

Critical news analysis Generic term for a wide-ranging and complex approach to the analysis of the presentation of NEWS in the mass media. Perhaps the most influential starting point in the UK for this critical analysis is the book by Stanley Cohen and Jock Young, eds, *The Manufacture of News: Social Problems, Deviance and the Mass Media* (Constable, 1973). They, along with other commentators of the time – such as Professor Stuart Hall and colleagues at the University of Birmingham, and research teams such as the GLASGOW UNIVERSITY MEDIA GROUP – contributed to a developing awareness that the news is *socially constructed* and that it is both a social and an *ideological* construct. In other words, news isn't neutral. Critical news analysis focuses on content, presentation and language.

Emphasizing the importance of the linguistic assembly of messages in his book *Language in the News: Discourse and Ideology and the Press* (Routledge, 1991), Roger Fowler says that 'there are different ways of saying the same thing, and they are not random, accidental alternatives'; thus there can never be 'a value-free reflection of "facts"'. Two processes occur: *selection* (see AGENDA-SETTING; GATEKEEPING; NEWS VALUES), followed by *transformation* according to the dictates of the MEDIUM and the influences upon all the encoders involved. See HEGEMONY; IMPARTIALITY; JOURNALISM; SAPIR-WHORF LINGUISTIC RELATIVITY HYPOTHESIS.

Cropping Photographs for publication are rarely printed exactly as they emerge from the original negative or electronic transmission. They are very often 'cropped', that is cut to fulfil certain objectives: the space requirements of a page; to maximize impact; to serve aesthetic or ideological criteria. Generally pictures are cropped to get rid of redundant detail that might detract from the central thrust and drama of the picture's message. See ANCHORAGE; PREFERRED READING.

Cross-media ownership That is, where a PRESS BARON or corporation owns a range of media, newspapers, TV and RADIO stations within what, in the US, are described as *designated market areas* (DMAs). Resistance to cross-media ownership acts on the principle that to own the press *and* BROADCASTING in any particular area – city, district or region – constitutes a threat to media diversity and hence to the PLURALITY of the media; and such resistance has been incorporated in many countries in regulations designed to prevent monopoly.

In contrast, the corporate position is that regulation of cross-media ownership is an unnecessary inpediment to business practice and the making of profits. It follows that corporate owners of media seek DEREGULATION by pressurizing governments to abandon rules (generally made in the public interest) in favour of the free market (generally operating to the advantage of the corporations).

The issue of cross-media ownership has become a matter of profound concern, at least among media-watchers if not the public, because it trails other critical issues, such as the maintenance of quality, the integrity and independence of information; in short, the preservation of *public service* in the media.

In the UK the job of regulating cross-media ownership rests with Ofcom, following the COMMUNICATIONS ACT (UK), 2003. It is a requirement that Ofcom report on the ownership-of-media situation every three years and to make recommendations to government. Usually these shift in the direction of relaxing rules of ownership, and are based upon complex criteria concerning overlapping ownership, these operating in a context of technological change and mergers of ownership.

Differention is made between *viewpoint plurality* and *ownership plurality*, the latter being easier to define than the former. Ofcom's *Review of Media Ownership Rules* (2006) states that 'ownership plurality does not necessarily ensure editorial or viewpoint diversity. Whilst diversity of ownership may have an effect on plurality, it may also be the case that different sources of news offer the same perspective'.

Rules of media ownership (MO) in the US, for example, prevent any one individual or organization from owning more than one of the main TV networks: ABC, CBS, Fox and NBC. In Australia, working on a 'national interest principle', foreign ownership is not permitted; this contrasts with the situation in Finland and Luxemborg, where there are no restrictions on foreign ownership.

In Sweden, periodical publication ownership is restricted to the European Economic Area, while in Denmark, licences for regional broadcasting are only granted if the majority of board members reside in the local area. All of the above are subject to constant pressures for change as traditional media grapple with the challenges and opportunities brought about by the Network Society. See PRIVATIZATION; OFCOM: OFFICE OF COMMUNICATIONS (UK); REGULATORY FAVOURS. See also *TOPIC GUIDES* under MEDIA: OWNERSHIP & CONTROL; NETWORK SOCIETY.

Cryptography Secret LANGUAGE; the transfer of messages into secret codes. A cryptograph is anything written in *cypher*. See DATA PROTECTION.

Cues See BARNLAND'S TRANSACTIONAL MODELS OF COMMUNICATION.

Cultivation As used by US communications analyst George Gerbner, the term describes the way the mass media system relates to the CULTURE from which it grows, and which it addresses. The media 'cultivate' attitudes and VALUES in a culture. For example, audiences are cultivated into rejecting certain acts of violence while at the same time being cultivated into accepting or tolerating others. See MAINSTREAMING.

Cultural apparatus 'Taken as a whole,' writes

C. Wright Mills in *Power, Politics and People* (Oxford University Press, 1963), 'the cultural apparatus is the lens of mankind through which men see; the medium by which they interpret and report what they see.' It is composed of 'all the organizations and *milieux* in which artistic, intellectual and scientific work goes on, and of the means by which such work is made available to circles, publics and masses'.

The cultural apparatus features large in the processes of guiding experience, defining social truths, establishing standards of credibility, image-making and opinion-forming, and is 'used by dominant institutional orders'. It confers prestige, and the 'prestige of culture is among the major means by which powers of decision are made to seem part of an unchallengeable authority'.

Wright Mills goes on to argue that, no matter how internally free the 'cultural workman', as he names the artist or intellectual, he/she is intrinsically part of the cultural apparatus which tends in every nation to become a 'close adjunct of national authority and a leading agency of nationalist propaganda'. CULTURE and authority overlap, and this overlap 'may involve the ideological use of cultural products and of cultural workmen for the legitimation of power, and the justification of decisions and policies'. See CONSENSUS; HEGEMONY; IDEOLOGICAL STATE APPARATUSES.

Cultural capital French philosopher Pierre Bourdieu (1930–2002) makes the distinction between economic capital and cultural capital – the latter being the knowledge, tastes, attitudes, VALUES and assumptions which individuals or groups possess with regard to various cultural artefacts and endeavours, in particular those of what might be termed legitimate culture – though definitions of such legitimacy are open to debate. An individual's cultural capital clearly may influence the way in which messages are encoded or decoded. Advertisers, for example, often make assumptions about the cultural capital of the target consumer groups when constructing advertising messages.

A popular record of the late 1960s may be used as the soundtrack in a television commercial not just because of its musical merits, but because its location within a particular youth culture may be felt to give the product connotational and ideological meanings related to the desire for freedom and independence. The messages may be read this way, though not necessarily accepted, by consumers familiar both with the song and with the youth culture, but is unlikely to be read as such by someone unfamiliar with either.

The notion of cultural capital is linked to CLASS, GENDER, ethnic identity and STATUS, in that some cultural capital is more highly valued than others by the dominant groups within a society – and indeed possession of such cultural capital is often widely taken as a sign of membership of these groups. There is among these groups a tendency to denigrate popular cultural capital. Popular cultural capital on the other hand can be seen as a rich source of responses to, including resistance to, social subordination. See CULTURE; HIGHBROW; TASTE CULTURES; YOUTH CULTURE.

▶ Pierre Bourdieu, *Distinction* (Routledge, 1984) and *The Field of Cultural Production* (Polity Press, 1993).

Cultural Indicators research project See MAINSTREAMING.

Cultural industry See FRANKFURT SCHOOL OF THEORISTS.

Cultural memory That which the community recalls, re-encodes in a process of making sense of the present. Cultural memory contrasts with what has been termed *instrumental* or *electronic* memory – that which can be numerically encoded and recorded, as on a computer. In *Communication, Culture and Hegemony: From the Media to Mediation* (Sage, 1993), Jesus Martin-Barbero writes, 'In contrast to instrumental memory "cultural memory" does not work with pure information or as a process of linear accumulation'; rather, it is 'articulated through experience and events. Instead of simply accumulating, it filters and weighs'.

It is not, says Martin-Barbero, 'a memory we can use, but the memory of which we are made'. What threatens cultural memory inflicts damage on culture itself, particularly in cultures where tensions exist, dramatically, between tradition and progress. Says Martin-Barbero, a part of whose book focuses on media development in South American countries, 'in the dilemma of choice between under development and modernization, cultural memory does not count and has no place': a situation he and other scholars of cultural change view with dismay.

Cultural metaphor Generally an image, or a series of images, seen to represent a culture. The expression 'An Englishman's home is his castle' attempts to classify the English – perhaps even stereotype them – by means of a dominant image or practice. In this case a number of characteristics are drawn together in the image of home as something to be defended as though it were a castle – private, self-contained, constructed to be resistant to outside intrusions and influences.

According to Martin J. Gannon and associates in *Understanding Global Cultures: Metaphorical Journeys Through 17 Countries* (Sage, 1994), the use of identifying metaphors can assist us in grasping the nature of our own and other cultures. The authors take the view that 'the dynamics of the culture of a particular nation can be best understood through the use of one dominant metaphor that reflects the basic values that all or most of its members accept without question or conscious thought'.

They cite the following metaphors that represent some of the cultures on their 'metaphorical journey': American football (US), the dance of Shiva (India), the family altar (China), the opera (Italy), wine (France), lace (Belgium), ballet (Russia), the symphony orchestra (Germany), the bullfight (Spain), the kibbutz (Israel), the garden (Japan), the stuga or summer home (Sweden), the market place (Nigeria) and the coffee house (Turkey). For Ireland, home of the Blarney Stone, the authors perhaps appropriately select as the country's presiding metaphor, conversation.

Cultural modes The *literate* mode is rooted in the written word; the *oral* mode is spoken or visual. Traditionally these have been aligned to CLASS differences; that is, the better-educated upper-classes have lived by a literate mode of cultural interaction – the *dominant* CULTURE – while the more 'untutored' classes have relied upon oral modes. With the advent of electronic media the oral mode has become increasingly assertive. It is essentially the mode of film and television, though both media still tend to be run by a class educated in the literate mode and whose perceptions are conditioned by such a mode.

Cultural or citizen rights and the media In 'Rights and representations: public discourse and cultural citizenship', in *Television and Common Knowledge* (Routledge, 1999), edited by J. Gripsrud, Graham Murdock poses the following citizen rights – what citizens have the right to expect from the mass media: (1) the right to information; (2) the right to have access to 'the greatest possible diversity of representations of personal and social experience'; (3) the right to knowledge, that is access to 'frameworks of interpretation' which facilitate understating of the links between issues, the causes that lead to effects, and the processes by which knowledge is assembled and represented to the public; and (4) the right to participation in a contemporary context where there is a demand from individuals and groups 'to speak about their own lives and aspirations in their own voice'.

The exercise of 'full citizenship', Murdock argues, depends upon the media fulfilling these rights of information, experience, interpretation and participation. See TOPIC GUIDE under MEDIA ETHICS; MEDIA ISSUES & DEBATES; MEDIA: VALUES & IDEOLOGY; REPRESENTATION.

Cultural racism See RACISM.

Culture The sum of those characteristics that *identify* and *differentiate* human societies – a complex interweave of many factors. The culture of a nation is made up of its LANGUAGE, history, traditions, climate, geography, arts, social, economic and political norms, and its system of VALUES; and such a nation's size, its neighbours and its current prosperity condition the nature of its culture.

There are cultures within cultures. Thus reference is made to working-class culture or middle-class culture. Organizations and institutions can have their own cultures (see ORGANIZATION CULTURES). We refer to cultural *epochs* resulting from developments – social, political, industrial, technological – that create cultural change. Mass production and the mass media have contributed immensely to cultural change, giving rise to what critics have termed 'mass culture' and disapprovingly portrayed as manufactured, manipulated, force-fed, marketed like soap powder and, because of its unique access to vast audiences, open to abuse of the mass by the powerful.

Alan Swingewood in *The Myth of Mass Culture* (Macmillan, 1977) argues, however, that there 'is no mass culture, or mass society; but there is an ideology of mass culture and mass society'. The ideology is real enough, but the thing itself he describes as myth: 'If culture is the means whereby man affirms his humanity and his purposes and his aspirations to freedom and dignity then the concept and theory of mass culture are their denial and negation.'

Culture is transmitted through SOCIALIZATION to new members of a social group or society. The media play an important role in this process. A central concern of culturalist studies of the media is the degree to which the media's output may both reflect and communicate the culture of the more powerful social groups in that society at the expense of the less powerful. By asserting one culture against others, the media help to nurture a *dominant culture* and relegate rival cultures to the realms of deviance.

Today's cultures have to be examined through the lens of the Network Society, which has brought about profound shifts in terms of the nature of communications. In the world of blogs (see BLOGOSPHERE), the rise and rise of the mobile phone and its multitude of applications (see MOBILIZATION), in a cyberspace populated by FACEBOOK and YOUTUBE, the traditional dominance of the mass media – their power to define, legimitimize and lead culture – is in rapid transition.

▶ Nick Stevenson, *Understanding Media Cultures* (Sage, 1995); Colleen Roach, ed., *Communication and Culture in War and Peace* (Sage, 1995); Andrew Tudor, *Decoding Culture: Theory and Method in Cultural Studies* (Sage, 1999); David Hesmondhalgh, *The Cultural Industries: An Introduction* (Sage, 2002); John Storey, *Cultural Studies and the Study of Popular Culture: Theories and Methods* (Edinburgh University Press, 2003); James Curran and David Morley, *Media and Cultural Theory* (Routledge, 2005); Jeff Lewis, *Cultural Studies* (Sage, 2nd edition, 2008); James Curran, ed., *Media and Society* (5th edition, Bloomsbury Academic, 2010); Graeme Turner, *Ordinary People and the Media: The Demotic Turn* (Routledge, 2010).

Culture: consumer culture Arguably consumer culture is the prevailing culture of late modernity in Western societies. Don Slater in *Consumer Culture & Modernity* (Polity Press, 1997) argues that 'it is more generally bound up with central values, practices and institutions which define Western modernity, such as choice, individualism and market relations'.

For Slater its 'defining feature' is that it 'denotes a social arrangement in which the relation between lived culture and social resources, between meaningful ways of life and the symbolic and material resources on which they depend, is mediated through markets'. The media and cultural industries obviously play a pivotal role in the operation of consumer culture, and the nature of this relationship is the focus of much research. See CONSUMERIZATION.

Culture: copyrighting culture In the global context of communication, and in view of the open-access properties of the INTERNET, a question of growing importance is – to whom does a TEXT or work belong? (See TEXT: INTEGRITY OF THE TEXT.) R.V. Bettig, in *Copyrighting Culture: The Political Economy of Intellectual Property* (Westview Press, 1996), addresses this concern, arguing that with information/knowledge becoming one of the chief commercial industries in the current age, the control of CULTURE has fallen to a number of transnational corporations (TNCs) through their ownership of copyright.

TNCs fear copyright piracy on a world scale and their ambition is to extend, globally, measures to protect intellectual property from piracy. The Berne Convention laid initial guidelines on protection that eventually materialized in the Agreement on Trade-related Aspects of Intellectual Property Rights (TRIPS) of the World Trade Organization. This included the extension of protection to databases, computer programs being classified as literary works and therefore subject to copyright.

Texts are not only protected, their universal access – working within a global free market – is also protected; thus, for example, the attempts by one country to protect its own cultural products from cultural 'invasion' becomes an area of contention. The result, fears Bettig, threatens to be an economic domination of the information-rich nations over the information-poor.

Economic dominance brings with it ideological influence. Copyright becomes a device for the privatization of knowledge where 'the views and accounts of the world held by the capitalist class and aligned class factions and groups are broadly disseminated and persistently publicized'. In practice, however, global agreements have a mother of all battles in the war against piracy. See DOWNLOADING; INFORMATION COMMONS.

Culture: globalization of Considered by many commentators as a paramount trend in the late twentieth century, in which cultures and cultural practices of chiefly Western nations – the US in particular – spread through the world, dominating native, home-grown cultures. The media are seen to be the channels through which the globalizing torrent has poured; and those channels have been largely under the direction and control of transnational corporations. Under the umbrella of globalization we encounter a couple of key, linked and interactive phenomena: CONSUMERIZATION and MEDIA IMPERIALISM.

With cultural dominance, fear some commentators, comes ideological dominance, and that IDEOLOGY centres around the processes of production and consumption and the targeting of audiences in their role of consumers. Todd Gitlin in his chapter 'Prime time ideology: the hegemonic process in television entertainment' in *Television: The Critical View* (Oxford University Press, 1994), edited by Horace Newcomb, was of the opinion that 'the dominant ideology has shifted toward sanctifying consumer satisfaction as the premium definition of "the pursuit of happiness"'.

Corporate domination of the economy extends to corporate dominance worldwide of CULTURE, at least those cultures through which profits may be obtained. It is not happiness alone that global corporatization promises, says Gitlin, but liberty, equality and fraternity: all can 'be affirmed through the existing private commodity forms, under the benign, protective eye of the national security state'.

The vision of a world dominated by American cultural products is challenged by observers who see in *localism* a force of resistance, or if not resistance, assimilation. Roland Robinson offers us a useful term in this respect – *glocalization* (in 'Globalization or glocalization?' in the *Journal of International Communication, 1* (1994)), that is the ability of people in their own cultures to deal in their own way with the cultural imports from the West; to absorb them, to adapt them, to glocalize them.

John B. Thompson in *The Media and Modernity: A Social Theory of Media* (Polity, 1995) urges us to see trends of dominance within historical perspectives: 'Rather than assuming that prior to the importation of Western TV programmes etc. many Third World countries had indigenous traditions and cultural heritages which were largely unaffected by external pressures, we should see instead that the globalization of communication through electronic media is only the most recent of a series of cultural encounters, in some cases stretching back many centuries, through which values, beliefs and symbolic forms of different groups have been superimposed on one another, often in conjunction with the use of coercive, political and economic power.'

Thompson maintains that the media-imperialist position underestimates the power of audiences to make their own meanings from what they read, listen to or watch. 'Through the localized process of appropriation,' Thompson believes, 'media products are embedded in sets of practices which shape and alter their significance.'

Evidence for the process of glocalization is offered by Tamar Liebes and Elihu Katz in *The Export of Meaning: Cross Cultural Readings of Dallas* (Oxford University Press, 1990; Polity, 1993). Their researches indicated that the American soap *Dallas* was read in quite different ways by people of different origins, cultures and outlooks. It was *Dallas* which was dominated, not the audience for *Dallas*.

Majid Tehranian in his chapter 'Ethnic discourse and the new world dysorder' in *Communication and Culture in War and Peace* (Sage, 1993), edited by Colleen Roach, argues that the levelling-out which is said to be a benefit of globalization is more apparent than real. In fact the 'levelling' has camouflaged 'a hege-monic project by a new modern, technocratic, internationalist elite' speaking 'the language of a new international, a new world order'. However, Tehranian perceives the 'periphery' reacting against the 'core' in a number of potentially conflicting, even explosive, ways.

He speaks of *countermodernization* as a significant contemporary trend, in which pressure GROUPS such as some traditional religions react against modern ideas and dominant ideologies – the resurgence, for example, of fundamentalist religion in the face of scientific and technological advances; while a contrary trend, *demodernization*, is expressed by the voices of environmentalists or feminists; and by those 'localites' (as contrasted with 'cosmopolites') whose advocacy is inspired by the notion that 'small is beautiful'.

The nature and degree of globalization of culture will continue to be fiercely debated, and such debate will inevitably have to take into account inequalities of wealth, provision and media technology across nations. See NEWS: GLOBALIZATION OF; INFORMATION GAPS; SLAPPS. See also *TOPIC GUIDE* under GLOBAL PERSPECTIVES.

▶ Peter Golding and Phil Harris, eds, *Beyond Cultural Imperialism* (Sage, 1996); Daya Kishan Thussu, ed., *Electronic Empires: Global Media and Local Resistance* (Arnold, 1998); Barry Smart, ed., *Resisting McDonaldization* (Sage, 1999); George Monbiot, *Captive State: the Corporate Takeover of Britain* (Macmillan, 2001); Mike Savage, Gaynor Bagnall and Brian J. Longhurst, eds, *Globalization and Belonging* (Sage, 2004).

Culture: intercultural communication See COMMUNICATION: INTERCULTURAL COMMUNICATION.

Culture jamming See GENRE.

Culture of deference In an article entitled 'Pressure behind the scenes' and subtitled 'A history of deference, and cosy relationships in Westminster, have made self-censorship acceptable' (*Index on Censorship 4 & 5*, 1991), journalist Richard Norton-Taylor writes of a 'deep-seated culture of deference' existing between many British editors and journalists in their relationship with those in authority (see POWER ELITE). This, Norton-Taylor claims, arises out of an anxiety to be accepted by and be a part of the Establishment. The deference has its 'origins in the centralization of the British state and in Britain's imperial past – where there was virtually unchallenged consensus about the Empire's "civilizing mission"'.

Deference, says Norton-Taylor, continues to be applied to institutions of the State such as Whitehall, the Monarchy, the courts and Parliament. This deference also helps create and supports CONSENSUS against 'enemies', against foreign rivals, in war or in business. See JOURNALISM.

Culture: popular culture Something of a redundant term in that all culture is to a degree 'popular'; otherwise, if it is 'unpopular' – that is, if it does not attract or involve an AUDIENCE – it vanishes. The term has come to mean the culture of 'ordinary people', of the working class, the non-elite majority as contrasted with so-termed *high* or *highbrow* culture. Popular culture generally signifies cohesion, high culture difference – difference, that is, from popular culture and those with whom it is associated.

Popular culture has traditionally been looked down on as something banal, trashy, unchallenging or even potentially harmful: an ELITE standpoint. In their time, theatricals, dancing, 'pulp fiction', the PRESS, POSTERS, postcards, COMICS, SOAP OPERA, the hit-parade and the cinema have varyingly been defined as the kind of culture which contains the potential for subversion – usually of 'standards'.

According to the French philosopher Pierre Bourdieu, popular culture is basically associated with that section of the population who lack both economical and CULTURAL CAPITAL. Since at least the 1960s popular culture has become the focus of critical attention and re-evaluation: it is studied – analysed, measured; in short, taken seriously.

In *Cultures and Societies in a Changing World* (Pine Forge Press, 1994), Wendy Griswold writes, 'Scholars examining previously despised works, genres and systems of meaning found them to contain complexities and beauties; at the same time, deconstructing previously esteemed works, genres and systems of meaning, they found widespread representations of class, hegemony, patriarchy, and illegitimate canonization.'

Culture, whether popular or 'elitist', *cultivates*, hence its fascination for researchers, commentators and students of media. Television, it has been claimed, has appropriated popular culture and by doing so redefined the term to mean 'that which is popular on TV'. The nature of participation by the populace in generating and taking part in popular culture has not been lost on TV programme-makers: audience participation is the key to popular quiz and competition programmes and to so-termed 'REALITY' TV series, in many cases turning that which traditionally has been private and intimate into public display. See AUDIENCE: ACTIVE AUDIENCE;

ETHNOGRAPHIC (APPROACH TO AUDIENCE MEASUREMENT); RESPONSE CODES.

▶ Dominic Strinati, *An Introduction to Studying Popular Culture* (Routledge, 2000); Graeme Turner, *Understanding Celebrity* (Sage, 2004); Annette Hill, *Reality TV: Audiences and Popular Factual Television* (Routledge, 2005); P. David Marshall, ed., *Celebrity Culture Reader* (Routledge, 2006); Anita Biressi and Heather Nunn, eds, *The Tabloid Culture Reader* (Open University, 2007); Sean Redmond and Su Holmes, eds, *Stardom and Celebrity: A Reader* (Sage, 2007); Matt Briggs, *Television, Audience and Everyday Life* (Open University, 2009).

Cultures of organizations See ORGANIZATION CULTURES.

Custom audience research That which is commissioned or undertaken by a company or client into AUDIENCE response to the media marketing of its product or services, generally targeting specific media outlets. Such studies produce rich, focused data while at the same time incurring doubts concerning the objectivity of that data. In contrast, *syndicated* studies are grander in scope as, like the Nielson ratings, they measure the audiences of multiple media outlets of audience response.

As Peter V. Miller says in 'Made-to-order and standardized audiences: forms of reality in audience measurement' published in *Audiencemaking: How the Media Create the Audience* (Sage, 1994), edited by James S. Ettema and D. Charles Whitney, 'the unique, made-to-order nature of the custom study is both its chief benefit and its major cost'. He goes on, 'The syndicated study offers comparative, longitudinal information about audiences that can be used to sell advertising space and time. Unlike the custom study, the syndicated effort provides the advertisers with a standard way to judge alternative vehicles for their messages.' See AUDIENCE MEASUREMENT.

Cybernetics The study of communication FEEDBACK systems in human, animal and machine. Taken from the Greek for 'steersman', the term was the invention of American Norbert Wiener, author of *Cybernetics: Or Control and Communication in the Animal and the Machine* (Wiley, 1949). Essentially an interdisciplinary study, cybernetics ranges in its interest from control systems of the body to the monitoring and control of space missions. Cybernetics concerns itself with the analysis of 'whole' systems, their complexity of goals and hierarchies within contexts of perpetual change. The Greek steersman used the feedback of visual, aural and tactile indicators to chart his passage through rough seas. Today we have computers: the potential for accuracy and rapidity of feedback and control is vastly greater, and so is the potential for disaster should the feedback systems go wrong.

Cyberspace See also INTERNET and NEW MEDIA. Term probably first used by William Gibson in his novel *Neuromancers* published in America by Ace Books in 1984. Gibson describes cyberspace as 'a consensual hallucination ... [People are] creating a world. It's not really a place, it's not really space. It's notional space'. By pressing computer keys, and by grace of a modem and telephone line, the operator has access to potentially infinite information and endless exchanges with other users.

According to Mark C. Taylor and Esa Saarinen in *Imagology: Media Philosophy* (Routledge, 1994), itself a mercurial sortie into cybergraphics, chief among cyberspace's characteristics is speed. 'Power,' the authors declare, 'is speed' and the 'swift will inherit the earth'. Much comment suggests that control, traditionally exercised by governments and powerful groups such as the transnational corporations, is shifting and will rapidly continue to do so. Cyberspace is seen as a force for dismantling patriarchal structures in society and altering existing gender relations.

Fears about the posting of information about paedophiles on the Net, of information-exchange between extremist factions, of freely available information on how to make weapons of mass destruction, have surfaced on public agendas to the point where, in many countries, those in authority have sought to 'fence in' the open prairies of cyberspace by legislation. Such moves have prompted many expressions of concern about the CENSORSHIP of the Net.

Equally, there are fears that the major CONGLOMERATES are intent on colonizing cyberspace, converting the open prairie into virtual shopping malls. Many analysts take the view that the Net is unlikely to be a bridger of the gap between information-rich and information-poor, that it is failing to redress the balance between core and periphery; and some are of the opinion that cyberspace is largely off-limits to the poor, the ill-educated and the unemployed. See CORE NATIONS, PERIPHERAL NATIONS; INFORMATION GAPS; REGULATION OF INVESTIGATORY POWERS ACT (RIPA) (UK), 2000; SURVEILLANCE SOCIETY; WIKI, WIKIPEDIA. See also *TOPIC GUIDE* under DIGITAL AGE COMMUNICATION.

Cylinder or rotary press The most important technical development in PRINTING history following the invention of movable type was the steam-driven cylinder press invented by Fried-

erich Koenig. Born in Saxony, Koenig moved to London in order to set up a works to manufacture the new machines (1812). He demonstrated that a cylinder press machine could take off impressions at the rate of over 1,000 copies an hour. On 28 November 1814 one of the presses was used to print *The Times*. Its editor, John Walter, described the cylinder press as 'the greatest improvement connected with printing since the discovery of the art itself'. As a result of its advantage in using Koenig's press, *The Times* became the dominant and most influential newspaper of the nineteenth century in the UK. See *TOPIC GUIDE* under MEDIA: TECHNOLOGIES.

D

DAB: Digital Audio Broadcasting The first DAB transmission took place in Germany, though the UK was the first to establish DAB radio broadcasting stations after pilot broadcasts were transmitted in several European countries in 1996. The first DAB receivers were being marketed by 1999. By 2001 there were more than fifty BBC and COMMERCIAL RADIO (UK) services. The World DMB (Digital Mutimedia Broadcasting) Forum represents over thirty countries worldwide.

Through multiplexing and compression, DAB is considered twelve times more efficient than analog-FM for national and regional networks. However, automatic tuning display has proved a harder drain on battery life and the jury is still out in terms of the quality and reliability of sound production.

DAB+ consitutes a major upgrade, but older transmitters cannot carry forward DAB+. DMB is suitable for mobile radio and TV and can be added to any DAB transmission. Digital Radio Transmission, sometimes referred to as *mobile TV*, can operate via satellite (S-DMB) or terrestrially (T-DMB), South Korea being a major pioneer in this field of development. Receivers are integrated into car navigation systems, laptop computers and digital cameras.

▶ See Wikipedia for full technical data and updates on development.

DA (Defence Advisory) Notices British government memoranda requesting the media not to publish or broadcast specific items of information considered by authority to pose a security risk if widely disseminated. Notices are issued by the Defence, Press and Broadcasting Advisory Committee. They have no binding force at law, even in wartime, but defiance of a DA Notice may incur a harsher response from government by having avenues of information, other than that which is classified, closed to offenders. However, the Notices have little chance of combatting information, pictures or film posted on the INTERNET. See CENSORSHIP; OFFICIALS SECRETS ACT (UK).

Daguerrotype Early photograph produced in the manner of Louis Daguerre (1789–1851), a French theatrical designer who teamed up with Joseph Nicéphore Nièpce (1765–1833), a founding father of photography, in 1830. Nièpce died three years later but Daguerre continued their work, fixing images on metal plates coated with silver iodide, which he treated with mercury vapour in a darkroom. Daguerre was eventually able to reduce the exposure time of a photograph from 8 hours to between 20 and 30 minutes. His Daguerrotype was taken up by the French government in July 1839 and revealed to the world at a meeting of the Académies des Sciences in August. No prints could be made from a Daguerrotype; thus Daguerre's method was a cul-de-sac in photography, though a vastly successful one at the time. See PHOTOGRAPHY, ORIGINS.

Dance's helical model of communication, 1967 The earliest communication models were linear; their successors were circular, emphasizing the crucial factor of FEEDBACK in the communication process. Frank E.X. Dance in 'A helical model of communication' in the book he edited, *Human Communication Theory* (Holt, Rinehart & Winston, 1967), commends the circular model as an advance upon the linear one, but faults it on the grounds that it suggests that communication comes back full-circle, to exactly the same point from which it started – an assumption which is 'manifestly erroneous'.

The helix or spiral, for Dance, 'combines the desirable features of the straight line and of the circle while avoiding the weaknesses of either'. He goes on, 'At any and all times, the helix gives geometric testimony to the concept that Communication while moving forward is at the same moment coming back upon itself and being affected by its past behaviour, for the coming curve of the helix is fundamentally affected by the curve from which it emerges'. Dance's spiral concept parallels theories of education put forward by Jerome Bruner, and generally referred to as the *spiral curriculum*. See *TOPIC GUIDE* under COMMUNICATION MODELS.

Data footprint Term describing the 'trail' INTERNET users leave in their wake, the evidence of their identity, online activity, what they communicate about and to whom. The data footprint provides clues to every interaction online or

via the use of the mobile phone. The evidence is open to the scrutiny of individuals and agencies, assisting all bodies, governmental or commercial, involved in the SURVEILLANCE of the public. For example, data footprints are a vital aid to targeted marketing, allowing companies to track a user's tastes and patterns of consumption. See CRYPTOGRAPHY; TOR.

Data mining In a 1998 publication *Data Mining: Staking a Claim on Your Privacy* (IPC), Ann Cavoukian, Ontario (Canada) Information and Privacy Commissioner, defines data mining as 'a set of automated techniques used to extract buried or previously unknown pieces of information from large data bases'. The Commissioner states that 'successful data mining makes it possible to unearth patterns and relationship, and then use this "new" information to make proactive knowledge-driven business decisions'.

The process illustrates the penetrative power of surveillance (see SURVEILLANCE SOCIETY) made possible by computer networking. Extensively used by governments and business, data mining identifies patterns and trends in the seemingly disparate activities of citizens; such patterns and trends being used as indicators of future policy and promotion. See JOURNALISM: DATA JOURNALISM; PRIVACY.

Data protection The increasing use of computers and sophisticated information technology has greatly magnified the harm to individual PRIVACY that can occur from any collection, storage or dissemination of personal information, and many countries have legislated against data abuse. Sweden, Denmark, Norway, Luxembourg, West Germany and France have all legislated to protect both the public and private sectors of society. In the US and Canada, data protection legislation only applies to the public sector and compliance with it is voluntary.

In the UK, the report of the Lindop Committee (*Report of the Committee on Data Protection*, 1978) urged the need for individuals to have a right of veto on what information was disseminated about them, and how this would operate in the context of 'the interests of the rest of society, which include the efficient conduct of industry, commerce and administration'. Becoming law in the UK in 1984, the DATA PROTECTION ACT began operation in 1987 (see next entry).

CRYPTOGRAPHY, or what in modern parlance is termed *privacy transformation*, can be employed to 'scramble' data prior to storage in order to guard against accidental or deliberate disclosures of information. The problem here is how the key or code to the scrambling process

D

is to be protected. In the US, the Hellman-Diffie method allowed for different keys for the scrambling and unscrambling processes.

An alternative to this is the so-called *electronic signature*, which works by reversing the roles of scrambling and unscrambling keys. Another mode is PIN – personal identity number, where everybody is issued with a personal key. PIN is already in use for the authorization of electronic funds transfers. See ECHELON. See also *TOPIC GUIDE* under MEDIA: FREEDOM, CENSORSHIP.

Data Protection Act (UK), 1984 The purpose of the Act is 'to regulate the use of automatically processed information relating to individuals and the provision of services in respect of such information'. From November 1987 the public has been able to check if any organization holds information on them; to see a copy of that information, known as personal data; to complain to the Data Protection Registrar about the way data has been collected or used; to have inaccurate computer records corrected or deleted in certain circumstances; and to claim compensation through the courts if the 'data subject' has suffered damage by the loss or destruction of personal data, or through an unauthorized disclosure or because of inaccuracy.

Designed to bring Britain into line with the Council of Europe Convention for the Protection of Individuals with regard to Automatic Processing of Personal Data, the Act provides for the establishment of a data watchdog, the Data Protection Registrar, and outlines eight DATA PROTECTION PRINCIPLES (see next entry).

The test of any act protecting the citizen is the size and scope of the exceptions. There are three unconditional exemptions from registration: personal data required to be exempt for the purpose of safeguarding national security; data which its user is required by law to make public; and personal data held by an individual and 'concerned with the management of his personal, family or household affairs or held by him only for recreational purposes'. Subject access is barred on matters of prevention or detection of crime, the apprehension or prosecution of offenders, or the assessment or collection of any tax or duty.

Data Protection Principles Listed in the DATA PROTECTION ACT (UK), 1984 are the following eight principles governing data protection for computer users handling personal data: computer users must (1) obtain and process the information fairly and lawfully; (2) register the purposes for which they hold the data; (3) not use or disclose the information in a way contrary to those purposes; (4) hold only information which is adequate, relevant and not excessive for the purposes; (5) hold only accurate information and, where necessary, keep it up to date; (6) not keep any information longer than is necessary; (7) give individuals access to information about themselves and, where appropriate, correct or erase the information; (8) take appropriate security measures. Persons feeling that any computer user has broken one or more of the above principles may complain to the Data Protection Registrar. See PRIVACY; SECRECY.

Decency: Communications Decency Act, 1996 See COMMUNICATIONS DECENCY ACT (US).

Decisive moment French photographer Henri Cartier-Bresson (1908–2004) used this term to describe the instant when pressing the shutter release button produced the desired image. Indeed, some critics believe that Cartier-Bresson's timing, his ability to be at the ready when destiny appeared to be bringing highly photogenic elements together, this instinct for the decisive moment, qualifies him to be considered the finest of all twentieth-century photographers.

Declaration on the Mass Media (UNESCO General Council, 1978) See MEDIA IMPERIALISM.

Decode The process of interpreting, analysing and understanding the nature of messages – written, spoken, broadcast, etc. This requires not just an understanding of the words, signs or images used but also a sharing of the VALUES and assumptions that underpin their encoding into a message by the transmitter. A focus for research in communication studies is the extent to which the receiver decodes the message in the way the encoder or sender would prefer. This is an important element in the debate on the power and influence of the media.

If the message is received by an AUDIENCE which does not share the same codes or values as the sender, it will be interpreted in an 'aberrant' way, that is a different meaning will be assumed to that which was intended; hence the term *aberrant decoding*. In short, it is a difference of 'reading' the message derived from a difference of experience, perception or evaluation. See PREFERRED READING. See also *TOPIC GUIDES* under COMMUNICATION THEORY; LANGUAGE/DISCOURSE/NARRATIVE.

Deconstruction The process of deconstruction, as a mode of textual and intertextual analysis, is chiefly associated with the ideas of the French philosopher Jacques Derrida and his method of 'close-reading' of minute particulars in a text. The search is not for an ultimate MEANING; on the contrary, Derrida sees meaning as *undecidable*: signifiers within linguistic contexts refer to further signifiers, texts to further texts in an infinite web of INTERTEXTUALITY. Deconstructors such as Derrida seek to pry behind the dominant expressions of a TEXT, regarding these as serving to exclude subordinate terms. The technique is to *reverse* and *displace*, thus bringing about an upending – an overthrow – of the hierarchies which rule all forms of expression.

In the words of Madan Sarup in *An Introductory Guide to Post-Structuralism and Postmodernism* (Harvester Wheatsheaf, 1993), 'deconstruction disarticulates traditional conceptions of the author and undermines conventional notions of reading and history ... It kills the author, turns history and tradition into textuality and' – we must gratefully note – 'celebrates the reader'. If *self* can be constructed as a text, then self is subject to deconstruction, which displaces the notion of a *stable* self (see EISENBERG'S MODEL OF COMMUNICATION AND IDENTITY, 2001). The only coherence, it would seem, is fragmentation, leading to the conclusion that there can be no meaning, only interpretation.

Sarup's phrase 'textual undecidability' usefully sums up the position of the deconstructors, as does the term 'labyrinth of deconstruction' used by Christopher Norris in *Deconstruction: Theory and Practice* (Methuen, 1982).

▸ Jacques Derrida, *Writing and Difference* (Routledge & Kegan Paul, 1976); Christopher Norris, *Derrida* (Collins, 1987).

Decreolization See COMMUNICATION: INTERCULTURAL COMMUNICATION.

Deep Dish TV See PAPER TIGER TV.

Deep focus Film-making technique in which objects close to the camera and those far away are both in focus at the same time.

Deep structure Though the term was first used by Charles Hockett, the concept was given widest currency by fellow US linguist Noam Chomsky in 'Current issues in linguistic theory' in J. Foder and J. Katz, eds, *The Structure of Language: Readings in the Philosophy of Language* (Prentice-Hall, 1964). In its original form, deep structure is an underlying abstract level of sentence organization, which specifies the way a sentence should be interpreted.

For Chomsky, the deep and surface structures, and the relationship between them, provide the essential bases of language which, far from being merely a sequence of words strung together,

is rather a series of organized structures (see STRUCTURALISM). This deep structure, or level, supplies information that enables the reader or listener to distinguish between alternative interpretations of sentences which have the same surface form, or sentences which have different surface forms but have the same underlying meaning.

When, for example, a publisher replies to a budding author, 'I will waste no time in reading your manuscript', he presents a surface structure with alternative possible meanings. Yet by altering the surface structure of the sentence 'The dog chased the cat' to 'The cat was chased by the dog', the underlying idea is not altered. The transformations that might occur between deep and surface structure can be passive ('My father was warned by the doctor to give up smoking'), negative ('My father was not warned to give up smoking'), in question form ('Was my father warned to give up smoking?') or as an imperative ('Father was told – "Stop smoking!"'). See TOPIC GUIDE under LANGUAGE/DISCOURSE/NARRATIVE.

▸ Noam Chomsky, *Language and Mind* (Harcourt Brace Jovanovitch, 1968).

Deep throat Journalists' parlance for 'anonymous sources'. Perhaps the most famous of these was the unknown telephone informant calling himself 'Deep Throat' who set *Washington Post* reporters Carl Bernstein and Bob Woodward on the trail in the WATERGATE scandal that eventually led to the resignation of President Richard Nixon. In 2005 Deep Throat revealed his identity, winning worldwide media attention. He was Mark Felt, at the time of the revelations number two at the American FBI, responsible for the investigation into the burglary at the Democratic National Committee HQ in the Watergate apartment in 1972. Felt kept his secret for 33 years.

Defamation The UK Defamation Act of 1952 made illegal any statement made by one person that is untrue and may be considered injurious to another's reputation, causing shame, resentment, ridicule or financial loss. In permanent form, such as expressed in print, records, films, tapes, photographs, images or effigies, defamation is classified as *libel*. In temporary form, such as in spoken words or gestures, defamation is classified as *slander*.

No legal aid is granted to plaintiffs or defendants in defamation cases; thus persons even with the most genuine case for grievance must think twice before deciding to incur vast legal expenses in defending their reputation.

Legal provisions against defamation apply

equally to transmissions on the Internet which, while representing a massive challenge in terms of monitoring, also opens up the communicative exchanges of individual Net users, bloggers, chat rooms, newsgroups, etc. to surveillance, not only in home countries but globally.

Prior to the Defamation Bill of 2011 it was illegal not only to communicate potentially defamatory material, but also to republish it. As well as the originator of the material, the website owner and the Internet Service Provider (ISP) have been liable. The culture of the Internet in its pioneering days was one which celebrated independence and free speech; insults, or 'flaming', between Net users was commonplace.

This culture has changed since cyberspace expanded to include young people and corporate involvement, the one requiring a degree of protection from defamatory language, the other sensitive about preserving the good name of the company or corporation. The first corporate e-mail libel case in the UK was filed in 1997.

A report by English PEN and *Index on Censorship* magazine, *Free Speech Is Not For Sale* (2009), talked of 'an intimidating complexity of English libel law' and argued that it 'has served to discourage critical media reporting on matters of serious public interest, adversely affecting the ability of scholars and journalists to publish their work'. The report asserted that 'the law was designed to protect the rich and powerful, and does not reflect the interests of modern democratic society', and made ten recommendations, including the case for excepting 'interactive online services and interactivity chat from liability'.

What has been termed *libel tourism* has concerned the way that the UK, world famous for its repressive libel laws and sky-high fines – Oxford University research has found that defending a libel case in the England and Wales is 140 times the European average – has become *the* place to launch a libel suit. Indeed, London has been named 'the town named sue'.

A case in point involved a book, *Funding Evil*, published in New York by Rachel Ehrenfeld: she and her publishers were sued in London by a named Saudi-Arabian businessman, even though only twenty-three copies of the book were located in the UK. The court awarded £130,000 damages to the businessman.

This case, referred to as Rachel's Law, prompted a number of states in America to pass legislation protecting American citizens against the consequences of such foreign rulings. In 2008 the New York Assembly passed the Libel Terrorism Protection Act, and the US House of Representatives launched a similar bill, the Free Speech Protection Act (2009).

The incoming UK coalition government (2010) recognized the archaic and punitive nature of existing defamation law and set in motion a new Defamation Bill in March 2011. Justice Minister Kenneth Clarke promised that new legislation would 'ensure that anyone who makes a statement of fact or expresses an honest opinion can do so with confidence', a key element being the introduction of a public interest defence. The Libel Reform Campaign deemed the proposals to be 'a great starting point' but urged parliament to go further in key areas. See CENSORSHIP; SUPER-INJUNCTION; SURVEILLANCE SOCIETY. Also, see *TOPIC GUIDE* under MEDIA: FREEDOM, CENSORSHIP.

Defensive communication Occurs when people hear what they do not wish to hear. DISSONANCE arises when messages cut across, or contradict, VALUES and assumptions; the reaction varies from not concentrating on the MESSAGE to deliberately misrepresenting or misunderstanding the sender's motive as well as his/her message.

Climates of threat create defensive tactics, just as supportive climates help reduce them. If we know that we are being tested or evaluated, for example, our communication response will be guarded. Equally we might resort to defensive tactics if we feel the communicator of the message is intent on winning control, exerting superiority. We are less defensive in situations in which spontaneity, empathy, equality and a sense of open-mindedness about the nature of the message are predominant.

Deference, culture of See CULTURE OF DEFERENCE.

Deliberative listening See LISTENING.

Democracy and the media Both the word democracy and the idea are of Greek origin. *Demos* means citizen body; thus democracy is rule by the citizens, suggesting the right of all to decide on what are matters of concern, and possessing the power to decide on those matters. Democracy implies a vote for every citizen of a certain age, regular elections, a genuine choice of parties to *represent* citizens, and a range of rights – free speech, security from arbitrary arrest, the freedoms of belief, movement and association.

The media can be seen – and they often see themselves – as WATCHDOGS of democracy; journalists as articulators and defenders of democracy, the eyes and ears of the public. In his analysis of whether new technologies, in particular computer networks, enhance or diminish democracy, Darin Barney in *Prometheus Wired: The Hope for Democracy in the Age of Network Technology* (University of Chicago Press, 2000) identifies three elements he considers essential in *any* serious definition of democracy – equality, participation and 'a public sphere from which sovereignty emanates'.

Barney speaks of equality of *ability* as well as opportunity; and participation that is meaningful rather than 'frivolous or merely symbolic'. By this he suggests that 'democratic participation must be clearly and decisively connected to the political decisions that direct the activity of the participants' community'. Participation is not, he argues, confined to freedoms of 'consumer choice', the preferred interpretation of democracy by business. In Barney's view many self-proclaiming democracies would not pass the test of equality, participation and power through 'collective decisions'.

It has often been suggested that the media, through argument and advocacy, made democracy possible (see JOURNALISM). From Thomas Paine's seminal work *Rights of Man* (Part 1 published 1791; Part 2 published 1792) through to the age of the Radical press during the nineteenth century, the cause of democracy was championed by journalists and editors, often risking life and liberty to make their case. Within a modern democracy, the media have an ongoing responsibility to exercise vigilance – to nurture, protect and celebrate a range of features that keep democracy healthy, preventing it from corruption, manipulation, misuse and apathy. These might be described as *satellites* of democracy, facilitators, the absence of which threatens the democratic process; and they include full and fair transmission of information; PLURALITY of opinions and diversity of media provision.

Their enemies are monopolization of media outlets by the few (see CONVERGENCE), the profits-generated insistence on treating people as consumers rather than citizens (see CONSUMERIZATION) and the consequent displacement or marginalization in media channels of information, critical analysis, debate and investigation. In this sense, considering the nature of media ownership (see *TOPIC GUIDE* under MEDIA: OWNERSHIP & CONTROL), the media are as likely to subvert democracy, or at least relegate it in importance, as to be its defender and advocate. See AGORA; CULTURE: POPULAR CULTURE; DEMOTIC TURN; DISCURSIVE CONTESTATION; DISENFRANCHISEMENT (OF READERSHIP); FRAMING; PUBLIC OPINION; PUBLIC SERVICE BROADCASTING (PSB); PUBLIC SPHERE. See also *TOPIC GUIDE* under MEDIA: POLITICS & ECONOMICS; MEDIA: VALUES & IDEOLOGIES.

▶ John Street, *Mass Media, Politics & Democracy* (Palgrave Macmillan, 2nd edition, 2010); James Curran, *Media and Deomcracy* (Routledge, 2011).

Democratization See DEMOTIC TURN.

Demographic analysis Seeks to explore and quantify those factors about consumers that might identify whether or not they are in the market for certain products or services. It is thus a key tool of consumer research. Key demographic variables include age, generation, gender, stage in family lifestyle, income and occupation. However, information on demographic variables only takes the marketer or advertiser so far in understanding the consumer; a *psychographic* profile of the consumer(s) is often also needed. Psychographic analysis seeks to explore why a consumer might buy a product, and looks at such factors as lifestyles, motivations, personality traits, self-image, values and aspirations. See ADVERTISING; AUDIENCE MEASUREMENT.

▶ Martin Evans, Ahmad Jamal and Gordon Foxall, *Consumer Behaviour* (John Wiley & Sons Ltd, 2009).

Demonization What the media do, particularly the popular PRESS, to those whose views they perceive to be dangerous, destabilizing, bad for business or subversive. The process of demonization begins with *personalization*, that is focusing on the personal characteristics or attributes (invariably negative) of the leader or spokesperson advocating a cause or raising an issue, which the demonizers do not support. Having rendered the cause or issue a 'personal' matter associated with an individual, the aim of the media concerned is to destroy the credibility of the spokesperson and by doing so undermine, in the public mind, the cause for which he/she speaks. See FOLK DEVILS; LOONY LEFTISM.

Demotic turn Term introduced by Graeme Turner in *Understanding Celebrity* (Sage, 2004), returned to and developed in *Ordinary People and the Media: The Demotic Turn* (Sage, 2010), describing the increasing visibility of ordinary people on TV – in particular the way 'ordinariness' is converted into celebrity by REALITY TV programmes such as *Big Brother, Pop Idol, The X-Factor, Wife Swap* and *Fame Academy.*

Turner writes (2010): 'I use the demotic turn as a means of examining what I argue as a significant new development in how the media participate in the production of culture.' The author examines the demotic turn in the context of claims that participant formats are empowering, or, contrastingly, exploitative. He sees the media as a force for identity-making (or identity-challenging) and draws the reader's attention to the impact of Western-generated programmes featuring the demotic turn on other cultures such as those in the Middle East, Malaysia and China, resulting in *localization* (or *indigenization*) or CENSORSHIP.

On the issue of populating the airwaves with 'ordinariness', seemingly giving power to the people as well as visibility, Turner is sceptical, seeing 'democratainment' as an 'occasional and accidental consequence of the "entertainment" part and its least systematic component'.

He reminds us that 'celebrity still remains a systematically hierarchical and exclusive category, no matter how much it proliferates'. Access may be broadened as far as ordinary people are concerned, but this does not necessarily connect with democratic politics: 'Diversity,' believes Turner, 'is not of itself intrinsically democratic irrespective of how it is generated and by whom.'

Denotation See CONNOTATION.

Dependency theory The degree to which audiences are dependent upon the mass media constitutes one of the chief debates about the functions and effects of modern communication systems. In 'A dependency model of mass media effects' in G. Gumpert and R. Cathcart, eds, *Inter/ Media: Interpersonal Communication in the Media* (Oxford University Press, 1979), Sandra J. Ball-Rokeach and Melvyn DeFleur believe that 'the potential for mass media messages to achieve a broad range of cognitive, affective, and behavioural effects will be increased when media systems serve many unique and central information systems'. The fewer the sources of information in a media world, the more likely the media will affect our minds and thoughts, our attitudes and how we behave. Further, that influence will have increased potential 'when there is a high degree of structural instability in the society due to conflict and change'.

However, just as the audience may be changed by the information/messages it receives, in turn the media systems themselves are changed according to AUDIENCE response. It is not one-way traffic. In the cognitive or intellectual sphere, the authors cite the following possible media roles: (1) resolution of ambiguity, and relatedly limiting the range of interpretations of situations which audiences are able to make; (2) attitude formation; (3) AGENDA-SETTING; (4) expansion of people's systems of beliefs (for example, the tremendous growth in awareness of ecological matters); (5) clarification of values, through the

expression of value conflicts (see DEVIANCE).

The media play a significant role in the establishment and maintenance of 'we feeling', that is communal solidarity and oneness; equally they may work towards the alienation of sections of the population who are traditionally discriminated against – women, blacks, asylum-seekers, etc.

At critical decision-making times, such as elections, people have become increasingly dependent on the media, especially TV, for election information and guidance. Ball-Rokeach and DeFleur argue that the greater the uncertainty in society, the less clear are people's frames of reference; consequently there is greater audience dependence on media communication.

With the coming of the INTERNET and its empowerment of individuals and groups, the role of traditional mass media as shapers and influencers is being examined, researched and questioned, particularly with regard to the challenge newspapers, TV and radio face from the Net's power to tap off readership and audience and, perhaps most critically, ADVERTISING. Dependency in terms of information and opinion could become a thing of the past, with only entertainment holding its own. See BALL-ROKEACH AND DEFLEUR'S DEPENDENCY MODEL OF MASS COMMUNICATION EFFECTS, 1976; BLOGOSPHERE; DEMOTIC TURN; EFFECTS OF THE MASS MEDIA; MOBILIZATION. See also *TOPIC GUIDE* under COMMUNICATION THEORY.

Deregulation Describes the process whereby channels of communication, specifically radio and TV, are opened up beyond the existing franchise-holders. Another term in current use, 'privatization', emphasizes the practical nature of the shift, from public to commercial control, driven by the development of VIDEO, CABLE TELEVISION and SATELLITE and accelerated by DIGITIZATION. Regulation is associated with public service communications, for example PUBLIC SERVICE BROADCASTING (PSB), deregulation with the ambitions and practices of the private sector of the communications industry. See COMMUNICATIONS ACT (UK), 2003; CONGLOMERATES: MEDIA CONGLOMERATES; CONSUMERIZATION.

Deregulation, five myths of In 'The mythology of telecommunications deregulation' (*Journal of Communication*, Winter, 1990), Vincent Mosco of Carleton University identifies five influential assumptions about the deregulation of telecommunications, which he describes as myths (see here Roland Barthes' definition of MYTH): deregulation lessens the economic role of government; benefits consumers; diminishes economic concentration; is widely supported; and is inevitable. Because deregulation is clearly in the interest of the non-public sector, particularly corporations profiting from the free market, it is in the sector's interest to establish the benefits of deregulation as a natural truth – unquestionably a good thing.

'Whatever their basis in fact', writes Mosco, 'these myths continue to reflect significant political and economic interests. Moreover, they help to constitute those interests with a shared belief system ... promoting the dismantling of a public infrastructure and massive income redistribution up the social class ladder.' Mosco goes on, 'In the long run they want to advance the transformation of information from a public resource into a marketable commodity and a form of social management control. Deregulation is more than a policy instrument; it serves as a cohesive mythology around which those who would benefit from these short- and long-run interests might rally.'

Desensitization Process by which audiences are considered to be made immune, or less sensitive to, human suffering as a result of relentless exposure to such suffering in the media. A constant media diet of violence, real or fictional, is widely believed to 'harden up' people's tolerance of violence. See COMPASSION FATIGUE.

Detachment, ideology of See IMPARTIALITY.

Determiner deletion A common stylistic practice of journalists whereby the characteristics of a person and the name are linked without use of 'the' or 'a', in the interests of verbal economy while at the same time having the effect of *labelling* the named person. An example might be: 'Ex-jailbird six-times married Joe Bloggs yesterday told the press ...' or '"Kiss-and-tell" Minister's former live-in lover claims ...' Allan Bell in *The Language of News Media* (Blackwell, 1991) describes this practice as a form of *titleness* that gives instant NEWS VALUE to the person being reported. See HYPHENIZED ABRIDGEMENT; LABELLING PROCESS (AND THE MEDIA).

Determinism See TECHNOLOGICAL DETERMINISM.

Developmental news That which developing nations consider will help rather than harm their prospects. 'Western news' is seen by developing nations as essentially the pursuit of 'bad' news; and bad news hurts. The term implies government monopoly of information-flow in the interests of giving a developing country a 'good name' and runs counter to Western notions of free comment. The aspirations to a reporting tradition of social responsibility rather than sensation-seeking are honourable; and the dangers, of press subservience to government, obvious. See INFORMATION SOCIETY; MEDIA IMPERIALISM. See also *TOPIC GUIDE* under NEWS MEDIA.

Deviance Social behaviour that is considered unacceptable within a social community is deviant; and the defining of what constitutes deviance depends upon what norms of conduct prevail at any given time in a society. Of primary interest in the analysis of deviance is the question – who defines deviance, and why? There are two main views on this: the first maintains that the definition of what is deviant behaviour stems from a general CONSENSUS within society; the second argues that it is the most powerful groups within a society who define as deviant that behaviour which may constitute a threat to themselves or their dominant position in society.

Deviance may then be in the eye of the beholder, as Erich Goode and Nachman Ben-Yehuda remind us in *Moral Panics: The Social Construction of Deviance* (Wiley-Blackwell, 2009); 'In other words, the very concept of what *constitutes* a threat is controversial, an expression of a diverse, socially divided, and multicultural society. Deviants are not "folk devils" to everyone, and what is regarded as wrongdoing or deviance is itself contested.' However, as they too acknowledge, there are some acts of behaviour (such as rape) that are almost universally defined as deviant.

Particular interest has been focused on the role of the media in shaping definitions of deviance and then responding to those. While from a moral standpoint the media may disapprove of deviant behaviour, there is at the same time a reliance upon it: normative behaviour rarely makes a good headline. Deviant behaviour, on the other hand, is a NEWS VALUE and it might be argued that if deviance did not exist, it would be necessary for the media to invent it.

Several studies of deviance have been concerned with the role of the mass media in both the definition and the amplification of deviance. Leslie Watkins first outlined the concept of *deviance amplification* in 'Some sociological factors in drug addiction control' in Daniel M. Wilner and Gene G. Kassebaum, eds, *Narcotics* (McGraw-Hill, 1965). He argues that the way in which a society defines and reacts to deviance may in fact encourage those defined as deviant to act in a more deviant manner. This would be particularly true for deviants excluded from or restricted in participation in normal social activities. If societal reaction to deviance is strong it can lead to greater deviance, which in turn may lead to stronger societal reaction and so on, establishing a deviance amplification *spiral* in which each increase in social control is met by an increase in the level of deviancy. The contribution of the mass media in precipitating and shaping such amplification spirals has proved a fruitful area of media research.

Perceptions of deviant behaviour are at the core of moral panics (see MORAL PANICS AND THE MEDIA). Erich Goode and Nachman Ben-Yehuda note in *Moral Panics: The Social Construction of Deviance* (Wiley-Blackwell, 2009), '... the key ingredient in the emergence of a moral panic is the creation or intensification of hostility toward and denunciation of a particular group, category or cast of characters. The emergence or the re-emergence of a deviant category characterizes the moral panic; central to this process is the targeting of new or past "folk devils"'. See FOLK DEVILS; MORAL ENTREPRENEURS.

▶ Yvonne Jewkes, *Media & Crime* (Sage, 2011).

Deviant See SLIDER.

Diachronic linguistics The study of language through the course of its history. In contrast, *synchronic linguistics* takes a fixed instant as its point of observation (chiefly a contemporary one). The distinction was first posed by Swiss linguist Ferdinand de Saussure (1857–1913).

Dialect A dialect is usually regionally based and is a variation within a language as regards vocabulary, pronunciation and grammar. For this reason Suzanne Romaine in *Language and Society* (Oxford University Press, 2000) argues, 'educated speakers of American English and British English can be regarded as using dialects of the same language'. In this case, she states, the differences are likely to be more evident in pronunciation and vocabulary than in grammar; for example the American English speaker using the word 'elevator' rather than 'lift'.

Though differences within Britain between the varying dialects of English may be declining, Simon Elms argues that the findings of the BBC Voices survey documented in his book entitled *Talking for Britain: A Journey through the Nation's Dialects* (Penguin Books, 2005) reveal that a considerable variation in dialect and ACCENT is still to be found across the country. For example, numerous regional variations in vocabulary continue to exist. Thus 'butty' might be used to refer to a friend in Wales, but to refer to a slice of bread and butter in Lancashire.

There also remain noticeable variations between what are sometimes termed standard and non-standard dialects. Martin Montgomery notes in *An Introduction to Language and Society* (Routledge, 1995) that typical differences include the use of vocabulary, pronouns, tenses, double-negatives and tags such as 'you know?'. Several authors have noted that there is greater use of non-standard dialects among those from lower socio-economic groups. In *Sociolinguistics: An Introduction to Language and Society* (Penguin, 2000) Peter Trudgill reminds us, however, that many individuals can switch between the use of standard and non-standard dialects depending on the social context.

In discussing the relationship between dialect, regional identity and social background, Suzanne Romaine comments that 'boundaries are, however, often of a social nature, e.g. between different social class groups. In this case we may speak of "social dialects" ... Social dialects say who we are, and regional dialects where we came from'. Dialects, though they add richness and variety to a language, can also, of course, form a barrier to communication. See ACCENT; COLLOQUIALISM; JARGON; REGISTER; SLANG. See also *TOPIC GUIDE* under LANGUAGE/DISCOURSE/NARRATIVE.

Diary stories See SPOT NEWS.

Diffusion The process by which innovations spread to the members of a social system. Diffusion studies are concerned with messages that convey new ideas, the processes by which those ideas are conveyed and received, and the extent to which those ideas are adopted or rejected. Appropriateness of CHANNEL to MESSAGE is particularly important. For example, mass media channels are often more useful at creating awareness – knowledge – of new ideas, but interpersonal channels are considered to be more important in changing attitudes towards innovations. The rate and success of diffusion is very much affected by the norms, VALUES and social structures in which the transmission of new ideas takes place. See EFFECTS OF MASS MEDIA.

Digital activism See BLOGOSPHERE; FACEBOOK; GLOBAL SCRUTINY; MOBILIZATION; NETWORKING: SOCIAL NETWORKING; TWITTER; YOUTUBE.

Digital Economy Act (UK), 2010 If you received a solicitor's letter this morning accusing you of breaching online copyright, demanding a substantial fine and threatening you with disconnection from the INTERNET, you could be a victim of the UK Digital Economy Act, made law in the dying days of the New Labour government in April 2010. Controversial and challenged in court by major broadband providers, the Act empowers companies to pursue illegal users of their product; those deemed to have made available to others, for copying, songs, TV programmes, movies, computer games, etc. Where there is proven evidence of piracy, companies can demand of Internet Providers (IPs) the e-mail addresses of users. Responsibility for monitoring and reporting on the operation of the Act is that of OFCOM in accord with an Initial Obligations Code and a Technical Obligations Code. The Act has forty-two sections and two schedules, the most contentious of which concern online breaches of copyright.

The Act aims to protect the UK's creative industries from piracy and the financial losses which result. Claims have been made that in 2008 alone, companies lost £1.2 billion to piracy. In brief, the Act empowers the industry to track down wrongdoers by making it a legal requirement that where there is evidence of breaches of copyright by individuals or groups, IPs must release details of e-mail addresses. Many fear that they are being cast in the role of online police.

Pursuit of wrongdoers is complex, gradual and with a number of safeguards, but as the process becomes routine the Act promises to be dynamic and ruthless: it begins with identification followed by warning, then legal action which may result in disconnection.

Dan Sabbagh in a *Guardian* online article, 'Digital Economy Act likely to increase households targeted for piracy' (12 April 2010) writes, 'The worry has to be that those keenest to use the Act to threaten people with disconnection will be ruthless operators who act for owners of content that nobody would describe as mainstream. If past experience is anything to go by, the number of complaints will rise, and miscarriages of justice will increase too.'

In a follow-up posting to Sabbagh's article, Cyberdoyle puts the issue more dramatically, declaring that 'the ambulance chasers have been given a golden goose with this stupid bill, but they will only persecute the innocent'. It is a genuine worry that the innocent will suffer as much as the intentionally guilty. For example, an illegal download in an Internet café by a passing stranger could make the café proprietor liable; equally, libraries, colleges and universities become legally responsible for the activities of users. See CENSORSHIP; SURVEILLANCE SOCIETY.

Digital natives, digital immigrants Neuroscientist Gary Small offers these definitions of INTERNET users in his book, written with Gigi Vorgan, entitled *iBrain: Surviving the Technological Alteration of the Modern Mind* (HarperCollins, 2008). Digital natives have inhabited the terrain of the Internet from childhood; they are those who have never known a world without e-mail, mobile phones and texting. They tend to be impressive multi-taskers, jugglers of information in all forms and from all sources. In contrast, digital immigrants came lately to Net communication, their hard-wiring having taken place in an age dominated by single, one-at-a-time source materials such as books.

Small and Vorgan argue that digital immigrants are better at reading facial expression and bodily gesture, that is real-life interactive situations (see NON-VERBAL COMMUNICATION). Instead of the digital native's multi-tasking approach to knowledge and information, the digital immigrant is more likely to take things step by step, addressing one thing at a time. The authors believe that this approach makes for deeper thinking and more reliable decision-making. See PLASTICITY: NEUROPLASTICITY AND THE INTERNET.

▸ Nicholas Carr, *The Shallows: How the Internet is Changing the Way We Think* (Atlantic Books, 2010).

Digital optimism Takes the view that online interactive exchange typified by the growth of blogging, social networking (see FACEBOOK; MYSPACE; NETWORKING: SOCIAL NETWORKING; YOUTUBE) and the rise of citizen journalism (see JOURNALISM: CITIZEN JOURNALISM) has had a profound and positive impact on traditional mass-media dominance and practices. Some commentators argue that celebration is ahead of the evidence. As Graeme Turner warns in *Ordinary People and the Media: The Demotic Turn* (Sage, 2010), 'Often without the support of empirical data or accounting for historical trends in the relevant locations, digital optimists move into futurological mode at the drop of a hat.'

▸ Matthew Hindman, *The Myth of Digital Democracy* (Princeton University Press, 2009).

Digitization The computer works digitally: information is broken down into a code of zeros and ones (*bits*). Today, all forms of electronic communication are converging through digital formats, and computer-mediated communication now applies to newspapers, telephone systems, BROADCASTING, film production as well as the INTERNET. Digitization makes for *profusion* – of TELEVISION and RADIO channels and, in terms of use and reception, *fragmentation*.

Such are the possibilities in the 'Digital Age' that each viewer or listener ceases to be, as in the past, part of a recognizable AUDIENCE. Specialized, more targeted provision comes at an extra price. Where once the annual licence fee was the only payment for radio and TV services, now reception depends more and more on subscriptions, smart-cards and digital conversion boxes. Viewing is becoming almost as expensive as a night at the opera.

Take up the new digital technology, and you pick up the cost of development and the rush for profits. Availability of what has been traditional screen fare for PUBLIC SERVICE BROADCASTING (PSB) – that is, programmes available for the entire nation to watch – rapidly diminished in the last decade of the twentieth century. British digital broadcasting began in 1998, with two rivals in the field, Ondigital and Sky Digital (in which News International has a 40 per cent stake), with government insistence that they must produce compatible technology to minimize consumer confusion.

Digitization is the ultimate form of CONVERGENCE, technically but also in terms of control. All texts converge in the bit, but the investment costs of turning the electronic world digital are enormous, meaning not only that the competition is to be between media giants, but that even the major operators will be continually at risk from their competitors.

At the same time there are serious worries that in terms of quality of programmes and schedules, more may turn out to be more of the same. A key question is whether segments of the population will be left behind in the new age of subscription and pay-per-view. Many commentators fear that digitization favours the already *information-rich* and widens the INFORMATION GAP between them and the *information-poor.*

Cees Hamelink in *World Communication: Disempowerment & Self-Empowerment* (Zed Books, 1995) identifies four major trends in world communications, citing digitization as the first, and interacting and interlocking with the others – *consolidation, deregulation* and *globalization.* The cost of developing digitization leads to consolidation of ownership and control, which in turn demands the minimum of regulation in order to expand and traverse the boundaries of nation states, and in particular regulations governing and protecting public-interest communication.

Finally digitization provides the technological basis for globalization 'as it facilitates the global trading of services, worldwide financial networks, and the spreading of high-technology research and development across the globe'.

Hamelink says that 'the digital age arrives with a monumental invasion of people's privacy' through the massive collection and sale of personal data, which he considers – referring to the proliferation of electronic monitoring by employers of their employees – to be 'a fundamental violation of human rights'. He believes that digital technology is creating 'transparent societies, "glass-house" countries that are very vulnerable to external forces and to the loss of their sovereign capacities'.

Digitization is seen to be both empowering (to the already powerful) and potentially disempowering (to those with less of it in the first place). In relation to the trend towards deregulation, Hamelink argues that 'tension between public good and private commodity is increasingly resolved to the latter's advantage'. Consequently the 'erosion of the public sphere by implication undermines diversity of information provision … everything that does not pass the market threshold because there is not a sufficiently large percentage of consumers, disappears. That may be good for markets, it may be suicidal for democratic politics and creative culture'. See COMMUNICATIONS ACT (UK), 2003; DISEMPOWERMENT; DOWNLOADING; JOURNALISM: PHONE-HACKING; MOBILIZATION. See also *TOPIC GUIDES* under MEDIA: TECHNOLOGIES; NETWORK SOCIETY.

▶ Jan van Dijk, *The Deepening Divide: Inequality in the Information Age* (Sage, 2005); Vincent Miller, *Understanding Digital Culture* (Sage, 2011).

Digital retouching Or electronic retouching; process whereby laser and computer technology are combined to retouch or re-create photographs. A laser beam scans and measures images and pigmentations, then reduces them into a series of 'pixels', or minute segments. These are then recorded in digital form and stored in the computer's memory for eventual reproduction, which permits the rearrangement of the picture, a re-creation – or just plain faking.

Digital video disc (DVD) Or digital *versatile* disc. One of a number of VIDEO compression systems, the size of a compact disc (CD) but holding up to twenty-six times more information. The DVD allows for four full feature-length films to be stored on a single disc, and permits wide-screen format. The cost of duplication is considerably less than that for VHS tape. DVDs can be encrypted, allowing the distributor to control viewing access, and in the case of parents to empower them, through the use of a program password, to restrict what their children view.

Originating in 1998, DVDs swiftly displaced

videos as the technology of popular choice, and with the introduction of Blu-ray, requiring high-resolution TV screens, the quality of picture was vastly improved. So far, while it is easy to lock in to specific scenes in a disc, DVD fails in targeting exact moments – something video tape can do. DVDs are now in dramatic competition with rival 'picture house' services such as web-enabled set-top boxes (see STREAMING), games consoles, the BBC's iPlayer and Apple's iPad.

Direct cinema Term used to describe the work of post-Second World War DOCUMENTARY film-makers in the US, such as Albert Maysles (*Salesman*, 1969 and *Gimme Shelter*, 1970), who coined the phrase, Stephen Leacock (*Don't Look Back*, 1968) and Frederick Wiseman (*High School*, 1968). New, lightweight equipment and improved synchronous sound recording facilities made the work of these observer-documentarists an inspiration for film-makers in many other countries. Direct cinema went out into the world and recorded life as it happened, in the 'raw'.

An earlier, and British, link with this mode of film-making was Free cinema, a short-lived 'collective' of directors in London, organized by Karel Reisz (*Momma Don't Allow*, 1956) and Lindsay Anderson (*O Dreamland*, 1953). Direct cinema film-makers had the technical edge on Free cinema because of the availability of superior sound recording. See CINÉMA VÉRITÉ.

Disconfirmation See CONFIRMATION/DISCOM-FIRMATION.

Discourse A form, mode or GENRE of LANGUAGE use. Each person has in his/her repertoire a whole range of possible discourses – the language of love, of authority, of sport, of the domestic scene. In a media sense, an example of a discourse would be the NEWS, reflecting in its choice of language and style of presentation the social, economic, political and cultural context from which the discourse emanates.

Gunther Kress in *Linguistic Processes in Socio-cultural Practice* (Deakin University Press, 1985) provides the following useful explanation of discourse: 'Institutions and social groupings have specific meanings and values which are articulated in language in systematic ways. Following the work particularly of Michel Foucault, I refer to these systematically-organized modes of talking as discourse. Discourses ... give expression to the meanings and values of an institution.

'Beyond that, they define, describe and delimit what is possible to say and not possible to say (and by extension what is possible to do or not to do) with respect to the area of concern of that institution, whether marginally or centrally. A discourse provides a set of possible statements about a given area, and organizes and gives structure to the manner in which a particular topic, object, process is to be talked about. In that it provides descriptions, rules, permissions and prohibitions of social and individual action.'

The analysis of discourses is central to the study of media, which is essentially about how TEXTS are encoded and how the MEANING of those texts, operating within and influenced by contexts, is decoded. Discourses are, in the words of John Fiske, 'socially produced' and a 'socially located way of making sense of an important area of experience'. Reality is a constant part of experience – how is it reconstructed into discourse? And how is it influenced by other discourses? (See INTERTEXTUALITY.)

All discourses are framed within *narratives* of one form or another. In news, or indeed in fiction, the story is what happens, the discourse how the story is told and the CONNOTATIONS or meanings embedded within it – the PREFERRED READINGS. Discourses struggle for attention; some are dominant and thus hold the public key to the definition of reality. They rigorously conform to *conventions* that work through mechanisms of information control (see AGENDA-SETTING; CONSENSUS; DISCOURSE OF POWER; GATEKEEPING) and are IDEOLOGY-driven (see CONFLICTUAL OPPOSITIONS; DEMONIZATION; NEWS VALUES; PHOTO-NEGATIVIZATION; WEDOM, THEYDOM).

Ultimately discourse is about ruling explanations and thus contributes to the nature of MYTH. Christopher P. Campbell in *Race, Myth and the News* (Sage, 1995) sees myth not as the 'grand storytelling tradition associated with ancient cultures' but in the 'sense of the stories that modern societies unwittingly create to reduce life's contradictions and complexities'. This is what the discourse of news does; it 'comprises continuing stories which uphold and consolidate myth which ultimately focuses on order and disorder'. Campbell argues that 'news is a way of creating order out of disorder, offering cultural meanings, resolutions and reassurances'.

Discourse serves (and services) myth, and the desired end-product is COMMON SENSE; in other words a state of affairs in which that which is defined by discourses is so patently commonsensical that it cannot be seriously contradicted. Campbell identifies the *divisive* rather than *cohesive* potential of commonsensical discourse: 'The danger of the commonsense claim to truth is in its exclusion of those who

D

live outside the familiar world it represents.' See DOMINANT DISCOURSE. See also *TOPIC GUIDE* under LANGUAGE/DISCOURSE/NARRATIVE.

Discourse analysis Form of MASS COMMUNICATION analysis that concentrates upon the ways in which the media convey information, focusing on the language of presentation – linguistic patterns, word and phrase selection (lexical choices), grammatical constructions and story coherence. In particular, discourse analysis sets out to account for the textual form in which the mass media present IDEOLOGY to readership or audience. See CONTENT ANALYSIS; MODES OF MEDIA ANALYSIS.

Discourse of power The French philosopher Michel Foucault (1926–84), wrote that *all* arguments as to the truth are driven by the will to power, that is to exert control. Clearly, in terms of the media, discourses are perceived as means of exerting influence and control over audiences. Foucault saw the field of a discourse in the same way that a physicist sees the electromagnetic field: it is defined not by its will to truth, but by its will to power. A discourse seeks power, and that is what marks out its range. See HEGEMONY; IDEOLOGY.

Discursive communication Susanne Langer in *Philosophy in a New Key* (Harvard University Press, 1942) differentiated between what she named *discursive* communication – prose and logic – and *non-discursive* communication, such as poetry, music and ritual.

Discursive contestation Situation, usually occurring in the transmission of NEWS, where the AUDIENCE is permitted room to challenge or disagree; where news TEXTS passing through *frames* of production are more open (to interpretation) than closed. News formats either facilitate discursive contestation or close down its potential.

Simon Cottle in 'Television news and citizenship: Packaging the public sphere', published in *No News is Bad News: Radio, Television and the Public* (Longman, 2001), edited by Michael Bromley, talks of how 'incredibly "restricted" some news formats are when reporting news stories'. Conventionalized TV news formats frame and discursively 'seal' the text from alternative interpretations. On the other hand, where 'words are spoken by accessed voices', that is by members of the public rather than media professionals, news texts are more open to discursive contestation.

Cottle argues that formats should work towards what he terms 'participatory control' or alternative frames where 'social actors are granted resources and news space to present in their own ways, and in their own words, their own frameworks of understanding'. See DISEMPOWERMENT; FRAMING: MEDIA.

Discursive gap Term used by Roger Fowler in *Language in the News: Discourse and Ideology in the Press* (Routledge, 1991). The 'gap' is that which exists between the mode of address of the newspaper – formal, bureaucratic – and that of the perceived reception mode of the reader, informal and personal, especially readers of the popular press. Fowler argues that 'the fundamental device in narrowing the discursive gap is the promotion of oral models within the printed newspaper text, giving an illusion of conversation in which common sense is spoken about matters on which there is consensus'.

He believes 'the basic task for the writer is to word institutional statements (those of the newspaper, and those of its sources) in a style appropriate to interpersonal communication, because the reader is an individual and must be addressed as such. The task is not only stylistic, but also ideological: institutional concepts have to be translated into personal thought'. In brief, the press employs a range of devices to simulate a sense of 'orality' which has the writer sitting next to the reader around the kitchen table or in the pub and joining in a process of 'co-production'; the product being CONSENSUS, an apparently shared vision of the world.

Disempowerment The taking away from individuals, GROUPS, communities or nations of the power to have control over their lives. In *World Communication: Disempowerment & Self-Empowerment* (Zed Books, 1995), Cees Hamelink describes disempowerment as 'the reduction of people's ability to define themselves and construct their own identities'. It can be the result of a deliberate strategy or the unintended outcome of developments locally, nationally or internationally. As a strategy, says Hamelink, disempowerment 'often employs the deceit of making people believe that existing conditions are desirable and preferred out of free will. The most perverse form of disempowerment makes people accept their own dependency and second rate position'.

The PRIVATIZATION of communications is seen as an agent of disempowerment: 'As knowledge is created and controlled as private property, knowledge as common good is destroyed'. For Hamelink, the inherent meaning of privatization is *private = to deprive*. Strategies of empowerment include regulation, the provision of power to people through human rights legislation (such as a freedom of information act or laws facilitating a RIGHT OF REPLY) or public-interest regulation (such as the Charter of the BBC).

Regulation can also be seen in national press councils, usually voluntary arrangements, created to protect the public against abuses committed by newspapers and journals. The weaknesses of these forms of empowerment are many and varied: voluntary WATCHDOGS can so easily end up dogs without teeth, without the power to insist that media perform according to empowerment principles; and all of this presupposes that the law itself is a force for equality, of access and treatment.

In the context of mass communication, a key tool of empowerment is media education – in Hamelink's words 'the need to make people critically aware of how media are organized, how they function, and how their contents can be analysed'. The author quotes Len Masterman in *Teaching the Media* (Comedia, 1985), who believes that 'media education is an essential step in the long march towards a truly participatory democracy, and the democratization of our institutions'. See FREEDOM OF INFORMATION ACT (UK), 2005; PEOPLE'S COMMUNICATION CHARTER.

Disenfranchisement (of readership) Researchers have commented on the extent to which some newspapers reflect an assumption – possibly that of the owners and editors – that their readership is totally uninvolved and uninterested in the political processes and events of the country. It is as if the readers were politically disenfranchised, not able to participate in the political process, and thus news of political affairs is of no concern to them. Such papers aim to entertain, to concentrate on stories of human interest and drama rather than to inform.

Disinformation Derives from the Russian, 'Dezinformatsiya', a term especially associated with the former Soviet Union's secret service, the KGB. It applied to the use of forgery and other techniques to discredit targeted governments, persons or policies. The process of disinformation is, of course, as old as mankind, and sowing the seeds of disinformation is matched by accusing the opposition of spreading disinformation. See EFFECTS OF THE MASS MEDIA; NEWS MANAGEMENT IN TIMES OF WAR.

Displacement effect In psychological theory, *displacement* is one of the major mechanisms of ego-defence identified by Sigmund Freud. Displacement occurs when an individual chooses an alternative focus for the expression of feel-

ings and emotions because he/she feels unable to express them towards their real target – the 'kick the cat' syndrome. The proposition that we unconsciously develop such defence mechanisms can be useful in the study of interaction. An example of how displacement may affect communicative behaviour is as follows: a waiter may feel that he has been unfairly treated by a customer, but also feels unable to do anything about this so instead later on picks an argument with a new and more junior member of staff in order to vent his feelings of frustration.

In relation to studying the media, displacement *effect* refers to the reorganization of activities that takes place with the introduction of some new interest or attention-drawer, such as TV or surfing the Net. Activities such as reading may be cut down, or stopped altogether; in the case of social networking, displacing face-to-face interaction with online exchange. New media 'displace' or adjust the placement of other media. Cinema-going habits have been substantially affected by competition from TV, and in turn television has been affected by video, DVD and the multi-task possibilities of the mobile phone (see MOBILIZATION). Travellers by train will have noticed how the potential for a chat with fellow passengers has largely been displaced by the prevalence of talk, gaming and film-watching on mobiles.

The notion of *functional similarity* has often been applied as a yardstick to measure the extent and nature of displacement: if the new is functionally similar to the old, then the old is likely to be displaced. Functionally dissimilar activities are likely to hold their own. The problem lies in establishing what functions a medium actually serves, which means that displacement is all the more difficult to assess.

As a result of TV, do people talk less, read less, go out with friends less, socialize less? Does the INTERNET mop up marginal activities, displace real with second-hand experience; does it displace 'day-dreaming'? Evidence concerning people's reactions to programmes is so open to influence from INTERVENING VARIABLES (IVs) that it is difficult to use it as a basis for reliable theory. See EFFECTS OF THE MASS MEDIA; USES AND GRATIFICATIONS THEORY. See also *TOPIC GUIDE* under COMMUNICATION THEORY.

Disqualifying communication A form of self-protection, or DEFENSIVE COMMUNICATION when, in a situation causing embarrassment, anxiety or uneasiness, people talk aimlessly about, say, the weather, or go into a variety of non-verbal responses in order to avoid direct communication. See INTERPERSONAL COMMUNICATION.

Dissolve A process in camera-work by which one picture fades out and the following scene fades in on top of it. Also called a 'mix'. See SHOT.

Dissonance Occurs when two COGNITIVE inputs to our mental processes are out of line. The result is a certain amount of psychological discomfort. Action is usually taken to resolve the dissonance and restore *balance*. Several strategies are commonly employed in order to achieve this: downgrading the source of dissonance; compliance with rather than acceptance of new expectations and ideas; changing one's previous ideas and attitudes; and avoidance of the source of dissonance.

All messages, particularly those conveyed to a mass AUDIENCE, are potentially a source of dissonance to someone. If they disturb the intended receiver(s), then they may well be ignored or rejected. The need for messages intended for a mass audience to be successful, however, ensures that such messages are often well 'laundered' in order to reduce their potential offensiveness. See COGNITIVE CONSISTENCY THEORIES; CONGRUENCE THEORY; NEWCOMB'S ABX MODEL OF COMMUNICATION, 1953; SELECTIVE EXPOSURE.

Distributed denial of service (DoS) Process by which computer HACKERS use special software to take control of other people's computers: a form of trespass or occupation in which endless – and spurious – requests for information block and disrupt the flow of genuine information exchange. The practice of DoS has affected the websites of individuals as well as those of corporate giants such as Amazon, Microsoft and Yahoo.

Diversification In media terms, the spread of ownership and control into a wide range of associated, and often unassociated, products and services. Thus newspapers have moved into TV share-holding and online services; TV companies into set rentals, bingo and social clubs and motorway catering services. In parallel, great corporations have moved into media ownership – oil companies buying up newspaper chains and investing in BROADCASTING interests, book publishing, record production and INTERNET platforms (see MYSPACE; YOUTUBE). The result of diversification is often, paradoxically, concentration of control, and a real danger to a newspaper, film company or publishing house of being just another 'product' on the shelf of the multi-national conglomerate whose objective is profit maximization above all other considerations. See CONGLOMERATES; DIGITIZATION.

D-Notices See DA (Defence Advisory) Notices.

Documentary Any mode of communication which, in addressing an AUDIENCE, documents events or situations – books, radio, theatre, photography, film or TV. Usually based upon recorded or observable fact, the documentary may aim for objectivity or PROPAGANDA; it may, however, in terms of human documentation, be highly subjective. 'Even when temperate,' writes William Stott in *Documentary Expression and Thirties America* (Oxford University Press, 1973), 'a human document carries and communicates feeling, the raw material of drama.'

British film director, producer and theorist John Grierson (1898–1972) is thought to have been the first to use the word 'documentary', in a New York *Sun* review (1926) of Robert Flaherty's film *Moana*, a study of the way of life of the South Seas islanders. In fact, 'documentary' is as old as the cinema itself. Louis Lumière's early short films of 1895 – one showing the demolition of a wall, another of a train coming into a station – can be described as documentaries.

The founding father of documentary filmmaking in the UK and later in Canada, Grierson never claimed scientific objectivity for such films. For him the documentary was far more than a straightforward reconstruction on film of reality. He spoke of the 'creative use of actuality' in which the director re-formed fact in order to reach towards an inner truth. Indeed when documentarists have felt it necessary to get at the truth of a subject as they perceive it, they have not held back from fictionalization, often using actors, often turning the real-life person into an actor re-creating a scene.

In the 1930s, FILM documentary ran parallel with RADIO documentary, the BBC showing considerable innovative enterprise in this field, especially its Manchester studio. In the US many publications combined documentary evidence with outstanding photography. The themes were often those of the Depression: concern at the plight of the poor, the unemployed, the alienated; and the mode was largely to have the people speak for themselves rather than distance the impact of their experience by using the mediation of a commentator.

The documentary approach has been a recurring feature in modern theatre, especially since the 1960s. Historical or contemporary events on stage are far from new: Aeschylus dramatized the victory of Marathon (490 BC) and Shakespeare reconstructed history, often to fit the perceptions of the Tudor monarchy, in a third of his output.

German dramatist Rolf Hochhuth won world-wide attention with his documentary drama *The Representative* in 1963, on the subject of the Papacy and the Jews during the Second World War (1939–45). He followed this up with *Soldiers* (1967) based upon the alleged involvement of British Prime Minister Winston Churchill in the wartime death of the Polish General Sikorski. In the UK, Peter Brook's highly successful *US* (1966) was an indictment of American involvement in the Vietnam war.

On-stage documentaries, in the US often termed the Theatre of Fact, have frequently been presented with the aid of official and press reports, original diaries, projected photographs, tape recordings and newsreel films. In the case of the Royal Court production *Falkland Sound* (1983), a moving and damning recollection of the Falklands War (1982) was presented through the letters home of a young naval officer killed in action.

Faction or drama-doc are terms mainly associated with TV documentaries in which actors re-create historical lives, such as in the BBC's *The Voyage of Charles Darwin* (1978), or play the part of famous people of the immediate past, such as Thames Television's *Edward and Mrs Simpson* (1978), Southern TV's *Winston Churchill – The Wilderness Years* (1981), and ITV's *Kennedy* (1983). To TV producers, faction has come to represent an ideal synthesis of education, information and entertainment, albeit highly selective and deeply coloured by contemporary perspectives.

Just as documentary has borrowed from fictional narratives, so fiction has taken on the 'guise' of documentary. Such works are described as 'mock' documentaries and they aim to examine the borderline between the real and the invented. A memorable example is Woody Allen's *Zelig* (1983) in which he achieved remarkable results by combining newsreels, stills and live footage (see Craig Hight and Jane Roscoe's *Faking it: Mock-documentary and the subversion of factuality*, Manchester University Press, 2001).

Early UK TV drama-docs of note are Ken Loach's *Cathy Come Home* (1965) and Peter Watkins's *Culloden* (1964) and *The War Game* (1965). The popularity of REALITY TV has in the New Millennium been matched by increased interest on the part of audiences in the genre, outstanding examples being Kevin Macdonald's *Touching the Void* (2003), Errol Morris's *The Fog of War* and Andrew Jarecki's *Capturing the Friedmans*, both of 2004, each with powerful stories to tell and conveying a dramatic sense of immediacy – indeed making the claims of authenticity made for reality TV pale in comparison.

Immensely popular on both sides of the Atlantic have been Michael Moore's documentaries, *Bowling for Columbine* (2002), a savage indictment of the US gun culture, and *Fahrenheit 9/11* (2004), a critical exploration of the Iraq war of 2003 and alleging links between President George Bush and top Saudi families including the Bin Ladens. *Fahrenheit 9/11* won the prestigious Palme d'Or award for best film at the Cannes Film Festival. It was the first time that a documentary had won the top prize since Jacques Cousteau's award for *Silent World* in 1956.

Inevitably drama-docs have stirred controversy. The BBC's *Dirty War* (2004), for example, was too close for comfort for some critics, being about a 'dirty bomb' explosion in London, while a few faint voices of protest were raised when Channel 4's *The Taking of Prince Harry* (2010) simulated the abduction of the Prince while on military duty in Afghanistan. See CINEMATOGRAPHY, ORIGINS; CINÉMA VÉRITÉ; DIRECT CINEMA; FLY-ON-THE-WALL; RADIO BALLADS; SOAPS: DOCU-SOAPS; WEB OR ONLINE DRAMA.

▶ John Caughie, *Television Drama: Realism, Modernism and British Culture* (Oxford University Press, 2000); Alan Rosenthal and John Corner, eds, *New Challenges for Documentary* (Manchester University Press, 2005); Sheila Curran Bernard, *Documentary Storytelling* (Focal Press, 3rd edition, 2011).

Dolly A trolley on which a camera unit can be soundlessly moved about during shooting; can usually be mounted on rails. A 'crab dolly' will move in any direction.

Domestication of the foreign See NEWS: GLOBALIZATION OF.

Dominant culture See CULTURE.

★**Dominant discourse** In a general sense, DISCOURSE is talk; converse; holding forth in speech and writing on a subject. Refers both to the content of communicative exchanges and to the level at which those exchanges take place, and in what mode or style as well as to whom the discourse is addressed. A dominant discourse is that which takes precedence over others, reducing alternative content, subordinating alternative approaches to 'holding forth'. All public discourse is socially and culturally based, thus it follows that the dominant discourse is usually that which emanates from those dominant in the social and cultural order. See ELITE; HEGEMONY; IDEOLOGY; POWER ELITE.

Dominant, subordinate, radical Three catego-

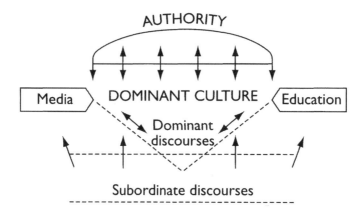

AUTHORITY

Media ⟩ DOMINANT CULTURE ⟨ Education

Dominant discourses

Subordinate discourses

Dominant discourse

ries of response in terms of the reading of media messages on the part of AUDIENCE are posed by Frank Parkin in *Class, Inequality and Political Order* (Paladin, 1972). Do we accept what we are told, only half accept it, or substantially reject it? Parkin argues that it is our place in the social structure which conditions our response. Stuart Hall in 'The determination of news photographs' in Stanley Cohen and Jock Young, eds, *The Manufacture of News* (Constable, 1st edition, 1973) supports Parkin's view, with the same categories but different terminology.

The dominant system of response (Hall calls it a *dominant code*) signifies that the dominant VALUES and existing society are wholly accepted by the respondent; the subordinate response (Hall's *negotiated code*) indicates general acceptance of dominant values and existing social structures, but the respondent is prepared to argue that a particular group – blacks, unemployed, women – within that structure may be unfairly dealt with and that something should be done about it. The radical response (Hall's *oppositional code*) rejects the PREFERRED READING of the dominant code and the social values that produced it.

David Morley's research into audience response, published in *The Nationwide Audience* (British Film Institute, 1980), gave substance to Parkin and Hall's division of response, but also emphasized other response-conditioning factors such as education, occupation, political affiliation, geographical region, religion and family. More recent commentators have expanded on the response codes mentioned here; for example, a *popular* response may be characterized by *inattention* on the part of audience or the rejection of media messages because 'they

have nothing to do with us'. See EFFECTS OF THE MASS MEDIA; ETHNOGRAPHIC (APPROACH TO AUDIENCE MEASUREMENT); POLYSEMY. See also *TOPIC GUIDE* under AUDIENCES: CONSUMPTION & RECEPTION OF MEDIA.

Double exposure Two pictures superimposed upon one another on the same piece of film. Like reverse motion, double exposure in filming began as a simple visual curiosity before it became a fully fledged means of artistic expression. It was first used in still photography, where double or multiple exposure images produced what was described as 'spirit photography'. Georges Méliès (1861–1938) used double exposure in his films from 1908; the technique has been employed to achieve many effects, chiefly that of suggesting the supernatural and of conveying the process of thought and spirituality.

Doughnut principle See ORGANIZATION CULTURES.

Downloading With DIGITIZATION facilitating the compression of electronic data, downloading has been characterized by exponential growth. As more and more people have invested in high-speed broadband transmission, the downloading of music, programmes from radio and TV and full-length feature films has had a massive impact on traditional modes of distribution.

Software enables users to download from a range of sources simultaneously, while compressing DVD data to a tenth of its original size. The result is lost revenue on the part of the producers, though significant profits for those who can adapt to what has caused a major shake-up in the communications industry.

Mobile devices such as digital music players are the must-have toys of the twenty-first century, but they are in competition for market share with the mobile phone (see MOBILIZA-TION). Digital download subscription services allow mobiles to store and play music in addition to their capacity to tune into broadcast news, watch TV or movie clips, listen to the news on radio, take pictures (moving and still), connect to the Internet – and, oh, make phone-calls. See PODCASTING.

Dramadoc See DOCUMENTARY.

Drama: television drama See TELEVISION DRAMA (UK).

Drama: web or online drama See WEB OR ONLINE DRAMA.

Dress Appearance and bodily adornment are important aspects of non-verbal communication, and play an especially significant role when people are forming first impressions of one another. These features can send a range of messages about an individual: for example about personality, cultural or group identity, GENDER, CLASS, STATUS, ethnicity, faith, wealth, age, roles, fashion-consciousness, STEREOTYPE, social context and historical context, to name but a few. In Ted Polhemus and UZi PART B, *Hot Bodies, Cool Styles: New Techniques in Self-Adornment* (Thames and Hudson, 2004), Polhemus argues that in Western cultures a wide variety of artefacts, adornments and styles from around the world are on offer in what he terms the 'global 24/7 supermarket of style'. The trend is for young people to experiment and construct a style that expresses personal rather than group identity, to display a sense of uniqueness rather than group solidarity. This 'DIY approach' is in contrast to an arguably earlier trend for style to signal membership of a youth SUB-CULTURE, such as those of the Mods, Rockers or Punks. However, it needs to be acknowledged that individuals are not always free to dress as they please. Norms, conventions and dress codes frame expectations in a number of circumstances and contexts. Many workplaces, for example, have a dress code.

An individual may consciously or unconsciously convey messages through dress, but receivers may not of course decode these messages in the way intended by the sender. While personal style may be an open text, uniforms often convey clear messages; unless of course those uniforms are worn in inappropriate circumstances – for instance, in the UK Prince Harry turned up to a fancy-dress ball in a Nazi uniform and prompted a blaze of reprimands in the nation's press. See COMMUNICATION, NON-VERBAL; OBJECT LANGUAGE. See also *TOPIC GUIDE* under INTERPERSONAL COMMUNICATION.

▶ Dick Hebdige, *Sub-Culture: The Meaning of Style* (Methuen, 1979; Routledge, 2002); Ken Gelder and Sarah Thornton, eds, *The Sub-Cultures Reader* (Routledge, 1997); and, all from Sage Publications: Angela McRobbie, *In the Culture Society: Art, Fashion and Popular Music* (1999); Stella Bruzzi and Pamela Church Gibson, eds, *Fashion Cultures: Theories, Explorations and Analysis* (2000); Chris Tilly, Webb Keane, Suzanne Kuechler, Mike Rowlands and Patricia Spyer, eds, *Handbook of Material Culture* (2005).

Dry-run TV programme rehearsal in which action, lines, cues, etc. are tried out prior to the final rehearsal.

Dub, dubbing In film-making, to blend speech, music, incidental sound and sound effects on to film or videotape. At a later stage, the language of the 'home' audience may be dubbed on to the sound track in preference to subtitles. See POST-SYNCHRONIZATION.

Duopoly A monopoly held by two organizations rather than one. In BROADCASTING, the term was used to refer to the duopoly once held in the UK by the BBC and the IBA (Independent Broadcasting Authority; succeeded in 1991 by the ITC – Independent Television Commission, in turn giving way to OFCOM in 2003). See MEDIA CONTROL.

DVD See Digital Video Disc (DVD).

DVD games See VIDEO/DVD GAMES.

Dyad A communication dyad consists of two persons interacting, and is the elemental unit of INTERPERSONAL COMMUNICATION.

Dynamic mediation See IMPARTIALITY.

E

Eady Plan, Eady Levy See BRITISH FILM PRODUCTION FUND.

e-book Published and read electronically, the e-book ranks as one of the outstanding developments in modern publishing. As early as 1971 the US Declaration of Independence was scanned into a Xerox mainframe computer by Project Gutenberg founder Michael Hart. Today, handheld electronic devices such as AMAZON's Kindle can hold hundreds of books, and new ones can be up loaded in seconds. Improvements in e-book readability – clarity and size of print – have resulted in rapidly increasing sales, giving both publishers and authors new and more flexible opportunities. According to the Association of American Publishers (AAP) the e-book market increased sales by 500 per cent between 2007 and 2010, this representing 15 per cent of trade sales in the US. There is evidence that e-reading is proving more attractive to young people in particular than the traditional print medium.

Echelon An automated global computer intelligence-gathering network run in partnership between the UK Government Communication Headquarter Agency (GCHQ) and the US National Security, using the intelligence agencies' own network of satellite and listening bases and also operated in Canada, Australia and New Zealand. It has been estimated that Echelon intercepts up to three billion communications a day. So-termed Echelon Dictionaries search intercepted messages according to target lists of subjects and people. See SURVEILLANCE.

▶ James Bamford, *A Pretext for War: 9/11, Iraq, and the Abuse of America's Intelligence Agencies* (Anchor, 2005); also his *The Shadow Factory: The Ultra-Secret NSA from 9/11 to the Eavesdropping on America* (Doubleday, 2008).

Echo chamber effect Web publics are subject to fragmentation, insulation from broader sources of information and comment, in danger of being a number of *enclaves*, talking between themselves and only to themselves, in a chamber that only echoes their own discourses. In 'The many faced "you" of social media' published in *Journalism and Citizenship: New Agendas in Communication* (Routledge, 2009), edited by Zizi Papacharissi, Sharon Meraz writes of 'the effect of limited argument pools and perspectives' in which the echo chamber effect can be seen as a threat to democracy 'because of negative informational cascades, which result when groups remain insulated and homogenous in both perspective and composition'.

The echo chamber effect, argues Meraz, 'can be exacerbated in social media environments that depend on friendships and social information filtering to determine popularity'. This can lead to 'collaborative filtering of news in some [blog] sites'. What has been described as the 'tyranny of the minority' can prove detrimental to the openly democratic selection and presentation of news and comment on Net sites. See POWER LAW PHENOMENON.

Effects of the mass media Can be broadly defined as any change induced directly or indirectly by the recording, filming or reporting of events. Analysts of effects, or impact, are concerned with the modification of attitudes and behaviour of individuals and GROUPS. The process of measuring these effects is immensely complicated as the ground upon which the measurements are taken is constantly shifting.

The actual effect of the media on audiences, so far as it can be ascertained, is arguably less significant than the *perceived* effect. In the

nineteenth century those in authority were of the view that access by the mass of the population to the printed word might turn docility into uprising. The new mass-medium of the cinema was similarly accused of a wide range of 'effects', while TV, in the eyes of some, is responsible for many of the ills of our time, as though such media could be somehow divorced from the social, political and cultural environment which produce them.

A few generalized hypotheses about effects can be tentatively posited: the media are probably more likely to modify and reinforce attitudes than change them; media impact will be greater among the uncommitted ('floating voters') than the committed; impact will be more influential if all the media are saying more or less the same thing at the same time (CONSISTENCY); equally, if the media are concentrating on a small rather than diverse number of stories (INTENSITY) and if they are repeating messages, images, viewpoints over and over again (FREQUENCY).

'The timing of communication processes,' writes Colin Seymour-Ure in *The Political Impact of Mass Media* (Constable, 1974), 'is probably one of the most important determinants of mass media effects.' If the timing is right, the media can often be the arbiters of crisis, by being in the most prominent position to define it. Because of their AGENDA-SETTING capacity, the media have influence upon the criteria which, in the public domain, decide what is important and what is not, what is normal and what is deviant, what is CONSENSUS and what is *dissensus*, what is significant, or newsworthy, and what is marginal.

No summary of effects, however brief, should neglect the role played, some would say most powerfully, by the media in supporting, reinforcing and cementing patterns of social control, not least by maintaining and sometimes fashioning the symbols of legitimate government. See *TOPIC GUIDE* under MEDIA: POWER, EFFECTS, INFLUENCE.

▶ Shearon A. Lowery and Melvyn L. DeFleur, *Milestones in Mass Media Research: Media Effects* (Longman, 1995); Michael Xenos and Patricia Moy, 'Direct and differential effects of the Internet on political and civil engagement' (*Journal of Communication*, December 2007); W. Lance Bennett and Shanto Lyengar, 'A new era of minimal effects? The changing foundations of political communication' (*Journal of Communication*, December 2008).

★**Eisenberg's model of communication and identity, 2001** In his article 'Building a mystery: toward a new theory of communication and identity' published in the *Journal of Communica-*

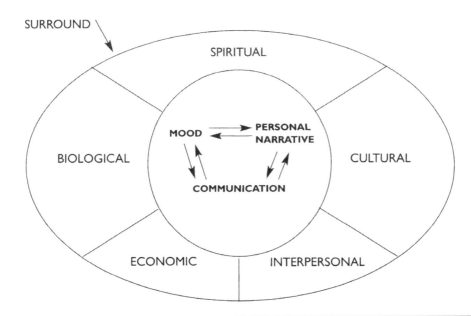

Eisenberg's model of communication and identity, 2001 (the identity process, with three subprocesses operating within a surround)

tion, September 2001, Eric M. Eisenberg opens with the comment that a 'primary challenge of human being is living in the present with the awareness of an uncertain future'. His focus is *identity*, the search for it, the establishment of it, and its shifting nature, as it relates to processes of communication within a modern-day context of flux and insecurity.

The aim of contemporary discourse should be to work towards stability without transforming that into dogma, into single truths. The author cites the many wars being fought across the globe 'over truth claims of one kind or another'. Just as there is a multiplicity of truths, so there is fluidity of identity, individual, group, communal or national.

The model demonstrates the interconnectedness of *surround*, that is a range of influences upon human beings in communities, and the process of communication, the dynamic of which arises from *mood* and *personal narrative*. Mood is how we feel about ourselves, our thoughts and emotions, our physical as well as psychological orientation to the world around us; to others within the context of that world. It concerns our sense of power – power to take hold of our lives, shape them, and this connects to the stories we construct about ourselves, our identity; facilitating (or otherwise) what Eisenberg terms our 'narrative possibility'.

The three core elements are interdependent and interactive, and the sense of empowerment will depend on the nature of communication, to put it briefly, less target-orientated, less occupied with the 'ideology of clarity', of objectivization, less individualized, less defensive of self, value and ideology and more communal, in essence, more connective; indeed orientated towards the cultivation of a 'planetary identity'.

While Eisenberg does not wish to minimize the importance of 'understanding' in communicative exchange, he sees in uncertainty its value as mystery, a vital counterbalance to strategies that endanger sympathetic communion with others; for as the author acknowledges, 'Despite unprecedented advances in science and culture, brutal dictatorships, medieval forms of torture and genocide persist' – all in the name of truth-assertion and the notion of identity as something fixed and permanent. The stories we tell ourselves, our construction of identity through self-narrative, are predicated on the nature of communication itself, its ability to accommodate the 'fundamental indeterminacy of the future' which, Eisenberg argues, 'is an essential quality of human experience'. See *TOPIC GUIDE* under COMMUNICATION MODELS.

Elaborated and Restricted Codes In *Class, Codes and Control Vol. 1* (Paladin, 1971), Basil Bernstein posed a now-famous classification of language codes, the Elaborated and Restricted codes based upon research into the language-use of children. Bernstein maintained that there are substantial differences in speech between middle-class and working-class children (see CLASS), the former using the Elaborated Code, the latter the Restricted Code.

The determinant of the code in each case is the nature of the social relationships and influences to which the child is exposed. A close-knit, traditional working-class community, Bernstein argues, has tended to use the Restricted Code because a high degree of shared MEANING is assumed. In the more typically loose-knit middle-class communities there are fewer grounds for making assumptions about shared meaning, and therefore a more explicit – Elaborated – code is used. This is not to say that the middle classes do not possess their own Restricted Codes in particular social or professional situations; the important point is that they have been able to move with ease from a Restricted to an Elaborated Code when it is socially or educationally necessary.

The Restricted Code tends to be less complex than the Elaborated, with a small vocabulary and simpler sentence structure; spoken rather than written. It is easy to predict (high in REDUN-DANCY) whereas the Elaborated Code is less easy to predict (high in *entropy*). The Restricted Code is orientated towards social relations, towards *commonality*, while the Elaborated Code represents an emphasis on individuality and individual differences.

The one is the language of the street, the home, the playground, the pub; the other, very largely, the language of school, the language of formal education. Thus, Bernstein indicates, within the educational context, the user of the Restricted Code can be placed at a disadvantage. He does not argue that the Elaborated Code is superior to the Restricted Code, only that it is different and more useful for upward social mobility.

Bernstein's claims prompted considerable debate, some of it critical, and a number of researchers argued that his classification is inflexible. Martin Montgomery, for instance, in *An Introduction to Language and Society* (Routledge, 1995) writes, 'There is, for example, in the final analysis hardly any linguistic evidence to support the division of speech into two mutually exclusive codes or speech variants. And by the same token, Bernstein's treatment of the social structure looks with hindsight somewhat rigid and schematic.' See *TOPIC GUIDE* under LANGUAGE/DISCOURSE/NARRATIVE; REPRESENTATION.

▶ Basil Bernstein, 'Social class, language and social-ization', an extract from his major work, in John Corner and Jeremy Hawthorn, eds, *Communication Studies* (Arnold, 1993).

Electronic Frontier Foundation (EFF) US donor-funded independent organization formed in 1990 to campaign for, and defend, public and consumer interest in the field of digital rights.

Electronic mail: e-mail The sending and receiving of e-mails – texts of all kinds through the 'postal' system of the computer – has become the fastest-growing means of communication in business, within institutions and between friends, families and total strangers across the world. It has proved a useful tool in the exchange of knowledge, the provision of advice, the two-way transmission of research data and the sharing across social and national boundaries of a myriad of problems. It serves as a link between GROUPS and communities of like interest, all at the price of a local phone-call.

In 1992 only 2 per cent of the American population used the e-mail service. This had risen in 1998 to 15 per cent. By 2010, 77 per cent of the North American population had e-mailing facility, an increase of of 146 per cent in the period 2000–2010, according to statistics published by Internetwordstatistics (www.internetworldstats.com). The figure for population penetration of e-mail use in Europe was 58 per cent, with Iceland topping the chart with 97 per cent compared with Sweden (92%), the Netherlands (88%), Denmark (86%), the UK (82%), Germany (79%) and France (68%). Albania's 43 per cent penetration marked a 59,900 per cent growth.

These figures contrast dramatically with Africa's 10 per cent penetration. While that of Tunisia was 34 per cent, Egypt 21 per cent and South Africa 10 per cent, e-mailing was all but a stranger to the majority of the population of Chad (1%), the Congo Democratic Republic (0.5%), and Ethiopia (0.5%). Somalia's 1 per cent represented a growth of 52,900 per cent.

The rise in what has been referred to as 'computer babble', both for business and leisure use, is such that e-mails now constitute a problem as much as an opportunity. The *Wall Street Journal* has gauged that a typical worker in a European company deals with an average of 150 e-mails a day. Allowing time to read these and reply, it would take some four to five hours to process – a dramatic example of information overload. The *Journal* reported that an executive returning to the States from a business trip in Europe found 2,000 e-mails waiting to be dealt with.

E-mails are also very public statements, open to the scrutiny of those not intended to read them. Then there has been the growth of junk e-mails – *spam* – and more seriously, *phishing*, using spam e-mails to redirect users of online banking to fake sites, often with devastating financial consequences for the victims. Even more serious still is *spoofing*, where spammers use header information to convince you that their message is genuinely from your bank or any other confidential source.

The effectiveness of Net industries will increasingly depend on systems of *authentication*, that is making sure that all communications sent are valid and legitimate, while at the same time blocking unwanted sources. See TOPIC GUIDES under DIGITAL AGE COMMUNICATION; MEDIA: TECHNOLOGIES.

Elite A small group within a society who may be socially acknowledged as superior in some sense, and who influence or control some or all sectors of that society. Several definitions of the term *elite* exist, and these influence the precise focus of research into the relationship between the media, elites, and society.

Early writers generally saw the elite as a ruling group or oligarchy whose power is general and affects most aspects of society. Writers such as Vilfredo Pareto (1848–1923) and Gaetano Mosca (1848–1941) regarded elites as being inevitable, whatever the political system. C. Wright Mills in a study of elites in US society entitled *The Power Elite* (Oxford University Press, 1956) points to the similarity of backgrounds, attitudes and VALUES, and power skills of the members of the three elites which, he argues, dominate American society: the *military*, the *economic* and the *political*. He also comments on the degree of personal and family contacts between elite members and the interchangeability of personnel between top posts in the military, economic and political elites from which the 'power elite' is recruited.

This concept of *elite cohesion* has been of interest to media researchers who have sought to investigate links between members of economic and political elites and those who own or control the media, and the effect such links might have on media output.

The notion of a ruling elite or oligarchy contrasts with the Marxist concept of a ruling CLASS. Whilst elite theorists point out the necessity for the elite to recruit from outside itself, to remain accessible to the influence of the non-elite and to maintain a CONSENSUS among the non-elite which legitimates the elite's right

to rule, Marxist analysis stresses the continuing and increasing polarization or separation of the ruling from the ruled class. Marxist analysis of the media therefore concentrates upon the role of the media in propagating the ideas of the dominant class in order to create a false consciousness, or to create HEGEMONY, which is instrumental in subjugating the rest.

The liberalist-PLURALIST school of analysis sees the media as a kind of FOURTH ESTATE pressuring governing elites and reminding them of their dependency on majority opinion. Other commentators have pointed to the role played by social elites in media *coverage*. The emphasis on the activities and perspectives of leading politicians, celebrities and the royal family would be examples here. In *Mass Communication Theory* (Sage, 2010) Denis McQuail discusses the study carried out by Bennett *et al* (2004) of media coverage of the 'Great Globalization Debate' during the World Economic Forum meetings held in 2001, 2002 and 2003; one finding was that the coverage focused disproportionately on the WEF elite as opposed to those of activists and protestors and, further, that coverage of the elite was significantly more positive in tone. See COMMANDERS OF THE SOCIAL ORDER; DOMINANT DISCOURSE; ESTABLISHMENT; GUARD DOG METAPHOR; NEWS VALUES; POWER ELITE.

▶ W.L. Bennett, V.W. Pickard, D.P. Iozzi, C.I. Schroeder, T. Lago and C.E. Caswell (2004), 'Managing the public sphere: journalistic constructions of the great globalization debate', *Journal of Communication*, 54 (3): 437–55.

Ellul's theory of technique See TECHNIQUE: ELLUL'S THEORY OF TECHNIQUE.

E-mail See ELECTRONIC MAIL: E-MAIL.

Emancipatory use of the media Term employed by Hans Magnus Enzensberger in 'Constituents of a theory of the media' in *Sociology of Mass Communication* (Penguin, 1972), edited by Denis McQuail, to contrast with what he defines as the *repressive* use of the media. He characterizes the emancipatory use of the media as follows: decentralized programme (as opposed to the repressive mode of a centrally controlled programme); each receiver a potential transmitter (as opposed to one transmitter, many receivers); mobilization of the masses (as opposed to immobilization of isolated individuals); interaction of those involved, and FEEDBACK (as opposed to passive consumer behaviour); a political learning process (as opposed to *depoliticization*); and collective production, social control by self-organization (as opposed to production by specialists, control by property owners or bureaucracy). See BLOGOSPHERE; DEMOCRACY; DOMINANT, SUBORDINATE, RADICAL; INTERNET; NETWORKING: SOCIAL NETWORKING.

Embargo Restriction set upon a news item, indicating when that item can be published or broadcast. A PRESS release from government or industry, for example, will be headed 'Not for publication/broadcasting until ... ' and give a specific date.

Embedded reporters With the invasion of Iraq in 2003 by American and British forces, the tactic of the authorities was to insist that reporters of the war were 'embedded' with allied military personnel – the aim being to exercise control over the movements of reporters and to ensure that reports were subject to CENSORSHIP. Equally, it was expected that reporters, attached to operative units, would identify with those units and subsequently develop an EMPATHY with them, an emotional bonding that would make overt censorship unnecessary.

The advantage embedded reporters have over independents, or 'unilaterals', is that they have the chance to witness battle at first-hand, share the experience of combat, learn with their soldier-comrades the nature of fear and stress in which each individual relies on others for survival. The downside is to be subject to military influence and control. The system is not new: reporters were embedded with British troops during the First World War (1914–18). See NEWS MANAGEMENT IN TIMES OF WAR.

Emblem See NON-VERBAL BEHAVIOUR: REPERTOIRE.

Emotive language To describe a crowd as a 'mob' or a 'rabble' is to be emotive, to convey not only information but also one's own attitude towards the crowd and one's intention of influencing the receiver's attitude towards it. Emotive language tells as much about the communicator as the message. It reveals *what* he/she thinks and very often *how* he/she thinks. IDEOLOGY is the root and inspiration of the media use of emotive language. Newspapers often use it on those they disagree with, who appear somehow to threaten what the newspapers wish to preserve. In times of national emergency such as a war, emotive language is used to whip up support and fervour for the cause and to forge a sense of national unity.

Empathetic listening See LISTENING.

Empathy The ability to put oneself into another person's position, into another person's shoes, and to attempt to understand his/her behaviour and perspectives without filtering them through one's own value system. It is not possible totally

to avoid such filtering, but to be empathetic requires that an individual make an effort to avoid judging others on the basis of his/her subjective experiences and perspectives – attempting to see things from the other person's point of view, whilst retaining his/her own perspectives, values and so on. Clearly empathy has an important role to play in effective interpersonal communication and in reducing barriers to communication.

Empirical Based upon experience. Empirical research in the social sciences centres upon fieldwork – the collection of evidence about observable human behaviour.

Its evidence may be used to establish an isolated proposition, to test certain theoretical analyses against observable behaviour, or to gain insight into certain behaviours. Such evidence may itself generate hypotheses, concepts, models and theories.

▶ David Deacon, Michael Pickering, Peter Golding and Graham Murdock, *Researching Communications: A Practical Guide to Methods in Media and Cultural Analysis* (Hodder Education, 2007).

Empowerment Giving to people, individually, as GROUPS or as communities or nations, power over their lives, of choice and decision. The role of the media in advocating, assisting, blocking or subverting empowerment is the subject of keen debate as the media increasingly operate on a global scale. Empowerment also refers to the ways in which AUDIENCE responds to media messages; the degree to which it is capable of resistive reading (see DOMINANT, SUBORDINATE, RADICAL). Those who are 'empowered' are firstly capable of interpreting for themselves the agendas and meanings of media communication. They are able to 'make use' of these agendas and meanings to further individual or communal needs, ultimately with a political purpose: the power is to change things.

There is currently much debate on the extent to which the INTERNET is a force for empowerment, offering opportunities for people to use Net platforms to comment, exchange views and campaign on agendas not set by authority or by mass media. See BLOGOSPHERE; DEMOTIC TURN; FACEBOOK; JOURNALISM: CITIZEN JOURNALISM; MOBILIZATION; MYSPACE; TWITTER; WEB 2.0; WIKILEAKS; YOUTUBE.

Encode We communicate by means of a variety of visual and aural signals which are assembled according to certain rules or codes. If Person A wishes to convey to Person B a MESSAGE that Person B is likely to understand, then that MESSAGE has to be encoded with Person B's ability to DECODE the message-carrying signals well in mind. The MEANING of a message is something the receiver assigns in the act of decoding, which is itself part of an interaction with the encoder.

A glance at the ANDERSCH, STAATS AND BOSTROM'S MODEL OF COMMUNICATION, 1969 helps here. This emphasizes the stages through which the act of encoding passes. There is a stimulus to a message, which is structured – put together – and evaluated for its possible effect on the receiver before it is transmitted. The same process occurs on the part of the receiver: the message is registered; it is reconstructed according to the decoder's perception of the message and of the encoder who has delivered the message; the response is then evaluated prior to transmission.

This is only the beginning of a continuing circle of sending and receiving, encoding and decoding. Contributory to the perceptions of encoder and decoder in the process of communication are such factors as previous experience, the current and future context of the interaction, and the feelings, opinions, assumptions and values of the encoder and decoder. The terms *encipher* and *decipher* are sometimes used instead of encode and decode. See DEEP STRUCTURE; ELABORATED AND RESTRICTED CODES.

Encrypt To 'scramble' signals – for satellite TV, for example, so that non-subscribers cannot tune into programmes.

Enculturation The process by which individuals acquire the VALUES, language, skills, ways of thinking and behavioural patterns of a particular CULTURE that enable them to function effectively within it. See ACCULTURATION, DECULTURATION; INTERCULTURAL COMMUNICATION; M-TIME, P-TIME; SAPIR-WHORF LINGUISTIC RELATIVITY HYPOTHESIS.

Enigma code See CODES OF NARRATIVE.

Entropy See REDUNDANCY.

Ephemera In communications terms, publications such as cigarette cards, PICTURE POSTCARDS, and POSTERS produced for the moment, conveying information for immediate use. Ironically such ephemera are now collectors' items, illuminating records of our past. See CIGARETTE CARDS: CULTURAL INDICATORS.

EPISTLE Developed from a well-used technique called PEST analysis, EPISTLE is a technique for analysing the context in which a corporation operates. In addition to analysing the political, economic, social and technological aspects of the context, attention should be given to the following: the environment and green issues that might arise from a corporation's operations;

the implications of a corporation's activities for access to and distribution of information; and the nature of the legal environment and its potential impact on the corporation's behaviour.

Establishing shot Opening shot or sequence showing the location of a film scene or a juxtaposition of characters who will be involved in the subsequent NARRATIVE.

Establishment The ELITE in society, comprising people who because of wealth, birth or position in government are able to exercise considerable power and influence. The term is often associated with a study of power in Britain in the 1960s conducted by Anthony Sampson and entitled *Anatomy of Britain* (1962). Sampson pursued this study until the early 2000s and published a number of updated versions of his original analyses.

The relationship between members of the establishment and elected politicians has been the focus of some debate. The latest and last version of Sampson's study is to be found in *Who Runs This Place?: The Anatomy of Britain in the 21st Century* (John Murray, 2005). Here he argues that since his series of studies began, power has shifted significantly in favour of the Prime Minister.

Certainly those who own and manage the various media organizations within society could be considered to figure among such an establishment. They may not necessarily be in or act in agreement, however, with those in powerful positions in other institutions of society, for example the City, large corporations, the Civil Service, the Law Courts, the Police, the Intelligence services, the Armed Forces, the Monarchy, and the Universities. However, the nature of the relationship between the mass media and other key institutions is the subject of much research. See HEGEMONY; POWER ELITE.

▶ Tom Lodge, *Ship that Rocked the World: How Radio Caroline Defied the Establishment, Launched the British Invasion and Made the Planet Safe for Rock & Roll* (Bartleby Press, 2010); Garrick Alder, *Diana: Unfinished Business – The Princess of Wales Versus the British Establishment* (Picnic Publishing Ltd, 2011).

Ethnic Term used in the social sciences to refer to a community of people possessing its own CULTURE. The characteristics that identify an ethnic group may include a common language, common customs, faith and beliefs, and a cultural tradition. A society may contain several ethnic groups, some of whom, but not all, may also be racial groups. The UK contains many ethnic groups: for example, Caribbean, Chinese,

Indian, English and Welsh. In a number of ways ethnic background and identity may affect the manner in which an individual communicates. Those from the Caribbean-British community may, for instance, use British Black English based on Jamaican Creole as a linguistic marker of ethnic identity.

Current areas of research within the media and communication field include the media's role in the representation and construction of ethnic identities, ethnicity and language, ethnic differences in the use of non-verbal communication, and the influence of ethnic background on social interaction. See ETHNOCENTRISM; HYBRIDIZATION; INTERCULTURAL COMMUNICATION; ORIENTALISM; OTHER; PREJUDICE. See also *TOPIC GUIDE* under MEDIA ISSUES AND DEBATES.

Ethnocentrism The use of one's own CULTURE, its norms and VALUES, as a yardstick by which to measure, to judge, the attributes and activities of other cultures. Such judgement bears the implicit or explicit assumption that one's own culture is superior. Harry C. Triandis in *Individualism and Collectivism* (Westview Press, 1994) is one of several researchers to argue that there is a tendency for all humans to be ethnocentric. If this is the case, then such a tendency could be expected to have considerable impact upon the way in which messages about other cultures are interpreted and the way in which other cultures are discussed in any one culture.

Stella Ting-Toomey in *Communicating Across Cultures* (Guildford Press, 1999), with reference to work of several research studies, proposes a continuum of communicative behaviour that ranges from ethnocentrism to ethnorelativism. At the far ethnocentric end is communicative behaviour that often disparages those from other cultures – the use of ETHNOPHAULISMS, for example names, nicknames and sayings used to belittle others, is found here; whilst at the far ethnorelativistic end is communicative behaviour that is supportive, inclusive and provides encouragement to those from other cultures.

Ethnocentrism is seen by many commentators on media performance to influence the coverage of NEWS. We see, and thus report, the world through the lens of our ethnocentric perception, often falling into the trap of envisioning that world in terms of *us* and *them* (see WEDOM, THEYDOM). It follows that OBJECTIVITY is often at the mercy of how we see the world rather than how it actually is. See AGENDA-SETTING; EVENT: AMERICANIZING OF; MEDIA IMPERIALISM; NEWS VALUES; OTHER; PREJUDICE; STEREOTYPE.

Ethnographic approach to audience research Ethnography has its roots in the research traditions of anthropology and urban sociology. David Deacon, Michael Pickering, Peter Golding and Graham Murdock in *Researching Communications: A Practical Guide to Methods in Media and Cultural Analysis* (Hodder Education, 2007) comment that ethnographic research is part of a tradition that seeks to explore 'the ways that people make sense of their social worlds and how they express these understandings through language, sound, imagery, personal style and social rituals'.

An important body of cultural research into the relationship and interaction between TV texts and audience has been described as *ethnographic*, that is describing a culture, emphasizing the native point of view. Ethnographic studies have, for example, revealed the fact that people respond to TV programmes much less along lines of social CLASS and in a much more varied way than some commentators have believed.

Ethnophaulisms See ETHNOCENTRISM.

Ethnorelativism See ETHNOCENTRISM.

Ethos In communication terms, the ethos of a communicator determines the image one has of him/her at any given time – either one person or a GROUP. In their paper 'A summary of experimental research in ethos', *Speech Monographs*, 30 (1963), Kenneth Anderson and Theodore Clevenger Jr refer to research findings that point to two general categories of ethos: *extrinsic* and *intrinsic*. The first is the image, say, of a speaker as it exists prior to a given speech; the second is the image derived from elements during the presentation of a speech, consciously or unconsciously provided by the speaker. The final impression is a mixture of extrinsic and intrinsic factors.

The prestige of a speaker, his/her appearance, likeableness, credibility, social CLASS, voice, etc. contribute to his/her ethos. Anderson and Clevenger assert that evidence from research proves 'that the ethos of the source is related in some way to the impact of the message' and that this applies 'not only to political, social, religious and economic issues but also to matters of aesthetic judgment and personal taste'.

Euphemism In polite circles, 'belly' is not referred to, but 'stomach' is acceptable. That is a euphemism, the rendering of blunt, harsh or unpleasant terms in mild, inoffensive or quaint LANGUAGE. Thus 'to die' may be rendered euphemistically as 'to pass away'; a 'bookie' may prefer to seek more status by calling him/herself a 'turf accountant'. In advertising, 'budget items' are preferred to 'cheap goods'. In business, people are not 'sacked' but 'the labour force is slimmed' or 'downsized'.

Some euphemism is justifiable in INTER-PERSONAL COMMUNICATION, for example at times of grief and tragedy; some is insulting to language and to human intelligence and dignity, such as the terminology of armed conflict where 'demographic targeting' means the destruction of cities in situations of war, 'support structure' is civilians, 'collateral damage' is dead civilians and an 'intelligence producing facility' is a torture chamber.

In their chapter 'Doublespeak' in *Weapons of Mass Deception: The Uses of Propaganda in Bush's War on Iraq* (Tarcher/Penguin; Constable and Robinson, 2003), Sheldon Rampton and John Stauber cite 'shaping the security environment' as polite language for controlling people at gunpoint, while 'critical regions' is doublespeak for 'countries we want to control'.

Euronet A consortium of national computer interests in a number of European countries, working towards the creation of a mutually compatible interconnection of European databases. Euronet is designed for reasons as much political as economical, as a method of ensuring that in the long term the economic control of Europe remains in European hands, and thus, inextricably, the control of information.

European Community and media: 'Television without frontiers' Title of a Council of Europe directive, October 1989, the first attempt by the European Community to regulate and institutionalize BROADCASTING between member states; revised in 1997. The directive requires EC members to guarantee unrestricted reception for audiences across Europe and to avoid any strategies likely to limit retransmission in their territory of any EC broadcasts that meet Community conditions. The directive lays down a policy of minimum regulation, granting equal rights to commercial operators and public service broadcasters while at the same time requiring no legal obligations to enhance public discourse.

Facing the TWF initiative in 2005 was the monumental task of legislating for the vast increase in INTERNET and mobile phone traffic. Pressure for further DEREGULATION came from major corporations such as Time Warner, News International, Bertelsmann and Microsoft, lobbying under the umbrella of the International Communications Round Table (ICRT). See FAIRNESS DOCTRINE (USA); PRIVATIZATION.

Europe: cross-border TV channels Since the 1980s the number of cross-border TV channels has risen to more than a hundred, some eighty of these holding a licence from the UK Independent Television Commission (ITC, replaced by OFCOM in 2003), whose licences are cheap and easy to obtain, the prime criterion being that such stations are based in the UK.

The expansion of cross-border transmission was made possible, and encouraged by, three key factors: (1) DEREGULATION, which occurred through Europe (and elsewhere) during the 1980s and 1990s; (2) the European Community's Television Without Frontiers directive (see above), Article 2 of which prevents member states barring broadcasting emanating from other member states; and (3) the possibilities brought about by SATELLITE TRANSMISSION. See LOCALIZATION.

Event The occurrence which gives rise to media coverage will have fulfilled one or more or an amalgam of NEWS VALUES. In the analysis of media, different forms of event can be identified. Primarily there is the *key event* triggering media and subsequently public attention. Such an event may, as in terrorist attacks in one country or city, trigger a worldwide sense of crisis.

In 'The impact of key events on the presentation of reality' in the *European Journal of Communication*, September 1995, Hans Mathias Kepplinger and Johanna Habermeier refer to events that are *key*, *similar* and *thematically related*. These can be seen as *genuine* (independent of the media), *mediated* (influenced by media) and/or *staged* (for the media).

Media coverage of events, especially if these give ground for concern about causes and consequences, stimulates the 'activities of pressure groups who see an opportunity of gaining media attention, since their concerns fit in with the established topic. The consequence is an increased number of mediated and staged events'.

Equally, such coverage tends to exert 'pressure upon decision-makers in politics, business, administration, etc.' The authors give the example of how safety-rules for petrol tankers may be changed as a result of media conjecture about possible, rather than actual, accidents. Coverage of key events will, say Kepplinger and Habermeier, enhance the coverage of similar or related events, and add interest and urgency to events thematically linked.

Of course the nature of coverage will vary between media, for example between daily and weekly newspapers or between broadsheets and tabloids. The authors note a tendency in the reporting of key events to give the impression of an *accumulation* of such events (hence the sense of crisis), whereas what is actually happening is an accumulation of another kind: similar stories, being gathered together from the past as well as the present, are being reinvigorated and intensified as they compound information about the new key event.

Key events thus trigger apparent waves of such events when in reality only one has occurred: 'Here one has to take into account that the news coverage creates a false impression that events accumulate and problems become more urgent.' See next entry.

Event: Americanizing of Practice, in the US, of reporting world events in relation to American interest or interests. As Susan D. Moeller points out in *Compassion Fatigue: How the Media Sell Disease, Famine, War and Death* (Routledge, 1999), 'the American filter, the notion of relevance to the United States, is very important.' Speaking of the American public, Moeller says, 'Since our knowledge about the lands outside our borders is minimal, even the abbreviated version of events which makes it into news has to be translated for us.' (See ETHNOCENTRISM.)

In her conclusion to her analysis of COMPASSION FATIGUE and how the media can strive to avoid creating or reinforcing it, Moeller believes that the Americanizing of events '(once called the "Coca-Colonization" of events) can be a positive force to attract the public's attention to a far-off event, but it should not be the defining characterization of that event', for 'once in play, the Americanization can become a crutch, simplifying a crisis beyond recognition, and certainly beyond understanding'.

The author concedes that 'Americans are already too self-involved' and she blames the media's 'entrenched news net and news priorities' as the cause 'of their neglect of certain events or countries'. See HISTORICAL ALLUSION.

Excorporation The process by which those who are not members of the dominant group(s) within society, for example members of YOUTH CULTURES and SUB-CULTURES, utilize the material resources provided by the prevailing system to fashion cultural statements that communicate their difference from or opposition to the dominant culture. See BRICOLAGE; COUNTER-CULTURE; STYLE.

Exnomination Roland Barthes uses this term in *Mythologies* (Paladin, 1973) to describe the assumption on the part of the communicator, usually the mass media, that certain VALUES are so basic and so widely shared, indeed so natural,

that they are beyond question and need not be referred to or justified. Exnomination is integral to the working of IDEOLOGY, representing the dominant code of a society. See COMMON SENSE; HEGEMONY; MYTH.

Exotica Interest in, and commodification of, ethnic differences; most strikingly demonstrated in fashion.

Expectation, horizons of Describes the 'readiness factor' of AUDIENCE in terms of its expectations concerning a communicative TEXT: is the audience well-primed for what is to come, or likely to be resistant out of unawareness, ignorance, prejudice; and is the audience likely to conform to the PREFERRED READING or *aberrantly decode* the text? (See DECODE.) The German literary critic Hans Robert Jans uses the phrase in *Towards an Aesthetic of Reception* (University of Minneapolis Press, 1982), referring to each reader of a text as approaching it with horizons of expectations shaped by previous literary, cultural and social experience. A text is interpreted on a basis of how it accords with or challenges expectations. Such expectations need to be seen in relation to, and generally arising from and interactive with, collective representations.

Expectations People come to have a collection of ideas about what is expected of them in terms of their behaviour in certain social situations and, in turn, of what they should expect concerning the behaviour of others and of their treatment in society generally. Research into human PERCEPTION has highlighted the important influence expectations have on an individual's perception of new information.

Expectations are formed from personal experience and by information received from various other sources. Information received from these other sources may modify previous expectations, or play a particularly crucial role in shaping expectations about persons or social situations of which the individual has no direct experience. An item of information will be more readily accepted if it is compatible with existing ideas and expectations; if it is not, then DISSONANCE may occur and the information may be rejected or ignored.

The media are an important source of information about many social and political events of which the individual has little or no first-hand experience. Several researchers have therefore sought to investigate the role played by the media in shaping an audience's expectations about certain persons, social GROUPS or social situations – those related to social unrest, for example – of which the audience has little or no direct experience against which to test the validity of the media's presentation.

The matter of concern here is that in such cases, individuals are more than usually vulnerable to PROPAGANDA. Also of interest is the role of the media in creating STEREOTYPES by engendering a set of expectations and beliefs about particular individuals, social groups or social situations.

Experimental group A research term for the group within an experiment to whom the experimental treatment is applied (for example, the group may be asked to conform to a particularly rigorous procedure of communication whilst performing a set task). The results from this group are then compared to those from a comparable *control group* which was not subjected to the experimental treatment. The control group provides the base-line against which the effectiveness of the treatment can be judged. Changes that take place in the behaviour of the experimental group but not the control group are likely to be seen as resulting from the treatment. See *TOPIC GUIDE* under RESEARCH METHODS.

Extracted information Youichi Ito, then Professor of Political and International Research at the University of Keio, Tokyo, in 'Climate of opinion, *kuuki*, and democracy' in William Gudykunst, ed., *Communications Yearbook*, No. 26 (Lawrence Erlbaum, 2002) used this term to describe that which the public draws from sources other than the mass media, for example from personal experience and observation, and talking to others.

The more people talk to each other, argues Ito, the less dependent they are on the mass media. Conversely, the less they talk among themselves, the more media agendas dominate the public's way of thinking and perceiving. 'If people depend heavily upon mass media for information,' writes Ito, 'and if personal influence in political communication is weak, then the political influence of mass media may be overwhelming.' See KUUKI.

Extrapersonal communication That which takes place without human involvement: machine-to-machine communication, for example; a major growth industry of communications with the coming of computers, increased automation and the development of robotics.

Eye contact and gaze Perhaps the most subtle and significant feature of non-verbal communication (see COMMUNICATION, NON-VERBAL). 'So complex is mutual eye contact,' notes C. David Mortensen in *Communication: The Study*

of Human Interaction (McGraw-Hill, 1972) 'that a whole vocabulary is necessary to distinguish among the ways people look at each other.' We stare, glower, peep, pierce, glance, watch, gaze and scan; and we do it directly or indirectly, provocatively or furtively, confidently or nervously. Eye contact and gaze play an important role in the regulation of social interaction.

Gaining eye contact is usually the first step in starting a social encounter, just as decreasing eye contact is typically one of the signs that an encounter is ending – although increased eye contact is often given as the encounter is actually concluded. During a conversation the listener usually indicates attention by frequent eye contact with the speaker. The speaker, however, looks less often at the listener but does use eye contact to check for feedback. Lack of eye contact on the part of the listener will often be read as a sign of lack of interest in what the speaker is saying. Listeners can therefore use lack of eye contact to make a speaker feel uncomfortable and to close a conversation down.

The smooth handing-over between speaker and listener within a conversation also involves the appropriate use of eye contact, according to Judy Gahagan in *Social Interaction and its Mangement* (Methuen, 1984). Michael Argyle notes in *Bodily Communication* (Methuen, 1988) that participants in a conversation tend to use more eye contact if placed further apart than if closer together. The topic of a conversation can also influence the use of eye contact: typically less eye contact is used if the topic is difficult. People also display less eye contact if they are sad or embarrassed. Those attempting to persuade may be more successful if they use increased eye contact.

Argyle argues that the nature of relationships can also be revealed in the use of eye contact. Prolonged looking is typically a sign of a close or intimate relationship but it can also be a sign of aggression and used to threaten or intimidate – for this reason we may be uncomfortable with prolonged gazes from those with whom we are not intimate. Factors of psychological dominance and submission are reflected in the extent and nature of eye contact. A single glance may be all that is required for an individual to assert him/herself over others, to take initiative or leadership, whereas gaze aversion can be a sign of submission.

Cross-cultural differences exist as regards the degree of eye contact or gaze regarded as normal in social encounters. Roger E. Axel in *Gestures: The Do's and Taboos of Body Language Around*

E

the World (John Wiley & Sons Inc., 1998) notes, for example, that whilst direct eye contact is expected in North America, Britain, Eastern Europe and in Jewish cultures, less direct eye contact is expected by West Indians, Asians and African Americans. See CIVIL INATTENTION; INDICATORS; PROXEMICS; REGULATORS. See also *TOPIC GUIDE* under INTERPERSONAL COMMUNICATION.

▸ Desmond Morris, *People Watching* (Vintage, 2002); Allan and Barbara Pease, *The Definitive Book of Body Language* (Orion, 2004).

F

Facebook One of the outstandingly successful social NETWORKS, with millions of subscribers, exponentially growing, its key feature being the gathering of 'Friends', facilitating not only scores if not thousands of contacts, but encouraging users to launch into their contacts' contacts and their contacts' contacts' contacts in an eternal chimera of apparently opening doors. As with most social exchange on the INTERNET, the dominant characteristic of exchanges is at the level of 'I'm not looking forward to work on Monday' kind of trivia; comments then prompting a response of followers, such as 'Nor am I'. One can 'like' what's being uploaded, and add a comment such as 'Tuesdays are worse for me'.

On a more serious note, Facebook users have influence. There are cases when users have moved beyond the homespun and the domestically bizarre to unite in some cause, to pressurize decision-makers. Campaigns are possible, but they remain leaderless and the tide of protest is rarely long-lived: individuals return to the specifics of everyday life. For some, Facebook may be seen as a dating agency; for others, self-promotion; for others an opportunity to explore online Net vistas by being something different from their real selves. What Facebook will rarely if ever do is match real friendship.

Launched in 2004, the creation of Mark Zuckerberg and fellow Harvard computer studies students Chris Hughes, Dustin Moskowitz and Eduardo Saverin, Facebook became by 2009 the most used social network in the Western world. From 2006 it was open to anyone over the age of thirteen with an e-mail address. It has encountered widespread blocking in a number of countries and, as with most of the premier online services, challenges concerning copyright as well as raising doubts concerning issues of privacy. It has been said that by its very nature it is prone to cyberstalking.

Facebook insists (unlike MYSPACE) on users operating as their true identities. Its services have diversified innovatively, with News Feed being introduced in 2006, followed by Photos, allowing unlimited photo-posting, Facebook Notes, Gifts, Marketplace and Facebook Messages. Over 150 million users access Facebook through mobile-phone devices in sixty or more countries.

Facebook plays on the 'flocking' nature of human beings and in this it is ideologically suited to derive SYNERGY from consumerism. Indeed the financial success of Facebook for its Silicon Valley masters is a triumph for consumerist ethics and on a global scale, a fact not overlooked by Digital Sky Technologies which owns 10 per cent of the company.

Despite having a hard ride in Ben Mezrich's book *Accidental Billionaires: The Founding of Facebook, A Tale of Sex, Money and Betrayal* (Doubleday, 2009), and something of a drubbing in the film based on the book, *The Social Network* (2010), directed by David Fincher, Mark Zuckerberg was deemed worthy of celebration as *Time* magazine's Person of the Year 2010. The ruthless competitiveness illustrated in book and film was on show in May 2011 when Facebook was revealed to have employed a PR firm to disseminate 'bad news' stories in the US press about Facebook's rival GOOGLE, with the specific intention, commentators believed, to undermine Google's social networking tool, Social Circle.

Facework In communicative encounters we often need to have some concern for the image or reputation of ourselves as well as that of others; facework strategies are commonly employed to achieve the desired outcome. There are however cultural differences in the manner in which facework is employed. Stella Ting-Toomey in *Communicating Across Cultures* (Guidford Press, 1999) argued that in Western cultures the emphasis typically tends to be on protecting one's own 'face', whereas in Asian cultures the emphasis is on protecting the face of others, principally by showing respect and consideration when in conversation. As several researchers have cautioned, ASSERTIVENESS is not a universally admired aspect of an individual's communicative style. See IMPRESSION MANAGEMENT.

Facial expression The face's main role in providing non-verbal communication is in the expression of emotions. Michael Argyle in *Bodily Communication* (Methuen, 1988) argues that the main facial expressions are those used to display happiness, surprise, fear, sadness, anger, disgust, contempt and interest. Facial expressions play a key role in providing FEEDBACK during conversations. However, Argyle comments that our awareness of what our facial expressions may reveal often leads us to control them, and that we can be quite successful in doing so. Thus there may be difficulties in accurately judging emotional reactions from facial expressions alone. Despite attempts to conceal our reactions, *leakage* may occur, that is other non-verbal behaviour, often in the lower half of the body, may reveal our true reactions. For example, whilst the face might be passive, a tapping foot might indicate that we are agitated by a message.

A number of studies suggest that the facial expressions used to convey these emotions are to a large extent universal, thus they are found across all human cultures. The cultural rules concerning the display of facial expressions may, however, vary. For example, Larry Samovar and Richard Porter in *Communication Between Cultures* (Wadsworth/Thomson Learning, 2004) note that in Korean culture, too much smiling can be interpreted as a sign of shallowness. See COMMUNICATION, NON-VERBAL.

▸ Stella Ting-Toomey, *Communicating Across Cultures* (Guildford Press, 1999); Allan and Barbara Pease, *The Definitive Book of Body Language* (Orion, 2004).

Facsimile Exact copy; today, facsimile (or fax) is the transmission of a printed or handwritten page or image by electronic means. As early as 1842 Scotsman Alexander Bain proposed the first facsimile system, though it was not until the 1920s that the process was generally employed for the transmission of news, photographs, weather maps and maps for military purposes.

Newspaper editions can be transmitted across continents for simultaneous publication; the pictures of wanted criminals can be relayed instantly to practically every police force in the world, while the facsimile machine can combine with the domestic TV receiver to provide a permanent record of news and other items appearing on the screen.

Faction See DOCUMENTARY.

Fade in Gradual emergence of a scene from blackness to clear, full definition. The term is used in RADIO as well as film and TV.

Fairness Doctrine (USA) A BROADCAST-ING regulation in the US until 1987 when the Federal Communications Commission (FCC), responsible for its observation, abolished it. The doctrine required broadcasters to devote time to controversial issues and to air varied opposed viewpoints. In the 1980s expansion in RADIO and TELEVISION channels, and a dominant ideology

which prized the private above the public, led to pressures to *deregulate* broadcasting. The FCC was persuaded that the broader and more diverse market-place would ensure plurality of opinion without regulation.

In *Democracy Without Citizens: Media and the Decay of American Politics* (Oxford University Press, 1989), Robert M. Entman voiced deep scepticism about the idea of leaving controversial matters in the hands of market forces. He writes of the 'dangers of basing public policy on the assumption that the economic market inevitably nourishes journalism's contribution to democratic citizenship'; indeed, 'decisions rooted in this premise, as the FCC's elimination of the Fairness Doctrine, might actually retard progress towards a freer press and citizenship'. See DEREGULATION; PRIVATIZATION.

Fatwa On St Valentine's Day 1989, Iran's Ayatollah Khomeini issued a 'fatwa', or edict, against the British novelist Salman Rushdie for his novel *Satanic Verses* (1988). The book was deemed blasphemous, guilty of containing scenes so insulting to the Islamic faith that every true Moslem had a bounden duty to kill the author. To carry out the fatwa would guarantee a place in heaven. Rushdie went into hiding, with police protection. The fatwa applied to all those involved in the publication of the novel. Bookshops were fire-bombed. The Japanese translator of the novel was attacked, beaten up and stabbed to death and an Italian translator stabbed. The Iranian government distanced itself from the fatwa death sentence in 1998, without actually withdrawing it officially. See CENSORSHIP.

Fax See FACSIMILE.

Federal Communications Commission (FCC) Set up by the US federal government in 1934; a body empowered to regulate interstate and foreign communications such as radio and TV. Its effectiveness in the role of protector of public sector broadcasting against the ambitions and predatory intentions of the private sector in the US has long been questioned. In 'An American view of UK terrestrial TV', published in *Free Press*, journal of the Campaign for Press & Broadcasting Freedom (CPBF), July-August 2002 edition, American documentary-maker and journalist Willams Rossa Cole states that US government 'regulation of content for the public interest has diminished consistently over the last decades'. He is of the view that the FCC 'is so passive in the realm of television content and ownership that it might as well shut its doors to save the taxpayer some money'.

He quotes the-then FCC chairman, Michael

Powell – 'thoroughly pro-deregulation and pro-market' – as stating on his first day in office that he 'had waited for a visit from the angel of public interest ... but she did not come'. See DEREGULATION; REGULATORY FAVOURS.

Feedback According to *Chambers Twentieth Century Dictionary* (ed. A.M. Macdonald, 1972), feedback is the 'return of part of the output of a system to the input as a means towards improved quality or self-correction of error'; in *A Dictionary of New English, 1963–1972* (eds, C.L. Barnhart, S. Steinmetz and R.K. Barnhart, Longman, 1973), feedback is 'a reciprocal effect of one person or thing upon another; a reaction or response that modifies, corrects, etc., the behaviour of that which produced the reaction or response'. Without feedback – the signal that is stimulated by an act of communication, biological, mechanical, human or animal – meaningful contact halts and cannot make progress.

Feedback is the regenerative circuit, or loop, of communication. A student who submits his/her essay to the teacher expects feedback in terms of comments and a mark. Unless this feedback occurs, the student lacks guidance for the future; more, he/she is likely to be demotivated and draw back from further communicative interaction. When the student's essay is returned it may contain *positive* or *negative* feedback: harsh comments, without encouragement, and a low mark might well be more demotivating than not receiving any feedback at all. Praise and supportive criticism on the other hand are likely to produce a positive response – of greater effort and motivation.

Central to the purpose of feedback is *control*; that is, feedback enables the communicator to adjust his/her message, or response, to that of the sender, and to the context in which the communicative activity takes place. At the interpersonal level feedback is transmitted by voice, expression, GESTURE, sight, hearing, TOUCH, smell, etc. The greater the distance between communicators, the fewer the 'senses' being employed to 'read' and return feedback, the more difficult it is to arrange and control, and the more difficult it is to assess its nature and meaning. See AUDIENCE MEASUREMENT; CYBERNETICS. See also *TOPIC GUIDE* under COMMUNICATION THEORY.

Feminism Though embracing different perspectives and schools of thought, fundamentally feminism is concerned with the advancement and achievement of equal social and political rights for women, and the fight against SEXISM. Feminism challenges many traditional, patri-

archal, assumptions about the behavioural difference expected of men and women and the assignment of social roles and STATUS that rests on them; and what it perceives as a widespread devaluing of women's attributes, experiences and perspectives.

One focus of current research is the exploration of the role played by the media both in fostering and reinforcing sexism and more generally notions of femininity and masculinity, and media coverage of women's rights issues and the feminist movement and its ideas. Another important research interest is the degree to which language and its use reflect and perpetuate sexism and assumptions about differences between masculine and feminine behaviour. See GENDER; PERFORMATIVITY. See also *TOPIC GUIDE* under GENDER MATTERS.

▶ Liesbet van Zoonen, 'Feminist perspectives' in James Curran and Michael Gurevitch, eds, *Mass Media and Society* (Arnold, 1996); Caroline Ramazanoglu and Janet Holland, eds, *Feminist Methodology: Challenges and Choices* (Sage, 2002); Jennifer Coates, *Women, Men and Language* (Pearson Education, 2004); Mary Crawford and Rhoda Ungar, *Women and Gender: A Feminist Psychology* (McGraw-Hill, 2004); Lana F. Rakow and Laura A. Wackwitz, eds, *Feminist Communication Theory* (Sage, 2004); Janet Holmes and Miriam Meyerhoff, *The Handbook of Language and Gender* (Blackwell, 2006); Charlotte Brunsdon and Lynn Spigel, eds, *Feminist Television Criticism: A Reader* (Open University Press/McGraw-Hill Education, 2008); Sue Thornton, 'Media and feminism' in James Curran, ed., *Mass Media and Society* (Bloomsbury, 2010).

Fibre-optic technology One of the wonder-products of the Information Age, fibre-optic cable is fine-spun glass, a mixture of silicon and oxygen, through which digital codes are passed in pulsing light. Its impact on telephone technology has been immense, and its potential for this, cable television, and many other purposes turns so rapidly into achievement and new possibilities that even the experts find it difficult to plan for fibre's accelerating capacity.

Fibre-optic cable can carry ten times further than coaxial without requiring a booster. Over 7,500 different channels can operate along a single pair of optical fibres, though the potential number lies in millions. Because fibre-optic transmission is free from electrical interference, cable can be cheaply laid along existing railway lines; it can follow existing electricity pylons, enclosed in the earth wire. Fibre-optic cable has crossed the English Channel and the Atlantic (1989).

All forms of cable are limited in terms of the span of the networks by the number of cable terminals. In contrast, satellite transmission has a global reception capacity: the extension of one is the opportunity of the other – the harnessing of cable and satellite within the same transmission systems. See TOPIC GUIDE under MEDIA: TECHNOLOGIES.

Fiction values These work with and as NEWS VALUES. Milly Buonanno in an article 'News-values and fiction-values: news as serial device and criteria of "fictionworthiness" in Italian fiction', published in the *European Journal of Communication*, June 1993, argues that the criteria for modern TV and film fiction parallel news values. She cites, for example, the high social STATUS of the protagonists (the ELITE value of news) and the emphasis on *proximity*, that which is 'happening in our own backyards' (an *ethnocentric* news value).

Film See ANARCHIST CINEMA; ANIMATION; BRITISH BOARD OF FILM CENSORS; BRITISH FILM INSTITUTE (BFI); BRITISH FILM PRODUCTION FUND; CATALYST EFFECT; CERTIFICATION OF FILMS; CINEMATOGRAPHY, ORIGINS; CINÉMA VÉRITÉ; DIRECT CINEMA; DOCUMENTARY; DOUBLE EXPOSURE; EMOTIONAL DYNAMIZATION; FILM NOIR; FLASHBACK; FLY ON THE WALL; HAYS OFFICE; HIGH-SPEED PHOTOGRAPHY; HOLLYWOOD; IMAX; KINETOSCOPE; KULESHOV EFFECT; MARCH OF TIME; McGUFFIN; MONTAGE; MULTIPLE IMAGE; MUSICAL: FILM MUSICAL; NATIONAL FILM ARCHIVE; NEWSREEL; NEW WAVE; OMNIMAX; PERSISTENCE OF VISION; RUSHES; SHOT; SLOW MOTION; SOVIET MANIFESTO, 1928; SPECIAL EFFECTS; SYNCHRONOUS SOUND; VAMP; VIDEO; WESTERN; WIPE; ZOOM LENS; ZOOPRAXOGRAPHY.

Film censorship See CENSORSHIP; CERTIFICATION OF FILMS.

Film noir Term used by French film critics, notably Nino Frank, to describe a particular kind of dark, suspenseful thriller. A classic of the GENRE is French director Marcel Carné's *Le Jour Se Lève* (1939) – 'Day Arises', starring Jean Gabin. We see the last doomed hours of a man wanted by the police for murder. He has barred himself in his attic bedroom in an apartment block. He is totally surrounded. He has no chance; but then, Carné makes clear, the man never did have a chance. At dawn he shoots himself and, as he lies dying, his alarm clock goes off, reminding him of his otherwise intolerable life as a worker.

Described as 'symbolism with a three o'clock in the morning mood', film noir gained substantial currency in the US, generally thriving between the early years of the Second World War and the late 1950s, and ranging from John Huston's *Maltese Falcon* (1941) to Orson Welles's *Touch of Evil* (1958). Hollywood film noir, says Michael Walker in the *Introduction to The Movie Book of Film Noir* (Studio Vista, 1992), edited by Ian Cameron, features 'heroes who are frequently victims of a hostile world'. Such movies are characterized by a 'distinctive and exciting visual style, an unusual narrative complexity' and 'a generally more critical and subversive view of American ideology than the norm'.

In the words of E. Ann Kaplan writing in *Women in Film Noir* (British Film Institute, 1980, edited by Kaplan), women are 'presented as desirable but dangerous to men'. They 'function as the obstacle to the male quest. The hero's success or not depends on the degree to which he can extricate himself from the woman's manipulations'. Billy Wilder's *Double Indemnity* (1941), with Fred MacMurray as the (willingly) manipulated male victim and Barbara Stanwick as the alluring manipulator, is a classic example of the genre.

▶ Foster Hirsch, *Film Noir: The Dark Side of the Screen* (Da Capo Press, paperback 1983 and later editions); James Chapman, ed., *The New Film History: Sources, Methods, Approaches* (Palgrave Macmillan, 2009).

First Amendment (US, 1791) The lynchpin of American freedom of speech and expression: 'Congress shall make no law respecting an establishment of religion, or prohibiting the free exercise thereof; or abridging the freedom of speech, or of the press; or the right of the people peaceably to assemble, and to petition the government for a redress of grievances.'

First impressions There is evidence that we tend to give too much attention to the initial information we may receive about an individual, and relatively less to later information that may be contradictory; that is, we are biased towards primacy effects (see PRIMACY, THE LAW OF). Evidence also suggests that negative first impressions in particular can be resistant to change.

First impressions can clearly count in situations where most of the information is received about a person in a fairly short, discrete period of time, as in an interview. In this instance there might be little opportunity for first impressions to be modified.

In some circumstances – as when a considerable time gap intervenes between sets of information received about an individual or when there is regular, close contact with that individual – first impressions can be modified. Here the later information received may have greater impact. This is known as the *recency effect*, because it is the more recent information that is the more influential. See TOPIC GUIDE under COMMUNICATION THEORY.

Five filters of the news process See CONSENT: MANUFACTURE OF.

Five myths of deregulation See DEREGULATION, FIVE MYTHS OF.

Flak Term used by Edward Herman and Noam Chomsky in *Manufacturing Consent: The Political Economy of the Media* (Pantheon, 1988; Vantage paperback, 1994), to describe a 'negative response to a media statement or programme, and this may resemble flak in its wartime sense: a blitz taking the form 'of letters, telegrams, phone calls, petitions, lawsuits, speeches and bills before Congress, and other modes of complaint, threat, and punitive action'.

The authors argue that 'if flak is produced on a large scale, or by individuals or groups with substantial resources, it can be both uncomfortable and costly to the media'. Used by the powerful such as the great corporations, flak is intended to inhibit media activity, or bring about the cessation of that activity. Flak can be aimed at media activity indirectly as well as directly 'by [in the case of corporations] complaining to their own constituencies (stockholders, employees) about the media, by generating institutional advertising that does the same, and by funding right-wing monitoring or think-tank operations designed to attack the media'. See CONSENT: MANUFACTURE OF.

Flashback A break in the chronology of a NARRATIVE in which events from the past are disclosed to the reader, listener or viewer, and which have a bearing on the present situation. Flashback was a device used very early in the history of the cinema: D.W. Griffith's epic *Intolerance* (1916) is made up of four flashbacks. Used with a narrator, the form achieved its greatest popularity in the cinema in the 1930s and 1940s. Orson Welles's *Citizen Kane* (1941) is made up entirely of a dazzling series of flashbacks; equally inventive is the flashback narrative of the Ealing comedy, Robert Hamer's *Kind Hearts and Coronets* (1949).

Flat earth news See CHURNALISM.

Fleet Street Until the 1980s, the home of most of Britain's major national newspapers; indeed the name had become the generic term for the nation's PRESS; a figure of speech (see METONYMY). The advent of new technology linked with the cost-cutting ambitions of newspaper owners, both of which led to bitter conflict with the print unions, caused an exodus from 'The Street' of all the major titles.

▶ Laura Melvern, *The End of the Street* (Methuen, 1986).

Flow See PROGRAMME FLOW.

Fly on the wall Popular title given to a GENRE of DOCUMENTARY film-making, for the cinema or TV, in which the camera remains concealed, or is handled so discreetly that the subjects forget they are being filmed. Richard Denton, producer of the BBC documentary series *Kingswood: A Comprehensive School* (1982) described the approach in 'Fly on the wall – designed to invade privacy', *Listener* (13 January, 1983), as attempting 'to remove the process of filming so far from the consciousness of the contributors that they will, in theory, forget its existence and so behave in a markedly more natural, truthful and realistic manner'.

Denton speaks of two distinct problems: 'The first concerns the question of accuracy and context ... The second, and probably more important, problem concerns privacy'. Outstanding examples of the fly-on-the-wall approach were the BBC's *Police* series (1982), the work of Roger Graef and Charles Stewart, and Channel 4's *Murder Squad* (1992). Of particular interest for fly-on-the-wall documentarists has been *family interaction*. First in the UK to win fame by exposing their lives to the eye of the camera were the Wilkenses of Reading, featured in the BBC series *The Family* (1974). In 1999 Granada Television screened the lives of a mixed-race family from Leeds, in *Family Life*. Later *observational documentaries* have meticulously and intrusively closed in on the lives and opinions of neo-Nazis (*100% White*, Channel 4, 2000), the 'realities' of giving birth in a hospital environment (*One Born Every Minute*, Channel 4, 2009) and SC4's documentation of the glories (and otherwise) of the Caernarvon Town FC (2010).

Sam Leith in a UK *Guardian* online article, 'Fly on the wall has become surveillance TV: Big Brother didn't die. Its many cameras are pointing at all of us' (21 November 2010) refers to 'rigged-up' documentaries, and compares current approaches to the genre, with the Panopticon conceived by nineteenth-century philosopher Jeremy Bentham.

This was a design for a prison (see PANOPTICON GAZE) in which every minute of an inmate's life was subject to constant scrutiny, the theory being that prisoners would modify their behaviour according to corrective expectations. However, in the case of fly-on-the-wall documentaries, there is the INTERVENING VARIABLE of the need for such films to be entertaining; in other words, misbehaviour (as in REALITY TV programmes) is more likely to capture audience attention than good behaviour; hence the distortion rather than replication of reality. See CINÉMA VÉRITÉ; DIRECT CINEMA; SURVEILLANCE SOCIETY.

Focus groups Focus groups are frequently employed in market research. Members of a group are brought together by a researcher to discuss aspects of a product, be it soap powder, a political party or a television programme. The group is often chosen to be a representative SAMPLE of all those who are thought to be the actual or potential consumers of the product. As a qualitative research method, use of focus groups allows for in-depth discussion and exploration of consumers' orientations towards and evaluations of a product. Focus groups are also widely used by governments and political parties as a gauge of public opinion on proposed or actual policies. See TOPIC GUIDE under RESEARCH METHODS.

Foe creation See WEDOM, THEYDOM.

Folk culture Term generally applied to the CULTURE of pre-industrial societies. Such societies have certain distinguishing features that are thought to affect the elements of their culture: work and leisure are undifferentiated; there is relatively little division of labour; the communities are small, and social action is normally collectivist as opposed to individualist. Thus folk songs, for example, are usually firmly rooted in the everyday experience and beliefs of both the AUDIENCE and the performer.

Folk devils Stanley Cohen in *Folk Devils and Moral Panics* (MacGibbon & Kee, 1972, 3rd edition 2002) argues that societies are subject to periods of moral panic in which certain groups are picked out as being a special threat to the VALUES and interests of society. The media and in particular the press play an important role in transmitting this sense of outrage to the general public.

Such groups or individuals are usually those transgressing the values of the dominant hierarchy. It is further argued by Cohen and others that the castigation of such groups, such folk devils, by the media is a mechanism by which adherence to dominant social norms is strengthened, along with support for the forces of law and order and an extension of their powers. See LOONY LEFTISM; MORAL PANICS AND THE MEDIA.

▶ Chas Critcher, ed., *Critical Readings: Moral Panics and the Media* (Open University Press/McGraw-Hill Education, 2006); Erich Goode and Nachman Ben-Yehuda in *Moral Panics: The Social Construction of Deviance* (Wiley-Blackwell, 2009).

Footage Length of film expressed in feet.

Footprint Term used to describe the area in which a signal from a communications satellite can be received. See SATELLITE TRANSMISSION.

Four stages in audience fragmentation See AUDIENCE: FRAGMENTATION OF.

Fourteen-Day Rule (UK) In the period after the Second World War (1939–45) the BBC entered into an agreement with government whereby it would not try to usurp the functions of the House of Commons as the supreme forum of the nation by BROADCASTING on issues due to be debated in Parliament. An embargo was placed upon all such issues until fourteen days after Parliament had debated them. It was a crippling intrusion upon the editorial rights of the corporation, and the BEVERIDGE COMMITTEE REPORT ON BROADCASTING (UK), 1950 called for the abandonment of the Rule. Nevertheless, successive governments held tenaciously to it. In 1956 the House of Commons set up a Select Committee to investigate the workings and effects of the Rule: it recommended a reduction to seven days. Pressure from broadcasters and the press continued unabated, and within a year the Rule was abandoned altogether (1957). See TOPIC GUIDES under MEDIA: FREEDOM, CENSORSHIP; MEDIA HISTORY.

Fourth Estate The eighteenth-century parliamentarian Edmund Burke (1729–97) is thought to have been the originator of this phrase describing the press and its role in society. According to Burke's definition, the other three 'Estates' were the Lords Spiritual (the church), the Lords Temporal (the judiciary) and the Commons. 'And yonder,' he is believed to have said in Parliament, 'sits the Fourth Estate, more important than them all.'

The implication is that the press, like the other estates, serves the State, as differentiable from government, and thus functions as a force for social, cultural and national cohesion. Underlying this argument is the assumption that while governments might be in error, the State is benign if not sacrosanct. A glance at states ancient and modern would suggest otherwise. The classifying of the press as the Fourth Estate points up the ambivalent role of the media in society: does it tell the truth, the whole truth and nothing but the truth; or, because the priorities of State seem to require it, manipulate, conceal or deny that truth? See ELITE; GUARD DOG METAPHOR; MEDIA CONTROL; POWER ELITE; WATCHDOGS. See TOPIC GUIDE under MEDIA HISTORY.

Fragmentation of audience See AUDIENCE: FRAGMENTATION OF.

F

Framing: interpersonal Conversations are often framed by METASIGNALS that let observers and participants know what kind of activity is going on so that they are better able to interpret the conversation. For example, is the conversation a serious argument or horseplay?

Such signals also allow people to recognize what Erving Goffman in *Frame Analysis* (Harper & Row, 1974) terms the *alignment*, that is the relative positions with regard to STATUS, intimacy and so on, being taken by the participants – themselves included. If A, for instance, explains something to B in a condescending manner, A is taking a superior alignment with regard to B.

In *You Just Don't Understand: Men and Women in Conversation* (Virago, 1992), Deborah Tannen argues that protective comments and gestures from men towards women 'reinforce the traditional alignment by which men protect women'. She goes on to argue that 'the act of protecting frames the protector as dominant and

the protected as subordinate'. However, arguably because men and women are fundamentally tuned to interpret some aspects of conversation differently, the difference in relative status signalled by such comments may be more apparent to men than women. Women may simply interpret them as indicating a desire to protect or be supportive rather than as indicative of women's traditionally subordinate status in society. See GENDER; GENDERLECTS.

★**Framing: media** The process by which the media place reality into frame; and the study of the process of framing is at the core of media analysis, hence the length of this entry. Framing constitutes a NARRATIVE device. What is *not* on the page of a newspaper is 'out of frame'; what does not appear within the frame of the TV is off the public agenda. For the NEWS, there is the world – and 20 minutes (or 24 hours) to put it in the frame. *Time*, then – the extent of it – is an important deciding factor. For a soap opera, time also poses problems of framing. There are

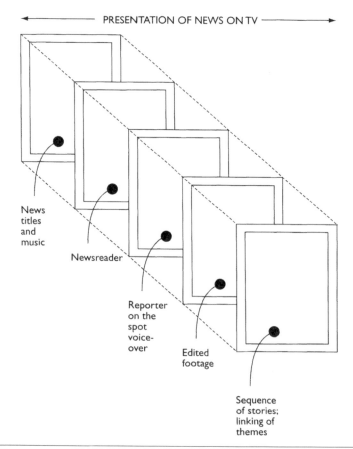

PRESENTATION OF NEWS ON TV

News titles and music

Newsreader

Reporter on the spot voice-over

Edited footage

Sequence of stories; linking of themes

Framing reality

30-minute slots to be filled, each to conclude with unfinished business, preferably dramatic and suspenseful, while not being so dramatically 'final' that the series cannot continue day by day, week by week. Presented with such a time-frame, soaps require many characters and many plots. To facilitate this requirement (and to capture and retain AUDIENCE attention) scriptwriters divide up the frame into quick-bite scenes – framing within frames.

What happens outside the creative frame – audience measurement, for example –influences the nature of the frame and what goes on inside it. Robert Entman in 'Framing: toward clarification of a fractured paradigm', in the *Journal of Communication*, 4 (1992), says that a crucial task of analysis is to show 'exactly how framing influences thinking' for 'the concept of framing consistently offers a way to describe the power of a communicating text'.

He argues, 'Analysis of frames illuminates the precise way in which influence over a human consciousness is exerted by the transfer (or communication) of information from one location such as speech, utterance, news report, or novel – to the consciousness'. Essentially, framing constitutes *selection* and *salience*; what is perceived to be most meaningful, the one serving the other. Entman suggests that framing serves four main purposes: (1) to define problems; (2) to diagnose causes; (3) to make moral judgments; and (4) to suggest remedies.

These will function varyingly according to the text, but they operate in four locations in the communication process: the *communicator*, the *text*, the *receiver* and the *culture*. Communicators 'make conscious or unconscious framing judgments in deciding what to say, guided by frames (often called schemata) that organize their belief systems'. Before we frame, we are *in* a frame. The text will not only be framed by the framer within a frame, it will also be shaped by a number of factors – requirements concerning format and presentation, aesthetic considerations, notions of professionalism and pressures to meet the expectations of convention.

When the text comes to be 'read', the frames as presented may be at variance with the frames that guide the receiver's thinking. For Entman, the culture is 'the stock of commonly invoked frames ... exhibited in the discourse and thinking of most people in a social grouping'. 'Framing in all four locations includes similar functions: selection and highlighting, and use of the highlighting elements to construct an argument about problems and their causation, evaluation and/or solution.'

This approach is useful in analysing the encoding of messages and gauging their effectiveness. It emphasizes the subjective nature of encoding by recognizing the 'invisible' schemata – psychological templates – which, however hard we try to be objective and impartial, deeply influence our actions.

For successful communication, that is winning the interest and attention of the audience, and perhaps even going beyond that in terms of gaining the audience's assent or approval, there seems to be a need for a meeting of schemata: a common ground. The communicator selects, then attempts to give salience to those parts of the story which may fit with the existing schemata in a receiver's belief system.

Much of what we know about the past, about history, is itself in frames – in ancient palaces and tombs, on triumphal arches, the walls and ceilings of great monasteries and cathedrals. These artefacts do not necessarily tell us what life was like in those days; rather, they tell us what was considered salient by those with power to make decisions. In *The Nature and Origins of Public Opinion* (Cambridge University Press, 1992), J.R. Zaller says that framing is a central power in the democratic process: it is political elites who control the framing of issues. Such framing, Zaller believes, not only influences public opinion but also is capable of defining it.

At a practical level, framing is governed by professional conventions, indeed by ritual: newspapers are framed by deadlines and publication times. TV news is framed with music, graphics, headlines and news readers. Each ritual presence reinforces and increases the salience of the frame, its dominance over alternative frames. The study of media is an example of what Entman calls *counterframing* in that it attempts to call the ritual frames into question by analysing them in the light of possible alternative frames.

In 'Framing European politics: a content analysis of press and television news', in the *Journal of Communication*, Spring 2000, Holli A. Semetko and Patti M. Valkenburg identify five key frames in which the media present the news – *attribution of responsibility*, *conflict*, *economic consequences*, *human interest* and *morality*. In their researches, the authors found less divergence between press and TV and more between serious and sensationalist press; the first operating within the attribution-of-responsibility frame, the second in the human-interest frame. See TOPIC GUIDE under MEDIA: PROCESSES & PRODUCTION.

F

▶ Dietram A. Scheufele, 'Framing as a theory of media effects', *Journal of Communication*, Winter 1999.

Franchise Contractual agreement; most commonly associated with the licensing to broadcast, for fixed periods, of commercial television and radio companies.

Franchises for Independent Television (UK) Royal Assent to the TELEVISION ACT, 1954 was received on 30 July, and on 4 August the Independent Television Authority (later to become the Independent Broadcasting Authority) was set up by the Postmaster-General under the chairmanship of Sir Kenneth Clark, and the first commercial television franchises were issued in 1955, with the Associated Broadcasting Company (ATV) beginning its first London transmission on 24 September 1955, and its first Midlands transmission on 17 February 1956.

Franchises from 1993 (UK) What the UK *Guardian* called 'the biggest shake-up in television's 36-year history', with an estimated loss of some 2,500 jobs, occurred in October 1991. The Independent Television Commission (ITC) chaired by George Russell announced the winners of the 'auction' for sixteen regional commercial TV franchises, including a breakfast TV licence, to extend over ten years and commencing on 1 January 1993.

Four existing stations lost their renewal bids: Thames Television (replaced by Carlton Communications), Television South (Meridian Broadcasting), Television South West (Westcountry Television) and the breakfast station TV-am (Sunrise Television). The stations empowered to continued broadcasting through the 1990s were: Granada Television (for the North West), London Weekend, Yorkshire, Anglia Television, Tyne-Tees (North East), Harlech Television (Wales), Ulster Television, Channel Television (Channel Islands), Central Television (Midlands) and the Scottish channels Grampian, Border and Scottish Television. Russell declared that though the process had caused 'undoubted turmoil' within ITV, 'the quality and the viewers will win out'. This point of view was not shared by George Walden in an article 'Is this merely a lottery, or is it a serious business?' (*Daily Telegraph*, 17 October 1991). 'Sadly,' he wrote, 'what has been at stake in this lottery is the quality of British television.'

The Times leader of 17 October called the whole affair an 'ITV auction fiasco' and said 'the government should never ask such a task again … auctioning terrestrial commercial television was always intended to benefit the Treasury not the television viewer. The result must be fewer resources available for programme-making and thus for competing with the cheap products on offer from the American television industry'.

The original plan of the Conservative government was to auction-off the franchises to the highest bidder in a blind sale. This was later modified by the introduction of a so-called 'quality threshold'. Eight of the sixteen licences did not go to the highest bidder and thirteen applications were judged not to have passed the quality threshold. One notable characteristic of the new franchise-winners was the declared policy of running lightly staffed publisher-broadcaster stations, on the lines of Channel 4, buying-in programmes from independent producers rather than the companies originating most of their own material.

Frankfurt school of theorists Founded in 1923, the Institute for Social Research in Frankfurt became the meeting point of several young Marxist intellectuals, among whom were Theodor Adorno, Herbert Marcuse and Max Horkheimer. The members of the 'school' placed at the forefront of their thinking and analysis the centrality of the role of IDEOLOGY in mass communication. When Hitler came to power in 1933, the Institute moved to New York and until 1942 it was affiliated to the Sociology Department of the University of Columbia. In 1949, Horkheimer led the Institute back to Frankfurt, though Marcuse remained in America.

The Frankfurt school posed the questions: why had the prospect of radical change in society so little popular or natural support? Why was there so little consciousness of the need for politically radical change – indeed how had that sense of need been apparently eliminated from popular consciousness? Marcuse, in *One Dimensional Man* (Sphere Books, 1968), contended that in advanced societies capitalism appears to have proved its worth; by 'producing the goods' it is deemed a successful system and therefore one which has rendered itself immune to criticism.

The Frankfurt school believed that culture – traditionally transcendent of capitalist ethic and thus in many ways potentially subversive of it – had been harnessed by the mass media (see HEGEMONY). Classical art had been popularized, yes; but in the process of media-adoption, it had been deprived of its *oppositional* values (see DOMINANT, SUBORDINATE, RADICAL). The Frankfurt school has had considerable influence upon thinking about the media and its power to shape cultures, but has been criticized for condemning existing reality without proposing how it might be changed for the better. See

AUDIENCE: ACTIVE AUDIENCE; CULTIVATION; CULTURAL APPARATUS; DOMINANT DISCOURSE. See also *TOPIC GUIDE* under COMMUNICATION THEORY.

▶ Rolf Wiggershaus, *The Frankfurt School: Its History, Theories and Political Significance* (Polity Press, paperback edition, 1995).

Freedom of Information Act (UK), 2005 The right of access by citizens to information of public interest is enshrined in legislation in many countries, in particular the United States. In the UK in 1994 the Conservative government under John Major took a tentative step towards creating a degree of open government with its Code of Practice on Access to Government Information. In opposition, the Labour government made no secret of its intention to end secret government, the future Labour Prime Minister Tony Blair promising that a Freedom of Information Act, should Labour be elected, would 'signal a new relationship between government and people; a relationship which sees the public as legitimate stakeholders in the running of the country'. The basis of this relationship was to be freedom of information.

Once elected, the New Labour government delayed implementing FOI (Freedom of Information) legislation, eventually producing an Act which a UK *Guardian* leader of 31 December 2004, described as 'a pale shadow of the 1997 white paper', *Your Right to Know.* The Act, which became law at midnight on 31 December 2004, gives the public rights of access to parliament, government departments, local authorities, the National Health Service and education, but not the security services or the courts. Coming into force at the same time as the Act were Environmental Information Regulations (EIRs), implementing an EU directive freeing-up previously closely guarded information about the environment and increased rights of access under the DATA PROTECTION ACT (UK), 1984.

A welcome step towards more open government, the Act nevertheless is cluttered with exemptions. The provision of information can be denied if it is likely to prejudice interests such as international relations, defence, the enforcement of the law, economic and commercial interests. As the *Guardian* leader points out, 'about 75% of the disclosures in the Hutton and Butler enquiries … would not be permitted under the new law'. See HUTTON REPORT (UK), 2004.

Freedom of information does not come cheaply. If the cost of finding and extracting information exceeds set limits, the authority is empowered to say 'No', though in many straightforward cases the service is free.

The Act also created the role of Freedom of Information Commissioner but drew back from granting him or her independent powers, subjecting the Commissioner's actions to the will of government ministers. A notable case of ongoing CENSORSHIP and resistence to open government was New Labour's refusal through 2004 and 2005 to make public the advice offered to Cabinet by Lord Goldsmith, the Attorney General, on the legality or otherwise of the invasion and occupation of Iraq in 2003. See HUMAN RIGHTS ACT (UK), 2000; ICELANDIC MODERN MEDIA INITIATIVE (IMMI); REGULATION OF INVESTIGATORY POWERS ACT (RIPA)(UK), 2000; SURVEILLANCE; TERRORISM: ANTI-TERRORISM, CRIME AND SECURITY ACT (UK), 2001. See also *TOPIC GUIDE* under MEDIA: FREEDOM, CENSORSHIP.

Frequency In a non-technical sense, and as used in relation to the media, frequency is the degree of repetition of topics of NEWS or information in the press, on RADIO or TV. The more frequently a topic inhabits news headlines and news stories, the more likely it is to continue to do so; to be defined and accepted as 'important', and to have media impact.

Negative frequency operates when stories are overlooked, or edged to the margins of attention. Consequently they rarely have the chance either to improve their status as news or impart the full weight of their argument. The term may also be used to refer to the way in which news items fit the frequency – the *time scale* – of the mode of communication. See CONSISTENCY; EFFECTS OF THE MASS MEDIA; IMMEDIACY; INTENSITY; NEWS VALUES.

Front See SELF-PRESENTATION.

Front region, back region See IMPRESSION MANAGEMENT.

Functionalist (mode of media analysis) Interprets social behaviour in terms of its contribution to the assumed overall goals of society, recognizing a CONSENSUS within society of common norms and VALUES. The main focus of functionalist analysis is upon the ways in which social systems maintain *equilibrium.* A functionalist would consider any social or cultural element in relation to its contribution to the survival, integration or stability of society. The communication process features as a major component in the 'servicing' of equilibrium.

Structural functionalism, a mode of analysis developed by US sociologist Talcott Parsons, identifies common features of a complex

F

industrial society that are central to its survival. These include the delineation and maintenance of boundaries (social, cultural, etc.); the definition of major structural units of society and the connections between them; and an overriding concern with system maintenance. This school of analysis has been particularly strong in the US.

Within the functionalist perspective, activities that contribute to the survival of a system are known as *eufunctions*; those which contribute to disturbance are known as *dysfunctions*. A distinction is also made between manifest and latent functions, the one intended and recognized by the participants, the other neither intended nor recognized.

The functionalist approach makes challengeable assumptions about consensus over the goals of society, leaving untouched important questions about the source of these goals and the degree to which an identified source may influence the nature of the social structure and social action. Its tendency is to legitimize the status quo and to emphasize the predominance of the whole over the parts, overlooking alternative means of achieving the same or similar functions. See MARXIST (MODE OF MEDIA ANALYSIS).

Functions of communication See COMMUNICATION, FUNCTIONS.

Functions of mass media See NORMATIVE THEORIES OF MASS MEDIA.

G

Gagging order Issued by judges to restrain the publication or broadcast of information where it is considered that such information breaches the law. Companies in the UK may seek gagging orders to prevent communication to the public that seems a threat to *commercial confidentiality*; individuals may seek the imposition of such orders to protect their personal PRIVACY.

The HUMAN RIGHTS ACT (UK), 2000, emanating from the European Convention of Human Rights forbids, for example, publication of details of a person's heath. Deemed a 'private matter', this nevertheless raises difficult questions when a person's individual heath – say if he/she is a health worker suffering from HIV – may have implications for the public. See *TOPIC GUIDE* under MEDIA: FREEDOM, CENSORSHIP.

Galtung and Ruge's model of selective gatekeeping, 1965 Whenever 'newsworthiness' is discussed and analysed, the names of Johan Galtung and Mari Ruge are likely to be mentioned before all others. Their article, 'The structure of foreign news: The presentation of the Congo, Cuba and Cyprus crises in four foreign newspapers' in the *Journal of International Peace Research*, 1 (1965) and reprinted in *The Manufacture of News* (Constable, 1973), edited by Stanley Cohen and Jock Young, has proved a focal point for those who ask the questions: What qualifies as news? What makes one item of news predominate over another?

World events stream towards a revolving door of criteria for news selection, these operating according to *media perception* and undergoing a process of GATEKEEPING. The more an event fulfils one or several of the criteria, the more likely it will be treated as news and the more it will continue to be regarded as newsworthy. For a diagrammatic representation of the model, see James Watson's *Media Communication: An Introduction to Theory and Process* (Palgrave Macmillan, 3rd edition, 2008), Chapter 5, 'The news, gates, agendas and values', page 158. For details of the criteria identified by Galtung and Ruge, see NEWS VALUES. See also *TOPIC GUIDE* under COMMUNICATION MODELS.

Games See TRANSACTIONAL ANALYSIS.

Gantt chart Named after Henry Lawrence Gantt and originally developed in the early twentieth century. The chart is still widely used in the communications field to plan and track the schedule of activities required for events, programmes or campaigns. Basically, activities are plotted from top to bottom (with the initial activity at the top and the last at the bottom) along the vertical axis against a time-frame plotted along the horizontal axis.

Gatekeeping To reach its intended target, every MESSAGE has to pass through many 'gates'; some will be wide open, some ajar, some tightly closed. At work, the boss's secretary is the archetypal gatekeeper. She may be under instruction to welcome callers or delay them, by letter, by telephone or physically by 'guarding' the boss's door (though it is interesting to conjecture on how far the mobile phone has impacted on this cosy arrangement).

Gatekeeping in the media involves the selection or rejection of material made according to NEWS VALUES which arise from the specific character and objectives of the medium (tabloid newspaper, TV, etc.) and of the organization through which the medium operates.

The process and effect of gatekeeping in the media have undergone substantial modification in the digital age. Traditional media no longer have the monopoly of channels of communication; the INTERNET now challenges newspapers, radio and TV as a multi-source not only of information, but also as a means of opening up the airwaves to the public as *communicators*. Consumers of communication now have at their fingertips the power to evade traditional modes of gatekeeping. Text, pictures, the latest movies, pop tunes have all become available for downloading online; and if gatekeeping has always been a process of manipulation by the communicators as well as selection, the consumer can do this too with the images and texts that he/she can summon up and print or broadcast (see YOUTUBE).

As populations access the Net in increasing numbers, there is the potential for a shift of control from producer to consumer, to the point when 'manning the gates' becomes near impossible and arguably pointless. Mass-media gates continue to exercise power within their own parameters, but out there is the BLOGOSPHERE – millions of content-providers competing with traditional media, and with each other, for user attention.

Further, news itself has lost dominance as demand for social networking (see NETWORK-ING: SOCIAL NETWORKING) has advanced in popularity, and as cost-cutting in the media industry has resulted in newspaper closures and the retreat of fact-based programmes in TV output.

The crowding-out of traditional gatekeeping also threatens to reduce the ability of governments to exercise intervention in the form of regulation and censorship, though not their desire to do so. The very freedom of expression that electronic data-exchange offers people worldwide prompts many governments to seek to curb this freedom by ever more sophisticated blocking devices, new legislation directed at service providers or covert deals in return for rights to operate. See AGENDA-SETTING; CONSENSUS; DIGITIZATION; DEMOTIC TURN; DISPLACEMENT EFFECT; GALTUNG AND RUGE'S MODEL OF SELECTIVE GATEKEEPING, 1965; MR GATE; MOBILIZATION; NETWORK NEUTRALITY; WHITE'S GATEKEEPING MODEL, 1950; YAROS' 'PICK' MODEL FOR MULTIMEDIA NEWS, 2009. See also *TOPIC GUIDES* under MEDIA: PROCESSES & PRODUCTION; NEWS MEDIA.
▶ Bu Zhong and John E. Newhagen, 'How journalists think while they write: a transcultural model of news decision making' (*Journal of Communication*, September 2009).

Gender Gender is a socio-cultural variable with considerable potential to influence behaviour. In recent decades there has been a significant

amount of interest in the way in which gender identity might influence and be influenced by communicative behaviour. Language, non-verbal behaviour and the conventions of everyday social interaction can be seen to carry many messages pertinent to the construction and display of gender identity.

Richard D. Gross in *Psychology: The Science of Mind and Behaviour* (Hodder Arnold, 2005) notes that whilst sex is the term often used to refer to 'the biological facts about us, such as genetic make-up, reproductive anatomy and functioning, and is usually referred to by the terms "male" and "female", gender, by contrast, is what culture makes out of the "raw material" of biological sex'.

Expectations of appropriate behaviour for males and females can vary from one CULTURE to another and, over time, within a particular culture or society. Debate exists within our own society regarding expectations of gender roles and such debate has the potential to spill over into conflict. The link between gender and male and female categories can be complex. A transvestite, for example, in playing out this role adopts the appearance and other aspects of behaviour usually associated with those of the opposite sex.

Several researchers have argued that interpersonal processes play a crucial role in establishing, maintaining and changing notions of gender. It is arguable that maintenance of a gender identity requires the individual to carry off a performance in line with expectations others hold of suitable behaviour for the identity claimed. Judith Butler, for example, in *Gender Trouble: Feminism and the Subversion of Identity* (Routledge, 1999) stresses the crucial importance of performance, and thus of verbal and non-verbal communication, in the construction of gender identity.

Mary Crawford and Rhoda Ungar in *Women and Gender: A Feminist Psychology* (McGraw-Hill, 2004) make a similar point: 'Gender is a kind of performance, and the actors must learn their lines and cues. Like acting, gender is best performed when it appears most natural.' These authors note that sociocultural expectations exist as regards appropriate performances and that social sanctions may be applied if these are challenged too much. However, whilst everyday performances may typically reinforce expectations, they also have the potential, over time, to change them.

Ideas about appropriate gender behaviour also lie at the heart of notions of femininity and masculinity and include assumptions about

G

sexual preferences. A current area of research focuses upon media portrayal of sexual preferences and, in particular, its portrayal of those preferences assumed to be minority preferences – for example those of lesbians and gay men. Larry Gross in 'Minorities, majorities and the media' in Tamar Liebes and James Curran, eds, *Media, Ritual and Identity* (Routledge, 1998) argues that traditionally in much of the US media, portrayals of lesbians and gay men have been limited and stereotypical, with the underlying message being that such identities are deviant. See FEMINISM; GENDERED GENRE; GENDERLECTS; HE/MAN LANGUAGE; MALE-AS-NORM; NEWS: THE 'MALENESS OF NEWS'; PATRIARCHY; PERFORMATIVITY; PLEASURE: ACTIVE AND REACTIVE; REPORT-TALK, RAPPORT-TALK; REPRESENTATION; SELF-IDENTITY; SELF-PRESENTATION; SEMIOTIC POWER; STEREOTYPE; QUEER THEORY.

▸ Jennifer Coates, *Women, Men and Language* (Pearson Education, 2004); Janet Holmes, *Gendered Talk at Work: Constructing Social Identity Through Workplace Interaction* (Blackwell, 2006); Janet Holmes and Miriam Meyerhoff, *The Handbook of Language and Gender* (Blackwell, 2006); Gavid Gauntlett, *Media, Gender and Identity: An Introduction* (Routledge, 2008); Paula Pointdexter, Sharo Meraz and Amy Schmitz Weiss, *Women, Men and News: Divided and Disconnected in the News Media Landscape* (Routledge, 2008); Mary Celeste Kearney, ed., *The Gender and Media Reader* (Routledge, 2011).

Gender and media monitoring Especially since 1995, when the United Nations Fourth Conference on Women took place in Beijing, China, women's groups have focused intensively on the degree to which media globally have asserted male over female interests; at the same time representing women in stereotypical ways. The Conference affirmed the need for systematic and ongoing monitoring of the media, judging that evidence was the key to influencing hearts, minds and practices. The weight of research evidence would be the driving force behind lobbying for fairer representation.

▸ Margaret Gallagher, *Gender Setting: New Agendas for Media Monitoring and Advocacy* (Zed Book, with the World Association for Christian Communication, 2001).

Gendered genre Term used in cultural analysis to denote GENRES of film or television which are seen to appeal to one GENDER rather than another. For example, SOAP OPERAS have traditionally been seen as primarily directed at female audiences, whilst crime series are perceived to appeal more to male audiences. Another example of a gendered genre would be the range of magazines that are targeted at either female or male readerships.

The TEXT and its NARRATIVE patterns typically reflect such differences in AUDIENCE and in part, though not uncritically, assumptions about gender roles and typical masculine and feminine behaviour. Soap operas, for instance, concentrate on the family and local neighbourhood and the interplay of interpersonal relationships within these contexts; whereas the crime series focuses on action, heroic deeds and male bonding. Some researchers have argued that the concept of gendered genre over-simplifies the potentially complex relationship between the text, its narrative form, its authors and its audience.

The term *gendered viewing* describes the different perspectives, ways of seeing, *between* genders in relation to cultural, social and historical contexts. This is not simply a matter of the ways in which men look, or perceive, compared with those of women, for as Mary Ellen Brown asserts in *Soap Opera and Women's Talk: The Pleasure of Resistance* (Sage, 1994), 'gender role characteristics of the one sex can be displayed by people of either sex'. Indeed, the 'simple delineations of masculine and feminine are also somewhat inappropriate because they imply masculinity as central and femininity as marginal'. See FEMINISM; GENRE; MELODRAMA; SEXISM. See also *TOPIC GUIDE* under GENDER MATTERS.

▸ Bethan Benwall, ed., *Masculinity and Men's Lifestyle Magazines* (Blackwell, 2003); Anna Gough-Yates, *Understanding Women's Magazines: Publishing, Markets, Readerships* (Routledge, 2003); Dorothy Hobson, *Soap Opera* (Polity Press/Blackwell, 2003); David Gauntlett, *Media, Gender and Identity: An Introduction* (Routledge, 2008); Mary Celeste Kearney, ed., *The Gender and Media Reader* (Routledge, 2011).

Genderlects In *You Just Don't Understand: Men and Women in Conversation* (Virago, 1992), Deborah Tannen argues that in conversation while men 'speak and hear a language of status and independence', women 'speak' and hear a language of 'connection and intimacy'. These fundamentally different orientations and their influence on perception are, she argues, important factors in creating confusion and misunderstanding in conversations between men and women.

These differences have led Tannen to conclude that men and women speak different *genderlects*, and her book examines examples of how male and female differences in orientation, and consequently in interpretation, can be observed in many different contexts. See REPORT-TALK, RAPPORT-TALK.

▶ Mary Crawford, *Talking Difference: On Gender and Language* (Sage, 1995); Jennifer Coates, *Women, Men and Language* (Pearson Education, 2004); Janet Holmes and Miriam Meyerhoff, *The Handbook of Language and Gender* (Blackwell, 2006).

Gender signals According to Desmond Morris, an important feature of our non-verbal behaviour is that it can transmit 'gender signals'. In *People Watching* (Vintage, 2002) Morris argues that such signals are prevalent in social interaction and provide 'clues that enable us to identify an individual as either male or female', helping to confirm gender identities. Morris views many of these signals as 'invented' rather than natural and thus as cultural markers of gender that can vary across time and cultures, as can be seen in styles of male and female dress, for example.

Genre Term deriving from the French, meaning type or classification. In literature the major classic genres were epic, tragedy, lyric, comedy and satire, eventually to be followed by the novel and short story. Genres, working at least approximately to basic ground rules of form and style, are categories to be found in all modes of artistic expression. In films there are genres of the WESTERN, gangster movies, FILM NOIR, science fiction, romantic comedy, horror, disaster, costume drama, etc. In TELEVISION there are SITCOMS, SOAPS, crime dramas and 'reality' programmes (see REALITY TV).

Genres are rarely discrete or singular entities. They are subject to influence by other genres, and are often a mixture of genre elements. Indeed part of the pleasure audiences derive from genre TEXTS is their inventiveness, the way the CODES of different genres have been knowingly manipulated, sometimes to satirical effect. In short, what attracts and fascinates is their INTERTEXTUALITY. Nick Lacey in *Narrative and Genre: Key Concepts in Media Studies* (Palgrave Macmillan, 2000) offers a useful guide to the analysis of media genres, listing six key aspects: *setting, characters, narrative, iconography, style* and *stars*.

Writing in *Acts of Literature* (Routledge, 1992), French philosopher Jacques Derrida is of the opinion that there is 'no genreless text'; thus the way is open to classify TV news, party political broadcasts, weather reports, quiz shows, chat shows and consumer programmes as genres.

In *The Sitcom* (Edinburgh University Press, 2010), Brett Mills argues that 'the more genres develop, the more they stay the same' (a good question for a media studies essay, perhaps).

This suggests that the boundaries of genre are elastic but have a natural tendency to return to the norm. Referring to the genre of TV sitcoms, Mills believes that traditional, conventional or basic formats will continue to appeal to writers, producers and audiences alike.

Online communication has seen the creation of a number of genres; among these are e-mailing, personal websites, blogs and online newspapers – their forms and purposes adapted and modified by users, according to technological availability and the possibilities and requirements of social contexts. Online genres are essentially dynamic; they are interactive and participative and very often operate as alternatives to traditional, media-dominated genres (see WEB OR ONLINE DRAMA).

Leah A. Lievrouw in *Alternative and Activist New Media* (Polity Press, 2011) cites a number of such alternative online genres. (1) *Culture jamming*. This 'critiques popular/mainstream culture, particularly corporate capitalism, commercialism and consumerism. Here media artists and activists appropriate and "repurpose" elements from popular culture to make new works with an ironic or subversive point – put another way, culture jamming "mines" mainstream culture to critique it'. Such jamming invites or provokes 'reverse jamming', where 'radical or oppositional messages and styles are reappropriated ... by mainstream marketers to give their products a cool, countercutural, or anti-establishment image'.

(2) *Hacktivism* where skilled users – sometimes referred to as 'outlaws', but largely with ethical intent – seek to expose corporate wrongdoing (see HACKER, HACKTIVIST; WIKILEAKS). This genre also includes 'the development of systems that elude or sabotage state or commercial surveillance and censorship, encrypt data and communications, or disable digital rights management or copy protection schemes, in the name of preserving users' privacy, government or corporate accountability, or freedom of information'.

(3) *Participatory journalism* takes the form of 'web-based alternative, radical or critical news outlets and services that adopt the practices and philosophy of public, civic, citizen, participatory or "open source" journalism to provide alternatives to mainstream news and opinion'. (4) *Mediated mobilization* 'takes advantage of web-based social software tools like social network sites, personal blogs ... to engage in live and mediated collective action'.

(4) *Commons knowledge*, writes Lievrouw

'relates to the content of culture itself – the nature of knowledge and expertise, how information is organized and evaluated, and who decides'. Traditional formations and taxonomies fall short of encompassing 'the sheer volume and idiosyncrasy of information online' which has 'driven the creation of new tools, such search engines and tags, that use searchers' own language rather than the predetermined *controlled vocabulary* (search terms or technical languages) approved by experts, to locate and retrieve relevant sources'.

Commons knowledge systems are 'bottom-up classification schemes for organizing and categorizing diverse, arcane, local, personal, or amateur information sources, which often challenge or critique expert disciplinary taxonomies'. See FACEBOOK; GOOGLE; NARRATIVE; PODCAST; TWITTER; WIKIPEDIA; YOUTUBE.

★**Gerbner's model of communication, 1956** This is described by Denis McQuail in *Communication*, (Longman, 2nd edition, 1993) as perhaps 'the most comprehensive attempt yet to specify all the component stages and activities of communication'. Below is a modified version of George Gerbner's model as presented in 'Towards a general model of communication', in *Audio Visual Communication Review*, 4. M is responder to E (event) and may be human or machine (such as a microphone or camera). Gerbner's emphasis is upon the considerable

variability in the perception of an EVENT by a communicating agent and also in the way the MESSAGE is perceived by a receiver. He speaks of the essential 'creative, interactional nature of the perceptual process'. Equally important is the stress placed upon the importance of context to the 'reading' of messages, and of the open nature of human communication.

For Gerbner the relationship between form and context in the communication process (S = Signal) is dynamic and interactive. It is also concerned with access and control, dimensions which inevitably affect the nature and content of communication messages – their selection, shaping and distortion. At the level of the mass media this is obvious, but access and control also operate at the level of interpersonal communication – teachers in classrooms, for example; speakers at public meetings, parents in the home situation.

Back on the horizontal axis, Gerbner stresses the importance of *availability*. A literate electorate may have the capacity to read all the facts about a political situation, all the pros and cons of an industrial dispute, but that capacity can only operate, and the pros and cons be properly weighed, if the necessary facts are made available. What Gerbner's model does not do is address itself fully to the problems of how MEANING is generated. The form or code of the message (S) is taken for granted, whereas the

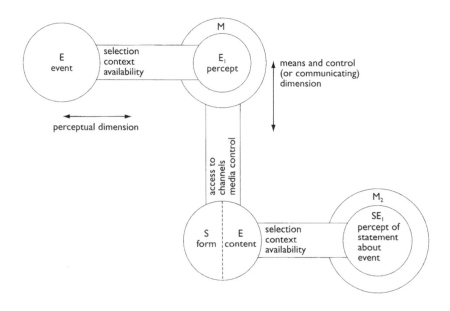

Gerbner's model of communication, 1956

advocate of SEMIOLOGY/SEMIOTICS would argue that meaning is of the essence. See TOPIC GUIDE under COMMUNICATION MODELS.

Gestural dance Term describing the way in which gestures are employed to achieve inter-actional synchrony (similar timing) between participants in an encounter. For example, the smooth handing-over of the conversational floor from speaker to listener is achieved by a combination of prolonged gaze, falling intonation, returning of the hands to a rest position and possibly the use of a gesture towards the listener to invite a contribution. The listener may have indicated a wish to speak by the use of rapid HEAD NODS.

Gestural echo See POSTURE.

Gesture Several different parts of the body may be used to make gestures – most typically the arms, feet, hands and head; HEAD NODS are usually classed as a gesture. Desmond Morris in *People Watching* (Vintage, 2002) notes that gestures can be 'Primary' or 'Incidental' as regards their communicative intent. 'Primary' gestures are those intended to communicate a message, such as pointing to the location of a shop when giving directions, whereas 'Incidental' gestures occur for non-communicative reasons: for example an individual may wink if he/she gets grit in their eye. To an observer, however, the wink may be interpreted as an intended act of communication: a message signalling a desire to interact.

Michael Argyle in *Bodily Communication* (Methuen, 1988) divides gestures and bodily movements into three main categories: *Emblems*, *Illustrators* and *Self-touching*. Emblems are movements, often hand movements, that can easily be translated into speech in terms of their MEANING (they may stand in for speech) within a particular GROUP or CULTURE. The use, in Britain, of the thumbs-up gesture would be an example. Illustrators are those gestures used to illustrate or accompany speech, often to aid explanation – for example gestures used when giving directions. Gestures can be used to regulate everyday interaction and to provide feedback; waving to a friend may indicate a desire to start a conversation, and during a conversation the listener may use rapid head nods to show agreement with the speaker's comments. Self-touching normally indicates information about an individual's emotional state, such as the scratching of a face when anxious, but can also be used in displays of courtship and grooming. Morris (2002) argues that self-touching can also be a displacement activity; for example a nervous passenger about to board a plane may frequently tug his/her earlobe.

Morris in *Manwatching: A Field Guide to Human Behaviour* (Jonathan Cape, 1977) offers six categories of gesture: (1) *Expressive*; shared by other animals as well as humans, and including facial expression and manual gesticulations. (2) *Mimic* gestures; exclusively human; 'the essential quality of a Mimic Gesture is that it attempts to copy the thing it is trying to portray'. This category Morris subdivides into *social* mimicry (or 'putting on a good face'); *theatrical* mimicry; *partial* mimicry (pretending your hand is a gun, for example); and what he terms *vacuum* mimicry – gestures to indicate hunger or thirst. (3) *Schematic* gestures are those in which imitations become abbreviated or abridged; a gestural shorthand. (4) *Symbolic* gestures represent moods and ideas, such as the SIGN to indicate that you consider someone is 'round the twist'. (5) *Technical* gestures constitute specialized signal systems recognized only by those in the trade or profession, such as those employed by a TV studio manager or a fireman to his colleagues. (6) *Coded* gestures are based upon formal systems, such as Deaf-and-Dumb Sign Language, Semaphore and the tic-tac signalling of the race-course.

Many gestures carry universal meaning, but in general the meaning of a gesture is dependent upon cultural context, timing and situation as well as other acts of verbal and non-verbal communication. Gestures are not often used in isolation. The meaning of a gesture can vary considerably across cultures; Morris (2002) uses the term '*multi-message* gestures' for such gestures. An example here is the 'thumbs-up' gesture mentioned earlier. In Britain this means that things are going well; in Australia, however, it means 'up yours'. As Roger E. Axel reminds us in *Gestures: The Do's and Taboos of Body Language Around the World* (John Wiley & Sons Inc., 1998), gestures should be used with care in unfamiliar cultures. See BARRIER SIGNALS; BATON SIGNALS; COMMUNICATION, NON-VERBAL; CUT-OFF; GESTURAL ECHO; METASIGNALS; NON-VERBAL BEHAVIOUR: REPERTOIRE; PROXEMICS; SALUTATION DISPLAY; SHORTFALL SIGNALS; TIE-SIGNS. See also TOPIC GUIDE under INTERPERSONAL COMMUNICATION.

▸ Allan and Barbara Pease, *The Definitive Book of Body Laguage* (Orion, 2004).

Ghost-writer One who does literary work for someone else, usually a celebrity, who takes the credit.

Glasgow University Media Group Set up with a grant from the UK Social Science Research Council, the Group has published research findings that have won considerable attention and not unexpectedly drawn fire from the media under investigation. By 1982 the Group had published three major works tabulating its exhaustive research into the way TV handles the NEWS. First came *Bad News* (Routledge & Kegan Paul, 1976), which exploded the generally held image of broadcasters being substantially more objective and reliable in news reporting than the PRESS.

'Our study,' wrote the eight authors of the original study, 'does not support a received view that television news is "the news as it happens".' The Group had monitored all TV news broadcasts over a six-month period, from January to June 1975. Notable among the Group's findings was evidence of a bias in TV against the activities of organized labour and a relentless emphasis upon effects rather than causes.

Later publications by the Glasgow University Media Group have been *More Bad News* (Routledge & Kegan Paul, 1980), *Really Bad News* (Writers and Readers' Publishing Co-operative, 1982) and *War and Peace News* (Open University Press, 1985) about media coverage of the Falklands War, the Miners' Strike of 1984 and Northern Ireland. The theoretical base from which the Group works may be summarized by a quotation from *More Bad News*: 'news is not a neutral and not a natural phenomenon: it is rather the manufactured production of ideology'.

The GUMG was back in the news again in 2002 with research findings suggesting that TV news has failed to inform young people about the Israeli-Palestinian conflict. Reporting on these in a UK *Guardian* article (16 April), 'Missing in Action', Greg Philo writes, 'If you don't understand the Middle East crisis it might be because you are watching it on TV news.' The research group interviewed 12 small audience groups involving 85 people with a cross-section of ages. These were asked a series of questions on the Middle East situation, and then the same questions were posed to 300 young people between the ages of 17 and 22. It was found that 'many of those questioned had little understanding of the reasons for the conflict and its origins'.

The conclusion drawn from this research was that the failure to place events into a historical *context* occurred as a result of TV news existing 'in a very competitive market' subject to anxiety about audience ratings: 'In this respect it is better to have great pictures of being in the middle of a riot with journalists ducking stones than to explain what the conflict is about.' The reluctance to contextualize, says Philo, also lies in the political roots of the conflict in which 'Israel is closely allied to the United States and there are very strong pro-Israeli lobbies in the US and to some extent in Britain.'

Bad News from Israel (Pluto Press) by Philo and Mike Berry was issued in 2004 to be followed, on the same theme and with the same dire message about how 'Israel continues to spin images of war', by *More Bad News from Israel* (Pluto) in 2011. See TOPIC GUIDE under RESEARCH METHODS.

Glasnost Openness; Russian term for greater freedom of expression and less state secrecy. The word became universal currency with the election to leadership in the Soviet Union of Mikhail Gorbachev, who welcomed rather than shunned world publicity and demonstrated an openness within the Russian nation and in communication with other countries not experienced since the early days of the Russian Revolution (and only fitfully experienced since). Linked with glasnost has been *perestroika*, meaning reconstruction – reform in relation to government practices and expectations.

Globalization (and the media) A term bandied about in all spheres – political, economic, cultural, environmental – yet rarely satisfactorily defined; or indeed defined at all. The clues are many: does it mean cross-border, cross-nation, cross-cultural? Does it essentially mean, as the Americans prefer the term, *international*; and what part in the advances in globalization do the media play? Is it about convergence or diversity, or both operating together; and how does globalization relate to such notions of the PUBLIC SPHERE as the AGORA, and thus ideas concerning *democracy*?

A scrutiny of the commentators on globalization reveals some fairly dramatic differences of viewpoint. There are those who have been called *hyperglobalizers* who predict the end of the nation state; *transformalists* who reckon that globalization is a driving force for change; and *sceptics* who claim that globalization is a myth. First it must be acknowledged that globalization is an all-purpose catchword requiring definition and redefinition. If we are referring to media (and other services) crossing borders, we need to identify what we mean by borders: between what borders; for example, would we discuss displaced populations, cultures within cultures, and are we talking about the flow of news or entertainment in particular across borders? And in the domain of *effects*, are we viewing processes of *homogenization* (sameness) taking place as a result of the flow of news and entertainment across nations and cultures, or *heterogenization* (difference), or both occurring simultaneously?

In short we are swimming in a sea of uncertainties. If we are considering the way globalization has been heading, we can discern what on the face of it appear to be contradictory trends – *convergence* and *diversity*. Convergence refers to ownership and control and focuses on multinational corporations extending their business across the globe. Diversity focuses on the ways in which individual communities adapt or *appropriate* the (predominantly Western) flow of news and entertainment to their own cultural uses and vision; what has been called 'the domestication of the foreign'.

Colin Sparks, in a paper entitled 'What's wrong with globalization?' presented to the International Communication Association in New York in 2007, argues that 'there is no theory of globalization that commands common consent'. The term gets mixed up with *modernity* and *media imperialism* and can mean 'anything that a given author wants it to mean'. What we have in place of evidence is opinions. Sparks is not among those commentators who see in globalization major shifts away from Western (particularly American) political, economic and cultural dominance. The centre of gravity continues to rest 'very firmly in the developed world'.

A critic of the perceived benefits to communities of globalization is Tehri Rantanan. In *The Media and Globalization* (Sage, 2005) the author writes that 'globalization is without doubt, a very uneven process, which brings much misery into people's lives, either because they are excluded from it or because they are part of it'. Rantanan believes media analysis should agree the 'response necessary to address the negative consequences of globalization' and engage with such issues as how far the lives of people (all people) worldwide are benefiting from globalization; what are the upsides and what are the downsides and what part do the media play in the process?

Perhaps the most serious questioning of the media's role in globalization comes from Kai Hafez in *The Myth of Globalization* (Polity, 2007, translated by Alex Skinner), who sees fact being mixed with 'exaggerated projections', fusing 'truth and falsehood'. This isn't to reject the 'myth' out of hand but to probe it with a view to reaching 'an undistorted view of the world'.

Hafez argues that 'casting light on the myth of "globalization" as it affects cross-border communication does not mean exposing it as pure fiction'; rather it demands more exhaustive

scrutiny seasoned with alert scepticism. Hafez's own scepticism arises from what so-called globalization is failing to achieve – connectivity and system change. Even where communities are equipped with the technologies that potentially bring about cross-border, cross-cultural fusion, there is as much chance of intolerance of *other* occurring as tolerance and the will to connect.

Referring to multiculturalism, which has often been named as one of the benefits arising from globalization, Hafez asserts that 'there is no causal relationship between integration and media. The recent assumption that the local is simply relocated through migration and globalization is just as misleading as the one that crossing borders works to open up cultures'. A key focus for commentators on globalization is the part that is played, and might be played, by the INTERNET in bringing about a world in which peoples are more tolerant of each other, exercise greater equality and benefit from cross-border interaction in what has been termed 'civil society'. Hafez is not convinced, referring to uncertainties of information flow which 'are generating an often "virtual" knowledge of the world, which is almost impossible to harmonize with verifiable reality'.

Sparks in 'What's wrong with globalization?' reminds us that 25 per cent of the world's population is without access to electricity: 'No electricity, no Internet'; and leaves his audience with the comment, 'A theory that is blind to the facts is blind to reality.' See CONGLOMERATES; CONSUMERIZATION; CONVERGENCE; CULTURE: GLOBALIZATION OF; EUROPE: CROSS-BORDER TV CHANNELS; GLOBALIZATION, THREE ENGINES OF; GLOBAL MEDIA SYSTEM: THE MAIN PLAYERS; GLOCALIZATION; LOCALIZATION; MEDIAPOLIS; WORKERS IN COMMUNICATION AND MEDIA. See also *TOPIC GUIDES* under GLOBAL PERSPECTIVES; MEDIA ISSUES AND DEBATES; MEDIA: OWNERSHIP AND CONTROL.

▶ Colin Sparks, *Globalization, Development and the Mass Media* (Sage, 2007).

Globalization: three engines of According to the Group of Lisbon publication *Limits to Competition* (MIT Press, 1995), the three engines seen to be driving globalization are *liberalization*, *deregulation* and *privatization*, the first permitting companies to move capital and operations to locations offering competitive terms (such as low wages). DEREGULATION allows liberalization and, as a consequence, leads to PRIVATIZATION of public utilities.

Ultimately, many commentators fear, these three engines of global financial and industrial activity undermine, if not dismantle altogether, the welfare state of individual nations. The authors of *Limits to Competition* argue that at the core of the dismantling process is the conviction that the more labour costs are cut and related social benefits reduced, the better will be the country's competitiveness. As the media are so substantially a part of the portfolios of TNCs (transnational corporations), the danger is that they will either advocate these trends or hold back from the public responsibility of subjecting them to critical scrutiny. See NETWORK NEUTRALITY.

Global media system: the main players Fewer than fifteen transnational corporations (TNCs) dominate world media ownership. The ranking of these is subject to rapid shifts resulting from mergers, but the current players at the top of the media tree are: Time Warner, Vivendi, Viacom, Disney, Sony, Bertelsmann, News Corporation, Segram (snapped up by Vivendi in 2000), Poly Gram and General Electric.

The giant of giants is Time Warner (owning *Time* magazine, Time Life Books, Warner Music Group, America On Line, Warner Brother films, HBO cable channel, CNN, etc.). A close challenger is Disney (ABC, film studios, theme parks, record production, book publication, global cable TV channels, etc.). Close business links between the media giants is a key feature of operations, alliances between them being more common than direct competition. Rupert Murdoch's NEWS CORP has equity joint ventures in long-term alliances with Time Warner, Viacom, EMI, Granada TV and Globo of Brazil. Disney is involved in joint ventures with Bertelsmann, NBC and Hearst Newspapers (not to mention Coca-Cola and McDonalds). Bertelsmann of Germany has joint enterprises with (in addition to Disney) Time Warner, Sony, Pearson publications (UK) and the BBC.

The objective of the great media corporations is expansion worldwide, linked with a policy of *customizing* or tailoring the media product to local needs, tastes and expectations; thus Disney's ESPN 24-hour-a-day sports channel broadcasts in over 20 languages to more than 160 countries (see EUROPE: CROSS-BORDER TV CHANNELS).

What applies to electronic communication applies in equal measure to publishing, now dominated by six major players – the largest, HarperCollins, being part of the Murdoch stable, while Random House belongs to Bertelsmann. Orion belongs to Hachette which in turn is owned by Lagadere Media linked with Vivendi.

It would be a mistake to regard these behemoths, as they have been described, as so massive and powerful that they are impervious to the tide of events. Time Warner's merger with AOL (American On Line) proved an ill-starred marriage, while Murdoch's News Corp acquisition of MYSPACE turned out a shaky business venture (it was sold off at a substantial loss in 2011). Indeed corporate ambition to colonize online social networking platforms has proved anything but a reliable, steady-state investment. See MEDIA MAGNATES: FOUR SOURCES OF CONCERN. See also *TOPIC GUIDE* under MEDIA: OWNERSHIP & CONTROL.

Global scrutiny Describes the vastly increased *visibility* of people and events on a global scale, largely as a result of TELEVISION. John B. Thompson in *The Media and Modernity: A Social Theory of the Media* (Polity, 1995) speaks of a 'regime of visibility created by an increasingly globalized system of communication'; and, however structured (see FRAMING), this power to scrutinize represents a 'significant historical development. For it means not only that political leaders must now act in an arena which is in principle open to view on a global scale, but also that recipients are able to see and experience distant individuals and events in a way that was simply not possible before'. See MOBILIZATION.

Global village See GLOBALIZATION OF MEDIA; MCLUHANISM.

Glocalization According to Roland Robinson in 'Globalization or glocalization?' in the *Journal of Communication 1* (1994), glocalization is a process that, arguably, often accompanies the process of GLOBALIZATION. Glocalization occurs when global media corporations adapt or localise their operations and output to accommodate local circumstances and culture. Richard Rooke in *European Media in the Digital Age* (Pearson, 2009), for example, discusses how pressure to maintain audience share against growing local competition and thus secure local advertising revenue led MTV to diversify. He notes that, 'Today MTV Networks Europe has regional channels in 26 different languages and considerable amounts of content are produced locally.' See HYBRIDIZATION; MCDONALDIZATION; MCWORLD VS JIHAD.

▶ Patrick D. Murphy and Marwan M. Kraidy, *Global Media Studies: Ethnographic Perspectives* (Routledge, 2003).

Golden pen of freedom Annual award by the International Federation of Newspaper Publishers (FIEJ) based in Paris.

Google Conceived by Stanford University

computer-science graduate students Larry Page and Sergei Brin in 1995 and launched in 1997, Google experienced almost instant and exponential growth, by 2000 becoming the world's largest search engine. The original name was BackRub. 'Googal' is a mathematical term coined by Milton Sirotta, nephew of the US mathematician Edward Kasner, for the number represented by 1 followed by 100 zeros; thus a 'google' stood for an extremely large number, reflecting the new company's ambition to provide vast amounts of information on the World Wide Web.

A cheque for US$ 100,000 from Sun Microsystems founder Andy Bechtolsheim made the launch of Google possible in 1998. One is tempted to say, 'And the rest is history.' Google now runs in excess of 150 million information searches a day. Shortly after its launch, Google was chosen by AOL (American On Line)/ Netscape as their web search service, traffic levels having risen to over 3 million.

In June 2000 the company entered into partnership with Yahoo! Growth was dynamic and brilliantly innovative. Image Search was launched in 2001 to be followed by G News (2002), a content-targeted advertising service (March 2003), Google Print and Google Book Search in the same year. In 2004 the launch of Orkut enabled Google to tap into the sphere of social networking (see NETWORKING: SOCIAL NETWORKING). Google Local followed, and also in 2004 users could begin keying into Google SMS (Short Message Service), Desktop Search and Google Scholar. There followed Google Maps, My Search Engine, Blogger Mobile, Mobile Websearch, Google Earth, Google Talk, Google Reader, Google Analytics, Gmail for Mobiles (2005), Google News for Mobiles, Google Finance, Google Trends, Google Checkout – all in the same year that Google acquired YouTube (2006).

Lateral thinking has been no stranger to Google: in 2009 the YouTube Symphony Orchestra played at New York's Carnegie Hall. All the way, Google has accumulated businesses such as Keyhole (2004), a digital mapping company whose technology proved the foundation for Google Earth. Others followed: Doubleclick (2008), reCAPTCHA (2009), Aardvark, Picnik, ITA, Slide and Widevine (2010). Acquisitions represented both Google's development needs and their perceived direction; for example, Widevine was a vendor of digital rights management software, enabling broadcasters to safely transmit video content online.

Google came in for widespread criticism in agreeing to conform to the Internet censorship requirements of the Chinese government. A 'cyber-attack' in December 2009, suspected as coming from within China and targeting Google's Chinese Gmail accounts, particularly those of human rights activists, proved the trigger for Google to threaten to pull out of China, even at the prospect of the loss of a vastly lucrative market.

David Drummond, corporate development and chief legal officer of the company, in a Google blog (12 January 2010) wrote, 'We have decided we are no longer willing to continue censoring our results on Google.cn … we will be discussing with the Chinese government the basis on which we could operate an unfiltered search engine within the law, if at all …' The Chinese government renewed Google's licence to operate in the summer of 2010, though in the view of Ted Dean of a Beijing-based company and reported by BBC New Business (9 July 2010), 'many of the issues around why Google shut down its Chinese search page in the first place are still there'.

▶ Randall Ross, *Planet Google: One Company's Audacious Plan to Organize Everything We Know* (Free Press, 2008).

Gossip Traditionally gossip has been ranked as 'woman's-talk' and, within DISCOURSES and social structures that are male-dominated, given low status in the order of exchange, or even disparaged. Gossip, to outsiders, usually male, appears to be 'going nowhere', 'undirected' and ultimately pointless if not damaging. Such judgments are essentially made from ideological positions which view communication as less an exchange of experience (a cultural exchange) and more a transmission of information: in short, 'man's talk'.

Gossip deserves more serious attention than is usually given to it. In 'Gossip: notes on women's oral culture' in *Women's Studies International Quarterly*, 3 (1980), Deborah Jones defines gossip as 'a way of talking between women in their roles as women, intimate in style, personal and domestic in topic and setting, a female cultural event which springs from and perpetuates the restrictions of the female role, but also gives the comfort of validation'. Jones lists four functions of gossip: *house-talk*, *scandal*, *bitching* and *chatting*. Such talk establishes and confirms the pleasures of interaction while at the same time working to give them value and validity. As such, it is potentially empowering.

Gossip networks A mode of resistance, by women, to male-dominated DISCOURSES. The term is used by Mary Ellen Brown in *Soap Opera* *and Women's Talk: The Pleasure of Resistance* (Sage, 1994). Brown discusses how gossip networks arise out of viewing SOAP OPERA, and the use of such entertainment as a means of constructing alternative meanings. The author asks, 'How can such a trivial or even exploitative genre as soap opera be associated with the notion of empowerment for its viewers?' She responds to the question by arguing that the answer 'lies in the invisible discourse networks it plugs into and helps solidify. Such discourse networks, or gossip networks, are important for women's resistive pleasure'.

Gramophone Originally the Phonograph, invented by Thomas Alva Edison (1847–1931), his first sketch of which was published in the *Scientific American*, 22 December 1877. His 'talking tinfoil' led to the creation in 1878 of the Edison Speaking Phonograph Company, and soon a single exhibition phonograph could earn as much as US$ 1,800 a week. Concurrently Edison designed different models including a disc machine with a volute spiral that anticipated later developments.

Commercial recordings began in 1890, though sound reproduction remained poor, the wax cylinders could only play for two minutes and there was no way of mass-producing them. Machines were driven by cumbersome, heavy-duty batteries and were very expensive to purchase, that is until Thomas Hood Macdonald, a manager of Graphophone, rival company to Edison's, put on sale the first mechanical phonograph (1894), retailing at US$ 75.

The Columbia company were the first to manufacture double-sided discs (1908), though the next major innovation was electrical recording, initiated by Lionel Guest and H.O. Merrimen in 1920 when they recorded, by electrical process, the Unknown Warrior burial service in Westminster Abbey. Bell Laboratories in the US proved substantial pioneers in this area, which they termed *orthophonic* recording.

The miraculous rise of the gramophone was eventually hit by the more popular mass appeal of RADIO and the 1930s were lean years, though the record industry in Europe did not plumb the depths to the extent it did in the US where, by January 1933, the record business was practically extinct. However, in September 1934, the RCA Victor sales department offered the Duo Junior, consisting of an electrically powered turntable and a magnetic pickup, primitive but popular; and by 1935 the notion of 'high-fidelity' was born. Station W2XR (later WQXR) in New York began 'high-fidelity broadcasting' in 1934, in truth, as

much high publicity as hi-fi.

The Second World War (1939–45) cut non-military use of shellac, the material for the discs and principally imported from India, thus record production was severely curtailed. 1944 saw the first examples of Decca's 'ffrr' sound reaching British ears. This was 'full frequency range reproduction' achieving standards of reproduction never previously heard.

In 1941, 127 million discs were sold; in 1947, 400 million, a year before Columbia Records in the US launched the unbreakable microgroove disc, with a playing time of 23 minutes per side. The LP (Long Playing) Record had arrived. It bore between 224 and 300 grooves per inch compared to 85 grooves on the ordinary disc; and it moved on the turntable at 33⅓rpm instead of the traditional 78. Not to be outdone, RCA Victor hit back with the 45rpm record, thus beginning the so-called Battle of the Speeds, diminishing trade in what turned out to be a period of consumer uncertainty. It was the period too when recording by magnetic tape was rapidly expanding. Neither ousted the other: in fact they proved complementary and expanded together in the dynamic growth period of Rock and Roll and the radio disc jockey.

Stereophonic sound, or 'two-eared listening', had been possible since the Bell Laboratories had put on binaural demonstrations at the Chicago World's Fair of 1933, and Walt Disney's film *Fantasia* (1940) showed the possibilities of multi-source music reproduction in a cinema. The stereo effect was caught first on high-quality magnetic tape. Then in 1957 the Westrex Company devised a successful method of putting two stereo channels into a single groove. By September of the following year every major record company in the US was offering stereo discs for sale.

The tape cassette emerged from Philips who demonstrated its potential at the 1963 Berlin Radio Show. They improved it substantially and in 1970 along came the Dolby system, just at the time when tape machines were becoming popular as in-car entertainment.

An innovation in gramophone technology which never quite caught on was Quadrophony, using four speakers rather than two, the additional channels intended to convey 'ambient' sound – fractionally delayed impulses reflected from the rear of the recording hall. Digital recording is now standard and the CD (Compact Disc) dominates the music market. However, vinyl is by no means a spent force; vinyl records are still manufactured, fulfilling the demands of independent musicians and a substantial number of enthusiasts who prefer the vinyl sound to the 'compression effects' of its more 'advanced' rivals. See TOPIC GUIDE under MEDIA HISTORY.

Grip Person in a film crew responsible for laying tracks, portable 'railway lines' for the smooth movement of the camera mounted on a DOLLY.

Groups A good deal of communication takes place within groups of one type or another. In *Group Processes* (Blackwell, 2000), Rupert Brown argues that 'a group exists when two or more people define themselves as members of it and when its existence is recognised by at least one other. The "other" in this context is some person or group of people who do not define themselves so'. The following criteria typically denote the existence of a group: common goals, interaction between members and a structure for that interaction, a measure of interdependence, a stable relationship among members, a sense of group identity and social integration.

Robert A. Baron and Donn Byrne in *Social Psychology* (Allyn & Bacon, 1994) suggest some common characteristics of groups: allocation of ROLES, generation of NORMS and group IDEOLOGY, cohesiveness and encouragement of conformity, and allocated roles may often have differing degrees of STATUS within the group. Common structures found in groups are those based on liking, role and status.

Charles H. Cooley, one of the initiators of research into group behaviour and communication, in his work *Social Organization* (Scribner, 1909) classifies groups into two main types. *Primary* groups such as the family are defined as groups in which there is face-to-face communication; in which norms and *mores* are produced; in which roles are allocated and in which a feeling of solidarity is enjoyed. *Secondary* groups, such as social class groups, are much larger aggregates. Several researchers have sought to determine the communication processes that take place within groups and in particular the inter-relationship between a group's CULTURE, ROLES, STATUS structure, cohesiveness, size, and type, and its communication processes.

It is also possible to classify groups as being in-groups or out-groups, as identified by Harry C. Triandis in 'Collectivism vs. Individualism' in G. Verma and C. Bagley, eds, *Cross-cultural Studies of Personality, Attitudes, and Cognition* (Macmillan, 1988). In-groups are those to which we belong and which we value, whilst out-groups are those to which we do not belong and we may view some of these in a negative light.

Rupert Brown in *Group Processes* (Blackwell, 2000) notes as regards in-groups, 'Since part of our self-concept (or identity) is defined in terms of group affiliation, it follows that there will be a preference to view these groups positively rather than negatively.'

Triandis also notes that in-groups are likely to have much more influence over their members in collectivist cultures than is the case in individualistic cultures. In-groups and out-groups may cooperate for mutual benefit but such groupings may also be a source of intergroup conflict. Brown argues that a range of studies reminds us that 'the readiness for people to show partiality for their own group (and its products) over outgroups (and theirs) is not confined to artificially created groups'. The resulting conflicts are, arguably, much in evidence.

The performance of individuals is often affected by group membership. Being in a group can enhance or inhibit individual performance, depending on such factors as the nature of the task, the degree of effective leadership, the cohesiveness of the group and the flexibility of its communication networks. These factors also determine the quality of group decision-making.

In certain circumstances individuals may feel they need to make less effort in a group situation and become social *loafers*; alternatively they may be motivated to work harder and become social *labourers*. At times individuals may be prepared to work harder to make up for their less energetic group members and thus contribute to social *compensation*.

Robert A. Baron, Donn R. Byrne and Nyla R. Branscombe in *Social Psychology* (Pearson Education, 2006) argue that 'contrary to popular belief, a large body of evidence indicates that groups are actually more likely to adopt extreme positions than are individuals making decisions alone' – a dynamic termed *group polarization*.

A small primary group particularly has the potential to influence the perceptions of its individual members and thus the way in which they interpret and respond to communication from sources both within and outside the group. Secondary groups are not without influence either, in the communication process. An individual's ACCENT and DIALECT, for example, can reflect their socio-economic background. See GROUPTHINK.

Groupthink Cohesiveness, or the desire for cohesiveness, in a group may produce a tendency amongst its members to agree at all costs. Sometimes the decisions brought about by such unanimity turn out to be disastrous.

Research by Irving Janis detailed in his study entitled *Victims of Groupthink* (Houghton Mifflin, 1972) demonstrated that what he termed 'groupthink' often leads to ineffective decision-making. Janis identified eight symptoms of groupthink, ranging from the group's 'illusion of invulnerability' to the existence within the group of 'self-appointed mind guards' – the latter being group members who shield the group from information and ideas that might challenge the consensus. When groupthink predominates, the group does not subject its ideas and decision-making to careful scrutiny. Janis identified other variables likely to promote groupthink: a strong dominant leadership that discourages open debate, a group's relative isolation from outside sources, the absence of strategies for evaluating decisions, and pressure being placed on the group to make decisions quickly. A number of subsequent studies have investigated the effects of groupthink. See GROUPS.

▶ G. Moorhead, R. Ference and C.P. Neck, 'Group decision fiascos continue: Space Shuttle Challenger and a groupthink framework' in R.S. Cathcart, L.A. Samovar and L. Henman, eds, *Small Group Communication: Theory & Practice* (Brown & Benchmark, 1996); Rupert Brown, *Group Processes* (Blackwell, 2000).

Grub Street Description of any form of literary or journalistic drudgery. According to Dr Johnson (1709–84), Grub Street was 'originally the name of a street near Moorfields in London, much inhabited by writers of small histories, dictionaries and temporary poems, whence any mean production is called grub street'.

Grunig and Hunt: four models of public relations practice, 1984 Proposed by James Grunig and Todd Hunt in *Managing Public Relations* (Harcourt Brace Jovanovitch, 1984), these models have been widely used for analysing public relations performance. Practices based on *The Press Agentry/Publicity* model focus activities on gaining publicity, on one-way communication with the audience through the mass media. There is little concern with gaining FEEDBACK and evaluating the effectiveness of messages. The *Public Information* model is seen to stem from the view of public relations propounded by Ivy Lee – an early public relations practitioner – which emphasizes informing the audience on issues by the presentation of facts, details and figures.

Additionally Grunig and Hunt argue that most practitioners of this model inform the public, 'with the idea of making the organization more responsible to the public'. Clearly however any presentation of information can be selective. This model does allow for two-way communication with the audience and is an approach much used by government institutions and agencies.

The authors make the case that the need for propaganda, mainly as a consequence of the first and second world wars, led to the development of the *Two-Way Asymmetric* model. This focuses upon the role of public relations in the process of persuading audiences to change their attitudes and behaviour and is associated strongly with another early public relations practitioner, Edward Bernays. The model acknowledges that research on human behaviour is useful for constructing persuasive programmes and campaigns.

In particular, research on the audience's existing interests, values and attitudes is considered important, as the audience is seen as best persuaded by messages in line with these. Finally there is the later *Two-way Symmetric* model associated with Scott Cutlip and Allen Center, as well as with Bernays. This model stresses the need to engage with the audience in order to establish a harmonious relationship: for example between an organization and its PUBLICS. This requires that, rather than just seeking to persuade its publics, the organization takes into consideration the needs and goals of its publics and adapts its own policies and practices to the feedback received from them. Whilst expressing a preference for the Two-way Symmetrical model, which is seen as a model of excellence for PR practice, Grunig and Hunt note that the choice of approach for any particular programme or campaign will be contingent upon situational factors.

The model has been open to criticism. One particular criticism is that it fails to acknowledge sufficiently the influence of vested interests on public relations activities. In response to such criticisms, Dozier, Grunig and Grunig developed the idea further in the following studies: David M. Dozier, James E. Grunig and Larissa A. Grunig, *Manager's Guide to Excellence in Public Relations and Communication Management* (Lawrence Erlbaum Associates, 1995); Larissa E. Grunig, James E. Grunig and David M. Dozier, *Excellent Public Relations and Effective Organizations: A Study of Communication Management in Three Countries* (Lawrence Erlbaum Associates, 2002). They employed aspects of game theory, and identified three models of practice, each of which denotes the degree of symmetry likely in the communication process and whose interests are likely to be served. The

Pure asymmetry model describes communication practices that are one way and likely to be used by an organization to dominate its public; the *Pure cooperation* model denotes a situation in which communication is used to convince the organization of the public's position; and in the *Two-way model*, communication is used to achieve a win-win outcome for both the organization and its public.

Guard dog metaphor A variation of (and in contrast to) the WATCHDOG metaphor; representing one of the traditional functions of mass media. The term suggests that the media perform as a *sentry*, not for the community but for special-interest GROUPS that have the power and influence to establish and maintain their own security systems (see POWER ELITE). In 'A guard dog perspective on the role of media' in the *Journal of Communication*, Spring, 1995, George A. Donohue, Phillip J. Tichenor and Clarise N. Olien of the University of Minnesota argue that the guard dog media 'are conditioned to be suspicious of all potential intruders, and they occasionally sound the alarm for reasons that individuals in the master households, that is, the authority structure, can neither understand nor prevent. These occasions occur primarily when authority within the structure is divided'. In communities where there is no apparent conflict within power structures, 'the media are sleeping guard dogs'.

The guiding principle appears to be: support the powerful unless the powerful are intruders. 'Where different local groups have conflicting interests,' say Donohue *et al*, 'the media are more likely to reflect the views of the more powerful groups.' Consequently the guard-dog role works towards internal cohesion. The metaphor contrasts with that of the media's perceived role as *watchdog*. The role in this case is one of surveillance of the powerful on behalf of and in the interests of the public. The media serve as freedom-seekers-and-defenders, hence the titles of so many early newspapers – *Sentinel*, *Voice of the People*, *Champion*, *Justice*, *Poor Man's Guardian*, *Observer*, *Enquirer* and *Advocate*.

A third 'dog' in the repertoire of the media is that of the lapdog. As Donohue *et al* point out, 'a lapdog perspective is a total rejection of the Fourth Estate view on all counts'. The lapdog is submissive to authority and oblivious 'to all interests except those of powerful groups', and serves to frame all 'issues according to the perspectives of the highest powers in the system'.

While the guard dog is characterized by deference as contrasted with submissiveness, at least it recognizes the existence of, and gives attention to, conflict. The greater the social differentiation within a community or nation, the more extensive is the reporting of conflict. Where there is 'power uncertainty' the media are likely to 'display a tendency to concentrate on individuals while accepting the structure. In doing so, the media are reinforcing the tendency within the culture to emphasize great men and personalities rather than individuals as actors in the system who are subject to the influence of social forces and processes'. See AGENDA-SETTING; NEWS VALUES.

Guide signs Actions indicating direction, sometimes called *deictic signals*: finger pointing, head pointing, eye pointing. Thumbs down and thumbs up come into this category, and all the gestures of beckoning as well as repelling. See NON-VERBAL BEHAVIOUR: REPERTOIRE.

H

Habitus See TASTE.

Hacker, hacktivist Just as the tomb robbers of ancient Egypt broke into seemingly impregnable pyramids and underground tombs, so the 'hacker' breaks into computer codes and computer systems. All the hacker needs is a personal micro, know-how and persistence, and some of the world's most closely guarded information banks can be penetrated. What has been termed a *hacktivist* is a hacker with a social or political agenda, wherein hacking becomes a form of protest. Chief among the targets of hacktivists is the nation state and the organization.

The hacktivist pursues a range of tactics, from simple e-mail protests to causing websites to crash and diverting visitors to other sites. Then there are 'bombs' – e-mails by the thousand directed at offending sites; and, of course, the spread of viruses.

In general hackers are in favour of open systems of communication, and their activities are directed towards supporting and maintaining online freedoms. They have been described as *white hat* (the good guys on the side of emancipation) and *black hat* (the bad guys who launch computer viruses, for example). A less emotive term to describe hacking is *alternative computing*.

As subversives for good or ill, hackers have long faced infiltration into their ranks by agents of authority such as, in the US, the Federal Bureau of Investigation (FBI). They operate either directly, by posing as hackers, or indirectly by enrolling existing hackers to spy and report on their peers. See GENRE; JOURNALISM: PHONE-HACKING; REGULATION OF INVESTIGATORY POWERS ACT (RIPA)(UK), 2001; WIKILEAKS.

▸ Tim Jordan and Paul Taylor, *Hacktivism and Cyberwars* (Routledge, 2004); Leah A. Lievrouw, *Alternative and Activist New Media* (Polity Press, 2011).

Halo effect One way in which our perceptions of others may be biased is through the operation of what has been termed the 'halo effect'. In initial encounters we tend to pick out one or two characteristics of a person and let these influence our general impression of them. For example, at an interview, it may be assumed that someone who is well qualified, neatly dressed and pleasant in manner will perform well in the job and work hard. Such generalizations from one or two characteristics are based on our implicit personality theory, that is our basic assumptions about which characteristics go together, and how people are likely to behave.

Hammocking Strategy used by TV schedulers to boost the viewing figures of a programme by placing it between two popular programmes.

Hankey Committee Report on Television, 1943 Set up under the Coalition War Government in the UK, chaired by Lord Hankey, the committee was requested to 'prepare plans for the reinstatement and development of the television service after the War'. Hankey recommended a re-opening on the 1939 basis of the 405-line system rather than waiting for the development of any new, improved version. The Report was of the view that 'it is in the televising of actual events, the ability to give the viewer a front-row seat at almost every possible kind of exciting or memorable spectacle, that Television will perform its greatest service'. Hankey's general conclusion was 'that Television has come to stay ...' See TOPIC GUIDE under COMMISSIONS/COMMITTEES/LEGISLATION.

Hard times scenario See VALS TYPOLOGY.

Harmonious interaction Fred Inglis uses this phrase in *The Imagery of Power: A Critique of Advertising* (Heinemann, 1972) to describe the friendly and mutually supportive relationship between the media and the forces of advertising. This 'harmonious interaction' of ADVERTISING and editorial styles consistently reproduces and endorses the consumer's way of life, argues Inglis.

Hays Office In the US for three decades the Hays Office meant CENSORSHIP. In 1922 leading figures in the film industry formed Motion Picture Producers and Distributors of America Incorporated (MPPDA) to protect their interests against a range of would-be film censors in a climate that had produced Prohibition (Volstead Act, 1919). Will H. Hays, Postmaster-General to the Harding administration, was invited to become president.

In 1930 Martin Quigley, a Chicago publisher, and Father Lord, Society of Jesus, reframed the Hays Office studio recommendations of 1927 into a Production Code (The Hays Office Code) to meet the even more restrictive demands emanating from the recently formed Legion of Decency, made up of leaders of the Roman Catholic church and other religious denominations. A Production Code Administration was prised out of the MPPDA under the direction of Roman Catholic Joseph I. Breen who, between 1934 and the anti-trust decree of 1948, supervised 95 per cent of films made in the US. Any film released without Breen's approval was liable to a US$ 25,000 fine and condemnation by the Legion.

Political as well as moral attitudes and behaviour were subject to severe censorship. The Legion, for example, supported the Fascists in the Spanish Civil War and generally opposed any production with Leftish leanings. The Hays Office Code remained operative until 1966. See HUAC: HOUSE UN-AMERICAN ACTIVITIES COMMITTEE. See also TOPIC GUIDE under MEDIA: FREEDOM, CENSORSHIP.

Head nods Head nods are an element of non-verbal communication and can be used to communicate a range of messages. They are commonly used to give positive FEEDBACK to the sender of a message by indicating both interest and/or approval on the part of the receiver; to indicate *floor appointment*, that is to signal whose turn it is to speak next; and to give emphasis to speech. See COMMUNICATION: NON-VERBAL.

▸ Allan and Barbara Pease, *The Definitive Book of Body Language* (Orion, 2004).

Hearsay See RUMOUR.

Hedges Utterances such as 'you know', 'sort of' and 'perhaps' would be examples of hedges. Jennifer Coates in *Women, Men and Language* (Pearson Education, 2004) notes that the precise function of hedges varies with the social context and the relationship of the interactors. Coates discusses the range of uses to which hedges may be put, such as expressing confidence, suggesting uncertainty and enabling face-saving to occur when sensitive topics are being discussed. Whilst women appear to use more hedges than men in conversation, the interpretation to be placed on this difference is a matter for debate.

Hegemony The concept of hegemony owes much to the work of Italian political thinker Antonio Gramsci (1891–1937). A state of hegemony is achieved when a provisional alliance of certain social groups exerts a CONSENSUS that makes the power of the dominant group appear both natural and legitimate. Hegemony can, however, only be maintained by the *won consent* of the dominated. It is therefore, like consensus, subject to renegotiation and ongoing redefinition. Also, the consensus may be broken as the ideologies of the *subordinate* cannot always be accommodated.

Institutions such as the mass media, the family, the education system and religion play a key role in the shaping of people's awareness and consciousness, and thus can be agents through which hegemony is constructed, exercised and maintained. The definition and workings of hegemony have obviously undergone adaptation since Gramsci's day. The power, reach and global penetration of the media as instruments of hegemony have intensified issues of control and influence, though these need to be viewed in relation to the impact over the last decade of INTERNET communication, which some commentators claim is in the process of undermining hegemony.

In the view of Todd Gitlin in his chapter, 'Prime time television: the hegemonic process in television entertainment' in *Television: The Critical View* (Oxford University Press, 1994), edited by Horace Newcomb, hegemony is sustained by the flexibility of its IDEOLOGY: 'In the twentieth century, the dominant ideology has shifted toward sanctifying consumer satisfaction as the premium definition of "the pursuit of happiness", in this way justifying corporate domination of the economy. What is hegemonic in consumer capitalist ideology is precisely the notion that happiness, or liberty, or equality, or fraternity can be affirmed through the existing private commodity forms, under the benign, protective eye of the national security state.'

In other words, consumerism and its playmate CELEBRITIZATION have become integral to a coalition of interests, including that of the state. On the face of it, the INTERNET has shown a maverick tendency to serve different purposes because of the opportunities it provides to individuals and self-generated groups largely free of authority and supervision.

The flexibility of hegemony both in principle and practice which Gitlin remarks on must, however, give us pause, for imperial ambitions exist as prominently on the Net as elsewhere. As ownership and control increasingly become global phenomena, hegemony is as likely to flex its muscles as suffer diminishment. See ELITE;

IDEOLOGICAL STATE APPARATUSES; MCDON-ALDIZATION. See also *TOPIC GUIDE* under MEDIA: VALUES & IDEOLOGY.

▸ Jacques Ellul, *The Technological Society* (Knopf, 1964); Antonio Gramsci, *Selections from the Prison Notebooks* (Lawrence & Wishart, 1971).

Helical model of communication See DANCE'S HELICAL MODEL OF COMMUNICATION.

Heliological metaphor See VISIONS OF ORDER.

He/man language Dale Spender in her book *Man Made Language* (HarperCollins, 1990 edition) refers to the principle by which for several centuries the terms *he* and *man* have been used to include women – for example, *man*kind. According to Spender, this principle has the effect not only of contributing to the perspective of MALE-AS-NORM – of males as more worthy – but also of helping to construct the invisibility of women in language, thought and reality. Not everyone, of course, either agrees with or employs this principle, and it has become the focus of some critical scrutiny in recent decades.

Herman and Chomsky's propaganda model See CONSENT, MANUFACTURE OF.

Hermeneutic code See CODES OF NARRATIVE.

Hermeneutics The science of interpretations or understanding. The word is taken from the Greek, *hermeneuein*, and derives from Hermes, messenger of the gods; it means to make things clear, to announce or unveil a MESSAGE. In film study, a hermeneutic code, or 'code of enigma', explains by one device or another the mysteries of the plot – the situation or predicament characters find themselves in – and indicates the process of resolution.

Heterophily See HOMOPHILY.

Hidden agenda When the underlying objective of an act of communication is different from that which is stated. See IMPRESSION MANAGEMENT.

Hidden needs Vance Packard in *The Hidden Persuaders* (Penguin, 1960, with updated editions) cites eight 'hidden needs' which the adman can cater for. These are: emotional security; reassurance of worth; ego-gratification; creative outlets; love objects; a sense of power; a sense of roots; and immortality. See ADVERTISING; HOT BUTTONS; MASLOW'S HIERARCHY OF NEEDS; VALS TYPOLOGY.

Hierarchy Classification in graded subdivisions. The hierarchy of a company starts at the top with the chairperson or managing director; a social hierarchy is dominated by the ELITE classes, who varyingly influence those CLASS divisions below them. In the media, the dominant hierarchy are the owners, top executives, major shareholders, boards of directors, etc. See ORGANIZATION CULTURES.

High and low context communication See COMMUNICATION: INTERCULTURAL COMMUNICATION.

Highbrow Someone considered to be a member of the intellectual and cultural ELITE, whose tastes are, by definition, considered to be aesthetically superior to those of the majority, is deemed a highbrow. Highbrow tastes are limited to the few. The terms middlebrow and lowbrow are used to indicate a level of intellectual capacity of cultural appreciation judged against the standards of the highbrow elite. See CULTURAL CAPITAL.

High fidelity See GRAMOPHONE.

High-speed photography One of the wonders of modern technology, but a preoccupation of photographers from the earliest pioneering days, the high-speed flash process slows down, or magnifies, time: the splash of a drop of water, the trajectory of a bullet, can be reduced to slow motion that permits astonishing revelations. Foremost among developers of ultra-high-speed electronic flash photography as a tool of scientific analysis was the American Harold Edgerton, inventor of the stroboscope.

The term *stroboscopic photography*, or strobe photography, refers to pictures of single or multiple exposure taken by flashes of light from electrical discharges, permitting objects moving at their natural speeds to be observed in slow motion – the rate of the slow motion depending on the frequency of the strobe and object. When the flash frequency exactly equals that of the rotation or vibration, the object is illuminated in the same position during each cycle, and appears stationary.

In contrast to high-speed photography, *time-lapse photography*, by taking pictures at timed intervals of seconds, minutes, hours or days, speeds up, or telescopes, time. In a few moments of film we can see the germination of a seed, the hatching of an egg, or blow-fly maggots consuming a dead mouse. Both high-speed and time-lapse photography are employed most widely to answer two questions: how is it done, and what went wrong? See PHOTOGRAPHY, ORIGINS.

Historical allusion The practice in NEWS reporting of making reference – alluding to – events in the past perceived as being similar to current events, recognized by AUDIENCE as such, and potentially capable of adding to the NEWS VALUE of a story. For example, a convenient (and often all-too-easy) way to demonize an 'enemy' leader is to compare him to Hitler, the

activities of 'enemy' peoples to Nazis, and to use past terminology such as 'holocaust' and 'death camps'.

Following the terrorist assault on the US Pentagon and the World Trade Centre in New York on 11 September 2001 (9/11), and the subsequent build-up to war by the US and UK, the British Prime Minister Tony Blair was compared in the media – varyingly and queryingly – with the pugnacious war-leader Winston Churchill, the nineteenth-century PM William Gladstone (whose mission was to 'pacify Ireland') and the gunboat-happy British Foreign Secretary Lord Palmerston. Blair's public performance following the London bombings of July 2005 was similarly described as Churchillian and recalling the London Blitz during the Second World War.

Such use of analogies and metaphors is seen generally to serve to place events into contexts familiar to the public. However, in *Compassion Fatigue: How the Media Sell Disease, Famine, War and Death* (Routledge, 1999), Susan D. Moeller issues a cautionary note on this practice. 'The effect,' she believes, has been 'that readers and viewers' have come to 'overlook the complexity' of reported conflicts, and 'to believe in the simplicity of comparisons'.

Historical revisionism Term addressed specifically to attempts in the US and Europe to write out of history the genocide of the Third Reich of Adolph Hitler; to deny that the atrocities ever took place.

Hollywood Centre of the US film industry, located in California, providing maximum sunshine for outdoor shooting and some magnificent scenery. In 1908 *The Count of Monte Cristo*, begun in Chicago, was completed in California and the first Hollywood studio was established in 1911. Within a year another fifteen film companies had set up in business. The Hollywood studio system reached its peak in the 1930s; its fortunes have since fluctuated, at first knocked sideways by the advent of TV, then restored by a simple philosophy of 'if you can't beat them, join them'. Today Hollywood plays a key role in the US television industries, while its film enterprises are profitably supplemented by global sales of movies on video and DVD.

▶ Janet Wasko, *Hollywood in the Information Age: Beyond the Silver Screen* (Polity Press, 1994); David Bordwell, *The Way Hollywood Tells It: Story and Style in Modern Movies* (University of California Press, 2006; also a University Press Audiobook, 2010); James Walters, *Alternative Worlds in Hollywood* (Intellect, 2008); Matthew Alford, *Reel Power: Hollywood Cinema and American Supremecy* (Pluto Press, 2010).

Holography With the invention of the laser in 1960 an intriguing new form of three-dimensional photography, named holography, became possible. Though the theory originated with Dennis Gabor as early as 1947, development was not possible until an intense source of 'coherent' light became available, which the laser supplied. Coherent light is light of 'pure' colour containing waves of a single frequency whose wave-fronts all move in perfect step.

Derived from the Greek, *holos*, or whole, and *gram*, message, the hologram is made without a lens by splitting a laser beam so that part of it is directed at the subject and part becomes a reference beam. When light reflected from the subject and light from the reference beam meet on the photographic plate, the wave-fronts create interference patterns which contain all the visual information needed to construct a three-dimensional image of the subject, amazingly lifelike, and viewable from different angles. Recent developments have enabled holograms to be made for viewing by ordinary white light.

Holography has proved a boon to the world of business. Machine-readable reflection holograms store digital information in hundreds of layers within the emulsion of a film or plastic card. The holographed data on a credit card, passport, security access card or ticket to a high-priced event, forming a three-dimensional pattern, can be read electronically, thus providing a formidable obstacle to counterfeiting.

Home Service Name of the BBC's prime talk RADIO channel, founded in 1939. The name was changed to BBC Radio 4 in 1967. See BBC DIGITAL; RADIO 1, RADIO 2, RADIO 3, RADIO 4, RADIO 5 LIVE.

Homo narrans See NARRATIVE PARADIGM.

Homophily Interacting individuals who share certain attributes – beliefs, VALUES, educational background, social status – are said to be *homophilous*. Communication is commonly believed to be closer when between people who are homophilous as they are more likely to share a common language-level and pattern of MEANING. On the other hand, *heterophily* refers to the degree to which interacting individuals differ in these attributes. Generally, heterophilic interaction is likely to cause some disturbance and confusion to the individuals concerned, and thus more effort is required to make communication effective. See COGNITIVE CONSISTENCY THEORIES.

Horizons of expectation See EXPECTATIONS, HORIZONS OF.

Horizontal integration See INTEGRATION: VERTICAL AND HORIZONTAL.

Horse-race story Approach to NEWS coverage of elections anchored in the metaphor of horse racing (or any other competitive sport), in which the political party ahead in the opinion polls is 'winning at a canter' or is losing ground to the opposition, which is coming up fast on the outside. Todd Gitlin in 'Bites and blips: chunk news, savvy talk and the bifurcation of American politics' in *Communication and Citizenship: Journalism and the Public Sphere* (Routledge, 1991), edited by Peter Dahlgren and Colin Sparks, calls this mode of campaign journalism an 'enchantment – with means characteristic of a society which is competitive, bureaucratic, professional and technological all in one ... This is a success culture bedazzled by sports statistics and empty of criteria for value other than numbers to answer the question, "How am I doing?" Journalists compete, news organizations compete, the channel aggression of the race is what makes their blood run'. See TOPIC GUIDE under NEWS MEDIA.

Hot buttons Barry Feig in *Hot Button Marketing* (Adams Media, 2006) argues that 'consumers buy from motivations they are not even aware of. Those motivations are the Hot Buttons of marketing ... Hot Buttons are the keys to the psyches of your customers'. He claims, 'People don't buy products and services. They buy the satisfaction of unmet needs'. Feig identifies sixteen such emotional hot buttons that can be pressed to hook into the motivations of consumers. These range from 'the desire for control' to the 'wish fulfillment' hot button. The choice of which hot button(s) to use will depend on factors such as the needs, interests, values, lifestyles and priorities of the consumer group being targeted. See HIDDEN NEEDS; MOTIVATION RESEARCH (MR); VALS TYPOLOGY.

Hot media, cold media Terms coined by Marshall McLuhan, author of *The Gutenberg Galaxy* (University of Toronto Press, 1962) and *Understanding Media* (Routledge & Kegan Paul, 1964), and forming a basic tool of his analysis of the media. For McLuhan, 'hot' media extend one sense-mode with high-definition data: examples of 'hot' media are RADIO and FILM. 'Cold' media provide, in contrast, low-definition data, requiring much more participation by the individual. Examples are TV, telephone and cartoons. As Ralph Berry queries in *Communication Through the Mass Media* (Edward Arnold, 1971), 'all this is highly controversial ... for example, the "hot-cold" metaphor runs speedily into difficulties (is the living theatre significantly different in the front or the rear stalls?)'.

H

HUAC: House Un-American Activities Committee

Inspiration for Arthur Miller's play, *The Crucible*, which explored the nature of community hysteria leading to the persecution of 'suspected witches'. In the case of HUAC, set up by the US Congress in 1938 (and not wound up until February 1969), the witches were Communists, alleged Communists or Communist sympathizers. Among the witch-finders were Richard Nixon, later Republican president, and the notorious Senator Joseph McCarthy.

Every section of society was scrutinized for suspects, not the least the entertainment industry. One committee member, John Rankin – a 'virulent bigot who equated Jews with Communists and Negroes with monkeys', as Godfrey Ryan describes him in his three-part series of articles, 'Un-American activities' (*Index on Censorship* 1, 2 and 3, 1973) – declared 'one of the most dangerous plots ever instigated for the overthrow of this government has its headquarters in Hollywood ... The information we get is that this is the greatest hot-bed of subversive activities in the United States'.

HUAC's pursuit of 'subversives' thrived in the years of the Second World War and flourished even more in the years of the so-called Cold War. In *Joe McCarthy and McCarthyism: The Hate That Haunts America* (McGraw-Hill, 1972), Roberta Fauerlicht writes, 'Since the government had to find subversives before they could subvert, people were punished not for what they did but for what they might do. Men and women found their loyalty questioned because they liked Russian music, because they had books on Communism in their libraries, or because they believed in equality for blacks or civil liberties for Communists.' One hundred and thirty-nine government employees were fired as a result of HUAC investigations, although not a single one was found guilty of subversive acts. Hearst newspapers were prominent in applauding the work of HUAC.

Perhaps the most insidious result of HUAC activities was *blacklisting*, whereby 'suspects' – often mysteriously – failed to gain employment or were laid off from work for specious reasons. Blacklisting was keenly felt in the movie industry and in broadcasting. It is a cruel irony that where accusations were publicly proved to be fraudulent, blacklisting increased rather than decreased.

Prominent victims of HUAC scrutiny were Arthur Miller himself (he was refused a passport by the State Department in 1956), the black singer Paul Robeson, Hollywood scriptwriters Ring Lardner and Dalton Trumbo, film directors Elia Kazan and Martin Ritt (see Ritt's movie of 1976, *The Front*, on the theme of blacklisting), writers Clifford Odets and Lillian Hellman, and actors Zero Mostel (star of *The Front*) and Edward G. Robinson. During the 1960s HUAC's dominance of the hearts and minds of the American nationals was repeatedly challenged. Indeed its momentum had been seriously checked by TV commentator Edward R. Murrow, who produced a *See It Now* documentary (1954) in which he suggested that McCarthy had repeatedly stepped over the fine line between investigating and persecuting.

The nightmare spell which McCarthy cast over a nation was mercifully broken when he died of liver failure in May 1957. In 1969 HUAC was reincarnated as the House Internal Security Committee which, learning the lessons of the past, opted for low-key activities, holding fewer sessions and avoiding unpleasant confrontations by not subpoenaing unfriendly witnesses. See USA – PATRIOT ACT (2001). See also TOPIC GUIDES under MEDIA ETHICS; MEDIA: FREEDOM, CENSORSHIP; MEDIA HISTORY.

Human Rights Act (UK), 2000

Incorporating into British law the European Convention on Human Rights, the Act has been described as the biggest change in UK law since the Bill of Rights of 1688. The Act guarantees freedom of thought, conscience and religion; freedom of expression, and this right 'shall include freedom to hold opinions and to receive and impart information and ideas without interference by public authority and regardless of frontiers'.

Freedom of expression is deemed to be subject to 'duties and responsibilities' and conditional upon 'restrictions and penalties as are prescribed by law and are necessary in a democratic society, in the interests of national security, territorial integrity or public safety'. That freedom is equally subject to criteria concerning 'the prevention of disorder or crime, for the protection of health and morals, for the protection of the rights of others, for preventing the disclosure of information received in confidence or for maintaining the authority and impartiality of the judiciary'.

Discrimination 'on any ground such as sex, race, colour, language, religion, political or other opinion, national or social origin, association with a national minority, property, birth or other status' is prohibited. The right to life, to a fair trial, to respect for private and family life, freedom of assembly, the right to marry are all confirmed. See TOPIC GUIDE under COMMISSIONS, COMMITTEES, LEGISLATION.

Human Rights Watch An independent, non-governmental organization funded by private individuals and foundations worldwide, with offices in New York, Washington, Rio de Janeiro and Hong Kong. Formed in 1978, the Human Rights Watch investigates and reports on the state of human rights in Africa, the Americas, Asia, the Middle East and the signatories of the Helsinki accord on human rights, scrutinizing such matters as arms transfers, women's and children's rights and prison conditions. The organization also makes grants to writers who have suffered from political persecution.

Hunt Committee Report on Cable Expansion and Broadcasting Policy (UK), 1982 Set up by the Conservative government, the three-man committee chaired by Lord Hunt, a former top civil servant, was required to report and make recommendations on the future of cable systems in the UK. In brief, the report, the result of a hurried investigation begun in March 1982 and finalized by September, recommended a future pattern of cable transmission systems marked by few regulations, many channels and as much ADVERTISING as operators could attract.

Pay-as-you-view TV was not given the green light by Hunt on the grounds that major national events, such as the Cup Final or Wimbledon, might be siphoned-off from national access and be seen only by those on cable and able to pay. 'Cherry picking' – cabling just for the well-off suburbs of a city, for example – was also to be barred. See CABLE TELEVISION.

Hutton Report (UK), 2004 In 2003, former Lord Chief Justice of Northern Ireland Lord Brian Hutton conducted an inquiry in public into the suicide of a UK government weapons-expert, Dr David Kelly. The terms of the inquiry were 'urgently to conduct an investigation into the circumstances surrounding the death of Dr Kelly'. The context was the second Iraq war; the issue, whether government claims that Saddam Hussein possessed weapons of mass destruction capable of being deployed on the UK within 45 minutes had been 'sexed up'.

The trigger for this controversial claim was an early-morning BBC radio report by journalist Andrew Gilligan. The source of Gilligan's information, kept secret by the journalist but brought into the public domain via government ministries, was Kelly, who was sceptical of claims relating to WMDs (Weapons of Mass Destruction). Faced by a barrage of publicity, and of a House of Commons panel of MPs asking sharp and often aggressive questions, Kelly had alleg-edly taken his own life.

Lord Hutton took evidence from 74 witnesses over 25 days and his report was 740 pages long. He completely exonerated the government, government communication services, the civil service and security services and directed the blame entirely towards the BBC. Ben Pimlott in a *Guardian* survey of opinions, 'Returning verdicts on the judge' (30 January 2004), spoke of the Report's prose style as 'exemplary', the clarity 'impeccable' and the judgments 'unambiguous', yet the author knew of 'no precedent for a major report so black-and-white in its conclusions, or quite so supportive of the powers that be'.

The publication of the report led to the resignation of the Chairman of the BBC, Sir Gavyn Davies, the Director General, Greg Dyke and Andrew Gilligan – and it stirred up a hornets' nest of protest and accusations that the report had been a 'whitewash'. See BUTLER REPORT (UK), 2004; PHILLIS REVIEW OF GOVERNMENT COMMUNICATIONS (UK), 2004.

Hybridization Described by James Lull in *Media, Communication, Culture* (Polity Press, 1995) as the 'fusing of cultural forms'. Travel and the global nature of much of the media and music industries enable a cultural form which originates in one culture to be disseminated quickly and easily to other cultures, where it may well be influenced by and merge with local cultural forms, thus producing a cultural *hybrid*. Lull gives the example of rap music that has travelled widely from its roots in US inner-city ghettos and has become incorporated into other kinds of popular music in a number of other countries. See GLOBAL VILLAGE.

In particular, TV is seen as a prime agency of hybridization (or *hybridity*). It represents a site of travel in which people draw images, IDEOLOGY and visions of lifestyles other than their own. Arguments over hybridity centre on whether TV as a travelling medium creates cultural *diversity* or results in cultural *homogeneity*, or sameness. In addition to TV, and perhaps more importantly, the INTERNET can be seen as an agency of hybridization.

Hyperreality Just as hyperactivity is enhanced or beyond-the-normal activity, hyperreality, in the age of mass production and reproduction, offers us reality-plus. Images, simulations of reality, serve to extend and heighten the realities they represent, to the point, in the view of some commentators, that they are more real than, and preferable to, actual realities. Both the French philosopher Jean Baudrillard and the Italian semiologist Umberto Eco cite Disneyland as having taken realities to a point where they achieve hyperreality – a substitute that supplants, even erases the original and replaces it with the 'reality' of simulation. In short, that which is imitating is more real, more significant, than that which is imitated.

Baudrillard, in *Selected Writings* (Polity Press, 1988), edited by Mark Poster, refers to the 'society of the image' in which the real is subsumed by 'all the entangled orders of simulation'. Eco does not go so far as to say that the hyperreal supplants the real, but in *Travels in Hyperreality* (Picador, 1986) he states that imitations are indeed coming to be preferred, by those who create them and those who consume them, to the original. He refers to such fakes as deriving from 'a present without depth'. He classifies Disneyland as the home of the 'total fake'. However, the real, he believes, can be reasserted through a sense of history that 'allows an escape from the temptations of hyperreality'.

Hypertext Electronic text on computer, interfaced with links or pathways to other, related texts. For example the text of a novel might be the primary text while a web of supplementary texts – background notes, critiques, biographies – can be instantly consulted and cross-referenced.

Hyphenized abridgement Herbert Marcuse (1898–1979) uses this term in *One-Dimensional Man* (Sphere Books, 1968) to describe the practice of the PRESS of concentrating information by bringing two or more descriptive facts together by using a hyphen. Thus: 'Georgia's high-handed-lowbrowed governor ... had the stage set for one of his wild political rallies last week'. Marcuse argues, 'The governor, his function, his physical features and his political practices are fused together into one indivisible and immutable structure' by the press employing this device, 'which in its natural innocence and immediacy, overwhelms the reader's mind. The structure leaves no space for distinction ... it moves and lives only as a whole'.

Hyphenized abridgement, used repeatedly and assertively, 'imposes images while discouraging, on the part of the reader, conceptualization; that is, it beats him/her with images, but impedes thinking; and thus the media define for us the terms in which we are permitted to think'. See DETERMINER DELETION; EFFECTS OF MASS MEDIA; FRANKFURT SCHOOL OF THEORISTS; PSEUDO-CONTEXT; TABLOIDESE.

Hypodermic needle model of communication More a METAPHOR representing a view of the effects of the mass media, the hypodermic needle 'model' has formed a point of general reference in crediting the media with power over audiences. The basic assumption is that the mass media have a direct, immediate and influential effect upon audiences by 'injecting' information into the consciousness of the masses.

The AUDIENCE is seen as impressionable and open to manipulation. Like other early models of communication flow from the media, it overlooks the possible effects of INTERVENING VARIABLES (IVS) in the communication process, and presents the masses as being unquestioning receptacles of media messages. This sense of the all-powerfulness of the media is a central feature of early mass-society research. It is now regarded as crude and simplistic. See AUDIENCE: ACTIVE AUDIENCE; COMMERCIAL LAISSEZ-FAIRE MODEL OF (MEDIA) COMMUNICATION.

Hypothesis The first step of the research cycle is the formulation of an hypothesis. This will usually be based on an idea or hunch gained by the researchers from their own reading of earlier studies and/or their own observations of society. Starting with this basic idea, a researcher usually proposes a working hypothesis that will guide the research. The hypothesis proposes a relationship between certain social phenomena: for example, that people from a higher-education background are more likely to read what is regarded as the quality press.

Not all hypotheses are expressed as formal statements: some can be a general collection of ideas about particular social phenomena. All hypotheses, though, must be capable of EMPIRICAL testing; that is, they must be capable of being proved or disproved by facts and argument. The hypothesis will determine the nature of the research design – the method of collecting the information that will prove or disprove the hypothesis.

Once this information has been collected and analysed, the hypothesis is reviewed. It may be proved, disproved or amended; indeed, in many cases the original hypothesis may have been modified during the data collection stage of the research. Alternatively it may be decided that further evidence is required before any conclusion is reached. See MEDIA ANALYSIS.

Hypothesis of consonance See NEWS VALUES.

I

Icelandic Modern Media Initiative (IMMI)
In 2008 the Icelandic parliament passed into
law an idealistic initiative gathering together
best practices from all over the world in furthering and protecting freedom of information.
Comparison has been made with off-shore tax
havens; only in the Icelandic case, what is being
given haven is information – access to it and the
reporting of it.

Model practices from a number of countries
have been incorporated, based upon the
presumption of the public's right to access
government documents and the notion that in
the context of global communication, the media
know no national boundaries. The initiative
arose following the banking collapse in Iceland
during which vital information was kept from
the people of the country. The situation led to
demands for transparency from banking, business and government. See TOPIC GUIDE under
MEDIA: FREEDOM, CENSORSHIP.

Iconic Describes a SIGN which, in some way,
resembles its object; looks like it, or sounds
like it. Picture-writing is iconic, as is a map.
ONOMATOPOEIA (word sounds that resemble real
sounds) is iconic. In SEMIOLOGY/SEMIOTICS the
iconic is one of three categories of sign defined by
American philosopher C.S. Peirce (1834–1914):
where the *iconic* describes or resembles, the
index is connected with its object, like smoke
to fire; while the *symbol* has no resemblance or
connection, and communicates MEANING only
because people agree that it shall stand for what
it does. A word is a symbol. The categories are
not separate and distinct: one sign may be made
up of all three categories. See TOPIC GUIDE under
LANGUAGE/DISCOURSE/NARRATIVE.

Id, ego, super-ego See SELF-IDENTITY.

Ideational functions of language The use of
language to explore, interpret, construct and
express views about ourselves and the world.
Another major function of language, the interpersonal function, is that of establishing and
maintaining relationships with others. Clearly
both functions are often present in communicative encounters and the two are often related.

Identification The degree to which people
identify with and are influenced by characters,
fictional or otherwise, in books, radio, films and
TV has fascinated media analysts, especially in
areas of behaviour where such identification
might lead to anti-social activity such as violence.
'To identify with' has two common meanings: to
participate in the situation of someone whose

plight has caught one's sympathy; and to incorporate characteristics of an admired person into
one's own identity by adopting that person's
system of values.

Identification is used in a more specific sense
when we discuss the degree of influence that
persons, institutions and the media may have on
others. In 'Processes of opinion change', *Public
Opinion Quarterly*, 25 (1965), Herbert Kelman
explores three basic processes of social influence
with reference to opinion change and to communication. These are *compliance, identification*
and *internalization.* The first position in this
'social influence theory' refers to the acceptance
of influence in the hope of either receiving a
reward or avoiding punishment. Identification
in this sense occurs 'when an individual adopts
behaviour derived from another person or a
group because this behaviour is associated with
a satisfying self-defining relationship to this
person or group'.

As with compliance, change or influence is reliant upon the external source and 'dependent on
social support'. Internalization occurs when the
proposed change, the influence, is fully believed
in, accepted, taken fully on board, because the
influenced person 'finds it useful for the solution
of a problem or because it is congenial to his
own orientation, or because it is demanded of
his own values'.

Linked to the analysis of the extent to which
identification takes place is the interest in how
we identify along lines of age, CLASS or GENDER.

Identity See SELF-IDENTITY.

Idents Channel identities; snapshot films,
reminding TV viewers in graphic, computer-
generated form which channel they are tuned to.
Idents are designed to establish an image of the
channel, a channel branding. The generic ident is
basically suitable for any programme introduction, while specific idents create images closely
reflecting the nature of particular programmes
or series.

Ideological presumption Term describing the
view that journalists and the NEWS media are
necessarily and unavoidably ideologically impli-
cated in the MESSAGE systems and DISCOURSES
to which they contribute. In *The Foucault Reader*
(Random House, 1984) the French philosopher
Michel Foucault states that the social relations
of power produce and constitute knowledge,
and that socio-economic power lies at the root
of what we are, what we believe and what we are
shown – through the media. The position locates
journalists as *cultural workers*, in the service of
those with power and authority.

The view is challenged by Matthew Kieron in 'News reporting and the ideological presumption' published in the *Journal of Communication*, Spring 1997. He declares that the 'presumption' is 'either false, incoherent or trivial'; it is 'overextended, misplaced and distortive'. Kieron argues that we should, in our scrutiny of journalism, acknowledge that in broadly free societies there are sufficient variables in interpretation and approach to escape the grip of the voice of authority.

Ideological state apparatuses This term derives from the work of the French philosopher Louis Althusser (1918–90). Ideological state apparatuses (ISAs) are those social institutions which, according to Althusser, help shape people's consciousness in a way that secures support for the IDEOLOGY of those who control the state; that is, the dominant ideology. Such institutions include education, the family, religion, the legal system, the party-political system and the mass media. The dominant ideology is thus represented as both natural and neutral. As a result it becomes almost unseen, taken-for-granted.

In contrast there is what Althusser calls the RSA (*Repressive State Apparatus*), comprising the law, police, military; these are brought into operation – using coercion or the threat of it – when the ISAs are failing to secure their objectives of social control through persuasion. Authority relies on the media to serve as an ISA and to support situations when the RSA is brought into action. See COMMON SENSE; DISCOURSE; ELITE; HEGEMONY; MYTH; POWER ELITE. See also *TOPIC GUIDES* under MEDIA: POLITICS & PRODUCTION; MEDIA: VALUES & IDEOLOGY.

Ideology An ideology is a system of ideas and beliefs about human conduct which has normally been simplified and manipulated in order to obtain popular support for certain actions, and which is usually emotive in its reference to social action. Karl Marx (1818–83) used the term to apply to any form of thought that underpins the social structure of a society and which consequently upholds the position of the ruling class. The twentieth-century French philosopher Louis Althusser (see above), drawing on the work of Marx, saw ideology as being an unconscious set of VALUES and beliefs that provide frames for our thinking and help us make sense of the world.

Ideology can often be found to be hiding (or hidden) under terms such as 'common sense', the 'common sense view', which Marx would claim was merely the view of the ruling CLASS

translated by repeated usage through channels of communication into wisdom as apparently natural as fresh air; a process sometimes referred to as *mystification*. Within society there may be a variety of contending ideologies at play, representing different sets of social interests, each seeking to extend recognition and acceptance of its way of making sense of the world, its own capacity to give order and explain social existence.

Language itself may be seen not as a neutral medium, but as ideological, thus in its use ensuring that ideology is present in all discourses. Each may seek to become the dominant ideology, and it can be argued that the capacity to make use of the channels of mass communication is crucial to either achieving or maintaining this position.

The use of the media in this respect is the focus of much research and analysis. German sociologist Karl Mannheim (1893–1947) in *Ideology and Utopia* (Routledge, 1936) distinguishes between ideas that defend existing interests, the status quo, which he terms *ideologies*, and ideas that seek to change the social order, which he terms *utopias*. See CONSENSUS; CULTURAL APPARATUS; DISCOURSE; DOMINANT DISCOURSE; HEGEMONY; IDEOLOGICAL STATE APPARATUSES; MALE-AS-NORM. See also *TOPIC GUIDE* under MEDIA: VALUES & IDEOLOGY.

▶ Mike Cormack, *Ideology* (Batsford, 1992); Tuen A. van Dijk, *Ideology: A Multidisciplinary Approach* (Sage, 1998).

Ideology of detachment See IMPARTIALITY.

Ideology of romance An aspect of HEGEMONY in which the perceptions and attitudes of women, in particular teenaged girls, are 'shaped' by DOMINANT DISCOURSES into accepting the roles of wife and mother within an essentially patriarchal social structure. Wendy Halloway in 'Gender difference and the production of subjectivity' in *Changing the Subject: Psychology, Social Regulation and Subjectivity* (Methuen, 1984), edited by Julian Henriques *et al*, calls this mode of communicative conditioning a 'to have and to hold' discourse which links acceptable behaviour with monogamous relationships.

The ideology of romance can be found expressed and reinforced in magazines, films, pop songs, ADVERTISING and SOAP OPERAS. It is, in the view of Mary Ellen Brown, author of *Soap Operas and Women's Talk: The Pleasures of Resistance* (Sage, 1994), an ideology that 'can leave young women few options'. At the same time the ideology of romance can be seen as a rational response to, and a means of coping with, material and economic subordination, encapsulated in the song *Diamonds Are A Girl's Best Friend*. Says Brown, 'Such romantic ideology positions young women in such a way that they can easily decide to buy into the system.' Most feminist writers would argue that the ideology of romance is coterminous with the notion of the *ideology of dependence*.

Ideology of silence The belief, held chiefly by governments, that the best way of 'getting things done' in, for example, attempts to win the release of political prisoners or hostages, is through secret, behind-the scenes diplomacy. The same rule would apply in cases where one government may feel obliged, perhaps through public pressure, to protest to another country. The problem in such cases is that there is no real proof that a protest has been made and consequently no evidence as to the nature of that proof.

In an article entitled 'Against silence' in *Index on Censorship* (February 1987), Jacob Timerman, formerly a political prisoner in Argentina, expands on the notion of the ideology of silence and concludes that 'the only way to solve problems of decency and civilization is to speak out'.

Idiolect An individual's personal dialect which incorporates the individual variations that exist between people in their use of punctuation, grammar, vocabulary and style. No two people are likely to express themselves in exactly the same way.

Idiot salutations See PHATIC LANGUAGE.

Image A likeness; a representation; a visualization. The term can have several meanings depending on the context in which it is used. It may refer to a visual representation of reality such as is seen in a photograph; it can also refer to a mental, imaginative conception of an individual, event, location or object as, for example, one conjures up an image of a character in a novel. The image does not merely reproduce, it interprets; it has added to it certain meanings. The writer, artist, architect, photographer and advertising image-maker all use assemblies of signs in order to represent or suggest states of mind, or abstractions. Van Dyck's equestrian portrait of Charles I portrays the monarch on a noble steed against a background suffused with dramatic light. All the details of this painting converge to create an image of kingship, thus a process of *symbolization* has taken place.

The purpose of image-creation obviously varies, but all images are devised in order to evoke responses of one kind or another, usually emotional. Images often serve as psychological triggers effecting responses that are not always easy to articulate. Advertisements regale us with images of the good life; they play upon our perceived needs (see HIDDEN NEEDS; MASLOW'S HIERARCHY OF NEEDS). Image is also something we present of ourselves – our best face, the way we want the world to perceive us. Politicians work at their images more than most, and these are portrayed to fit in with the image appropriate to a public figure whose aim is to impress voters by his/her qualities of leadership and trustworthiness.

Sometimes we talk of a person whose image has 'slipped', which seems to indicate a connection between image and *performance* (see IMPRESSION MANAGEMENT) and that it relates to an ideal. For the artist, whatever his/her medium, imagery is central to expression. It is a part of STYLE and a key to the construction of MEANING. See METAPHOR. See also *TOPIC GUIDE* under REPRESENTATION.

Image, rhetoric of In its contemporary use, the word *rhetoric* is interchangeable with persuasion or PROPAGANDA; thus the rhetoric of the image indicates the use of images as a means of persuasion; of inculcation or reinforcement of ideological positions. The power of the image is employed, particularly in the NEWS, to *empower* the overt or covert MESSAGE. Such images have the effect of closing off, by their dramatic and emotional nature, alternative ways of reporting and interpreting realities.

IMAX Canadian film-projection system developed in the 1970s, notable for the vastness of its screen for 70mm film; installed in the UK in 1983 at the National Museum of Photography, Film and Television in Bradford, and later in London. See OMNIMAX.

Immediacy A prime NEWS VALUE in Western newspaper, radio and television news-gathering and presentation. At the centre of decision-making and of news control is the time factor, usually related to the daily cycle. In his article 'Newsmen and their time machine', in *British Journal of Sociology* (September 1977), Philip Schlesinger points out that in industrialized societies an exceptional degree of precision of timing is necessary in our working lives. 'Especially noteworthy are those who operate communication and transport systems ... Newsmen ... are members of a stopwatch culture.'

Immediacy shapes and structures the approach to news-gathering. The report of an event must be as close to the event as possible, and ideally the event should be reported as it happens; the pure type of immediacy would be the live broadcast. News, says Schlesinger, is 'hot' when it is most immediate. 'It is "cold", and old, when it can no longer be used during the newsday in question.' Immediacy is not only a vital factor in the selection of a story for treatment; it also helps fashion that treatment. Pace is what counts in presentation, especially in TV news where the priority is to keep the audience 'hooked'.

The danger with such emphasis on immediacy is that news tends to be all foreground and little background, all events and too little context, all current happening and too little concentration on historical and cultural frameworks. Schlesinger rounds off his article by saying that it is plausible to argue 'that the more we take note of news, the less we can be aware of what lies behind it'. See EFFECTS OF MASS MEDIA. See also *TOPIC GUIDE* under NEWS MEDIA.

Immersion The degree to which the virtual, the invented – as in VIRTUAL REALITY – submerges the real perception system of the user. The more that VR works to the exclusion of contact with the real, physical world, the more it is classified as being immersive. The prospect of near-total immersion, on the part of some users, is a matter of interest and concern. As Frank Biocca says in 'Communication within virtual reality: creating a space for research' in *Journal of Communication*, Autumn 1992, 'If people eventually use VR technology for the same amount of time that they spend watching television and using computers, some users could spend 20 or more years "inside" virtual reality.'

Impact of the mass media See EFFECTS OF THE MASS MEDIA.

Impartiality Just as Professor Stuart Hall doubts the existence, in media terms, of OBJECTIVITY, so Philip Schlesinger, in a remarkable study of the workings of BBC News, has cast doubt on the possibility of impartiality. Between 1972 and 1976, Schlesinger had a unique research opportunity to conduct in the newsrooms of Broadcasting House and the Television Centre, London; fieldwork which attempted 'to grasp how the world looks from the point of view of those studied' – the reporters, correspondents, editors and managing editors in the most prestigious media organization in the world. He interviewed more than 120 members of BBC news staff and spent 90 days in observation. His findings were published in *Putting 'Reality' Together: BBC News* (Constable, 1978; Methuen/University paperback, with new Preface, 1987).

Several key words framed the basic principles of news production: *balance, objectivity, responsibility, fairness* and *freedom from bias*; and these were, in the 'ordinary discourse of newsmen' for the most part 'interchangeable'. They could be gathered under one banner, that of impartiality – what Schlesinger refers to as the central mediating factor in news-processing at the BBC, 'the linchpin of the BBC's ideology'.

Schlesinger found this a notion 'saturated with political and philosophical implications' and classifies the 'ideology of detachment' as in essence an example of 'latter-day Mannheimianism'. In *Ideology and Utopia* (Routledge, 1936), Karl Mannheim explained how a 'socially unattached intelligentsia' could play a role in society that was above all conflict, capable of representing to society all relevant views.

It is a theory which has regularly been condemned as an unrealistic dream, though the doctrine has remained persistently attractive: by virtue of their education, argued Mannheim, the intellectuals, *déclassés*, are exposed to the 'influence of opposing tendencies in social reality'; thus theirs is the potential to improve social integration, to produce a new CONSENSUS by means of 'dynamic mediation'.

The theory implies that it is possible to view the world in a value-free way, and to act accordingly. Schlesinger calls value-freedom 'a myth', yet one that in terms of the BBC's aspiration to impartiality, to being above the fray, 'is believed by those who propagate it' as well as being 'essential for public consumption'. Such beliefs, Schlesinger argues, 'anchor news production in the status quo'. What the BBC produces as news is 'structurally limited by the organization's place in Britain's social order' and the main consequence of that position is that 'the outputs of broadcasting are, in general, supportive of the existing social order'.

Schlesinger's findings were a snapshot in time, and it would be interesting to survey them in relation to the trouble the BBC encountered with government in 2003 in their reporting of the war in Iraq and their questioning of official claims concerning weapons of mass destruction. See HUTTON REPORT (UK), 2004. See also *TOPIC GUIDE* under MEDIA ISSUES & DEBATES.

Imperialism in information systems See MEDIA IMPERIALISM.

Implication In the production of TEXTS, particularly the NEWS, much is left implicit: assumptions about prior knowledge, expectations about response are implied rather than made manifest, and this implication is generally if not always *ideological*. As Tuen van Dijk says in 'Media contents: the interdisciplinary study of news as discourse', in *A Handbook of Qualitative Methodologies for Mass Communication Research* (Routledge, 1991), edited by Klaus Bruhn Jensen and Nicholas W. Jakowsky, 'The analysis of the "unsaid" is sometimes more revealing than the study of what is actually expressed in the text.' This would suggest a key aspect of the study of media – a focus on what is omitted, or *absent*, as well as what is included and present.

Impression management Technique of self-presentation defined by Erving Goffman in *The Presentation of Self in Everyday Life* (Anchor, 1959; Penguin, 1971). Because most social interaction requires instant judgments, alignments and behaviour, the individual must be able rapidly to convey impressions of him/herself to others, highlighting favourable aspects, and concealing others.

Goffman argues that impression-management has the character of drama: all social ROLES, he believes, are, in a sense, performances in which it is important to set a scene and rehearse a role, and this means coordinating activities with others in the 'drama'. Thus we put up a front, 'that part of the individual's performance which regularly functions in a general and fixed fashion to define the situation for those who observe the performance'.

Our formal, public selves Goffman calls *front region* and our more informal, relaxed selves, *back region*. Indeed Goffman believes that all our roles depend upon the performer having a back region; equally all front-region roles rely upon keeping the audience out of the back regions.

Teams as well as individuals operate in front and back regions: in a restaurant, for example, the front-stage conduct of the team of waiters and other staff subscribes to formal rules and rituals, even a mystique. Behind the scenes, however, the performers relax. The need to unify in sustaining an expected version of reality – of smartness, politeness, professionalism – gives way to a back-stage reality where individual differences can be freely aired without letting the team, or the performance, down. See SELF-PRESENTATION.

Independent Television (ITV), UK The broadcasting monopoly held by the BBC since the inception of broadcasting in Britain ended with the UK Television Act of 1954. This set up the Independent Television Authority (ITA), its responsibility to establish, control and review independent commercial television (ITV). The service opened in London in 1955 and in the Midlands and North England the following year, each region having its own programme-producing studios.

ITV companies are licensed to broadcast for limited periods (see FRANCHISES FROM 1993, UK;

FRANCHISES FOR INDEPENDENT TELEVISION, UK). They are currently licensed and supervised by Ofcom (see OFCOM: OFFICE OF COMMUNICATION, UK) born of the COMMUNICATIONS ACT (UK), 2003. The ITV landscape has altered substantially from the early days of commercial television, largely in the direction of concentration of company ownership. For example, in 1992 Yorkshire TV bought up Tyne Tees TV, only to become part of Granada TV in 1997.

South England witnessed similar convergence. Following the collapse of ITV Digital in face of competition from BSkyB (see BRITISH SKY BROADCASTING, BSKYB), the remaining major players, Carlton and Granada, merged and became ITVplc (2004). Of the fifteen regional broadcasters in the UK, the ITV Network controls eleven.

Concentration has been one trend; another has been the weakening of ITV's commitment to the principles and practices of public service broadcasting (see PUBLIC SERVICE BROADCASTING (PSB)). What remains an imperative is the requirement to provide regular national and local news; provided nationwide by Independent Television News (ITN).

Referred to as Channel 3 in order to differentiate it from the BBC's Channels 1 and 2, and Channel 4, ITV programming is in the main entertainment-based, targeting the kind and size of audiences likely to appeal to commercial TV's taskmasters, the advertisers. Programmes with high audience-ratings such as *Who Wants to Be a Millionaire?* and *X Factor*, and soaps such as *Coronation Street* and *Emmerdale*, are the dominant and highly profitable fare of ITV; the loss has been the demise of quality current affairs programmes such as *World in Action* (Granada) and *This Week* (Rediffusion/Thames).

In February 2011 PRODUCT PLACEMENT was permitted in programme content for the first time in the UK (for all broadcasters), offering rich pickings for provider and advertiser alike but marking a worrying incursion of commerce into the creative process (see CONSUMERIZATION; CULTURE: GLOBALIZATION OF).

ITV was closely involved with the BBC in the launch of Freeview in 2002 and Freesat in 2008. After suffering dramatic losses in advertising revenue during the economic recession in the UK in 2009, ITV sprang back to profit in 2011, though success in the highly competitive field of commercial broadcasting depends on the sustainability of current popular programmes and the audience drawing-power of new ventures.

▶ Wikipedia: comprehensive and reliable entries.

Index Short for *Index librorum prohibitorum*, a list of proscribed books. The Council of Trent, in attempting to turn the tide against the Protestant Reformation, drew up a set of rules about what Roman Catholics should, or rather should not, read. In accordance with these rules the Index was published by authority of Pope Paul IV in 1559. In its current form, the Index is a list not only of works prohibited in their entirety to the faithful but also of works not to be read unless or until they are corrected.

The *Index expurgatorius*, or Expurgatory Index (1571), specifies passages to be expurgated in works otherwise permitted. Appropriately, the word has been used in the title of the UK magazine whose chief aim is to counter such repressions of information and expression, *Index of Censorship*.

Index as a sign See SIGN.

Indicators In INTERPERSONAL COMMUNICA- TION the means by which one communicator conveys his/her attitude and response to another – feelings of attraction or rejection, of evaluation or esteem of the other person. Proximity, for example, is an ideal indicator of liking (unless, of course, it becomes a SIGN of threat or intimida- tion). Also important as indicators are frequent eye contact, body orientations and spontaneous gestures. See PROXEMICS.

Inductive reasoning Involves the drawing of conclusions from collected observations and data; from evidence. The acceptability of the conclusions drawn depends upon whether or not the type and quantity of evidence can reason- ably be said to support them. It is important to recognize how limited such conclusions may be. Someone unfamiliar with traffic observing traffic flow between 10am and 2pm for one week, in a busy street, may for example note that when the red traffic light is illuminated, cars in front of the light stop.

He/she may conclude that the illumination of the red traffic-light caused the cars to stop – certainly at the times at which he/she was observing the traffic. The observer, however, could not reasonably draw conclusions about why this was the case, or whether or not this occurred at times when he/she was not observ- ing the traffic. That would require further investigation.

Deductive reasoning involves the application of an already accepted generalization or gener- alizations to an individual case. It is the reverse of inductive reasoning. Someone who has accepted, for example, that drinking too much alcohol before driving is dangerous might as a consequence regulate the intake of alcohol at a party if he/she were driving home – a decision based upon deductive reasoning. See EMPIRI- CAL; HYPOTHESIS.

Indymedia Exemplifing open-platform, activist journalism, Indymedia are usually volunteer- run, their aim to build a fairer and just society and involve citizens more fully in public life. The first IMC (Independent Media Centre) was created in Seattle, Washington, in 1999 in advance of the the World Trade Organization (WTO) conference of that year, with a view to counteracting the bland, uncritical reporting of such events by traditional mass media. Within two years the number of IMCs grew to 60, and by 2009 there were 170 worldwide.

Global liaison led to the formulation of a set of Principles of Unity (POU) in San Francisco in 2001 based on equality, decentralization and local autonomy, favouring open-exchange and open access, 'allowing individuals, groups and organizations to express their views, anony- mously if desired'.

As with all volunteer-run enterprises, Indyme- dia need funding to survive and develop, hence impermanence is built into their DNA. See BLOGOSPHERE; GENRE; JOURNALISM: CITIZEN JOURNALISM.

Inference According to Gail Myers and Michele Myers in *The Dynamics of Human Commu- nication* (McGraw-Hill, 1985), 'A statement of inference is a guess about the unknown based on the known.' We often *infer*, that is make assump- tions, about people, events, behaviour and so on. In doing so we add these inferences to our observations. For example if we saw a young man running away from an elderly woman, we might infer that he had stolen her purse; however we might be quite wrong and he might be running for a bus.

We automatically make inferences and in doing so rely on a range of factors such as past experiences, stereotyping, VALUES, attitudes and beliefs. Yet inferences can mislead both ourselves and others if they stray too far from our actual observations or accepted facts. Clearly, in communication we need to be careful to distinguish between statements of fact and statements of inference.

Inflection The patterns of alteration or modula- tion in the pitch of a person's voice.

Influence of the mass media See EFFECTS OF THE MASS MEDIA.

Info-rich, info-poor See INFORMATION GAPS.

Information blizzards Traditionally, a nation's citizens have been granted too little information on which to base decisions and choices; yet by the late twentieth century, that position appeared to have been reversed: nowadays there is too much information – blizzards of it – and the result is not undernourishment but confusion. John Keane in *The Media and Democracy* (Polity Press, 1991) writes, 'The world seems so full of information that what is scarce is citizens' capacities to make sense of it. The release of new opinions through the media rarely shatters unaccountable power. Publicity better resembles the throwing of snowballs into a blizzard – or the blowing of bubbles into warm summer's air.'

The term 'blizzard' has also been used to describe the multiple and interacting images we encounter daily, brought to us with ever-new associations by the media (see TEXT). For the French cultural critic Jean Baudrillard, the sheer volume of signifiers in the contemporary world of mass communication, so readily and regularly detached from their original SIGNIFICATION, results in meaning itself being too lost in the blizzard to be worth the trouble of attempting to define it. Consequently in this cultural blizzard, anything can be made to mean anything. See Chapter 5, 'Baudrillard's blizzards' in Nick Stephenson's *Culture, Social Theory and Mass Communication* (Sage, 1995), in which Baudrillard's 'irrationalism' is challenged. See INFORMATION SURPLUS.

Information commons Equivalent to 'common land', that is space or territory accessible, by right, to the public, without charge; thus information commons relate to public space, or the public *domain*, with regard to information and expression. Some commentators fear that the public domain as typified by our shared culture has long been subject to a process of *enclosure*, or PRIVATIZATION, in which cultural artefacts and practices, once part of the information commons, have been turned into private property accessible only as commodity.

A particular area of concern is copyrighting, which has extended far beyond the protection of the works of writers, artists, musicians, etc. into images, sounds, acronyms and names. In a tom. paine.com online article (1 August 2002) entitled 'Stopping the privatization of public knowledge: the endangered public domain', David Bollier of the Annenberg School of Communications, Philadelphia, talks of 'content autocrats' dedicated to copyright enforcement operating in an atmosphere of 'fully fledged cultural pathology'. The enforcement of copyright in the courts has proved a serious intrusion upon the freedoms of cultural expression, believes Bollier. He cites McDonald's threatening 'every food business that uses "Mc" in their names' or Mattel threatening 'legal action against art photographers who use images of Barbie dolls to comment on American beauty ideals'. See CULTURE: COPYRIGHTING CULTURE; NEW MEDIA.

Information gaps Many scholars have focused their studies on the inequality in the distribution of information among different groups in societies. Such inequalities are mostly the result of educational or social CLASS differences, with the advantage being enjoyed by the better-educated and those in the higher-status groups. The role of the mass media in creating, widening or narrowing information gaps has prompted widespread concern.

There are differing kinds of gaps depending on the nature of the information.

Gaps – between *information-rich* and *information-poor* – may close or widen with time. It had been thought that the increasing flow of information from the mass media might help to narrow such gaps, but the evidence here is mixed. Whilst the media may have the potential to close gaps, it seems that an advantage remains with those with most communication potential and that new gaps open as old ones are closed. Gaps exist between groups within the same societies, but the greatest inequalities are between developed and less developed nations, most of the channels of global communication being controlled by the former.

This means that not only have the developed nations the potential to acquire and disseminate more information, but they also have the potential for considerable control of the flow and content of the information going to less developed nations. Thus the majority of information flowing from info-disadvantaged countries is *raw*, compared with the *mediated* information that flows in the other direction. Information gaps can also be generated, reinforced or modified through patterns of INTERPERSONAL COMMUNICATION.

Current research interest focuses on the contribution the INTERNET makes to traditional information gaps. In theory and much practice, the Net and the possibilities brought about by networking, both informational and social, represent powerful forces for bringing about access to information as well as participation in the exchange of information worldwide – not the least of the potential contributors to gap-closure being the mobile phone. See DIFFUSION; DISCURSIVE GAP; INFORMATION SURPLUS;

I

J-CURVE; MEDIA IMPERIALISM; MISINFORMED SOCIETY; MOBILIZATION.

Information society The Japanese were the first to apply the tag to this stage in the growth of the industrial era in which information has become the central and most significant 'commodity'. Through the development of computers and associated electronic systems, such aspects of national and international life as class relationships, government, economics and diplomacy are being visualized as functions of information transfer. Indeed we are at the point when information and wealth are practically one and the same thing.

With the development of satellite surveillance it is now possible for a country highly advanced in informatics to know more about the topography of, say, a developing nation than that country's own government does. And information is power that crosses national boundaries with greater ease than invading armies.

Information is not only a commodity but also a social and cultural resource, raising questions of social allocation and control, with such associated problems as PRIVACY, access, commercial privilege and public interest.

Information suburbs See TECHNOLOGICAL DETERMINISM.

Information surplus Any situation in which there is more information available than is necessary, called-for or manageable, but most relevantly for the study of communication, the availability of information on the INTERNET. In the age of digital distribution and reception of information, surplus is standard; often to the point of being information *overload*. The problem of over-abundant information is compounded by the fact that online, it is generally free and fast.

What is in short supply – from the point of view of traditional media communication and equally of online communicators (bloggers, contributors to YOUTUBE and websites across the board) – is *attention*. Users may only amount to scores or hundreds; they may also amount to millions; but how can their attention be captured and preferably retained? – this in the context of dramatic reductions in newspaper readership wherever online activity has increased.

A regular complaint concerning online news and entertainment websites is that they undercut traditional mass media, draw off audiences, subvert the market for information and threaten professional standards (see JOURNALISM: CITIZEN JOURNALISM). Not only does much online purveying of news and views come free to the user, there is also the alluring potential for *interactivity* to the point where the user becomes the producer.

The more enterprising traditional media have already taken on board the need for diversification of approaches, for nurturing FEEDBACK and providing for interactivity, and professional journalists these days operate their own blogs. Further, the press offer free access to their own online news, comment and information services. Rather than fighting off the 'blogger opposition' they now scout the BLOGOSPHERE for news feeds and comment.

A problem for the future is whether news organizations can continue to provide a slice of their services for free. In 2010, Rupert Murdoch's News International decided that the online news services of *The Times* would only be available on subscription. The jury remains out on whether users could be persuaded to pay for what they formerly had for free.

Prevailing worries concerning information surplus, audience fragmentation and competition for attention relate to such trends as the switch of attention by online users – especially among young people, for whom newspaper reading in particular is in decline – from news to entertainment.

Information technology (IT) Micro-electronics plus computing plus telecommunications equals IT. Its formal definition is framed as follows in a UK Department of Industry publication (1981) for Information Technology Year (1982): 'The acquisition, processing, storage and dissemination of vocal, pictorial, textual and numerical information by a micro-electronics-based combination of computing and telecommunications.'

Information Technology Advisory Panel (ITAP) Report on Cable Systems See CABLE TELEVISION.

Infotainment Term used to describe the trend towards enhancing the entertainment value of factual programmes in order to increase their popularity with audiences. There are concerns, expressed by a number of analysts, that NEWS and current affairs coverage may become trivialized by such an approach. See DOCUMENTARY.
▶ Daya Kishan Thussu, *News as Entertainment: The Rise of Global Infotainment* (Sage, 2008).

Inheritance factor The TV programme which captures a viewer's attention paves the way for those that follow.

Inner-outer directed See VALS TYPOLOGY.

Inoculation effect In the processes of persuasion, a relative immunity in an AUDIENCE may be induced by 'inoculation' prior to a concerted exercise in persuasion: if an audience is fore-warned about an attempt to persuade it, when that attempt occurs, they are more capable of defence against influence. Studies have also shown that the inoculation effect can be achieved by generating counter-arguments in people, through exposure to a mild version of arguments against their opinions as well as to arguments supporting their existing views. This seemed to 'inoculate' them against being persuaded later by more robust arguments against their beliefs, opinions and attitudes.

Insert shot In film, a close-up inserted into a dramatic scene, usually for the purpose of giving the AUDIENCE a view of what the character on the screen is seeing, such as a newspaper head-line, the title of a book, a cigarette, a letter, etc. See SHOT.

Institution The term *institution* is generally applied to patterns of behaviour which are estab-lished, approved and usually of some perma-nence. Such patterns of behaviour are normally rational and conscious. The term can be applied to both the *abstract* – for example, religion – and the *concrete* concept of an institution, such as a media organization. The patterns of behaviour to which this term is applied can vary, from simple routine acts to large complexes of standardized procedures governing social relationships in a large section of the population.

All institutions embody a particular complex of norms, VALUES, ROLES and role structures. They also, often, evolve relationships with other institutions. FUNCTIONALIST analysis tends to represent institutions as performing the func-tions essential to the maintenance of society, and views them as being mutually sustaining. Some research has, however, indicated the relative *autonomy* of most institutions and the often conflicting goals to be found within them. Much research into the mass media has concentrated upon their *corporate* role as major social institu-tions; upon their norms, values and relationships with other major social institutions.

Insult signals Generally defined as those signals which are always insulting, no matter what the context in which the signal has been made; though these do vary substantially between nationality and nationality. Such signals may communicate disinterest, boredom, superiority, contempt, impatience, rejection and mockery. *Dirt signals* appear to be universal and refer to human and animal waste-products on the basis, presumably, of: cleanliness – good; filth – bad. Picking the nose with forefinger and thumb in

Syria means 'Go to the blazes' while in the UK a gesture of derision is to pull an imaginary lava-tory chain at the same time as holding the nose. In Greece, pushing the flat of the palm towards another's face is the ultimate insult signal; called the *moutza*, the signal represents a thrusting of filth into the opponent's face, and has ancient roots (see RELIC GESTURES).

Beyond the insult signal is the *threat signal*, an attempt to intimidate without, necessarily, having recourse to blows. Threat signals are mostly substitutes for rather than prologues to violence, because such signals are checked, held back, and distance is maintained between threatener and threatened. Also, such signals are often redirected – to the insulter's own body, such as mock strangulation.

Of *obscene signals*, the phallic-displaying gesture is as old as civilized man. The Romans, for example, referred to the middle finger as the impudent and obscene finger. The more expressive forearm jerk is common throughout the Western world and is employed particularly in France, Italy and Spain as a threatening insult by one male towards another; however, in the UK, the signal tends to be more a crude sexual comment than a direct insult. The V-sign, with palm facing the communicator, is the most potent gestural insult in Britain along with its single-finger variant. See COMMUNICATION, NON-VERBAL (NVC); NON-VERBAL BEHAVIOUR: REPERTOIRE.

Integrateds See VALS TYPOLOGY.

Integration New ideas and behaviour vary in the degree to which they are incorporated into the continuing operations and way of life of members of a SOCIAL SYSTEM or sub-system. The term *communication integration* is used to describe the degree to which the members/units of a social system are interconnected by INTER-PERSONAL COMMUNICATION channels.

Integration: vertical and horizontal Vertical integration occurs when an enterprise owns and controls all the processes and stages involved in production. An example is where a film company initiates ideas and facilitates all aspects of production, marketing and ADVERTISING, as well as having direct or associate interest in product dissemination and consumption, including related promotional merchandise. In contrast, horizontal integration indicates concentration of ownership across rather than within products and producers – in media terms, CROSS-MEDIA OWNERSHIP and control.

Integrity of the text See TEXT: INTEGRITY OF THE TEXT.

Intellectual property See CULTURE: COPY-RIGHTING CULTURE; TEXT: INTEGRITY OF THE TEXT.

Intensity Some NEWS stories receive much more concentrated, more intense, coverage by the media than others, and tend to dominate or stifle competing stories. Intensity, if appropriate in terms of timing, and if given the promise of frequency, abetted by consistency of coverage, equals *influence*, at least in the sense of making audiences aware.

General elections provide useful illustrations of the intensity of media coverage. National attention is focused on the event (usually more on personalities than issues) and the legitimacy of the event is given substance and flavour. In contrast, local elections derive neither substance nor flavour from the media, who largely ignore them. See DISPLACEMENT EFFECT; EFFECTS OF THE MASS MEDIA; NEWS VALUES.

Interaction The reciprocal action and communication, verbal or non-verbal, between two or more individuals, or two or more social groups. Successful negotiation of social interaction requires considerable mastery of the verbal and non-verbal communication deemed appropriate to the social situation and the social ROLES being performed. As Judy Gahagan comments in *Social Interaction and its Management* (Methuen, 1984), 'The mere presence of others introduces a degree of control over our demeanour that we do not display when we are alone ... This control over demeanour suggests we follow quite strict sets of rules of conduct.' Most of these rules however are unwritten and learned, often unconsciously, through the process of SOCIALIZATION.

There are arguably more ritual and rules involved in our everyday social interaction than we realise. Gahagan notes that 'we are in fact quite unaware of their existence until someone does something "odd"'. See IMPRESSION MANAGEMENT; INTERPERSONAL COMMUNICATION; SELF-MONITORING; SELF-PRESENTATION.

★**Interaction Process Analysis, 1950** Robert F. Bales devised an influential scheme for the recording and analysis of interaction within groups, known as Interaction Process Analysis or IPA. The aim of IPA is to track the acts of communication that take place within an observed group discussion; the assumption being that group discussion is typically focused on the completion of some kind of task. Bales and his fellow researchers identified twelve main types of communicative acts that commonly occur during group interaction. These twelve

types were then organised into four main categories relating to socio-emotional and task behaviour, as illustrated in the diagram on the following page.

An example here might be:

Speaker 1 How do we all feel about these proposals? (8)

Speaker 2 They are far too complex. Can anyone explain them? (11)

Bales argued that IPA tracked not just the patterns of group interaction, but also the relationship between communicative acts and roles. For example, if an individual scores highly in the task categories, and especially in types 4–6, it may be evidence that they are the task leader of the group. He also identified common problems encountered within groups – communication, evaluation, control, decision-making, tension reduction, and reintegration – and argued that IPA can monitor the way in which these are dealt with by the group.

▶ Robert F. Bales, *Interaction Process Analysis: A Method for the Study of Small Groups* (Chicago University Press, 1950).

Interactive television Allows viewers to respond to programmes in ways ranging from seeking further programme information to making contact with programme-makers or providing instant FEEDBACK to questions put to them. The familiar red button invites the viewer into more specialized scenarios, many of which end up as marketing ploys. Early predictions for interactive TV suggested a new age of instant public response, of quick-fire referendums, of election and other polls 'going electronic'.

The greater potential for interactivity of the Internet may have checked if not stalled the use of TV as an interactive device – unless of course the TV and computer are one and the same as typified by the multi-functional mobile phone (see MOBILIZATION). However, for the majority of users the sophisticated mobile serves as an entertainment centre, interactivity focusing on the personal and the popular rather than issues of social or political concern. See REALITY TV.

Intercultural communication See COMMUNICATION: INTERCULTURAL COMMUNICATION.

Internal credits See SPONSORSHIP OF BROADCAST PROGRAMMES (UK).

Internalization See IDENTIFICATION.

Internationalization of Media Studies See MEDIA STUDIES: THE INTERNATIONALIZATION OF MEDIA STUDIES.

International Commission for the Study of Communication Problems Report, 1980 See MCBRIDE COMMISSION.

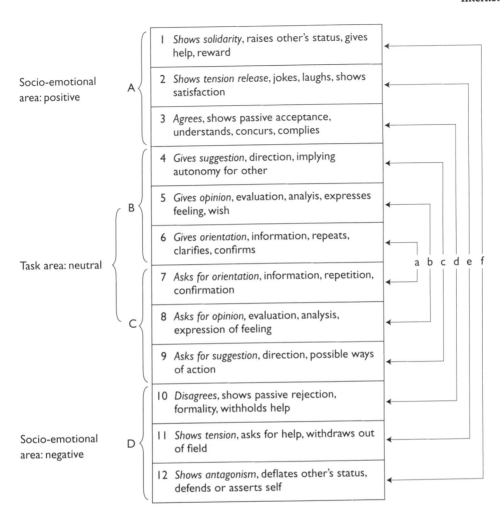

1 *Shows solidarity,* raises other's status, gives help, reward

2 *Shows tension release,* jokes, laughs, shows satisfaction

3 *Agrees,* shows passive acceptance, understands, concurs, complies

4 *Gives suggestion,* direction, implying autonomy for other

5 *Gives opinion,* evaluation, analyis, expresses feeling, wish

6 *Gives orientation,* information, repeats, clarifies, confirms

7 *Asks for orientation,* information, repetition, confirmation

8 *Asks for opinion,* evaluation, analysis, expression of feeling

9 *Asks for suggestion,* direction, possible ways of action

10 *Disagrees,* shows passive rejection, formality, withholds help

11 *Shows tension,* asks for help, withdraws out of field

12 *Shows antagonism,* deflates other's status, defends or asserts self

Socio-emotional area: positive — A

Task area: neutral — B, C

Socio-emotional area: negative — D

a b c d e f

Note: The coding categories in interaction process analysis and their major relations: (a) problems of communication; (b) problems of evaluation; (c) problems of control; (d) problems of decision; (e) problems of tension reduction; (f) problems of reintegration; (A) positive reactions; (B) attempted answers; (C) questions; (D) negative reactions.

Interaction Process Analysis, 1950

International Federation of Journalists (IFJ) Organization whose testament is that 'the promotion of a new world order of information is first and foremost the business of journalists and the trade unions and not of states, governments or any pressure group of whatever kind'. The IFJ is made up of chiefly Western journalists and was formed to monitor and counteract moves through the United Nations Educational, Scientific and Cultural Organization (UNESCO) to 'impose', through government legislation, a new world information order. See MCBRIDE COMMISSION; MEDIA IMPERIALISM; WORLD PRESS FREEDOM COMMITTEE.

International Law Enforcement Telecommunications Seminar (ILETS) See INTERNET: MONITORING OF CONTENT.

International Programme for the Development of Communication (IPDC) See MCBRIDE COMMISSION; MEDIA IMPERIALISM.

Internet The introduction to the Internet Society's *A Brief History of the Internet* states: 'The Internet has revolutionized the computer and communications world like nothing before. The invention of the telegraph, telephone, radio, and computer set the stage for this unprecedented integration of capabilities. The Internet is at once a world-wide broadcasting capability, a mechanism for information dissemination, and a medium for collaboration and interaction between individuals and their computers without regard for geographic location.'

Basically, the Internet is the story of computers being linked up and sharing information – a story that began in the 1960s in the US, the ideas and the developments emerging out of the universities but driven by the US government's Advanced Research Project Agency (ARPA), which was anxious to link computers at research establishments and to form a network of information distribution which could survive a nuclear attack.

In 1961 Leonard Kleinrock of the Massachussets Institute of Technology (MIT) published 'Information flow in large communication nets', the first paper on packet-switching (PS) technology. The following year another MIT scientist, J.C.R. Licklider, proposed a global network of computers to share information in research into scientific and military fields. Lawrence Roberts, also of MIT and later of the University of California (UCLA), connected the two universities using dial-up telephone lines. In 1966 Roberts' paper 'Towards a cooperative network of time-shared computers' outlined what would become ARPANET, the precursor of the Internet as we know it. This became a reality, coming online in 1969 with four computers connecting universities, then swiftly increasing.

The term 'Internet' was not in general use before 1974, but two years earlier e-mailing had become a familiar practice across the distribution network. Already by 1971 Project Gutenberg, started up by Michael Hart, was making electronically available copyright-free books, the first being the text of the US Declaration of Independence. The first computer 'chat' was conducted at UCLA in 1972.

The first desktop workstation was introduced in 1983 and the Domain Name System introduced the following year. In 1989 British scientist Tim Berners-Lee and others at the Geneva laboratories of the European Organization for Nuclear Research (CERN) proposed common protocols for computer intercommunication globally. The basic idea of the WORLD WIDE WEB (www) was to merge the technologies of personal computers, computer networking and hypertext into an easy-to-use global information system. Formed in 1994, the World Wide Web Consortium was born not only of the vision of Berners-Lee, but also that of US scientist Michael Dertonzos, whose notion of the Information Marketplace contributed to the creation of the Web.

Commercial interchange began in 1992, Delphi being the first commercial online service, followed by America On Line (AOL), Prodigy and CompuServe, to be dramatically followed in the browser, server and Internet service provider market by the arrival of Microsoft (see MICROSOFT WINDOWS).

In many ways the Internet has evolved into a global AGORA, an open space in which public DISCOURSE can be conducted without the MEDIATION of those in authority and without the GATEKEEPING and AGENDA-SETTING of the mass media. Citizens speak to citizens, groups to groups, across geographical and political boundaries (see BLOGGING; BLOGOSPHERE; NETWORKING: SOCIAL NETWORKING; WEB: WORLD WIDE WEB; WEB 2.0), and certainly governments are worried about the freedom of access to and use of information which computer-mediated communication allows.

Worries are regularly expressed about such issues as privacy, spam, identity theft and the mental and physical health hazards of spending 'too much time on the Net', especially now that networking is no longer tied to computers but is available through smart phones wherever and whenever the user feels inclined.

The Internet makes for speed, for instant exchange, but no old-fashioned postbox ever accumulated the mountain of e-mails which is the common lot of the majority of Net users. Such mountains, however, are indicators of the shifts in practice and activity in traditional media systems, marketing and advertising: the Internet has become the global marketplace, the world's shopping mall.

Remarkable is how free the Internet continues to be, that is in terms of being charge-free, though on this the tide is slowly beginning to change. *Paywalls* to free access are increasing, since providing information and entertainment comes at a price that even online advertising does not sustain.

The Internet has thrived on freedom and it has also been viewed as a force for equality: there are few financial, social or linguistic barriers to access and participation; a fact that increasingly concerns those organizations doing business on the Net (see NET NEUTRALITY). Concerns of another kind are exemplified by widespread state CENSORSHIP of Net activity in many countries worldwide. Paywalls are exceeded in height by *firewalls* – blocking of messages, surveillance and repressive legislation which in some countries, such as China, condemns those whose online comments are considered dissident to lengthy terms of imprisonment.

Naturally crime has taken to the Internet with relish, prompting in 2001 the European Council to draw up a cybercrime treaty. Few countries have resisted bringing in legislation attempting to exercise control over Net use (see INTERNET: MONITORING OF CONTENT; REGULATION OF INVESTIGATORY POWERS ACT (RIPA), UK).

A regular focus of research is the issue of how far the Internet is a *leveller*; that is, through the ease of exchange, helping to level up opportunities for peoples of different economic, cultural and political status. Does the Net help the poor – individuals, communities and nations – or does it somehow threaten to increase the INFORMATION GAP (or digital gap) between them and better-off individuals, communities and nations?

In 'The Internet and knowledge gaps: a theoretical and empirical investigation' (*European Journal of Communication*, March 2002), Heinz Bonfadelli focuses on the *digital divide*, identifying four barriers preventing people from benefiting fully from the information society. These Bonfadelli lists as (1) a continuing lack of basic computer skills 'and connected fears and negative attitudes especially among older and less educated people'; (2) restrictions on *access* to the necessary hardware and software – in short, expense; (3) the lack of user-friendliness; and (4) the actual use of the Net. Bonfadelli quotes research that suggests the 'higher the educational background [of the user], the more people use the Internet in an instrumental way, and the lower the educational background, the more people seem to use the Internet only for entertainment purposes'.

A UK report in 2010 by the charity Thee-Learning Foundation confirmed an increasing gap between the educational performance of rich and poor pupils in Britain, a million children from poorer families having no access to a computer at home and two million with no Net access. The Chief Executive of the Foundation, Valerie Thompson, said that 'without the use of a computer and the ability to go online at home, the attainment gap that characterizes children from low-income homes is simply going to get worse'. The findings were made public at the same time as Michael Gove, Minister of Education of the UK Conservative-Liberal Democrat coalition government, had cut £100 million from

a fund earmarked for new school computers and broadband facilities.

The overall picture offered by Internet practices and development is dichotomy typical of public perspectives on new technologies – the optimistic versus the pessimistic. E.M. Uslander in 'Trust, civic engagement and the Internet' published in *Political Communication* (No. 21, 2004) believes the Net is 'neither the tool of the Devil nor the new Jerusalem'. Where particular attention might be concentrated is on the online habits of the younger generation, where there is evidence that the Net is used for purposes of entertainment and social interaction without the compensating grace of online (or offline) seeking of information and debate.

The Internet Society's *Brief History* concludes: 'The most pressing question for the future of the Internet is not how the technology will change, but how the process of change and evolution itself will be managed ... With the success of the Internet has come a proliferation of stakeholders – stakeholders now with an economic as well as an intellectual investment in the network. We now see ... a struggle to find the next social structure that will guide the Internet in the future.

'The form of that structure will be harder to find, given the large number of concerned stake-holders. At the same time, the industry struggles to find the economic rationale for the large investment needed for the future growth ... If the Internet stumbles, it will not be because we lack for technology, vision, or motivation. It will be because we cannot set a direction and march collectively into the future.' See DIGITAL NATIVES, DIGITAL IMMIGRANTS; PLASTICITY: NEUROPLASTICITY AND THE INTERNET; MOBILIZATION.

▶ Lucy Kung, Robert G. Picard and Ruth Towse, eds, *The Internet and the Mass Media* (Sage, 2008); James C. Witte and Susan E. Mannon, *The Internet and Social Inequalities* (Routledge, 2010); Tim Wu, *The Master Switch: The Rise and Fall of Information Empires* (Borzoi Books, 2011).

Internet: denial of service (DoS) Internet service providers have the power to censor, and indeed they are often under a legal requirement to do so (see REGULATION OF INVESTIGATORY POWERS ACT (RIPA)(UK), 2000). When in 2010–11 WIKILEAKS made public sensational documents produced by US ambassadorial staff around the world, a number of Net platforms 'denied' Wikileaks access, and more critically for the survival of the organization, use of its funds; in other words they froze its assets or refused to pay its bills. The action proved a risk for the 'deniers' as Net commanders quickly organized an anti-denier campaign. This does not remove the ongoing danger to Net users of denial, as the defence of Wikileaks arose from its celebrity.

Internet: monitoring of content The 'freedom' of the Net has long been a matter of public concern, on the one hand by those in authority anxious about websites preaching political and racial hatred or providing PORNOGRAPHY, and on the other hand by those fearful of ambitions held chiefly by governments, to censor network exchange. Some commentators have argued that the key to network systems is not freedom but SURVEILLANCE. As Darin Barney points out in *Prometheus Wired: The Hope for Democracy in the Age of Network Technology* (University of Chicago Press, 2000), 'networked computers have emerged as surveillance technology par excellence'.

In May 1999 it was reported that European Commission ministers were planning to require manufacturers and operators to build in 'interception interfaces' to the Internet and all future digital communication systems. Details are set out in Enfopol 19, a restricted document leaked to the Foundation for Information Policy Research, based in London. In an article entitled 'Intercepting the Internet' in the UK *Guardian* (29 April 1999), freelance writer Duncan Campbell reports on plans requiring 'the installation of a network of tapping centres throughout Europe, operating almost instantly across all national boundaries, providing access to every kind of communications including the net and satellites'.

According to Campbell, the plans were formulated by an organization founded in 1993 by the American FBI, the International Law Enforcement Telecommunications Seminar (ILETS), made up of police and security agents from some twenty countries. ILETS has had success in persuading the European Community to adopt its recommendations contained in a document drawn up in Bonn in 1994, the International Requirements for Interception. These have become law in the US.

At meetings in subsequent years, ILETS has tightened further its monitoring requirements. So far, the major obstacle to the fulfilment of the demands listed in Enfopol 19 has been the cost of enforcement. However, the ease with which governments introduce laws of restriction, and the determination of those governments to spy on the Net, promises a serious reining-in of Internet freedoms. See REGULATION OF INVESTIGATORY POWERS ACT (RIPA)(UK), 2000.

See also TOPIC GUIDE under MEDIA: FREEDOM, CENSORSHIP.

▶ Jan van Dijk, *The Network Society* (Sage, 2nd edition, 2005); Stephen Cole and Jay G. Blumler, *The Internet and Democratic Citizenship: Theory, Practice and Policy* (Cambridge University Press, 2009).

Internet: wireless Internet The use of the Net without cables or wires; transmission of Internet messages by wireless technology. Developed in the late 1990s, 'wi-fi' (wireless fidelity) serves to connect computers, smart phones and digital audio to the Internet via access points (WAP, wireless access points) or 'hotspots'. These can be located over a few square miles or in a single building, area, or even a garden shed.

Originally used in rural areas where cabling proved too costly, wi-fi soon moved into cities. Although it has liberated digital users from wires and cables, wi-fi suffers from interference and sudden disconnection, and data transmission is insecure. It is also subject to *piggybacking* where, without the subscriber's permission or knowledge, wi-fi trespassers get their transmissions for free. See MOBILIZATION.

Interpersonal communication Describes any mode of communication, verbal or non-verbal, between two or more people. While the term MEDIO COMMUNICATION has often been used to specify interpersonal communication at a greater than face-to-face distance, such as when the communication is by letter, e-mail or telephone, it is most useful to keep the definition as wide and unprescriptive as possible.

Michele and Gail Myers in *The Dynamics of Human Communication* (McGraw-Hill, 1985) write, 'Interpersonal communication can be defined ... in relation to what you do with it. First, you can use communication to have an effect on your "environment", a term which means not only your immediate physical surroundings but also the psychological climate you live in, the people around you, the social interchanges you have, the information you want to get or give in order to control the questions and answers of your living. Second, you use communication to improve the predictability of your relations with all environmental forces, which act on you and on which you act to make things happen.'

A great many factors affect the sending and receiving of MESSAGES within the process of interpersonal communication, only some of which can be mentioned here. In constructing a message the sender may be influenced by his/her SELF-CONCEPT and perception of the receiver(s) and the knowledge, beliefs, attitudes, VALUES, assumptions and experiences on which they rest;

his/her personality; the role he/she is playing at the time; the state of his/her MOTIVATION; his/her communicative competence; and the context in which the communicative encounter takes place. All of these factors and others affect decisions about SELF-PRESENTATION. They also influence the receiver(s) and how he/she will interpret messages sent.

Barriers often arise in interpersonal communication, and these are categorized by Richard Dimbleby and Graeme Burton in *More Than Words: An Introduction to Communication* (4th impression, Routledge, 2007) into three main types: *mechanical* (physical barriers such as a noisy environment); *semantic* (barriers arising from an inability to understand the signs, verbal or non-verbal, being used by one or more of the persons involved in the transaction); and *psychological* (barriers caused by a range of psychological factors, for example the message may be perceived as a threat to one's values). Common errors made in the process of social perception, such as stereotyping, also constitute psychological barriers to effective communication.

Speech and non-verbal communication are the main means by which messages are sent in interpersonal communication; non-verbal communication being particularly important in providing FEEDBACK and in regulating interaction. Interpersonal communication is also affected by the context in which it takes place – in GROUPS or organizations, for example – and factors found there such as norms, MORES, power relationships and so on. Good interpersonal communication skills are valued and many techniques have been developed to try to improve them, ASSERTIVENESS TRAINING and TRANSACTIONAL ANALYSIS being but two examples. There is of course a rich interplay between the messages received in interpersonal and MASS COMMUNICATION and our reflection on them in the process of INTRAPERSONAL COMMUNICATION. To complicate matters further, most of the factors influencing the process of interpersonal communication are formed and shaped through that process. See *TOPIC GUIDE* under INTERPERSONAL COMMUNICATION.

▶ Michael Argyle, *Bodily Communication* (Methuen, 1988); Richard Ellis and Ann McClintock, *If You Take My Meaning: Theory Into Practice in Human Communication* (Edward Arnold, 2003); Graeme Burton and Richard Dimbleby, *Between Ourselves: An Introduction to Interpersonal Communication* (Hodder Arnold, 2006); Anne Hill, James Watson, Danny Rivers and Mark Joyce, *Key Themes in Interpersonal Communication* (Open University Press/McGraw-Hill, 2007); J. Devito, *Human Communication: The*

Basic Course (Pearson International Education, 2008).

Interpretant C.S. Peirce (1839–1914), generally regarded as the founder of the American strand of SEMIOLOGY/SEMIOTICS, used the word *interpretant* in his model defining the nature of a SIGN, which 'addresses somebody, that is, it creates in the mind of that person an equivalent sign, or perhaps a more developed sign. The sign which it creates I call the interpretant of the first sign. The sign stands for something, its object' (from J. Zeman, 'Peirce's theory of signs' in T. Sebeok, ed., *A Perfusion of Signs*; Indiana University Press, 1977). The interpretant, then, is a mental concept produced both by the sign itself and by the user's experience of the object. Peirce's sign and interpretant find a parallel in the *signifier* and *signified* of the father of the European strand of semiology, Swiss linguist Ferdinand de Saussure (1857–1913).

Intertextuality See TEXT.

Intervening variables (IVs) Those influences which come between the encoder, the message and the decoder are referred to as *intervening variables*, mediating factors which influence the way in which a MESSAGE is perceived and the nature and degree of its impact. Time of day, mood, state of health can all constitute intervening variables. More importantly, family, friends, peer groups, respected persons, opinion leaders, etc. are capable of significant mediation between what we are told and what we accept, believe or reject.

Whilst people may act as intervening variables between media messages and audience, the media may also be intervening variables between people. The TV socializes the child, as do parents; it also 'comes between them' in the sense that it can stop interaction, modify it, improve it, rechannelize it (not to mention the DISSONANCE it might cause in a family when, for example, it provokes controversy). See S-IV-R MODEL OF COMMUNICATION. See also *TOPIC GUIDE* under COMMUNICATION MODELS.

Intervention Chiefly describes the policy and practice of governments to 'intervene' in, and attempt to control, the nature and flow of information. Intervention operates through laws, regulations and SURVEILLANCE. From earliest times governments have, with justification, believed that communication is power and an agent of change. Such power is a threat to existing power structures. Intervention remains high on the agenda of contemporary governments apprehensive about the freedoms of access and expression brought about by online communication. See CENSORSHIP; CLIPPER CHIP; ENCRYPT;

INTERNET: MONITORING OF CONTENT; NEWS MANAGEMENT.

Interviews Though there are many forms of interview and many different reasons for conducting them, the common goal is that of gaining more information from and understanding of other people, through a planned process of questions and answers. PRESS and television journalists use interviews as a means of collecting information and opinions. Interviews can be used to provide entertainment, as in chat shows; they are the most common means of selecting people for jobs or students for courses; they are a major method of data collection in the social sciences.

The kinds of questions widely used in interviews are: (1) open questions; these are broad, usually unstructured and often simply introduce the topic under discussion in a way that allows the interviewee a good deal of freedom in answering; (2) closed questions; these are restrictive, offering a fairly narrow range of answers from which the interviewee must choose; (3) primary questions; these introduce the subject or each new aspect of the subject under discussion; (4) subsidiary or secondary questions; these follow up the answers to primary questions; (5) neutral questions; these do not suggest any preferred response; and (6) leading questions, which suggest a preferred response and are not normally used in research interviews. See *TOPIC GUIDE* under RESEARCH METHODS.

Intrapersonal communication That which takes place within ourselves: our inner monologues; our reflection upon ourselves, upon our relationships with others and with our environment. What goes on inside our heads (or hearts) is conditioned and controlled by our *self-view*, and that self-view has emerged from a vast complex of past and present influences – on the view we perceive others holding about us, on our past achievements and failures, on memory-banks of good, bad and neutral actions and impressions.

Our concept of self interacts with our view of the world. Having been formed by experience, it is shaped and modified by subsequent experience, though rarely straightforwardly. The psychologist, for example, speaks of the *extravert* personality and the *introvert* personality. On the face of it, the extravert is characterized by a confidence in public performance that may indicate inner assurance, while the introvert may demonstrate a public shyness or guardedness reflective of inner uncertainty.

However, the outer confidence may well be a role, as in a play or performance, which may conceal an altogether different inner image or performance. The so-called introvert, on the other hand, may, through the richness or assurance of inner resources, have opted out of public role-playing, or selected the role of introvert as a public defence mechanism.

Arising from both inner and outer stimuli, intrapersonal communication is a convergence, a coming-together, of both. A piece of music stirs in us, perhaps, previous memories; these memories of people or places may join with immediate impressions of events to create an ongoing DISCOURSE, between ourselves in the past and our current selves, perceiving and perceived.

Through intrapersonal communication we come to terms (or fail to come to terms) with ourselves and with others. Through it we create bridges or battlements; we make connections or we sever them; we open ourselves up or we establish self-defences. Most of us, it is important to note, are, as it were, on our own side. We use intrapersonal communication as a means of self-assurance, of confidence-building or confidence-maintenance as well as self-discovery (or indeed self-delusion). It is what makes us unique as individuals.

Investigatory Powers Act (RIPA) (UK), 2000 See REGULATION OF INVESTIGATORY POWERS ACT (RIPA) (UK), 2000.

Invisibility That is, invisible to the public as represented by media. The case is put by many commentators that certain sections of the population are overlooked, neglected, denied rightful attention by media, as though they did not exist. Ethnic minorities are seen to be 'invisible' or 'absent' in mainstream representations, except when they are viewed as a 'problem', in which case the spotlight of attention is trained upon them. Nations as well as individuals and groups are cloaked in invisibility, fulfilling NEWS VALUE only when there is trouble, conflict, a perceived threat to order.

Visibility then comes at the price of STEREOTYPING and the nurturing of 'us and them' (or WEDOM, THEYDOM attitudes). Tuen van Dijk in *Racism and the Press* (Routledge, 1991) writes that 'minorities continue to be associated with a restricted number of stereotypical topics, such as immigration problems, crime, violence (especially "riots"), and ethnic relations (especially discrimination), whereas other topics, such as those in the realm of politics, social affairs and culture are under-reported'. See *TOPIC GUIDE* under MEDIA ISSUES & DEBATES.

Involvement See YAROS' 'PICK' MODEL FOR MULTIMEDIA NEWS, 2009.

Issue proponents GROUPS or individuals, often SIGNIFICANT OTHERS, who promote, or help determine, the ranking of an issue on the media agenda. See AGENDA-SETTING.

Issues Those social, cultural, economic or political concerns or ideas which are, at any given time, considered important, and which are the source of debate, controversy or conflict. What is an issue for one social group may not be considered such by another. Environmental issues have arguably grown out of middle-class concern, in particular among the younger, often college-educated members of that class.

Of vital interest to the student of communications are such questions as: how are issues disseminated? Why do some issues 'make it' to the national forum of debate while others fall by the wayside? What are the characteristics of a 'successful' issue? What prolongs an issue? What factors, other than the resolution of the issue, are involved in the decline in attention paid to an issue? And, running through all these questions, what role do the processes of communication play in the definition, shaping and promoting of issues?

The media are, of course, themselves an issue, like all institutions wielding power and influence, and the issues involving the role of the media in society are meat and drink for the student of communication. This has been given due acknowledgment in communication and media study syllabuses. Among the many issues of current interest involving the media are: censorship; media ownership and control, including the role of conglomerates in world-wide media activity; the part played by the media in the REINFORCEMENT of the STATUS QUO in society; in SOCIALIZATION; in their claim to act as the so-called FOURTH ESTATE; in policing the boundaries of social and political dissent; in being largely unquestioning advocates of the capitalist consumer-orientated society. Increasingly the issue dominating media debates concerns the impact on traditional mass media of the INTERNET and the relationships between them. See DEVIANCE AMPLIFICATION; EFFECTS OF THE MASS MEDIA; JOURNALISM: CITIZEN JOURNALISM; LABELLING PROCESS (AND THE MEDIA); MAINSTREAMING; McCOMBS AND SHAW'S AGENDA-SETTING MODEL OF MEDIA EFFECTS, 1976; MEDIA CONTROL; MEDIA IMPERIALISM; NEWS VALUES. See also *TOPIC GUIDE* under MEDIA ISSUES & DEBATES.

ITV (UK) See Independent Television (UK).

J

J-Curve One focus of communications research has been the part played by personal contact in the diffusion of information about NEWS events featured in the mass media. The assassination of President Kennedy in 1963 and the speedy diffusion of the news of the EVENT gave an impetus to this research.

The J-Curve arose from the conclusions of Bradley S. Greenberg, and stems mainly from work on the Kennedy assassination when Greenberg investigated the first sources of knowledge about eighteen different news events. It represents the relationship between the overall extent of awareness people have of such an event and the proportion of those learning of it through interpersonal sources.

Greenberg argues that news events can be divided into three groups as regards the manner of their diffusion and the involvement of personal contact in it. Type 1 events are important to the few people who may be affected by them, but are of little concern to the general public. Such events, though reported in the media, will be most generally diffused by personal contact – the announcement of an engagement, for example. Type 2 events such as those in typical main news stories are generally regarded as important and command the attention of a large number of people.

News of such events is not likely to be passed on as information through personal contact, although they may be discussed, as it will be taken for granted that most people will either know of such news or that it is not of vital interest to them. An example here might be an earthquake in another country. Type 3 events are dramatic, important and of very wide interest. Such events, like the assassination of President Kennedy, the death of Diana, Princess of Wales, the destruction of New York's World Trade Centre by passenger planes hi-jacked by terrorists or the London bombings of 2005, get speedy and all-enveloping coverage from the media. They also mobilize interpersonal sources, and the proportion of those who learn of the events from personal sources will be considerably higher than for type 2 news items.

Such events are, however, rare and are usually related to crisis situations. In the case of the Kennedy assassination, Greenberg and Parker found that the extent and speed of diffusion was amazing: 99.85 per cent of the US population knew of the event within five hours of its occurrence. About 50 per cent of people first heard about it through personal sources, and of these a fairly high proportion were strangers – revealing the degree to which people departed from established communication patterns.

By plotting the proportion of people eventually aware of all types of events against the proportion who heard about them first from personal contacts, it was possible to group them into five categories, and the line joining these five categories was J-shaped. It can be seen from the J-Curve that the size of the total audience increases progressively, but the proportion of those receiving information from interpersonal sources does not and depends on the type of event. That proportion is higher for some of type 1 events than for type 2, but highest for type 3 events. See TOPIC GUIDE under COMMUNICATION THEORY.

▶ Bradley S. Greenberg and Edwin B. Parker, eds, *The Kennedy Assassination and the American Public: Social Communication in Crisis* (University of Stanford Press, 1965).

Jakobson's model of communication, 1958

A linguist, Roman Jakobson was concerned with notions of meaning and of the internal structure of messages. His model is a double one, involving the *constitutive factors* in an act of communication; each of these factors is then locked on to the *function* it performs.

Thus the constitutive factors are:

	Context	
Addresser	Message	Addressee
	Contact	
	Code	

The functions form an identically structured model:

	Referential	
	(Reality orientation of message)	
Emotive	Poetic	Conative
(Expressive)	Phatic	(Effect of a message on addressee)
	Metalingual	

Phatic here refers to the function of keeping the channels of communication open, and Metalingual is the function of actually identifying the communication code that is being used. See REDUNDANCY. See also TOPIC GUIDE under COMMUNICATION MODELS.

Jargon The specialist speech of groups of people with common identity – of religion, science, medicine, art, trade, profession, political party, etc. We can have educational jargon, cricket jargon, sociological jargon – that is, the in-language of people with specialist knowledge or interest. For those creating and operating jargon, it is a useful if not vital means of communicating quickly between expert and expert. For those outside, jargon appears to be an unnecessarily complicated alternative to plain speaking, and a barrier to good communication. Without the growth of jargon words and expressions in Communication and Media Studies, this dictionary would not have been deemed necessary.

JICNARS scale Administered by the Joint Industrial Committee for National Readership Surveys in the UK, JICNARS measures AUDIENCE according to social CLASS, occupation and perceived economic status: *Category A* (upper middle class; business and professional people, considerable private means); *Category B* (middle class, senior people of reasonable affluence; respectable rather than luxurious lifestyle); *Category C1* (white-collar workers, tradespeople, supervisory and clerical jobs); *Category C2* (blue-collar, skilled workers); *Category D* (semi-skilled or unskilled members of the 'blue collar' class); and *Category E* (those at the lowest level of subsistence, casual workers, those unemployed and/or dependent on social-security schemes).

This classification has come under increasing criticism over the years, especially regarding its emphasis upon targeting the occupation of the head of a household, traditionally male. More 'with it' methods of gauging patterns of consumption have concentrated on the notion of lifestyle as reflected in people's aspirations. The best known of these is VALS (Values and Lifestyles). See HICT PROJECT.

Jingoism Extreme and uncritical form of national patriotism. The word derives from G.W. Hunt's song, written at the time of the Russo-Turkish War (1877–78) when anti-Russian feeling in the UK was running high and the Prime Minister, Benjamin Disraeli, ordered the Mediterranean fleet to Constantinople: *We don't want to fight, but by Jingo if we do/We've got the ships, we've got the men, and got the money too.* The Falklands War of 1982 stirred up similar sentiments in Britain's popular press, which used language as declamatory and as sensational as anything employed during the Boer War, the two World Wars or the British invasion of Suez (1956).

From the *Sun* ('The paper that supports our boys'): '74 Days That Shook the World!', 'Lions Who Did The Impossible – By land, sea and air, our boys never faltered in their fight against tyranny' and, on the front page, in three-inch-high type, 'We've Won!' (15 July 1982). With the NATO bombing of Serbia in 1999, the *Sun* showed that it had not lost its jingoist panache. Under the resounding headline 'Clobba Slobba' (referring to the Yugoslav leader Slobadan Milosevic), the paper trumpeted 'Our boys batter Serb butcher in Nato bomb blitz'. And at the foot of the page, 'We go in: See pages 2, 3, 4, 5, 6, 7 and 8'. Again from the *Sun* during the allied invasion of Iraq, 2003: 'How Major Dunc's Rats Raised Hell', and 'Harriers KO Nest of Vipers' (24 March 2003). In contrast, the *Sun's* rival, the *Daily Mirror*, took a critical rather than a jingoistic stance: 'This War's NOT Working' (1 April 2003). See TOPIC GUIDE under MEDIA: VALUES & IDEOLOGY.

★**Johari Window** The term Johari Window is derived from the first names of those who devised the model in 1955, Joseph Luft and Harrington Ingram, who were working together in the US on the analysis and development of self-awareness. Effective interaction depends largely on the degree and growth of understanding between the individuals concerned. Luft's theory of the Johari Window, expounded in his work entitled *Of Human Interaction* (National Press Books, 1969), is a useful way in which to look at such factors of INTERPERSONAL COMMUNICATION as SELF-DISCLOSURE and FEEDBACK and the way these may influence our SELF-CONCEPT. The model, shown below, represents a way of analysing the self.

The *free area* represents the public self: information about yourself that is known to you and to others, such as your GENDER or race. There is a free and open exchange of information in this area. The *blind area* contains information about yourself that is not known to you but which is known to others, such as any irritating mannerisms you might have. The *hidden area* contains things you know about yourself but wish to keep hidden from others, such as your lack of confidence in certain situations. You normally take action to protect this area from the scrutiny of others. The *unknown area* contains information that neither you nor others are fully conscious of but which might still be influencing your behaviour – unconscious fears, for example.

The model can be used to analyse many aspects of interpersonal behaviour. Through interpersonal communication we can come to understand ourselves better, increasing the size of the free area and decreasing the size of the other three. For example, self-disclosure can reduce the hidden area and increase the free area, and thus enhance communication with others.

Feedback from others has the potential to reduce the blind area – although possibly at some cost to self-esteem – and further increase the free area. The degree to which we may be willing to make such changes to the relative size of the areas will of course vary with the situation and relationship. Generally speaking the greater the free area in any given situation, the easier the interaction.

Journalese A manner of writing that employs ready-made phrases and formulas and which

The Johari Window

breeds its own short-cut language and clichés, rarely without some catchy word-rhythm: 'Tory, Tory, Hallelujah' proclaimed the UK *Daily Express* in 1982; in 1900, the paper's headlines were equally ringing: 'The Boers' Last Grip Loosened'. The aim is to squeeze out the most dramatic expression with the minimum use of words. The higher the pressure on space, the more pronounced the journalese. See TABLOI-DESE.

Journalism While many professions feature in the public eye, journalism can be said to *be* the public eye. Journalism reports to the public, conveying to it information, analysis, comment and entertainment while equally purporting to represent the public; to speak for it in the public arena.

At the same time journalism is in the business of representing to the public 'the reality out there'. It is only at first sight a curiosity that journalists refer to the reports they write, edit or present as 'stories', yet many commentators have drawn close comparisons between journalism and fiction. In an article entitled 'The nature of aesthetic experience' published in the *International Journal of Ethics* 36 (1926), George Herbert Mead defined two models of journalism, the *information model* and the *story model*, stating that 'the reporter is generally sent out to get a story not the facts'. Of course journalists are not always happy to be described as storytellers; after all, the job of the serious journalist is to provide information and analysis and not to turn news into entertainment.

Yet subsequent commentators have confirmed Mead's definition. John Langer in 'Truly awful news on television' published in *Journalism and Popular Culture* (Sage, 1992), edited by Peter Dahlgren and Colin Sparks, argues that 'serious news is also based around the story model'. However, 'it pretends that it is not – it declares that it is concerned with imparting the important information of the day'. Langer is of the view that 'the world of fact and the world of fiction are bound more closely together than broadcasters are prepared to have us believe'.

The implication here is that journalism has a storytelling function that has much to do with VALUES, telling stories about who we are, how we have become what we are and what we should become. The journalist to a degree is a maker, or at least an upholder, of *myth* in the sense that the French philosopher Roland Barthes has used the word: mythologizing is essentially a mode of explaining things – a giver of meaning, albeit simplified and clarified. As Barthes puts it in

Mythologies (Paladin, 1973), myth 'abolishes the complexity of human acts'.

By a process of elimination and emphasis, the journalist *frames* meaning (see FRAMING). In the study of media we are as interested in what does not appear in the frame as what does; what is *absent*. The frame can also be seen as a set of boundaries which journalism defines and patrols. Cultural, social or political DEVIANCE is defined and labelled by the journalist. There are those – people, movements, ideas – that are DEMONIZED, defined as dangerous to the security of the community (see LOONY LEFT-ISM). It might even be suggested that the media have a policing role in society and that journalists, at least some of them, carry out the part of 'copper's nark'.

The relationship between the role of the journalist and the exercise of power and control has been a keen focus of study. In *Visualizing Deviance: A Study of News Organizations* (Open University, 1987), Richard Ericson, Patricia Baranak and Janet Chan speak of news journalists as a 'deviance-defining elite' who 'provide on-going articulation of the proper bounds to behaviour in all organized spheres of life'. American media analyst David Barsamian refers to journalists as 'stenographers of power' in *Stenographers of Power: Media and Propaganda* (Common Courage, 1992), meaning basically that journalists are largely servants of the state, taking down verbatim their script from the POWER ELITE. This could be described as the 'Poodle to the Powerful' model.

While not being so dismissive, Alan Bell in *The Language of News Media* (Blackwell, 1991) acknowledges that 'news is what an authoritative source tells a journalist ... The more elite the source, the more newsworthy the story'. In contrast, believes Bell, 'alternative sources tend to be ignored: individuals, opposition parties, unions, minorities, fringe groups, the disadvantaged'. In certain situations, particularly of national crisis such as wartime, the editors of *Media, Crisis and Democracy: Mass Communication and the Disruption of Social Order* (Sage, 1992), Marc Raboy and Bernard Dagenais, argue that the media become an 'extension of the state'.

They quote Anthony Lewis of the *New York Times* describing the press during the first Gulf War (1991) as 'a claque applauding the American generals and politicians in charge'; while television behaved as the 'most egregious official lapdog during the war' – an accusation that proved equally as relevant during the second Allied invasion of Iraq in 2003.

The contrasting model to the Poodle is that of the Watchdog, where journalism stands guard over the public interest, tirelessly snapping and snarling at injustice, corruption and abuse. Since the birth of the printed word in 1450 (in the West, that is; the Chinese had developed printing much earlier) there have been ample cases of conformity and rebellion (if not revolution) in journalism.

In the nineteenth century the courageous editors of the radical press, such as William Cobbett, Richard Carlile and Henry Hetherington, spent long years in prison for writing about and publishing beliefs that ran counter to those of the ruling elite. In the twentieth century hundreds of journalists and news photographers have been killed while reporting events throughout the world, and the twenty-first century has seen no diminution in the death-toll of the bringers-of-news.

In journalism there will always be the biased and the spurious; there will continue to be invasion of PRIVACY, nationalist hype, shameless and malicious STEREOTYPING, wallowing in scandal – all examples of contemporary journalism in action. There will also continue to be high-quality investigative journalism which, in the words of John Keane in 'The crisis of the sovereign state' (in Raboy and Dagenais), 'seeks to counteract the secretive and noisy arrogance of the democratic Leviathan'; which 'involves the patient investigation and exposure of political corruption and misconduct'; which sets out to 'sting political power, to tame its arrogance by extending the limits of public controversy and widening citizens' involvement in the public spheres of civil society'. See DEMOCRACY; EMBEDDED REPORTERS; JOURNALISM: CITIZEN JOURNALISM; JOURNALISM: DATA JOURNALISM; JOURNALISM: PHONE-HACKING; JOURNALISM: 'POSTMODERN JOURNALISM'; MEDIASPHERE; NEWS MANAGEMENT IN TIMES OF WAR; PATCH; PUBLIC SPHERE; WATCHDOGS; YAROS' 'PICK' MODEL FOR MULTIMEDIA NEWS, 2009. See also *TOPIC GUIDES* under MEDIA ETHICS; MEDIA: FREEDOM, CENSORSHIP; MEDIA: ISSUES & DEBATES; NEWS MEDIA.

▸ Alan McKee, *The Public Sphere: An Introduction* (Cambridge Uiniversity Press, 2005); Brian Winston, *Messages: Freedom, Media and the West from Gutenberg to Google* (Routledge, 2005); Chris Atton and James F. Hamilton, *Alternative Journalism* (Sage, 2008); Kevin Williams, *Get Me a Murder a Day! A History of Media and Communication in Britain* (Bloomsbury Academic, 2nd edition, 2009); Dan Hind, *The Return of the Public* (Verso, 2010); Denis McQuail, *McQuail's Mass Communication Theory* (Sage, 6th edition, 2010); Graham Meike, *News Online* (Palgrave, 2010); Steven Barnett, *The Rise and Fall of Television Journalism: Just Wires and Lights in a Box?* (Bloomsbury Academic, 2011).

Journalism: celebrity journalism The preoccupation in modern print journalism with recording the activities, sayings, scandals of celebrities; described by Peter Hamill in *News is a Verb* (Ballentine, 1998) as a virus, and 'the most widespread phenomena [sic] of the times'. Hamill is of the view that 'true accomplishment is marginal to the recognition factor. There is seldom any attention paid to scientists, poets, educators or archeologists'.

Big names are the constant focus of attention to the exclusion of other subjects. The obsession with celebrity worries many media watchers, for coverage of celebrity *displaces* the reporting of events, the analysis of ISSUES which are *in* the public interest as contrasted with being *of* interest to the public; the issue here being the swamping of important information by populist entertainment.

▸ Sean Redmond and Su Holmes, eds, *Stardom and Celebrity: A Reader* (Sage, 2007); Marina Hyde, *Celebrity: How Entertainers Took Over the World and Why We Need an Exit Strategy* (Vintage, 2010); Fred Inglis, *A Short History of Celebrity* (Princeton University Press, 2010).

Journalism: citizen journalism With the advent of the multi-purpose mobile phone, in particular its capacity to transmit instantly online images, still and moving, newsgathering has been opened up to the man and woman in the street. Citizen journalism is about being close to, or involved in, events as they happen and transmitting pictures to the mass media, often ahead of professional news teams. The capacity and potential of citizen-reporting of news as it breaks was most dramatically illustrated during the terrorist bombings in London, the first wave of which occurred on 7 July 2005.

Within minutes of the carnage of 7/7, newsrooms in and around the capital were swamped with images and video footage, some of the material actually transmitted by the victims. Mobile footage was on national news within 30 minutes, while still pictures were soon to dominate the front pages of the press worldwide.

Commentators have seen in citizen journalism a shift in power from mass communication, dominated as it is by corporate ownership, towards more democratic, more popular involvement in the news process. At the same time, concern has been registered at the possible unreliability of images published from unsolicited, unchecked sources, as well as issues of privacy.

Of particular interest to researchers is how professional journalists react to 'competition' from citizen journalists. Reporting her research findings in 'The Internet, mobile phones and blogging', published in *Journalism Practice* 2 (2008), Rena Kim Bivens records that the professionals are increasingly ready to make space for citizen contributions which supplement their own work, and that they themselves operate in the BLOGOSPHERE. Says Bivens, 'the readily accessible blogosphere greatly expands potential sources and knowledge of a wider range of discourses, and journalist blogging increases engagement with audiences while amplifying and extending the production process'.

There remain 'credibility concerns, followed by antagonistic attitudes towards citizen-produced content and occasionally a lack of technological knowledge'. Citizen journalism is largely *event-driven* rather than *institution-driven*, and Bivens points out that 'despite all these developments, news organization remains firmly embedded within traditional power structures, with ownership control and elite political power restricting the limits of permissible debate and preserving narrow news agenda'. See PATCH; YAROS' 'PICK' MODEL FOR MULTIMEDIA NEWS, 2009; YOUTUBE.

Journalism: data journalism That which focuses on delving into statistical data to produce news stories, and with a view to holding governments, organizations, institutions and local authorities to account. An outstanding example of this was the revelation over months, in 2009–10, by the UK *Daily Telegraph* of the widespread exploitation by members of parliament (and of the House of Lords) of the system of parliamentary allowances. Offenders were named from all parties and included government ministers (the minister responsible for immigration was found to have claimed for nappies, women's clothes and panty liners).

The *Telegraph*'s team of data diggers also found that more than a hundred peers claimed in excess of £50,000 each for their work in the Lords. The revelations seriously damaged the reputation of the UK parliament, and indeed of Britain itself. Transparency International, the leading global index of corruption, placed the UK 20th in their annual league-table of 'clean countries', a drop of six places from 2006.

In a speech in November 2010, Sir Tim Berners-Lee, father of the World Wide Web, said he believed that the future of journalism is 'going to be about poring over data' and employing 'the tools to analyse it', with a view to 'seeing where it all fits together, and what's going on in the country'. In 2011 London's City University launched an MA course in interactive journalism, part of its curriculum being data journalism.

▶ www.city.ac.uk/study/courses/arts/interactive-journalism-ma.html.

Journalism: investigative journalism Of all journalistic forms, investigative journalism is the one most at risk, even though the best investigative journalism is the jewel in the crown of media communication. Today we have 24-hour news demanding not better, more thorough, more penetrating work from journalists, but more and faster. Time is money, and more and more media organizations are cutting back on the time-consuming practices of investigating a story.

The November-December issue of the UK *Free Press* carried an article entitled *Public Interest Journalism: Who'll pay the price?* by Adrian White, General Secretary of the International Federation of Journalists, who laments that 'commercial news publishers are less and less willing to spend the money needed for the proper in-depth reporting that citizens need in a democracy'. White writes, 'The media obsession with celebrity and entertainment at the expense of analysis and scrutiny of public affairs has created an information vacuum', raising the question, 'if commercial media no longer want this kind of story, who will provide them in future – and who will pay?'

Is the INTERNET the answer? White is not optimistic, stating that 'it is increasingly clear that no amount of tweeting and social networking will fill the void caused by the decline of thorough investigative journalism'. One possibility which White addresses is public funding, quoting Dan Hind, who in his *The Return of the Public* (Verso, 2010) proposes public trusts to share out funds to worthy investigative causes. Models of support of this kind would seem to raise new problems, particularly of journalistic independence, but White believes 'they deserve consideration because without fresh thinking about the institutional framwework for the independent and democratic dispersal of public money, the initiative will rest with governments alone' – representing the biggest threat of all to independence. See JOURNALISM: CITIZEN JOURNALISM; NEWS ELEMENTS: BREAKING, EXPLANATORY, DEEP BACKGROUND.

Journalism: participatory journalism See GENRE.

Journalism: phone-hacking The pressure on journalists to 'bring home the bacon', to produce news stories, particularly about royalty and celebrities, can lead to practices which break the law. With the advance of e-mailing and the use of mobile phones, the risk to personal privacy from prying reporters has greatly increased. Obviously phone-hacking is a secret activity and victims are seldom aware that their passwords, their e-mail address books and their online messaging are being probed, tracked and potentially converted into hard copy and possible headlines.

In the UK the most notorious case of phone-hacking has involved the *News of the World*, a Sunday paper in the Rupert Murdoch NEWS CORP stable. A private investigator working for *NoW*, Glenn Mulcaire, hacked into the mobile phones of members of the royal household at the behest of the paper's royal editor, Clive Goodman. Both were jailed in January 2007.

NoW's defence was that this was a one-off case, while the editor of the paper at the time, Andy Coulson (later to be appointed Director of Communications to the new Prime Minister David Cameron), declared that he had not been party to the hacking or known about it. Following the suspension of Ian Edmondson, *NoW*'s assistant editor (news), the pressure on Coulson increased. He resigned from his government post in January 2011 as court cases began to line up from a range of celebrities, including John Prescott, former deputy prime minister, football analyst Andy Gray, comedian Steve Coogan and actress Sienna Miller, alleging breaches of privacy.

Revelations that News Corp had paid hefty sums in out-of-court settlements to Gordon Taylor, Chief Executive of the Professional Footballers' Association, and PR agent Max Clifford challenged *NoW*'s case that the hacking was simply the work of a 'rogue reporter'. Persistent enquiries and further revelations by the *Guardian* newspaper proved that hacking was common practice for *NoW*, and soon both paper and corporate owner, News Corp, were engulfed in a scandal that led to the dramatic closure of the paper on 7 July 2011. The final edition of the 168-year-old paper appeared on Sunday 10 July.

The hacking story emerged as far back as 2003, but other than the *Guardian* (and the *New York Times*) the media showed little interest until it became clear that the paper's law-breaking practices were systemic and were intrusive beyond the limits of royalty and celebrity. Evidence of police collusion – payment of police personnel for supplying information on people in the news – proved a compelling sub-plot.

8 July 2011 was a field-day for newspaper headlines: 'Hacked To Death' (*The Times*), 'Paper That Died of Shame' (*Daily Mail*), 'Shut In Shame' (*Daily Express*), 'Goodbye Cruel World' (*Daily Telegraph*) and 'World's End' (*Sun*).

Of public concern is the extent of phone-hacking, for there is widespread belief that *NoW* cannot be the only media outlet guilty of using information illegally obtained by electronic means. Further, criticism was addressed at the apparent ineffectualness of the newspaper-industry-funded PRESS COMPLAINTS COMMISSION (UK), which Ed Miliband, leader of the Labour opposition, described as a 'toothless poodle'. In the light of phone-hacking revelations, Prime Minister David Cameron announced the establishment of a public inquiry chaired by Lord Justice Leveson into lawbreaking by the press, the system of independent regulation and the issue of cross-media ownership.

Journalism: 'postmodern journalism' A broad and overarching term to describe a trend in journalism away from serious reporting; in particular emphasizing the personal over the political. It can be summed up as more *tabloid*, more *consumerist*, and focuses on discontinuities, celebrating difference over commonality and stressing the confessional over the reportorial.

'This confessional and therapy style of news,' write Deborah Chambers, Linda Steiner and Carole Fleming in *Women and Journalism* (Routledge, 2004), 'is characterized by a profoundly selective tolerance of some people's failings and misfortunes. It usually taps into sympathy for victims drawn largely from white, middle-class, heterosexual social groups of the same nationality as the national or regional newspapers and broadcast programmes. It ignores the misery and distress of migrants and refugees, drug addicts or prostitutes and of millions of people in developing nations suffering from starvation and war.'

Postmodern journalism works towards the decontextualization of events, and by skirting issues of power, it takes politics out of everyday life. In the words of Chambers *et al*, it 'systematically devalues issues concerning economic, social and cultural power and techniques of critical engagement and investigation'. Ultimately, what happens in this postmodernist scenario is the conversion of news into entertainment. See POSTMODERNISM.

Jump cut Where two scenes in a TV news

report are of the same subject, taken from the same angle and distance, the 'jump cut' is to be avoided; to get round this 'jump' from one shot to another that is virtually the same – usually of someone being interviewed – a 'cutaway' shot is inserted, that is a reaction shot from the interviewer.

K

Katz and Lazarsfeld's two-step flow model of mass communication and personal influence See ONE-STEP, TWO-STEP, MULTI-STEP FLOW MODELS OF COMMUNICATION.

Kepplinger and Habermeier's Events Typology See EVENT.

Kernal and satellite See NARRATIVE: KERNAL AND SATELLITE.

Kindle See e-BOOK.

Kineme A segment or fraction of a whole communicative GESTURE; a kinetic parallel to a *phoneme* (element of verbal language). The term was invented by Ray Birdwhistell. In *Kinesics and Context* (University of Philadelphia, 1970), Birdwhistell draws up a vocabulary of sixty kinemes which he found in the gestural/postural/expressive movements of American subjects. He maintains that these kinemes combine to form large units (*kinemorphs*) on the analogy of *morphemes* (or words). An example would be waving a fist or prodding the air with a finger while at the same time smiling or looking angry. See KINESICS.

Kinesics The study of communication through GESTURE, posture and body movement. In *Communication* (Open University, Block 3, Units 7–10, 1975), the OU course team loosely classify kinesics under five headings: (1) information (indicating, for example, welcome or 'keep away'); (2) communication markers (head and body movements to give emphasis to a spoken message); (3) emotional state (as expression of feeling); (4) expression of self (in the way you sit or walk or hold yourself); and (5) expression of relationship (revealing attitude to others by how close you stand to someone, how you angle, tilt, shift your body in relationship to others or by the way hair or clothes are touched, a tie adjusted). See COMMUNICATION, NON-VERBAL; NON-VERBAL BEHAVIOUR: REPERTOIRE; PROXEMICS; TOUCH.

Kinetoscope Early form of film projection invented in 1887 by Thomas Alva Edison (1847–1931) and his assistant K.L. Dickson. On 14 April 1894, the first 'Kinetoscope Parlor' was opened on Broadway, New York. The Kinetoscope was a wooden cabinet furnished with a peep-slit and an inspection lens through which a single person could view the endless loop of celluloid film that passed below it. It was driven by a small electric motor and illuminated by an electric lamp. Edison's lasting contribution to cinematography was his use of celluloid film 35mm wide, with four perforations for each picture. See CINEMATOGRAPHY, ORIGINS.

'Kite' co-orientation approach See MCLEOD AND CHAFFEY'S 'KITE' MODEL, 1973.

Knowns, unknowns In *Deciding What's News* (Pantheon, 1979), Herbert Gans says that those who are famous in society, *knowns*, appear at least four times more frequently in TV news bulletins than do *unknowns*. The POWER ELITE and celebrities generally tend to be both the source and subject matter of news stories; and by being so they further qualify themselves to appear on the news as knowns. Gans states that fewer than fifty individuals regularly appear on US news. It is not only the actions of knowns that qualify as newsworthy, but also their speech. As Allan Bell says in *The Language of News Media* (Blackwell, 1991), 'Talk is news only if the right person is talking.' Meanwhile the dominance of the headlines by knowns, by the elite, leads to other actors, other talk, being ignored. See NEWS VALUES.

KPFA Radio In the US, the first listener-supported independent RADIO station, founded by Lewis Hill in 1949, broadcasting from Berkeley, California. Sister stations were later introduced – KFPK in Los Angeles (1959) and WBA1 in New York (1960). Working under the umbrella link of the Pacific Foundation, the outspokenness of the stations proved a thorn in the side of government and the establishment in America. In 1970 KFPT went on air in Houston, Texas; it was firebombed twice by the Ku Klux Klan, but broadcasts continued. See RADIO: MICROPOWER RADIO.

Kuleshov effect Lev Kuleshov (1899–1970) was in at the sunrise of Russian cinema. He was film designer, film-maker and film theorist. In 1920 he was given a workshop to study film methods with a group of students. His Kuleshov effect, demonstrated in 1922, proved how, by altering the juxtaposition of film images, their significance for the audience could be changed.

In 1929 he wrote, 'The content of the shot in itself is not so important as the joining of two shots of different content and the method of their connection and their alternation.' An experiment, aimed at proving his theory, showed a close-up of an actor playing a prisoner. This is linked to two different shots representing what the prisoner sees: first a bowl of soup, then the open door of freedom. Audiences were convinced that the expression on the man's face was different in each instance, though it was the same piece of film. See MONTAGE; SHOT.

Kuuki Japanese term, shared by the Chinese and Koreans, meaning a *climate of opinion requiring compliance*. In an article entitled 'The future of political communication research: a Japanese perspective' published in the *Journal of Communication*, Autumn 1993, Youichi Ito, Professor at Tokyo's Keio University, emphasizes that kuuki refers less to generalities than specifics. In 'Climate of opinion, kuuki, and democracy' in William Gudykunst, ed., *Communications Yearbook*, No. 26 (Lawrence Erlbaum, 2002), the author states that kuuki, the pressure towards compliance, refers 'to a certain specific opinion, policy, or group decision'; and this is usually accompanied by 'threats and social sanction'.

As the author points out, the phrase 'climate of opinion' has a long history and was probably first used in the seventeenth century by the English philosopher Joseph Glanville (1638–80). Ito suggests a parallel with the German term 'zeitgeist', meaning spirit of the times. He cites the Russo-Japanese war of 1905, in which the climate of opinion became in Japan one of fervent popular support for the war. The circulation of the pro-war newspapers at the time grew dramatically, while that of the anti-war press shrank. Because kuuki, like zeitgeist, is more spirit than the corporeal, it is neither as predictable nor as controllable as more customary shaping devices. However, when the climate is right, kuuki's power can carry a nation. Ito sees a strong connection here with Elisabeth Noelle-Neumann's 'spiral of silence' (see NOELLE-NEUMANN'S SPIRAL OF SILENCE MODEL OF PUBLIC OPINION, 1974).

Kuuki can work for good or ill. When it is fired by JINGOISM 'it can be undemocratic and destructive ... The most dangerous case,' writes Professor Ito, 'is when kuuki is taken advantage of by undemocratic groups or selfish and intolerant political leaders. Even if the situation is not as bad as this, kuuki can make people's viewpoint narrower and limit their policy options.'

Ito explains how kuuki may be nurtured by the media, by government or by the strength of public opinion. Each is a source of influence upon the others, operating in a tripolar way. Where two of the major actors work in unison, or alliance, the dominant partnership can force the third actor into line. Ito lists five conditions in which kuuki operates to powerful effect: when (1) the majority opinion accounts for the

majority in more than two of the three sectors, government, mass media and the public; (2) when the majority opinion accounts for the majority across the three sectors; (3) when the majority opinion increases over time; (4) when the majority opinion is escalating; and (5) when the subject-matter 'tends to stir up the "spirits" inherent in individuals such as basic values, norms, prejudices, antagonism and loyalty to the collective or patriotism'.

Ito states, 'When these conditions are met and kuuki is created, it functions as a strong political or social force, resulting in the minority side becoming ever-more silent and acquiescent and changing or modifying its opinion on policy, or its members resigning from their positions.'

L

Label libel A MCLUHANISM. Marshall McLuhan (1911–80), media guru of the 1960s, wrote of the way in which the mass media stick labels on people, trap them in STEREOTYPES, typecast them, pigeon-hole them to the point that such generalizations become invidious and thus a mode of DEFAMATION.

Labelling process (and the media) Howard Becker in a classic study, *The Outsiders: Studies in the Sociology of Deviancy* (Free Press, 1963), analyses the process by which certain social actions or ideas and those who perform or express them come to be defined as DEVIANT; and which he calls 'the labelling process': 'The deviant is one to whom the label has successfully been applied; deviant behaviour is behaviour that people so label.'

Becker's work highlights the role that powerful social groups and individuals play in defining the limits of acceptable and unacceptable behaviour through the labelling process. He argues that certain groups within society – moral entrepreneurs – are particularly able to shape, via the mass media, new images of deviancy and new definitions of social problems. See CRISIS DEFINITION; ISSUES.

Language See TOPIC GUIDE under LANGUAGE/DISCOURSE/NARRATIVE.

Language pollution According to Gail and Michele Meyers in *The Dynamics of Human Communication* (McGraw-Hill, 1985), 'when language is used by people to say what in fact they do not believe, when words are used, sometimes unwittingly, sometimes deliberately, to cover up rather than to explain reality, our symbolic world becomes polluted. This means that language becomes an unreliable instrument for adapting to the environment and for communicating'. Hence language pollution occurs.

The authors identify three main types of language pollution and their common characteristics: *confusion* (unknown meanings), characterized by the use of foreign languages, unfamiliar words, technical JARGON and misused terminology; *ambiguity* (too many meanings), characterized by vagueness, the use of words with multiple definitions and the use of very general imprecise statements, or terms; and *deception* (obscured meanings), characterized by outright lies, distortion, and giving incomplete information or non-answers to questions.

Langue and parole In his *Cours de Linguistique Générale* (1916), published after his death, Ferdinand de Saussure (1857–1914) defined *La langue*, or language, as a system, while *La parole* represented the actual manifestations of language in speech and writing. The former he conceived as an 'institution', a set of interpersonal rules and norms; the latter, events or instances, taking their MEANING from, or giving meaning to, the system.

▶ De Saussure, *Course in General Linguistics* (English translation; Fontana/Collins, 1974).

Lasswell's model of communication, 1948 A questioning device rather than an actual model of the communication process, Harold Lasswell's five-point approach to the analysis of the mass media has nevertheless given enduring service. It remains a useful first step in interpreting the transmission and reception of messages.

In 'The structure and function of communication in society' in Lymon Bryson, ed., *The Communication of Ideas* (Harper & Row, 1948) Lasswell suggests that in order to arrive at a due understanding of the MEANING systems of MASS COMMUNICATION, the following sequence of questions might be put:

Who
Says *what*
In which *channel*
To *whom*
With what *effect*?

Assuming that the last question would include the notion of FEEDBACK, Lasswell's model could still do with an additional question: in what *context* (social, economic, cultural, political, aesthetic) is the communication process taking place? Also Lasswell makes no provision for INTERVENING VARIABLES (IVs), those mediating factors that impact on the ways in which messages are received and responded to. It is useful to compare Lasswell's list to the verbal version of GERBNER'S MODEL OF COMMUNICA-

TION, 1956. In 'Towards a general model of communication' in *Audio-Visual Communication Review*, 4 (1956), George Gerbner offers the following formula:

1 Someone
2 perceives an event
3 and reacts
4 in a situation
5 through some means
6 to make available materials
7 in some form
8 and context
9 conveying content
10 with some consequence.

See TOPIC GUIDE under COMMUNICATION MODELS.

Latitudes of acceptance and rejection The greater the gap between an attitude a person already holds and that which another wants to persuade him/her to adopt, the less likely it is that any shift in attitude will occur. Carol W. Sherif in *Attitudes and Attitude Change* (Greenwood Press, 1982) argues that our responses to attempts to challenge or change our attitudes are divided into three main types: (1) An individual's *latitude of acceptance* contains the opinions, ideas and so on about an issue that a person is ready to agree with or accept; (2) The *latitude of non-commitment* contains the range of opinions and ideas on the same issue that the individual is neutral about; (3) The *latitude of rejection* contains those ideas and opinions about an ISSUE that the individual finds unacceptable. Further, unacceptable statements tend to be interpreted as even more hostile and unfavourable than they really are – the *contrast effect*; while those that are not far removed from the latitude of acceptance may gradually be incorporated into it – the *assimilation effect*. See BOOMERANG EFFECT.

Laugh track Recorded laughter used on radio and TV programmes, chiefly sitcoms (see SITCOM). It functions as a stimulus to AUDIENCE laughter with the hint that all of us listening or watching are finding the programme funny. There is no room on the laugh track for the dissenting sounds of those who wish to express a contrary view.

In *The Sitcom* (Edinburgh University Press, 2010), Brett Mills writes that the laugh track 'presents the audience as a mass, whose responses are unambiguous and who signal a collective understanding of what is or isn't funny'. It 'not only ignores alternative readings of a comedy text, but also suggests there is pleasure to be had in going along with the rest of the crowd'. In other words, it has ideological connotations. At the same time, says Mills, the laugh track reminds individual viewers that they are, in certain circumstances, responding differently from the crowd. See PREFERRED READING.

Law of minimal effects Point of view that the media have little or no effect in forming or modifying the attitude of audiences. See EFFECTS OF THE MASS MEDIA.

LBC: London Broadcasting Corporation The first COMMERCIAL RADIO station to come on air in the UK, in October 1973; followed a few days later by Capital Radio.

Leadership Leaders can generally be defined as individuals within GROUPS, or organizations who have influence, who provide focus, coordination and direction for the activities of the group. It may be argued that the purpose of leadership is to enable the group to function effectively and achieve its goals, although in practice leadership may not always have this effect. Leadership may be (and often is) invested in one person, but it can also be shared.

Leaders may be emergent or appointed. An emergent leader is one who comes to acquire the role of leader through the process of group INTERACTION; he/she may, for example, be the person with the best ideas or communication skills. An appointed leader is one who is formally selected; leaders in work situations are often appointed to their position.

A considerable amount of research has been conducted with the aim of trying to ascertain the qualities and interpersonal skills required for effective leadership, as well as the type of leadership needed for the optimum performance of groups or organizations. An early perspective was the *trait* approach to leadership, which argues that individuals who become leaders have certain personality traits or characteristics enabling them to cope well with leadership. The suggestion is that leaders are born, not made. However, this approach has been widely criticized for being simplistic and lacking in any hard evidence to substantiate its claims. The *functional* approach to leadership focuses on identifying the behaviour needed from leaders so that particular groups and organizations may achieve their goals. The implication here is that individuals can improve their leadership abilities.

Another approach examines the varying *styles* of leadership that may be adopted and the characteristics of each style. An example here would be represented by the work of Robert Likert. In *The Human Organization* (McGraw-Hill, 1967), Likert identifies four main styles of leadership:

Automatic, Persuasive, Consultative and *Democratic*. Research into leadership styles tends to point towards the democratic leadership style as being superior to the others. However the *Contingency* approach to leadership argues that effective leadership depends on a leader being able to adjust his/her style to suit the context. Factors in the context that are thought to influence the appropriate choice of style include the nature of the tasks, the position power held by the leader, and the nature of the relationships between the leader and subordinates.

Another theory within the Contingency approach is the *Situational Leadership Theory* proposed by Paul Hersey and Ken Blanchard (1988). This maintains that key factors affecting the choice of effective style are the level of guidance and support a leader is willing to provide, and the degree of readiness among subordinates as regards performance of the tasks.

Examples of key situational factors identified by a number of theorists as determining suitable leadership styles include the nature of the task, the characteristics of the group and the organizational CULTURE. More recently Daniel Goleman (2000) has identified six leadership styles: *Coercive, Authoritative, Affiliative, Democratic, Pacesetting* and *Coaching*. Goleman argues that effective leaders are able to use all of these styles depending on the situation. He stresses the importance of *emotional intelligence* in the deployment of these styles.

In *Organizational Behaviour* (Prentice-Hall, 2007), Andrzej Huczynski and David Buchanan identify two trends in contemporary thinking about leadership. One gives 'recognition of the role of heroic, powerful, charismatic, visionary leaders', whilst the other gives 'recognition of the role of *informal leadership* at all levels'. Lucy Kung in *Strategic Management in the Media* (Sage, 2008) notes the work of Annet Aris and Jacques Bughin (2005), who 'propose two leadership styles for media organisations: an inspirational, charismatic, hands-on style; and a performance-orientated, structured style, involving systematic setting of strategic corporate and individual goals'.

One point all approaches are agreed on is that a good leader has to be a good communicator.

▶ Annet Aris and Jacques Bughin, *Managing Media Companies: Harnessing Creative Value* (Wiley, 2009).

Leakage See FACIAL EXPRESSION.

Leaks A time-honoured way in which governments disseminate information, often through 'sources close to' the president or the prime minister; a way of authority manipulating the

L

media. Leaks can always be denied. Sometimes, of course, leaks are genuine, that is they are true divulgences of information which those in authority would wish to be withheld. Here, those close to the centres of power, perhaps disagreeing with decisions about to be made or affronted at the potential mismanagement of power, disclose information with the intention of causing embarrassment and, through publicity, a change of policy. See DEEP THROAT; SECRECY; WIKILEAKS.

Legislation See *TOPIC GUIDE* under COMMISSIONS, COMMITTEES, LEGISLATION.

Legitimation/delegitimation In *Ideology: A Multicultural Approach* (Sage, 1998), Tuen A. Van Dijk states that 'legitimation is one of the main social functions of ideologies'. It is the process whereby a group, society or nation gives a status of acceptance – legitimizes – ways of doing or saying things. By the same token, a process of delegitimation occurs in which the 'We' or 'Us' of a situation seek overtly, or covertly, to deny acceptance to *other*, or what Van Dijk refers to as 'outgroups'. Reference, for example, to 'illegal' immigrants has the effect of delegitimating a host of different 'other' and, in the public mind, creates antipathy, fear (of the 'foreigner') and rejection.

Legitimation is very much about being a member of a group and relies in some part upon a recognition of what differentiates Us from Them (those who are not part of the group). Van Dijk speaks of an 'ideological square' in which four main positions are taken in relation to legitimation/delegitimation. The square serves as a) a positive SELF-PRESENTATION and b) a negative 'other' presentation. The positions are as follows: (1) express/emphasize information that is positive about Us; (2) express/emphasize negative points about Them; (3) suppress/de-emphasize information that is positive about Them; and (4) suppress/de-emphasize information that is positive about Us.

Communicative strategies employed in legitimation/delegitimation DISCOURSES are numerous, depending on the nature of the communication and the contexts in which it takes place. They work through the *implicit*, by assumption; by implication, presupposition, assertion and manipulation; and their aim is the maintenance of power through the creation of compliance and consent. See HEGEMONY; IDEOLOGY.

Lexis Linguist's term to describe the vocabulary of a language: a unit of vocabulary is generally referred to as a *lexical* item or *lexeme*. A complete inventory of the lexical items of a language constitutes a dictionary, a lexicon. Lexicography is the overall study of the vocabulary of language, including its history.

Libel See DEFAMATION.

'Libel tourism' See DEFAMATION.

Liberal Press theory Liberal Press theory echoes the principles of the *laissez-faire* ('leave well alone') model of the economy associated with classic nineteenth-century Liberalism. The key principle of the *laissez-faire* model is that of the need for a free marketplace (that is, free from government interference) in goods and services, in which producers compete with one another to sell their products and services to consumers. Thus with regards to the media sector of the economy, media corporations are viewed as having to compete for the attention and loyalty of their consumers, the audience. Supporters of this model argue that the consumer is sovereign, and thus that media corporations have to tailor their products to suit consumer wishes, tastes and needs.

David M. Barlow and Brett Mills in *Reading Media Theory: Thinkers, Approaches, Contexts* (Pearson Education Limited, 2009) argue that 'concepts such as "freedom of the press", "freedom of speech" and the "Fourth Estate" have informed – and continue to underpin – what is variously referred to as the liberal theory of the press, or liberal press theory. This theory holds that "the freedom of the press" is rooted in the freedom to publish in the free market'. Thus the public interest is seen as best served by a free market in newspapers, magazines and so on. As James Curran points out in James Curran and Jean Seaton, *Power Without Responsibility: Press, Broadcasting and the Internet in Britain* (Routledge, 2009), this model is not without its critics. Theorists have pointed out contemporary disadvantages such as the intrusion into personal privacy in some reporting, the concentration of ownership within the press, the potential influence of owners over content, and the difficulty of radical voices being heard. See FOURTH ESTATE; PRESS, FOUR THEORIES OF.

▶ Denis McQuail, *Mass Communication Theory* (Sage, 2010).

Life positions In his book, *I'm OK, You're OK* (Harper & Row, 1969), Thomas Harris identifies four *life positions* that can be used in TRANSACTIONAL ANALYSIS for exploring and examining people's feelings, attitudes or positions towards themselves and others, and the way in which these influence their social interaction. The 'I'm OK, You're OK' position is one in which an individual believes in his/her own worth and that of others; in which we accept ourselves and other people, and base our transactions on this orientation. Harris argues that to reach this position requires conscious decision and effort.

Harris believes many people hold an 'I'm not OK, You're OK' position as a result of early socialization which, in attempting to shape an individual's behaviour into a pattern that is socially acceptable, contains a lot of messages critical of the individual – that is, not OK messages. This position may lead to a feeling of inferiority that shows itself in defensive communication, such as game-playing.

Experiences in early childhood, especially abuse and neglect, may result in an individual forming the perspective that whilst he/she is OK, other people are not; hence the 'I'm OK, You're not OK' position, which may show itself in a characteristically hostile or aggressive communicative style. 'I'm not OK, You're not OK' is the position of those who feel that neither they nor others are OK; this negative perspective may show itself through a despairing and resigned attitude when communicating with others. Life positions influence the kinds of life SCRIPTS that individuals write for themselves. See TOPIC GUIDE under INTERPERSONAL COMMUNICATION.

▶ Ian Stewart and Vann Joines, *TA Today* (Lifespace, 1987); Amy and Thomas Harris, *Staying OK* (Arrow Books, 1995); Abe Wagner, *The Transactional Manager* (London: The Industrial Society, 1996).

Lifestyle See STYLE; VALS TYPOLOGY.

Light Programme One of three BBC radio channels until the introduction of Radio 1 in 1967, and a change of names for the rest: Light became Radio 2, Home Service became Radio 4, and the Third Programme became Radio 3. The Light Programme, for general entertainment RADIO, was created in the year the Second World War ended, 1945.

Lindup Committee Report on Data Protection, 1978 See DATA PROTECTION.

Linguistic determinism The proposition that the language of a culture determines the way in which the world is perceived and thought about. Thus in acquiring a language, an individual is also acquiring a particular way of thinking about the world; a particular world-view. The two linguists closely associated with this position are Benjamin Lee Whorf and Edward Sapir, whose Linguistic Relativity Hypothesis helped to establish this particular view on the relationship between language and thought. Though their proposition that language actually determines thought has been much questioned, many would accept that the language at an individual's disposal influences the way he/she thinks about the world. See SAPIR-WHORF LINGUISTIC RELATIVITY HYPOTHESIS.

Linguistics The scientific study of language. *Diachronic* or *historical* linguistics investigates how language-use has changed over time; *synchronic* linguistics is concerned with the state of language at any given point in time; *general* linguistics seeks to establish principles for the study of all languages; *descriptive* linguistics is concerned with the analysis of the characteristics of specific language; *contrastive* linguistics explores the contrasts between different languages or families of languages; and *comparative* linguistics concentrates on common characteristics. Among a profusion of other linguistics-related studies are *anthropological* linguistics, *biolinguistics*, *psycholinguistics* and *sociolinguistics*. See PARADIGM; SEMIOLOGY/ SEMIOTICS; STRUCTURALISM.

Linotype printing Patented in 1894 by German immigrant to Baltimore, US, Ottmar Mergenthaler. The operator uses a keyboard similar to that of a typewriter. As each key is depressed, a brass matrix for that particular letter drops into place. When the line is complete, the row of matrices is placed over a mould and the line of type is cast, the molten lead alloy setting almost at once. See MONOTYPE PRINTING; PRINTING.

Listening Though often taken for granted, listening is a crucial element of human communication, and poor listening can often lead to a breakdown in communication. Effective listening may not always be that easy, given the number of potential distractions in a typical social encounter: examples here might be pressure of time, frequent interruptions or background noise. The nature of the relationship we have with the speaker(s) may affect the attention we pay to what is being said. The content of the message may challenge our attitudes, VALUES and beliefs and we may, therefore, be reluctant to listen with an open mind. There is some evidence that in a group situation we may listen less carefully as each of us leaves the task of careful listening to others.

A number of researchers have identified different listener preferences, and another problem is that we may stick with our preference even though it may not be the most appropriate way to listen in all situations. In *Small Group Communication: Theory and Practice* (Brown and Benchmark, 1996), R.S. Cathcart, Larry A. Samovar and L. Henman (with reference to the work of Watson, Barker & Weaver) identify

L

four listener preferences: People-Oriented, Action-Oriented, Content-Oriented and Time-Oriented, each of which has their own 'pros and cons'. The key to being a good listener, they argue, is to understand our own preference and those of others, and to be willing to adapt to the most suitable listening preference for the situation. We need also to adapt our delivery to the listening preferences of others: 'Just as we tend to get in the habit of listening in only one way, we also tend to speak to others in habitual ways. To make the most of interactions, think of the best ways to package information so others will listen.'

Lithography Printing from stone, slate or a substitute such as zinc or aluminium, with greasy ink; invented in 1798 by Alois Senefelder.

Lloyd's List The oldest international daily newspaper, founded in 1734; perhaps most noted for its role as almanac of world shipping movements and casualty reports.

Lobbying Lobbying is a term usually used to refer to the various activities undertaken by individuals, groups and organizations in order to influence the public policy-making processes of local and central government. Lobbying is at the core of the activities of PRESSURE GROUPS. As Ralph Tench and Liz Yeomans note in *Exploring Public Relations* (Pearson Education Limited, 2009), lobbying can be done by ordinary citizens or by professional lobbyists.

Professional lobbying developed considerably in the 1980s and 90s in the UK, and in his book entitled *An Introduction to Political Communication* (Routledge, 2007), Brian McNair describes political lobbying as a 'huge industry throughout the world'; it is also one in which many PUBLIC RELATIONS (PR) practitioners are involved. As Ralph Tench and Liz Yeomans explain, '*Public Affairs* is the much used PR specialism that seeks to influence public policy making through lobbying, done either privately or publicly, along with media relations, or by combining both routes.' Many powerful interest groups see professional lobbying as an essential part of their strategies of persuasion.

It is also the case that some former lobbyists become politicians and former politicians become lobbyists; further, that a significant number of politicians maintain their connections with interest or pressure groups whilst in power. Lobbying may be an integral aspect of the political process in many countries, but concerns exist about the relationship between lobbyists – especially those representing powerful interests – and politicians. In their study *A*

Century of Spin (Pluto Press, 2008), David Miller and William Dinan make the following comment on the situation in the UK: '... it is clear that those in power or likely to assume power in Britain are in the grip of business ideologues, in the grip more precisely of the professional idea warriors, the think-tankerati, the spinners, the lobbyists.'

Lobby Practice A book of rules of conduct written by, and abided by, UK parliamentary lobby correspondents who operate from offices in the House of Commons and whose access to the centres of power is highly prized. The lobby system in the British House of Commons goes as far back as 1886. Correspondents meet daily at Downing Street, the home of the prime minister, and weekly on Thursdays in the Commons for a briefing by the PM's press secretary.

The system has been subjected to considerable criticism on the grounds of its secrecy, alleged cosiness and danger of collusion between government and privileged lobby correspondents. It has been varyingly called 'an instrument of closed government' and the 'real cancer of British journalism'. At the heart of the criticism is the fact that the lobby correspondents receive no more information than government wishes them to know; if they break the rules of Lobby Practice, they know their privileges will be withdrawn. See PHILLIS REVIEW OF GOVERNMENT COMMUNICATIONS (UK), 2004.

Localization The process by which global media tailor their products for local markets and local audiences. The 1980s and 1990s saw a dramatic expansion of TV channels crossing national borders, and this trend was nowhere more manifest than in Europe. Companies such as MTV, CNN, Sky News, BBC Prime, BBC World and National Geographic reached out for pan-European audiences.

Initially, channels such as MTV (launched in the US in 1981 and in Europe in 1987) operated in a global capacity, that is in the sense of an increasingly homogenous culture, offering a single brand regardless of national and regional differences. They were swiftly to recognize the importance of catering to local tastes.

Jean K. Chalaby in 'Transnational television in Europe: The role of Pan-European channels' in the *European Journal of Communication* (June, 2002) writes that 'these cross-border players awoke to the reality of national boundaries and cultural and linguistic markers and realized that there were limits to the exportability of their programmes'.

Localization became an imperative, at first by opening local ADVERTISING windows, then by adapting programming itself, especially of entertainment, to local needs. Chalaby is of the view that while the 'necessity for localization can be interpreted as evidence of the limits of cultural globalization', it nevertheless 'accelerates the process of globalization, notably because it allows global players to operate in a multi-national environment': true, the 'music may become local' but the 'expansion plan remains global'.

Localization is less evident in NEWS services such as CNN and BBC World. For them, the reporting of international events is their key function. In contrast, channels dedicated to children's entertainment, such as Fox Kids or the Cartoon Network, demand localization, the originating language being converted to the 'home' language directly or through dubbing or subtitling.

Chalaby believes that 'localized channels are not so much a "hybrid" cultural form' as a 'bridge that helps the global reach the local'. See EUROPE: CROSS-BORDER TV CHANNELS.

Looking behaviour See CIVIL INATTENTION; EYE CONTACT.

Lookism The theory that the better-looking you are, the more successful you will be in life. The term was first used as early as 1978, in the *Washington Post Magazine*, but more recently has been written about at length by American psychologist Nancy Etcoff in *Survival of the Prettiest: The Science of Beauty* (Little, Brown, 1999). In an age of images, the image dominates our perceptions, our thoughts and our judgements. According to Etcoff, even mothers love their offspring just a little bit less if they are less than handsome. In the world of work, says Dr Etcoff, 'good looking men are more likely to get hired, at a higher salary than unattractive men'. She compares 'Looking' with sexism and racism.

However these are conscious, easily recognized attitudes, while Lookism works at a subconscious level. We are largely unaware of favouring the beautiful. Robert Cialdini in *Influence: Science and Practice* (London: Pearson, 2009) discusses a number of studies that demonstrate the advantages of physical attractiveness, and notes that we are also more likely to be persuaded by those we find physically attractive.

Loony Leftism In the 1980s in the UK a mythology was created by local and national newspapers about the policies of Labour-led councils, particularly those in Greater London. 'Loony' became the catchword whenever councils such as Hackney, Haringey or Islington were mentioned; the accusation arose from rumours

that were simply untrue. For example, *The Daily Star* printed a headline-story declaring that the Hackney council, in its attempt to stamp out racism and racist language in the borough, had banned the singing of 'Baa, Baa, Black Sheep' in playschools.

Hackney had never considered banning the nursery rhyme; however, newspapers throughout the country and in the rest of the world picked on this example of 'Loony Leftism'. Once in print, the story gained momentum and credence: even Labour MPs took on board the Loony Left slogan. Similar press treatment was handed out to the authors of the Congestion Charge Scheme which came into force in London in February 2003. Prior to this, the press subjected the scheme, and its architect, Mayor Ken Livingstone, to villification and scare-stories.

The tabloid paper the *Sun* called Livingstone 'the madcap mayor', 'crazy', 'loopy', 'potty', 'barmy' and a 'crackpot'. Reference to 'Red Ken' appeared in the *Sun* twenty-nine times and the 'Loony Left' ten times between January 2002 and May 2003. The broadsheet *Daily Telegraph* referred to 'Red Ken' thirty-one times and the 'Looy Left' seven times, while the London *Evening Standard* referred to the 'Loony Left' fourteen times. For detailed research-findings on this topic, see *Culture Wars: The Media & the British Left* (Edinburgh University Press, 2005) by James Curran, Ivor Gaber and Julian Petley. See WIKILEAKS.

Lord Chamberlain (UK) Until they were abolished in 1968, the powers of the Lord Chamberlain to censor plays in the British theatre went as far back as the reign of James I, though such powers were not defined by statute until 1737. All plays, except those performed by theatre clubs, were obliged to obtain a licence from the Lord Chamberlain's office. Each script was vetted for bad language, subversive ideas and any criticism of monarchy, parliament, the church, etc.

In 1967 a Joint Committee on Censorship of the Theatre was set up by government. This recommended freedom for the stage 'subject to the overriding requirements of the criminal law', and that managements and dramatists should be protected from 'frivolous or arbitrary' prosecutions. These recommendations formed the basis of Labour MP George Strauss's private member's bill that became law, liberating the theatre from the Lord Chamberlain in the Theatres Act of September 1968.

Lowbrow See HIGHBROW.

LP See gramophone.

M

MacBride Commission International Commission for the Study of Communication Problems, chaired by Sean MacBride, former Secretary General of the International Commission of Jurists. Its purpose was to deliberate on aspects of media interaction between Western and developing nations. In particular, the Commission was to report on the impact of Western media technology, and the subsequent flow of Western-orientated information, upon developing nations.

Set up by the United Nations Educational, Scientific and Cultural Organization (UNESCO) in 1978 with a committee of 'fifteen wise men and one woman', including Colombian novelist Gabriel Garcia Marquez and Canadian media guru Marshall McLuhan, the Commission produced a 484-page report in 1980.

This urged a strengthening of 'Third World' independence in the field of information-gathering and transmission, and measures to defend national cultures against the formidable one-way flow of information and entertainment from Western capitalist nations, chiefly the US. Faced with the antipathy and resistance of such nations, the Commission's recommendations, and their vision of a new world information order, were left dead in the water. See CHAPULTE-PEC DECLARATION, 1994; INFORMATION GAPS; MEDIA IMPERIALISM; TALLOIRES DECLARATION, 1981; YAMOUSOUKROU DECLARATION. See also *TOPIC GUIDE* under GLOBAL PERSPECTIVES.

Machinery of representation In modern societies, the various forms of mass media have been named the 'machinery of representation' by Professor Stuart Hall in his chapter on media power and class power in *Bending Reality: The State of the Media* (Pluto Press, 1986), edited by James Curran, Jake Ecclestone, Giles Oakley and Alan Richardson. Hall writes of the 'whole process of reporting and construction' through which reality is translated into media forms – forms that the AUDIENCE is expected to recognize as reality.

Yet reality, argues Hall, is not simply transcribed in 'great unassimilated lumps through our daily dose of newspapers or our nightly diet of television'. He is of the opinion that the media 'all work using language, words, text, pictures, still or moving; combining in different ways through the practices and techniques of selection, editing, montage, design, layout, format, linkage, narrative, openings, closures – to represent the world to us'.

They exercise 'the power to represent the world in certain ways. And because there are many different and conflicting ways in which meaning about the world can be constructed, it matters profoundly what and who gets represented, what and who regularly and routinely gets left out; and how things, people, events, relationships are represented'. See DISCURSIVE GAP; HEGEMONY; LEGITIMATION/DELEGITIMATION; POWER ELITE; PREFERRED READING.

Magnum International cooperative agency of photo-journalists, formed in 1947. Among its early members were Henri Cartier-Bresson, Robert Capa, Marc Bresson and Inge Morath. Magnum's objectives have been: top-quality photography, independence, objectivity and control – by the members – over the use of their pictures.

▶ William Manchester, *In Our Time: The World as Seen by Magnum Photographers* (Andre Deutsch, 1989).

Mainstreaming George Gerbner and a team of researchers at the Annenberg School of Communications, University of Pennsylvania, conducted a massive and ongoing research project throughout the 1980s on the impact of TELE-VISION BROADCASTING on cultural attitudes and attitude formation. A process is identified that Gerbner calls *mainstreaming*, whereby television creates a coming-together, a CONVERGENCE of attitude among viewers. In their article, 'The "mainstreaming" of America: violence profile No. 11' in *Journal of Communication* (Summer, 1980), Gerbner, Larry Gross, Michael Morgan and Nancy Signorielli write, 'In particular, heavy viewing may serve to cultivate beliefs of otherwise disparate and divergent groups towards a more homogeneous "mainstream" view.'

The authors' opinion is that TV's images 'cultivate the dominant tendencies of our culture's beliefs, ideologies, and world views' and that the 'size' of an 'effect' is far less critical 'than the direction of its steady contribution'. The light viewer is more likely to hold divergent views and the heavy viewer more convergent views: 'For heavy viewers, television virtually monopolizes and subsumes other sources of information, ideas and consciousness.' Convergence in this sense is to the world as shown on television.

Returning to this theme in an article for the American magazine *Et cetera* (Spring, 1987), Gerbner writes, in 'Television's populist brew: The three Bs', 'The most striking political difference between light and heavy viewers in most groups is the collapse of the liberal position as the one most likely to diverge from and challenge traditional assumptions.' The three *Bs* referred to in Gerbner's article are the processes by which television brings about mainstreaming. First, television *blurs* traditional social distinctions; second, it *blends* otherwise divergent groups into the mainstream; and thirdly it *bends* 'the mainstream in the direction of the medium's interests in profit, populist politics, and power'.

In a study conducted in the UK in 1987, researchers from the Portsmouth Media Research Group, Anthony Piepe, Peter Charlton and Judy Morey (see their article 'Politics and television viewing in England: hegemony or pluralism?' in the Winter 1990 edition of the *Journal of Communication*) found that British television 'does not cultivate a single mainstream around which a heterogenous audience converges', as in the US, but that it contains two message systems and constructs two audiences: that for essentially news-related programmes, which keep pluralist options open, and that for soaps which do, the researchers confirm, hasten a mainstreaming tendency, particularly when heavy viewing is involved.

In 1994 a study of TV influence on political attitudes in Italy was published by Luca Ricolfi of the University of Turin. According to his findings summarized in 'Elections and mass media. How many votes has television moved?' (*Il Mulino*, 356), TV, public and commercial, had influenced 10 per cent of the Italian electorate and the commercial channels had significantly assisted the shift of voters from the Left and Centre to the Right. See CULTIVATION; EFFECTS OF THE MASS MEDIA; GLASGOW UNVERSITY MEDIA GROUP; MACHINERY OF REPRESENTATION; MEAN WORLD SYNDROME; RESONANCE; SHOWBUSINESS, AGE OF; VIOLENCE ON TV: THE DEFENCE.

Male-as-norm In her introduction to *Man Made Language* (Routledge & Kegan Paul, 1980) Dale Spender says, 'One semantic rule which we can see in operation in the language is that of the male-as-norm. At the onset it may appear to be a relatively innocuous rule for classifying the objects and events of the world, but closer examination exposes it as one of the most pervasive and pernicious rules that has been encoded.'

The rules of society are man-made, and so, Spender argues, is the language we use – the 'edification of male supremacy'. Thus women are allotted a *negative semantic space*, illustrated by the way in which women are often referred to when they occupy a role traditionally the preserve of men. Suzanne Romaine in *Language and Society: An Introduction to Sociolinguistics*

(Oxford University Press, 2000) comments that in the British National Corpus of 1995, 'I found the following usages: *lady* doctor (125 times), *woman* doctor (20 times), *female* doctor (10 times), compared to *male* doctor (14 times)'. Other terms used for male-as-norm in relation to language are *androcentralism* (male centred) and *masculist*, as well as *patriarchal*. See TOPIC GUIDE under GENDER MATTERS.

★**Maletzke's model of the mass communication process, 1963** What is so useful about the model constructed by German Maletzke and presented in *The Psychology of Mass Communications* (Verlag Hans Bredow-Institut, 1963) is the comprehensiveness of the factors operating upon the participants in the mass communication process, and at the same time of the complex interaction of such factors.

The SELF-IMAGE of the communicator corresponds with that of the receiver: both act upon and are influenced by the message, which is itself constrained by the dictates of the medium chosen. To add to the complexity, the message is influenced by the communicator's image of the receiver and the receiver's image of the communicator. Maltetzke's is a model suggesting that in the communication process many shoulders are being looked over: the more shoulders, the more compromises, the more adjustments.

Thus not only is the communicator taking into due regard the medium and the nature of AUDIENCE, and perceiving these things through the filter of self-image and personality structure, he/she is also keenly responsive to other factors – the communication team, with its own special set of values (see NEWS VALUES) and professional practices. Beyond the team, there is the organization, which in turn has to look over its shoulder towards government or the general public (see IMPARTIALITY).

Just as the communicator is a member of a team within an organizational environment, so the receiver is part of a larger context of reception: he/she is subject to influences other than the media message. Those influences may start in the living room of a family home, and the influencers might be the viewer's or reader's family, but there are contextual influences beyond that in the pub, at work, in the community.

Maletzke's model provides students of the media with a structure for analysis. By its complexity, by suggesting an almost limitless interaction of variables, it also indicates the enormous difficulty faced by research into the EFFECTS OF THE MASS MEDIA. See *TOPIC GUIDE* under COMMUNICATION MODELS.

M

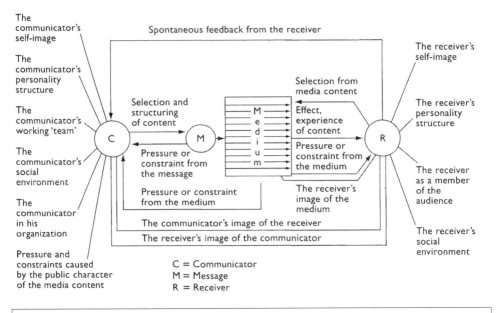

The communicator's self-image

The communicator's personality structure

The communicator's working 'team'

The communicator's social environment

The communicator in his organization

Pressure and constraints caused by the public character of the media content

Spontaneous feedback from the receiver

Selection and structuring of content

Pressure or constraint from the message

Pressure or constraint from the medium

The communicator's image of the receiver

The receiver's image of the communicator

Selection from media content

Effect, experience of content

Pressure or constraint from the medium

The receiver's image of the medium

The receiver's self-image

The receiver's personality structure

The receiver as a member of the audience

The receiver's social environment

C = Communicator
M = Message
R = Receiver

Maletzke's model of the mass communication process, 1963

Manufacture of consent See CONSENT, MANU-
FACTURE OF.

March of Time Famous US newsreel series of the
1930s, and a classic example of media interaction. Roy Larsen, one of Henry Luce's aides on
Time magazine, had arranged to have items from
the magazine broadcast on RADIO, and these
newscasts became so popular among listeners that they were developed into a network
programme, *The March of Time*. One attraction
was that the programme dramatized the news;
actors played 'memorable scenes from the news
of the week'.

In 1934, Louis de Rochement, under Larsen's
supervision, adapted the radio format to film
which, after early uncertainties, made a notable
impact. The monthly film panoramas of American and international events alerted the public
to the growing menace of Fascism. They carried
an Academy award-winning report on life inside
Nazi Germany (1938) and an even more powerful
one on refugees. In 1935, 432 US cinemas were
showing *The March of Time*, with its famous
end-of-programme words, 'Time ... marches on!'
and by 1939 the number had trebled. The series
continued until 1953. See DOCUMENTARY. See
also *TOPIC GUIDE* under MEDIA HISTORY.

Marginality See DISPLACEMENT EFFECT.

Marketing Defined on the website of the Chartered Institute of Marketing (UK) in 2005 as 'the
management process responsible for identifying,
anticipating and satisfying customer require-

ments profitably'. The site goes on to state: 'The
central premise of marketing is that in order to
be successful, and effectively satisfy customers,
there are certain marketing fundamentals that
you need to address.' These have been called the
Ps of marketing: (1) the *product* or service must
satisfy customer needs; (2) the *price* should be
competitive and appropriate to the quality of the
product and customers' pockets; (3) there will
need to be effective *promotion* of the product
or service to customers through the appropriate employment of a range of communication
strategies and activities such as ADVERTISING,
PUBLIC RELATIONS, sales promotion, personal
selling, and direct marketing activities; (4)
the product or service must be available in
the right *place*, at the right time. Similarly any
promotional communication with the customer
must be accurately located; (5) *people* are also a
key element of the marketing process. All those
who deal with the customer have the potential
to influence the customer's perception of the
product or service. Thus the Chartered Institute
argues, 'This means that they must be appropriately trained, well motivated and the right type
of person.' Good INTERPERSONAL COMMUNICA-
TION skills are crucial here; (6) the *process* of
marketing involves a myriad activities, many
of them communication activities focused on
delivery of the product or service to the satisfaction of the customer; (7) it is also important to
provide customers with *physical evidence* that

reflects the benefits and quality of the product, given that they are not able to experience the product in advance.

The *Ps* need to be appropriately considered, with reference to the product, service and consumers, but 'together they form the basis for any marketing plan'. According to the Institute, the first five are important for the marketing of a product and all are important to the marketing of a service. Four of them – Price, Product, Place, Promotion – are often described as being at the core of the MARKETING MIX.

Frances Brassington and Stephen Pettitt in *Essentials of Marketing* (FT/Prentice-Hall, 2007) discuss the rise of a contemporary approach to marketing known as *relationship marketing* – one that focuses on building the relationship between buyer and seller. This is typical of marketing activity in the business-to-business sector, where longstanding relationships between buyers and sellers is seen as a significant factor in the decisions made about purchases. It is also increasingly used in other sectors. New technology and the rapid growth of online marketing have facilitated direct communication with individual consumers, the building of closer relationships with the ordinary customer and the nurturing of consumer loyalty.

Brassington and Pettitt point out that, 'Although relationship marketing over time focuses on customers' needs and attitudes as important points of concern, it can also embrace social and ethical concerns ...' This may be the case especially where an organization has developed a Corporate Social Responsibility programme. A number of organizations have such programmes as a means of enhancing their reputation with both consumers and the wider national and international community. In part such programmes reflect a growing awareness that a significant number of consumers are concerned about the ethical behaviour, or otherwise, of companies. See CULTURE: CONSUMER; MARKET RESEARCH.

▶ Terence A. Shrimp, *Integrated Marketing Communications in Advertising & Promotion* (Thomson South-Western, 2009).

Market liberalism IDEOLOGY dominant in Western countries, adopted worldwide after the fall of Soviet communism as a normative way of state, industrial and commercial governance; its key principle – *leave to market forces*. It is essentially *capitalist*, resistant to attempts to restrict free enterprise by state control or regulation; these are considered to be ill-judged, an interference with the 'natural order of things'. Ownership of the means of production is essentially private: the 'public' denomination of private corporations has nothing to do with the public; rather, it denotes shareholding by other 'public' bodies and private individuals. Out of market liberalism has sprung the concept of the free press; policies urging PRIVATIZATION of all mass communication (not to mention other public services such as education, health and transport); and DEREGULATION.

John Keane in *The Media and Democracy* (Polity Press, 1991) says that many market liberals 'love to talk of the need for a free communications market without censorship'. However, 'they are ... unsympathetic or hostile to citizens' attempts to extend the role of law, to reduce the arbitrariness and secrecy of political power'. Thus two competing principles are at work. The 'free market' process coexists within 'a powerful, authoritative state which acts as an overlord of the market'. This amounts to a position where there is liberty for some but not necessarily for all.

Keane believes market liberalism 'succours the old doctrine of sovereignty of the state – permission for the state to defend itself by any means should it feel threatened, including controlling and regulating the liberties of the public'. Should there at the same time appear to be a threat to the free market, then the free market will collude with the state in seeking out and identifying 'enemies of the state'. Private sector media, in particular the PRESS, will have taken on the role of GUARD DOG. See COMMERCIAL LAISSEZ-FAIRE MODEL OF (MEDIA) COMMUNICATION; KUUKI; HEGEMONY.

Market research A term that covers the wide range of research activities that may be undertaken to investigate aspects of an existing or potential market. It may have a number of aims: for example, to discover whether there is a need for a proposed new service; to ascertain consumers' views on the need to modify an existing product; to test out ideas for promotional activities; or to evaluate responses to a CAMPAIGN.

With regard to its use in marketing activities, Brassington and Pettitt in *Essentials of Marketing* (FT/Prentice-Hall, 2007) comment that, 'Decisions on product range, packaging, pricing and promotion will all arise from a well-understood profile of the different types of need in the market'. It is the role of market research to help construct such profiles. Typical research methods include observational techniques, QUESTIONNAIRES, INTERVIEWS and FOCUS GROUPS. See CONSUMPTION BEHAVIOUR; SAMPLING; SEGMENTATION.

▸ Terence A. Shrimp, *Integrated Marketing Communications in Advertising & Promotion* (Thomson South-Western, 2009).

Market threshold Decisions on media production – whether to initiate, go ahead or continue with media enterprises – depend more and more on whether there is a sufficiently large percentage of consumers to warrant investment. The market threshold is the critical point at which a media artefact justifies, financially, its existence; and the greater the competition within the market, the more critical that threshold becomes.

Marxist (mode of media analysis) Focuses on social conflict, which is seen as being essentially derived from the mode of production in capitalist societies. Karl Marx argued that the CULTURE – and communication process – of a capitalist society reflects the NORMS and VALUES of that section of the community which owns the means of production: out of the dominant CLASS springs the dominant IDEOLOGY which the media serve to disseminate and reinforce in the 'disguise' of CONSENSUS.

Marxist analysts have employed three main strategies of research (also used by other, non-Marxist commentators): *structuralist, political/economic* and *culturalist*. The structuralist approach examines the ideology embodied in media content, concentrating on 'text' and the source of the ideology. The political/economic approach investigates the location of media power within economic processes, and the structure of media production. The culturalist approach commences from the standpoint that all societies are made up of a rich variety of group cultures, but seeks to indicate that some groups, therefore some cultures, receive a disproportionate representation in the media in the process of shaping and defining consensus and obscuring the roots of genuine conflict. See FUNCTIONALIST/SOCIAL ACTION (MODES OF MEDIA ANALYSIS); MACHINERY OF REPRESENTATION. See also *TOPIC GUIDE* under RESEARCH METHODS.

Maslow's hierarchy of needs According to Abraham Maslow in his highly influential book, *Motivation and Personality* (Harper & Row, 1954), human behaviour reflects a range of basic needs that form a hierarchy. 'For the man who is extremely and dangerously hungry,' writes Maslow, 'no other interests exist but food.' When that need is satisfied, 'new (and still higher) needs emerge'. In what he terms a holistic-dynamic theory of MOTIVATION, Maslow cites the following basic needs: *physiological* needs; *safety* needs; *belongingness* and *loving* needs; *esteem* needs; and the need for *self-actualization*.

Among the physiological needs are food, water, sleep and sex. Safety needs include security, stability, protection, freedom from fear, from anxiety and from chaos; the need for structure, order, law, limits; the preference for the familiar over the unfamiliar, the known rather than the unknown; for religion.

Maslow writes that the threat of chaos or humiliation can be expected in most human beings 'to produce a regression from any higher needs to the prepotent safety needs, so that a common, almost expectable reaction, is the easier acceptance of dictatorship or of military rule' and this is 'most true of those living near the safety line'. Such people are 'particularly disturbed by threats to authority, to legality, and to the representatives of the law' (see MAINSTREAMING). Belongingness and loving needs include the 'deeply animal tendency to herd, to flock, to join, to belong'.

Maslow's highest-order need is self-actualization, where a person seeks and finds fulfilment: 'A musician must make music, an artist must paint if they are ultimately to be at peace with themselves.' 'What a man can be, he must be.' The term self-actualization was coined by Kurt Goldstein in *The Organism* (American Book, 1939), and means, in Maslow's words, 'to become everything that one is capable of becoming'.

The fulfilment of needs, Maslow argues, depends on essential preconditions, obviously at the physiological level the availability of food and water, but at the higher levels such conditions as 'freedom to speak, freedom to do what one wishes so long as no harm is done to others, freedom to express oneself, freedom to investigate and seek for information, freedom to defend oneself'. In Maslow's view 'secrecy, censorship, dishonesty, blocking of communication threatens all the basic needs'.

An essential part of the process of self-actualization is the desire to know and to understand, 'to systematize, to organize, to analyse, to look for relations and meanings, to construct a system of values' and these aspects too tend towards a hierarchy: to know leads us to want to understand. Within this frame too are aesthetic needs. Maslow speaks of some individuals who 'get sick (in special ways) from ugliness, and are cured by beautiful surroundings'.

The hierarchy as cited by Maslow is dynamic and capable of reversal. Some people for example may go for esteem before love (though at the same time these individuals may 'seek self-assertion for the sake of love rather than self-esteem itself'). There are artists who put creation before all else; there is the psychopathic personality suffering from a permanent loss of the love needs; and there is the potential reversal caused by the undervaluing of a long-satisfied need: 'Thus a man who has given up his job rather than lose his self-respect, and who then starves for six months or so, may be willing to take his job back even at the price of losing his self-respect.'

The hierarchy is at its most reversible in situations involving 'ideals, high social standards, high values, and the like. With such values people become martyrs'. Torture victims who defy their oppressors also confound Maslow's hierarchy. It is further acknowledged by Maslow that human behaviour is prompted by multiple motivations.

It would be theoretically possible, he says, 'to analyse a single act of an individual and see in it the expression of his physiological needs, his safety needs, his love needs, his esteem needs, and self-actualization'. Equally, not all behaviour is motivated; and motivation must also be considered in the light of the 'external field', the pressures placed upon people to react in certain ways. See SELF-CONCEPT; VALS TYPOLOGY. See also *TOPIC GUIDE* under COMMUNICATION THEORY.

Mass communication Traditionally a term describing institutionalized forms of public-message production and dissemination, operating on a large scale, involving a considerable division of labour in their production processes and functioning through complex mediations of print, film, recording tape and photography. However, as Denis McQuail points out in *Mass Communication Theory* (Sage, 2010), 'Mass communication, in the sense of a large-scale, one-way flow of public content, continues unabated, but it is no longer carried only by the "traditional" mass media. These have been supplemented by new media (especially the Internet and mobile technology) and new types of content and flow are carried at the same time. These differ mainly in being more extensive, less structured, often interactive as well as private and individualized.' Mass communication systems are deeply involved in the processes and debates surrounding CULTURE, politics and economics.

With the advent of the INTERNET and the arrival of the mobile phone with its capacity for instant text and picture transmission, the media institutions that once held a monopoly of national and global communications have been challenged by what has been termed *mass self-communication*, that is a new world of BLOGGING, indeed a BLOGOSPHERE in which thousands of ordinary people and groups have modified, if not as yet substantially altered, the landscape of mass communication.

Mass self-communication is characterized by horizontal flows of activity, of communicative autonomy opening up a scenario which Manuel Cassells in an article entitled 'Communication, power and counter-power', published in the *International Journal of Communication* (Vol. 1, 2007), says is 'self-generated in content, self-generated in emission and self-generated in reception by many that communicate with many'.

Faced with competition from horizontal networking, corporate media have responded by following policies of coexistence leading to absorption: at vast expense, social networking sites such as YOUTUBE (Google), MYSPACE (Murdoch's NEWS CORP, until sold off at a considerable loss in 2011) and Flickr.com (Yahoo!) become part of the porfolios of corporate giants who, in Cassell's words, 'understood the need to enter the battle in the horizontal networks ... buying social networking sites to tame their communities, owning the network infrastructure to differentiate access rights, and endless other means of policing and framing the newest form of information space'. See CULTIVATION; CULTURAL APPARATUS; DEMOTIC TURN; MASS COMMUNICATIONS: SEVEN CHARACTERISTICS; MOBILIZATION; NORMATIVE THEORIES OF MASS MEDIA; WEB 2.0.

▶ James Curran, ed., *Media and Society* (5th edition, Bloomsbury Academic, 2010).

Mass communications: seven characteristics In *Towards a Sociology of Mass Communications* (Collier-Macmillan, 1969), Denis McQuail cites the following features of mass communications: (1) they normally require complex formal organizations; (2) they are directed towards large audiences; (3) they are public – the content is open to all and the distribution is relatively unstructured and informal; (4) audiences are heterogeneous – of many different kinds – in composition, people living under widely different conditions in widely differing cultures; (5) the mass media can establish simultaneous contact with very large numbers of people at a distance from the source, and widely separated from one another; (6) the relationship between communicator and audience is addressed by persons known only in their public role as communicators; (7) the audience

M

for mass communications is 'collectively unique to modern society'.

It is an 'aggregate of individuals united by a common focus of interest, engaging in an identical form of behaviour, and open to activation towards common ends', yet the individuals involved 'are unknown to each other, have only a restricted amount of interaction, do not orient their actions to each other and are only loosely organized or lacking in organization'.

What occupies current media analysis is how far the INTERNET has modified the seven pillars of mass communications – indeed, shaken those pillars, fragmented the 'common focus of interest and threatened the very notion of collective experience'.

Massification However large the population, it is made up of individuals. *Massification*, a US term, is the process by which the population is regarded as, and treated as, a lumpen mass with similar if not identical tastes and attitudes. Massification serves as an excuse by society's privileged and ELITE to regard the mass as 'only capable' of benefiting from art, education, information, entertainment if it is presented in its simplest, most unchallenging form. Massification only makes headway when large numbers of people accept the image of themselves as projected by the purveyors of mass culture. See ADVERTISING; PUBLIC SERVICE BROADCASTING (PSB).

Mass manipulative model of (media) communication See COMMERCIAL LAISSEZ-FAIRE MODEL OF (MEDIA) COMMUNICATION.

Mass media See MASS COMMUNICATION.

Mass media effects See EFFECTS OF THE MASS MEDIA.

Mass Observation An organization founded in 1937 by Charles Madge and Tom Harrisson with the purpose of furthering the scientific study of human behaviour in the UK. Large numbers of volunteer observers were used, recruited through advertisements in the national press; at one time it is estimated that there were over 1,000 such volunteers. The object of Mass Observation was ultimately the 'observation of everyone by everyone, including themselves'. Data that has been collected is to be found in the Tom Harrisson Mass Observation Archives in the University of Sussex. See MEDIA ANALYSIS.

Mass self-communication See MASS COMMUNICATION.

Mathematical theory of communication See SHANNON AND WEAVER'S MODEL OF COMMUNICATION, 1949.

Max Headroom The first male computer-generated television personality; followed by Roxscene, the first female. The *Max Headroom Show* on the UK's CHANNEL 4 won the Royal Television Society's Original Programme Award in 1986.

McCombs and Shaw's agenda-setting model of media effects, 1976 The process and effects of AGENDA-SETTING have been a central interest for media research and study. Two important contributions to our understanding of agenda-setting theory have been articles by Maxwell E. McCombs and Donald L. Shaw, 'The agenda-setting function of mass media' in *Public Opinion Quarterly*, 36 (1972) and 'Structuring the "Unseen Environment"' in the *Journal of Communication* (Spring, 1976). Shaw followed these up with 'Agenda setting and mass communication theory' in the *Gazette* XXV, 2 (1979).

In their 1976 publication, the authors write, 'Audiences not only learn about public issues and other matters through the media, they also learn how much importance to attach to an issue or topic from the emphasis the mass media place upon it. For example, in reflecting what candidates are saying during a campaign, the mass media apparently determine the important issues. In other words, the mass media set the "agenda" of the campaign'. Thus in the view of McCombs and Shaw, the media are highly influential in shaping our perceptions of the world: 'This ability to affect cognitive change among individuals is one of the most important aspects of the power of mass communication'. (See EFFECTS OF THE MASS MEDIA.)

Issues and events are given an X, and each X is subject to *differential media attention*. Accordingly, the amount of media exposure an event or issue receives governs the size of the X in the perceptions of the public. In other words, what the media treat as important is consequently regarded as important by the public (a large X); and what the media neglect, or fail to report, remains a miniscule X.

Some writers have been critical of this model for oversimplifying the process of media influence, as it takes no account of influences other than the media in setting personal agendas in relation to public issues. Another problem with the McCombs and Shaw model is highlighted by Denis McQuail and Sven Windähl in *Communication Models for the Study of Mass Communications* (Longman, 5th impression, 1998).

They identify not one, but a range of agendas: 'We can speak of the agendas of individuals and groups or we can speak of the agendas of institutions – political parties and governments. There is an important distinction between the notion of setting personal agendas by communication directly to the public and setting an institutional agenda by influencing the politicians and decision makers.' McQuail and Windähl perceive here a dual role for the media – influencing public opinion, and influencing the ELITE: 'In reality there is a continuous interaction between elite proposals and public views, with the media acting as carrier as well as source.'

A third criticism of McCombs and Shaw's model relates to the actual intentions of the media: do they initiate and select the issues which they go on to amplify; climb aboard a 'bandwagon' of nascent public interest; or respond chiefly to the promptings of the power elite? Further, it was early in the day for McCombs and Shaw to key into the shifts in public attention and activity brought about by the INTERNET and the online opportunities it has provided for greater participation and interactivity.

For a diagrammatic representation of the model, see James Watson's *Media Communication: An Introduction to Theory and Process* (Palgrave Macmillan, 3rd edition, 2008), Chapter 5, 'The news: gates, agendas and values', page 151. See BLOGOSPHERE; CONSENT, MANUFACTURE OF; GUARD DOG METAPHOR; INTERVENING VARIABLES (IVS); MAINSTREAMING; MEAN WORLD SYNDROME; MOBILIZATION; NOELLE-NEUMANN'S SPIRAL OF SILENCE MODEL OF PUBLIC OPINION, 1974; ONE-STEP, TWO-STEP, MULTI-STEP FLOW MODELS OF COMMUNICATION; ROGERS AND DEARING'S AGENDA-SETTING MODEL, 1987; SIGNIFICANT OTHERS. See also *TOPIC GUIDE* under COMMUNICATION MODELS.

▸ McCombs and Shaw, 'The evolution of agenda setting research: twenty-five years in the marketplace of ideas', *Journal of Communication* Spring, 1993; James W. Dearing and Everett M. Rogers, *Agenda-Setting* (Sage, 1996).

McDonaldization Term formulated, and introduced in his book *The McDonaldization of Society* (Pine Forge Press, 1992, revised edition, 1996), by George Ritzer, and with the subtitle 'An investigation into the changing character of contemporary social life'. As Ritzer points out, the book is not about the fast-food business, but rather serves as a major paradigm of a 'wide-ranging process I call McDonaldization' – the 'process by which the principles of the fast-food restaurants are coming to dominate more and more sectors of American society as well as of the rest of the world'; these effects are felt throughout CULTURE, in 'education, work, health care, travel, leisure, dieting, politics, the family, and virtually every other aspect of society'.

Ritzer sees McDonaldization as showing every sign 'of being an inexorable process by sweeping through seemingly impervious institutions and parts of the world'. McDonalds *is* America, and wherever the Big Mac and fries are consumed, so is the American way of life, the American dream. The author analyses his subject through the frame of ideas posed by the German social theorist, Max Weber (1864–1920), on the workings of bureaucracy in the creation of an 'iron cage' of rationality, that is a bureaucratic sameness of normative behaviour from which it is impossible to escape.

In Ritzer's view, the universalization, the rationalization of eating and other behaviours, as represented and driven by the McDonald's empire, is based upon four 'alluring dimensions' of irresistibility: *efficiency* ('the optimum method for getting from one point to another'); *calculability* ('quantity has become the equivalent to quality'); *predictability* ('there is great comfort in knowing that McDonald's offers no surprises'); and *control*, a production/service discipline which applies equally to the customer as to those who serve them.

Crucial in the exercise of control is the use of technology, 'the soft-drink dispenser that shuts itself off when the glass is full, the french fries machine that rings and lifts itself out of the oil when the fries are crisp'. This technology, says Ritzer, 'increases the corporation's control over workers'.

Ritzer acknowledges that McDonaldization has 'powerful advantages', but he argues that the foundations of its success as mentioned above 'can be thought of as the basic components of a rational system'; his view is that 'rational systems inevitably spawn irrationalities' and 'irrational consequences', not the least of them being matters of ecological concern. Ritzer's book focuses on the 'great costs and enormous risks of McDonaldization'; its purpose is to help alert the public to these and 'to stem its tide' while fearing that 'the future will bring with it more rather than less McDonaldization'. See SLAPPS. See also *TOPIC GUIDE* under GLOBAL PERSPECTIVES.

▸ Barry Smart, ed., *Resisting McDonaldization* (Sage, 1999).

McGregor Commission Report on the Press (UK), 1977 Under the chairmanship of Professor Oliver Ross Gregor, the Royal Commission produced an interim report in 1976. Concerned about the shaky finances of newspapers, the Commission proposed that the State should give

M

interest-relief on loans which papers would need if they were to modernize their printing methods and cut costs. Like so many inspired ideas emerging from royal commissions, the proposal got nowhere.

In its final report (1977), the Commission recognized the anti-Labour bias in most of the nation's press: 'We have no doubt that over most of this century, the press had treated the beliefs and activities of the Labour movement with hostility.' The Commission recommended that the Press Council be strengthened, its influence increased; that, for example, its lay members be equal in number to its press representation. This recommendation was accepted, though the Council demurred at other advice. See COMMISSIONS/COMMITTEES ON THE MEDIA.

McGuffin Film director Alfred Hitchcock (1899–1980) was fond of using this expression to describe any device or element of plot that captures the attention and interest of the audience, but which is intended to be, and acknowledged to be, merely a means to an end: an amiable red herring. Hitch himself described the McGuffin as 'that which spies are after (in films) but the audience don't care'. See NARRATIVE.

★**McLeod and Chaffee's 'kite' model, 1973** This is best studied in conjunction with NEWCOMB'S ABX MODEL OF COMMUNICATION, 1953. Newcomb focuses on interpersonal links in relation to ISSUES, believing that each element (Person A and Person B) forms a triangular dynamic in relation to X (the issue). McLeod and Chaffee take this model and apply it to MASS COMMUNICATION. In 'Interpersonal approaches to communication research' in the *American Behavioural Scientist*, 16 (1973), they too refer to a 'co-orientational approach'.

In their model there are three major 'players' forming the frame of the kite – the ELITE, the public, and, in a MEDIATING role, the media – orientated towards each other and to the tail of the kite which represents current NEWS, and issues in the news – an endless stream of new matter which the media process with the elite and public in mind, and serving, as it were, both. Such a balanced, symmetrical arrangement is closer to the ideal than a reflection of realities, for quite clearly the elite (see POWER ELITE) have considerably more influence over media performance than the public; indeed ownership and control of media lie largely with the elite in one form or another.

To obtain a more accurate representation of the co-orientational nature of the relationship between the key players in the drama of media, it would be necessary to shift the axis a little, with the media being in much closer proximity to the elite than to the public. However, the kite metaphor remains a useful one, in that the situation in which all the players find themselves is unstable, and it is the stream of Xs – EVENTS, innovations, developments, changes – which causes that instability. This model should also

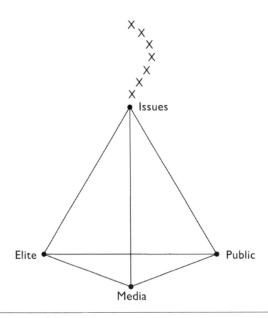

McLeod and Chaffee's 'kite' model, 1973

be looked at in relation to AGENDA-SETTING models. See *TOPIC GUIDES* under COMMUNICATION MODELS; COMMUNICATION THEORY.

McLuhanism The archpriest of media analysis in the late 1960s was the Canadian professor, Marshall McLuhan (1911–80), creator of the Centre for Media Studies in Toronto. His headline-catching assertions and prophesies about the effect of the new media, particularly TV, on society as we know it were aided and abetted by inspired phrase-making. Described by Northrop Fry as a 'manic depressive roller-coaster of Publicity', McLuhan foretold the annihilation of the printed word by the electronic media, yet his books sold (and were read) in thousands.

The most quoted McLuhanism is his phrase, *the medium is the message*, used as the heading of Chapter 1 in *Understanding the Media* (Routledge & Kegan Paul, 1964; Routledge, 2002). McLuhan was convinced that with electronic transmission, especially TV, content was everywhere swamped by *process*. Equally he was concerned at the irre-

sistible cultural spread that RADIO, TELEVISION and FILM made possible throughout the world, turning it into a *global village*. Radio he called the Tribal Drum, photography was the Brothel-without-walls, TV the Timid Giant, the motor car the Mechanical Bride.

Perhaps McLuhan's most valuable analysis is to be found in his examination of the impact of printing on civilization in *The Gutenberg Galaxy: The Making of Typographic Man* (Routledge & Kegan Paul, 1962). See HOT MEDIA, COLD MEDIA.

★**McNelly's model of news flow, 1959** An improvement upon WHITE'S GATEKEEPER MODEL, 1950. In 'Intermediary communicators in the international news' in *Journalism Quarterly*, 36 (1959), J.T. McNelly identifies several intermediary stages through which a NEWS item passes from EVENT to presentation in mass communication form. The author follows the progress of a newsworthy event (E) taken up by a foreign correspondent (CI) and then passed through several agencies where the report of E

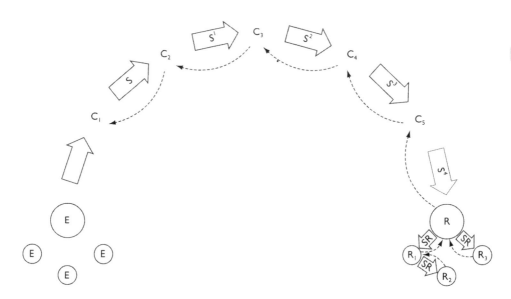

Keys to symbols in diagram:
E = Newsworthy event
C₁ = Foreign agency correspondent
C₂ = Regional bureau editor
C₃ = Agency central bureau or deskman
C₄ = National or regional home bureau editor
C₅ = Telegraph editor or radio or TV news editor

S, S¹, S², etc. = The report in a succession of altered (shortened) forms
R = Receiver
R₁, R₂, etc. = Family members, friends, associates, etc.
S – R = Story as modified by word-of-mouth transmission
Dotted line = Feedback

McNelly's model of intermediary communicators in news flow, showing news passing different 'gatekeepers' (after McNelly, 1959)

is shaped and shortened (rather like the game of Chinese Whispers, though, hopefully, not with the same hilarious results).

McNelly illustrates a very complex process of MEDIATION which continues beyond the production/presentation stage when readers or viewers pass on the news to others by word of mouth. What the model does not do is address the criteria for news selection, the NEWS VALUES which operate the operators of the GATEKEEPING process. See GALTUNG AND RUGE'S MODEL OF SELECTIVE GATEKEEPING, 1965. See also TOPIC GUIDE under COMMUNICATION MODELS.

McQuail's accountability of media model, 1997 In a number of books and periodical articles, Denis McQuail has written searchingly on the responsibilities of media to society. His model illustrating the relationship between media freedom, responsibility and accountability is published in the *European Journal of Communication*, December 1997, and analysed in the article 'Accountability of media and society: principles and means'.

The model is underpinned by principles of public service, that is the 'best interests' of society in its broadest sense, and this framework includes people as voters and citizens as well as consumers. Free media have responsibilities and obligations, and they are answerable for their performance. *Assigned* obligations may be discerned, for example, in the broadcasting charters of PUBLIC SERVICE BROADCASTING (PSB), while *contracted* obligations may relate to those bodies that commission and pay for media services. All the while *self-imposed* obligations work according to professional aims and practices and the organizational contexts that influence them.

Media have responsibilities to source, to AUDIENCE, to the public at large, to minorities, and obligations in relation to community and nation. Liability for harm caused can be seen to operate when the media are brought to court on charges of DEFAMATION, though ensuring answerability in relation to quality of performance is obviously more problematic.

McQuail believes 'we face a major dilemma in reconciling the interests of society with current trends of media development'. More than ever, control over the media has become difficult to exercise, partly because of media's proliferation into many models – brought about by new technology – and because of the *trans-nationalization* of media ownership: 'Modern mass media are less inclined to make voluntary commitments to society, less able to have any

meaningful relationship with their audiences and those whom they affect, less ready to enter into dialogue'. McQuail sees accountability as being in a state of crisis. His article examines possible ways of achieving accountability and suggests how principles and practice might cope with present and future developments.

Concluding his analysis, McQuail cautions against overstating the 'crisis of accountability'; after all, 'the performance of media reflects the imperfections of society as much as their own failings'. We must realize that 'free media have the right to be "irresponsible" and that some perceived "misuses" of autonomy will be a necessary price for potential benefits of invention, creativity, opposition, deviation and change'.

▶ Denis McQuail, *Media Performance: Mass Communication in the Public Interest* (Sage, 1992); *McQuail's Mass Communication Theory: An Introduction* (Sage, 6th edition, 2010).

McQuail's four stages of audience fragmentation, 1997 See AUDIENCE, FRAGMENTATION OF.

McWorld Vs Jihad A global conflict in cultures, represented by the transnational corporation bringing to the world 'sameness' and the counterforces of localism. Benjamin R. Barber in *Jihad Vs McWorld* (Times Books, 1995) investigates the dynamic scenario of *localite* resistance to the burgeoning power of all-encompassing cultures emanating chiefly from the United States (and sometimes referred to as *Americanization*). McWorld is characterized by 'fast music, fast computers and fast food – MTV, Macintosh and McDonald's – pressing nations into one homogenous global theme park ...' (see MCDONALDIZATION).

Jihad on the other hand celebrates tribalism. The resistance is seen to take the form of adoption and assimilation of dominant imported cultures; what Roland Robinson has called *glocalization*, turning the global into the local. See his article 'Globalization or glocalization?' in *Journal of International Communication*, 1 (1994).

With the terrorist destruction of the Twin Towers of the World Trade Centre in New York on 11 September 2001, what had been perceived as essentially a *cultural* conflict passed into a new sphere of crisis, in which the government of the US, aided by that of the UK, declared a jihad (holy war) ostensibly on terrorism, but in the view of many commentators effectively deepening cultural and political divisions globally, in particular along fault-lines between Western and Muslim nations.

In his book *The Clash of Civilizations and the Remaking of World Order* (Simon & Schuster, 1997), Samuel P. Huntington, whilst acknowledging the tensions between Muslim and Western nations, presents a more nuanced view of the fault-lines between cultures or civilizations. He defines a civilization as 'a culture writ large' and argues that 'the post-Cold War world is a world of seven or eight major civilizations. Cultural commonalities and differences shape the interests, antagonisms, and associations of states. The most important countries in the world come overwhelmingly from different civilizations'. Thus 'global politics has become multipolar and multicivilizational'.

Huntington identifies the following contemporary civilizations: Sinic (China, and Chinese communities in Southeast Asia and other locations outside of China, as well as Vietnam and Korea); Japanese; Hindu (mainly in India); Islamic (whose subcivilizations include Arab, Turkic, Persian and Malay); Orthodox (located mainly in Russia); Western (located mainly in Europe, North America, Australia and New Zealand); Latin American; and African (although North Africa belongs to the Islamic civilization, and much of the continent has been subjected to Western influences). He further argues that 'religion is a central defining characteristic of civilizations', noting that four of the five major world religions are linked to the major civilizations: Christianity, Islam, Hinduism and Confucianism; the exception is Buddhism.

Huntington questions the view that popular culture and consumerism are necessarily significant factors in relationships between civilizations, arguing that 'the essence of Western civilization is the Magna Carta not the Magna Mac. The fact that non-Westerners may bite into the latter has no implications for their accepting the former'.

Meaning In communication terms, a dynamic interaction between reader/viewer/listener, etc. and the MESSAGE. As John Fiske puts it in *Introducing Communication Studies* (Methuen, 1982; see also 3rd edition, Routledge, 2010), 'A reader is constituted by his socio-cultural experience and thus he is the channel through which message and culture interact. This is meaning.'

When we say something is 'a question of semantics', we are referring to the hazardous nature of actually pinning down, with any exactitude, the meaning of what a person has communicated. The word 'freedom' on some lips has quite a different CONNOTATION than if expressed by others.

There is a ready tendency to consider words as the actual embodiment of the meaning they attempt to describe; in fact, they are approximations. Just as paper money has no intrinsic value, words have no intrinsic meaning: rather they are accredited with value or meaning by common consent. Like currency, word-meanings are subject to devaluation and manipulation. Ultimately you can paper the walls with debased currency; debased language becomes a weapon against meaning.

A prevalent assumption is that an act or work of communication has to mean *something*. Thus a bemused spectator in front of, say, a work of abstract art, might declare, 'But what does it mean?' The short answer is that our spectator is unfamiliar with (or resistant to) the nature of the DISCOURSE that has, in the first instance, taken place between the artist, his/her medium and his/her environment (in place and time). Unless the spectator can 'tune into' the CODES operated by the artist, unless the spectator can recognize that a discourse is actually taking place, then the art he/she witnesses – for him or her, not necessarily anyone else – is meaningless.

On the other hand, the spectator might instinctively warm to a work of art, be attracted by its colour, shape, texture, and still be at a loss to grasp its meaning. In this case, common ground between artist, work of art and spectator has been found. Communication has begun, and so, arguably, has meaning.

Meaning, obviously, has to be worked at. The codes or practices of specific communicative discourses have to be recognized and eventually understood, the relationship between speaker/writer/artist/musician actor/dancer, etc. and the forms and conventions of the chosen medium of communication responded to, preferably sympathetically and with EMPATHY.

Meaning can be said to be in a perpetual state of reworking or renegotiation. The artist's meaning may never be the spectator's meaning; but meaning is the property of neither. Indeed, to regard meaning as something universally determinable and fixed is to create MYTH and to deal in PROPAGANDA. See DECONSTRUCTION; DEEP STRUCTURE; PARADIGM; POLYSEMY; SEMIOLOGY/SEMIOTICS.

Meaning systems See DOMINANT, SUBORDINATE, RADICAL.

'Mean world' syndrome It has been argued by commentators such as the American media analyst George Gerbner that the more people watch television, the more likely they will consider that out there is a 'mean world'. On the small screen, content analysis tells us, crime rages about ten times more often than in real life. Heavy viewers (see MAINSTREAMING), according to Gerbner in a series of published analyses since 1980, overestimate the statistical chance of violence in their own lives (see RESONANCE) and consequently harbour a heightened mistrust of strangers. However, Gerbner's conclusions have been challenged by recent researchers.

While granting that Gerbner's scenario of TV *cultivating* in viewers a fear of crime is interesting, Guy Cumberbatch and Dennis Howitt in *A Measure of Uncertainty: The Effects of the Mass Media* (Broadcasting Standards Council/John Libbey, 1989) write, 'All in all, few empirical studies lend full support to the original Gerbner hypothesis, while there are many failures to replicate.'

This position is reinforced by Jib Fowles in *The Case for Television Violence* (Sage, 1999), who refers to 'substantial studies done outside laboratories and with large numbers of respondents that could find no evidence of a relationship between television violence and real-world aggression'; further, such evidence indicated that 'exposure on a large scale to violence was linked to reduced aggressiveness and criminality'. The debate continues. See EFFECTS OF THE MASS MEDIA.

Media accountability See MCQUAIL'S ACCOUNTABILITY OF MEDIA MODEL, 1997.

Media activism A term that in the main refers to a variety of online critiques, protests and revelations directed at authority, big business, corporate practices and mainstream media – by either individuals (as for example in blogs – see BLOGOSPHERE) or by groups operating websites, online newspapers, etc., the nature of such protests being satirical, iconoclastic and subversive; often employing modes of popular culture in order to subvert it.

An offline example of activism would be the addition of graffiti comments on public posters, the adding of words or images to existing text or image, thus appropriating the original, *official* message. Online activist tactics such as *culture jamming* (see GENRE) and *hactivism* (see GENRE; HACKER, HACTIVIST) tend to be the work of issue-committed groups possessing advanced computer skills and seeking to get their message across in face of the traditional dominance of mass media; hence the need to shock, startle, provoke, entertain (sometimes to sabotage) with a view to creating a swift and growing volume of popular support.

Media activism is essentially about *interven-*tion – cultural, political, economic, social, aesthetic and, in terms of prevailing systems of communication, more guerilla warfare than something preplanned and formalized; it tends to be DIY action, 'micromedia' being a useful label. What activist groups have in common is a commitment to bringing about change in society; they see themselves as agents of change, their aim to draw public attention to issues, their target to convert attention into public action. Their endeavours are generally small-scale, collective, often ephemeral and dependent for success on the *media literacy*, or awareness, of potential users, subscribers and followers. See BRICOLAGE; FACEBOOK; GLOBAL SCRUTINY; MOBILIZATION; NETWORKING: SOCIAL NETWORKING; OPEN SOURCE; TWITTER; WIKILEAKS; YOUTUBE.

▶ Jill Posener, *Spray It Loud* (Routledge & Kegan Paul, 1982); Dick Hebdige, *Subculture: The Meaning of Style* (Routledge, 1979); John D.H. Downing (with Tamara Vallareal Ford, Geneve Gil and Laura Stern), *Radical Media: Rebellious Communication and Social Movements* (Sage, 2001); Jonah Peretti, 'My Nike media adventure', *The Nation* (9 April, 2001); Chris Atton, *Alternative Media* (Sage, 2001); Sean Cubitt, 'Tactical media' in Katharine Sarikakis and Daya Kishan Thussu, eds, *Ideologies of the Internet* (Hampton Press, 2006); Manuel Castells, *Communication Power* (Oxford University Press, 2009); Leah A. Lievrouw, *Alternative and Activist New Media* (Polity, 2011).

Media control Four categories of media control are generally recognized: *Authoritarian, Paternal, Commercial* and *Democratic*. They can apply to an individual communications system, such as ownership of a newspaper, or to a state pattern of control. The first indicates a total monopoly of the means of communication and control over what is expressed. The second is what Raymond Williams in *Communication* (Pelican, 1966) terms 'authoritarianism with a conscience', that is authority with VALUES and purposes beyond those concerning the maintenance of its own power. The third relates to control by market forces: anything can be said, provided that you can afford to say it and that you can say it profitably.

Democratic control is the rarest category, implying active involvement in decisions by the workforce and, indeed, the readership or audience. Control works at different levels – at the *operational* level (editors, producers, etc.), at the *allocative* level (of funds, personnel, etc.) and at the *external* level (government, advertisers, consumers).

Trends in media control have been towards greater concentration of ownership; towards ownership by CONGLOMERATE organizations and subsequently a series of ever-diversifying control NETWORKS in which international finance has fingers in practically every communications pie, from newspapers to cinema, from records to satellites and, in the opening decades of the twenty-first century, ownership of online services and platforms.

Running parallel with these trends has been the development of multi-marketing of media products – books, films, TV series, video cassettes, with such products being packaged for worldwide consumption. Economies of size have allowed conglomerates to incoporate marketing and advertising of their diverse products at costs well below what smaller competitors can match. Where conglomerates fall short of monopoly, they synergize with other giants in the field, making market alliances that become more exclusive the more powerful they grow. See GLOBAL MEDIA SYSTEM: THE MAIN PLAYERS; NEW MEDIA; NORMATIVE THEORIES OF MASS MEDIA; PAYWALL; SYNERGY; WORLD TRADE ORGANIZATION (WTO) TELECOMMUNICATIONS AGREEMENT, 1997. See also *TOPIC GUIDE* under MEDIA: OWNERSHIP & CONTROL.

Mediacy Term first given public prominence at the 1983 British Association conference by Michael Weiss and Carol Lorac of the Communication and Social Skills Project at Brighton Polytechnic. Deemed as important, in the education curriculum of the future, as literacy and numeracy are today, mediacy is defined by Weiss and Lorac as 'the ability to understand and manipulate recorded sound and vision. Information technology and video are the machinery of mediacy: its pen and paper'.

▶ Kathleen Tyner, ed., *Media Literacy: New Agendas in Communication* (Routledge, 2010); Elliot Gaines, *Media Literacy and Semiotics* (Palgrave Macmillan, 2011).

Media effects See EFFECTS OF THE MASS MEDIA.

Media: hot and cold See HOT MEDIA, COLD MEDIA.

Media imperialism Term used by some theorists to refer to the activities of the Western media by which they attempt to dominate developing countries through global communication operations. Crucial to the notion of media or *cultural* imperialism is the understanding of the relationship between economic, territorial, cultural and informational factors. In the age of Western economic colonialism in the nineteenth century the flow of information was a vital

process of growth and reinforcement. Where the trade went, so followed developing media practice and technology, reflecting the VALUES and assumptions of those who owned and manned the service.

As developing countries reached independence, much concern was felt at the degree of penetration by Western media. In 1972, the General Conference of the United Nations Educational, Scientific and Scientific Organization (UNESCO) drew attention to the way in which the media of the richer sections of the world were a means towards 'the domination of world public opinion or a source of moral and cultural pollution'. Subsequently the movement towards a new world information order grew in vigour and strength.

In 1973, in Algiers, a meeting of heads of state of non-aligned countries agreed to take concerted action to promote a fairer, more balanced exchange of information among themselves, and to release themselves from dependence upon the experts of the richer nations, demanding the 'reorganization of existing communication channels which are the legacy of the colonial past ...' By 1978, the UNESCO General Council agreed its new *Declaration on Mass Media*, emphasizing the 'balanced' aspect of a concept of information based on the principle of 'free and balanced flow'.

Developing countries have long held a heartfelt belief that Western agencies only report the bad news of what happens in their countries, and that this bad news – based upon what Anthony Smith in his book *The Geopolitics of Information* (Faber, 1980) terms 'aberrational' criteria for news selection – causes serious harm, especially when such countries are in need of Western financial support and investment.

One proponent of the imperialist thesis, Herbert Schiller, writing in the late 1960s, saw American television exports as part of an attempt by the American military industrial complex 'to subjugate the world'. He argued that the declining European empires had been replaced by an emergent US empire; one arm of this empire being the US-based, transnational communications industries which Schiller saw as working in collaboration with Western (predominantly US) political and military interests.

These communications industries were for the most part funded privately by advertising revenue and were thus extensively tied to commercial interests. The cultural artefacts exported – mainly from the US – to other countries were seen as promoting the values

M

of consumer capitalism. As such they could be seen as either reinforcing these values where they already existed, as for example in Western European countries, or as undermining traditional values and supplanting them with those of consumer capitalism in countries, such as Third World countries, where capitalist modes of production were non-existent or less developed. It was, for Schiller, a means by which the US could encourage, among other things, demand for its own products.

Schiller's thesis has met with some criticism. John B. Thompson in *The Media and Modernity* (Polity Press, 1995), for example, argues that it overlooks the *multipolar* nature of the global economy in which Europe, Japan, South-East Asia and China have played an increasingly important role. Thompson believes that, 'It would be quite implausible to suggest that this complex and shifting field of global power relations could be analysed in terms of the thesis of cultural imperialism. The thesis is simply too rigid and one-dimensional to do justice to a global situation which is in considerable flux.'

Further, argues Thompson, the thesis tends to overlook the fact that whilst messages may be diffused on a global scale, many factors within the locale of their reception can affect the way in which they are *appropriated* by the audience. Both senders and receivers contribute to the construction of their meaning. Tamar Liebes and Elihu Katz, for example, in their classic study of audience reception of episodes of *Dallas*, the American SOAP OPERA, *The Export of Meaning: Cross-cultural Readings of 'Dallas'* (Polity Press, 1993), demonstrate the impact that cultural variables can have on the reading of television texts.

Schiller in later writings did acknowledge some of these criticisms of his thesis. Whilst there are now a number of large multimedia corporations based outside of the US, it is still the major player within the globalized media market.Whatever the criticisms of the media imperialism thesis, the concentration of symbolic power mainly in the US as a result of the ongoing process of GLOBALIZATION of ownership within the media and cultural industries cannot be denied.

Denis McQuail in *Mass Communication Theory* (Sage, 2010) notes that numerous theorists view the process of globalization as being accompanied by the process of GLOCALIZATION; a process in which 'international channels, such as CNN and MTV, adapt to the circumstances of regions served'. He goes on to argue that 'the "problem" of potential cultural damage from transnationalized media may well be exaggerated. Globally, many distinct regional, national (and subnational) cultures within Europe and other regions are still strong and resistant'. However, as McQuail points out, this does not mean that the media imperialism thesis has ceased to be valid, for 'many features of the world media situation attest to the even more powerful grip of the capitalist apparatus and ethos on media nearly everywhere, with no place left to hide'.

What is not in dispute are inequalities of wealth and therefore of cultural and media provision between so-called core nations and peripheral nations (see CORE NATIONS, PERIPHERAL NATIONS) and the serious and ongoing INFORMATION GAPS between them; gaps which are unlikely to be bridged until the *structures* of deprivation are removed.

It is not only the inequalities in the distribution of information which cause concern, but also the *flow* of that communication. Cees Hamelink in *World Communication: Disempowerment and Self Empowerment* (Zed Books, 1995) says: 'Information flows across the globe are imbalanced, since most of the world's information moves among the countries in the North, less between the North and the South, and very little flows among the countries of the South,' and that this 'differential access to the management of information has put the developing countries at a serious disadvantage in the world political-economy.' This situation 'compromises their national sovereignty' and in so far as developing nations have increased 'their import capacity for communication technology, they have become more dependent upon the economic forces of the North'.

More recent contributions to the media imperialism debate focus on the impact that the INTERNET is having on traditional structures of communication and association, assessing the nature and potential of more popular, diffuse interactivity, of far more 'bottom-up' activity, less vertical and more horizontal, less organizational and more individualized. See BLOGOSPHERE; DEMOTIC TURN; GLOBAL MEDIA SYSTEM: THE MAIN PLAYERS; INTERCULTURAL INVASION; HYBRIDIZATION; MACBRIDE COMMISSION; MEDIASPHERE; MOBILIZATION; NEWS AGENCIES; NEWS AID?; NEWS VALUES; NON-ALIGNED NEWS POOL; TALLOIRES DECLARATION; WORLD PRESS FREEDOM COMMITTEE. See also *TOPIC GUIDES* under GLOBAL PERSPECTIVES; MEDIA ISSUES & DEBATES; MEDIA: OWNERSHIP & CONTROL.

▸Edward S. Herman and R.W. Chesney, *The*

Global Media: The New Missionaries of Corporate Capitalization (Cassell, 1997); James Lull, *Media, Communication, Culture: A Global Approach* (Polity Press, 2000); George Monbiot, *The Capitalist State: the Corporate Takeover of Britain* (Macmillan, 2001); Tehri Rantanen, *The Media and Globalization* (Sage, 2005); Kai Hafez, *The Myth of Media Globalization* (Polity Press, 2007); Colin Sparks, *Development, Globalization and the Mass Media* (Sage, 2007); Zizi Papacharissi, ed., *Journalism and Citizenship: New Agendas in Communication* (Routledge, 2009); Jonathan Benthall, *Disasters, Relief and the Media* (Sean Kingston Publishing, 2010).

Media moguls: four sources of concern The issue of global media ambitions on the part of transnational corporations (TNCs) prompts debate between those alarmed by the CONVER-GENCE of ownership across the world, and others who accept its inevitability while at the same time arguing that 'media moguls' are not as all-powerful, or their progress as inevitable, as some commentators believe.

Such a debate was conducted on the Open Democracy website (www.opendemocracy.net) by analysts on both sides of the Atlantic. One contributor to this debate is James Curran who, in an online article, 'Global media concentration: shifting the argument' (23 May 2002), as relevant today as it was when written, discusses what he perceives as four sources of concern in relation to what he sees as a 'pattern of domination'.

First, Curran believes that 'the private concentration of symbolic power potentially distorts the democratic process'. He cites the example of Italian media mogul Silvio Berlusconi, whose media empire helped catapult him 'into the premiership of Italy without having any experience of democratic office ... Berlusconi would not be ruling Italy now if he did not dominate a massive media empire that enabled him to manufacture a political party'.

The second concern 'is that the power potentially at the disposal of media moguls tends to be exerted in a one-sided way', usually rightist and consumerist-orientated. Curran refers to Rupert Murdoch, who 'may have presided over the subversive *Simpsons* but he is also the man who bullied his British journalists to follow a right-wing agenda ... part of a more general pattern in which shareholder interventions sometimes advance conservative or market-friendly positions, but more rarely their antithesis'.

Curran's third concern is that 'the concentration of market power can stifle competition'. He believes that a 'fundamental reason for the long-standing deficiencies of the British national press ... is that it has been controlled so long by an oligopoly'. Leading on from this is the fourth concern, a 'one-sided protection of our freedoms'; on the one hand 'a state of constant alert against the abuse of state power over media, reflected in the development of numerous safeguards', yet on the other hand 'not matched by an equivalent vigilance and set of safeguards directed against the abuse of shareholder power over the media'.

In other words, in the conflict between media power and public interest the latter is likely to lose out. One consequence of what Curran describes as 'the current quiescence' (in the face of the media's assertion of its own freedoms) 'is that media conglomerates have been able to persuade governments around the world to ease monopoly controls'. See BERLUSCONI PHENOM-ENON; CROSS-MEDIA OWNERSHIP; GLOBAL-IZATION (AND THE MEDIA); GLOBAL MEDIA SYSTEM: THE MAIN PLAYERS; JOURNALISM: PHONE-HACKING; MURDOCH EFFECT; NEWS CORP; OFCOM: OFFICE OF COMMUNICATIONS (UK); REGULATORY FAVOURS. See also *TOPIC GUIDE* under MEDIA: OWNERSHIP & CONTROL.

▶ James Curran, *Media and Democracy* (Routledge, 2011).

M

Media-Most Media empire in Russia after the fall of Communism and the shift in that country towards a capitalist and democratic system. The 'Rupert Murdoch' of Media-Most was Vladimir Gosinsky, whose independence, and indeed criticism of the state government under Vladimir Putin, led to the group's destruction and dismemberment. 'Through the selective application of tax and criminal law,' writes Jonathan Becker in 'Lessons from Russia: A neo-author-itarian media system' in the *European Journal of Communication* (June 2004), 'including the invasion of Media-Most premises by hooded and heavily armed tax police, the direct pressure of the Ministry of Press, Radio and Television and boardroom intrigue, Medi-Most collapsed.' In Becker's view, 'The timing, form and tenacity of governments actions sent a chill through non-state media, contributing to uncertainty and, no doubt, self-censorship.' See CENSORSHIP.

Media: new media See NEW MEDIA.

Mediapolis 'Polis' is Greek for city, thus the term envisages a city of media, but one that is global in reach and influence. It links with McLuhan's notion in the 1960s of the media turning the world into a global village. The mediapolis is the AGORA, that open space in which community and communication come together, where the people and their leaders deliberate on 'the affairs of state', and ideally contribute, together, to decision-making.

Roger Silverstone in *Media and Morality: On the Rise of the Mediapolis* (Polity, 2007) describes the mediapolis as 'a site for the construction of a moral order ... commensurate with the scope and scale of global interdependence'. It is an ideal founded in the principle of *one world* based upon equality and civility; a very different scenario from that which currently exists.

Silverstone sees 'no integrity within the contemporary midiapolis. The public space which it constitutes', he believes, 'is fractured by cultural difference and the absence of communication, as much as it is by the homogenization of global television and genuine, if only momentary, collective attention to global events, crises and catastrophes'. What we have is something 'manifestly ... embryonic and imperfect; and even in its potential can never be imagined as fully realizable'. However, 'it has to be seen as a necessary starting point for the creation of a more effective global space'.

What Silverstone is suggesting is a new moral order, one that challenges 'the inequities of representation and persistence of exclusion' characteristic of the exercise of media power 'both by capital and the state, and within the ideological and prejudiced frames of unreflexive reporting and storytelling'. Key is 'our relationship to the other, to the stranger'; our obligation 'to welcome the stranger ... to listen and to hear', and thus to acknowledge the need for the creation of 'space for effective communication'. See ACCESSED VOICES; DEMOCRACY AND THE MEDIA; EMANCIPATORY USE OF THE MEDIA; EMPOWERMENT; GLOBALIZATION (AND THE MEDIA); INFORMATION GAPS; OPEN SOURCE; PEOPLE'S COMMUNICATION CHARTER; PUBLIC SPHERE; WEDOM, THEYDOM.

▶ Shuang Liu, *Introducing Intercultural Communication: Global Cultures and Contexts* (Sage, 2010); Alexander G. Nicolaev, ed., *Ethical Issues in International Communication* (Palgrave Macmillan, 2011).

Media research centres See RESEARCH CENTRES.

Mediasphere Term posed and defined by John Hartley in *Popular Reality: Journalism, Modernity, Popular Culture* (Arnold, 1996) to describe the positioning of media, its range and breadth of influence, in relationship to the PUBLIC SPHERE, and the notion of the *Semiosphere* put forward by Yuri Lotman in *The Universe of the Mind: A Semiotic Theory of Culture* (University of Indiana Press, 1990). Hartley sees the semiosphere – the sphere of cultural expression

and cultural MEANING – as being in a constant process of interaction with the mediasphere and public sphere. He images the relationship as resembling Russian dolls: the public sphere fits within the mediasphere, which in turn fits within the semiosphere.

The most salient feature of these interlocking spheres, argues Hartley, is JOURNALISM. It was journalism that originated and nurtured concepts of freedom, of human rights, within societies. It served a key function in, and in turn was served by, the success of the American and French revolutions. The public sphere of the nineteenth century was created by journalism. Hartley believes 'there would be no public' and consequently no progress towards the sovereignty of the people without the aid of journalistic writing. This served, and continues to serve, as a counterforce to subordination; indeed it is 'the mechanism for making these [democratic] discourses generally available, and also for articulating the different forms of resistance'.

Ultimately, though, journalism's power to define and further the public sphere depends on readership. The changing nature of readership also alters the nature of the public and private spheres. Hartley believes that we have moved from the traditional *adversarial* mode of journalism, with its public, political and masculine bias, to a POSTMODERNIST phase, driven in particular by popular journalism (described by Hartley as 'the textual system of modernity').

This gives emphasis not to public life 'but to private meaning'. He identifies the following shifts in the nature of readership: from male to female; from old to young; from militant to meditative; from public to private; from governmental to consumerist; and from law-making to identity-forming. Hartley describes the mediasphere as 'suffused with images and issues which connect popular readerships and popular meanings together ... the mainstream of contemporary journalism is fashion, gossip, lifestyle, consumerism and celebrity, and "news" is private, visual, narrativized and personalized'. It follows that the icon of the contemporary mediasphere is 'not the superpower but the supermodel'.

The shifts mentioned here are not, however, to be seen as having become disengaged from the past of journalism/readership: modern journalism is, populist, yes. Yet it remains in the tradition of the radical journalism that helped give birth to the American and French revolutions. See DEMOCRACY AND THE MEDIA.

Media Studies: the internationalization of

Media Studies Media Studies took its early dominant form from US-UK perspectives; it was essentially English language-based, working along largely Western parameters; and study of media by and about the rest of the world either did not exist, or operated in the margins of course programmes more enthnocentric than global in scope. In 2000 James Curran and Myung Jin-Park edited a seminal book, *De-Westernizing Media Studies* (Routledge). Its several contributors argued the case, expressed in the book's introduction by Curran, that the study of media be broadened 'in a way that takes account of the experience of countries outside the Anglo-American orbit'.

In 2009 Routledge published another influential work, *Internationalizing Media Studies*, edited by Daya Kishan Thussu. In his introductory chapter, 'Why internationalize Media Studies and how?', Thussu writes that 'meaningful endeavours at providing comparative models of media systems have ignored analysis beyond the Euro-American ambit, despite the extraordinary expansion of the media, especially in Asia'. Any meaningful examination of the internationalization of media study, states Thussu, 'must take into account the rapid growth of China and India ... which are increasingly making their presence felt on the global scene'.

Thussu talks of 'a moral imperative to internationalize', for despite 'the exponential expansion in media in the non-Western world, its study in non-metropolitan centres remains largely insignificant, not to say tokenistic'.

▶ Katharine Sarikakis, *British Media in a Global Era* (Bloomsbury Academic, 2004); Daya Thussu, *International Communication: Continuity and Change* (2nd edition, Bloomsbury Academic, 2006); Gerard Goggin and Mark McLelland, eds, *Internationalizing Internet Studies: Beyond Anglophone Paradigms* (Routledge, 2009).

Media technology See TOPIC GUIDE under MEDIA: TECHNOLOGIES.

Media theory: purpose and uses In his introduction to *Understanding Media Theory* (Arnold, 2003), Kevin Williams says that the purposes of media theory are fourfold: to answer the question 'What is going on?'; to explain how and why; to suggest what might happen next; and, taking prediction into account, to serve as a guide to future behaviour and performance. He identifies three *levels* of theory, each of which interacts with, influences and is influenced by the others in the contexts where communication takes place.

There is *commonsense theory* in which 'people have implicit understandings or ideas with which they make sense of the media'. Such a theoretical level is important because of the role it plays in public debate on the media, though often leading 'to simplistic portrayals of the role and influence of the media'. *Practioner theory* relates to the ideas which media practitioners have about their world. It is also referred to as *operational theory*, covering 'the accumulated practical wisdom found in most organizational and professional settings'.

Academic theory – the primary focus of Williams's book, and indeed of the study of media from GCSE and A level to degree work and beyond – is what occupies scholarship, and as far as media study is concerned, involves a broad range of academic fields, including, as Williams lists them, sociology, psychology, social psychology, literary studies, anthropology, sociolinguistics, economics, political science, philosophy, history, law, rhetoric and speech communication, group and systems theory, 'and even mathematics'.

In the light of this diversity, says Williams, 'it is not surprising that there are conflicts over the assumptions, *foci* and methods of analysis in the field and that contradictory hypotheses and theories are put forward'. This, of course, is part of the fascination, indeed the open-endedness, of the study of media. Theories must be examined and re-examined, subjected to close and insistent scrutiny; in other words tested in terms of relevance and reliability, and it must not be seen as something 'detached from the day-to-day issues of ordinary men and women'.

Theory 'guides research by helping scholars organize how they gather facts and observe the world. But good theory should also help us to understand and make sense of our personal experience and the wider structures and processes of daily life, and how they shape our interaction with other people'. For Williams, the ultimate test of any theory 'is the extent to which it furthers our understanding of the world we live in'. As well as assisting us to develop our knowledge of mass media, theory helps us 'challenge the misleading ideas that have come to dominate public debate about their influence and involvement'.

In terms of subject interest, theory focuses in the main on the *production* side of texts, the *texts* themselves (see SEMIOLOGY) and the *reception* of those texts, all within the cultural, political, economic, technological and environmental contexts in which communication takes place. During the early days of media study and

M

research, the 1940s and 1950s, attention centred almost exclusively on the communicators, and there was the assumption that what was transmitted was simply received. With the advent of USES AND GRATIFICATIONS THEORY the audience became important and it became plain that audiences put media to many uses, not always the ones intended by the communicators.

At around the same time, in the 1960s and 1970s, textual analysis came into its own (see DENOTATION, CODES, CONNOTATION, SIGNS). *Deconstruction* of texts became a key activity. Eventually interest turned to deconstructing the audience itself, using research methods such as those pioneered in ethnography (see ETHNO-GRAPHIC APPROACH TO AUDIENCE MEASURE-MENT). Today there is general agreement that to focus on one area of study to the neglect of others is to produce skewed results, and the validity and reliability of theory suffers. Ultimately, however, the purpose of theory can be summed up in one phrase – the search for MEANING. See *TOPIC GUIDE* under COMMUNICATION THEORY.

▶ Stephen W. Littlejohn, *Theories of Human Communication* (Wadsworth, 7th edition, 2002); Em Griffin, *A First Look at Communication Theory* (McGraw-Hill, 5th edition, 2003); Steve Duck and David T. McMahon, *The Basics of Communication: A Relational Perspective* (Sage, 2008); Denis McQuail, *McQuail's Mass Communication Theory* (Sage, 6th edition, 2010).

Mediation Between an EVENT and the reporting or broadcasting of it to an AUDIENCE, mediation occurs, that is a process of interpretation – shaping, selecting, editing, emphasizing, de-emphasizing – according to the perceptions, expectations and previous experience of those involved in the reporting of the event; and in accordance with the requirements and characteristics of the means of reporting. Between the event of a car accident or a murder and the report of such an event a whole series of inter-mediating actions takes place. The event is translated into words or pictures; it is processed according to the demands of the MEDIUM – for headlines, for good pictures – and pressures such as time, space and contending messages.

Even when, in INTERPERSONAL COMMUNI-CATION, person A communicates a message to person B which B conveys to person C, a process of mediation inevitably takes place: B may rephrase the message, give parts of it prominence and understate other parts, supplement or distort the information. Mediation is inescapable: much of our knowledge of life and the world comes to us at second hand, through

the mediation of PRESS and TV; our perceptions of events are coloured by the perceptions, preoccupations, VALUES, of the mediators.

However, the *construct* of events is far from a monopoly of the mass media; it is further mediated, and the process modified or altered altogether, by those around us who exert influence – friends, relatives, work colleagues, etc. – and other so-called INTERVENING VARIABLES (IVs) such as personal mood, time of day or state of health.

The term takes on fresh dimensions and direction when applied to network communication (see NEW MEDIA; NETWORKING: SOCIAL NETWORKING). In the digital age mediation is characterized by the participation and interaction of network users; patterns of mediation are more horizontal than vertical, more a process of exchange in which users become their own message-makers and mediators; thus the scenario is more fragmented, individualized and in a perpetual state of flux.

In *Alternative and Activist New Media* (Polity Press, 2011), Leah A. Lievrouw writes that 'mediation is comprised of two interrelated modes of communicative action that contrast with the production-consumption dynamics and linear "effects" or feedback models of associated with mass media'.

Reconfiguration describes how users 'modify and adapt media technologies and systems as needed to suit their various purposes or interests'. *Remediation* (a term originated by Jay Bolter and Robert Grusin in *Remediation: Understanding New Media*, MIT Press, 1999) occurs when 'content, forms and structures of communication relationships' are mediated by users when they 'borrow, adapt or remix existing materials, expressions, and interactions to create a continually expanding universe of innovative new works and ideas'. Lievrouw cites these as 'hallmarks of contemporary communication processes, creative work and media culture'.

Reconfiguration and remediation 'allow people to work around the fixity of traditional media technologies and institutional systems, and to negotiate, manipulate, and blur the boundaries between impersonal interaction and mass communication'. See AUDIENCE: ACTIVE AUDI-ENCE; BLOGOSPHERE; OPEN SOURCE; S-IV-R MODEL OF COMMUNICATION; WEB 2.0.

▶ Neil Washbourne, *Mediating Politics: Newspaper, Radio, Television and the Internet* (Open University, 2007); Philip M. Napoli, *Audience Evolution: New Technologies and the Transformation of Media Audiences* (Columbia University Press, 2011).

Mediatization Process whereby political or indeed any public activity, having become reliant for its audience/electorate upon the media for its messages to be communicated, adopts the principles and methods of media communication. In particular TV has become the medium and channel of political communication. Consequently political communication pays greater attention to entertainment value as practised by TV, for example PERSONALIZATION, simplification and an emphasis on using 'media-*genic*' players (see LOOKISM) and stressing image over content.

Media user ethics See TEN COMMANDMENTS FOR MEDIA CONSUMERS.

Media workers See WORKERS IN COMMUNICATION AND MEDIA.

Medio communication That mode of communication taking place between direct, face-to-face address and MASS COMMUNICATION; into this classification comes communication by letter, e-mail, fax or telephone.

Medium The physical or technical means of converting a communication message into a signal capable of being transmitted along a given channel. TV, for example, is a medium that employs the channels of vision and sound. John Fiske in *Introduction to Communication Studies* (Methuen, 1982; see 3rd edition, Routledge, 2010) divides media into three categories: (1) *Presentational* media: the voice, face, body; the spoken word, GESTURE; where the medium is actually the communicator. (2) *Representational* media: books, paintings, photographs, etc., using cultural and aesthetic conventions 'to create a "text" of some sort'; they become independent of the communicator, being *works* of communication (whereas presentational media are *acts* of communication). (3) *Mechanical* media: telephone, radio, TV, film, etc., and they are *transmitters* of (1) and (2). The properties of the medium determine the range of CODES which it can transmit, and considerably affect the nature of the message and its reception.

Medium is the message One of the classic quotes of media literature and perhaps the best-known of Marshall McLuhan (1911–80). 'The medium is the message' is the first chapter heading in his book, *Understanding Media: the Extensions of Man* (Routledge & Kegan Paul, 1964; Routledge, 2002). What is said, McLuhan believes, is deeply conditioned by the MEDIUM through which it said. The particular attributes of any medium help to determine the MEANING of the communication, and no medium is neutral. See McLUHANISM.

Message That which an act, or work, of communication is *about*. For purposes of definition and analysis it is sometimes necessary to treat the message as something separable from the *process* of communication; but ultimately a message can only meaningfully be examined in the context of other elements, all of which are interlinked and interacting.

It is important to distinguish between the actual signal that carries the message and the message itself: a wink is a signal but what is its message? The answer depends on many factors – for example, who is winking, to whom and in what context? (See SIGN.) While message-signals in the form of visual or aural CODES may be sent, the message may not be understood. Thus an ambiguous smile may represent the signal that a message is being conveyed, but the receiver may fail to understand the message while recognizing the signal.

The message may draw its initial shape or purpose from the Sender or Communicator: it will be similarly influenced by the nature of the medium in which it is sent. The Receiver of a message may be close at hand, in sight of the Communicator, or some distance away. If the message involves INTRAPERSONAL COMMUNICATION, the Communicator and the Receiver may be one and the same. Both the signal and the intended message may encounter NOISE, that is physical or psychological interference that will affect its meaningfulness. The message may elicit FEEDBACK, which will further modify the message and indeed create a new communication situation and new signals and messages.

We can rarely, if ever, be certain of how other people will interpret our signals, or whether we will 'get our message across'. Thus the message sent may be quite different from the message received, and while we think we are communicating a single message we may, unconsciously, be putting across all sorts of other messages too.

We are 'selecting in' and 'selecting out' a barrage of message-carrying signals all the time, and we give attention to them if we are *motivated* to do so. The effectiveness of a message depends, at a basic, instrumental level, on the weight it carries in competition with other signals and messages, but equally it depends upon the significance attached to it by the receiver(s).

This in turn depends upon the 'set', or preparedness, of the receivers for the Sender/Message/Medium. The message of a satirical cartoon, for example, might be completely lost if the reader knows nothing about the particular circumstances to which the cartoon refers. Even a knowledge of the facts may not be enough to facilitate the intended interpretation, because this may only occur if the reader shares the social, political or cultural values of the cartoonist. In short, whether we 'get our message across' depends partly upon the context in which it is received; and the VALUES, attitudes, perceptions and knowledge of the receiver at a crucial part of that context. See DOMINANT, SUBORDINATE, RADICAL; INTERVENING VARIABLES (IVS); METAMESSAGE; POLYSEMY; PREFERRED READING.

Metamessage The underlying message in a communicative act. This may differ from what on the surface appears to be the message. The metamessage is conveyed both verbally and, often more crucially, non-verbally. The metamessage carries information about the relationships of those involved in an encounter, and the attitudes they have towards each other and the topic in question.

The interpretation of the metamessage is usually influenced by the way in which the message is communicated; non-verbal communication thus plays a vital role in the sending and receiving of metamessages. A simple question such as 'May I help you?' asked by someone in a higher-status ROLE, for example, can be interpreted as a friendly gesture or as an accusation of incompetence depending, in part, on the tone of voice adopted.

Metamessages can also help to frame a conversation, as they help to define the nature of the encounter by, for example, defining the seriousness of the conversation and the relationships of those taking part.

Metaphor A figure of speech or a visual device that works by transporting qualities from one plane of reality to another: 'the camel is the ship of the desert'; 'life for Mary was a bed of roses'. Without metaphor there would be no scope for the development of either visual or verbal language; it would remain clinical and colourless.

Metaphor is not merely an expressive device but an integral part of the function of language as a *definer* as well as a reflector of reality. As a rhetorical device metaphor is central to the way in which media define reality, structure, maintain and monitor DISCOURSE, uphold (and sometimes challenge) hierarchies, service (and sometimes undermine) HEGEMONY. Metaphor provides us with the pictures by which we envision the world: we define time by metaphor ('time is money'); we view the public as inhabiting a 'space' (see AGORA); we define public argu-

ment and debate using metaphors of conflict, and the notion of argument as 'war' is built into the CULTURE we inhabit.

Even where peace is being referred to, the media are more than likely to express it in military terms: 'War breaks out over classroom peace plans'. Press language is riddled with the bombast of conflict: things are axed, chopped, smashed, slashed; knives are constantly out; prime ministers stick to their guns; oppositions are routed.

We use metaphor to define the nature of communication as *transmission* or as *ritual*. We talk of *homo narrens* (see NARRATIVE PARADIGM), casting the human being as the storytelling animal; or, with Erving Goffman, we may use the *dramaturgical* model, the metaphor of life as a stage.

In *An Introductory Guide to Post-Structuralism and Postmodernism* (Harvester Wheatsheaf, 1993), Madan Sarap states 'that metaphors determine to a large extent what we think in any field. Metaphors are not idle flourishes – they shape what we do. They can help make, and defend a world view'. As well as being 'productive of insights and fresh illuminations', metaphors, according to Sarap, 'can encapsulate and put forward proposals for another way of looking at things'. They can serve as agents of change as well as weapons of reinforcement (see STEREOTYPE).

'Through metaphor,' says Sarap, 'we can have increased awareness of alternative possible worlds'. The so-called *mixed metaphor*, beloved of politicians seeking by their RHETORIC to attract media attention, contains in a statement two or more ineptly linked images: 'Lame ducks will be barking up the wrong tree if they think government is going to bail them out every time profits take a hammering.' Though the metaphorical allusions may be all over the place, the statement's underlying IDEOLOGY is, however, crystal clear.

Few contemporary media phenonema have prompted so many and such varied metaphors as the INTERNET. In addition to the World Wide Web (see WEB: WORLD WIDE WEB (WWW)), the Net has been described as an open prairie or a superhighway of information, an ocean to be surfed, a mail pigeon, an uncatalogued library, an amusement park, a maze, a bottomless pit, a collective nervous system and a global village, each term attempting, constructively or destructively, to get a grasp of exactly what the Internet is, and how we perceive it.

Because of the Net's lack of physicality, we translate its infinite spaces into familiar imagery, such as transport; thus we refer to crashes, fast and slow lanes and blocked traffic; or we opt for the experience of markets – shopping malls or even the more humble flea-market. The competition for labelling the Net is significant. What names it goes by has an impact on the ways in which communities view and use it. See EUPHEMISM; METONYMY; VISIONS OF ORDER. See also *TOPIC GUIDE* under LANGUAGE/DISCOURSE/NARRATIVE.

Metasignal A signal that makes a comment about a signal, or a set of signals: it directs us to their accurate meaning. For example, two people appear to exchange blows: is the fight real or make-believe? Their smiling faces form the metasignal which indicates that, at least on the surface, what we are seeing is a play-fight.

Body posture is among the chief metasignals. Equally, *uniform* serves effectively in this capacity; we react differently to the policeman in uniform than we might to the same person in off-duty jeans and tee-shirt. Desmond Morris in *Manwatching: A Field Guide to Human Behaviour* (Jonathan Cape, 1977) says that 'in a sense the whole world of entertainment presents a non-stop Metasignal, in the form of the proscenium arch around the stage of a theatre, or the edge of the cinema or TV screen'. Audiences, he believes, can tolerate, and gain entertainment from, films and plays featuring dollops of death and mayhem because of the metasignals which indicate that 'this isn't real'. Morris argues that though the actors may aim at maximum reality in their dark deeds, 'no matter how convincing they are, we still carry at the back of our minds (even as we gasp when the knife plunges home) the Metasignal of the "edge" of their stage'.

▸ Desmond Morris, *People Watching* (Vantage, 2002).

Metonymy A figure of speech in which the thing meant is represented by something that is an attribute of the original. When we talk of the newspaper business, we refer to the press – something that stands for the whole.

As far as images are concerned, the metonym is a selection of one of those available to represent the whole; and from that selection flows our interpretation or understanding of the whole. Thus the selection of a piece of film of young people lounging at a street corner, or strike pickets in combat with the police, acts as the 'trigger of meaning' for the way the teenager or the striker is defined. For this reason, metonyms are powerful conveyors of reality; indeed they are so powerful that they can come to be accepted as reality – as the way things actually are.

Microsoft Windows The personal computer (PC) software that has bestrode the computer world like the proverbial colossus. Harvard graduates Bill Gates and Paul Allen, later joined by Steve Ballmer, were among the first entrepreneurs to spot the future of personal computers. They formed a business partnership in 1975, naming it Microsoft (microcomputer software). By 1980 they were able to offer the world, via the IBM company, M-DOS (Microsoft Disk Operating System), the first personal, desktop computer (1981).

By 1983, the new Windows System (1.0) described by Bill Gates as 'unique software designed for the serious PC user' hit the market, followed by Windows 2.0 (1987) with expanded memory and increased desktop facility. There followed, each an advance upon the last, fifteen editions of Windows, among them Windows 3.0 (1990) and 3.1 (1992), this with advanced graphics and add-on games such as Solitaire.

Windows 95 (1995) came complete with built-in INTERNET support, dial-up networking and Plug and Play facilities, and featured for the first time the Start menu and task bar. Major improvements to networking and support for mobile computing and USB devices came with Windows 2000. Released in 2001, Windows XP carried new design features and enhanced digital photo capabilities. Windows XP Professional was followed between 2006 and 2008 with Windows Vista (with advanced Windows Media Player, known as Longhorn) available in thirty-five languages. Windows 7 introduced the capacity for users to stream (see STREAMING) music, videos and photos from the PC to a TV or stereo system.

The Microsoft company celebrated its twenty-fifth anniversary in 2010. Over those twenty-five years it encountered problems – and was faced with court cases – concerning copyright. For example, in 1990 rival APPLE MACINTOSH cited 189 examples of what it claimed were copyright infringements, the judge reducing these to ten instances. In 2001 the company was obliged by the American Department of Justice to share (rather than hog) systems with a panel of experts.

In 2003 the European Commission demanded that Microsoft produce a Windows package without Windows Media Player and to create a version without Internet Explorer; all in all, moves to counteract Microsoft's perceived monopoly of the market. Microsoft initially began such a version but then scrapped it in favour of a 'browser ballot' allowing users to make a choice between providers.

Windows has struggled to establish itself

M

in the mobile consumer market, faced by the entrepreneurial genius of APPLE MACINTOSH with all its ground-breaking innovations in the field. However, diversification has always been key to Microsoft's ambitions. The company took a US$ 240 million equity stake in FACEBOOK in 2007 and attempted to buy the platform in 2010. It created Bing search engine to rival GOOGLE and this is now integrated with Facebook, allowing users to see, directly from search results, what their friends have 'liked'. From 2010 Bing powered YAHOO! searches in the US and Canada.

Micro-myth, macro-myth Philip Schlesinger in *Putting 'Reality' Together: BBC News* (Constable, 1978; Methuen/University Paperback, 1987) examines the BBC news machine at work, and identifies what in his view are two myths entertained by those who work in BBC news: the *micro-myth*, that production staff are permitted autonomy within the organization; and the *macro-myth*, that the BBC is an independent organization, largely socially unattached. See IMPARTIALITY.

Milieu The social environment of the individual, group, CULTURE or nation.

Milton's paradox On the one hand the English poet John Milton (1608–74) is famous for his stalwart defence of the freedom of expression (see AREOPAGITICA); on the other, Milton did not entirely practise what he preached. Dominant in Milton's own life was anti-Catholicism. The paradox arises from the difference between principle and practice: during the period of the Interregnum, 1649–60 (the Commonwealth of Oliver Cromwell) Milton was an official censor, though apologists argue that the poet was less involved in CENSORSHIP than in editing and supervision.

In 'Milton's paradox: the market-place of ideas in post-Communist Bulgaria', in the *European Journal of Communication*, September 1997, Ekaterina Ognianova and Byron Scott believe that 'in a simplistic way at least, Milton represents a perennial conflict between general beliefs and specific behaviour, between concepts and practice when it comes to the question of how much freedom to permit'.

Mimetic/semiosic planes In NARRATIVE, the mimetic is the plane of *representation*, the semiosic the plane of *meaning* production. See CODES OF NARRATIVE; CONNOTATION; NARRATIVE PARADIGM; PROPP'S PEOPLE; SEMIOLOGY/SEMIOTICS.

Minneapolis City Council inquiry into pornography See PORNOGRAPHY.

Minority Report of Mr Selwyn Lloyd This was attached to the Majority BEVERIDGE COMMITTEE REPORT ON BROADCASTING, 1950, and, contrary, to Beveridge, who supported a continued monopoly of broadcasting for the BBC, argued that independent, and commercial, competition would be a good thing. Author of the Minority Report was Conservative MP Selwyn Lloyd, who produced a scheme for a Commission for British Broadcasting to be set up which would license a number of rival broadcasting stations.

Lloyd wrote, 'Having considered these arguments put forward by the BBC on behalf of monopoly, I am of the opinion that independent competition will be healthy for broadcasting.' His view had considerable support in the Tory party and in the business world: commercial broadcasting in the UK was on the horizon. See TOPIC GUIDE under BROADCASTING.

Miracle of Fleet Street Description by Lord Northcliffe (1865–1922) of the redoubtable UK *Daily Herald* (1912–64), a sometimes swashbuckling radical paper which, despite having a substantial circulation and vast readership, received little ADVERTISING. This was as a result partly of its left-wing views, but perhaps more importantly because of its insistence on thorough reporting of political issues, considered at that time to appeal more to male readers. When other national popular papers were priced at one penny, the *Daily Herald* was forced to charge two pence. Yet it lost very little in circulation, due to the energy and leadership of its greatest editor, George Lansbury, MP (1859–1940).

The *Herald* was the first newspaper in the world to reach a circulation of 2 million – in mid-1933 – though it was soon overtaken by Beaverbrook's *Daily Express*. By the time the *Herald* had reached its peak circulation of 2.1 million in 1947, the *Daily Mirror* and *Daily Express* were pushing 4 million and by 1960, sales had tumbled to 1.6 million. The *Herald* struggled on until 14 September 1964. See TOPIC GUIDE under MEDIA HISTORY.

Misinformed society As the means of communication expand, the assumption that more and diverse information equates with better-informed citizens has been challenged by many commentators. In asking the question, How far have media succeeded/failed to provide information for citizenship?' Peter Golding argues that the so-termed information society 'is a myth'. In 'Telling stories: sociology, journalism and the informed citizen' in the *European Journal of Communication* (December 1994), Golding believes that we live in a media society, in which information is available at a price, or not at all', and that a more accurate term for today would be the *mis*informed society: 'Wherever we look, in coverage of race, industrial relations, welfare, foreign relations, or electoral politics, the media have failed democracy. We live in a society in blinkers.'

For Golding, the 'information age' constitutes not a devolution of the message systems reaching ever wider into every part of society, but a scene made up of media monoliths and a society which has become increasingly centralized in terms of decision-making and the 'reach' of vital information. Golding's misinformed society is marked by a narrowing range of media ownership, a reduction in the number of newspapers (especially in the US), the casualization of labour in media industries, and wholesale redundancies.

In terms of programming, Golding warns of the marginalization of serious information programmes on TV and an obsession with maximizing ratings that threaten the range and diversity of broadcasting. He sees the current flow and quality of information as fragmenting rather than unifying society, furthering not equality but inequality. The media of today render a 'flawed account of social reality' and shirk the abiding principle of a self-respecting media, 'to tell the truth and make things better'. See GLOBALIZATION (AND THE MEDIA); INFORMATION BLIZZARDS; JOURNALISM: CITIZEN JOURNALISM; JOURNALISM: INVESTIGATIVE JOURNALISM; PRIVATIZATION; SURVEILLANCE SOCIETY.

Mix, mixing In film-making a *mix* is a gradual transition between two shots where one dissolves into another. It is a soft fade, often used to denote the passage of time (see MONTAGE; SHOT; WIPE). *Mixing* is the process of re-recording all original dialogue, music and sound effects on to a single master sound track. See SYNCHRONOUS SOUND.

Mobile concept of communication See MOBILIZATION.

Mobile phone See next entry.

Mobilization An important capacity of the media is to mobilize public opinion, that is to arouse sympathy or concern about certain issues to the point where *action* is taken by the public themselves, or by those in authority. The classic example is the role played by the media in the preparation of a nation for war. In such a case, the media are instrumental in informing the public about the situation, arguing the case for action and then, when the action takes place, reporting it – usually – from a strictly partisan point of view. Their role becomes that of propagandist.

A twenty-first-century alternative, but nicely linked, definition of mobilization refers to the remarkable expansion, until it has become a cultural phenomenon, of the use of the mobile phone linked with the INTERNET. Few technological advances have become so much part of modern communication at every level of society and so rapidly as the mobile, to the point where reference is made to the *m-generation*, to *m-commerce* and to the *m-future*, in which the dominance of the computer as the hub of network transactions is seen to be giving way to the mobile, with all its manifold functions from simple telephoning and texting to Internet use, DOWNLOADING, listening to radio and watching TV.

Of particular interest to the study of aspects of mobilization – or in this case, as Manuel Cassells terms it, *mass self-communication* – is the way public opinion can be mobilized across nations and globally. In an article entitled 'Communication, power and counter-power in the Network Society', published in the *International Journal of Communication* (Vol. 1, 2007), Cassells writes: 'The spread of instant political mobilizations by using mobile phones, supported by the Internet, is changing the landscape of politics.'

Cassell states that it 'becomes increasingly difficult for governments to hide or manipulate information. The manipulation plots are immediately picked up and challenged by a myriad of "eye balls", as debate and mobilization are called upon by thousands of people, without central coordination, but with a shared purpose, often focusing on asking or forcing the resignation of governments or government officials'.

The rapid escalation of popular protests against government in a number of North African countries in 2010 and 2011 (the so-called African Spring) was substantially aided by what is termed *digital activism*. No longer is information confined to the authoratitive few: today news spreads instantly via mobile phones to thousands and within hours or days vast numbers can be informed, united in a cause and organized into action.

The brutal killing, caught on camera, of Khaled Said by Egypt's security forces in June 2010 received widespread Internet coverage, sparking protests that led to the January 2011 uprising that toppled the country's president, Hosi Mubarak. As one Egyptian activist tweeted during the protests, 'We use Facebook to schedule the protests, Twitter to coordinate, and YouTube to tell the world.'

In her *Index on Censorship* (No. 1, 2011) editorial, 'Playing the long game', Jo Glanville writes,

M

'The invitation to the blogger Slim Amamou to join the interim government in Tunisia was one of the most remarkable acknowledgments of the role of digital activists in civil society, not to mention the symbolism of his appointment in a country that has stifled free speech for decades.'

Less sanguine about the 'tweeting power' that brings about revolution is Evgeny Morozov. In *The Net Delusion: How Not to Liberate the World* (Allan Lane, 2011) Morozov offers a counterview to that of the 'cyber utopians' as he terms them, believing that online mobilization has 'often strengthened rather than undermined authoritarian rule'. Dissident voices become 'outed' and thus open to surveillance, playing into the hands of authority. Morozov believes that 'many analysts fall into the trap of equating liberalization with democratization'. See GLOBAL SCRUTINY; JOURNALISM: CITIZEN JOURNALISM; ONLINE CAMPAIGNING; OPEN SOURCE.

▸ Gerard Goggins and Larissa Hjorth, eds, *Mobile Technology: From Telecommunications to Media* (Routledge, 2009).

Modality The use of the words 'may' or 'might' are referred to by linguists as *modal auxiliaries*, part of the modal system of language. Modality serves to insert 'yes but' into definitions, for example of truth or reality. Modality can be confirming or disconfirming by means of its degree of affinity with that which is described, within the system or contexts in which it is described. Thus affinity between a speaker and a listener will condition the degree of modality: they may agree, 'This is true' or 'This is real' and agreement gives both a sense of security and status.

Robert Hodge and Gunther Kress in *Social Semiotics* (Polity Press, 1988) write that 'a high degree of affinity indicates the expression of solidarity between participants'. The authors define affinity as 'an indicator of relations of solidarity or of power: that is, relations orientated towards the expression of solidarity or of power (difference)'. Thus 'modality points to the social construction or contestation of knowledge-systems'. Agreement confirms the status of 'truth' and 'reality', disagreement disconfirms or undermines that status. 'Modality is consequently one of the crucial indicators of political struggle. It is a central means of contestations, and the site of the working out, whether by negotiation or imposition, of ideological systems.'

Model In social science research, a model is a tentative description of what a social process – say, the communication process – or system might be like. It is a tool of explanation and analysis, very often in diagrammatic form, that attempts to show how the various elements of a situation being studied relate to each other. Models are not statements of reality; only after much further research and testing would the model be considered viable. It could then develop into a theory.

The term can also refer to a familiar process or object that is used as a point of reference when an attempt to explain the unknown is being made. An analogy is made showing the similarities between the phenomenon to be explained and one that is well known, i.e. the model.

Additionally, a model can be a person whose behaviour others wish to imitate; on whom they wish to model themselves – a ROLE MODEL. The desire to model oneself on other people is particularly strong in one's teenage years, and the mass media play a significant part in presenting teenagers with a variety of such models. See HYPOTHESIS; IDENTIFICATION. See also *TOPIC GUIDE* under COMMUNICATION MODELS.

Modem Device for converting *analogue* signals to *digital* signals and from digital to analogue. Modem is short for modulator/demodulator.

Modes of media analysis See FUNCTIONALIST (MODE OF MEDIA ANALYSIS); MARXIST (MODE OF MEDIA ANALYSIS); SOCIAL ACTION (MODE OF MEDIA ANALYSIS). See also *TOPIC GUIDE* under RESEARCH METHODS.

Monofunctional In a media sense, the term ascribing to a work – of literature, RADIO, film, TV – a single function; for example, to entertain. Research findings over the years have seriously challenged assumptions that particular forms of content are monofunctional. Adults declare a considerable interest in NEWS programmes, yet functional studies have shown that for many viewers, the primary function of news is not informational. The news broadcast is, apparently, more closely related to habit; it also affords to the individual, feelings of security and of social contact. See EFFECTS OF THE MASS MEDIA; SURVEILLANCE.

Monopoly, four scandals of According to the BEVERIDGE COMMITTEE REPORT ON BROADCASTING (UK), 1950, these were 'bureacracy, complacency, favouritism and inefficiency' – indicators that the Committee saw in the performance of the BBC as monopoly-holder of British airwaves. Nevertheless, Beveridge recommended that the Corporation's licence be renewed, because the alternative – US-style commercial TV – promised a system that was considered to be much worse.

Monotype printing Invented in 1889 by American Tolbert Lanston. The machine is in two parts.

The first, operated by the keyboard, punches coded holes into a paper tape; the second has the tape fed into it and the code controls the casting operation. In monotype casting, unlike linotype printing, every letter and space is cast separately.

Monroe motivated sequence Five-step sequence advocated by American Professor Alan Monroe in *Principles of Speech Communication* by Douglas Ehninger, Bruce E. Cronbach and Monroe (Scott Foresman, 1984) for use in organizing speeches, especially those with an intent to persuade. The first step is to command, and maintain, audience *attention* by some eye- or ear-catching device (such as a lively story, anecdote or dramatic set of statistics). The second step is to fulfil an audience *need,* achieved through making the speech relevant. What follows is *satisfaction,* where possible solutions are proposed and examined. The speaker then proceeds to *visualization*, where the audience is persuaded to see more clearly how the speaker's information or ideas will help them. Step five is *action*, a plea for response, for the taking-up of the speaker's points.

Montage From the French, 'monter', to assemble; the process of cutting up film and arranging – editing – it into the screened sequence. The Russian film director Sergei Eisenstein (1898– 1948) explained montage as putting together camera shots which, in combination, made a greater impact than did the sum of the parts – a creative juxtaposition. Separate elements combine to produce a new MEANING. Montage is the *synthesis* that gives film its unique character.

Montage is used as a *narrative* device and an *expressive* device, the one concerned with sequencing, ensuring the smooth continuity of action, the other with the intention of producing a particular effect by the clash, comparison or contrast of two or more images, often symbolic or metaphoric in meaning. This use of montage is often compared with *collage* in art, in that it draws attention to itself as an exercise in construction: it says, 'Look at me as film, not reality.' See ALIENATION EFFECT; KULESHOV EFFECT; SHOT.

Moral economy See HICT PROJECT.

Moral entrepreneurs Howard Becker first used this term in *Outsiders: Studies in the Sociology of Deviance* (Free Press, 1963) to describe those members of the community who take upon themselves the role of GUARD DOG, vigilant against alleged attempts to subvert public morals. Such individuals often try, sometimes with success, to use the media to gain public support for their views; or latterly to aim their messages directly to the online public by using the various avenues of expression offered by the INTERNET, such as blogging and tweeting.

▶ Stanley Cohen, *Folk Devils and Moral Panics* (Routledge, 2002); Chas Critcher, ed., *Critical Readings: Moral Panics and the Media* (Open University Press/ McGraw-Hill Education, 2006); Erich Goode and Nachman Ben-Yehuda's note in *Moral Panics: The Social Construction of Deviance* (Wiley-Blackwell, 2009).

Moral panics and the media Individuals and social GROUPS can by their activities emerge as a focus for outrage expressed by influential members of society who perceive these activities as seriously subverting the MORES and interests of the dominant CULTURE. Such reactions are, says Stanley Cohen in *Folk Devils and Moral Panics* (MacGibbon & Kee, 1972, edited by Cohen and Jock Young; 3rd edition, Routledge, 2002), disseminated by the mass media usually in an hysterical, stylized, and stereotypical manner, thus engendering a sense of moral panic. Generally such panics have occurred in relation to OTHER, for example when immigrants or asylum-seekers are perceived, via media coverage, and the repetition of that coverage over time and by agencies with political motivation, as a threat; a problem about which those in authority seem to be doing nothing, or too little.

In the 2002 edition of his book, Cohen argues that over the years, 'the objects of moral panic belong to seven familiar clusters of social identity'. The clusters and related fears are categorized as follows: Young, Working-class, Violent Males; School Violence: Bullying and Shootouts; Wrong Drugs: Used by Wrong People at Wrong Places; Child Abuse, Satanic Rituals and Paedophile Registers; Sex, Violence and Blaming the Media; Welfare Cheats and Single Mothers; and Refugees and Asylum Seekers: Flooding our Country, Swamping our Services. The individual or group exemplars of these are the folk devils in an (otherwise) ordered society and perceived as a threat to that ordered society.

Just as the focus for a moral panic may be predictable, so too, argues Cohen, are the essential features of the way in which panics are constructed. Specific panics may be seen as new but also as 'camouflaged versions of traditional and well-known evils'. Panics are of concern in their own right, but are also seen as '… *warning signs* of the real, much deeper and more prevalent condition'. Panics are '*transparent* … but also *opaque*' and 'accredited experts' are engaged to explain the hidden dangers to the public.

Erich Goode and Nachman Ben-Yehuda in

Moral Panics: The Social Construction of Deviance (Wiley-Blackwell, 2009) examine a number of moral panics and identify three theories of moral panic. The 'grassroots' model explains moral panics as stemming from unplanned, popular responses to perceived societal threats, whilst the 'elite-engineered' model on the other hand views moral panics as generated and manipulated by members of powerful elites for their own purposes. The 'interest group' model locates the source of moral panics in interest groups from 'somewhere in society's middle strata: professional associations, journalists with a mission, religious groups, social movement organizations, educational institutions, in fact middle-level associations, organizations, groups, and institutions of every description.'

In his introduction to the 3rd edition of *Folk Devils and Moral Panics*, Stanley Cohen speaks of moral panics as 'condensed political struggles to control the means of cultural reproduction. Studying them is easy and lots of fun. It also allows us to identify and conceptualize the lines of power in any society, the ways we are manipulated into taking some things too seriously and other things not seriously enough.'

Anxiety has been widely expressed that modern society is in a near-permanent state of panic. Cohen notes that between 1984 and 1991 there were eight citations of moral panics, and between 1994 and 2001, an average of over a hundred a year. In his BBC Online blog (11 September 2009), 'When panic shapes policy', Mark Easton worries about the broad social and political impact of targeting 'folk devils': 'Our democracy is regularly buffeted by panics which make rational, considered discussion impossible until the dust settles years later.' See DEVIANCE (for *deviance amplification spiral*); FOLK DEVILS; LABELLING PROCESS (AND THE MEDIA); PREJUDICE.

▸ David Altheide, *Creating Fear: News and the Construction of Crisis* (Aldine de Gruyler, 2002); Chas Critcher, ed., *Critical Readings: Moral Panics and the Media* (Open University Press/McGraw-Hill Education, 2006); Frank Furedi, *Politics of Fear: Beyond Left and Right* (Continuum, 2006); Sean Hier, ed., *Moral Panic and the Politics of Anxiety* (Routledge eBook, 2011).

Moral rights (in a text) See TEXT: INTEGRITY OF THE TEXT.

Mores Those social rules concerning acceptable behaviour which it is considered wrong to break. Such rules play an important part in the maintenance of social order and cohesion; consequently breaches of mores usually meet with the imposition of sanctions by society, formally through laws, informally through, for example, social rejection.

Some mores are particular to a specific society; others can be found in most societies. A majority of societies respects the sanctity of human life, though this is varyingly weighed against the sanctity of social order. Also, within a society different social GROUPS may have different mores. Traditionally it is against the unwritten law of school life for pupils to tell tales to teacher; the sanction against those who do may be their temporary isolation or ejection from the group, or reprisals after school.

Mores may often prescribe both the tone and content of communication. Differences in sexual mores, for example, underpin many of the arguments about the dissemination of PORNOGRAPHY.

Morphing In film-making, seamlessly joining together different images; special effects most notably used in horror movies, when images – faces, for example – 'metamorphose' into one another or change dramatically in appearance. Also employed in popular music videos.

Morphology Study of the structure or forms of words, traditionally distinguished from SYNTAX which deals with the rules governing the combination of words in sentences. Generally morphology divides into two fields: the study of inflections and of word-formation.

Morse Code See TELEGRAPHY.

Mother tongue A term used to refer to an individual's language of origin or native language – one learnt from birth, from the mother or other primary caregivers, and passed on through the generations. The mother or other primary caregivers may of course provide a bilingual or multilingual experience for the child. In a culturally diverse society there is likely to be a range of mother tongues used, and therefore it may be the case for a considerable number of people that their mother tongue differs from the prestige or official language of that society. Such differences in perceived status can be the cause of resentment.

Keeping the mother tongue alive can be an important aspect of ethnic identity for a community. In 'Mothers and mother tongue: perspectives on self-construction by mothers of Pakistani heritage' in Aneta Pavlenko and Adrian Blackledge (eds), *Negotiation of Identities in Multilingual Contexts* (Multilingual Matters Ltd, 2004), Jean Mills discusses a study she undertook with Asian mothers in the West Midlands. She found that linguistic competence in the 'mother tongue' (Urdu, for example) was regarded as an important element of Pakistani-British identity. The mothers felt they had a responsibility to ensure that their children had competency in the 'mother tongue' as well as in English. The 'mother tongue' was widely used within the family – indeed it was crucial for communicating with the older generation and relatives in Pakistan – and the local community.

Motion capture See ANIMATION.

Motivation The concept of motivation is relevant to several areas of communication and media studies. As Richard Dimbleby and Graeme Burton remind us in *More Than Words: An Introduction to Communication* (Routledge, 2007), 'People must have a reason for communicating. It is worth remembering that when people communicate, they may be fulfilling more than one purpose at the same time.' Motivation theories can then help to provide a range of ideas about why people want to communicate.

In *Psychology: The Science of Mind and Behaviour* (Hodder Arnold, 2005) Richard Gross notes that essentially, 'motivation is concerned with why people act and think the way they do' and that 'motivated behaviour is *goal-directed*, *purposeful* behaviour'. Numerous theories seek to explore the mysteries of human motivation. Whilst the sources of motivation are varied and complex, there is general agreement that motivation arises from a desire to satify needs. A range of research has sought to define these needs and the relative importance that individuals attach to them (see MASLOW'S HIERARCHY OF NEEDS).

Of relevance here is William Schutz's theory of interpersonal needs. Schutz, in *The Interpersonal World* (Science and Behaviour Books, 1966), identifies three basic interpersonal needs which he argues underlie most interpersonal behaviour: the need for *inclusion*, the need for *control* and the need for *affection*. These then are the needs one might wish to have satisfied in INTERPERSONAL COMMUNICATION. Situations in which others satisfy one or more of your needs are likely to be valued; those situations in which your needs are not met may well be avoided.

Another example of the use made of the concept of motivation is in the consideration of why and how people might be influenced or persuaded to act in certain ways, by certain messages. Much effort is expended in the ADVERTISING and PUBLIC RELATIONS (PR) industries trying to devise strategies for selling products, services or people, by appealing to what are thought to be the motivations of the general public. See HIDDEN NEEDS; HOT BUTTONS; MOTIVATION RESEARCH (MR); VALS TYPOLOGY.

See also *TOPIC GUIDE* under COMMUNICATION THEORY.

Motivation research (MR) The key question in MR is – what motivates people to buy, or in media terms, what motivates them to tune in, to read, to watch; in short, to respond; and how might that motivation be influenced in order for them to continue responding? MR's traditional mechanisms of questionnaires, interviews and focus groups have long been supplemented by electronic devices such as the *pupilometer* to measure respondents' eye movements and the degree of 'stopping power' of, for example, an audience member's response to a TV advertisement.

There are machines which offer voice-pitch analysis; machines to tabulate brain waves. Not only is psychology wheeled into action in the service of MR, but so are the findings of psycholinguists, who study the mental processes governing the learning and use of language. MR is involved in an ever-restless process of seeking more and more sophisticated ways of 'reading' consumption, but it is seen by some commentators as being more and more into the business of *shaping* or manipulating responses, not the least in the arena of politics. The arrival of the INTERNET presented MR with new challenges, in particular with regard to social networking (see NETWORKING: SOCIAL NETWORKING). By 2011, online advertising in many consumerist areas was showing traditional ad locations a clean pair of heels. See ADVERTISING: INTERNET ADVERTISING; AMAZON.COM; BLOGOSPHERE; DIGITAL OPTIMISM; FACEBOOK; HOT BUTTONS; GOOGLE; MOBILIZATION; TWITTER; YOUTUBE. See also *TOPIC GUIDE* under ADVERTISING/ MARKETING.

▶ Vance Packard, *The Hidden Persuaders* (Ig Publishing, 2007 edn with introduction by Mark Crispin Miller); Martin Evans, Ahmed Jamal and Gordon Foxall, *Consumer Behaviour* (John Wiley & Sons, 2009).

MP3 Digitized music file with the potential to revolutionize the music industry, and in the words of David Edwards in a UK *Daily Mirror* article, 'CD R.I.P. Why your shiny new album collection is being made obsolete by the March of MP3', promises to change for ever 'the way people buy and listen to music'. The initial reaction by the music industry to the MP3 file, which allows for music to be downloaded from the INTERNET, free of charge, was to resist it. Napster, a company offering free music on the Net, was shut down following legal action by the Recording Industry Association of the US. It was a pyrrhic victory and soon the industry was offering music and other downloads to subscribers. See DOWNLOADING.

Mr Gate American media analyst David Manning White in 1950 investigated the process of GATEKEEPING by studying the editing selections by a copy-editor, 'Mr Gate', from the (then) three major American news agencies on a 30,000-circulation daily newspaper in the US midwest. 'Mr Gate' in one week used 1,297 column inches – about one-tenth of the 11,910 column inches supplied. 'Mr Gate' confessed to a few prejudices which might well cause him to put items on the spike (reject them), and to a preference: 'I go for human interest stories in a big way'; but White also perceived how important the pressure of time was on the selection process. The nearer the next edition of the newspaper came, the stronger in NEWS VALUE a story had to be not to be rejected. See WHITE'S GATEKEEPER MODEL, 1950.

M-time, P-time Edward Hall in *The Dance of Life: Other Dimensions of Time* (Doubleday, 1983) contends that cultures tend to adopt either a *monochronic* (M-time) or *polychronic* (P-time) perspective to managing time. The M-time perspective focuses on the clock: time is measured into units; time should be used productively; punctuality and meeting deadlines are viewed as important; time is represented as having a linear pattern; and the focus is on doing one thing at a time.

In contrast the P-time perspective focuses on people and events, not the clock: time is fluid and flexible; activities have an evolving timescale; deadlines and appointments are not rigidly adhered to; several activities may be undertaken at the same time; and tasks and conversations are likely to be interrupted. There is a tendency for individualistic cultures to be driven by M-time and for collectivistic cultures to embrace the P-time perspective (see COMMUNICATION: INTERCULTURAL COMMUNICATION).

Such differences can be the cause of misunderstanding and friction in intercultural encounters. Stella Ting-Toomey in *Communication Across Cultures* (Guilford Press, 1999) discusses the problems that differences in time rhythms can cause; to take one example from conflict-management situations: 'M-time people want to establish a clear timetable to achieve specific conflict goals and objectives; P-time people want to spend more time building up trust and commitment between the conflict parties. Different M-time and P-time rhythms ... can further polarize individualists

and collectivists ...'

MTV Music Television; worldwide popular music video broadcasting service created by Robert Pittman in the US in 1981, to take advantage of initially free programming provided by popular VIDEO. Transmitted via satellite and cable television, MTV is financed by advertising and sponsorship.

Multi-actuality The meaning of communication signs – language – is not fixed but subject to differing interpretations according to context. The term originated with Valentin Volosinov in *Marxism and the Philosophy of Language* (Seminar Press, 1973; first published in Russian, 1929–30), who argued that the prevailing MEANING of a word or expression, such as democracy or freedom, works towards the suppression of multi-actuality, except in terms of 'social crises or revolutionary changes'. In other words, the dominant hierarchy will strive to impose its own meaning – one meaning as opposed to many. Signs, therefore, Volosinov believes, may become the 'arena for the class struggle' as the dominant group of interpreters of meaning strive to eradicate alternative meanings. See HEGEMONY; IDEOLOGY; METAPHOR.

Multicultural London English (MLE) A new dialect of English being studied by researchers at Lancaster University and Queen Mary College, University of London. MLE is spoken by young people in inner city areas of London, particularly those from ethnic minority backgrounds. It is strongly influenced by British Black English but contains a mixture of other linguistic influences from West Asia and Africa. See www.lancs.ac.uk/fss/projects/linguistics/innovators/.

Multiplane Walt Disney (1901–66) used this word to explain an innovation in the process of ANIMATION, illustrated in *Fantasia* (1940). Instead of building up a drawing by laying 'cells' one directly on top of another, an illusion of depth was achieved by a space being left between the celluloid images of foreground, background and principal figures.

Multiple image A number of images printed beside each other on the same film frame, often showing different camera angles of the same action, or separate actions. Abel Gance (1889–1981) used this device to stunning effect in his masterpiece of 1926, *Napoleon*.

Multiplier effect Where CULTURE as a commodity – usually in the form of films and TV programmes – exported to other countries, opens up markets for other goods. See MEDIA IMPERIALISM.

Murdoch effect Arising from the dominance of

the media by Rupert Murdoch and his global organization NEWS CORP, the term relates to processes of acquisition, control, expansion and the targeting of rivals in the fields of media, entertainment and sport which are seen to characterize the Murdoch approach to business. In terms of competition, it is ruthless; in terms of ideology, rightist; in media approach, populist. It is also visionary and decisive.

Murdochization is a related term describing the broader effect of Murdoch's impact on the nature and processing of news and comment. In a UK *Guardian* interview with Stephen Moss ('I'm very pessimistic about the future of the BBC', 15 March 2010), veteran reporter John Simpson stated that Murdoch 'and the newspapers he's run have introduced an uglier side, an abusive side, into journalism and life in general in this country'.

He has 'introduced an ugly tone which he has now imported into the US and which we see every day on Fox News, with all its concomitant effects on American public life – that fierce hostility between right and left that never used to be there, not to remotely the same extent'.

More pro-Murdoch commentators argue that Murdoch's often-ruthless entrepreneurialism has benefited the media industry, showing the way for others to follow (or fall by the wayside, if not into Murdoch's lap). From the outset Murdoch proved a predator, identifying companies that had grown feeble through complacence, and targeting them.

Not the least of the features that make up the Murdoch effect is the mogul's high level of risk-taking. Between 1990 and 1993 News Corp was close to bankruptcy, yet in 1992 BSkyB (British Sky Broadcasting) outbid ITV for UK Premier League soccer broadcasting rights. In the following year Murdoch swiped American football from under the nose of the NBC network.

For many, the most worrying aspect of the Murdoch effect is the mogul's perceived influence on politics and politicians. In the UK both the Labour administration and its Conservative-Liberal Democrat successor (2010) have been accused of bending the knee to Murdoch in return for a favourable press. In 2011 Murdoch's ambition to increase his 39 per cent stake in BSkyB to 100 per cent looked certain to be accepted by Culture Minister Jeremy Hunt, until the phone-hacking scandal engulfing the *News of the World* (and the paper's dramatic closure in July) put Murdoch's plans on hold. See ANTICIPATORY COMPLIANCE; BERLUSCONI PHENOMENON; CONGLOMERATES:

MEDIA CONGLOMERATES; GLOBALIZATION OF MEDIA; OFCOM: OFFICE OF COMMUNICATIONS (UK); PREDATORY PRICING. See also *Dictionary* Preface.

▸ Michael Wolff, *Autumn of the Moguls* (Flamingo, 2004); Bruce Dover, *Rupert's Adventures in China* (Tuttle Publishing, 2008); *A Chance for Change* (Campaign for Press and Broadcasting Freedom, 2011), pamphlet dealing with questions of media and democracy, ownership and regulation.

Musical: film musical Essentially the invention and hallmark of the US, and of Broadway, New York in particular. Though *The Jazz Singer* (1927) was not by any means the first film to be accompanied by music, it is nevertheless classified as the first film musical as well as the 'talkie' that made the break-through for SYNCHRONOUS SOUND. The first all-talking, all-singing, all-dancing film was *The Broadway Melody* (1929).

Colour in musicals was used with earliest success in *The Wizard of Oz* (1939).

The hey-day of the musical stretched glitteringly from the 1930s to the end of the 1950s, when vastly increased production costs and the decline in mass audiences made musicals uneconomical. They were replaced in their extravagance with musical stories such as *Oklahoma!* (1955), *West Side Story* (1961) and *My Fair Lady* (1965), with *The Sound of Music* (1965) capping all at the box-office. Imitations failed, though *Cabaret* (1972) proved that old forms and old patterns could be creatively extended; while, against the odds, *Moulin Rouge* (2000), directed by the Autralian Baz Luhrmann, proved both a critical and a box-office success.

Music Television See MTV.

MySpace Social networking service launched in Beverly Hills, California, in 2003; purchased in 2005 by News Corp Digital Media (the Murdoch empire, see NEWS CORP) for US$ 580 million, only to be sold off for an estimated US$ 35 million (£21m) to Specific Media in June 2011. As with other social sites such as Bebo and Friends United, MySpace failed to hold its own against the rise in popularity of FACEBOOK; a third of its workforce was laid off in 2009. New services, like MySpace Karaoke, were added in order to turn the business around, but January 2011 saw further substantial job losses. See NETWORKING: SOCIAL NETWORKING; YOUTUBE.

Mystification See HEGEMONY.

Myth The generally accepted meaning of myth is of a fictitious (primitive) tale, usually involving supernatural characters embodying some popular idea concerning natural or historical phenomena, and often symbolizing virtues or other timeless qualities. In everyday parlance, a myth is something invented, not true. For analysts of the communication process, myth has more specific connotations. Myth is an interpretation of the way things are; a justification. For Claude Levi-Strauss, myth is a force generated to overcome *contradictions*. Either way, at the heart of myth is IDEOLOGY, chiefly the value-system of those at the top of society.

The French philosopher Roland Barthes (1915–80) ascribes myth to the second order of SIGNIFICATION, that is, CONNOTATION, but connotation with a very special task – that of distorting the truth in a particular direction. For Barthes, myth is a weapon of the bourgeoisie which it uses to regenerate its cultural dominance.

In *Mythologies* (Paladin, 1973), Barthes writes, 'Myth does not deny things, on the contrary, its function is to talk about them; simply, it purifies them, it makes them innocent, it gives them a natural and eternal justification, it gives them a clarity which is not that of an explanation but that of a statement of fact.'

Myth defines 'eternal verities' that may be neither eternal nor verities. And myth acts economically, 'it abolishes the complexity of human acts, it gives them the simplicity of essences, it does away with all the dialectics, without any going back beyond what is immediately visible, it organizes a world which is without contradictions because it is without depth, a world wide open and wallowing in the evident, it establishes a blissful clarity: things appear to mean something by themselves'.

According to Richard Cavendish in his introduction to *Mythology: An Illustrated Encyclopaedia* (Little Brown, 1999; Silverdale Books, 2003), myth is a 'charter of authorization for groups, institutions, rituals, social distinctions, laws and customs, moral standards, values and ideas ... [Myths] authorize the present state of affairs' and their power 'transcends rational argument'. Myth succours and supports the *status quo*; its chief inspiration is *order* and its communication mode is RHETORIC. See SEMIOLOGY/SEMIOTICS. See also *TOPIC GUIDES* under MEDIA: POLITICS & ECONOMICS; MEDIA: POWER, EFFECTS, INFLUENCE; MEDIA: PROCESSES & PRODUCTION; MEDIA: VALUES & IDEOLOGIES; REPRESENTATION.

▶ Jonathan Cuffer, *Barthes* (Fontana, 1983).

Myths of deregulation See DEREGULATION, FIVE MYTHS OF.

N

Narcotizing dysfunction Term used as early as 1948 by Paul H. Lazarsfeld and Robert K. Merton in 'Communication, taste and social action' published in *The Communication of Ideas* (Harper & Row, 1948), edited by Lyman Bryson, to describe what they saw as one of the chief social consequences of AUDIENCE exposure over time to the mass media. This rather awful-sounding affliction, of first being subdued, or 'drugged', and then put out of action, comes about, believed the authors, because audiences are reduced to 'mass apathy' by a heroic effort to keep up with the vast amount of information placed before them.

The authors feared that 'mass communications may be included among the most respectable and efficient of social narcotics ... increasing dosages of mass communications may be inadvertently transforming the energies of men from active participation into passive knowledge'. See COMPASSION FATIGUE; EFFECTS OF THE MASS MEDIA; USES AND GRATIFICATIONS THEORY; MAINSTREAMING.

Narration In, for example, a TV documentary, what the narrator or the voice-over tells the AUDIENCE helps structure both programme and response. Narration is the intermediary between 'raw information' and the ordered DISCOURSE or TEXT. In his monograph *Television Discourse and History* (British Film Institute, 1980), Colin McArthur argues that the 'central ideological function of narration is to confer authority on, and to elide contradictions in, the discourse'. Narration, therefore, serves to identify and help further an ideological base.

Narration is as much a technical convenience as an ideological mechanism. It is a time-saver; permits summary; allows for efficient transition; is custom-built for an expensive, time-conscious medium. Given creative independence, many programme producers have reduced the dominance of narration or done away with it altogether, as much as possible letting the world 'speak for itself' by using sound and vision without comment; allowing camera and microphone to eavesdrop on activities free from FRAMING.

Of course the process of MEDIATION is ultimately unavoidable: cameras have to be set up in one place or another; pointed in one direction rather than another; decisions have to be made about long-shot and close-up and finally the film has to be edited. A text has been *constructed*. See CODES OF NARRATIVE; NARRATIVE; NARRATIVE PARADIGM; SYMBOLIC CONVERGENCE THEORY.

Narrative In *Narratives in Popular Culture, Media, and Everyday Life* (Sage, 1997) Arthur Asa Berger defines narrative as 'a story, and stories tell about things that have happened or are happening, to people, animals, aliens from outer space, insects – whatever. That is, a story contains a sequence of events, which means that narratives take place within or over, to be more precise, some kind of time period. This time period can be very short, as in a nursery tale, or very long, as in some novels and epics'. As Berger picturesquely puts it, our lives are 'immersed in narratives. Every day we swim in a sea of stories and tales ... from our earliest days to our deaths'.

The study of communication is very much concerned with the study of narratives – how they are put together, what their functions are and what uses are made of them by those who read, listen to or watch stories. In the view of Michel de Certeau in *The Practice of Everyday Life* (University of California, 1984), narratives 'articulate our existences'; indeed we as social, communal animals, are 'defined by stories' (see MYTH).

At the level of denotation, narratives tell us what happened to whom and in what circumstances; at the CONNOTATIONAL level we enter the realm of MEANING, of signification: what is the story really about? This applies as much to NEWS stories as to fictional stories; indeed the news can be classified as a GENRE, that is a mode of narrative which conforms (for the most part) to a set of particular rules.

In 1926 George Herbert Mead (in 'The nature of aesthetic experience' in the *International Journal of Ethics*, 36) defined two models of JOURNALISM, the information model and the story model, stating that 'the reporter is generally sent out to get a story not the facts'. The storyness theme is taken up by Peter Dahlgren in his *Introduction to Journalism and Popular Culture* (Sage, 1992, edited by Dahlgren and Colin Sparks). He writes that 'storytelling ... is a key link which unites journalism and popular culture ... narrative is a way of knowing the world', and goes on: 'Journalism officially aims to inform about events in the world – analytical mode – and does this most often in the story mode' which both 'enhances and delimits the likely range of meanings'.

Above all, like social rituals generally, the story mode has the power to bring about a sense of shared experience and shared VALUES. This, it might be said, is the 'story' of news, its connotational function: it is about cohesion-making as much as it is about information-transmission (see STRUCTURE OF NEWS: REASSURANCE).

In this multi-media age, narratives more than ever before interact and overlap but for convenience, of analysis and study, they continue to be classified under the heading of genres, each with its own narrative rules and traditions, each with recognizable FRAMING devices. In some genres the frame is tight, highly restrictive to the point of being ritualistic. Other genres have 'flexible' framing and offer the potential for change and development.

SOAP OPERAS have this potential, situation comedies (sitcoms) less so, contends Jasper Rees in the UK *Independent*, reviewing the second festival of sitcoms run by the UK's Channel 4. In his article 'Slap 'n' tickle', 30 July 1996, Rees says, 'In a play, events take place which irrepressibly alter the relationship between the characters. Whatever happens in a sitcom, you always go back to square one at the start of a fresh episode; the idea of stasis is built into the design. No doubt sooner or later a writer will come along and create a sitcom which breaks new ground, though this will depend as much upon external framing mechanisms such as programming and popularity as the nature of the genre itself.'

Each genre contains a range of *signifiers*, of conventions that audiences recognize and come to expect while at the same time readily accepting experiment with those conventions. Knowledge of the conventions on the part of audience, and recognition when convention is flouted, suggests an active 'union' between the encoder and the decoder. Audience, as it were, is 'let in on the act'; and this 'knowingness' is an important part of the enjoyment of narrative genres. When the hero in a Western chooses not to wear a gun (a great rarity), audience (because we are familiar with tradition) recognizes the salience of this decision. Such recognition could be said to constitute a form of participation.

We use our familiarity with old 'routines' as a frame for reading this new twist of narrative. We wonder whether convention will be flouted altogether as the story proceeds, or whether the rules of the genre will be reasserted by the hero taking up the gun to bring about a resolution to the story. For a soap opera *time* is a key element in the framing process. There are 30-minute slots to be filled, each to conclude with unfinished business, preferably dramatic and suspenseful, while not being so dramatically 'final' that the series cannot continue into an indefinite future.

Soap narratives need time to bed down, to unfold, and in their own time they reflect the timescales of audience. In some cases, the time-frame of the soap is as important as the time-frames within it. The soap 'frame', thus amply provided with time, requires many characters and many plots. The narrative template or mould out of which soaps emerge is, give or take an adjustment, the same or similar to that which produces popular narratives of all kinds, including the news. They must attract and hold attention. They must gratify both COGNITIVE (intellectual) and affective (emotional) needs. They must facilitate IDENTIFICATION, personal reference as well as diversion (see USES AND GRATIFICATIONS THEORY). They must meet the needs of a certain type of audience at a certain time of day while at the same time fulfilling such criteria as commercial viability, which in turn is conditional upon ratings and audience share.

Another key element of narratives is what is termed *binary* framing, that is the story being structured in terms of opposites – heroes/villains; good/evil; kind/cruel; tolerant/intolerant; beautiful/ugly. In *Narratives* Asa Berger talks of 'central oppositions'. Stories are built around protagonists who are archetypal, with character-traits that are readily recognized – heroes, heroines, villains and victims (see PROPP'S PEOPLE). Something happens, an event producing a state of *disequilibrium*, of imbalance, which has to be corrected or resolved; and in the resolution we may read a MESSAGE, a moral, about valour or self-sacrifice.

Robert C. Allen, writing in *Channels of Discourse: Television and Contemporary Criticism* (Routledge, 1987, edited by Allen), differentiates between what he calls the *Hollywood narrative mode* and the *Rhetorical mode*. The first hides the *means* by which the text is created. It invites audience to believe that what they are seeing is real: one is absorbed into the text without being, as it were, addressed by it. In contrast, the rhetorical mode directly addresses the viewer. The news, Allen sees presented in this way – the news reader looks directly out at us; and similar formats can be recognized in cooking, sports and gardening programmes on TV: 'The texts are not only presented for us, but directed out at us.'

Asa Berger concludes his book by affirming the importance of narrative analysis in the study of communication: 'We used to think of the stories we read, listen to, and watch as little more than trivial amusements to "kill time". Now we know that people learn from stories, are emotionally affected by them, and actually need stories to lend colour and interest to their everyday lives.' See CODES OF NARRATIVE; NARRATIVE: KERNEL AND SATELLITE; NARRATIVE PARADIGM; WEB OR ONLINE DRAMA. See also *TOPIC GUIDE* under LANGUAGE/DISCOURSE/NARRATIVE.

Narrative codes See CODES OF NARRATIVE.

Narrative: kernel and satellite Terms defined by Seymour Chatman in *Story and Discourse: Narrative Structure in Fiction and Film* (Cornell University Press, 1978) to describe structural elements in narrative. The *kernel* is an event crucial to the advance of the plot, serving to direct the story's progress and development. A *satellite* is a minor feature of the story that embellishes the plot, adding detail, fleshing out the narrative.

Chatman writes of kernels as 'narrative moments that give rise to cruxes in the direction taken by events. They are nodes or hinges in the structure, branching points which force a movement into one of two (or more) possible paths'. Satellites are secondary elements that feed into the kernal; their loss would not seriously hinder the plot development. Without kernels, however, there would be no story.

Narrative paradigm Theory that sees people as essentially storytellers, defining humankind as *homo narrans*. A substantial section of the Autumn 1985 edition of the *Journal of Communication* was devoted to an analysis, by a variety of contributors, of the notion that if storytelling is central to human DISCOURSE and interaction, then the paradigm provides an important METAPHOR for communications research, which has its own story – its own narrative-base – rooted in beliefs about truth and falsehood, fact and fiction and the nature of reason.

In 'The narrative paradigm: in the beginning', Walter R. Fisher, Professor of Communication Arts and Sciences at the University of Southern California, believes that rationality in humans is determined by the nature of persons as narrative beings: by 'their inherent awareness of narrative probability, what constitutes a coherent story, and their constant habit of testing narrative fidelity, whether the stories they experience ring true with stories they know in their lives'. He goes on, 'The world is a set of stories which must be chosen among to live the good life in a process of continual recreation.'

Narratives: grand narratives See POSTMODERNISM.

Narrowcasting As contrasted with *broad*casting; the term describes the process whereby programme-makers and advertisers aim at specialized-interest (or *niche*) audiences, from gardening to golf, from astronomy to cookery; or at special levels of AUDIENCE distinguished by, for example, social CLASS, education or spending power. The INTERNET has proved fertile ground for narrowcasting.

National Film Archive (UK) Founded in May 1935, the NFA is the largest division of the BRITISH FILM INSTITUTE (BFI). Its role is to acquire, preserve and make available for study a collection of films and TV programmes of all kinds exhibited or transmitted in the UK from any source and of any nationality. Particular emphasis is placed on British productions, which may have lasting value as works of art, as examples of film or TV history, or as valuable records of past and present socio-cultural behaviour.

National Viewers' and Listeners' Association (NVLA) See 'CLEAN UP TV' MOVEMENT.

Naturalistic illusion (of television) The visual qualities of TV can lead to the assumption that it is merely a window on the world, showing life as it really is. Stuart Hall in 'The rediscovery of "ideology"' in M. Gurevitch, T. Bennett, J. Curran, and J. Woollacott, eds, *Culture, Society and the Media* (Methuen, 1982) refers to this phenomenon as the 'naturalistic illusion'. TV programmes are in fact the result of considerable planning and research. Elaborate procedures of FRAMING, editing and the matching of images with dialogue have to be undertaken in order to present an exposition.

During these procedures decisions are taken that may significantly affect the finished presentation. Different impressions can be given, for example, of a mass demonstration depending upon when or where the film is taken and how it is edited. In short, what TV produces is a *construct* of reality as perceived by those with the power to represent it, and transmit it to the public. See IDEOLOGY.

Necessity, supervening social necessity (technology) See SUPERVENING SOCIAL NECESSITY.

Needs See MASLOW'S HIERARCHY OF NEEDS.

Negative news values See NEW VALUES.

Negative semantic space See MALE-AS-NORM.

Negativization See VISIONS OF ORDER.

Negotiated code See DOMINANT, SUBORDINATE, RADICAL.

Neologism The invention or usage of a new word, or giving an old word a new MEANING, such as 'viewer' from the French 'voyeur' to indicate someone who views other people's sometimes illicit activities. One of the most picturesque neologisms in the area of media is COUCH POTATO.

Net See INTERNET.

★**Network** Channels of communications that are interconnected are termed *networks*, to be found in all communication in which numbers of people are involved, such as GROUPS and organizations. In essence a communication network consists of linked dyads in which the *receiver* in one DYAD is the source in the next. Such networks will vary in size, and not all members of the network will necessarily have equal access to information or participation.

A communication structure is a network in which some channels are systematically neglected. Generally speaking the greater the number of links between members, and the closer the distance between them, the more

N

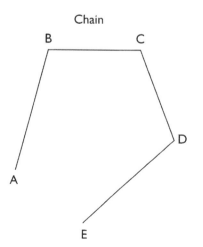

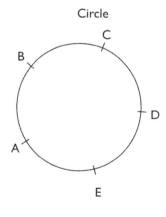

Examples of communication networks

likely it is that information is distributed equally – assuming that all members communicate through all the links at their disposal.

In a network with a high level of centrality it is likely that some members will possess more information than others. Communication networks may take several forms, such as the two illustrated. Networks may vary as to the ease with which individual members can be isolated from fellow members, and some networks will suffer more than others from the removal of a member or a link. If a member or link is missing from a chain network, for example, the effect is likely to be more serious than if either were missing from a circle network. A network may also spawn a sub-network: a sub-network can be said to exist when the number of links between certain members is greater than the number of links between these members and others.

The term network is used in BROADCASTING to describe the pattern of connection of the broadcasting stations of a broadcasting company or companies. Such a connection allows the simultaneous broadcast of the same programme. To 'network' a programme means to broadcast it to the widest number of TV/radio stations both within one network and in other networks. In the US, the term is used more specifically: the Networks are those companies that commission programmes and programme-series.

Perhaps the most familiar use of the term 'network' applies to those established *electronically*. Computer networks (see INTERNET) are key to practically every aspect of modern life, at the personal, national and global levels, while *social networking* constitutes a whole new dimension for the term – see the next entry.

Networking: social networking The INTERNET has rapidly fulfilled the prophecy of media guru Marshal McLuhan that electronic communication would turn the world into a global village; indeed it can be said that, with the exponential growth of social networking, it has become a global backyard. Basically, social networking is hundreds and thousands of people e-chatting and message-exchanging via the Net and sites such as FACEBOOK, LiveJournal, MYSPACE and Bebo. These are used for communicative exchange both with people you know – old school or college friends, for example – and with new people you would like to get acquainted with. Potentially these may extend into hundreds or thousands, each serving as a node to future personal, group and organizational connections.

As Jill Walker Rettberg says in *Blogging* (Polity Press, 2010), one of the reasons why

social network sites are so popular 'is that they appeal to our instinct for collecting'. There is also something of the herd instinct in expanding Net acquaintance. Rettberg writes, 'Once enough of your friends have joined a social network site, social pressure can make it very difficult *not* to participate.'

The Wikpedia definition of a social network is a 'structure made up of individuals (or organizations) called "nodes" which are tied (connected) by one or more specific types of interdependency, such as friendship, kinship, common interest, financial exchange, dislike, sexual relationships or beliefs, knowledge or prestige'. J.A. Barnes is credited with using the term in 1954 to describe the nature and process of patterns of association.

Social network analysis has become a rapidly expanding field of study, producing a new generation of commentators and gurus matching optimistic with pessimistic visions of the impact of social networking on users. The optimism of American writer Clay Shirky shines through the title of his book published by Allen Lane in 2010, *Cognitive Surplus: Creativity and Generosity in a Connected Age*. In an interview with the UK *Guardian*'s Decca Aitkenhead ('If there's a screen to worry about in your house, it's not the one with the mouse attached', 5 July 2010), Shirky says the popularity of online social media proves that 'people are more creative and generous than we have ever imagined, and would rather use their free time participating in amateur online activities such as Wikipedia – for no financial reward – because they satisfy the primal human urge for creativity and connectedness ... Instead of lamenting the silliness of a lot of social online media, we should be thrilled by the social activism also emerging'.

Shirky talks of the 'civic value' of this activism and sees it as potentially revolutionary. He acknowledges the downsides of Net anonymity, which allows users to 'behave more meanly', but predicts a time when 'we are slowly going to set up islands of civil discourse' in which norms are established that encourage people to use their real names or some well-known handle. The challenge for social networking is how 'to maximize' the Internet's 'civic value'. See BLOGOSPHERE; DIGITAL NATIVES, DIGITAL IMMIGRANTS; MOBILIZATION; WEB 2.0; YOUTUBE.

▶ Jan van Dijk, *The Network Society* (Sage, 2nd edition 2006, reprinted 2010); Gerard Goggin, *Global Mobile Media* (Routledge, 2011); Leah A. Lievrouw, *Alternative and Active New Media* (Polity Press, 2011).

Network neutrality Means 'open' and 'equal' – that is, open to all without discrimination, and equal in terms of access; in short, all Net postings, whether corporate or personal, must be treated alike and move at the same speed over the network. 'No tolls on the Internet' was the headline of a Washingtonpost.com article (13 June 2006) by Lawrence Lessig and Robert W. McChesney, in which they ask whether network neutrality can be preserved, 'Or will we let it die at the hands of network owners itching to become content gatekeepers?' The authors argue that the 'implications of permanently losing network neutrality could not be more serious'.

On 14 January 2007, in an article entitled 'Protecting Internet democracy', the *New York Times* asserted that 'on the information superhighway, net neutrality should be a basic rule of the road', echoing what has become the battlecry of millions of Net users across America – that Net neutrality is the equivalent of the First Amendment guaranteeing freedom of speech for all.

The struggle to preserve network neutrality against corporate ambitions to introduce a first class/second class post-style realignment of network content continues. 'Backroom corporate deals won't protect Net Neutrality' was the title of an August 2010 posting by the Free Press website, calling on the Federal Communications Commission of the US to act before 'Industry players carve up the Open Internet'.

Aparna Sridhar feared that 'Industry titans will propose rules that serve only their own interests … it's time for the FCC to take back its role as a policymaking body and act quickly to re-establish its authority over broadband and to adopt meaningful rules to protect the openness of the Internet for all Americans'.

As feared, Google and the Verizon Internet service provider came to a private agreement which threatened to terminate the once-sacred tenet that no form of content is favoured over others. In the UK the Conservative-Liberal coalition government breached the dam within

months of coming into power; in November 2010, Communications Minister Ed Vaisey announced a 'two-speed' Internet on the basis of the more you pay, the quicker you transmit. In response to the announcement Open Rights Group director Jim Killock protested that 'removing Net neutrality is likely to reduce innovation' and curtail 'people's ability to exercise their freedom of speech'. See CONGLOMERATES: MEDIA CONGLOMERATES; PAYWALL.

▶ Tim Wu, *The Master Switch: The Rise and Fall of Information Empires* (Borzoi Books, 2011).

★**Newcomb's ABX model of communication, 1953** In contrast to the linear structure of the SHANNON AND WEAVER'S MODEL OF COMMUNICATION, 1949, Theodore H. Newcomb's model is triangular in shape, and is the first to introduce as a factor the role of communication in a society or a social relationship. A and B are communicators and X is the situation or social context in which the communication takes place. Both the individuals are orientated to each other and to X, and communication is conceived of as the process that supports this *orientational* structure. Symmetry or balance is maintained between the three elements by the transmission of information about any change in circumstance or relationship, thus allowing adjustment to take place.

For Newcomb, the process of communication is one of the interdependent factors maintaining *equilibrium*, or as Newcomb himself puts it in 'An approach to the study of communicative acts' in *Psychological Review*, 60 (1953), 'communication among human beings performs the essential functions of enabling two or more individuals to maintain simultaneous orientation to each other and towards objects of an external environment'. See CONGRUENCE THEORY; DISSONANCE; MCCOMBS AND SHAW'S AGENDA-SETTING MODEL OF MEDIA EFFECTS, 1976; MCLEOD AND CHAFFEE'S 'KITE' MODEL, 1973; WESLEY AND MACLEAN'S MODEL OF COMMUNICATION, 1957.

N

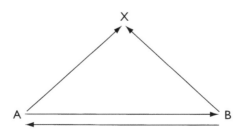

Newcomb's ABX model of communication, 1953

New media Term referring specifically to the possibilities brought about by computers and telecommunication, encompassing the INTERNET and all its manifest applications. New media includes the mobile phone (see MOBILIZATION) and is characterized by technological CONVERGENCE and, contrastingly in terms of its reach, DIVERGENCE.

New media differ from 'old' media in a number of ways. Traditionally, control of any communicative transmission beyond the field of the personal has rested in the hands of institutions, both public and private. To communicate with hundreds and thousands it was necessary to own such institutions or work for them. Now fresh territories have opened up for groups and individuals; communication is possible free of institutional control. The airwaves buzz with bloggers (see BLOGGING; JOURNALISM: CITIZEN JOURNALISM); it is as easy to tune into, and be active with, cyber-journalists, cyber-philosophers, as it is to pick up a newspaper.

New media are interactive; they are two-way, multiple-way, where traditional media have tended to be one-way means of information and entertainment. No longer are we entirely reliant for news and comment on the press, radio or TV. The traditional vertical structure of communications has tilted, and continues to tilt, towards the horizontal.

What has been created by new media is a 'downloading culture'; and the impact of being able to download texts of all kinds, from music to movies, is seen as both a marvellous opportunity and a threat. If everything is for free, who pays the piper in the first place? Across the board, communications industries are having to adjust to the challenges of DOWNLOADING.

Not least, new media is characterized by the speed of its development, matched by the pace of absorption by the public, young people in particular. The 'old' media have not, of course, been left behind. Now we can read newspapers online; popular photography has creatively and profitably embraced the digital; our mobile phones are fast becoming 'infotainment centres'. In schools, electronic whiteboards are taking over from chalk and duster; in higher education, text-messaging is being given academic status and respectability with new courses.

New media have made possible the rise of new voices, new modes of communication – essentially, but not always, personal; expressions of individuality. It remains to be seen how far these expressions can move, consistently, beyond the personal to the communal. One thing is for certain, new media have made possible communication across space more accessible to a wider section of the population, both national and international, than would have been dreamed of a decade or so ago. The world of knowledge, once limited to books and libraries, once guarded by the secrecy of officialdom, once a 'property' accessible only to the privileged, has been prised wide open.

In her introduction to *Alternative and Activist New Media* (Polity Press, 2011), Leah A. Lievrouw cites four factors which make 'new media' new: (1) *Recombination*, that is the way users of media technology make up, as it were, their own menus and forms of communication, producing hybrids or recombinations. What emerges is 'the product of people's ideas, decisions and actions, as they merge the old and new technologies, uses and purposes'. (2) Design and use based on *networks* (and networks of networks), the hyperlink being 'the quintessential feature of new media'. (3) *Ubiquity*, 'the seeming presence of new media everywhere, all the time which affects everyone in societies where they are, whether or not every individual uses them directly' (see INFORMATION GAPS). (4) *Interactivity* characterized by the participation by users in innovative as well as traditional intercommunicative ways.

These factors are mutually influencing, each helping to shape the others, subject to 'change more rapidly than media systems have in the past'. They 'resist stablilization of "lockdown" and change continuously ...' See AUDIENCE: ACTIVE AUDIENCE; BRICOLAGE; DEMOTIC TURN; GENRE.
▶ Martin Lister *et al, New Media: A Critical Introduction* (Routledge, 2nd edition, 2009); Jan van Dijk, *The Network Society* (Sage, 2nd edition, 2010).

New media genre theory See GENRE.

News The study of news is central to most, if not all, courses in communication and media studies. Like information itself, the news is a vital component of the life of individuals, GROUPS, communities and nations. News brings us information 24 hours a day. Whether it is in print or broadcast form, the news re-presents to us the world – reality; and every student soon learns that the news is a process, or rather an amalgam of many processes, which mediate information: select it, edit it, emphasize some parts of it, distort it, even manipulate it. News, that is the raw information that is eventually constructed as news, is turned into NARRATIVE, a mode of storytelling, which by the application of certain professional practices – conventions – establishes what has come to be termed news DISCOURSE.

In this sense, news can actually be described as 'olds': what has by precedent been counted as news continues to be classified and used as news. We become acutely aware of the *selective* nature of news, of the fact that, for example, the ELITE – persons, societies, nations – appear more often in the news than ordinary people or less prestigious societies and nations. And there is a reciprocal nature about inclusion in the news: if you are important, the news covers what you do or say; if the news covers what you do or say, what you do or say becomes better known. You become a Known instead of an Unknown.

The focus of study will shift from the analysis of news *sources*, to the predisposition, reportorial approach, and the constraints upon that approach, of the *practitioners* of news; and their activities will be examined in micro and macro situations. At the micro level we would scrutinize the relationship of practitioners to the organization that employs them and thus directs and influences their professional activities.

At the macro level we would study the influences from outside the organization, from society itself: what part in shaping news content and presentation does big business have, or government, or the law? What social, cultural, economic or political pressures are brought to bear on news production that will influence the shape and tenor of it as it reaches the audience?

We would be equally interested in how the news is put together, how decisions are made about what is considered important or less important. This might lead us into an investigation of AGENDA-SETTING, in turn providing us with a useful guide to the processes of GATE-KEEPING. The agenda controls the gate; but what controls the agenda? We would need to explore the basic principles of what information, at any given time, is considered *newsworthy*. We would focus on the NEWS VALUES which both practitioners and media analysts have identified as influencing decision-making.

Very importantly, we would be interested in investigating how news is *received* by AUDIENCE. We would attempt to discover how audiences actually *use* the news; how far it actually does inform them, and whether it influences them. We soon understand that news reconstructs the world according to the *perceptions* of those who produce the news, and those who employ or influence the news producers; and we would be interested in discovering to what extent audiences take on board the 'reality' presented by news.

In examining the approaches to news produc-tion and presentation, we would be alert to the capacity of audience to choose *alternative* readings to the realities with which they are being presented. We will most certainly have noted how news presentation has developed over the years; that it is more lively than ever before in style and content; that it is more entertaining. We might need to ask whether such developments have increased or decreased audience comprehension of the matters being presented: how much of what is read or seen on TV news is fully grasped, *contextualized*; indeed, how much of it has been retained as meaningful information?

No form of public communication has a higher profile than news production and management, and issues relating to this concern a number of high aspirations – *objectivity*, *balance* and *impartiality* – each difficult to define both in theory and in practice. Many commentators would argue that a more pressing issue is the nature of ownership and control and whether, in any given society, there is a *plurality* in the ways in which information and opinion are presented.

Finally, news and news production have to be seen in relation to trends – the impact of new media technologies, the *transnationaliza-tion* of media ownership, the *privatization* of public media services and the *globalization* of message/meaning systems. See BLOGGING; BLOGOSPHERE; CHURNALISM; JOURNALISM; JOURNALISM: CELEBRITY JOURNALISM; JOUR-NALISM: CITIZEN JOURNALISM; JOURNALISM: DATA JOURNALISM; JOURNALISM: INVESTIGA-TIVE JOURNALISM; JOURNALISM: 'POSTMODERN JOURNALISM'; NEW MEDIA; NEWS: AUDIENCE EVALUATION, SIX DIMENSIONS OF; NEWS: AUDI-ENCES FOR NEWS; NEWS PROVISION: THREE ELEMENTS; NEWS: STRUCTURE OF REASSUR-ANCE; NEWS: THE 'MALENESS' OF NEWS; NEWS WAVES. For a full listing, see *TOPIC GUIDE* under NEWS MEDIA.

▶ Daya Kishan Thussu, *News as Entertainment: The Rise of Global Infotainment* (Sage, 2008); Stuart Allan, *News Culture* (Open University, 3rd edition, 2010); Graham Meikle and Guy Redden, eds, *News Online: Transformations and Continuities* (Palgrave Macmillan, 2010); Kaitlynn Mendes, *Feminism in the News: Representations of the Women's Movement Since the 1960s* (Palgrave Macmillan, 2011).

News agencies 'The invention of the news agency,' writes Anthony Smith in *The Geopoli-tics of Information* (Faber, 1980), 'was the most important single development in the newspaper industry in the early 1800s, apart from the rotary press.' The early agencies – Reuter, Havas and

N

Wolff – carved up the world into spheres of activity in much the same way as imperialist nations parcelled out 'Third World' territories between them.

In 1869 the major agencies signed an Agency Alliance Treaty. Reuter was 'granted' the British Empire and the whole of the Far East; Havas, a French agency, was granted Italy, Spain, France and the Portuguese empire; and the Germany-based Wolff received Austria, Scandinavia and Russia. America was awarded jointly to Havas and Reuter.

Today, the biggest agencies are The Associated Press (AP), the Press Association (PA, created as early as 1868), Reuters and the United Press International.

Out of the traditional, print-centred news agencies have developed international television news agencies distributing TV news material around the clock, both 'raw' footage and complete news stories ready for transmission.

Concern has focused on the role of international news agencies in giving world news a Western 'slant' through the operation of NEWS VALUES reflecting the IDEOLOGY of Western nations' news flow; that is, the degree to which that flow is *mediated* and the dominant direction of that flow. What has been termed *raw* news flows from the periphery to the centre, but on the way it becomes *cooked* news – constructed according to Western production criteria; while the flow of information from the centre is almost invariably cooked, shaped, according to Western news values. See EVENT; MEDIA IMPERIALISM; NON-ALIGNED NEWS POOL.

News Aid? Paul Harrison and Robin Palmer use this term in their book *News Out of Africa: Biafra to Band Aid* (Hilary Shipman, 1986), to illustrate the ambivalent relationship between the media's coverage of the dramatic and distressing effects of famine in the 'Third World', particularly Africa. The authors note the media's long-term reticence, in news or current affairs programmes, to participate in a DISCOURSE about the underlying causes of such famine and ways in which famines might be prevented. Such reticence begs the question of whether or not coverage of the effects of famine, however galvanizing of public opinion and action in the short term, really aids finding a solution to the problem.

Indeed some commentators argue that the media's tendency to concentrate reporting of 'Third World' countries around issues of natural disasters or conflict leads to the perpetuation of negative and stereotypical images of those countries' citizens. Liam Kane in 'Media Studies and images of the "Third World"', in the Spring 1994 edition of *Media Education*, comments that '"Third World" people tend to be portrayed very negatively, as passive victims of an unexplained poverty'. The consequence, he goes on to argue, is that we can 'easily blame poverty on a combination of "natural disasters" and the supposed ignorance, laziness or backwardness of Asians, Africans, and Latin Americans'.

What are often overlooked are the structural causes of these problems; in both national and international inequalities in the distribution of resources and power. Also undervalued or not reported at all are the resilience and achievement of 'Third World' citizens despite their often formidably adverse circumstances. Another fear, of course, is that concentration on the symptoms rather than the causes of disasters, like war and famine, may lead ultimately to a dulling of the audience's sensibility to them. See COMPASSION FATIGUE.

News: audience evaluation, six dimensions of In 'Research note: The effects of live television reporting on recall and appreciation of political news' in the *European Journal of Communication*, March 2000, Roland Snoeijer, Claes H. de Vreese and Holli A. Semetoko examine 'the evaluative judgment that viewers make of television news'. They pose six *evaluative dimensions*: Credibility, Importance, Involvement, Attractiveness, Immediacy and Comprehensibility.

TV news scores highly in terms of audience belief in its credibility, in part because viewers not only see what is happening, but, as a result of SATELLITE TRANSMISSION, can also see events as they are actually happening. 'The concept of importance', write the authors, 'refers to the implications or impact that a story is believed to have for society as a whole', viewers taking their cue from 'the importance of a story defined by newsmakers' (see AGENDA-SETTING). Involvement relates to NEWS VALUES and centres around personal likes and dislikes, interests and geographical proximity.

'Information', consider the authors, 'is found to be attractive if it is vivid, lively and attention grabbing', though perceptions and responses vary in impact, some GROUPS of people 'finding it very attractive, others disturbing'; and this dimension, as with credibility, applies to both the content and the presentation of the news.

The speed at which TV news can report events – its immediacy – is highly appreciated by the audience for news. Finally, viewers need to believe that 'they have received the information in a comprehensible way' and the success in this relates to the way news stories are structured and the way they tackle the complexity of events. See FRAMING: NEWS.

News: audience for news The Pew Research Center of the US in a phone survey conducted between April and May 1998 identified six groups of news consumers in America. The results, stated the Center's research report, indicated 'how differently the generations are responding to the information explosion'. The news-consuming groups identified were (1) the *Mainstream news* audience, deemed to have 'middle-of-the-road' preferences; newspaper readers who also regularly tune into local and networked TV news shows; (2) the *Basically broadcast* audience, relying primarily for its news on TV; (3) the *Very occasional* audience which 'only follows the news when something major is happening'; (4) the *Constant* audience 'that watches, reads and listens to just about everything – seemingly indiscriminately'; (5) the *Serious news* audience, equally committed but more selective; and (6) the *Tabloid* audience which 'rejects broadcast news and favours the *National Enquirer*, tabloid TV and the tell-all talk show ...'

'Ironically,' the Pew report states, 'the daily newspaper, the oldest format, is the only news source used regularly by a majority of all groups.' See *TOPIC GUIDE* under AUDIENCES: CONSUMPTION & RECEPTION OF MEDIA.

News consensus See CONSISTENCY.

News Corp One of the world's largest and most diverse media corporations, News Corporation was created by Australia-born Rupert Murdoch in 1979. Its portfolio includes newspapers, book publishing, film production, TV and satellite broadcasting, cable networking, integrated marketing and information services.

In the US, News Corp controls 20th Century Fox and Fox News, Fox Interactive Media, *The Wall Street Journal*, the *New York Post*, the online game store Direct2Drive, the recruiting agency Milkround and much more.

News Corp owns many national, metropolitan and regional newspapers in Australia (not to mention the Papua New Guinea *Post-Courier* and the *Fiji Times*). The organization's expansionary trajectory extends into cooperative ventures with other media conglomerates, such as Disney and NBC Universal: for example in 2009 Fox's Interactive Media TV's immensely popular *American Idol* was translated into *The American Idol Experience* at Disney's Hollywood Studios theme park in Florida (see SYNERGY).

As well as providing popular film and TV entertainment, News Corp's services are most closely identified with sport – in the UK, premier league football and test cricket in particular; areas seen by some commentators (and rivals) as veering dangerously towards News Corp monopoly (see MURDOCH EFFECT). News Corp makes large donations to the Republican Governors' Association and the US Chamber of Commerce.

As well as BSkyB in the UK (see BRITISH SKY BROADCASTING, BSkyB), News Corp either owns or has a substantial stake in Sky Deutschland, Sky Italia, Star TV of India and Greater China and Tata Sky, India. The main subsidiary of News Corp in Britain is News International, responsible for *The Times, Sunday Times, Sun* and (until it was dramatically shut down as a result of sensational revelations of phone-hacking – see JOURNALISM: PHONE-HACKING) the *News of the World.*

The foundations of the News Corp empire were badly shaken in July 2011 by the *NoW* scandal. The chief executive of News International, Rebekah Brooks resigned and she, Rupert Murdoch and his son James were summoned to appear before a UK House of Commons select committee while the government launched a public inquiry to be chaired by Lord Justice Leveson. News Corp's ambition to secure full control of BSkyB was put on hold.

News elements: breaking, explanatory, deep background In an article 'Public broadcasting: imperfect but essential' posted on the openDemocracy website (www.openDemocracy.net), 26 June 2001, Jean Seaton identifies three central elements of news provision: (1) *Breaking* news, what she describes as 'attention-grabbing top stories that are often visually dramatic ... that attract audiences by virtue of their drama'; (2) *Explanatory* or 'understanding' news – longer-format news programmes such as the UK's Channel 4 early evening news, 'which provides some context to understand headlines and breaking news'; and (3) *Deep background* news formats 'that track issues to the root.'

In Seaton's view, examples of element (3) 'are rare – that's part of the problem', for she sees, in the light of new technologies, of digital CONVERGENCE and remorseless pressures of competition, the threat of cost-cutting and the undermining of deep background, investigatory JOURNALISM. She considers that 'mainstream broadcast news is wilting under the pressure of the market and is losing intelligence, style, authority and audience', and argues that 'in a world of globalized corporate power, full-scale detailed investigation is essential to provide the public with the truth about what is going on'. See DEREGULATION; NEWS, GLOBALIZATION OF; JOURNALISM: INVESTIGATORY JOURNALISM.

News: flat earth news See CHURNALISM.

News frameworks Consist of a shared set of assumptions by reporters and editors about what is newsworthy. These assumptions influence the selection of items for investigation and reporting, and to some extent how they will be presented. This set of assumptions also enables journalists and editors to relate news items to an image of society in order to give them MEANING. Thus the framework can provide a 'ready reckoner' for constructing as well as selecting news that allows deadlines to be met. See FRAMING: MEDIA; NEWS VALUES.

News, globalization of Satellite technology coupled with trends in transnational media ownership and control have created global patterns of information transmission characterized by both CONVERGENCE and diversity. TV news services worldwide show marked similarities of content and narrative approach when stories of international dimensions are being reported. In contrast, diversity is maintained when national and local stories are dealt with.

In 'The global newsroom: convergences and diversities in the globalization of television news' in *Communication and Citizenship: Journalism and the Public Sphere* (Routledge, 1991), edited by Peter Dahlgren and Colin Sparks, Michael Gurevitch, Mark R. Levy and Itzhak Roeh write that convergence is in part predicated by the availability, worldwide, of pictures, and reinforces what the authors term a measure of 'shared professional culture', a certain 'commonality in news values and news judgments, across all services'.

However, diversity asserts itself in 'lesser items', suggesting 'that this sharing of news values is not complete and that national social and political differences, as well as journalistic norms between nations, also play a part in shaping patterns of news coverage'. Examples are cited of how globally available film footage is actually harnessed to national meanings – same pictures, different reading. This in the opinion of the authors is a practice offering 'an important antidote to "naive universalism" – that is, to the assumption that events reported in the news carry their own meanings, and that the meanings embedded in news stories produced in one country can therefore be generalized to news stories told in other societies'.

Gurevitch *et al* identify what they call the 'domestication of the foreign': stories from abroad are 'told in ways which render them more familiar, more comprehensive and more compatible for consumption by different national audiences'. TV news, then, anchored as it generally tends to be 'in narrative frameworks that are already familiar to and recognizable by news men as well as by audiences situated in particular cultures ... simultaneously maintains both global and culturally specific orientations'. The domestication of the foreign serves as a 'countervailing force to the pull of globalization'. See AUDIENCE: ACTIVE AUDIENCE; COMMODITIZATION OF INFORMATION; CONGLOMERATES; CONSUMERIZATION; GLOBALIZATION (AND THE MEDIA); MEDIAPOLIS; NEWS CORP.

▸ Daya Kishan Thussu, *International Communication: Continuity and Change* (Hodder Arnold, 2006); Thussu, ed., *Media on the Move: Global Flow and Contra-Flow* (Routledge, 2007); Robert M. McChesney, *The Political Economy of Media: Enduring Issues, Emerging Dilemmas* (Monthly Review Press, 2008).

News-literate Term used by John Hartley in *Understanding News* (Methuen, 1982) to describe the ability of a reader, listener or viewer to comprehend the norms, codes and conventions of news programmes; to intelligently scan the news, 'recognize its familiar cast of characters and events' and to be able to spontaneously 'interpret the world at large in terms of the codes we have learnt from the news'.

News management Refers to the tactics employed by those – usually in government or important positions in society – who wish to shape the news to their own advantage, or to control events in such a way as to win favourable publicity. In recent years the operative word to describe news management is *spin*. The so-termed 'spin doctors', drawn almost invariably from the ranks of professional JOURNALISM, are essentially in the business of PROPAGANDA, that is talking up the good news and concealing as far as possible the bad news.

Where the communication of bad news is unavoidable, a favourite ploy of the spin doctors is to issue that bad news when other events are attracting media and public attention. The danger that accompanies the use of spin is risk of public exposure and consequently cynicism, and eventually disillusion with those who manage the news. See next entry.

News management in times of war One of the most famous quotations about the management of information in times of war is encapsulated in the title of a book by Phillip Knightley, *The First Casualty: A History of War Reporting* (Harcourt Brace Jovanovich, 1975). This was revised and updated in 2000, issued by Prion in paperback (reprinted 2004), with the new title of *The First Casualty: The War Corespondent as Hero and Myth-maker from the Crimea to Kosovo*; the first casualty being the *truth*.

Since the first Iraq War (1999), followed by the Al-Qaeda attack on New York and the Pentagon, and the second invasion of Iraq by American and British forces (2003), the examples of war news management have been plain to see; and if they have not been obvious, there have been books, articles, TV and radio programmes and films to analyse these for the public.

Knightley bundles with news managament 'lies, manipulation ... propaganda, spin, distortion, omission, slant and gullibility of the coverage of ... war' and believes 'the sad truth is that in the new millennium, government propaganda prepares its citizens for war so skilfully that it is quite likely they they do not want the truthful, objective and balanced reporting that good war correspondents once did their best to provide'.

Basically, the strategy on the part of the authorities – governments – in times of war is to exert control over what the media can and cannot say about current military action. This can be done by direct CENSORSHIP of reporting (as happened during the Falklands War of 1982). However, as the media have become global in reach, as media outlets have multiplied, as INTERNET communication bypasses national frontiers, censorship has become increasingly difficult to sustain.

A better strategy is to win the media to your side by providing access to the war situation, only in strictly regulated ways (see EMBEDDED REPORTERS). The aim is PROPAGANDA for the home side, and the home public; yet the more complex a war situation, the more public opposition there is to it (as was the case in Britain and to a lesser extent in the US, concerning the 2003 invasion of Iraq and the military occupation of Afghanistan), the greater the pressures to win a 'good press'. However, support for war can be created and sustained if the public is starved of the kind of information and analysis that allows them to make up their own minds.

In the US, there was a CONSENSUS of media support for the second war in Iraq. Government propaganda, supported by the media themselves, had made the war a prime issue of patriotism and loyalty; criticize the war, and you were deemed disloyal to the flag. Patriotism

(as it has done from time immemorial) became a successful marketing strategy. At the same time, the American media looked timorously over their shoulders at the nature of those who controlled them: who paid the piper called the tune, and US corporations, counting as they did most of American media in their business portfolios, favoured the war.

In the UK the government of Prime Minister Tony Blair could not expect the media to fall into line so easily with war plans – until presented with convincing evidence that war was justified. This evidence came in the form of allegations of Weapons of Mass Destruction (WMDs) capable, so Blair claimed, aided and abetted by Britain's MI5, of putting the UK in peril within 45 minutes. These, later referred to by critics as weapons of mass *deception*, were never found, but by this time (if not long before) decisions to invade Iraq had already been made. The truth had been rendered irrelevant.

Once war is underway, action, rarely analysis, feeds the headlines. Violence sells, as does compassion for victims. There are heroes (on our side) to be feted; atrocities to be downsized or explained away as the inevitable consequences of war; and, very importantly, there is the need to support 'our' troops in times of combat.

Eventually, despite the efforts by news managers to supress it, the truth will out; although usually too late for anything but recrimination. President George Bush was re-elected by the American people in 2004, and Tony Blair was returned to government, albeit with a reduced majority, in 2005. In other words, even though truth eventually made its escape from the concrete bunker of news management, the managers, at least in the short-term, had won the day.

▶ Greg McLaughlin, *The War Correspondent* (Pluto Press, 2002); Sheldon Rampton and John Stauber, *Weapons of Mass Deception: The Uses of Propaganda in Bush's War on Iraq* (Constable & Robinson, 2003); John Simpson, *News from No Man's Land: Reporting the World* (Pan, 2003); Andrew Hoskins, *Television War: From Vietnam to Iraq* (Continuum, 2004); David Miller, ed., *Tell Me Lies: Propaganda and Media Distortion in the Attack on Iraq* (Pluto, 2004); John Pilger, ed., *Tell Me No Lies: Investigative Journalism and its Triumphs* (Cape, 2004); Mark Connelly and David Welch, eds, *War and the Media* (I.B. Tauris, 2005); Judith Sylvester and Suzanne Huffman, eds, *Reporting from the Front: The Media and the Military* (Rownan & Littlefield, 2005); Andrew Hoskins and Ben O'Loughlin, *War and the Media: The Emergence of Diffused War* (Polity Press, 2010); Richard M. Perl-

N

off, *The Dynamics of Persuasion: Communication and Attitudes in the Twenty-First Century* (Routledge, 4th edition, 2010); Susan L. Carruthers, *The Media at War* (Palgrave Macmillan, 2nd edition, 2011); Garth S. Jowett, *Propaganda and Persuasion* (Sage, 5th edition, 2011).

Newspaper price wars See PREDATORY PRIC-ING.

Newspapers, origins The earliest newspapers in Britain were far more internationalist in outlook and interest than they tend to be today. The reason for this was the extensive CENSORSHIP of home news by monarch and council. As early as the seventeenth century there was the so-called *Relation*, the publication of a single news story, usually related long after the events. The *Coranto* served to join individual Relations into a continuity, though still not appearing regularly. The *Diurnall* was a step forward, providing a weekly account of occurrences over several days. Like the others before it, the *Mercury* appeared in book-like form, but bore more prominently the individual stamp of writers and tended to be more immediate and more diverse. During the Civil War (1642–46) Mercuries appeared in great abundance, even on Sundays.

Contemporaneous with the Mercury was the *Intelligencer*, usually more formal, aspiring to be 'official'; a notable example was *The Publick Intelligencer* published with the blessing of Protector Oliver Cromwell. Indeed the street journalism of all kinds that emerged in the heady days of the English Civil War laid the basis for the popular journalism we recognize today. In the twenty years between 1640 and the restoration of the monarchy under Charles II, 30,000 news publications and pamphlets emerged in London alone.

The date usually cited for London's first regular daily paper is 1702. The intention of Samuel Buckley's *Daily Courant* was 'to give news, give it daily and impartially', and it continued for 6,000 editions. By 1750 London had five daily papers, six thrice-weeklies, five weeklies and several other periodicals, all amounting to a circulation of 100,000 copies a week.

The Stamp Act of 1712 heralded over a century of increasing concern on the part of the authorities about the proliferation and influence of newspapers. Government agents reported on the contents of newspapers and there was a bristling array of laws to use against the press, such as seditious libel and profanation.

Of dubious legality but considerable effectiveness was the general warrant enabling arrests and seizures of unnamed persons to be made by the King's Messengers, practically at their discretion. Though several warrants were no longer legal after 1766, the Stamp Duty and other taxes on knowledge were burgeoning until the middle of the nineteenth century, when massive and sustained press and popular pressure led to the reduction and eventual abolition of the duties.

New technology, the growth of ADVERTISING and a more literate general public contributed to a massive expansion of newspapers in the latter half of the nineteenth century. In 1821 there had been 267 newspapers, including weeklies, in the UK; by 1861 there were 1,102. Newspaper trains, which began running in 1876, meant that the London papers could reach all parts of the country, while TELEGRAPHY speeded news, increasingly provided by the NEWS AGENCIES (Paul Julius Reuter opened his London office in 1851). By 1880 London had eighteen dailies; in the English provinces there were ninety-six dailies, four in Wales, twenty-one in Scotland and seventeen in Ireland.

The most dramatic example of the rise in the popularity of newspapers was the boom in Sunday papers, whose audience, writes Anthony Smith in *The Newspaper: An International History* (Thames & Hudson, 1979), 'came increasingly to consist of the newly literate who could not afford six papers a week and were interested in non-political news. The Sunday journals traded in horrible murders, ghastly seductions and lurid rapes, but they were combined with a distinct brand of radicalism'. Edward Lloyd's *Weekly News*, founded in 1842, was the first periodical to reach a circulation of a million, leaving the highest-selling daily paper, the *Daily Telegraph*, with a 200,000 circulation – well behind.

The pattern for the future was set: new technology facilitated (and made economically necessary) massive print runs; journalism aimed for vast readerships; advertising became more and more the staple financial support of the press; ownership rested with very rich individuals or joint stock companies; readership patterns hardened along lines of social CLASS; and competition became increasingly desperate. See DEMOCRACY AND THE MEDIA; JOURNALISM; NORTHCLIFFE REVOLUTION; PHOTO-JOURNALISM; PRESS BARONS. See also *TOPIC GUIDE* under MEDIA HISTORY.

Newspeak As opposed to Oldspeak in George Orwell's novel *Nineteen Eighty-Four* (1949), where private thought and individual language were crimes against the totalitarian state of

Oceania, and where the TV screen could actually hear what viewers were saying and see whether they were indulging in one of the worst of all crimes, private reading. Guardian of Newspeak, the official language divested of all superfluities by the meaning defined by the State, was the Ministry of Truth (which, incidentally, had a sub-section called Pornsoc).

Orwell's appendix to the novel, *The Principles of Newspeak*, explains that Newspeak was 'not only to provide a medium of expression for the world-view and mental habits proper to the devotees of Ingsoc (English Socialism), but to make all other modes of thought impossible'. Though the word 'free' would be retained in Newspeak, its meaning applied in the sense of 'This dog is free from lice'.

News: public relations news (PRN) Defined by Karmen Erjavec in an article entitled 'Hybrid public relations news discourse' in the *European Journal of Communication* (June 2005) as pertaining 'to all published news that contains basically unchanged PR [public relations] information, that appears without citing the source and attempts to promote or protect certain people or organizations'. The author talks of a 'colonization of news discourse by PR', its typical feature being 'the fact that commercialization dictates its nature and prescribes the limits of public interest', a judgment echoed by a number of media analysts. See CONSENT, MANUFACTURE OF.

News: rage inducement What happens if a news service trades in emotions – those of the audience – rather than facts and reason? You are likely to have 'rage inducement'; that is, the way the news is slanted, the way it plays on anxiety, fear and prejudice both stirs those sentiments in the audience and offers a justification for having them. Commentators cite Fox News in the US (part of the Murdoch NEWS CORP stable) as an exemplar of this approach. Rage inducement could, in this sense, be regarded as a NEWS VALUE.

Newsreel The Lumière brothers fathered newsreel film at the birth of the cinema, from 1895, but the first regular newsreel, *Pathé-Journal*, began in 1908, and French influence upon news on film was considerable for many years.

The First World War (1914–18) gave impetus to newsreel especially in Germany, and with the Revolution in Russia (1917) propaganda-newsreel (see AGITPROP) was regarded by the Communist government as being of vital importance in the war for hearts and minds. Dziga Vertov's *Kino-Pravda* newsreel series ran from 1922 to 1925.

Companies in the US were the first to add sound to newsreels, and in the UK British Movietone was the first to adopt sound (1928). In the 1930s the outstanding newsreel in the US was the MARCH OF TIME series. News on TV eventually put an end to cinema newsreels. See CINEMATOGRAPHY, ORIGINS; DOCUMENTARY.

Newsroom, The Museum, research and educational centre set up in Farringdon Road, London, in 2002 by the Scott Trust, telling the story of the Trust's sister papers, the *Observer* (the world's oldest Sunday newspaper, over 200 years old) and the *Guardian*. The Newsroom contains exhibitions of photo-journalism, documents, diaries, etc. kept by some of the most distinguished of the papers' writers; features a permanent interactive exhibition telling the history of the two papers, and an oral history recording staff recollections going back several decades; and has a 90-seat lecture theatre. Students have the opportunity to use the archive's resources, and student groups are encouraged to produce their own newspapers using the latest technology.

News selection See AGENDA-SETTING; GALTUNG AND RUGE'S MODEL OF SELECTIVE GATEKEEPING, 1965; NEWS VALUES; PROTO-TYING CONCEPT; ROGERS AND DEARING'S AGENDA-SETTING MODEL, 1987.

News: structure of reassurance In *Representing Order: Crime, Law And Justice in the News Media* (Open University Press, 1991), Richard Ericson, Patricia M. Barnek and Janet B.L. Chan argue that in the construction of reality in news production, a guiding function of the journalist and editor is to render things 'plausible' and thus 'provide a familiar discourse, based in common sense and precedent'. This plausibility 'in turn provides a structure of reassurance, a tool of acknowledging the familiar': by asserting the plausible-become-familiar the news construction process silences alternative definitions.

News: the 'maleness' of news? If the news is to be ascribed a gender classification, some commentators argue that it is essentially 'male': male-orientated in terms of decisions over content, over NEWS VALUES and in the practical matter of who gathers, reports, edits and presents the news.

In *Feminist Media Studies* (Sage, 1994, new edition 2000), Lisbet van Zoonen argues that women journalists are often expected, by male colleagues and by the organizations employing them, to perform professionally in a manner different from men; to subscribe to expectations of 'femininity'. 'Women,' writes van Zoonen, 'are confronted by social and cultural

N

expectations of femininity and at the same time are expected to meet criteria of professionalism.' While there is no evidence that women constitute a different group of professionals from their male colleagues, there were differences in the topics and issues that women were selected to cover.

Sue Curry Jansen in 'Beaches without bases: the gender order' published in *Invisible Crises: What Conglomerate Control of the Media Means for America and the World* (Westview Press, 1996), edited by George Gerbner, Hamid Mowlana and Herbert I. Schiller, states that conditions and prospects for women are equally disadvantaged in the United States. For Jansen, the news generally, and international news in particular, needs to be viewed through the 'prism of gender'.

She talks of an institutionalized bias towards maleness: 'In the United States men write most of the front-page newspaper stories. They are the subject of most of those stories – 85 per cent of the references and 66 per cent of the photos in 1993. They also dominate electronic media, accounting for 86 per cent of the correspondents and 75 per cent of the sources for US network television evening programmes.'

In international news coverage, 'women not only are marginal but also normally absent'. Jansen says, 'Under the present global gender order, policymakers and journalists find it more manly to deal with guns, missiles, and violent conflicts than with matters like female infanticide in China' or 'the increased trade in children in the sex markets of Manila and Bangkok in the wake of the AIDS epidemic ...'

Jansen's views received support from data published in April 1997 by the UK Fawcett Society. During a week's monitoring of election coverage during main news bulletins on the BBC, ITN and Channel 4, it was found that 80 per cent of news gathering and presentation was carried out by male journalists; and the number of women featured as spokespersons in the news was similarly in a minority. Of twenty-six government officials asked for their views, none was a woman.

The picture in the twenty-first century so far has arguably improved, at least in terms of the number of women journalists who work in the most dangerous places on earth to report war, atrocity, famine and persecution. A glance at the International Women's Media Foundation (IWMF) list of winners of the Courage in Journalism awards not only illustrates how women journalists and photographers work in the eye of

the storm, but also reveals the geographical and cultural breadth of women in media.

Tsering Woeser, in 2010 awarded the prize for her reporting of events and conditions in Tibet, stated in her acceptance speech that she saw herself as a 'weapon of the powerless' and that she had suffered on their behalf at the hands of the authorities. Other winners have worked in countries dangerous for independent-minded women and dangerous for the trade of journalism: freelancer Vicky Ntetema reporting on the persecution of albinos in Tanzania; Jila Baniyaghoob, reporter and website editor, beaten, arrested and imprisoned in Iran; Belarus reporter Iryna Khalip, arrested, beaten and subjected to all-night interrogation; Agnes Tailo, human rights reporter in Cameroon, abducted, beaten and left for dead in a ravine.

Among Western winners of the Courage in Journalism award is *Christian Science Monitor* reporter Jill Carroll of the US, abducted in 2006 while reporting in Baghdad and kept prisoner for eighty-two days. Indeed, if ever there was a grim test of the equality of the sexes in a profession (in the front line, not in organizational hierarchies) it is demonstrated by the fact that women journalists receive no 'special treatment' by those who punish journalists officially or covertly. Russian journalist and outspoken critic of government Anna Politkovskaya was shot dead in 2006 in the lift of her apartment block, and TV journalist Olga Kotovskaya 'fell' to her death from a fourteenth-storey building in Kaliningrad in 2009, only months after freelancer Anastasia Buburova was shot dead on a Moscow street.

As far as the UK is concerned, Brian McNair was already writing in 1999, in *News and Journalism in the UK* (Sage), that 'as a new generation of women enters the profession from university ... young female journalists ... actually appear to be doing better than men of the same age'. McNair is of the opinion that while sexism is far from eradicated, it 'appears to be on the retreat, with consequences not just for the gender structure of the profession but the form and content of journalism'.

▶ Penny Colman, *Where the Action Was: Women War Correspondents in World War II* (Random House, 2002); Deborah Chambers, Linda Steiner and Carole Fleming, *Women and Journalism* (Routledge, 2004).

News values According to Harold Evans, former editor of the UK *Sunday Times* and *The Times*, in his book *The Practice of Journalism* (Heinemann, 1963), 'news is people'. Long-time journalist and later, politician, Denis MacShane in *Using the Media* (Pluto Press, 1979) sums up what journalists are on the look-out for with five tenets: *conflict*; *hardship* and *danger* to the community; the *unusual* (oddity, novelty); *scandal*; and *individualism*. He quotes Lord Northcliffe (1869–1922), one of the original PRESS BARONS, who once declared, 'News is what somebody somewhere wants to suppress; all the rest is advertising.' Stuart Hood in *Hood on Television* (Pluto Press, 1980) refers to news sense as 'the ability to judge the language and attitudes permissible within the opinion-forming organization of our society'; well within CONSENSUS thinking.

One of the most succinct and influential explanations of news values is that of Norwegian scholars Johan Galtung and Mari Ruge. In 'Structuring and selecting news', first published in the *Journal of International Peace Research* (1965), the authors state that events will be more likely to be reported if they fulfil any, some or several of the following criteria. (1) *Frequency*: if the event takes a time approximate to the frequency of the medium. A murder, for example, is more newsworthy than the slow progress of a 'Third World' country. (2) *Amplitude*: the bigger, the better, the more dramatic, the greater is the likelihood of the story achieving what the authors call 'threshold value'. (3) *Unambiguity*: the more clear-cut and uncomplicated the events, the more they will be noticed and reported. (4) *Familiarity*: that which is ethnocentric, of cultural proximity, and that which is relevant; so things close to home matter most, unless things close to home are affected by faraway events. (5) *Correspondence*: that is, the degree to which the events meet with our expectations – our predictions, even. In this case, say Galtung and Ruge, 'news' is actually 'olds'. They term this the 'hypothesis of consonance' – that which is familiar is registered; that which is unfamiliar is less likely to be registered. (6) *Surprise*: this forms an antidote in terms of criteria to (4) and (5), and works to the benefit of good news: 'Events have to be unexpected or rare, or preferably both, to become good news.' (7) *Continuity*: that which has been defined as news – which has hit the headlines – will continue to be newsworthy even if amplitude is reduced. (8) *Composition*: the need for a 'balance' in a news-spread leads the producer or editor to feed-in contrasting elements – some home news if the predominant stories have been foreign; a little good news if the news has generally been gloomy.

Galtung and Ruge draw the following generalizations: the more events concern elite nations or elite people, the more events can be seen in personal terms; and the more negative the event is in its consequences, the greater the likelihood of selection. Consequently, once a news item has been selected, what makes it newsworthy will be accentuated (the authors call this stage *Distortion*). Selection and distortion will, it is argued, take place at all steps in the chain from event to reader (*Replication*).

Although Galtung and Ruge's study deals only with newspaper content, Jeremy Tunstall in *Journalists at Work* (Constable, 1971) adapts the Galtung and Ruge thesis to the analysis of TV news values. He itemizes four points of difference. (1) In TV the *visual* is given pre-eminence. The possession of film footage of an event will often increase the prominence given to a news story. (2) News items which include film of 'our own reporters' interviewing or commentating on a story are preferred. (3) TV makes use of a small fraction of the number of stories the newspapers carry, and even major TV items are short compared with newspaper coverage. (4) There is preference for 'hard' stories or ACTUALITY on TV news.

In 'The global newsroom: convergences and diversities in the globalization of television news' published in *Communication and Citizenship: Journalism and the Public Sphere* (Routledge, 1991), edited by Peter Dahlgren and Colin Sparks, Michael Gurevitch, Mark R. Levy and Itzhak Roeh write that 'in a pictures-driven medium, the availability of dramatic pictures competes with, and often supersedes, other news considerations'.

They also argue that for an event to be judged newsworthy 'it must be anchored in narrative frameworks that are already familiar to and recognizable by news men as well as by audiences situated in particular cultures'; for 'different societies tell themselves – on television and elsewhere – different stories'.

The news values posited by Galtung and Ruge have had a justifiably long life and a number of them still operate in an age of immensely greater media diversity. Paul Brighton and Dennis Foy in *New Values* (Sage, 2007) cite a number of major trends which have altered the media landscape since Galtung and Ruge's time – the INTERNET, SPIN DOCTORING, ROLLING NEWS, citizen journalism (see JOURNALISM: CITIZEN JOURNALISM) and advances in interconnectivity, between communicators and AUDIENCE and between modes of transmission and reception. Not the least of the new phenomena since the 1960s is what Brighton and Foy call 'the burgeoning of celebrity, an all-encompassing term that can be

N

applied to everybody from politicians to pop musicians and soap opera "stars"'.

Brighton and Foy acknowledge that the hypotheses of Galtung and Ruge 'were absolutely fine for their time and in their intended context of social and behavioural studies ... But as Bob Dylan once put it, *Things Have Changed*'. Quite simply, media communication has become global with the 'emergence of borderless broadcast and publishing operations'.

Fresh values are called for, applying to a multiplicity of media; and these values, in the view of Brighton and Foy, 'will vary from medium to medium, and from each individual package to the next'. The authors offer their own listing of seven values. (1) *Relevance* (the significance of a news item to the viewer, listener or reader). (2) *Topicality* (is it new, current, immediately relevant?). (3) *Composition* (how a news item fits with other items that surround it). (4) *Expectation* (does the consumer expect to be told about this?). (5) *Unusualness* (what sets it apart from other events that are not reported?). (6) *Worth* (does it justify its appearance in the news?). (7) *External influences* (is the content of a news item pure, or has it been corrupted by pressure from outside, such as a proprietor, an advertiser or a politician?).

The authors are also of the view that 'positioning, inclusion or exclusion, and juxtapositions [of news items] are all filtered through aesthetic criteria to an extent greater than is widely appreciated'. See GALTUNG AND RUGE'S MODEL OF SELECTIVE GATEKEEPING, 1965; IMMEDIACY; IMPARTIALITY; NEWS MANAGEMENT IN TIMES OF WAR. See also *TOPIC GUIDES* under COMMUNICATION THEORY and NEWS MEDIA.

▶ James Watson, *Media Communication: An Introduction to Theory and Process* (Palgrave/Macmillan, 3rd edition, 2008), Chapter 5, 'The news, gates, agendas and values'.

News waves Media coverage of an event 'makes waves', that is causes a momentum of its own; the coverage becomes its own headlines. In a *European Journal of Communication* article, December 2005 entitled 'Media hype: self-reinforcing news waves, journalistic standards and the construction of social problems', Peter L.M. Vasterman writes of a '*mismatch* between these news waves and the *real world* the media are supposed to cover ... During these news waves, the media not the event seem to be governing the coverage'. Consequently 'the media sometimes create a chain of events that would not have taken place without their involvement'.

New visibility See DEMOTIC TURN; PANOPTICON GAZE; PORNOGRAPHY.

New Wave In the year 1959–60 an astonishing sixty-seven new directors made their film debut in France: this was the *nouvelle vague* as Françoise Giroud described it. At the crest of the wave were critics writing for the film magazine *Cahiers du Cinéma*, including François Truffaut (1932–84), Jean-Luc Godard (b. 1930) and Claude Chabrol (b. 1930). Their films were made cheaply, often with unknown actors, improvization, hand-held cameras and location shooting, and without huge teams of technicians.

The New Wave were always a loose-knit grouping of individual directors, and it was individualism – the belief in the film director as auteur – which was their common characteristic. They reacted against the studio product and produced films of extraordinary richness and variety. Others in the Wave have been Alain Resnais, Chris Marker, Eric Rohmer, Jacques Rivette, Louis Malle, Roger Vadim and Agnès Varda.

N-Gen Short for Net-Generation, a term describing young people familiar with, and users of, the INTERNET and digital technology in general. The 'N-Geners' are characterized by a level of MEDIACY that marks them out from their parents' generation.

'Niche' audiences In the digital age where in terms of programming and advertising the INTERNET has made inroads into traditional media operations, audiences have become more fragmented, less easy to target and arguably respond with higher and more specific expectations; hence the increasing need for more closely tailored approaches. The problem is not only locating more specifically identified audiences, but also tracking an essentially volatile market and ensuring that the 'niche' is sufficiently broad to match investment and future prospects.

Nickelodeon An early and primitive form of cinema, of immense popularity in the US by 1905, usually consisting of a long, narrow room furnished with wooden bench seats and very basic equipment for film projection; frequently converted from a shop or store. The term is thought to have been used by showman John P. Harris, combining the Greek for theatre with the slang expression for the five cents charged for admission. The English equivalent was the *penny gaf*.

Soon the Nickelodeon gave way to the more stately film-houses. In 1913, Mitchell L. Mark bought the Strand Theatre, a 3,000-seater on Broadway, New York, and set in motion a fashion for neo-Baroque splendour. The movies had moved upmarket. Much later, the jukebox got referred to as the nickelodeon; a translation in meaning testified in the post-Second World War hit song, 'Put another nickel in/In the Nickelodeon ...'

Nielsen ratings AUDIENCE MEASUREMENT figures produced by the US company A.C. Nielsen, the best-known and most influential ratings information business.

Nine American lifestyles See VALS TYPOLOGY.

Noelle-Neumann's spiral of silence model of public opinion, 1974 In her paper, 'The spiral of silence: a theory of public opinion' published in the *Journal of Communication*, 24 (1974), German professor of communications research Elisabeth Noelle-Neumann examines the interplay between three communicative factors: the mass media, INTERPERSONAL COMMUNICATION and an individual's PERCEPTION of his/her own standpoint in relation to others in society.

The model is based upon the belief that people are uneasy, suffer DISSONANCE, if they feel themselves to be *isolates* with regard to general opinion and attitude: that they are the odd one out. In response to a situation, we tend to ask, what do other people think; what is the majority or dominant opinion? A person may find 'that the views he holds are losing ground; the more this appears to be so, the more uncertain he will become of himself, and the less he will be inclined to express his opinion'. This is the spiral of silence.

The dominant view which the mass media express (see ELITE; HEGEMONY; POWER ELITE) exerts pressure to conform, to step into line; and the more this view is expressed, the more the dominant view is reinforced; the more dominant it appears, the more difficult it becomes to hold a contrary view. In a sense, Noelle-Neumann's model is a spiral within a spiral, the one an assertion, the other a withdrawal into a silence as the assertion grows stronger.

The spiral tapers towards silence under the influence exerted by opinion expressed as dominant by the mass media. Thus a spiral of silence on the part of individual members of the public reflects the spiral of dominance represented by the media. At the same time counter-influence can come to bear from interpersonal support for deviant opinion.

Professor Noelle-Neumann's definition of public opinion is that 'which can be voiced in public without fear of sanctions and upon which action in public can be based ... voicing opposite opinions, or acting in public accordingly, incurs the danger of isolation'. The model prompts the question whether the public merely holds back

from expressing diverging or contrary views, but continues to hold them, or whether attitudes have actually been changed as a result of dominant media voices. See KUUKI. See also TOPIC GUIDE under COMMUNICATION MODELS.

▸ Kurt Neuwirth, Edward Frederick and Charles Mayo, 'The spiral of silence and fear of isolation' (*Journal of Communication*, September 2007); Andrew F. Hayes, 'Exploring the forms of self-censorship: on the spiral of silence and the use of opinion expression avoidance strategies' (*Journal of Communication*, December 2007). An outstanding example from fiction on the theme 'of keeping silent' in the face of isolation and duress is Hans Fallada's *Alone in Berlin* (Penguin, 2011), translated by Michael Hoffman.

Noise Impedance or barrier between the sending and receiving of communication signals. Claude Shannon and Warren Weaver in *The Mathematical Theory of Communication* (University of Illinois Press, 1949) posit two levels of noise problems: level A, *engineering noise* and, at the higher level, B, *semantic noise*. Level A is physical and technical and is defined as any distortion of MEANING occurring in the communication process which is not intended by the source, but which affects the reception of the MESSAGE-carrying signals and their clarity. The semantic level is 'noise' or impedance in terms of CODES – linguistic, personal, psychological, cultural, etc. Later writers have identified *psychological noise* as a category in its own right: examples here could include lack of motivation, personality clashes and lack of shared experiences.

▸ Richard Dimbleby and Graeme Burton, *More Than Words: An Introduction to Communication* (Routledge, 2007).

Non-verbal behaviour: repertoire A useful classification scheme for the repertoire of non-verbal behaviour is suggested by American authors Paul Ekman and Wallace V. Friesen in 'The repertoire of nonverbal behaviour: categories, origins, usage and coding' in *Semiotica* 1 (1969). Their five categories of non-verbal movement are: emblems, illustrators, affect displays, regulators and adaptors.

Emblems are non-verbal behaviours that directly suggest specific words or phrases, usually without vocal accompaniment. Thus the beckoning first finger is the emblem for 'Come here'. Emblems are short-cut communication signals useful in many ways, especially where verbal communication is difficult or inappropriate, for example when a person is thumbing a lift.

Illustrators accompany and reinforce verbal messages: the nod of the head, a supportive smile, leaning forward to show interest, sketch-

N

ing something in the air with finger or hand, to give a point emphasis or clarity. Illustrators tend to be less culture-specific than emblems. *Affect displays* are movements of the face and body that hold emotional meaning: disappointment, rage, happiness, hopefulness, shock, etc.; indeed our whole body language constitutes affect displays.

For Ekman and Friesen, *regulators* are non-verbal actions that monitor and control the communication of another individual. These can take the form of encouragement of the other person to go on speaking, to explain more fully, to quicken up, slow down, or get to the point. Here we use nods, smiles, grunts, ah-ha's; we shake our heads, we glance away, blink, pucker lips. Equally we can employ regulators in a negative sense by using non-verbal behaviours to discourage the other person from talking.

Adaptors are generally habitual behaviours used to make a person feel more at ease in communication interactions: twisting a lock of hair, scratching, stroking (the hair, the chin, etc.), wringing hands, turning a ring round the finger, fiddling with jewellery, playing with matches – actions which are more private than public and are likely to undergo some modification when the private actions extend into a public domain. See COMMUNICATION, NON-VERBAL; GESTURE; PROXEMICS. See also *TOPIC GUIDE* under INTER-PERSONAL COMMUNICATION.

Non-verbal communication See COMMUNI-CATION, NON-VERBAL.

Non-verbal vocalizations In communication a number of sounds are used that are not speech but which convey important information contributing to the overall MEANING of the message being conveyed. At times these sounds communicate a message without the need for accompanying speech.

Michael Argyle in *Bodily Communication* (Methuen, 1988) identifies some of the main non-verbal vocalizations. There are those that aid the understanding and regulating of speech. These include *prosodic signals*, like the raising of pitch to indicate that what is being said is a question; *synchronizing signals*, such as the lowering of pitch to indicate that one has finished speaking for the time being; and *speech disturbances* such as stutters and repetitions.

Some are more independent of speech but communicate emotions, attitudes or other social information that may affect the encoding and decoding of the message. These include emotional noises such as cries and laughter; paralinguistic noises that convey emotional information by such means as pitch, volume and

speed; and aspects of the personal voice quality and ACCENT.

Larry A. Samovar, Richard E. Porter and Edwin R. McDaniel in *Intercultural Communication: A Reader* (Thomson Wadsworth, 2006) note a range of cultural differences in the use of non-verbal vocalizations; for example, 'Members of cultures with strong oral traditions, such as African Americans and Jews, tend to speak with more passion; Italians and Greeks talk much more and more loudly than Asians, who appreciate silence as a way of showing politeness.'

Normative theories of mass media In *Mass Communication Theory: An Introduction* (Sage, 1983), Denis McQuail posits six normative theories of the mass media: (1) Authoritarian Theory; (2) Free Press Theory; (3) Social Responsibility Theory; (4) Soviet Media Theory; (5) Development Media Theory; and (6) Democratic-Participant Theory.

By normative, we mean how the media should be, what is to be expected of them rather than what necessarily happens in practice; and it is out of the political, cultural and economic context that the normative principles arise. Central to the normative theory is the way the media 'behave' in relation to the state, and the dominant expectations that the state has of the role of the media.

The *Authoritarian Theory* thus appertains in a state in which press or BROADCASTING freedoms not only do not exist, but are not considered by those in power, or those who support them in power, desirable even as ideals. What Siebert *et al* call 'Libertarian theory' McQuail terms the *Free Press Theory*, which is considered the chief legitimating principle for the print media in liberal democracies. Free and public expression is, implies this theory, the best way to arrive at the truth and expose error. It is a principle enshrined in the First Amendment of the American Constitution. This states that 'Congress shall make no law ... abridging the freedom of speech of the press'. McQuail's analysis of this principle in practice is well worth noting, for he asks searching questions about *whose* freedom; about monopolistic tendencies; about the close identification of notions of freedom with profit and private ownership.

The *Social Responsibility Theory* believes in freedom provided that it is harnessed to responsibility: independence is desirable only so long as it is reconcilable with an obligation to society. In this sense, the media are perceived as fulfilling a role of public stewardship. They are the WATCH-DOGS of the common good against government or private abuse of power or corruption. There is an emphasis on neutrality and balance; most of all, a belief in media accountability to society (see MEDIAPOLIS).

Soviet Media Theory (worth noting even though the Soviet system has passed away) derives from the postulates of Marx, Engels and Lenin. Here, the media serve the interests of the socialist state, the state being an embodiment of all the members of a classless society. Because the media are of the people, they belong to the people. In practice, of course, they belonged to the people's leadership. The tasks of media are to socialize the people into desirable NORMS as defined in Marxist doctrine; to educate, inform, motivate and *mobilize* in the aims and aspirations of a socialist society. (See CLASS.)

Development Media Theory has arisen out of special needs in the 'Third World' developing nations (see MACBRIDE COMMISSION; MEDIA IMPERIALISM). This theory eschews bad news theory and favours positive reporting on the grounds that for developing nations, often struggling for economic survival in competition with Western industrialized countries, reporting of disasters and setbacks can substantially injure the process of nation building.

The *Democratic-Participant Media Theory* emphasizes the individual rights of access, of citizen and minority GROUPS, to the media, in fact the right to *communicate*; to be served by the media according to a more democratic determination of need (see DEMOCRACY AND THE MEDIA). Thus the theory opposes the concentration of ownership and rejects the role of AUDIENCE as tame receiver. Media should be answerable, free of government or big-business intervention, small-scale, interactive and participative (see CAMPAIGN FOR PRESS AND BROADCASTING FREEDOM; COMMUNITY RADIO; RIGHT OF REPLY).

In a later publication, 'Mass media in the public interest: towards a framework of norms for media performance' in *Mass Media and Society*, edited by James Curran and Michael Gurevitch (Edward Arnold, 1991), McQuail re-examines the validity of normative models because 'attempts to formulate consistent "theories" of the press' become increasingly difficult to sustain 'when media technologies and distribution systems are multiplying and when there is less consensus about basic values than in the past'. The dissolution of the Soviet Union is a case in point, though it is arguable that the 'Marxist' Media Theory continues to apply in China and Cuba.

McQuail proffers a set of defining principles by which media performance can be judged, and these relate to community values. He cites the following as Public Communication Values: (1) *Freedom*, acquiring its public definition through the independent status of the media, public access to channels and diversity of supply; (2) *Equality*, which concerns openness, access and OBJECTIVITY (characterized by neutrality, fairness and truth); and (3) *Order*, a classification relating to order both in the sense of solidarity and in the sense of control (the one operating bottom upwards, as it were, the other top downwards).

The principles interrelate, interact and are obviously in constant conflict with one another. McQuail acknowledges 'deep fissures and inconsistencies, depending on how they [the principles] are interpreted'. However, the application of these principles to the changing patterns of media operation provide 'the essential building blocks for a quite comprehensive, flexible and changing "social theory of media", relevant to our times and of practical value in the ever widening circle of public discussion of the role of mass media in society'. See JOURNALISM: CITIZEN JOURNALISM; MCQUAIL'S ACCOUNTABILITY OF MEDIA MODEL, 1997.

▶ Denis McQuail, *McQuail's Mass Communication Theory* (Sage, 6th edition, 2010).

Norms Shared expectations or standards of behaviour within a particular social group or society. Any type of established group will have norms, both peculiar to itself and shared with the wider community. Of those norms widely accepted in a society, some will operate on a high, some on a low CONSENSUS. Any individual's PERCEPTION and interpretation of experience will be influenced by the norms of the social groups and society to which he/she belongs. Individuals generally take such norms for granted. Communication between individuals likewise reflects certain norms, such as those of grammar and style of writing or norms of conduct that guide social INTERACTION.

Norms arise from such interaction between various individuals and social groups; once developed, they are passed on through SOCIALIZATION to new members. Norms are not static: they are subject to renegotiation. They play a significant part in maintaining the social position of particular groups and individuals and constitute an influential agent of informal social control.

The media, as agents of communication and socialization, are in a position to both reinforce general societal norms and to express the norms of certain social groups. In addition, the media have the potential to *shape* expectations of behaviour, particularly with regard to individuals or groups with whom the viewer, listener or reader is unfamiliar. It is this potential that has aroused considerable research interest. See CULTURE; MALE-AS-NORM; VALUES.

Northcliffe revolution New schooling in the late nineteenth century in the UK, following the Foster Education Act of 1870, created a rapidly expanding readership of literature and news. Alfred Charles William Harmsworth (1865–1922), later Lord Northcliffe, perhaps the most dynamic and extraordinary of the PRESS BARONS, built a press empire on the new flood-tide of literacy. Creator of the *Daily Mail* (1896) and the *Daily Mirror* (1903), Northcliffe combined a 'popular-educator' emphasis with a marketing sense that was energetic, imaginative, daring and ruthless. Northcliffe represents the fundamental shift towards the exploitation of, and increasing dependence upon, ADVERTISING as a means of newspaper finance.

Publicity was everything. Rivalry between papers, in terms of sensation-seeking and attention-grabbing stunts, resembled (as it continues to do today) the Battle of the Titans. Raymond Williams in *The Long Revolution* (Chatto & Windus, 1961) says, 'The true "Northcliffe Revolution" is less an innovation in actual journalism than a radical change in the economic basis of newspapers, tied to the new kind of advertising.' By 1908 Northcliffe's press empire included the *Mail*, the *Mirror*, *The Times*, two Sunday papers (*Observer* and *Dispatch*) and an evening paper (*News*), plus a host of periodicals such as *Tit-Bits* and *Answers* (whose circulation had leapt from 12,000 at its inception to 352,000 two years later).

Though the so-called Northcliffe revolution was chiefly characterized by the employment of new technology, the drive for mass circulations and the wholesale reliance on advertising as the prime source of press revenue, the 'flavour' of that revolution must not be overlooked, that is the style and content emanating from the Press Barons themselves. James Curran and Jean Seaton in *Power Without Responsibility: The Press and Broadcasting in Britain* (Routledge, 6th edition, 2003; see 7th edition, 2010, *Power Without Responsibility: Press, Broadcasting and the Internet in Britain*), write that 'Northcliffe and Beaverbrook shaped the entire content of their favourite papers, including their lay-out.' When *The Times* changed the place in the paper of the weather report, Northcliffe raged,

'... if it's moved again, whoever does it is fired.' Curran and Seaton speak of how the personal tastes of the Barons influenced the popular journalism of the time: 'Northcliffe had a lifelong obsession with torture and death: he even kept an aquarium containing a goldfish and a pike, with a dividing partition, which he would lift up when he was in need of diversion.' He told staff of the *Daily Mail* to find 'one murder a day'.

Meddling with the content by newspaper proprietors was not, of course, new. It had gone on throughout the nineteenth century, but then interference had focused mainly upon political matters. What was different with Northcliffe and his ilk was that the new proprietors meddled in everything. See NEWSPAPERS, ORIGINS. See also *TOPIC GUIDE* under MEDIA HISTORY.

▶ Kevin Williams, *Get Me A Murder a Day! A History of Mass Communication in Britain* (2nd edition, *Get Me a Murder a Day! A History of Media and Communication in Britain*, Bloomsbury Academic, 2009).

N-step theory See OPINION LEADER.

NVC See COMMUNICATION, NON-VERBAL (NVC).

Object See SIGN.

Objectivity Professor Stuart Hall has expressed the view that objectivity, 'like impartiality, is an operational fiction' (in 'Media power: the double bind', *Journal of Communication*, Autumn 1984). In examining the media, analysts encounter the 'Famous Four': balance, CONSENSUS, IMPARTIALITY and objectivity, upon which all good reporting is said to be based. The questions arising from this precept are: balance between what and what? Consensus among whom? Impartiality in what sense? Objectivity in whose eyes? Considering the complex processes of MEDIATION between an event and its report in media form, is it possible to have value-free information?

'All edited or manipulated symbolic reality,' says Hall, 'is impregnated with values, viewpoints, implicit theorizings, commonsense assumptions.' When there are differences between what is objective and what is not, whose opinion wins the day?

Hall says of consensus that it is 'structured dominance'. The prevailing definition usually rests with the POWER ELITE, the 'power-ideology complex' in any society whose control of and influence upon the media gives them a dominant say in the definitions of objectivity. See CULTURAL APPARATUS; ELITE; HEGEMONY; MACHINERY OF REPRESENTATION.

Object language According to Gail and Michele Myers in *The Dynamics of Human Communication* (McGraw-Hill, 1985), this term refers to 'the meanings you attribute to objects with which you surround yourself'. These objects might be items of clothing, hairstyle, fashion accessories, your house, your furniture, your car and so on; and they may say something about you to others – forming part of your SELF-PRESENTATION. The objects may not always convey to others the MESSAGE you wish them to: people can be unaware of their symbolic value or simply read into them different meanings from the ones intended. And of course you yourself might not be conscious of the messages you are sending through the objects you possess.

Object language can be particularly important when people are forming first impressions of one another. A great deal of ADVERTISING certainly works on the assumption that consumer objects have as their main appeal a *symbolic* rather than a purely functional value.

As Jib Fowles comments in *Advertising and Popular Culture* (Sage, 1996), 'The individual looks at advertising imagery and the associated commodity in the attempt to find those pleasing signs that will define oneself in distinction to others. Still, those signs *must* be readable by others, so what the solitary consumer is buying is not so much self-definition in isolation as participatory symbols.'

In their book *Understanding and Sharing: An Introduction to Speech Communication* (Brown, 1979; reprinted 1985), authors Judy Cornelia Pearson, Paul Edward Nelson and Donald Yoder use the term *objectics*, the study of 'clothing, adornments, hairstyles, cosmetics and other artefacts that we carry with us or possess'. Object language conveys information about our age, sex, status, role, personality, relationships with groups and with other people, psychological and emotional state, self-concept, and the 'physical climate in which we live'. See COMMUNICATION, NON-VERBAL (NVC); SELF-CONCEPT.

Obscene signals See INSULT SIGNALS.

Obsolescence Generally, anything passing out of date or out of use. In a communications sense, it refers to the link between social habits and media-using habits. Obsolescence can be defined as the abandoning of formerly institutionalized modes of conduct related to some established cultural activity.

Oeuvre French for 'work', generally the complete works of an artist, writer, composer, etc. The word refers to the work of the mind as well as of hand and eye. Thus we may refer to the *oeuvre* of Pablo Picasso (1891–1973) and mean not only the items of his work – paintings, sculpture, pottery – but also, by implication, the nature or character of that work. See OPUS.

Ofcom: Office of Communications (UK) A 'super regulator' born of the COMMUNICATIONS ACT (UK), 2003, and assuming its responsibilities on 29 December 2003; inherited the duties of the Broadcasting Standards Commission (BSC), the Independent Television Commission (ITC), the Office of Telecommunications (Oftel), the Radio Authority and the Radio Communications Agency.

Such issues as telephone silence calls, copyright infringement and broadband speed-up are dealt with by Ofcom, which is a member of the recently formed BEREC (Body of European Regulators in Electronic Communications) comprising twenty-seven regulators of the European Union, which held its inaugural meeting in January 2010.

Ofcom has responsibilities across the spectrum of broadcasting and telecommunications in Britain, and is required by statute to 'further the interests of citizens and consumers by promoting competition and protecting consumers from harm or offensive material'. Ofcom consults, researches, produces codes and policies and deals with complaints.

In May 2005 Ofcom published its Broadcasting Code for television and radio. This acknowledges Euro-Community directives relating to TV, and incorporates aspects of the Human Rights Act of 1998, in particular articles of the Convention relating to the rights to freedom of expression, thought, conscience and religion; personal privacy; and freedom from discrimination. Section One of the Code lays down broadcasting benchmarks to protect the under-18s and deals with programme scheduling; the coverage of sexual and other offences in the UK involving under-18s; drugs, smoking, solvents and alcohol; violence and dangerous behaviour; offensive language; sex and nudity; and excorcism, the occult and the paranormal.

Other sections of the Code deal with Harm and Offence; Crime ('To ensure that material likely to encourage and incite the commission of crime or lead to disorder is not included in television or radio services'); Religion; Impartiality and Due Accuracy; Elections and Referendums; Fairness ('To ensure that broadcasters avoid unjust or unfair treatment of individuals or organizations in programmes'); Privacy; Sponsorship and Commercial References; and Other Matters.

Of key and regular interest to the press and

public – and students of communication – are Ofcom reports. These are wide-ranging and address such matters as PRODUCT PLACEMENT and paid-for references to brands and products on radio (December 2010), NET NEUTRALITY (June 2010), and the deregulation of commercial local radio (April 2010).

Ofcom has clout: in November 2010 it revoked the licences of four stations (Tease Me, Tease Me TV, and Tease Me 2 and 3) run by Bang Channels Ltd and Bang Media (London) 'following serious breaches of the broadcasting code'. This followed a £157,250 fine imposed on the companies in July. In its judgment Ofcom referred to a 'wholly inadequate compliance system' that amounted to 'manifest recklessness'.

At the close of 2010 the regulator fined London-based Continental Telecom £50,000 for failing to provide information to Ofcom as part of its investigation into the firm for landline mis-selling.

In a more benign mood Ofcom celebrated small community radio stations which it considered bring far-reaching benefits to communities – both to audiences and to the thousands of unpaid volunteers (40,000 of them nationwide) who help man the 181 stations (November 2010). The report cited one such, Diverse FM of Luton, which broadcasts in Bengali, Hindu, Gujarati, Urdu, Pahari, Polish, Arabic, Swahjili and Patura.

Ofcom's power over UK broadcasting is, however, far from absolute. In 2011, the Conservative-Liberal Democratic coalition government ignored Ofcom's recommendation that Rupert Murdoch's NEWS CORP application to increase its holding in BSkyB from 39.1 per cent to 100 per cent be sent to the Competition Commission. The Secretary of State for Culture Jeremy Hunt was 'mindful' to give Murdoch the go-ahead based upon an offer to suspend direct control of BSkyNews for a period of ten years; a deal described by the UK *Daily Telegraph* as 'little more than a carefully choreographed capitulation' (Leader comment, 'A body blow to the notion of a vibrant, diverse press', 4 March).

However, such ambitions were dramatically put on hold as the Murdoch media empire was engulfed in scandal as revelations became public of extensive and systemic phone-hacking on the part of the *News of the World* (see JOURNALISM: PHONE-HACKING). The 168-year-old, highly profitable Sunday paper was shut down in July 2011, swiftly followed by the establishment by government of a public inquiry headed by Lord Justice Leveson.

The decision by Hunt to ignore Ofcom advice

was widely seen as arbitrary and unwise and an indication of government being 'in the pocket' of a seemingly all-powerful media mogul and his empire. Clearly part of Leveson's remit will be to consider the power, or lack of it, of Ofcom to assert principles of public interest and media regulation.

The watchdog took the initiative of announcing a review of whether those responsible for and running News Corp would qualify as 'fit and proper' persons to run public media. The head of Ofcom, Ed Richards, said the regulator would 'consider any relevant conduct of those who manage and control' licences to broadcast. See BRITISH SKY BROADCASTING (BSkyB); MURDOCH EFFECT; PRESS COMPLAINTS COMMISSION; PREDATORY PRICING; REGULATORY FAVOURS.

Official Secrets Act (UK) Born in a spy scare during the Agadir crisis of 1911, reinforced in 1920 during the Troubles in Ireland, and given further power as war broke out in 1939, the Act censors information – access to and expression of it – which might be of use to the nation's enemies. It is easier to define what the Act doesn't cover than what it does; without question, it is the single most comprehensive weapon of CENSORSHIP with regard to the activities of government in the UK, and has few parallels in the 'free' world.

For a time, the saving grace of the Act was the possibility of defending individual, group or media breaches of secrecy on the grounds that such a breach was in the *public interest*. This was excised from the Act by the Conservative government in 1990 and subsequent New Labour administrations made no move to put it back.

Brian Raymond, solicitor to the civil servant Clive Ponting who was unsuccessfully prosecuted under the Act for revealing information about the sinking by a British submarine of the Argentinian battleship Belgrano, with the loss of hundreds of lives during the Falklands War (1982), said: 'The obliteration of the public interest defence ... amounts to a licence to cover up Government wrong-doing.' See D-NOTICES; FREEDOM OF INFORMATION ACT, 2005; REGULATION OF INVESTIGATORY POWERS ACT (RIPA), 2000; SECRECY; SPYCATCHER CASE. See also *TOPIC GUIDE* under MEDIA: FREEDOM, CENSORSHIP.

Oligopolization Oligarchy is government by a small exclusive CLASS or group; in media terms, oligopolization is the process of communication systems falling into the hands of a small exclusive group of owners or corporations.

Omnimax Spectator-surrounding film projection technique developed, like IMAX, in Canada from a system invented by an Australian, Ron James. Though there are several Omnimax screens in North America, the first in Europe, with the largest screen in the world, operates at the 55-hectare Paris exhibition complex, Cité des Sciences et de L'Industrie at Porte de la Villette, which opened in 1986.

La Géode offers a projection screen covering 10,000 square feet and surrounds spectators with a complete hemisphere, exceeding the normal field of vision. Like Imax, Omnimax uses 70mm film which passes through the camera horizontally, producing a 5cm × 7cm film image – approximately nine times the image area on ordinary cinema film. Camera and projector use a 25mm fish-eye lens with a scope of 172 degrees. A massive light source is required to project such a gigantic picture and Omnimax has a 15 kW water-cooled xenon lamp.

One-step, two-step, multi-step flow models of communication Basically these are refinements of the HYPODERMIC NEEDLE MODEL OF COMMUNICATION. The one-step model ignores the role of the OPINION LEADER in the flow of communication and presents the view that the mass media communicate directly to a mass AUDIENCE. There is no suggestion, however, that the messages reach all receivers equally or that they have the same effect on each individual in the audience. The model takes into account the influence of an individual's PERCEPTION, memory and SELECTIVE EXPOSURE on his/her particular interpretation of a MESSAGE.

A study conducted by Paul Lazarsfeld and others of the 1940 presidential election in the US threw doubt on the validity of the one-step theory. Reporting in *The People's Choice* (Duell, Sloan & Pearce, 1944), the authors found little evidence of the direct influence of the media; indeed people seemed more influenced by face-to-face contact with others. Lazarsfeld and his fellow researchers suggested that the flow of communication to the individual is often directed through an opinion leader, who plays a vital role in both spreading and interpreting the information.

They thus proposed a *two-step model* of communication flow which later research has found to be generally useful. In highlighting the importance of the social context of the receiver in the process of the interpretation of mass communication messages, this model differs significantly from earlier ones. It presents the mass audience as being composed of interact-

ing and responsive individuals rather than of the socially isolated, passive atoms of earlier theories.

The *multi-step model* is a development of the other two, allowing for the sequential relaying of a message. It is not specific about the number of steps there will be in the relaying process; nor does it specify that messages must originate from a source and then pass straight through the agencies of the mass media. The model suggests a variable number of relays in the communication process and that the receivers may receive the message at various stages along the relay network. The exact number of steps in the process depends upon the following: (1) the intentions of the source; (2) the availability of the mass media; (3) the extent of audience exposure to agencies of communication; (4) the nature of the message; (5) the importance of the message to the audience.

The model allows the researcher to account for different variables in different communication situations. It may usefully be applied to communications on the INTERNET where messages pass between scores, hundreds or thousands of users, each with the opportunity of modifying that message. See MEDIATION. See also *TOPIC GUIDE* under COMMUNICATION MODELS.

Online campaigning Widely acknowledged as a form of people power, online campaigning came into its own in 2011 when human rights agencies such as 38 Degrees (UK) and its US sister, Avaaz, mobilized popular protest – by mass online petitions, activist protests and demonstrations – which influenced government decision-making and corporate activity.

Free Press, the journal of the UK CAMPAIGN FOR PRESS AND BROADCASTING FREEDOM, in its July/August 2011 edition was of the opinion that online campaigners such as 38 Degrees were instrumental in forcing the abandonment by NEWS CORP, the empire of Rupert Murdoch, of its ambition to obtain total control of BSkyB (British Sky Broadcasting), following the hacking scandal involving *News of the World* journalists. 38 degrees is the angle of slope when avalanches take place; in this case, when avalanches of protest command the attention of the powers that be.

Online drama See WEB OR ONLINE DRAMA.

Onomatopoeia Words that imitate actual sounds are onomatopoeic, such as bang, thud, crackle, hiss, quack and TWITTER. They are mostly invented words. The first ever attempts at spoken language were probably onomatopoeic and such words continue to be invented, not a few of them (zap, for example) starting life in comics and cartoons.

Open, closed texts Italian semiologist Umberto Eco has made this useful separation between TEXTS that are varyingly articulated, to either permit little or no interpretation on the part of AUDIENCE (*closed texts*) or to allow plenty of room for interpretation (*open texts*). A work of art – a poem, a painting, a piece of sculpture, for example – would represent an open text in that the intention of the writer, painter or sculptor is to express ideas or feelings which may be interpreted in different ways and at different levels.

The open text invites a sense of participation in the reader or viewer, and the interaction that occurs between creator, creation and audience is one in which 'right answers' are less important than the possibility of a proactive response; and this may be subject to flux in differing instances and at varying times. PROPAGANDA would constitute closed text in that there is a rigorously PREFERRED READING: the decoder is expected to receive the message, and register its MEANING as intended by the communicator. Any divergence from acceptance would, to quote another term of Eco's, represent *aberrant decoding*. See ANCHORAGE; DECODE.

Open source Works on the principle of free access to information, including computer software and the practice of user participation – a classic example of online open source being WIKIPEDIA, which allows users to write their own definitions and make adjustments or alterations to existing entries without prior clearance.

Such open platforms of communication have been pioneered by, for example, Independent Media Centres (IMCs), generally referred to as Indymedia. Their mission is to bypass traditional mass media and the control mechanisms of governments and corporations, their working aspirations being the furtherance of equality and democracy.

Existing regulation such as copyright rules are rejected. Public interest is favoured over privacy rights and new technologies are regarded as tools of intervention. Open source is almost invariably the product and process of *collaboration* in which committed people, usually highly skilled in the use of new technologies, seek to inform, influence and activate public opinion. The key is MOBILIZATION, which is accomplished, writes Lea A. Lievrouw in *Alternative and Activist New Media* (Polity, 2011), 'by cultivating collective identities, shared values, and a sense of belonging among people linked in diffuse, decentralized social and community

networks'. See BLOGOSPHERE; INTERNET; MEDIA ACTIVISM; MEDIATION; NETWORKING: SOCIAL NETWORKING; WEB 2.0.

Opera omnia Latin for 'All his works', the term denotes a total ban on an author's writings imposed by the Roman Catholic *Index Librorum Prohibitorum*, first issued in 1559. A few such prohibited writers have been David Hume, Émile Zola, Jean-Paul Sartre and Alberto Moravia. See CENSORSHIP; INDEX.

Opinion leader Someone able to influence informally other individuals' attitudes and/or behaviour in a desired way with relative frequency. He/she is a type of informal leader. Opinion leadership is earned and maintained by the individual's technical competence, sociability and conformity to the NORMS of the social system. When such leaders are compared to their followers, several characteristics are of note: opinion leaders are more exposed to all forms of external communication; more *cosmopolite*; of a higher social status; and more innovative.

Opinion leaders are widely thought to play a vital role in the spreading of new ideas, VALUES and beliefs. As Paul Lazarsfeld has noted in several studies, opinion leaders can be important intermediaries in the process of communication, including mass communication, in that they have the potential to influence reaction, among those around them, to messages received.

An opinion leader whose range of influence is limited to one specific topic exercises *monomorphic* opinion leadership. This type of leadership is thought to be typical of modern, industrial societies, as the complex technological base of such societies results in a sophisticated division of labour and considerable specialization of roles. Monomorphic opinion leadership can be related to what Randy Bobbitt and Ruth Sullivan in *Developing the Public Relations Campaign* (Pearson, 2005) term *N-step theory*. This proposes that 'individuals seldom receive information from only one opinion leader. Instead, they are likely to turn to different opinion leaders for each issue on which they form an opinion'.

An opinion leader whose influence covers a wide range of topics exercises *polymorphic* opinion leadership. This is generally thought to be more common in traditional societies. A respected, elderly member of a village, for example, might be consulted on a variety of matters ranging from marriage problems to methods of harvesting. See ONE-STEP, TWO-STEP, MULTI-STEP MODELS OF COMMUNICATION.

Opinion poll The process or processes by which public opinion is researched, the findings of which are widely and regularly published and broadcast, and are seen not only as evidence upon which governments, oppositions, public bodes, etc. might act, but also as an influence in their own right. For example, in election campaigns, poll results are seen as vital indicators of the way the public intends to vote, but the headlines such opinion polls produce are also seen to influence the electorate, particularly if the findings suggest a CONSENSUS of opinion. For this reason, some countries ban the publishing of poll results in the immediate run-up to elections.

Oppositional code See DOMINANT, SUBORDINATE, RADICAL; POLYSEMY.

Optical fibre cable See FIBRE-OPTIC TECHNOLOGY.

Opus Latin for 'work', a term most often applied to musical compositions in order of their creation; for example, Beethoven's 9th Symphony is Opus 125.

Oral culture An oral CULTURE or SUB-CULTURE is one in which essentially, most communication is by word of mouth. Pictures may also be used as a supplement but reading and writing play a minor role in the communication process.

Orality: primary and secondary In *Orality and the Technology of the Word* (Cornell University Press, 1982) Walter Ong, in investigating the nature of the shift between oral and literate cultures, differentiates between 'primary' and 'secondary' orality. The first refers to and describes *preliterate* societies; the second results from the introduction of electronic media into *literate* societies.

Order, visions of See VISIONS OF ORDER.

Organization cultures Andrej A. Huczynski and David A. Buchanan in *Organizational Behaviour* (Pearson Education, 2007) define organizational culture as 'the collection of relatively uniform and enduring values, beliefs, customs, traditions and practices that are shared by an organization's members, learned by new recruits and transmitted from one generation of employees to the next'. Such cultures do however change over time. It should be noted that not all theorists accept there is such a thing as organizational culture.

Edgar H. Schein in *Organizational Culture and Leadership* (John Wiley & Sons Inc., 1985) developed a widely known model of organizational culture. The model identifies three different levels of culture that interact with one another: *Surface manifestations*, such as organizational rituals, legends, myths, norms or language (level 1); *Values*, for example co-operation, equality of opportunity and community relations (level 2); and *Basic assumptions* about organizational practices and relationships – these tend to be unstated, not obvious and 'taken-for-granted' (level 3). It is these basic assumptions, Schein argues, which constitute the organization's culture.

Huczynski and Buchanan (2007) discuss a number of typologies of organizational cultures that have been developed by various theorists. One well-known typology is that developed by Handy and Harrison and outlined by Charles Handy in *Understanding Organizations* (Penguin, 1993). (1) The *power culture* depends upon a central power source, with 'rays of power, influence' (and communication) spreading out from the central figure. An example of such a culture could be found within the company of a self-made businessperson (see BERLUSCONI PHENOMENON; MURDOCH EFFECT). Without such a 'spider', the web structure of the culture would collapse. (2) The *role culture* is found in the classic bureaucracy comprised of functional roles organized into a hierarchy. Here the communication process following lines of authority is vertical and chiefly one-way. The BBC would be a good example of a role culture. (3) Handy argues that the *task culture* is a skills or ability-oriented culture in which what a person is capable of doing is more important than who they are in terms of position or role. The culture is centred on task completion. The model is net-shaped and made up of interdependent strands. LEADERSHIP is exchangeable according to the task in hand. (4) The *matrix structure* is characterized by very flexible channels of communication, horizontal rather than vertical in direction, and is responsive to change. Examples from the media world of a task culture would be a creative ADVERTISING agency, or the kind of small company that produces DVDs or designs websites. (5) The *person culture*, in terms of business organizations, is the rarest of them all; here the organization exists only to serve the individuals within it. The model is a cluster, a galaxy of individual stars, without hierarchical structures, constantly interchanging in form. Cooperatives found in the creative arts sector can be examples of organizations that embrace the person culture (see MAGNUM).

In *The Empty Raincoat* (Arrow Books, 1995) Handy discusses a new model for organizations, based on what he terms the *doughnut principle*. This, he argues, reflects the way in which the traditional models and cultures have changed and will continue to change in order to survive shifts in the technological and economic environment. The doughnut consists of a *core* surrounded by *bounded space*. It is 'an inside-out doughnut, one with the hole on the outside and the dough in the middle'; a 'conceptual dough-nut, one for thinking with, not eating'. The core contains 'necessary jobs and necessary people'.

These full-time employees often organize the activities of the bounded space that contains many other people working for the organization as flexible workers tied to the organization by flexible and often short-term contracts. Thus organizations will become much smaller in terms of the number of people they employ directly; consequently it is likely that more people will be self-employed or freelance workers. Within the television industry, for example, this method of working is now well established (see CASUALIZA-TION; PRODUCER CHOICE).

Lucy Kung in *Strategic Management in the Media* (Sage, 2008) examines a range of cultures and sub-cultures found within the media indus-try. She argues, for example, that the successful introduction of BBC News Online can in part be explained by the fact that the project resonated with 'Pan-BBC cultural assumptions' such as the importance of meeting the needs of licence-fee payers and remaining a 'dominant media player in the UK'.

▸ Annet Aris and Jacques Bughin, *Managing Media Companies: Harnessing Creative Value* (Wiley, 2009).

Ordinariness See DEMOTIC TURN; REALITY TV.

Orientalism Concept posed by Edward Said describing the stereotypical image of Asia held by those in European cultures. Representation of the Orient arises from ETHNOCENTRIC atti-tudes with an imperialist ancestry, and results in a projected image of Asia and Asians as being exotic ('the lure of the Orient'), indolent, untrust-worthy and devious; in short a misrepresenta-tion by Western commentators and analysts, of OTHER. In *Orientalism* (Routledge and Kegan Paul, 1978), Said raises the question whether anything can be truly or objectively represented. See also Said's *Culture and Imperialism* (Chatto & Windus, 1993).

The potency of the term has been reinforced by New Millennium events such as the war on ('Arab') terrorism conducted by the US in Afghanistan and, following 9/11 in 2001, the invasion of Iraq in 2003 by US and British forces. This was seen by many critics as underscored by Orientalist attitudes manifested by an ignorance of the complexities of Arab culture and a seeming indifference to the remonstrations of the Arab world. A chilling example of this came when,

having totted up their own war dead, the Allies saw it as no business of theirs to count those of the 'enemy', whether they were combatants or innocent civilians. Ultimately, Orientalism is about valuing some 'bodies' over others.

In August 2005, when the Israeli army expelled illegally settled Israelis from the Gaza Strip, massive publicity in the Western media focused on the heart-rending sight of residents forced from their homes. It was pointed out by some observers that no comparable attention had been paid to the expulsion of Palestinians and their families driven from their homes, often without warning, and with no compensation, over a number of years. It could equally be pointed out, taking NEWS VALUES into account, that the extra newsworthiness of the story arose from the surprising or the unexpected – clear-ance of Israelis by Israelis.

Orientation See SPATIAL BEHAVIOUR.

Other According to Edward Said in *Orientalism* (Routledge and Kegan Paul, 1978), Western cultural identity is often defined in relation to the 'Other' that is people from the 'Orient' and especially India and the Middle East. He called this perspective *Orientalism*, a perspective that defines the West as all that the 'Orient' is not: superior, developed, modern, universalistic, rational and powerful. This perspective thrives on stereotypical opinions about the 'Other'. The concept is widely used not just to comment on representations of the 'Orient', but also of those seen as the 'Other' within Western societies. David Morley and Kevin Robins in *Spaces of Identity* (Routledge, 1995) argue that the recent trends of globalization and migration have resulted in a considerable number of those once seen as the 'Other' now living within Western societies. This change has brought with it challenges to the ethnocentric assumptions of 'Orientalism'.

In more general terms the 'Other' may be perceived simply as those who are not like us – a person, group, community, ethnic group, gender or nation – and who are defined by their difference from us; yet who by that difference contribute to our concept of self. 'Other' in general media use represents, by and large, those we disapprove of, dislike, fear; and the popular media use of 'Other' works in *binary* fashion (see WEDOM, THEYDOM). In everyday communication, 'Other' plays a key role in jokes – Irish jokes, Scottish jokes, etc. – each one relying for its effect upon a CONSENSUS about the negative qualities of the butt of that joke (see ETHNOPHAULISMS).

In TABLOID press headlines, name-calling is a favourite device to put down 'Other' and consequently boost the sense of superiority of Us over Them. When 'Other' is perceived as a threat, the demarcation lines become more forcible; and of course in sport, 'Other' is always the opposition – at which point Germans become 'Krauts' and the French become 'Frogs'. 'Other', then, is almost invariably those in opposition; those who are different in appearance or CULTURE and are seen in some way as a challenge to 'our' ways.

Outer-inner directed See VALS TYPOLOGY.

Out-take Piece of film that is not actually used in the completed version.

Overhearing Kurt H. Wolff in *The Sociology of Georg Simmel* (Free Press, 1950) uses this expression to describe how recipients of messages may proceed, usually below the level of awareness, to select certain parts for special attention, often distorting them while at the same time overlooking ('overhearing') other parts entirely. In short, the human organism perceives to a considerable degree what it wants to perceive. See COCKTAIL PARTY PROBLEM; PERCEPTION; SELECTIVE EXPOSURE.

Overkill signals See SHORTFALL SIGNALS.

Ownership and control of mass media See BERLUSCONI PHENOMENON; GLOBALIZATION: THREE ENGINES OF; GLOBAL MEDIA SYSTEM: THE MAIN PLAYERS; MEDIA CONTROL; MURDOCH EFFECT; PRESS BARONS. See also *TOPIC GUIDE* under MEDIA: OWNERSHIP & CONTROL.

Oz Trial The longest-ever obscenity trial in the UK, lasting twenty-six days in the summer of 1971 and centred on the *Oz School Kids Issue* (*Oz* 28). The three editors, Richard Neville, Felix Dennis and Jim Anderson, were eventually acquitted on the most serious charge, that of conspiring to corrupt the morals of children, but a majority of ten to one of the trial jury found *Oz* guilty of publishing an obscene article, sending such articles through the post and having such articles for profit and gain.

Oz Publications Ink Ltd received a total fine of £1,000 with costs of £1,250. Neville got a 15-month jail sentence and a recommendation that he be deported (he was Australian); Anderson received 12 months, and Dennis 9 months. See CENSORSHIP; SPYCATCHER CASE. See also *TOPIC GUIDE* under MEDIA: FREEDOM, CENSORSHIP.

P

Packaging The style and the framework within which TV programmes are presented on our screens: good-looking announcers or interviewers, titling, music, the tailoring of programmes to suitable lengths; indeed any form of image-making for a media product. The word gives emphasis to the connection between the manufacture and sale of goods and the making and presentation of media products. Stuart Hood in *Hood on Television* (Pluto Press, 1980) refers to TV announcers as the 'sales people of the air'. See LOOKISM.

Panopticon gaze A metaphor used by Michel Foucault (1926–84) in *Discipline and Punish* (Penguin, 1979) to describe the exercise of power through the numerous and often subtle disciplinary practices and technology embedded within modern Western organizations and societies. The Panoptican (see also SURVEILLANCE SOCIETY) was originally a design, conceived by nineteenth-century social philosopher Jeremy Bentham (1748–1832), for establishments in which people could be be kept under supervision. The basic principle is that inmates, confined to separate compartments or cells, can be observed at any time but have no way of knowing when and if they are being observed. Consequently the feeling of being under constant surveillance is produced, even though the observer will not in fact observe any one inmate continuously.

As Foucault writes, the result is 'to induce in the inmate a sense of conscious and permanent visibility that assures the automatic functioning of power. So to arrange things that the surveillance is permanent in its effects, even if it is discontinuous in its actions; that the perfection of power should tend to render its actual exercise unnecessary'. Foucault argues that the use of surveillance in the exercise of power and control has become widespread and has helped to create 'the disciplinary society'; further, that the use of disciplinary practices to control the individual within prisons, organizations and societies share common features.

Contemporary examples of such practices within organizations might include performance-related pay, targets, monitoring of phone calls, e-mails, deadlines and schedules. These practices arguably operate to produce a sense of a *panopticon gaze*, which in turn leads people to become self-disciplining through anticipation of the considerable degree of monitoring and surveillance of their activities.

These practices are potentially powerful

instruments of socialization, ensuring conformity and order, particularly as they may often be taken for granted. It is arguable that within the wider society much modern communications technology, especially computer technology, facilitates the operation of the panopticon gaze, for example speed cameras and CCTV cameras.

Surveillance is also a recurrent theme running through the mass media: the tabloid press surveys the activities of celebrities; on REALITY TV shows like *Big Brother*, surveillance is presented as a form of entertainment whilst other programmes, for example *Crimewatch*, focus on enrolling the public's help in detecting criminals. Such coverage can be seen to contribute to a general sense, among the public, of being watched, scrutinized; a situation accepted more and more as the norm.

While the panopticon gaze is about the visual relationships between authority and people, the one subjecting the other to surveillance, what has come to be referred to as the *new visibility* is much more of a two-way process. This *balancing* (to a degree) of surveillance has been made possible by the availability to the public of digital technologies making reception and transmission of information and images instant and global (see FACEBOOK; MOBILIZATION; ONLINE CAMPAIGNING; TWITTER). In an article entitled 'The new visibility' in the periodical *Theory, Culture and Society* (Vol. 22, 2005), John B. Thompson writes of 'a new world of mediated visibility' in which 'spatial distance is irrelevant, communication instantaneous'. He examines the way in which modern-day politicians can manage their public performance to maximum public effect, yet that management – stage-management – now meets with a public visibility brought about by multimedia technologies allowing swift, instant and global transmission of texts and images, generated not so much by top-down authority as by bottom-up public activity.

The NETWORK SOCIETY has made possible a *public* panopticon, an audio and visual apparatus of record that turns the spyglass (or to be more exact, the mobile phone linked to online transmission) on statesmen, politicians and the old guardians of the traditional panopticon, the police and surveillance services.

Multimedia equipment now allows us to actually witness, in real time, events as they are happening – hijacked planes hurtling into the skyscrapers of New York or London police beating G20 protestors: they are on camera, on record, no longer the business of the mass media alone, but of individuals participating in the events they are filming. Thanks to networked media, states Thompson, 'the capacity to outmanoeuvre one's opponents is always present'.

The social, cultural and political implications of two-way surveillance are far-reaching, providing a rich field for communications research. A phenomenon increased and diversified as a result of easy-access and available technology is 'playing to the camera', where the camera, whatever its form, is a performer in and sometimes the instigator of the event itself; the promise of media notoriety often being the motive force, this in turn prompting 'copycat' behaviour. The new visibility in Thompson's view is both an opportunity and a danger enabling users to bring down walls of censorship but also to invade privacy.

Paparazzo Aggressive, prying and often unscrupulous freelance photographer who specializes in taking pictures of celebrities; pursuing them wherever they go, armed with thick skin and zoom lenses. The word is an Italian – Calabrian – surname. It was suggested by writer Ennio Flaiano as a name for a character in Federico Fellini's film *La Dolce Vita* (*The Sweet Life*), made in 1960. Paparazzi were accused of hounding Diana, Princess of Wales, to her death in 1997 and the press at that time made a number of resolutions to curb the use of 'intrusive' pictures.

Paradigm (paradigmic) Commonly used in the social sciences, the term refers to a framework of explanation within which theories from various schools of thought in a discipline are located and from which research operates. In *linguistics*, paradigm describes the set of relationships that a linguistic unit, such as a letter or a word, has with other units in a specific context. The word is applicable in all SIGN systems, verbal, numerical, musical, etc. The alphabet is a paradigm, or set of signs, from which a choice is made to formulate the message. A *syntagm* is a combination of the chosen signs, a chain that amounts to MEANING. In language we can describe the vocabulary we use as *paradigmic*, and the sentence that vocabulary is formed into, *syntagmic*.

All messages, therefore, involve selection from a paradigm and combination into a syntagm. All the units in a paradigm must share characteristics that determine the membership of that paradigm, thus letters in the alphabetic paradigm, numbers in the numerical paradigm, notes in the musical paradigm.

Each unit within the paradigm must be clearly differentiable from other units; it must be characterized by distinctive features. Just as the paradigm is governed by shared characteristics and distinctive features, so the syntagm is determined by rules or conventions by which the combination of paradigms is made – rules of grammar and syntax or, in music, rules of harmony. See PARADIGMS OF THE MEDIA; SEMIOLOGY/SEMIOTICS.

Paradigms of the media James Curran in 'Rethinking the media as a public sphere' in *Communication and Citizenship* (Routledge, 1991), edited by Peter Dahlgren and Colin Sparks, has identified three *paradigms* (see previous entry) that seek to explain the relationship between the mass media and the POWER structure of societies in which they operate: the *Marxist* or *Neo-Marxist*, the *Liberal-Pluralist* and the *Radical Democratic* paradigms.

The Marxist or Neo-Marxist school argues that it is those who own and control economic capital who are at the heart of a society's power structure, and that such a position allows them to exercise power over cultural institutions such as the mass media in order to better pursue their economic goals. Media professionals may view themselves as autonomous but, it is argued, they have been socialized into and have *internalized* the NORMS and VALUES of the dominant CLASS.

Thus from this perspective, a key ideological contribution made by the mass media is that it provides the audience with frameworks for interpreting messages which encourage it to construct readings that are consistent with the interests of the dominant class. Critics of this tradition have argued, though, that it overlooks the degree of leeway which does exist for journalists to ask awkward questions, as well as the need to consider the AUDIENCE and the audience's role in constructing the MEANING of mass media messages.

A competing paradigm is that offered by the Liberal-Pluralist tradition of media research, which argues that the mass media is and should be composed of a number of competing groups operating within a free market, though subject to state intervention when this is deemed in the public interest. Groups within the mass media tend to be seen as in competition for power and influence within society.

Media professionals, such as journalists, are seen to enjoy a considerable degree of *autonomy* over the production of media artefacts. Within this tradition, some perceive the media to have a responsibility within society to behave as a WATCHDOG whose role it is to provide an arena for wide public debate about civil issues, facilitating the articulation of a *plurality* of views and values and, in so doing, to allow private

individuals to exercise a form of informal control over the state.

This tradition has, however, been subject to much criticism for its failure to address the narrow social base from which media professionals are often drawn, resulting in those from working-class and/or ethnic backgrounds being under-represented; and the degree to which the political economy of media ownership, the CULTURE of media organizations, and the place of these organizations in the political economy of a society influence the content and reading of media artefacts.

The Radical Democratic paradigm, according to James Curran, offers a synthesis between the other two. Whilst this paradigm acknowledges the links between the ownership and control of media institutions and that of other key institutions, and the fact that the free market tends to be skewed in favour of the dominant class, it does not perceive the links to be so close that the media could be conceived as an arm of the ruling class. Rather, the media is seen as 'caught in the crossfire', providing 'a battleground between contending forces. The way in which the media responds to and mediates this conflict affects the balance of social forces and, ultimately, the distribution of rewards within society'.

Journalists and media professionals are viewed as having day-to-day autonomy that allows them to make a difference and opens up the possibility for the committed radical journalism which would allow the media to act as a countervailing force and to further the cause of the less powerful. It also recognizes that not all journalists and media professionals work in media organizations which have one dominant owner, and argues that those working in BROADCASTING and in commercial media where ownership is dispersed among a number of shareholders, may enjoy considerable freedom to criticize the powerful. The structure of the media, however, is seen as being in need of reform if it is to achieve its potential for providing diverse debate within a democratic society. See DEMOCRACY AND THE MEDIA. See also *TOPIC GUIDE* under MEDIA INSTITUTIONS.

Paralanguage See NON-VERBAL VOCALIZATIONS.

Parental Guidance (PG) See CERTIFICATION OF FILMS.

Participant observation Some research evidence is collected by the researcher becoming a member of the group or social situation under observation. The researcher participates fully in the situation, and those being observed may be unaware that he/she is a researcher. The advantage of this method of data collection is that the greater involvement of the researcher may facilitate an increased insight into and greater understanding of the behaviour being investigated. The role of participant observer may require the researcher to have the competence and experience to undertake a professional role within the context being observed. David Deacon, Michael Pickering, Peter Golding and Graham Murdock in *Researching Communications: A Practical Guide to Methods in Media and Cultural Analysis* (Hodder Education, 2007) note that this has been the case with a number of studies of journalistic practice. See ETHNOGRAPHIC (APPROACH TO AUDIENCE MEASUREMENT). See also *TOPIC GUIDE* under RESEARCH METHODS.

▸ Philip Schlesinger, *Putting 'Reality' Together: BBC News* (Routledge, 1992).

Partisan An adherent of a particular party or cause. The term is also used to describe actions as well as allegiances. Within media studies, much research has focused upon the political partisanship of the press and TV companies, that is upon the degree to which they may support one or other political party or faction, and colour their political coverage accordingly. If such coverage gives space to the views of two factions or parties it is generally described as being *bi-partisan*; if its tone is one of general disinterest, of being above party politics, it is described as being *anti-partisan*. Partisan perspectives may not, though, permeate political coverage only; they may pervade media presentations generally. See EFFECTS OF THE MASS MEDIA.

Participatory journalism See GENRE.

Passivity One influential and widely held PERCEPTION of the mass AUDIENCE is that it is largely passive and unreflective. There is little evidence for this, though assumptions carry weight, and are noticeable in content selection and approach, regardless of evidence. Modern media commentators insist on the diversity of response of audiences. Determinants of response are complex and largely unpredictable, influential factors being age, culture, social class and status, gender, race, belief and education, sickness and health, not to mention wealth (or the lack of it) and a multitude of other distractions.

At the same time commentators have expressed concern at the amount of time members of the public spend in front of TV and computer screens, raising questions as to whether computer gaming and surfing the Net take time away from personal relationships or participation in community activity.

An August 2010 report by Ofcom entitled 'Consumers spend almost half their waking hours using media and communications' presents a picture of a population getting their exercise by pressing buttons: people are sending four times as many texts a day than in 2004. The use of smart phones has accelerated this trend, and not just among the under-25s, for 'the over-55s are catching up, with half now having broadband at home – the fastest growing age group'.

Busy as we are on our mobiles, we still, says the report, have time to watch TV for an average 3 hours and 45 minutes a day, 'consumers being as attached to their TVs as they ever were and [are] hungry for more channels and better picture quality'. See AUDIENCE: ACTIVE AUDIENCE; AUDIENCE MEASUREMENT; EFFECTS OF THE MASS MEDIA; EMPOWERMENT; INTERACTIVITY; PLEASURE: ACTIVE AND REACTIVE; RESISTIVE READING.

Patch A community-specific news and information platform initiated in February 2009 by the AOL company (America On Line), with plans to create 500 communities within a year across the US. Professional editors and freelancers form a local nucleus which makes use of contributions by people in the locality – comments, stories, photographs; participation in one form or another (BLOGGING, for example). Warren Webster, President of Patch Media, celebrating the launch of the one-hundredth site in August 2010, told the press, 'We believe that Patch is a revolutionary and efficient approach to producing relevant, quality local journalism.' *www.patch.com*

Paternity of the text See TEXT: INTEGRITY OF THE TEXT.

Patriarchy Society ruled by or dominated by men; patriarch means father, thus patriarchal relates to a CULTURE shaped and governed in the interests of men, with women in a subordinate, and in some cases, subject, role. Patriarchy is reflected in customs, NORMS and VALUES, the law, education, commerce, industry, the arts, sport and, not least, language. Many commentators have also identified patriarchy as being assertively alive in the media, though at least at the *operative* (rather than the *managerial*) level, substantial advances have been made by women in JOURNALISM and BROADCASTING. See NEWS: THE 'MALENESS' OF NEWS.

Patriot Act (US), 2001 See USA-PATRIOT ACT (2001).

Pauper press See UNDERGROUND PRESS.

Paywall The INTERNET created a tradition of freely available information and content; and though the press charged for copies of the newspapers it published, online information services were generally free. In July 2010 Rupert Murdoch's News International introduced charges for previously free access to the UK *Times, Sunday Times* and *News of the World* with the intention of turning a profit from Net provision and the hope that the rest of the British press would follow suit.

Decisions to charge for what has been previously free reflect a number of major changes in the media scene: newspaper sales are in decline (indeed in many cases their online news is sampled by more readers than the paper-and-ink versions); the prime funding source of the press, advertising, is itself in difficulties if not recession; and the availability of news, etc. on mobile devices and tablets is perceived as a growing threat to the industry. In particular, the teen and twenties generation, brought up in the Network Society, make online data their first, and sometimes only, point of call.

PeaceNet See TELEDEMOCRACY.

'Pencil of Nature' Title of the first book ever illustrated with photographs, published in England in 1844, the work of William Henry Fox Talbot (1800–77), inventor of the CALOTYPE process of photo-printing. The range of photographs pasted into *The Pencil of Nature* was extraordinary and included intimate, informal studies of Talbot's household at his home, Laycock Abbey. See PHOTOGRAPHY, ORIGINS.

People's Communication Charter Proposed by Cees Hamelink in *World Communication: Disempowerment and Self-Empowerment* (Zed Books, 1995) in the light of his vision that the GLOBALIZATION of communication threatens to further divide the information-rich from the information-poor, at the personal, community and national levels. The Charter provides a valuable text in which issues are highlighted and rights and responsibilities spelt out.

The preamble to the Charter opens with the affirmation that 'communication is basic to the life of individuals and peoples and that communication is crucial in the issues and crises which affect all members of the world community'. It is mindful 'that communication can be used to support the powerful and to victimize the powerless and that communication is fundamental to the shaping of the cultural environment of every society'.

Disempowerment is seen as a major trend; and it occurs through the 'withholding of informa-tion, by distorting information, by overwhelming people with overloads of information, or by obstructing people's access to communication channels'. In consequence the Charter urges support to enable people to develop their own communication channels through which they can speak for themselves. Under General Standards, Article 1 declares the 'conviction that all people are entitled to the respect of their dignity, integrity, equality, and liberty'. Article 2 asserts freedom of expression, but aligned with that 'there should be free and independent channels of communication' on the basis that 'Free media are pluralist media'.

Article 3 speaks of the right to receive information 'about matters of public interest' and 'this includes the right to receive information which is independent of commercial and political interests'. Article 7 concerns the RIGHT OF REPLY; Article 8 speaks of the need to nurture a 'diversity of languages' and the need to 'create provisions for minority languages in the media'. Article 9 argues for the protection of people's cultural identity. See MEDIAPOLIS. See also *TOPIC GUIDE* under MEDIA ETHICS.

Perception The process of becoming aware and making sense of the stimuli received from our environment by the senses: sight, hearing, smell, taste, and TOUCH. *Social perception* refers to the application of this process to our attempts to explain, understand, make judgments about and predict the behaviour of other people.

Perception is selective. We are surrounded by many sensations but we tend to direct our attention to only a few of these. Our decision as to what to attend to can be influenced by environmental and personal factors: for example, environmental factors can include the intensity, size, motion or novelty of the stimuli whilst personal factors can include present needs and drives, physiological features, past experiences and learning – *perceptual set* – as well as personality.

The influence of personal factors explains why individuals may pay attention to different stimuli, to different messages or parts of a message. See ATTITUDES; CULTURE; EMPATHY; EXPECTATIONS; FIRST IMPRESSIONS; HALO EFFECT; LABELLING PROCESS (AND THE MEDIA); MALE-AS-NORM; MORES; MOTIVATION; NORMS; PROJECTION; SAPIR-WHORF HYPOTHESIS; SELECTIVE EXPOSURE; SELF-CONCEPT; SELF-FULFILLING PROPHECY; STEREOTYPE; SUBCULTURE; VALUES.

Performance See SELF-PRESENTATION.

Performance capture See ANIMATION.

Performatives Action words that indicate the

nature of action through talk: *announce, insist, declare* or *denounce*. In the reporting of speech in NEWS, performatives often embody evaluative connotations, indicating approval or disapproval on the part of the encoder. 'The Prime Minister declined to comment' carries with it marginally less disapproval than the statement 'The Prime Minister refused to comment'. The word *say* may be classified as a *neutral performative* unless it is contrasted with a performative used disapprovingly; thus 'The Management say their pay-offer is final, while the unions claim their actions will bring about further concessions'.

Periodicity Describes the timescale of the schedules of NEWS organizations; thus a daily newspaper has a 24-hour periodicity. The more the timescale of a potential item of news coincides with the periodicity of the news organization, the more likely it is that the story will 'make the headlines'. Information that can be gathered, processed and dramatized within a 24-hour cycle (such as bombings, assassinations, clashes with the police, the speeches of politicians) stands a better chance of breaking through the news threshold than news which is gradual and undramatic. See NEWS VALUES.

Persistence of vision The realization that the eye retains an image for a split second after the object has passed gave birth to the cinema. The principle was first illustrated, and proved marketable, with toys of the nineteenth century such as the THAUMATROPE, a disc with images on each side; when the disc was spun round, the images merged into a single action. The ZOETROPE was a drum with illustrations of figures inside which, when spun round, conveyed the impression of movement. See CINEMATOGRAPHY, ORIGINS.

Persona See PARASOCIAL INTERACTION; SELF-PRESENTATION.

Personal idiom Or idiosyncratic language; occurring in interpersonal relationships; serves the function of building relationship cohesiveness. Results of research into the use of personal idiom were published in an article, 'Couples' personal idioms: exploring intimate talk' in the *Journal of Communication* (Winter, 1981) by Robert Hopper, Mark L. Knapp and Lorel Scott. Such idioms, they found, take the form of a range of idiomatic exchanges: partner nicknames; expressions of affection; labels for others outside the relationship; for use in confrontations; to deal with requests and routines; sexual references and euphemisms; sexual invitations and teasing insults (or 'kidding').

Personal space See SPATIAL BEHAVIOUR.

Personalization One of the chief conventions of

media reportage. Where a potential NEWS item can be personalized it has a greater chance of being included than if it is difficult to translate into personality terms. The preference is for elite personalities (see NEWS VALUES).

John Lloyd in an article entitled 'The death of privacy: J'accuse!' (*New Statesman*, 5 March 1999) argues that this emphasis on the personal has been at the expense of an exploration of policy and ISSUES. He acknowledges that within TV news and current affairs it is 'a received wisdom that only by personalizing a story can it be given meaning for a mass audience. Thus a story about public spending must find someone in pain on a hospital waiting list'. Lloyd warns, 'the hazard of such stories is that the feeling swamps the understanding'. See JOURNALISM: PHONE-HACKING.

Personalization, involvement, contiguity, 'kick-outs' See YAROS' 'PICK' MODEL FOR MULTMEDIA NEWS, 2009.

PEST This is a well-used device for analysing aspects of a company's operating environment which could have a potential impact on its activities: **P**olitical, **E**conomic, **S**ocial and **T**echnological. Political aspects of the environment could include government attitudes towards private enterprise, whilst economic aspects might include the rate of inflation. Social aspects of the environment could include, for example, a trend towards an ageing population, and the widespread use of FACEBOOK would be an example of a technological aspect.

PEST analysis can be used to scan factors within the current situation and also to consider possible future developments, to anticipate the following: changes in the market; emerging environmental issues that might affect an organization's reputation; the need for the repositioning of a product; and consequent changes in promotional strategies. See EPISTLE.

Phatic (language) Derives from the Greek, 'phasis', meaning *utterance*. The term finds its modern connotation in the phrase 'phatic communion' coined by anthropologist Bronislaw Malinowski (1884–1942), meaning that part of communication which is used for establishing an atmosphere or maintaining social contact rather than for exchanging information or ideas. Phatic words and phrases have been called 'idiot salutations' and, when they comprise dialogue, 'two-stroke conversations'. Comments about the weather, enquiries about health, and everyday exchanges including nods, smiles and waves are part of the phatic communion essential for 'oiling' or maintaining channels of communication.

Phatic language is central to human relationships; its significance can be best noted by its absence: you give a cheery 'hello' to a friend passing in the street, only to be greeted by stony silence; you halt your car to permit another motorist to go ahead of you, and he/she does not acknowledge your gesture. From such phatic neglect might spring responses out of all proportion to the MEANING of the exchange, or lack of it. See JAKOBSON'S MODEL OF COMMUNICATION.

Phoneme The smallest unit in the sound system of a language. Each language can be shown to operate with a relatively small number of phonemes, some having as few as fifteen, others as many as fifty. Phonemics is the study of the basic sounds of language.

Phone-tapping See JOURNALISM: PHONE-HACKING; PRIVACY.

Phonetics The science of human sound-making, especially sounds used in speech. Phonetics includes the study of articulation, acoustics or perception of speech, and the properties of specific languages.

Phonodisc First-ever VIDEO recording, developed by John Logie Baird (1888–1946) in 1928. This was a 10-inch 78rpm record, in every way similar to the acoustic discs already being produced for conventional sound recording. Despite its novelty, the Phonodisc, coming so early in the age of the development of TV, failed to succeed commercially.

Phonograph See GRAMOPHONE.

Phonology A branch of LINGUISTICS which studies the sound systems of languages. Its aim is to demonstrate the patterns of distinctive sound in spoken language, and to make as general statements as possible about the nature of sound systems in languages throughout the world.

Photographic negativization See VISIONS OF ORDER.

Photography, origins Joseph Nicéphore Nièpce (1765–1833) and his brother Claude were the first to fix images of the CAMERA OBSCURA by chemical means in 1793, though the light sensitivity of silver nitrate had been known and written about as early as 1727 when Johann Heinrich Schulze, Professor of Anatomy at the University of Altdorf, published a paper indicating that the darkening of silver salts was due not to heat but to light.

1826 is generally recognized as the year in which the first photographic image was captured. Joseph Nièpce's reproduction of a roof-top scene, on a pewter plate, he called Heliographie – sun drawing. In 1830 he teamed up with Louis Daguerre (1789–1851), theatrical designer and co-inventor of the diorama. The death of Nièpce three years later left Daguerre to lead the field in France. He discovered that an almost invisible latent image could be developed using mercury vapour, thus reducing exposure time from around 8 hours to between 20 and 30 minutes.

His DAGUERROTYPE was taken up by the French government in 1839, and elicited from Paul Delaroche the immortal line, 'From today, painting is dead!' In the UK, astronomer Sir John Herschel (1792–1871) read a paper entitled 'On the art of photography' to the Royal Society, accompanied by twenty-three photographs. In 1840 he was the first to use the verb *to photograph* and the adjective *photographic*, to identify *negative* and *positive*, and twenty years later to use the term *snap-shot*.

William Henry Fox Talbot (1800–77) won fame and fortune with his Calotype (1841), the true technical base of photography because, unlike the Daguerrotype, its negative/positive principle made possible the making of prints from the original photographs. The inventions and discoveries that followed helped to improve the effectiveness of the photographic process. Frederick Scott Archer's *collodion* or wet-plate process, details of which were published in 1851, greatly increased sensitivity; the use of gelatine silver bromide emulsion, invented in 1871 by Dr Richard Leach Maddox, and later improved upon by John Burgess, Richard Kennett and Charles Bennett, proved a considerable advance on the collodion method, and ushered-in the modern era of factory-produced photographic material, freeing the photographer from the necessity of preparing his/her own plates.

Celluloid was invented by Alexander Parkes in 1861 and roll film made from celluloid was produced by the Eastman Company in the US from 1889. By 1902, Eastman, manufacturers of Kodak, were producing between 80 and 90 per cent of the world's output. Very swiftly photography became the hobby of the man in the street. Every tenth person in the UK – 4 million people – was estimated to own a camera by 1900.

Colour film photography hit many technical snags in its development. A colour screen process was patented as early as 1904 by the Lumière brothers. They introduced their Autochrome plates commercially in 1907, when good panchromatic emulsion was available. However, exposure was about forty times longer than that for black and white film.

Modern methods based on multiple-layer film

P

and coupling components were simultaneously introduced by Kodak and Agfa. In 1935, Kodachrome, created by two American amateurs, Leopold Godowsky and Leopold Mannes, was marketed, a year ahead of Agfacolor. In both, transparencies were obtained suitable for projection as well as reproduction. Electronic flash was invented in 1931 by Harold E. Egerton. See CAMERA, ORIGINS; FILMLESS CAMERA; HIGH-SPEED PHOTOGRAPHY; PHOTO-JOURNALISM; PHOTOMONTAGE; TIME-LAPSE PHOTOGRAPHY. See also *TOPIC GUIDE* under MEDIA HISTORY.

Photogravure Engraving by photography, for purposes of printing, was invented by Englishman William Henry Fox Talbot (1800–77) in 1852. It was not until 1947 that the first machine to do a complete typesetting job by means of photography was invented.

Photo-journalism Despite the popularity of photography among the general public, the press were curiously slow to realize the possibilities of photographs. The *Daily Mirror* was first in the field in the UK at the turn of the twentieth century, but the use of photographs did not become commonplace till the end of the First World War (1914–18). In June 1919, the New York *Illustrated Daily News* at last fully acknowledged a vital means of communication thirty-nine years after the feasibility of printing a half-tone block (reproducing light and shade by dots of different sizes and densities) alongside type had been demonstrated by Stephen H. Horgan in the New York *Daily Graphic*. It was not until the 1920s that photo-journalism in the modern sense began, with the introduction of the Ermanox camera and ultra-rapid plates.

Among the fathers of photo-journalism were Erich Saloman, Felix H. Man and Wolfgang Weber. With a camera hidden in his top hat, Arthur Barrett secretly took court photographs of the suffragettes, and, in February 1928, Saloman took sensational pictures of a Coburg murder trial. Man pioneered the picture story in, for example, *A Day in the Life of Mussolini*, 1934, and it was Man who founded *Weekly Illustrated* in the same year. He became chief photographer for *Picture Post*, founded in 1938, a position he held until 1945.

Photo-journalism was given increasing status over the years by many outstanding photographers. Henri Cartier-Bresson photo-reported visits to Spain (1933) and Mexico (1934); Robert Capa won undying fame with his war photography, especially his pictures taken during the Spanish Civil War (1936–9); Bill Brandt photographed the *English at Home* (1936) while

Margaret Bowke-White, in *You Have Seen Their Faces* (1937), portrayed the conditions in the South of the US, in particular the negro chain-gangs. Suppression of the photo-reportage of Bert Hardy from the Korean War (1950–53) by the proprietors of *Picture Post* led to the resignation of the magazine's outstanding editor, Tom Hopkinson.

Talented, fearless and concerned photo-journalists continue to the present, even in the age of TV and the closure of photo-papers. Don McCullin has photo-reported war, oppression, hardship and carnage all over the world in a vast array of unforgettable images. He was, incidentally, one of the photographers refused permission by the Ministry of Defence to cover the Falklands War (1982).

In *A Concise History of Photography* (Thames & Hudson, 1965; 3rd edition by Helmet, 1986), Helmet and Alison Gernsheim write, 'No other medium can bring life and reality so close as does photography and it is in the fields of reportage and documentation that photography's most important contribution lies in modern times.' Not the least of their achievements, photography and photo-journalism have proved powerful agents in the awakening of social conscience. They place images in the collective consciousness which resonate across cultures and time. Examples are Joe Rosenthal's picture of marines raising the Stars and Stripes at Iwo-Jima; Nick Ut's image of the Vietnamese girl, her shoulders burning with napalm; and Eddie Adams's photograph of an officer executing a Vietcong prisoner with a pistol to the head.

Photo-journalism records images that people prefer not to see; images that upset and depress. At the same time there are powerful arguments that photograph serves as an antidote to war and violence. Loup Langton in *Photojournalism and Today's News* (Wiley-Blackwell, 2008) writes: 'Visual images inform people about the world and about life in ways that words cannot. And the best images can motivate people to work towards a better world.'

In his preface to a Committee to Protect Journalists (CPJ) report, 'Attacks on the press, 2009', Fareed Zakaria writes: 'Unable to afford foreign bureaus, more newspapers and magazines are relying on freelancers abroad. These stringers look just as suspicious to dictators and military groups – and they are distinctively more vulnerable.' Photographers have ranked among the 847 journalists killed worldwide between 1992 and 2010. Zakaria points out that as 'publications and TV networks continue to shed staff and look for ways to cover conflicts more affordably' the number of journalist deaths, beatings and imprisonments is 'going to grow'.

Today photo-journalism competes with pictures of altogether different genres – fashion and celebrity. Fewer newspapers and TV stations now go to the expense of sending their reporters and photographers to areas of conflict, to the point where freelancing seems, for many photo-journalists, the only way forwards in their careers. See DOCUMENTARY; JOURNALISM: CITIZEN JOURNALISM; MEDIASPHERE.

▶ John Hartley, *The Politics of Pictures: The Creation of the Public in the Age of Popular Media* (Routledge, 1992).

Photomontage Process of mounting, superimposing, one photograph on top of another; a method almost as old as photography itself. The Dadaists and Surrealists experimented with photomontage to produce visionary pictures. Laslo Moholy-Nagy (1895–1946) combined several picture components in the production of a new work and termed his approach 'photolastics'. Malik of Berlin were the first publishers to use photomontage for book jackets. Most extensively, the process has been employed in ADVERTISING, though the British artist Peter Kennard has created many unforgettable – and satirical – images using photomontage. See PICTURE POSTCARDS.

Phototypesetting Method that bypassed the traditional metal-type stage of print production by PRINTING type photographically from an optical or electric store of individual characters. Though the first photocomposing machine was created as early as 1894, it was not until it could be 'manned' by computers, in the 1960s, that the process became widespread. Modern typesetting allows operators to lay out pages on VDUs: this means that the same person can enter copy, make up the pages and check errors; then, one touch of a button and a high-quality proof is produced. See *TOPIC GUIDE* under MEDIA: TECHNOLOGIES.

Phillis Review of Government Communications (UK), 2004 Examined the relationship between British government information services, the media and the public, identifying a lack of trust on the part of the public in the communications performance of government. The report by an independent committee chaired by Bob Phillis, Chief Executive of the Guardian Media Group, declared that favouritism, partisanship, collusion and distortion have become the key features of the relationship between government and media. The Govern-

ment Information and Communication Service (GICS) was considered 'no longer fit for [its] purpose' and ought to be disbanded.

The report criticized the lobby system (see LOBBYING; LOBBY PRACTICE) in which some media are favoured over others, chiefly because they can be relied on to provide the government with a 'good press'. It urged more *transparency*, more openness, as against briefings in 'a closed, secretive and opaque insider process' behind closed doors.

The report also voiced serious concern about the role of the civil service in the communications process, perceiving an erosion of impartiality brought about by government pressure. As for the response of government information services to the public, the Phillis Review urged a speeding-up of the official response rate to enquiries by members of the public, citing a case in which the Ministry of Defence took six years to respond to a query.

The public should, recommended Phillis, be guaranteed a reply to enquiries within twenty days of receipt, a move the report believed could, along with other measures – such as reducing the power of ministers to veto the provision of information – address the problem of the lack of trust on the part of the public, and its current disenchantment with government information services.

In its *Media Manifesto*, 2005, the CAMPAIGN FOR PRESS AND BROADCASTING FREEDOM describes the government's response to Phillis as 'lamentable', failing to act on the recommendation to cap the number of political advisers or limit their powers; 'in the face of opposition from political correspondents at Westminster, the Downing Street press office has backed away from changing the rules in order to allow lobby briefings to be televised'. See FREEDOM OF INFORMATION ACT (UK), 2005.

Picture postcards German Heinrich von Stephan is generally considered to have thought up the idea of a postcard, in 1865, though Emmanuel Hermann ran him close, persuading the director-general of the Austrian Post to issue the first government postcard, in 1869. It was called a 'Correspondence Card'. In 1870 the first government postcard was issued in the UK; 70 million such cards were sold in the first year. The US government followed suit in 1872.

Since then the picture postcard has provided a treasure house for the analysis of contemporary interests and attitudes: art, fashion, new technology, warfare, royalty, exploration, history, travel; ideas of patriotism and Empire, of family,

P

entertainment, comedy, etc. The title Mail Art has been given to a practice widespread in the late 1970s and 1980s of artists exchanging visual ideas by postcard.

During the same period the postcard became popular in a propagandist role, especially among protest groups of the Left. A classic piece of photomontage in postcard form is Peter Kennard's version of the painting by the nineteenth-century British painter, John Constable, *The Haywain*. Kennard superimposes cruise missiles on the horse-drawn wagon as it passes through a tranquil Suffolk landscape. Such cards use cartoons, photographs, photograffiti and quotations.

Inevitably cards of past ages have become collectors' items; the word Deltiology (from the Greek, *deltion*, small picture) was coined by American Randall Rhoades for picture-postcard collecting and study. See CIGARETTE CARDS: CULTURAL INDICATORS; POSTERS.

Pidgin See COMMUNICATION: INTERCULTURAL COMMUNICATION.

Piggybacking See INTERNET: WIRELESS INTERNET.

PIE chart A model proposed by Randy Bobbitt and Ruth Sullivan in *Developing the Public Relations Campaign* (Pearson, 2005) to outline the three-step process required for the development of a public relations campaign. These are as follows: '*Planning*. Research and analyse the problem in order to determine how to most effectively respond to it. *Implementation*. Execute the response. *Evaluation*. Measure the effectiveness of the response and determine what needs to be done next.'

Pilkington Committee Report on Broadcasting (UK), 1962 Set up under the chairmanship of Sir Harry Pilkington in 1960, the Committee's chief concern in a strongly worded 297-page deposition was the nation's cultural and intellectual life, and the effect upon these of broadcasting now that commercial television had been on the scene since 1954: 'Our conclusion,' declared the Committee, 'is that where it prevails it operates to lower general standards of enjoyment and understanding.'

The BBC emerged unscathed, and not a little praised, from the Committee Report: 'The BBC knows good broadcasting and by and large they are providing it.' The 'villain' of the scenario was ITV. So dissatisfied with ITV programmes were the Committee that one of their recommendations (never put into practice) was that the Independent Broadcasting Authority (IBA) take on responsibility for the planning of programmes.

Pilkington expressed disquiet at the portrayal of physical violence in TV programmes and of a 'comprehensive carelessness about moral standards generally'.

Most of the Report's recommendations were ignored, yet it did have its effect, giving the BBC, staggering from the impact of ITV competition, a shot in the arm. And it was through Pilkington that the BBC was the first to receive a second channel (BBC2, 1964). John Whale in *The Politics of the Media* (Fontana, 1977) says Pilkington 'aimed at large effects and missed them'. Nevertheless, Pilkington established a set of judgmental criteria, albeit elitist-cultural, which have formed a rallying point ever since for broadcasting reformers. See TOPIC GUIDES under COMMISSIONS, COMMITTEES, LEGISLATION; MEDIA INSTITUTIONS.

Pilot study A preliminary testing or 'experimental experiment' in which the researcher seeks to try out a new idea, system or approach; to determine whether an intended study is feasible, to clarify assumptions and improve instruments of measurement.

Pirate radio The monopoly of RADIO BROADCASTING held in the UK by the BBC was colourfully challenged in the 1960s by 'pirate' stations broadcasting from ancient forts and ships anchored in the North Sea. They played non-stop popular music, collected ADVERTISING revenues, paid no royalties on the music they played and thus made substantial profits.

In 1964 Radio Caroline, from a ship called the Caroline, took to the air on 28 March, one of a long line of pirates. Founder Ronan O'Rahilly received over 20,000 letters in the first ten days of broadcasting. The Duke of Bedford was the first advertiser, for Woburn Abbey – his advertisement brought in 4,500 people the next day.

War on the pirates was initially conducted in the Council of Europe. The European Agreement for the Prevention of Broadcasts transmitted outside National Territories, signed by member states in Strasbourg in 1965, sought to outlaw pirate broadcasting throughout the countries of the Common Market.

This was followed, in the UK, with the Labour government's Marine, etc. Broadcasting (Offences) Act, which became law in 1967. Among sections of the broadcasting and political establishment there was fear that the pirates might not only undermine existing systems of broadcasting, but also have an 'undesirable' cultural and even political impact. The 1967 Act made it an offence to direct unlicensed broadcasts into the UK and to buy advertising time on illegal channels.

With the apparent defeat of the pirates, and the dismantling of their stations, there was clearly a gap to be filled in the pattern of official broadcasting services. At the end of 1966 the Labour government issued a White Paper containing proposals that opened the way for the creation of Radio 1.

That was not the end of pirate radio. A widespread enthusiasm for radio broadcasting independent of the duopoly was sustained through the 1970s, and in the 1980s pirates began popping up all over, making illegal broadcasts from unlicensed transmitters in woodlands, on hilltops, in back bedrooms, in garages or even on the move. Today's pirates continue, with no less ingenuity, to evade the efforts of authority to curtail their activities, though the majority of today's 'piracy' is only an INTERNET website away. See BLOGGING; COMMERCIAL RADIO; COMMUNITY RADIO; PODCASTING. See also TOPIC GUIDE under BROADCASTING.

Pistolgraph See CAMERA, ORIGINS.

Plagiarism From the Latin, 'plagiarius', meaning kidnapper; the act of stealing from others their thoughts or their writings and claiming them as one's own.

Plasticity: neuroplasticity and the Internet Refers to the way in which stimuli can work on and alter the activity of the brain. In relation to media, concern has been expressed by a number of writers that the INTERNET can, with prolonged and intensive use, rewire the circuits of the brain. American neuroscientist Gary Small with Gigi Vorgan published an influential but much-challenged treatise on the effects on plasticity of Net use in *iBrain: Surviving the Technological Alteration of the Modern Mind* (HarperCollins, 2008), stating that 'perhaps not since early man first discovered how to use a tool has the human brain been affected so quickly and so dramatically'. The authors' view is that, 'As the brain evolves and shifts its focus towards new technological skills, it drifts away from fundamental social skills.'

The case was taken up in 2010 by another neuroscientist, Nicholas Carr, in *The Shallows: How the Internet Is Changing The Way We Think, Read and Remember* (Atlantic Books). Carr writes: 'Dozens of studies by psychologists, neurobiologists, and educators point to the same conclusion: When we go online, we enter an environment that promotes cursory reading, hurried and distracted thinking, and superficial learning. Even as the Internet grants us easy access to vast amounts of information, it is turning us into shallower thinkers, literally changing the structure of our brain.' See DIGITAL NATIVES, DIGITAL IMMIGRANTS.

Play theory of mass communication In *The Play Theory of Mass Communication* (University of Chicago Press, 1967), William Stephenson counters those who speak of the harmful effects of the mass media by arguing that first and foremost the media serve audiences as play-experiences. Even newspapers, says Stephenson, are read for pleasure rather than for information and enlightenment. He sees the media as 'a buffer against conditions which would otherwise be anxiety producing'. The media provide communication-pleasure.

Stephenson argues that what is most required by people within a national culture is something for everyone to talk about. For him, mass communication 'should serve two purposes. It should suggest how best to maximize the communication-pleasure in the world. It should also show how far autonomy for the individual can be achieved in spite of the weight of social controls against him'.

The theory finds ready connection with practices and reception in the online age of information. In the words of Graeme Turner in *Ordinary People and the Media: The Demotic Turn* (Sage, 2010), 'entertainment has become the most pervasive discursive domain in twenty-first-century popular culture'. The burgeoning trend has been to equate pleasure with public participation, to reposition information as entertainment by stressing audience engagement and interactivity largely within the frame of consumption. See CONSUMERIZATION. See also TOPIC GUIDE under COMMUNICATION THEORY.

▶ Johan Huizinga, *Homo Ludens: A Study of the Play Element in Culture* (Paladin, 1970); Pat Kane, *The Play Ethic: A Manifesto for a Different Way of Living* (Macmillan, 2004).

Pleasure: active and reactive Mary Ellen Brown in *Soap Opera and Women's Talk* (Sage, 1994) speaks of the active and reactive pleasure of women viewers of soap operas. She argues that 'active pleasure for women in soap opera groups affirms their connection to a woman's culture that operates in subtle opposition to dominant culture'. It is this 'cult of the home and of women's concerns,' says Brown, 'recognized but devalued in patriarchal terms, that provides a notion of identity that values women's traditional expertise'.

On the other hand, reactive pleasure, 'while not rejecting the connection women often feel towards women's cultural networks and concerns, also recognizes that these concerns

P

often arise out of women's inability to completely control their own lives'. Consequently they are able to 'recognize and to feel at an emotional level the price of oppression'.

Key to resistive soap opera groups is *talking*, the very act of which 'indicates the importance of connectedness to others'. Brown acknowledges that soaps are a genre 'designed and developed to appeal to women's place in society' and largely to keep her in that place, yet 'although soap operas work at isolating women in their homes and keeping them busy buying household products, in fact many observations indicate that they actually bring women together'; thus, it would seem, paradoxically undermining HEGEMONY while aiming to underpin it.

Pluralism, pluralist The view that modern industrial societies have populations that are increasingly *heterogeneous*, that is different in kind, divided by such factors as ethnic, religious, regional and CLASS differences. Such heterogeneity, it is argued, produces a diversity of NORMS, VALUES interests and personal perspectives within such societies. Technological developments, such as those fostered by the digital revolution, make it increasingly possible for the media and cultural industries to address and access the heterogeneous nature of audiences, niche advertising being but one example of this.

It can also be argued that a plurality of groups compete for power and influence within society. Power is seen, therefore, as being increasingly diffuse in terms of its distribution within these societies. This perspective is not without its critics. Some GROUPS are likely to have more power than others and will be in a better position to impose their values upon other groups. As far as the field of media studies is concerned, recent concentrations in media ownership throw some doubt on the degree to which power is becoming more diffuse in its distribution.

However, as populations increasingly embrace the digital age and communicate with potentially vast audiences via the INTERNET, as they post comments and news on FACEBOOK, set up blogs, tweet comments on TWITTER or transmit their images on YOUTUBE, bypassing traditional modes of interchange, it could be argued that the Net – at least potentially – serves the advance of pluralism (see BLOGOSPHERE; MOBILIZATION; NET NEUTRALITY).

The term *pluralist* means many modes, many alternatives; in media terms, *diversity* – of ownership, style, content and standpoint. A pluralist society is one in which there are many choices and many interpretations of MEANING. It follows that the Internet is a pluralist medium, at least for the present. In recent years it has been the target for conglomerate ownership ambitions; in the view of some commentators putting the freedoms enjoyed by the Net at risk through acquisition and control based on the search for profitability.

Operators in media services seek control by extending ownership. This allows for a wide range of cost benefits – TV, for example, supporting an organization's press, its online services drumming up publicity for its TV channels. Cross-promotion, bundling of content (a newspaper to go with a TV subscription) and favourable advertising terms constitute vital benefits in highly competitive markets. See BRITISH SKY BROADCASTING (BSKYB); MURDOCH EFFECT.

Podcasting 'Pod' derives from the APPLE MACINTOSH iPod DOWNLOADING music system. A podcast is a RADIO equivalent of BLOGGING. It allows individuals and groups to run their own radio broadcasting service, downloadable onto the INTERNET. As Ken Young points out in a UK *Guardian* article, 'One-man band' (21 July 2005), 'with podcasting, the one man radio station was born'. Podcasts can be delivered by an automatic news feed system known as Really Simple Syndication (RSS) enabling broadcasts to be automatically downloaded whenever a station is being broadcast. Problems concern copyright on music and the risk that the authorities will seek to impose licensing regulations.

Polarization Refers to the tendency to think and speak in terms of opposites (see WEDOM, THEYDOM) or what have been termed *binary oppositions*. The English language abounds with terms denoting opposition. Reality, however, is more complex, and arguably few things can be seen meaningfully in terms of polar opposites. Our language then may tempt us into misleadingly simple perspectives.

As Gail and Michele Myers in *The Dynamics of Human Communication* (McGraw-Hill, 1985) argue, 'Our language supports dividing the world into false opposites. Polarization consists of evaluating what you perceive by placing it at one end of a two-pole continuum and making the two poles appear to be mutually exclusive ... If you are honest, you cannot be dishonest'.

Whilst there are situations in which genuine opposites are found, what we should be wary of is applying this perspective when it is not appropriate; and in so doing denying the complexities of a situation, or debate, and the range of alternatives that can or may exist. See VISIONS OF ORDER.

Politics of accommodation (in the media)
Potential conflict between various individuals and GROUPS within media corporations and between these corporations and a central social authority is seen by some commentators to be mediated by what Tom Burns in *The BBC: Public Institution and Private World* (Macmillan, 1977) calls a 'politics of accommodation'. This is a negotiated compromise in which notions such as professional standards and the public interest are used as trading pieces. Negotiations of this type can be conducted at several levels: between the professionals and the management; between one corporation and another; and between a corporation and the government.

Even between rival media empires there can exist, temporarily at least, what might be termed *reciprocal silence*, an agreement to censor information that may be, if publicized, damaging to one or other sides. A case in point is the silence exercised by the UK *Daily Mail* and its sister paper the *Mail on Sunday* over the controversial take-over of the *Mail*'s rival, *Express* newspapers by porn-king Richard Desmond, head of the Northern and Shell company. The Labour government's approval in 2002 of this takeover was explained by some commentators – though not in the *Mail*, among Labour's harshest critics – as being linked with Desmond's £100,000 contribution to Labour Party funds.

Associated Newspapers (AN), owners of the *Mail* and *Sunday Mail*, turned out to have a legal agreement with Northern and Shell – a pact of reciprocal silence – not to report the controversy in return for the *Express* group's silence concerning allegations about the Rothermere family, owners of AN. Margaret McDonagh, the-then Labour Party General Secretary who banked the £100,000 for Labour, joined Northern and Shell shortly afterwards. See CONSENSUS; ELITE; ESTABLISHMENT; HEGEMONY; MEDIA CONTROL; MEDIATION; REGULATORY FAVOURS; STRATEGIC BARGAINING. See also *TOPIC GUIDES* under MEDIA INSTITUTIONS; MEDIA: POLITICS & ECONOMICS.

Polysemy Has a number of meanings; broadly used, the term describes the potential for many interpretations in media TEXTS, or the capacity of AUDIENCE to read into such texts their own meanings rather than merely the PREFERRED READING of the communicators. For some commentators, audience is the 'victim' of media messages; for others, it is perceived as being capable of making its own diverse responses (see AUDIENCE: ACTIVE AUDIENCE; DOMINANT, SUBORDINATE, RADICAL). There is CONSENSUS among researchers that the extent of polysemy is to be viewed with caution.

The use of this term in media and communication analysis arguably reflects the influence of theoretical approaches from the field of cultural studies, and particularly those from theorists, such as John Fiske, who argue that the meaning of a text is produced in the act of reception and that it is essentially subject to differing interpretations. Thus most, if not all, texts would be polysemic in nature. As Denis McQuail notes in *Mass Communication Theory* (Sage, 2010), from this perspective, 'mass media content is thus in principle *polysemic*, having multiple potential readings for its "readers" (in the generic sense of audience members)'. It is also the case that texts can be intentionally constructed to be more or less open to interpretation, that is to have the capacity to be more or less polysemic. See OPEN, CLOSED TEXTS; OPINION LEADER; SIGNIFICANT OTHERS.
  ▶ John Fiske, *Television Culture* (Methuen, 1987).

Pool system Practice, particularly in wartime, of governments channelling media access to NEWS events through a regulated 'pool' of reporters; and consequently the 'pooling' of information for publication or broadcasting. This strategy of NEWS MANAGEMENT effectively censors journalists by corralling them, while at the same time claiming to offer prompt and reliable information on events. The first Gulf War (1991) offered a classic example of control through pooling. For a similar exercise in the control of war reporting, this time during the second Gulf War (2003), see EMBEDDED REPORTERS.

Poor Man's Guardian Title of perhaps the most influential radical newspaper in Britain during the nineteenth century, edited by Bronterre O'Brien, published by Henry Hetherington. It appeared between 1831 and 1835, and was described by George Jacob Holyoake, a campaigner against the Taxes on Knowledge levied by government on the press, as 'the first messenger of popular and political intelligence which reached the working classes'. Other radical papers of this turbulent period were Richard Carlile's *Gauntlet* (1833–34), Robert Owen's *Crisis* (1832–34), James Watson's *Working Man's Friend* (1832–33) and Fergus O'Connor's *Northern Star* (1837–52), principal organ of the Chartist movement. See STAMP DUTY; UNDERGROUND PRESS. See also *TOPIC GUIDE* under MEDIA HISTORY.

Popular culture See CULTURE: POPULAR CULTURE.

Populism According to some theorists, one of the distinguishing features of a Mass Society is its populist nature. Legitimacy is given to those persons, ideas or actions that are thought to best express the popular will or meet the most widely shared expectations. One result, such theorists claim, is that a premium is placed upon the capacity of those in leadership positions, to both create and placate popular opinion. The mass media tend to be seen as the agents through which such leaders control and exploit the masses.

Pornography Word originates from the Greek, 'writing of harlots'. Two sorts of pornography are usually differentiated: *erotica*, concentrating on physical aspects of heterosexual activity; and *exotica*, focusing on abnormal or deviationist sexual activity. Attitudes to pornography reflect a society's permissiveness, its current 'tolerance threshold', and also cast a light on prevailing social values.

Tolerance of pornography only makes sense if there is no felt risk; if pornography is thought to be linked with the abuse of women and children and the degradation of human relationships and family life, pornography will be fought against whether the link is proved or not. In any case, pornography itself often makes the link between sexuality and violence: hard porn is, by general definition, a DISCOURSE in dominance expressed through violence which, at the very least, poses examples of possible behaviour.

Of interest and concern is the indisputable fact that in many countries pornography is big business. Civic concern about the possible link between porn and violence was registered by the Minneapolis City Council in 1983. Exhaustive public hearings took place to provide a basis of information for a decision whether or not to add pornography as a 'discrimination against women' to existing civil rights legislation. The transcript of the Minneapolis hearings was published in 1988 and has ongoing relevance.

Quoting evidence from academic and clinical research on the effect of pornography on ordinary men, the report stated that, exposed to pornography, men become desensitized; they see themselves as more likely to commit rape, less likely to respond sympathetically to women who are victims of rape, or more likely to be lenient in their response to men who commit rape. According to the Minneapolis transcript, pornography which portrays women enjoying rape or violence or humiliation is the most damaging kind.

As a result of the hearings the City Council passed a civil rights law enabling female victims of pornography to bring civil rights actions against the pornographers. However, the law was vetoed by the mayor and never implemented. A similar situation arose in Indianapolis, where pornographers claimed they were being denied their constitutional right to free speech (under the First Amendment). Thus, in the courts, free speech took precedence over women's equality and safety from physical abuse.

In a UK *New Scientist* article, 'Flesh and blood' (5 May 1990), on the effects on men of pornography, Mike Baxter writes, 'The weight of evidence is accumulating that intensive exposure to soft-core pornography desensitizes men's attitudes to rape, increases sexual callousness and shifts their preferences towards hard-core pornography. Similarly, the evidence is now strong that exposure to violent pornography increases men's acceptance of rape myths and of violence against women ... Many sex offenders claim they used pornography to stimulate themselves before committing their crimes.'

The arrival and expansion of the INTERNET, with its relative freedom from control and overview, has offered global opportunities for pornography, along with the pornography of race hatred. Any system that combines the privacy of output and input with potentially universal access will be abused. It has been argued that for women exercising their right to explore the Net, there is as much danger from online predators as there is on the streets at night.

In *Pornland: How Porn Has Hijacked Our Sexuality* (Beacon, 2010), US sociology professor Gail Dines sees porn as having entered the mainstream of contemporary culture, affecting 'the way women and girls think about their bodies, their sexuality and their relationships'. She argues that rather than sexually liberating or empowering us [as the highly profitable porn industry presents itself as doing], porn offers us a plasticized, formulaic, generic version of sex that is boring, lacking in creativity and disconnected from emotion and intimacy'.

Dines believes that 'in today's image-based culture, there is no respite' from the power of porn 'when it is relentless in its visibility'. She fears that women today 'are still held captive by images that ultimately tell lies about women', the biggest of these being that conformity to a 'hypersexualized image will give women real power in the world ... not in our ability to shape the institutions that determine our life chances but in having a hot body that men desire and women envy'. In much of today's popular culture, women's pleasure 'is derived not from being a desiring subject' but a 'desired object'.

A particular concern of Gail Dines is the affect porn has on young lives; the way it is in danger of becoming the main form of sexual education for boys who are at risk of being desensitized by degrading images. Indeed porn is seen as being damaging to the point where it has become a public health issue.

In a UK *Guardian* article 'All authentic desire is rendered plastic by this multi-billion dollar industry' (5 January 2011), Dines says that 'the porn business is embedded in a complex value chain, linking not just film producers and distributors, but also bankers, software producers, credit card companies, internet providers, cable companies, and hotel chains', and that it is 'no accident' that the International Consumer Electronics Show takes place in Las Vegas 'at exactly the same time' as the Adult Entertainment Expo, the world's biggest porn convention: 'Porn has helped drive the technologies that expand its own market.' See CENSORSHIP; DESENSITIZATION; LOOKISM; MOBILIZATION; REGULATION OF INVESTIGATORY POWERS ACT (RIPA)(UK), 2000; STEREOTYPE; SYNERGY.

Postcards See PICTURE POSTCARDS.

Post-Colonial theory Focuses on an examination and exploration of the cultural production, activities and experiences of those societies that were, until recently, colonies – that is, subject to European colonisation. The term can be used broadly, but in *The Post-Colonial Studies Reader* (Routledge, 2005) Bill Ashcroft, Gareth Griffiths and Helen Tiffin, eds, argue 'that post-colonial studies are based in the "historical fact" of European colonialism, and the diverse material effects to which the phenomenon gave rise'. They note that this varied field of study encompasses 'discussion about experience of various kinds: migration, slavery, suppression, resistance, representation, difference, race, gender, place, and responses to the influential master discourses of imperial Europe'. They also remind us that the impact of colonialism is not just to be found in the past: 'All post-colonial societies are still subject in one way or another to overt or subtle forms of neo-colonial domination, and independence has not solved this problem.' See GLOBALIZATION; GLOCALIZATION; MEDIA IMPERIALISM; ORIENTALISM.

▸ Edward Said, *Culture and Imperialism* (Vintage Books, 1994); Bill Ashcroft, Gareth Griffiths and Helen Tiffin, *Post-Colonial Studies: The Key Concepts* (Routledge, 2007).

Posters Printed posters have had a short but vivid history, dating from the 1870s when the perfection of techniques in colour LITHOGRAPHY first made mass production possible. Posters have been described as the art gallery of the street, and indeed the form has appealed to many artists, such as Henri Toulouse-Lautrec (1864–1901), members of the Art Nouveau movement and the graphic designers of the Bauhaus and the De Stijl group. Posters have served every mode of PROPAGANDA, social, political, religious, commercial. The arresting clarity of their images, combined with words used dramatically, emotively, humorously have often continued to impress long after the ideas, events or products they relate to have faded from attention.

So immediate and memorable are posters, and so widely recognized, that they have formed a regular inspiration for image-makers: they have been imitated, reproduced, turned into cult objects, transmuted into other meanings. For example, many different uses have been made of Alfred Leete's famous poster of 1914, 'Your Country Needs You', in which Lord Kitchener points out towards the audience, offering a formidable challenge to all those who have not yet volunteered for the First World War.

In peacetime, between elections, ADVERTISING dominates the poster contents of the billboards, sometimes with bold, witty and memorable images such as the Guinness adverts or Benetton's striking socio-political images. Posters come into their own in times of protest or revolution; some of the finest posters were designed and printed during and after the Russian Revolution of 1917, while the Spanish Civil War (1936–39) stimulated the production of hundreds of hard-hitting, passionate and often tragic images. See *TOPIC GUIDE* under MEDIA HISTORY.

Postmodernism Term referring to cultural, social and political attitudes and expression characteristic of the 1980s and 1990s, following the modernist period of psychoanalysis, functional, clean-line, machine-inspired architecture, abstract art and stream-of-consciousness fiction. Wendy Griswold in *Cultures and Societies in a Changing World* (Pine Forge Press, 1994) writes, 'Many people believe that society has entered this new stage beyond modernity, a postindustrial stage of social development dominated by media images, in which people are connected with other places and times through proliferating channels of information.'

If hope and anxiety were features of modernism, says Griswold, 'the postmodern person is characterized by a cool absence of illusion.

P

Modern minds were sceptical, Postmodern minds are cynical'. The prevailing cynicism is wary of traditional attempts at explaining the evolution of society. It discards the affirming or 'grand narratives' (*metanarratives*) of the past that subscribed to the view of the inevitability of human progress; what might be described as the Enlightenment position. Reality itself is an uncertainty: being a creation of language and existing in socially produced DISCOURSE, it represents an infinitely movable feast.

Marxism, for example, has been rejected by postmodernist thinkers such as Michel Foucault, Jacques Derrida, Jean-François Lyotard and Jean Baudrillard as having 'totalizing ambitions', that is offering grandiose explanations of reality which cannot be sustained. They therefore reject the central tenet of Marxism, its belief in the emancipation of humanity.

The postmodernist position derives much of its vision from the German philosopher Friedrich Nietzsche (1844–1900), in particular his profound antipathy to any system and his rejection of the view expressed by an earlier German thinker, Georg Wilhelm Friedrich Hegel (1770–1831), of history as progress. Instead of such totalizing, postmodernism embraces *fragmentation* (and this includes views on the fragmentation of time itself, and therefore of concepts of the past and present). It hones in on micro-situations; the stress is on the local. Taking a deeply sceptical position, postmodernists declare that progress is a MYTH. If there are no unities, then nothing figures; if nothing figures, nothing matters, and if nothing matters then anything goes.

Thus in architecture postmodernism scorns traditional forms while unapologetically plagiarizing them. It has varyingly been described as a culture of surfaces, of self-aware superficiality characterized by the ephemeral and by discontinuity. In the postmodernist approach, writes Norman K. Denzen in a review, 'Messy methods of communication research' in the *Journal of Communication* (Spring, 1995), all 'criteria are doubted, no position is privileged'.

Taken to a logical conclusion, such a standpoint facilitates cultural freedom and unshackled PLURALISM; it could also unhinge freedom from responsibility on the grounds that a definition of responsibility could only be arrived at on a personal, micro-level; hence the accusation made in some quarters that postmodernism is the cultural arm of the *commoditization* of information and knowledge.

Madan Sarup in *An Introductory Guide to Post-Structuralism and Postmodernism* (Harvester Wheatsheaf, 1993) says of Baudrillard, 'Personally I find many of his insights stimulating and provocative but, generally, his position is deplorable. In Baudrillard's world truth and falsity are wholly indistinguishable, a position which I find leads to moral and political nihilism'. The danger for a postmodernist world resides in a view expressed by Lyotard: that power has increasingly become the criterion of – the *synonym* for – truth.

A key and resonating criticism of postmodernist writers focuses on the density and complexity of their language; to the point where some commentators view it as meaninglessly obscure (or obscurely meaningless!). The case is summarized by Alan Sokal and Jean Bricmont in *Intellectual Impostures* (Profile Books, 1998). First published in French, the book makes a full-frontal attack on both the language and the meaning of aspects of postmodernism.

Professors of physics, Sokal and Bricmont direct their critique at the postmodernists specifically in terms of their invoking concepts from physics and mathematics. For example, they target the French philosopher Lacan as follows: ' ... although Lacan uses quite a few key words from the mathematical theory of compactness, he mixes them up arbitrarily and without the slightest regard for their meaning. His "definition" of compactness is not just false: it is gibberish'.

In a review of Sokal and Bricmont's book, 'Postmodernism disrobed' (*Nature*, 9 July 1998), Richard Dawkins wonders whether 'the modish French "philosophy" whose disciples and exponents have all but taken over large sections of American academic life, is genuinely profound or the vacuous rhetoric of mountebanks and charlatans'. See SOKAL HOAX.

▶ J.F. Lyotard, *The Postmodern Condition* (Manchester University Press, 1984); David Harvey, *The Condition of Postmodernity: An Inquiry into the Origins of Cultural Change* (Blackwell, 1990); Frederic Jameson, *Postmodernism Or The Cultural Logic of Late Capitalism* (Verso, 1991); Christopher Norris, *Uncritical Theory: Postmodernism, Intellectuals and the Gulf War* (Lawrence & Wishart, 1992); Angela McRobbie, *Postmodernism and Popular Culture* (Routledge, 1994); John Hartley, *Popular Reality: Journalism, Modernity, Popular Culture* (Arnold, 1996); Stuart Sim, ed., *The Routledge Companion to Postmodernism* (Routledge, 2001); Christopher Butler, *Post-Modernism: A Very Short Introduction* (Oxford University Press, 2002); Richard Appignanesi and Chris Garrett, *Introducing Postmodernism*

(Icon, 2004); Mike Featherstone, *Consumer Culture and Postmodernism* (Sage, 2nd edition, 2009).

Post-synchronization Or *dubbing*. In film-making, the process of adding new or altered dialogue in the original language to the sound track of a film after it has been shot. See SYNCHRONOUS SOUND.

Postulates of communication To define the fundamental attributes of the communication process is possibly a more fruitful area of analysis than struggling for an all-embracing and acceptable definition of communication. C.D. Mortensen in *Communication: The Study of Human Interaction* (McGraw-Hill, 1972) poses a single, basic postulate, that 'communication occurs whenever persons attribute significance to message-related behaviour'. He then follows this up with five secondary postulates.

These are: (1) Communication is dynamic. (2) Communication is irreversible. (3) Communication is proactive (as opposed to *reactive*). Mortensen says here, 'The notion of man as a detached bystander, an objective and dispassionate reader of the environment, is nothing more than a convenient artefact. Among living creatures man is the most spectacular example of an agent who amplifies his environment'. We are shapers, not mere recipients. (4) Communication is interactive. (5) Communication is contextual. See TOPIC GUIDE under COMMUNICATION MODELS.

Postural echo See POSTURE.

Posture A range of messages, especially those about emotional states and relationships, can be communicated through posture. Michael Argyle in *Bodily Communication* (Methuen, 1988) provides some examples: fear, depression, dominance, submission, confidence and happiness. Optimism, confidence and dominance, for example, are often associated with an upright posture, whereas depression tends to be associated with a slouching, shrinking posture. Posture can play a role during interaction regulation and can be used to provide feedback. Positive feelings towards others are often shown by leaning forwards in conversation and by POSTURAL ECHO. Conversely negative feelings can be indicated by leaning back from others during a conversation and may indicate a desire to end it. Shifts in posture can be used to mark stages in a conversation.

Postural and GESTURAL ECHO occur during interaction when the participants enjoy a good rapport and signal this, typically without being aware that they are doing so, by mirroring each other's postures and gestures. Mirroring of this kind is thought to encourage a positive and friendly encounter. Whilst postural and gestural echo occur naturally within a good relationship, in other situations attempts may be made to manipulate such mirroring activity: for example, to build a false sense of rapport when trying to persuade another person. Alternatively, efforts can be made to destroy rapport by deliberately displaying mismatched postures and gestures.

There are some culturally specific uses of posture. Desmond Morris in *People Watching* (Vintage, 2002) notes that in some cultures – those found in Germany and Japan, for example – bowing is still used in greeting rituals. Roger E. Axel in *Gestures: The Do's and Taboos of Body Language Around the World* (John Wiley & Sons Inc., 1998) notes that in several countries, showing the soles of your feet to others is considered offensive – in Arab countries, Nigeria, Malaysia, Pakistan, India and Turkey, for example – and thus care needs to be taken with the posture adopted when seated.

▶ Allan and Barbara Pease, *The Definitive Book of Body Language* (Orion, 2004).

Power This has been defined, and written about at length, by many theorists in many different disciplines, but a useful working definition is that provided by John B. Thompson in *The Media and Modernity: A Social Theory of the Media* (Polity Press, 1995): power is 'the ability to act in pursuit of one's aims and interests, the ability to intervene in the course of events and to affect their outcome. In exercising power, individuals employ the resources available to them; resources are the means which enable them to pursue their aims and interests effectively'. Whilst the individual may be the basic building-block of the power structure of any society, some blocks are arguably a lot bigger than others, since some individuals have considerably more personal resources than others.

Further, as Thompson argues, 'While resources can be built up personally, they are also commonly accumulated within the framework of institutions, which are important bases for the exercise of power. Individuals who occupy dominant positions within large institutions may have vast resources at their disposal, enabling them to make decisions and pursue objectives which have far-reaching consequences'.

A concept closely related to that of power is *influence*. Charles B. Handy in *Understanding Organizations* (Penguin, 1993) describes the relationship between power and influence thus: 'Influence is the process whereby A modifies the attitudes and behaviour of B. Power is that

P

which enables him to do it.' As well as resources, the exercise of power and influence requires a *power base* and at the same time the selection of appropriate methods of influence. In turn this is predicated to a considerable extent on the acceptance of, or acquiescence in, the exercise of power by those subjected to it.

John B. Thompson offers a distinction between the differing *sources* of power and categorizes these into four main types: *economic, political, coercive* and *symbolic*. Of course these often overlap, and the way in which they do so is in itself an indication of the often complex and at times mutually supportive relationships that exist within the overall power structures.

Varying forms of power are often concentrated in institutions. *Economic power* is based in ownership or control of those resources required for the productive activity involved in transforming human, material and financial resources into goods and services, for sale or exchange in a market in order to generate a means of subsistence. This might also be described as *corporate power*.

Political power stems from the authority, usually of governments and those bodies invested with authority, to organize the activities of individuals, GROUPS or organizations and nations. *Coercive power* expresses itself through the use of force and can be found in a diverse range of power relationships. Most states, whatever their form of government, have resources that underscore their political power with the ability to employ physical force when the exercise of power by persuasion seems likely to fail.

Very different, but not necessarily less effective, is *symbolic power*, which Thompson defines as stemming from 'the activity of producing, transmitting and receiving meaningful symbolic forms'. He sees such activity as being 'a fundamental feature of social life ... Individuals are constantly engaged in the activity of expressing themselves in symbolic forms and in interpreting the expressions of others; they are constantly involved in communicating with one another and exchanging information and symbolic content'.

To do so, individuals draw upon the various 'means of information and communication', such as access to the channels of communication, communicative competence, knowledge and acknowledged expertise in areas of symbolic exchange. The mass media serve as key operators of symbolic power.

The pivotal role that the media play in transmitting information about politics and politicians to a wide audience, in *power-broking*, has resulted in their being referred to as the FOURTH ESTATE; that is, they rank alongside the judiciary, the church and government as exercizers of power and influence. Indeed it is the media who play an essential role in communicating to the public the nature, location and distribution of power in the community and the power-relationships operating within it; hence the central interest among media analysts and researchers in the media's capacity to influence, shape, reinforce or undermine the exercize of power at all levels of society, and the degree to which public attitudes and behaviour may be influenced. See DEMOCRACY AND THE MEDIA; EFFECTS OF THE MASS MEDIA. See also *TOPIC GUIDES* under MEDIA: ISSUES & DEBATES; MEDIA: OWNERSHIP & CONTROL; MEDIA: POLITICS & ECONOMICS; MEDIA: POWER, EFFECTS, INFLUENCE; MEDIA: PROCESSES & PRODUCTION; MEDIA: VALUES & IDEOLOGY.

Power elite Term used by C. Wright Mills in his seminal analysis *Power, Politics and People* (Oxford University Press, 1963) to describe those members of a society who combine social and political privilege with power and influence. See CULTURAL APPARATUS; ELITE; ESTABLISHMENT; HEGEMONY.

PR See PUBLIC RELATIONS (PR).

Pragmatics Adam Jaworski and Nikolas Coupland in *The Discourse Reader* (Routledge, 2006) note that 'closely related to semantics, which is primarily concerned with the study of word and sentence meaning, pragmatics concerns itself with the meaning of utterances in specific contexts of use'. Numerous factors within the context of a communicative act can affect its meaning: for example, the purpose of the interaction; expectations as regards relevant or suitable topics for conversation; the nature of the relationships between the communicators; and expectations concerning politeness. See ASSERTIVENESS; FACEWORK; COMMUNICATION: INTERCULTURAL COMMUNICATION.

Predatory pricing In relation to the PRESS, reduction in the price of a newspaper in order to undercut the competition, and in the long run to put the competition out of business.

Preferred reading Stuart Hall poses this concept in 'The determination of news photographs' in Stanley Cohen and Jock Young, eds, *The Manufacture of News* (Constable, 1973). Here the preferred reading of a photograph – preferred, that is, by the transmitter of the photograph – is one, Hall believes, that guides us to an interpretation which lies within the traditional social, political and cultural VALUES of the time, symbolizing and reinforced by the interests of the dominant HIERARCHY.

The framing, cropping, captioning and juxta-position of the photograph with TEXT all serve to close-off the reader from lateral, or independent, interpretations of the picture – from ABERRANT DECODING of the MESSAGE. Thus *closure* is achieved. The term has come to be applied to message systems generally. See DOMINANT, SUBORDINATE, RADICAL; MEDIATION; POLYSEMY. See also *TOPIC GUIDE* under AUDIENCES: CONSUMPTION & RECEPTION OF MEDIA.

Prejudice Phillip G. Zimbardo and Michael R. Leippe in *The Psychology of Attitude Change and Social Influence* (McGraw-Hill, 1991) define prejudice as 'a learned attitude towards a target object that typically involves negative affect, dislike or fear, a set of negative beliefs that support the attitude and a behavioural intention to avoid, or to control or dominate, those in the target group'. Such an attitude may be directed towards ideas, objects, situations or people. Prejudice is arguably of greatest concern when it is negative and directed towards other people. In this instance prejudice is often accompanied by negative STEREOTYPES of its targets.

The targets of prejudice tend to be those who are the relatively powerless members of GROUPS, organizations, or societies as well as those who are perceived as being deviant. It is of course possible to be both. One aspect of media research is the exploration of whether or not the media plays a role in promoting prejudice against some groups, cultures or nationalities.

Gordon Allport in *The Nature of Prejudice* (Addison-Wesley, 1954) identifies five stages in the behavioural component of prejudice: *anti-locution*, *avoidance*, *discrimination*, *physical attack* and *extermination*. Examples of anti-locution include insults and so-called jokes (in which the intention is to denigrate the subject). Avoidance of communication, though a more passive demonstration of prejudice, will tend to ensure that negative beliefs and attitudes are unchallenged by contact. The term *discrimination* is normally used to describe the acting-out of prejudice, which often shows itself in communicative behaviour. Rejection shown in communicative behaviour may be a precursor to physical attack and extermination. See DEVIANCE; ETHNOCENTRISM; FOLK DEVILS; GENDER; LABELLING PROCESS (AND THE MEDIA); MORAL PANICS AND THE MEDIA; NORMS; OTHER; RACISM.

▶ Julian Petley and Robin Richardson, eds, *Pointing*

the *Finger: Islam and Muslims in the British Media* (One World, 2011).

Press See JOURNALISM; NEWS VALUES; NEWSPAPERS, ORIGINS; NORTHCLIFFE REVOLUTION; PHOTOJOURNALISM; PRESS BARONS. See also *TOPIC GUIDES* under AUDIENCES: CONSUMPTION & RECEPTION OF MEDIA; MEDIA HISTORY; MEDIA INSTITUTIONS; MEDIA ISSUES & DEBATES; MEDIA: POWER, EFFECTS, INFLUENCE; NEWS MEDIA.

Press barons As early as 1884, Scots-American steel magnate Andrew Carnegie headed a syndicate that controlled eight daily papers and ten weeklies. In the UK Edward Lloyd owned the mass-circulation *Daily Chronicle* and the blockbuster Sunday paper *Lloyd's Weekly*, the first periodical to sell a million copies. As the costs of founding and running newspapers grew, leaving ownership a privilege of none but the very rich, or joint stock companies, the trend towards chain ownership accelerated.

In *The Life and Death of the Press Barons* (Secker and Warburg, 1982), Piers Brendon points out that 'the press barons of the New World, stimulated by the tradition of freedom and protected by constitutional guarantees, were wilder beasts than their Old World counterparts'; but they shared characteristics with UK press barons, being 'vicious, unstable, despotic …' and sharing a 'ruthless quest for wealth, power and independence'. However, in Brendon's view, 'their refusal to endure restraints on journalistic freedom was a real boon', despite their being 'armour-plated sabre-toothed behemoths'.

James Gordon Bennett (1795–1872), perhaps the first press baron, compared himself to Moses, Seneca, Socrates and Martin Luther, and ranked his own genius as a newspaper baron with Shakespeare, Scott, Milton and Byron. He handed over the New York *Tribune* in 1868 to his son of the same name: James Gordon Bennett Jr matched his father's outrageous eccentricity as well as demonstrating, in Brendon's words, 'flair, enterprise and decision'.

Then came the heavyweight contestants Joseph Pulitzer (1847–1911), proprietor of the New York *World*, referred to as His Majesty by his staff, and William Randoph Hearst (1863–1932) whose *Journal* and other newspapers, spreading as they did throughout America, made their owner 'the most vilified press baron in history'.

Generous supplies of egotism, eccentricity and paranoia were to be found in UK press barons, such as Alfred Harmsworth, later Lord Northcliffe (1865–1922), whose admiration for Pulitzer was reciprocated to the point where Pulitzer

P

offered Harmsworth editorship of the *World* for one day, 1 January 1900. Harmsworth produced a twelve-page four-column 'tabloid', about half the *World's* normal size. Of this publication, William Randolph Hearst confessed, 'We all thought it was a clever stunt, but few of us realized the vital importance of the principle'; and this was – by any means – to provide reading material that would attract and hold the interest of the masses.

In 1888 Harmsworth had launched a weekly journal, *Answers*, modelled on George Newnes's *Tit-Bits*, comprising jokes, puzzles, 'sound-bites' of odd news and information but, advancing on *Tit-Bits*, encouraging reader involvement, in particular, with competitions for prizes. In 1890, *Answers*, which had now reached a circulation of over 200,000, was supplemented by *Comic Cuts*, followed by *Illustrated Chips, Home Chat, The Marvel, Wonder* and *Union Jack*. Harmsworth bought and rejuvenated the *Evening News* in 1898, and in 1896 he founded the *Daily Mail*, following the 'Harmsworth way', containing condensed news, gossip, sports reports and striving to prove through rising circulation Harmsworth's dictum that 'most of the ordinary man's prejudices are my prejudices'.

Harmsworth was a publicist of genius but he owed much to the business acumen of his brother Harold, later Lord Rothermere, who eventually inherited and continued the Northcliffe media stable. For his services to the Conservative party, in particular the support offered the Tories by the *Daily Mail*, Harmsworth was offered a peerage, becoming Lord Northcliffe in 1905. By 1921 he controlled *The Times*, the *Daily Mail*, the *Weekly Despatch* (later a Sunday paper) and the *London Evening News*. Brother Harold controlled the *Daily Mirror*, the *Sunday Pictorial*, the *Daily Record* and several other papers. Together they owned the large magazine group Amalgamated Press, while brother number three, Sir Lester Harmsworth, owned a string of papers in the southwest of England. Between them these baronial brothers owned papers with an aggregate circulation of over 6 million. Their dominance was rivalled by another larger-than-life press baron, Lord Beaverbrook (1879–1964). His *Daily Express* led all its competitors in the late 1930s. His four papers reached a joint circulation of 4.1 million by 1937.

Regional newspaper chains displayed similar baronialist tendencies. The Berry brothers, Lords Camrose and Kemsley, pushed their tally from four daily and Sunday papers in 1921 to twenty daily and Sunday papers by the outbreak of the Second World War in 1939. As newspapers fell into fewer hands, circulation expanded dramatically. Between 1920 and 1939 the circulation of national dailies went from 5.4 million to 10.6 million, while Sunday paper circulations rose from 13.5 million to 16 million. In the US, Hearst, by 1942, ran seventeen daily and twelve Sunday papers, at the time the biggest media business in the world.

Almost to a man, the press barons were autocratic, eccentric and immensely ambitious, exerting far-reaching editorial control and involving themselves minutely in the day-to-day running of a newspaper business. Competition was savage and unrelenting. Politics were important, but profits came first. In fact the British political establishment viewed the press barons with dislike and suspicion, for they were not as easily 'bought' or persuaded as their predecessors had been.

Of course this did not stop them meddling in politics. Between 1919 and 1922 Rothermere and Northcliffe put all their press backing behind policies advocating public-spending cuts. Their Anti-Waste League won three parliamentary by-elections in 1921. During the 1930s Rothermere's papers the *Daily Mirror* and *Daily Mail* supported the British Union of Fascists for a brief period and were rabidly anti-Red. Patriotism, a deep emotional attachment to Empire, ill-concealed racialism, hatred of foreigners; these – along with their inveterate antisocialism – characterized the 'voice' of press baronage in the inter-war years.

The post-war period saw new styles of press leadership as the one-product newspaper tycoons gave way to multi-marketing trends, conglomerate ownership and more self-effacing, though no less far-reaching, control. Today, 'baronialism' is more powerful because it is more global in reach and influence, and barons such as Rupert Murdoch think and act globally, aiming to extend ownership and control across the whole field of mass communication, including the INTERNET. In addition to owning newspapers worldwide, the Murdoch empire counts among its portfolio of ownership film studios, publishing houses, TV stations such as Sky TV, and SATELLITE broadcasting. Compared to Murdoch's holdings in 175 newspapers worldwide, nine TV networks and an estimation that his media reach one in three of the world's population, the imperialism of Hearst and Northcliffe (with whom Murdoch developed a close friendship) pale in comparison. See BERLUSCONI PHENOMENON; COMMANDERS OF THE SOCIAL ORDER; CONGLOMERATES; GLOBAL MEDIA

SYSTEM: THE MAIN PLAYERS; MEDIA CONTROL; NEWSPAPERS, ORIGINS. See also TOPIC GUIDE under MEDIA HISTORY.

▶ Roy Greenslade, *Maxwell's Fall* (Simon & Schuster, 1992); Nicholas Coleridge, *Paper Tigers* (Heinemann, 1993); Tom Bowyer, *Maxwell: The Final Verdict* (HarperCollins, 1996); Gillian Doyle, *Media Owner-ship: Concentration, Convergence and Public Policy* (Sage, 2002); James Curran and Jean Seaton, *Power Without Responsibility: Press, Broadcasting and the Internet* (Routledge, 7th edition, 2010).

Press commissions See TOPIC GUIDE under COMMISSIONS, COMMITTEES, LEGISLATION.

Press Complaints Commission (UK) Body created by the UK newspaper industry, begin-ning its duties on 1 January 1991, and replacing the Press Council – Lord McGregor being appointed the Commission's first chairman. The PCC operates on the basis of a Code of Practice, the 'five commandments' of which concern privacy, opportunity for reply, prompt correc-tion and appropriate prominence, the conduct of journalists and the treatment of race. The Code warns newspapers against publishing 'inac-curate, misleading or distorting material' as well as recommending them 'to distinguish clearly between comment, conjecture and fact'.

The PCC's effectiveness as an independent regulator of the press has been subject to ongo-ing criticism; arguably its biggest failure relates to the phone-hacking scandal in 2011 involving NEWS CORP's *News of the World*. The PCC, in face of revelations by the *Guardian*, insisted that there was insufficient evidence to take action. A scandal that quickly became an issue of national and international concern led the leader of the UK Labour opposition, Ed Miliband, to call the PCC a 'toothless poodle'.

Public and parliamentary outrage at the *NoW*'s systemic phone-hacking (see JOURNALISM: PHONE-HACKING) and the paper's dramatic closure in July 2011 led to the establishment by Prime Minister David Cameron of a public inquiry to be headed by Lord Justice Leveson, part of whose remit would be an investigation into press and broadcasting regulation. The future of a watchdog created and funded by the industry it was supposed to watch over was in the balance. See CALCUTT COMMITTEE REPORTS ON PRIVACY AND RELATED MATTERS, 1990 AND 1993; OFCOM: OFFICE OF COMMUNICATIONS (UK).

Pressure groups Also known as interest groups or lobbies, pressure groups aim to influence central and local government and its actions in certain, limited areas of policy. They do not usually seek formal political office, although some pressure groups do sponsor elected individuals. Pressure groups can be usefully divided into two main types: those which act to protect their members' interests, and those that are concerned to promote a cause which they believe will be in the general interests of society.

Pressure groups vary not only in the focus of their concern, but also more crucially in the degree of influence they have. In some cases a government may consult relevant pressure groups before introducing or amending legisla-tion or policies, and some groups enjoy relatively easy access to government.

According to Wyn Grant in *Pressure Groups, Politics and Democracy in Britain* (Harvester Wheatsheaf, 2000), pressure groups involved in LOBBYING activities can be divided into Insider and Outsider groups depending on their relative ease of access to government. An example of an Insider group would be the Confederation of British Industry, whereas the National Union of Students could be considered as an Outsider group. Insider groups usually have better access because they have expertise, influence and resources valued by a government and thus the groups are seen as potentially useful contribu-tors to that government's activities. As David Miller and William Dinan warn in a *A Century of Spin* (Pluto Press, 2008), such access may, however, lead to undue influence and corrup-tion. With less access, Outsider groups are more likely to use public appeals and protest in order to put pressure on those in power.

To be successful, pressure groups need well-planned strategies of communication, or campaigns. The methods used vary but include letter-writing, gaining interviews on local or national radio, using radio 'phone-in' slots, the distribution of literature, advertisements, demonstrations and gaining television cover-age. The INTERNET has proved a key means of disseminating information by pressure groups. Its capacity for *interactivity* in particular has facili-tated planning and organization across national borders, often bypassing traditional channels of mass communication. See LOBBYING.

▶ Spinwatch: www.spinwatch.org.

Primacy, the law of The view that whichever side of a case or argument is presented first will have greater impact on an AUDIENCE than anything which follows. F.H. Lund is considered to have been the first to advance this theory in 'The psychology of belief' in the *Journal of Abnormal and Social Psychology* (1925). There are those, however, who espouse the law of

P

recency, asserting that that which is most recent is the more likely to have greatest impact and retention.

Primacy puts its faith in first impressions, recency in last impressions; both are marginal factors in the real context of debate where *who* goes first or last, and *what* is said first or last, in what *situation* and by what *means*, are more fundamental criteria.

Primary groups See GROUPS.

Primary, secondary definers In relation to events, primary definers are those such as the police who are in a position to speak authoritatively in matters of crime and public order; who are structurally dominant in terms of their potential for defining reality. The media are secondary definers, either re-presenting, interpreting or rejecting the dominant definition. The position becomes complicated when the field of definition is occupied by rival definers, such as when employers and unions are in conflict.

Primary, secondary texts See TERTIARY TEXT; TEXT.

Prime time US term to describe the peak TV viewing period: generally between 8pm and 11pm.

Printing John of Gutenberg (c.1400–68) introduced printing using movable type in 1450, though the Chinese had developed print technology centuries before. Printing made the mass production and dissemination of knowledge and information possible for the first time, and had a revolutionary impact on the conduct of business, commerce, government, learning, literature, politics, the recording of history, the advance of technology and the sciences.

Gutenberg's system, still widely practised today despite sophisticated advances in computer-generated texts, worked by the application of ink, and subsequently paper, to a raised surface, a process called *relief printing*. Other methods are *planographic* and *intaglio* or *gravure*. With the former, the design to be printed and its background are in one flat surface; in intaglio printing the part to be printed is etched or cut into the plate, the exact reverse of relief printing.

Bavarian actor/playwright Alois Senefelder in 1798 found that some kinds of stone absorb both oil and water. He drew on the stone with a greasy crayon and then dampened the stone, which absorbed the water only where there was no crayon design. He then made an ink of wax, soap and lamp-black which stuck to the crayon and came off on paper, producing a print. *Lithography*, from the Greek 'lithos', stone, was born.

Today zinc or aluminium sheets are used and the design to be printed is applied to the plates by a photographic process.

Off-set lithography, the main process of planographic printing employed today, came about as a result of an accident by American printer Ira W. Rubel who had allowed the rubber covering of the impress cylinder to become inked. He discovered that the perfect impression it transferred to the sheet of paper was of better quality than that produced by direct contact with the plate. The first patent for a system of printing using *photocomposition* was taken out by William Friese-Greene in 1895, though typesetting by photography was not in commercial use until the early 1950s. See CYLINDER PRESS; LINOTYPE PRINTING; MONOTYPE PRINTING; NEWSPAPERS, ORIGINS; UNDERGROUND PRESS. See also *TOPIC GUIDE* under MEDIA HISTORY.

▸ Asa Briggs and Peter Burke, *A Social History of the Media: From Gutenberg to the Internet* (Polity, 2002).

Prior restraint Legal term describing the rights in some countries for CENSORSHIP to be exercised before publication. In the United States, where the Second Amendment of the Constitution protects freedom of speech, there is no such thing as prior restraint. In the UK, however, it was prior restraint, on the grounds of confidentiality, that prevented the publication of Peter Wright's book, *Spycatcher* (see SPYCATCHER CASE).

In February 1999 New Labour's Home Secretary, Jack Straw, attempted to impose prior restraint on the *Sunday Telegraph* when he received information that the paper intended to publish extracts, three days before its official release, of the Macpherson Report into police conduct in the case of the murdered teenager, Stephen Lawrence. Justice Rix at first imposed a court order, then 24 hours later removed it again. A *Guardian* leader, headed 'A very British farce', declared prior restraint 'as fundamentally inimical to free speech'. See SUPER-INJUNCTION. See also *TOPIC GUIDE* under MEDIA: FREEDOM, CENSORSHIP.

Privacy A keenly debated issue of our time is the perceived threat to, or indeed loss of, individual privacy. Our privacy is at risk from those in authority who hold information about us, and from the media, part of whose mission is to make public the private; to uncover dark secrets, to bring illumination to facts held from view. The right to privacy obviously clashes with the right to know, and there is a long and colourful history of actions by those in the public eye, from politicians to celebrities, who wish to protect their privacy (when it suits them) at the same time seeking publicity (when it suits them).

What might be deemed of public interest is often simply mistaken for what interests the public. We may be indifferent to matters of this kind until we experience our own loss of privacy. As never before, the privacy of ordinary citizens is seen by many commentators as being at risk from surveillance on the part of those who hold data on us (see SURVEILLANCE SOCIETY); a risk in the New Millennium compounded by the so-termed 'war on terror'. With the declared objective of targeting suspects, governments have extended their powers to monitor the population as a whole.

The French philosopher Michel Foucault, in *Discipline and Punish* (Pantheon, 1990), refers to 'technologies of power' which reach into the very hearts of our lives; while Mark Poster in *The Mode of Information: Poststructuralism and Social Context* (Polity, 1990) fears that the 'populace has been disciplined to surveillance and to participating in the process' willingly, without coercion: 'Social security cards, drivers' licences, credit cards, library cards and the like – the individual must apply for them, have them ready at all times, use them continuously. Each transaction is recorded, encoded and added to databases. Individuals themselves in many cases fill out the forms; they are at once the source of information and the recorder of the information.'

Home networking constitutes 'the streamlined culmination of this phenomenon: the consumer, by ordering products through a modem connected to the producer's database, enters data about himself or herself directly into the producer's database in the very act of purchase'. In this sense, the population participates in 'the disciplining and surveillance of themselves as consumers'.

A practice that came dramatically to the fore in 2011 was phone tapping, in particular the secret and illegal extracting of information by journalists in pursuit of headlines (see JOURNALISM: PHONE-HACKING). Revelations of the systemic hacking of the phones of people in the news led to the closure of the Murdoch Sunday paper, the *News of the World*, and the debate about public and private, about inadequate legal protection and redress (see PRESS COMPLAINTS COMMISSION) became a pressing issue for government and the UK press.

It must be acknowledged that surveillance and the loss of privacy are not entirely one-way. The performance of a nation's leaders, civil servants, business people – people whose activities have traditionally been shielded from public gaze – is now more *visible* to the public than ever before. John B. Thompson in *The Media and Modernity: A Social Theory of the Media* (Polity, 1995) says that 'the development of communication media provides a means by which many people can gather information about a few and, at the same time, a few can appear before many; thanks to the media, it is primarily those who exercise power, rather than those over whom power is exercised, who are subjected to a certain kind of visibility'. Thompson believes the visibility made possible by communication media makes it 'more difficult for those who exercise political power to do so secretively, furtively, behind closed doors'.

The power of intrusion remains, however, with those in authority. The results of a survey of conditions of privacy conducted by Privacy International and the Electronic Privacy Information Centre, US, and published in 2002, cited UK government and authorities as one of the most ineffective of fifty countries in protecting rights to privacy. The UK government in recent years has not only increased practices of surveillance in Britain, but has also been instrumental in pushing the European Community in the same direction. According to Simon Davies, director of Privacy International, government ministers in the UK have mounted a 'systematic attack' on the right to privacy by introducing laws extending mass surveillance. His belief is that 'the UK demonstrates a pathology of antagonism towards privacy', declaring that, for example, the UK Data Protection Act 'is almost useless in limiting the growth of surveillance'.

Personal privacy is at its most vulnerable online, yet for the pleasure of social networking (see NETWORKING: SOCIAL NETWORKING) many users of networking bases such as FACEBOOK and MYSPACE are happy to disclose facts about themselves in the ready knowledge that those facts might be exploited. In the age of MOBILIZATION, loss of privacy would seem to be a price well paid for connecting and interacting with others. See BLOGOSPHERE; CALCUTT COMMITTEE REPORTS ON PRIVACY AND RELATED MATTERS, 1990 AND 1993; DATA PROTECTION ACT (UK), 1984; DEFAMATION; DIGITAL ECONOMY ACT, UK (2010); FREEDOM OF INFORMATION ACT (UK), 2005; HUMAN RIGHTS ACT (UK), 2000; NEW VISIBILITY; PRIVACY: PRESS COMPLAINT'S COMMISSION CODE OF PRACTICE (UK), 1997; REGULATION OF INVESTIGATORY POWERS ACT (RIPA), UK, 2000; SUPER-INJUNCTION; USA – PATRIOT ACT, 2001; WIKILEAKS; YOUTUBE. See also *TOPIC GUIDES*

P

under MEDIA: FREEDOM, CENSORSHIP; MEDIA ISSUES & DEBATES.

Privacy: Press Complaint's Commission Code of Practice (UK), 1997 Following the death of Diana, Princess of Wales in a car crash in Paris, and the widespread belief that this had been caused in part by the hounding of her by PAPARAZZI, the UK Press Complaints Commission issued in December 1997 a Code of Practice concerning privacy and PRESS harassment. Clause 3 of the Code declares that 'everyone is entitled to respect for his or her privacy and family life, home, health and correspondence. A publication will be expected to justify intrusion into any individual's life without consent'. Taking pictures of people 'in private places without their consent is wholly unacceptable', a private place being 'public or private property where there is a reasonable expectation of privacy'.

On harassment, Clause 4 urges that journalists and photographers 'must neither obtain nor seek to obtain information or pictures through intimidation, harassment or persistent pursuit' and this extends to 'telephoning, questioning, pursuing or photographing individuals after having been asked to desist'. The Code also sets out rules concerning intrusion into the lives of children, banning press payment to minors.

The Code is self-regulatory, without the power of law, being the creation of the newspaper industry. It draws upon the European Convention for the Protection of Human Rights and Fundamental Freedoms, Article 8 of which, having asserted the right of the citizen to respect for his/her privacy and family, home and correspondence, then lists the exceptions to the rule of personal privacy: 'There shall be no interference by a public authority with the exercise of this right except such as is in accordance with the law or is necessary ... in the interests of national security, public safety or the economic well-being of the country, for the prevention of disorder or crime, for the protection of health or morals, or for the protection of the rights and freedoms of others.'

An unenforcible code is a code that can be conveniently broken. The most notorious recent case of this was the involvement of the UK *News of the World* (a Murdoch newspaper) in a phone-hacking scandal (see JOURNALISM: PHONE-HACKING).

Privatization Dominant trend in media organization throughout the 1980s and 1990s, in which public-owned media utilities were sold off into private hands; specifically into those of the great transnational companies (TNCs); and with it the privatization of information itself; or as some commentators have put it, the *commoditization* of information. In fact the process commenced with the expansionism of multi-national, multi-product corporations after the Second World War.

It was soon perceived that in the developing Age of Information, information was profitable. Corporations which were not already owners of media, bought into media. Private ownership and its dominance of cultural and social expression, whether in the arts, education, the museums service, libraries, sport or entertainment generally, came up against a major competitor: the public sector. In this domain, information was treated as a public right available to all rather than essentially a saleable commodity.

Such rivalry in an increasingly competitive world was considered bad for private business. It became, then, corporate policy to pressurize governments into dismantling the public sector. Rightist governments in the 1980s and 1990s (the US under Ronald Reagan and George Bush Sr, the UK under Margaret Thatcher and John Major) made privatization the driving-force of political and cultural change. Notions of 'public good' or 'public interest' were to become conditional upon the requirements of 'market forces'; as was social responsibility. See COMMUNICATIONS ACT (UK), 2003.

At a global level, privatization has been linked with financial and technical aid. The World Bank and International Monetary Fund (IMF), for example, have refused economic assistance to developing nations wishing to update their telecommunications systems unless these have first been privatized. Telmex, the Mexican state-owned telecommunications system, privatized in 1990, increased the local telephone rate by over a thousand percent in the next decade.

The chief beneficiaries of cross-world privatization of previously state-run systems have been American-owned tele-corporations. These hold substantial and increasing investments in operations in more than thirty-six countries. Corporate ambitions have made substantial headway in the world of the INTERNET, which itself has given burgeoning life to corporate giants (see GOOGLE; FACEBOOK). What incoming corporations are not happy about is the tradition of the Net to supply most services to users free of charge. Commentors express fears that gradually, cyberspace will echo to the sound of cash-tills (see PAYWALL).

Support in the European Community for PUBLIC SERVICE BROADCASTING (PSB), and indeed the competitive edge which PSB services have demonstrated in the face of the commercial sector, have checked if not stayed the hand of privatization – for the moment, though the influence of the POWER ELITE in the private sector will continue to bring pressure on governments to serve private media interests over public interests. See COMMANDERS OF THE SOCIAL ORDER; CROSS-MEDIA OWNERSHIP; DEMOCRACY AND THE MEDIA; DEREGULATION; MEDIAPOLIS; NETWORK NEUTRALITY; OFCOM, OFFICE OF COMMUNICATIONS (UK); PUBLIC SPHERE; REGULATORY FAVOURS. See also *TOPIC GUIDES* under GLOBAL PERSPECTIVES; MEDIA INSTITUTIONS; MEDIA ISSUES & DEBATES; MEDIA: OWNERSHIP & CONTROL.

Pro-con, con-pro In capturing the attention of an AUDIENCE, is it best to put good news or good points (*pro*) before the bad (*con*), or after them? Researchers have indicated that pro-con generally works best. See PRIMACY, THE LAW OF.

Producer choice The term used to describe the operation of an internal market system within, for example, the BBC for the purchase of the services and facilities needed in programme-making. Since 1993 producers have had control over their budgets and have been free to buy the services and facilities they need, such as post-production, from the most cost-effective provider. The BBC's previous in-house providers of such services and facilities thus have had to compete with other providers for contracts from programme-makers. The designer of the scheme, Sir John Birt, then Director General of the BBC, argued that the system would create a more cost-effective and less bureaucratic organization and thus enable more resources to be channelled into creative areas.

Criticisms of the system are that it has contributed to a reduction in staffing levels; that it has accelerated the trend, partly attributable to the increasing use of independent producers, towards freelancing and CASUALIZATION of employment in the TV industry; that it threatens the long-term prospects of in-house providers and thus ultimately of the BBC itself as an organization concerned with making programmes as opposed to commissioning them; and that it may eventually result in a considerable loss of expertise within the organization, thus a lowering of standards in programme-making. See INDEPENDENT PRODUCERS.

Product placement A branch of modern ADVERTISING, especially in the US, where agencies place, in films and TV programmes, the products of clients – brightly lit, facing camera

and in clear focus – and pay programme-makers considerable sums for the privilege of doing so. In the movie *Days of Thunder* (1990), Tom Cruise wore black Levi 501s throughout and sales of the garment went up considerably. Perhaps the classic *coup* in terms of product placement in movies occurred when, in *Independence Day* (1996), Jeff Goldblum saves the world, threatened by an invasion of aliens, using his Apple Power Book.

Once an artefact is featured 'in shot', the company then draws further publicity by advertising the fact in its commercials. As the worlds of big business and entertainment grow closer and interlock – *synergize* – and as budgets for films and TV grow tighter, product placement threatens to become more assertive throughout the media. It has been estimated that in the US, companies' expenditure on product placement exceeds the GDP of Paraguay; some US\$ 10 billion a year, and growing.

Product placement was forbidden in UK public broadcasting until 2005, when the Office of Communications (OFCOM) signalled a future loosening of regulation with a consultation paper. In December 2010 the organization published 'Rules for product placement on TV and paid-for references to brands and products on radio'. The Audiovisual Media Services (Product Placement) Regulations of 2010 amended the 2003 Communications Act, the case being put that the Rules for TV and radio 'will enable commercial broadcasters to access new sources of revenue, whilst providing protection for audiences'. The new regulations came into force in February 2011.

Restrictions are placed on the types of products that can be placed, the types of programme in which products can be placed, and the limits of ways in which products can be seen and referred to in programmes. Product placement is permitted in films (including dramas and documentaries), TV series (including soaps), entertainment shows and sports programmes, but not in children's and news programmes or in UK-produced current affairs, consumer affairs or religious programmes.

Prohibited is product placement of alcohol, gambling, tobacco, food or drinks that are high in fat, salt or sugar, medicines and baby milk banned by UK legislation. The ban extends to products and services not permitted in UK TV advertising. The rules state that 'product placement must not impair broadcasters' editorial independence and must always be editorially justified'. This means that programmes cannot be created or distorted so that they become vehicles

P

for the purposes of featuring product placement.'

Promotion and endorsement are not permitted and a logo at the beginning and end of a programme will signify the use of product placement. Programme sponsors will in future be able to include their own products and services in those programmes which they sponsor, while sponsors' logos 'will be able to appear as brief sponsorship credits during programmes'.

Commercial references are now permitted to be 'integrated within programming' on radio. 'However, broadcasters will have to ensure that listeners are always aware when promotions are paid-for.' See www.ofcom.org.uk.

Produser That is, prod-user: in the age of network communication, a term coined to describe how users also produce and transmit online material. See YOUTUBE.

Profane language The Latin derivation of profane is *pro fana*, meaning 'outside the temple'. Profanity referred to anyone refusing to be initiated into the ways of the temple, thus showing a contempt for that which is sacred. Profane language takes three main forms: religious, excretory or sexual; and the questions asked about such language are, why do people use profanities, and what are the effects upon AUDIENCE of the use of profanity?

J.D. Rothwell in 'Verbal obscenity: time for second thoughts' in *Western Speech*, 35 (1971) lists five reasons for using profane language: (1) to create attention; (2) to discredit someone or something; (3) to provoke confrontations; (4) to provide a type of *catharsis* or emotional release for the user; and (5) to establish interpersonal identification. Profanity depends for its impact on who is actually using it and in what circumstances.

Geoffrey Hughes in *Swearing: A Social History of Foul Language, Oaths and Profanity in English* (Penguin, 1998) argues that there has been a shift in the focus of swearing in Western societies, from the use of words linked to religion to those associated with sexual and bodily functions and the use of national and racial insults – although the latter are not generally tolerated now. This trend, he argues, is a reflection of 'the increasing secularization of Western society'. Attitudes to the use of such language have become more relaxed and he comments that there is a 'profusion of foul language and swearing in modern times'. Of course tolerance for the use of such language does depend to some extent on context. John Berger recounts in a recent work, *Bento's Sketchbook* (Verso, 2011), that in 2008 he was asked to leave the National Gallery for

having uttered aloud a well-known and fairly strong profanity.

Professionalization (of political communication) Describes the ways in which governments and political parties have adopted the practices of professionals in media communication, especially practices from the fields of public relations, advertising and marketing. Indeed a significant number of such professionals are now employed in the transmission of policies, the nurturing of favourable images in the minds of the public and of putting a 'spin' on aspects of news. In short, NEWS MANAGEMENT – slick presentation, use of the latest communication technologies; not just at times of elections but as elements of a permanent, ongoing campaign.

Leon Mayhew (1997) comments in 'The new public: professional communication and the means of social influence' in Ralph Negrine and James Stanyer, eds, *The Political Communication Reader* (Routledge, 2007) that political communication can be seen as dominated by these professional specialists and their tactics of 'civic persuasion', such as 'sound-bite journalism, thirty second political advertising, *one-way* communication, evasive spin control by public figures who refuse to answer questions'. David Farrell, Robin Kolodny and Stephen Medvic (2001) in an article entitled 'Parties and campaign professionals in a digital age', also to be found in Negrine and Stanyer (ibid), argue that it is of some concern that the replacement of 'party bureaucrats' by such specialists is at the expense of party philosophy and the involvement of ordinary members.

Such professionalization of communication risks public cynicism, a factor which inevitably leads to fraught re-examinations of current strategies of persuasion and a hunt for new ways to win public trust. See NEWS MANAGEMENT IN TIMES OF WAR. See also *TOPIC GUIDE* under MEDIA: POLITICS & ECONOMICS.

▶ Brian McNair, *An Introduction to Political Communication* (Routledge, 2007); Nick Davies, *Flat Earth News* (Chatto & Windus, 2008); David Miller and William Dinan, *A Century of Spin* (Pluto Press, 2008); Spinwatch – www.spinwatch.org.

Programme flow 'In all developed broadcasting systems,' writes Raymond Williams in *Television: Technology and Cultural Form* (Fontana, 1974), 'the characteristic organization, and therefore the characteristic experience, is one of sequence or flow.' Williams believed flow to be a chief principle of programming; the process of organizing a pattern of programmes, each one leading on to the next; each one being a 'tempter' for the

AUDIENCE to stay tuned to a particular channel. Programme boundaries, Williams points out, are constantly being obscured by advertisements and/or trailers for other programmes, to counteract the itchy finger on the remote control button and the much-feared viewer indulgence in ZAPPING. However, the major obstacles to effectively managing programme flow in recent years are the diversity of competing channels and the empowerment, through new technologies, of audiences to select and record and view at their own convenience.

Proiaretic code See CODES OF NARRATIVE.

Projection A throwing outwards or forwards; term commonly used within several areas of communication and media studies. The ability to *project* oneself is an important communication skill. Here projection has been achieved when a person, in giving a talk, making a speech or acting a part on stage, has reached the whole AUDIENCE both with words and with his/her personality. Voice, posture, eye contact, facial expression, GESTURE combine in creating effective projection.

The term can be used in a psychological sense: when people tend to project on others – *transfer* to others – their own motives for behaviour, in particular those which cannot be gratified or which are regarded as unacceptable; in other words, to assume in others the same motives. We may be more inclined to make such assumptions about those we like and perceive as being similar to ourselves. Clearly projection can lead to errors in PERCEPTION and to misunderstandings in the communication process.

Projection of pictures A German Jesuit, Athanasius Kircher (1601–80), professor of mathematics at the Collegio Romano in Rome, is generally thought to have been the first person to project a picture on to a screen. His apparatus was crude but effective, containing all the essentials – a source of light with a reflector behind it and a lens in front, a painted glass slide and a screen. Kircher's astonished audience spoke of black magic. Undaunted, the inventor published a description of his findings.

The projection of moving pictures was first demonstrated by Baron Von Uchatius (1811–81) in 1853. He used a rotating glass slide, a rotating shutter and a fixed lens. An improved version contained a rotating light source, fixed slides and a series of slightly inclined lenses whose optical axes met on the centre of the screen. See CINEMATOGRAPHY, ORIGINS.

Project of self In *The Media and Modernity: A Social Theory of the Media* (Polity, 1995), John B.

Thompson refers to the 'project of self' in relation to how members of the audience for media connect their personal development – the story of themselves – to *lived* and *mediated* experience. Equally, media practitioners – journalists, broadcasters or INTERNET bloggers – experience a constant process of self-formulation, negotiating a passage between personal needs and aspirations and the pressures and demands of the media world and those of the real world. Thompson writes, 'Individuals increasingly draw on mediated experience to inform and refashion the project of self … The growing availability of mediated experience thus creates new opportunities, new options, new arenas for self-experimentation.'

Above all, the Net has not only created possibilities for the development of self, but has also allowed self to become a multiplex of identities; the emphasis often becoming *projection*, that is the use of new media technologies to launch one's image, persona, ambitions, passions, creativity as well as one's opinions, beliefs, prejudices through innumerable social networking platforms – even to the point where the project of self relies more on the mediated than the real world for its definition and recognition. See BLOGOSPHERE; FACEBOOK; MYSPACE; NETWORKING: SOCIAL NETWORKING; SELF-CONCEPT; SELF-IDENTITY; TWITTER; WEB 2.0; YOUTUBE.

Prolefeed The rubbishy entertainment and spurious news piped to the proletariat by the Party in George Orwell's novel *Nineteen Eighty-Four* (1949).

Propaganda Usually deliberate manipulation by means of symbols (words, gestures, images, flags, monuments, music, etc.) of thoughts, behaviour, attitudes and beliefs. The word originates with the Roman Catholic Congregation for the Propagation of the Faith, a committee of cardinals in charge of missionary activities of the church since 1622. Propaganda works through emphasizing some factors and excluding others, often emotively appealing to anxieties, fears, prejudices and ignorance of the true facts. Propaganda can be blatant (see RADIO DEATH) or work by stealth, often using entertainment as a means of 'sugar-coating' messages.

In the world of contemporary politics, propaganda takes the form of NEWS MANAGEMENT or *spin*; and a profession of *spin-doctors* now 'doctor' facts in ways intended to favourably propagate to the public the ideas, policies and performance of government. Propaganda, whether it is that of governments, companies, institutions, charitable organizations or the

P

world of sport, aims to create in the public mind a favourable impression; this might be termed *white* propaganda. In contrast, propaganda that sets out to create in the public mind a bad impression – of other countries, for example, or other ethnic groups, foreigners, asylum seekers and minorities, defining them as 'enemy' – might be termed *black* propaganda.

Garth S. Jowett and Victoria O'Donnell in *Propaganda and Persuasion* (Sage, 1999) identify three forms of propaganda: *white, black* and *grey.* 'White propaganda comes from a source that is identified correctly, and the information in the message tends to be accurate ... Although what listeners hear is reasonably close to the truth, it is presented in a manner that attempts to convince the audience that the sender is the "good guy".

'Black propaganda on the other hand,' explain the authors, '... is credited to a false source and spreads lies, fabrications and deceptions. Black propaganda is the "big lie", including all types of creative deceit.' DISINFORMATION would be an example of black propaganda. Grey propaganda lies 'somewhere between white and black. The source may not be correctly identified, and the accuracy of the information is uncertain.'

Sheldon Rampton and John Stauber in *Weapons of Mass Deception: The Uses of Propaganda in Bush's War on Iraq* (Constable & Robinson, 2003) write, 'Whereas democracy is built upon the assumption that "the people" are capable of rational self-governance, propagandists regard rationality as an obstacle to efficient indoctrination. Since propaganda is often aimed at persuading people to do things that are not in their own best interests, it frequently seeks to bypass the rational brain altogether and manipulate us on a more primitive level, appealing to emotional symbolism.'

The authors talk of 'corporate spin doctors, think tanks and conservative politicians' who have 'taken up the rhetoric of fear for their own purposes'. See ADVERTISING; CONSENT, MANUFACTURE OF; DEMONIZATION; EFFECTS OF THE MASS MEDIA; LOBBYING; NEWS: RAGE INDUCEMENT; PSYOPS; PUBLIC RELATIONS (PR); RHETORIC; RADIO 'SHOCK-JOCKS'. See also *TOPIC GUIDE* under LANGUAGE/DISCOURSE/NARRATIVE.

▶ David Miller, ed., *Tell Me Lies: Propaganda and Media Distortion in the Attack on Iraq* (Pluto Press, 2003); Garth S. Jowett and Victoria O'Donnell, *Propaganda and Persuasion: New and Classic Essays* (Sage, 2006); Noam Chomsky & Gilbert Archer, *Perilous Power* (Penguin, 2007).

Propaganda model of mass communication See CONSENT, MANUFACTURE OF.

Property: intellectual property See CULTURE: COPYRIGHTING CULTURE.

Propinquity A significant determinant of group membership, propinquity is liking through *proximity*; when people are close together physically there is a strain towards amicability which aids group formation, more reliably than with physically distant persons. See GROUPS.

Propp's people In a study of Russian folk tales, Vladimir Propp classified a range of stock characters identifiable in most NARRATIVES (see his *Morphology of the Folk Tale* published in 1968 by the University of Texas Press). These may be individualized by being given distinguishing character traits, but they are essentially functionaries enabling the story to unfold. Propp describes a number of archetypal story features: the *hero/subject* whose function is to seek; the *object* that is sought; the *donor* of the object; the *receiver*, where it is sent; the *helper* who aids the action; and the *villain* who blocks the action.

Thus in one of the world's best-known folk tales, Red Riding Hood (heroine) is sent by her mother (donor) with a basket of provisions (object) to her sick granny (receiver) who lives in the forest. She encounters the wolf (villain) and is rescued from his clutches – and his teeth – by the woodman (helper).

This formula can be added to and manipulated in line with the requirements of the GENRE, but it does allow us to differentiate between *story level* and *meaning level*, between the denotive and the connotive, between the so-termed *mimetic plane* (the plane of representation) and the *semiosic plane* (the plane of MEANING production). See CODES OF NARRATIVE.

Prosodic signals Timing, pitch and stress of utterances to convey MEANING.

Proxemics See SPATIAL BEHAVIOUR.

PR: Public relations See PUBLIC RELATIONS (PR).

PSB (Public Service Broadcasting) See PUBLIC SERVICE BROADCASTING (PSB).

Pseudo-context In his sharply critical assessment of the impact of TV on society, in *Amusing Ourselves to Death* (Methuen, 1986), American author and communications professor Neil Postman says of a pseudo-context that it is 'a structure invented to give fragmented and irrelevant information a seeming use'. However, the pseudo-context offers us no useful function for the information in terms of action, problem-solving or change. TV is the culprit in this fragmenting process. All that is left for what

Postman calls the 'decontextualization of fact' by the non-print media, particularly TV, is to amuse. All knowledge, having been fragmented, is reduced to a trivial pursuit. See EFFECTS OF THE MASS MEDIA.

PSI Para-social identification; that is, members of an AUDIENCE associate with fictitious characters as portrayed in the media, or with well-known personalities whom they regularly 'meet' through the mediation of radio, TV, etc. See PARASOCIAL INTERACTION.

Psychographic analysis See DEMOGRAPHIC ANALYSIS.

Psycholinguistics The study of the interplay between language acquisition, development and use and other aspects of the human mind.

Psychology This discipline seeks to explore the way in which individual behaviours are linked together to form a 'personality'. Its focus is upon the experience and behaviour of the individual, upon the individual's reaction to certain physiological and/or social conditions. Some areas of social psychology are concerned with the behaviour of individuals in small groups or crowds; here there is some overlap between this discipline and that of SOCIOLOGY.

▶ Valerie Walkerdine and Lisa Blackman, *Psychology and the Media* (Macmillan, 1999); Nigel Benson, *Introducing Psychology* (Icon Books, 2007); Richard Cross, *Psychology* (Hodder Education – Hodder Arnold, 6th edition 2010); Pamela Regan, *Close Relationships* (Routledge Academic, 2011).

Psychological Reactance theory See Cognitive Consistency theories.

Psyops US shorthand for 'psychological operations'; the equivalent UK term, 'information support'; an arm of PROPAGANDA. Psyops work in a number of ways to promote 'fact' and 'truth' in support of state action, especially times of conflict and war. David Miller in 'The propaganda machine', a chapter in the book he edited entitled *Tell Me Lies: Propaganda and Media Distortion in the Attack on Iraq* (Pluto, 2004), writes that such operations are 'entirely outside of democratic control'. They appear 'not to be constrained by adhering to any standard of truthfulness', operating 'on the basis that anything goes so long as it is calculated that it can be got away with'.

The author is of the view that the use of psyops shows contempt for the process of democracy, 'since the lies are constructed to misinform and persuade – in part – the electorate of the US and UK as well as world opinion'. He is referring in particular to the techniques and processes of persuasion which supported the invasion and occupation of Iraq in 2003 by American and British forces; alluding in particular to the 'evidence' put forward to the public of weapons of mass destruction that posed a threat to the invading nations – weapons which were never found.

In the digital age, such propagandist activity is increasingly difficult to sustain in face of the INTERNET's capacity to expose previously secret data and to broadcast that data instantly and globally. See WIKILEAKS.

Public Affairs See LOBBYING.

Public cues See BARNLUND'S TRANSACTIONAL MODELS OF COMMUNICATION, 1970.

Public Interest Disclosure Act (UK), 1999 See WHISTLE BLOWING.

Public Occurrences Both Foreign and Domestic Title of the first American newspaper, founded in Boston on 25 September 1690 by Benjamin Harris. The paper survived one issue only, being immediately suppressed by the Governor and Council of the-then British colony.

Public opinion The Greek AGORA is traditionally seen as the birthplace and location of public opinion. It was an open space where free citizens gathered to discuss and ideally shape the affairs of state. By its nature, public opinion lacks the structure of, for example, ELITE opinion and there are difficulties both of definition and identification. The modern-day OPINION POLL tests samples of the whole public; market and audience research have pursued increasingly sophisticated, technology-aided modes of opinion measurement. For such research, measurement is of TASTES, expectations, needs, VALUES and behaviour as well as opinions. For the student of media, the public is examined from the point of view of how the media *represent* public opinion, purport to speak for it, indeed, to define it; and to shape it especially in the light of perhaps the most important and specific expression of public opinion – voting.

Susan Herbst and James R. Beniger in 'The changing infrastructure of public opinion' published in *Audiencemaking: How the Media Create the Audience* (Sage, 1994), edited by James S. Ettema and D. Charles Whitney, explore the connections between the concept of public opinion and the means by which public opinion is measured, the one being influenced by the other; thus what public opinion is in any situation is to a degree defined by how it is defined and measured. The authors say that 'both polling and voting embrace a conception of public opinion as the aggregation of individual opinions

P

and both provide means for elite management of those opinions.

They identify three historical phases in the evolution of public opinion infrastructures. The first was located in the salons of mid-eighteenth-century France (see SALON DISCOURSE). Here the political and intellectual elite gathered socially to discuss all matters from art to philosophy, not least the affairs of state and the nature of government. This elite model of public opinion found a modestly downmarket parallel in the coffee houses of London, presided over by such 'agorans' as Dr Samuel Johnson (1709–84). These 'spaces' for DISCOURSE were only one aspect of the infrastructure; what formed an extension of them were the writings of those novelists, poets, scientists and philosophers who attended the salons or met in the coffee houses.

Towards the middle of the nineteenth century the press became the dominant residence of public opinion, but the newspapers were increasingly reflecting, both in the UK and the US, the development of political parties. Herbst and Beniger believe that 'in concert with the newspapers that shared their ideologies, political parties were a critical component of the late-19th century American infrastructure of public opinion expression and assessment'. In fact PRESSURE GROUPS of all kinds, including trade unions, contributed to the group-based model of public opinion.

New media technology such as RADIO and more efficient measurement practices contributed to what Herbst and Beniger term 'a shift from publics to audiences'. What had, until the emergence of audience-measurement techniques (such as the Audimeter-based NIELSEN RATINGS in the States), been an aggregate of opinions was now a profile of *differences*, leading to what in ADVERTISING terms was to become SEGMENTATION. The ability to discriminate between shades of opinion as far as this audience model is concerned indicates advancing degrees of rationalization, and this, state Herbst and Beniger, 'works best for those at the top of a given system'.

With the advent of INTERNET communication, and particularly social networking (see NETWORKING: SOCIAL NETWORKING), opinion is varyingly to be found on platforms such as FACEBOOK, where public issues are not only aired but campaigns launched free of initiation by the POWER ELITE. In this sense, the Net has become the most interactive of public spaces, the agora of the twenty-first century, often challenging traditional media but just as frequently drawing the media in its wake. See BLOGOSPHERE; DEMOTIC TURN; INFORMATION COMMONS; MEDIASPHERE.

Public radio Term used in Australia to refer to COMMUNITY RADIO.

Public relations news (PRN) See NEWS: PUBLIC RELATIONS NEWS (PR).

Public relations (PR) According to the Chartered Institute of Public Relations website (2005), 'Public Relations is about reputation – the result of what you do, what you say and what others say about you ... Public Relations is the discipline which looks after reputation, with the aim of earning understanding and support and influencing opinion and behaviour. It is the planned and sustained effort to establish and maintain goodwill and mutual understanding between an organization and its publics.'

Many companies and institutions in both the public and private sector have PR departments dedicated to creating and sustaining their good image and reputation with a variety of publics: for example, shareholders, taxpayers, clients, customers and employees. Public relations personnel may work alongside those in ADVERTISING and MARKETING but their role is essentially focused on building relationships and fostering the two-way communication channels required to achieve this aim.

Shirley Harrison in *Public Relations: An Introduction* (Routledge, 1995) writes that 'the most common public relations activities undertaken by practitioners are media relations, publicity and publications, corporate public relations and provision of information'. See BERNSTEIN'S WHEEL; EPISTLE; GRUNIG AND HUNT MODEL, 1984; JOHNSON AND SCHOLES: STAKEHOLDER MAPPING; LOBBYING; OPINION LEADER; PEST; PIE CHART; PUBLIC AFFAIRS; PUBLICS; STAKEHOLDERS; SWOT; PROFESSIONALIZATION (OF POLITICAL COMMUNICATION); PROPAGANDA.

▶ David Miller and William Dinan, *A Century of Spin: How Public Relations Became the Cutting Edge of Corporate Power* (Pluto Press, 2008); Sandra Cain, *Key Concepts in Public Relations* (Palgrave Macmillan, 2009); Bob Franklin, Mike Hogan, Quentin Langley, Nick Mosdell and Eliot Pill, *Key Concepts in Public Relations* (Sage, 2009); Ralph Tench and Liz Yeomans, *Exploring Public Relations* (Pearson Education Limited, 2009).

Publics A term used within PUBLIC RELATIONS (PR) practice to refer to specific groups that are or might become an intended audience for communication activities: pressure groups, customers, competitors, local communities, and opinion leaders. As Paul Baines, John Egan and

Frank Jefkins note in *Public Relations: Contemporary Issues and Techniques* (Elsevier Butterworth-Heinemann, 2004), 'the identification of the "publics" of public relations is fundamental to the planning of a PR programme, for unless the publics are defined it is impossible to select the media that will best convey our messages to them'.

Relevant publics will vary from one organization or individual client to another and from one programme or campaign to another; they will also vary over time. As with any communication activity, knowledge of the public (audience) is crucial when making decisions about the construction as well as the delivery of messages. A PR activity may, of course, have a number of publics, each of which might need to be approached, to some extent, in a different manner. The concept can also be used in identification of potential future publics.

A number of researchers have proposed means of classifying publics. James Grunig and Todd Hunt in *Managing Public Relations* (Harcourt Brace Jovanovich, 1984) note the four categories derived from James Grunig's studies. Grunig divided up publics in terms of their levels of likely activity as regards a PR programme, and identified four main types: (1) publics that are active on all of the issues; (2) publics that are apathetic on all issues; (3) publics interested in single issues; and (4) publics that are active only on issues that involve nearly everyone in the population, that is controversial topical issues. Any one individual's position may of course change over time, and one aim of a campaign, for example, might be to convert apathy into some form of active engagement.

Ralph Tench and Liz Yeomans in *Exploring Public Relations* (Pearson Education Limited, 2009) point out that there have been a number of criticisms of Grunig and Hunt's typology; one such is that it does not sufficiently take account of variables like cultural differences or power relationships, both of which have considerable potential to affect communicative behaviour. See BERNSTEIN'S WHEEL, 1984; GRUNIG AND HUNT: FOUR MODELS OF PUBLIC RELATIONS PRACTICE, 1984; OPINION LEADER.

▶ Allen H. Center and Patrick Jackson, *Public Relations Practices* (Prentice-Hall, 2003); Scott M. Cutlip, Allen H. Center and Glen. M. Broom, *Effective Public Relations* (Prentice Hall, 2006).

Public service broadcasting (PSB) Term refers to any BROADCASTING system whose first duty is to a public within a DEMOCRACY, serving to inform, educate and entertain, and to regard AUDIENCE as constituting citizens, members of communities and individuals rather than merely consumers. PSB is essentially the creation of government in the first instance, though for this reason safeguards are built into the system so that its operation is (relatively) free of government control and influence. Financing of PSB is usually through some form of taxation or licence, subject to periodic revision by government; or in the case of COMMERCIAL TELEVISION, by means of ADVERTISING.

The BBC in the UK represents for many the classic example of public service broadcasting (see BBC, ORIGINS). It was created by act of Parliament and is subject to *regulation* laid down by Parliament. The importance of John Reith's tenure as first Director General of the BBC is that, arguably, he forged the philosophy of public service broadcasting. As noted by Paddy Scannell and David Cardiff in *A Social History of British Broadcasting: Volume 1, 1922–39: Serving the Nation* (Blackwell, 1991), the core principles of this philosophy were set out by Reith in a memorandum written to the Crawford Committee in 1925.

They can be summarized as follows: that broadcasting should serve the interests of the general public; that it should be accountable to the public but independent from government whilst being subject to government regulation; that audiences should be treated as citizens, usually of a democracy; that it had a duty to not only entertain but also to inform and educate the audience and contribute to public debate within society in an impartial and balanced manner; that broadcasting should offer a mixture of programmes; that broadcasting activities should be publicly funded; and that it should foster and reinforce national identity.

Commercial TV in the UK has been equally subject to regulation, but will cease to have a PSB obligation once the broadcasting services in Britain switch completely to digital transmission (see COMMUNICATIONS ACT (UK), 2003).

Regulation aims, for example, to achieve BALANCED PROGRAMMING, that is balance between information and entertainment, preserving the one against the possible encroachment of the other. Regulation serves to guarantee a balance between the serious and the popular, between programmes that appeal to minorities and programming designed to attract mass viewing.

Since the 1990s PSB has suffered diminishment in the face of commercial competition, greater diversity of provision brought about by

P

new technology and dominant ideologies working towards the PRIVATIZATION of the airways, to the point at which some commentators fear for its future.

Pressure on governments by multi-national corporations seeking to extend their media portfolios (see MURDOCH EFFECT), and viewing PSB as an obstacle to their ambitions, has been unrelenting (see BRITISH MEDIA INDUSTRY GROUP). As long ago as 1991, Peter Golding and Graham Murdock in 'Culture, communications, and political economy' in *Mass Media and Society* (Edward Arnold, 1991), edited by James Curran and Michael Gurevitch, were writing that assaults on PSB are 'part of a wider historical process whereby the state in capitalist societies has increasingly assumed a greater role in managing communicative activity'. This process, the authors point out, has occurred hand in glove with big business: modern communication media are significant for their 'growing incorporation into a capitalist economic system'.

That PSB continues to be defined as an issue rather than a crisis is partly due to a determination to maintain a central place in AUDIENCE use of broadcasting, and this has meant matching the commercial sector in terms of programme popularity and thus of *ratings* (see AUDIENCE MEASUREMENT). The fear is that *quality* programming (a vital principle of PSB) will be sacrificed in the pursuit of *quantity*. Debate over what has been termed the *dumbing-down* of PSB has been lively but generally inconclusive.

What might be seen as the greatest opportunity and at the same time the greatest hazard facing PSB have been the profound changes brought about through DIGITIZATION and the energy with which PSB has carried the battle with private sector broadcasting on to the INTERNET. The online services offered by the BBC led the field until cutbacks were forced on the Corporation in 2011.

The degree to which governments support PSB in future, and the degree to which governments concede to the demands of media corporations, will continue to dominate the scenarios of broadcasting throughout the European community. See AUDIENCE FRAGMENTATION; DEMOCRACY AND THE MEDIA; DEREGULATION, FIVE MYTHS OF; MCQUAIL'S ACCOUNTABILITY OF MEDIA MODEL, 1997; MEDIASPHERE; MEDIAPOLIS; OFCOM: OFFICE OF COMMUNICATIONS (UK); PUBLIC SPHERE; RADIO BROADCASTING. See also *TOPIC GUIDE* under BROADCASTING.

▶ Petros Iosifides, ed., *Reinventing Public Service Communication: European Broadcasters and Beyond* (Palgrave Macmillan, 2010); Richard Rudin, *Broadcasting in the 21st Century* (Palgrave Macmillan, 2011).

Public sphere With the development of capitalism in the mid-seventeenth century, argues Jürgen Habermas, a public sphere of debate and communicative interchange was opened up, mainly among the bourgeoisie, in Western society. Economic independence provided by private property, the expansion of published literature such as novels that encouraged critical reflection, and the growth of a market-based press created a new public awareness of politics and involvement in public debate.

The public sphere existed between the economy and the state and represented a nascent form of supervision of government. However, Habermas believed that from the middle of the nineteenth century the public sphere came to be dominated by the expanded state and organized economic interests. The media ceased to be agencies of EMPOWERMENT, surrendered much of their role as a WATCHDOG and became a further means by which the public were sidelined and PUBLIC OPINION manipulated. According to Habermas, the public sphere ceased to be a 'neutral zone'.

Today, commentators see the INTERNET as a welcome extension of the public sphere, while at the same time expressing doubts as to how long this AGORA will remain a space of free exchange for communities of interest in the face of corporate ambitions to occupy – to commercialize – that space. At the same time that space is seen as being increasingly subject to government surveillance. See BLOGGING; BLOGOSPHERE; INFORMATION COMMONS; MEDIASPHERE; MEDIAPOLIS; SURVEILLANCE SOCIETY.

▶ Jürgen Habermas, *Communication and the Evolution of Society* (Beacon, 1979); Habermas, *The Structural Transformation of the Public Sphere* (Polity, 1989); Peter Dahlgren and Colin Sparks, eds, *Communication and Citizenship: Journalism and the Public Sphere* (Routledge, 1993); John Hartley, *Popular Reality: Journalism, Modernity, Popular Culture* (Arnold, 1996); Michael Bromley, ed., *No News is Bad News: Radio, Television and the Public* (Longman, 2001); Bob Franklin, ed., *British Television Policy: A Reader* (Routledge, 2001); James Watson, *Media Communication: An Introduction to Theory and Process* (Palgrave Macmillan, 3rd edition, 2008); (Zizi Papacharissi, ed., *Journalism and Citizenship: New Agendas in Communication* (Routledge, 2009).

Pulitzer prizes for journalism American awards made annually for breaking news, national reporting, criticism, editorial writing and feature photography; named after Joseph Pulitzer (1847–1911), Hungarian-born newspaper proprietor and rival of William Randolph Hearst (1863–1932), model for Orson Welles's film *Citizen Kane*, 1943.

Q

Quadrophony See GRAMOPHONE.

Quality press See BROADSHEETS.

Queer theory Views sexual identity as essentially fluid, ambiguous and unstable. In examining the dynamics of sexual identity it explores, as Annamarie Jagose notes in *Queer Theory: An Introduction* (New York University Press, 1996), the 'mismatches between sex, gender and desire'. Queer theory challenges the view that heterosexual desire is 'natural', unproblematic and to be regarded as the norm. Indeed it challenges the view that there can be any 'natural' and stable sexual identity or orientation.

Its concerns include not only lesbian and gay sexual orientations but, according to Jagose, 'cross-dressing, hermaphroditism, gender ambiguity and gender-corrective surgery'. Further, according to Paul Burston and Colin Richardson, editors of *A Queer Romance: Lesbians, Gay Men and Popular Culture* (Routledge, 1995), it 'seeks to locate Queerness in places that had previously been thought of as strictly for straights'. In *A Critical Introduction to Queer Theory* (Edinburgh University Press, 2003) Nikki Sullivan discusses examples of 'queer' readings of a number of texts ranging from *Batman Forever* to *Austin Powers, International Man of Mystery*.

An influential perspective informing the development of the theory is that provided by Judith Butler in *Gender Trouble: Feminism and the Subversion of Identity* (Routledge, 1990, 1999). Butler argues that GENDER categories and notions of identity and sexual orientation associated with them are not natural, but rather are social constructs which rely heavily upon everyday performances and interaction with others.

Such performances are often repeated and typically are framed by social expectations of what constitutes appropriate behaviour. It is through the repetition of performances that notions of gender and gender identity are constructed. The process of 'performativity', not nature, is at the heart of gender categories. Butler's theory of performativity facilitates examination of a range of possibilities that may exist as regards gender, identity and sexual orientation.

▶ Iain Morland and Annabelle Willox, *Queer Theory* (Palgrave Macmillan, 2005).

Questionnaires A popular method of data collection, a questionnaire basically consists of a series of questions designed to obtain factual information and/or information about people's attitudes, VALUES, opinions, or beliefs about a particular subject or issue. A questionnaire can also be constructed so as to contain questions about a *range* of topics or issues. They are regularly used as a tool of market research and are central to AUDIENCE MEASUREMENT.

Because it is not usually possible to give a questionnaire to all those who make up the group in which you are interested, questionnaires are normally given to a sample (see SAMPLING); care needs to be taken to ensure that the sample represents the total population, that is the total number of people in that group in all significant respects. Questionnaires are useful for gathering large amounts of data but may be less useful for investigating an issue in depth; here PARTICIPANT OBSERVATION or INTERVIEWS may be more useful. Further, constructing an unambiguous, unbiased and productive questionnaire is not easy, nor is the impartial analysis of the responses collected. See *TOPIC GUIDE* under RESEARCH METHODS.

QWERTY Arrangement of letters on the traditional TYPEWRITER and COMPUTER keyboard, devised in 1873 to overcome jamming problems on the world's first production machine, a Remington.

R

Rachel's Law See DEFAMATION.

Racism Discrimination against individuals or GROUPS of people on the basis of assumed racial differences. The term is problematic in that there is some argument as to whether the concept of race is useful anyway in describing biological differences between people. Racism, though, rests on the belief that different races with specific characteristics can be meaningfully identified. At an individual level such discrimination takes the form of PREJUDICE, whereas the term racism is often used to describe the way in which such discrimination is embedded into the structure of a society. *Cultural* racism refers to the perpetuation, consciously or unconsciously, of such discrimination and the beliefs and VALUES on which it rests through the cultural institutions of a society, for example education and the mass media.

As Stuart Hall notes in 'The whites of their eyes: Racist ideologies and the media' in *The Media Reader* (BFI Publishing, 1990), edited by

Manuel Alvarado and John O. Thompson, 'the media are ... part of the dominant means of ideological production. What they "produce" is precisely representations of the social world, images, descriptions, explanations and frames for understanding how the world is and why it works as it is said and shown to work. And, amongst other kinds of ideological labour, the media construct for us a definition of what race is, what meaning the imagery of race carries, and what the "problem of race" is understood to be. They help to classify out the world in terms of the categories of race'.

In *Learning the Media* (Macmillan, 1987) Manuel Alvarado, Robin Gutch and Tana Wollen pose four main categories in which black people are portrayed on television. (1) The *exotic*, for example coverage of tribal dancing used to welcome members of the Royal Family when visiting various Commonwealth countries. (2) The *dangerous*, for example coverage of immigration as an issue that presents coloured immigrants and asylum seekers as a threat. (3) The *humorous*, where humour may well serve to reinforce notions of racial differences to the detriment of coloured people. (4) The *pitied*, for example media coverage of famines in Africa and of Western attempts to provide aid, which tend to represent famine as resulting from the inadequacies of the people and their governments rather than as a legacy of Western colonialism.

One important focus of current media research is the role that the media play in shaping and perpetuating racism and racist STEREOTYPES. Research suggests that negative and stereotypical images of ethnic minorities abound and present an image of them as inferior, marginal and a potential source of social problems. Simon Cottle in *Ethnic Minorities and the Media* (Open University Press, 2000), edited by Cottle, argues that 'Over recent decades a considerable body of research conducted in both the UK and the US has examined the media's representations of ethnic minorities.

'The collective findings of this research effort generally make depressing reading. Underrepresentation and stereotypical characterization within entertainment genres and negative problem-orientated portrayal within factuality and news forms, and a tendency to ignore structural inequalities and lived racism experienced by ethnic minorities in both, are recurring research findings.'

Tuen A. van Dijk in 'New(s) racism: A discourse analysis approach', published in Cottle's *Ethnic Minorities and the Media*, analyses the contribution news coverage in the press makes to *new racism*, which opts for a more subtle negative portrayal of ethnic groups rather than the more obvious and open racism of the past. Van Dijk writes that 'most mentions of "terrorists" (especially also in the US press) will stereotypically refer to Arabs. Violent men who are our friends or allies will seldom get that label.

'For the same reason, "drug barons" are always Latin men in South America, never the white men who are in the drugs business within the US itself'. New racism extends to selection of stories for news coverage, and van Dijk argues that as regards news about immigrants and ethnic minorities, there is 'a preference for those topics that emphasize Their bad actions and Our good ones'. The consequence, he concludes, is that 'systematic negative portrayal of the Others, thus vitally contributed to negative mental models, stereotypes, prejudices and ideologies about the Others, and hence indirectly the enactment and reproduction of racism'.

Another fairly recent study reported in *Race in the News* by Ian Law (Palgrave, 2002) examined coverage of race news across radio, television and the press during six months from 1996 and 1997. The study found that there had been a shift towards an anti-racist stance in news coverage, a willingness to expose racist attitudes and behaviour and a more inclusive representation of British identity, one that acknowledged the multi-cultural and multi-ethnic nature of contemporary British society. However, in a later publication entitled *Racism and Ethnicity: Global Debates, Dilemmas, Directions* (Pearson, 2010) Law points to continuing concern over the representation of race in media coverage of such topics as inner-city gangs and violence, educational performance, dysfunctional families, unemployment, sport, Muslim issues, Gypsies, Travellers and asylum seekers.

The limited ethnic diversity among media practitioners also continues to be an issue. Law points to a recent report published by the Committee for Racial Equality entitled *Why Ethnic Minority Workers Leave London's Print Media* (CRE, 2006), which found numerous examples of racism and discrimination towards journalists from ethnic-minority backgrounds within the print news media. See BIGOTRY; COMPASSION FATIGUE; ETHNOCENTRISM; MEDIA IMPERIALISM; OTHER. See also TOPIC GUIDE under MEDIA ISSUES & DEBATES.

▶ Steve Fenton, *Racism, Class and Culture* (Macmillan, 1999); Sarita Malik, *Representing Black Britain: Black and Asian Images on Television* (Sage, 2001);

Norman K. Denzin, *Reading Race* (Sage, 2002); John Downing and Charles Husband, *Representing Race* (Sage, 2005); Kjartan Sveinsson, *A Tale of Two Englands, Race and Violent Crime in the Media* (Runnymede Trust, 2008); Rosalind Brunt and Rinella Cere, eds, *Postcolonial Media Culture in Britain* (Palgrave Macmillan, 2010); Gilbert B. Rodman, *The Race and Media Reader* (Routledge, 2010).

Radical press See MEDIA ACTIVISM; OPEN SOURCE; UNDERGROUND PRESS.

Radical suppression of potential (technology) See SUPERVENING SOCIAL NECESSITY.

Radio See RADIO BROADCASTING.

Radio ballads Form or GENRE of musical DOCUMENTARY inspired in the UK by radio producer Charles Parker, and compiled by folk-singers Ewan McColl and Peggy Seeger, beginning in 1958 with *The Ballad of John Axon*. The introduction of high-quality portable tape recorders to the BBC enabled Parker and his team to create new patterns of vocal sound, interlaced with sound effects (real, not studio-simulated) which served as an 'impressionistic' means of describing the lives and work of ordinary people. John Axon was a train driver, killed in a crash, and the nature of his life was re-created in ballad and recollection. *Singing the Fishing* (1960), taking for its theme the hard life of the North Sea fisherman, won the Italia Press award. The BBC withdrew financial support from this pioneering team in 1964. See RADIO DRAMA; WEB OR ONLINE DRAMA.

Radio broadcasting The First World War (1914–18) had given impetus to the development of radio for military purposes, and the training of wireless operators. Visionaries of the age saw the possibility of wireless programmes as an exciting extension of wireless messages – a 'household utility' which would create a world of sound, of voices and music; which would annihilate distance and offer undreamed-of opportunities for CULTURE, entertainment and information. With the ending of the war, crystal sets tuned in by their 'cat's whisker' became immensely popular. The valve, called the 'magic lantern of radio', developed between 1904 and 1914, soon usurped the crystal.

The first 'broadcast' of music and speech was made by an American, R.A. Fissenden, in 1906. The American Radio and Research Company was broadcasting concerts twice and three times a week as early as 1916, though KDKA of Pittsburg won the earliest renown as a pioneer in the field (on air, 1920).

A ban imposed on 'amateur' radio in Britain at the outbreak of the First World War was not lifted until 1919, but in February 1920 the Marconi Company in the UK began broadcasting from Writtle/Chelmsford, though later in the year the Post Office withdrew permission for these broadcasts. However, on 14 February 1922 the first regular broadcasting service in Britain was again beamed from Writtle, organized by the Experimental Section of the Designs Department of Marconi. Their London station, 2LO, began broadcasting on 11 May of the same year.

The Post Office, faced with nearly 100 applications from manufacturers who wanted to set up broadcasting stations, and realizing the need to have some sort of control of the airways, proposed a consortium of companies to centralize broadcasting activity: the British Broadcasting Company was born, and John Reith appointed its Managing Director (see BBC, ORIGINS). The BBC, set up by Royal Charter, came into existence 1 January 1927. It was to hold a monopoly of broadcasting in the UK until commercial radio was legalized in the SOUND BROADCASTING (UK) ACT, 1972 (see COMMERCIAL RADIO, UK).

From its beginning, radio broadcasting in the US was financed by ADVERTISING; from its beginning, radio broadcasting in the UK was free of advertising; the one was predominantly local, the other a national public service and eventually a national institution. No study of the evolution of broadcasting in the UK can avoid also being an analysis of the philosophy, vision and practices of the BBC's Managing Director and later Director General John (later Sir John) Reith. Varyingly called the Napoleon of Broadcasting, and Prospero, the all-powerful magician, Reith disliked politics and politicians, and viewed commerce with disdain (and commercialism with contempt). He forged a definition of PUBLIC SERVICE BROADCASTING (PSB) that dominated broadcasting, both radio and TV, for generations and which, even in the age of the dispersal of control, affects us still.

Radio newsreaders wore dinner jackets and bow-ties to read the NEWS, a symbol of the aloofness and distancing characteristic of Reith and much of the output of the BBC. There was even a Pronunciation Committee. Yet the Corporation resisted criticisms from the popular press that its tastes were too elitist. It was to give drama and classical music, as well as many other forms of music, a new structure and a new popularity. Equally, there was room for developing the potential of radio in outside broadcasts, drama documentary, discussion programmes, and fireside talks.

R

The greatest fear of the broadcasters was, and continues to be, government interference. Reith's caution was as monumental as the extent of his control. His desire to render the BBC beyond political reproach led to the Corporation often censoring itself so as to be one step ahead of being censored. The risks to the BBC were not imagined. During the General Strike of 1926 Winston Churchill wanted the government to commandeer the Corporation, a move Reith managed to resist – but at a price: during the strike no representative of organized labour was permitted to broadcast, and the leader of the Opposition, Ramsay MacDonald, was also banned.

With the introduction and swift public take-up of television, radio lost dominance and for a time looked as if it would be displaced as a major player on the stage of mass communication. In the 1990s and into the New Millennium, both the BBC and commercial radio responded to the challenge, diversified, took audience tastes into account as never before, introduced new channels, new programme modes, adopting digital broadcasting with alacrity. Radio acquired a dynamic new profile, not only for music but also for talk programmes, sport, the arts, drama and comedy. See WIRELESS TELEGRAPHY. See also TOPIC GUIDE under BROADCASTING.

▶ Asa Briggs, *The History of Broadcasting in the United Kingdom* (Oxford University Press, four volumes, 1961, 1965 and volumes 3 and 4, 1979); P.M. Lewis and J. Booth, *The Invisible Medium: Public Commercial and Community Radio* (Macmillan, 1989); Paddy Scannell and David Cardiff, *A Social History of British Broadcasting: Vol. 1 1922–1939: Serving the Nation* (Blackwell, 1991); Andrew Crissell, *Understanding Radio* (Routledge, 1994) and *An Introductory History of British Broadcasting* (Routledge, 1997); Stephen Barnard, *Studying Radio* (Arnold, 2000); Caroline Mitchell, ed., *Women and Radio* (Routledge, 2000); Michele Hilmes, ed., *Radio Reader: Essays in the Cultural History of Radio* (Routledge, 2001); Asa Briggs and Peter Burke, *A Social History of the Media: From Gutenberg to the Internet* (Polity, 2002); Guy Starkey and Andrew Crissell, *Radio Journalism* (Sage, 2008); Hugh Chignell, *Key Concepts in Radio Studies* (Sage, 2009).

'Radio Death' Or 'Hate Radio'; nickname given to Rwanda's *Radio Television Libre des Milles Collines* (Thousand Hills Television Radio) which, following the assassination of President Juvenal Habyarimana, conducted an intensive campaign of hatred against the minority tribe, the Tutsis (9 per cent of the population as against 90 per cent Hutu). RTLM proved the power of radio in a land almost without TV and with an illiteracy rate of over 50 per cent of the population. A broadcast in April 1994 claimed that 'by the 5th May the elimination of the Tutsis should be finished'. In the first week of the killing spree, upwards of 200,000 people were murdered as Hutu militia combed the countryside.

In 1995 REPORTERS SANS FRONTIÈRES (Reporters Without Borders), a Montpellier-based group of journalists set up in 1987 to defend press freedom worldwide, initiated a civil law suit in Paris against the founders and organizers of Radio Death alleging their responsibility for genocide, violation of humanitarian law and crimes against humanity.

In response to the torrents of hatred emerging from RTLM, Radio Gatashya was formed and took to the air for the first time in August 1994 in Goma. Its own nickname was 'Humanitarian Radio', and it provided an information service of help and support for the thousands of refugees. In June 2000 a Belgian-born announcer on 'Radio Death', Georges Ruggiu, was sentenced by an international criminal tribunal to twelve years' imprisonment on two counts of inciting the Hutu massacres of Tutsis in Rwanda.

Radio drama The first ever radio play was Richard Hughes's *Danger* (1923), about a couple trapped in a mine, but the play that appears to have had the most substantial impact as a work in a new MEDIUM was Reginald Berkeley's *The White Chateau*, broadcast by the BBC to an audience of over 12 million on Armistice Day, 1925 and telling an extremely harrowing story of the trench-war.

Since that time hundreds of writers have been given a start in their professional lives by radio, one of whose many virtues is cheapness: today, a 30-minute radio play requires one day's studio time; an hour-long play, two days. The radio playwright need not concern him/herself with the massive costs of scene-changes; there is little need to keep costs down by writing plays for two people and an armchair. The whole world of time and space is at the writer's command.

Most importantly, there is the awaiting imagination of the listener. The best radio plays take listeners on a journey into their imagination, where the play is given its own unique setting, the characters a unique appearance – all with the help of voices, sound effects and silence; an art form, as the poet W.H. Auden once said, that is 'not spoiled by any collision with visual reality'.

Radio drama possesses the characteristic of intimacy: it has made the interior monologue, the soliloquy, a dramatic device perhaps more convincingly acceptable than on the stage; at the same time, because its stage is contained by no proscenium arch or screen-frame, because its 'stage-set' is actually the mind of the listener, radio also lends itself successfully to epic drama: Shakespeare can be marvellous on radio.

Among writers who took an early interest in radio as a serious art form was the Irish poet Louis MacNeice (1907–65). His verse plays broadcast during and after the Second World War, such as *The Story of My Death* (1943) and *The Dark Tower* (1946), impressively explored the potential of radio, while in 1953 another poet, Welshman Dylan Thomas (1914–53), gave to the world one of the best known and most loved plays for radio, *Under Milk Wood*. The play was first broadcast on 25 January 1954, with a distinguished all-Welsh cast and produced by Douglas Cleverdon.

For thirty years Val Gielgud as Head of Radio Drama at the BBC guided the evolution of the radio play, himself producing and writing. Throughout its history, radio drama has witnessed a strong tradition of able producers such as Cleverdon, Lancelot Sieveking, Donald McWinnie and Alfred Bradley, nurturing writers who later became famous: Harold Pinter, Stan Barstow, Giles Cooper, Allan Prior, Alun Owen, William Trevor, Henry Livings, Peter Terson, Alan Plater, David Rudkin and Tom Stoppard.

Despite its creative potential, radio as a dramatic medium has acquired less status, and been paid less attention than other, more glamorous, media; and less than it deserves. However, the BBC continues to broadcast between 200 and 300 radio plays a year, classical drama as well as new works. See TELEVISION DRAMA; 'WAR OF THE WORLDS'; WEB OR ONLINE DRAMA.

Radio: Independent radio; Radio Luxembourg; Radio Normandy See COMMERCIAL RADIO: ORIGINS.

Radio Northsea PIRATE RADIO station, UK, which began broadcasting off the coast of Essex immediately prior to the General Election of 1970. Mindful of the Labour government's antipathy to commercial radio and the Conservatives' support for it, Radio Northsea broadcast pro-Tory propaganda at an election in which the 18–21 age group were voting for the first time.

Many constituencies in London and the south-east were marginal seats. Labour lost the election; in the constituencies nearest Radio Northsea, the swing against Labour was greatest. At the Royal Opening of Parliament on 2 July 1970, the Queen's Speech confirmed that legislation would be introduced for local radio

stations 'under the general supervision of an independent broadcasting authority.'

Radio 1, Radio 2, Radio 3, Radio 4, Radio 5 Live (BBC) Radios 1 to 4 have broadcast in their present form since 1967; Radio 5 took to the air in August 1990, to be revamped into Radio 5 Live in March 1994. Prior to 1967 there was the Home Service, catering for news, plays, talks, comedy shows and magazine programmes – the Talk channel; the Light Programme, largely for popular music and entertainment; and the Third Programme serving the world of classical music and drama. During the 1960s PIRATE RADIO invaded the airways with pop music, which attracted large audiences; the Marine Broadcasting (Offenders) Act, 1967 made such stations illegal. BBC's Radio 1 was created to meet the new demand and successfully competes with commercial radio stations for the attention of popular music fans.

Radio 2 took on a similar if not identical role to that of the Light Programme, Radio 3 that of the Third Programme, and Radio 4 became Britain's premier talk radio channel. For its richness, diversity and sheer quality of output, Radio 4 must rank among the world's finest radio services. Faced with competition from CLASSIC FM Radio, Radio 3 has proved itself responsive to audience needs without sacrificing quality.

Radio 5 was to be a speech-led service catering for the needs of children and young people, sharing airtime with news and sport. Just when this pioneering new channel was beginning to win listeners and produce programmes of originality, the BBC abandoned it and opted for Radio 5 Live, more general in orientation, often crossing lines with Radio 4 but in terms of its sports coverage, unexcelled. See BBC DIGITAL. See also *TOPIC GUIDE* under BROADCASTING.

Radio: Rokker Radio The UK's first radio programme for gypsies and travellers, broadcast by the BBC's Three Counties Radio, covering Bedfordshire, Hertfordshire and Buckinghamshire and then extending to BBC Radio Cambridgeshire, BBC Radio Essex and BBC Radio Norfolk. Rokker Radio closed in 2008, but traveller news and views are still obtainable at Travellers' Times Online launched on International Roma Day, 8 April 2009.

Radio 'shock-jocks' Populist radio talk hosts trading in strong, sometimes sensationalist opinions, generally taking Rightist viewpoints and purporting to speak on behalf of ordinary citizens; to be heard mostly in the US and Australia, where PUBLIC SERVICE BROADCASTING (PSB) regulations are less restricting than,

R

for example, in European broadcasting.

Following the removal from radio regulation of the 'Fairness Doctrine' in the US by the Reagan administration in 1987, the green light was given to the kind of talk radio exemplified by Rush Limburgh (nicknamed 'The Most Dangerous Man in America'). His show is broadcast on over 600 radio stations nationwide with an estimated 20 million listeners. Prejudiced, often intolerant of contrary opinions, demagogic and frequently anti-democratic in tone, shock-jock radio has displaced other journalistic formats such as current affairs, at the same time having marginalized traditional principles of balance and objectivity in content and presentation.

Random sample See SAMPLING.

Ratings See AUDIENCE MEASUREMENT.

Reaction shot When a person is being interviewed on television there are regular *in-cuts* where the viewer is offered a glimpse of the reactions of the reporter or interviewer – nodding, smiling, acknowledging. When interviews take place on location rather than in the studio, such reaction shots are usually filmed separately and edited-in later. See SHOT.

Readership See MEDIASPHERE.

Reading Just as, in modern usage, we refer to TEXT as any human-made artefact, rather than merely a printed text, so we refer to reading as a process which is a response to all texts. Use of this term suggests a more positive, attentive and interpretative reaction to a text rather than merely looking. We read critically; we analyse, while at the same time modern usage accepts the more open nature of 'readings' – their POLYSEMY (or many-meaningness). A *work*, as Roland Barthes has defined it, emanates from a creator, an encoder – writer, artist, composer, for example – but the *text* belongs in the sphere of reading and thus becomes, as it were, the property of the decoder. So readers may produce different interpretations, different texts from the same work, and their interpretations may all differ from that intended by the author.

It does not necessarily follow that all readings are of equal value, for inevitably there are informed as contrasted with uninformed readings. Recognition of *competence* has to be considered, and this would involve what Noam Chomsky has termed 'linguistic competence', as well as knowledge, experience, training and a degree of EMPATHY. The study of media communication is largely about learning to read competently, with PERCEPTION and understanding. See TOPIC GUIDE under TEXTUAL ANALYSIS.

▶ Jonathan Silverman and Dean Radar, *The World is*

a Text: Writing, Reading and Thinking About Visual and Popular Culture (Pearson/Prentice Hall, 2009); John Fiske, Henry Jenkins, Kevin Glynn, Jonathan Gray and Pamela Wilson, *Reading the Popular* (Routledge, 2011).

Realism That which is portrayed as 'reality' in art, literature, theatre, film fiction or documentary and photography. It constitutes an imitation of *perceived* reality, a simulation. Because it is the result of a range of choices concerning subject-matter and aesthetics, realism is a *construct* of reality rather than a reproduction of it, influenced by VALUE and IDEOLOGY and convention. Socialist realism in Russian cinema, for instance, focused on the realities of the lives of workers, on the land or in factories, but such portraits of reality were highly charged with the ideology of the Soviet system in the ways that labour was idealized rather than portrayed by means of a critical READING of the system.

Susan Strehle in *Fiction in the Quantum Universe* (University of Carolina Press, 1992) suggests the use of the term 'actualism' rather than 'the old mechanistic reality' because it has 'its roots not in things [or facts] but in acts, relations and motions'. The term corresponds to ACTUALITY, an approach pioneered by early radio DOCUMENTARY-makers to allow real situations to be communicated with a minimum of intervention from the programme-maker. Yet however absent seems to be the hand of MEDIATION, it is (in actuality) ever-present.

Peter Dahlgren in *Television and the Public Sphere: Citizenship, Democracy and the Media* (Sage, 1995) says of TV texts that 'realism' (his inverted commas) is a 'very central feature' but one which is highly problematical. We should constantly remind ourselves, Dahlgren believes, that 'all representation involves construction'. In discussing TV, the author talks of the 'pleasure of verisimilitude'. Essentially TV is 'mimetic', imitating reality rather more than interpreting it. In Dahlgren's view this limits the potential TV has for POLYSEMY and thus, in this context, the representation of alternative realities.

In 'Reading realism: audiences' evaluations of the reality of media texts', *Journal of Communication* (December 2003), Alice Hall poses six tests of the authenticity of realism – whether the text is plausible; whether it it typical and factual; whether it convinces in terms of emotional involvement; whether it achieves narrative consistency; and whether it is sufficiently persuasive of audience perceptions of what is real. See TOPIC GUIDE under REPRESENTATION.

Reality TV Perhaps best described as 'live documentary'; a prime example being, in the UK, Channel 4's *Big Brother*, versions of which have been produced in many other countries worldwide. While participants in Reality TV are real people (rather than actors), and while the story of their interactions is unscripted and not known in advance, such programmes are essentially *contrivances* of reality – highly mediated by the TV production team, and highly manipulated from start to finish.

The participants are painstakingly vetted prior to selection. Once chosen, although they are 'real' people, they are placed into a situation that requires *performance.* They become actors in front of cameras and millions of viewers, knowing full well that the performance of the realities of self-presentation will be judged by a 'participatory' audience.

Such programmes as *Big Brother*, the BBC's *Castaway* or ITV's *Popstars* have been described as docu-soaps with gameshow appeal, and they chiefly target younger-generation audiences. Their popularity, the unscripted sensation-seeking of many participants, and the encouragement of such sensationalism on the part of the popular press, have provoked criticism and a degree of righteous indignation, in part because they take up so much TV time.

Generally, Reality TV shows such as *American Idol*, *The X Factor*, *Survivor*, *Wife Swap* and *Hell's Kitchen* are cheap to produce (the participants queue in thousands to take part, for the lure of fame and fortune). They are about success and failure; success for a few and failure, and very often audience derision, for the many.

Reality TV is a classic bad effects/good effects scenario, giving rise to questions such as what exactly is meant by 'success'; and for those who achieve it, what is the long-term future for what have been called 'nonebrities' or 'Z-list celebrities'? Critics argue that the price of failure is both damaging to the participant and brings out the worst in audences. Media analyst Tom Alderman has written that 'there is a subset of Reality TV that can only be described as Shame TV becauses it uses humiliation as its core appeal'.

In a blog posted to SF Gate website of the *San Francisco Chronicle* (31 January 2011) entitled 'Reality TV is NOT Reality', psychiatrist Jim Taylor, focusing on US Reality TV, argues that 'Reality TV has become the public executions of our times. We sit on the edge of our seats waiting eagerly for the guillotine to fall, yet don't want the end to come too quickly. We want to savour the lingering death of humiliation and rejection'. It would seem, according to Dr Taylor, that the

'symbolic deaths' of contestants serve as questionable therapy for the watchers (or voyeurs?): we return to 'our lives feeling somehow better' knowing that we 'are "survivors" of our own reality show called Life'.

On the other hand, in a London *Evening Standard* online article (3 July 2009), Brian Sewell argues that Reality TV 'is the modern equivalent of Aesop's Fables ... in drawing morals from such programmes they are every bit as instructive as examples of how we should behave in what is left of our still fundamentally Judo-Christian society'. We obtain glimpses of 'society as it now really is'.

When we turn to actual research evidence rather than cursory impression, as exemplified by broadcaster John Humphrey's view expressed at the Edinburgh Festival that Reality TV is 'mind numbing, witless vulgarity', we encounter a different picture. Annette Hill, author of *Reality TV: Audiences and Popular Factual Television* (Routledge, 2005), countered Humphrey's opinion in a *New Humanist* article, 'Witless vulgarity' (November/December 2004). Hill's research indicated that audiences for Reality TV were often proactively questioning. They 'gossip, speculate and judge how far people can portray themselves and stay true to themselves in the spectacle/performance environment'.

Hill states that viewers are well aware 'of how far the reality shows are planned and directed. And if they are aware of the constructed nature of these formats, they are also aware of the staging of reality in other types of factual programmes, such as documentary, or even news. In other words, these audiences are truly media literate'. She argues that 'if the debunkers of reality TV actually listened to the people who watch such programmes they'd realise that rather than "mind numbing, witless vulgarity", *Big Brother*, *I'm a Celebrity* ... and even *Too Posh to Wash* can actually foster a new kind of intellectual engagement'.

The treatment of women in Reality TV programmes is a keen focus of attention for analysts. In 'Outwit, outlast, out-flirt? The women of Reality TV' published in *Featuring Females: Feminist Analyses of Media* (American Psychological Association, 2005), edited by Ellen Cole and Jessica Henderson Daniel, Laura S. Brown writes, 'Reality shows do a remarkable job of reflecting the social construction of gender within dominant culture. In that regard, no matter how contrived the story lines, the stereotypes of women on reality shows appear highly consistent with those seen in other aspects of popular media. These images arise from the decision of

R

producers and editors about who will appear and how they will appear" See EFFECTS OF THE MASS MEDIA. See also *TOPIC GUIDES* on MEDIA ISSUES & DEBATES; MEDIA: POWER, EFFECTS, INFLUENCE; MEDIA: VALUES & IDEOLOGY.

▸ Richard Kilborn, *Staging the Real: Factual TV Programming in the Age of Big Brother* (University of Manchester Press, 2003); Mark Andrejevic, *Reality TV: The Work of Being Watched* (Rowan & Littlefield, 2004); Annette Hill, *Restyling Factual TV: Audiences and News, Documentary and Reality Genres* (Routledge, 2007).

Received Pronunciation (RP) That mode of pronunciation in English which is free of regional ACCENT and aspires to a generally accepted standard; derives from the speech of the court and of public schools; traditionally the 'vocal sign' of the educated person, adopted as the norm for BBC broadcasters, and eventually being termed 'BBC English'. RP no longer has the prestigious status or the dominance it once had. Regional accents have been 'in' since the 1960s, though RP has retained a substantial foothold in national broadcasting.

Receiver See SENDER/RECEIVER.

Recency effect See FIRST IMPRESSIONS; PRIMACY, LAW OF.

Reception studies In recent years, particular research emphasis has been placed upon the ways in which AUDIENCES receive media messages; how they react to their reading, listening and viewing; and what audiences do with that experience, what MEANINGS they make of it. Such reception studies have, as far as television is concerned, shifted from a prime focus on audience response to news and current affairs to the investigation of audience reception of popular GENRES, such as REALITY TV and SOAP OPERAS. Of particular interest is the way online activity links with TV viewing experience: does one detract from the other, or does a process of SYNERGY take place? See AUDIENCE MEASUREMENT. See also *TOPIC GUIDE* under AUDIENCES: CONSUMPTION & RECEPTION OF MEDIA.

▸ Tony Wilson, *Watching Television: Hermeneutics, Reception and Popular Culture* (Polity Press, 1995); Sonia Livingstone, *Making Sense of Television: The Psychology of Audience Interpretation* (Routledge paperback, 1998); Pertii Alasuutari, ed., *Rethinking the Media Audience* (Sage, 1999); Nick Couldry, *Inside Culture: Reimagining the Method of Cultural Studies* (Sage, 2000); Nick Couldry, Sonia Livingstone and Tim Markham, *Media Consumption and Public Engagement* (Palgrave, 2007).

Reconfiguration; remediation See MEDIATION.

Record player See GRAMOPHONE.

Redundancy In communication terms, redundancy refers to that which is conventional or predictable in any message. Its opposite is *entropy*, that which is unexpected and surprising, of low predictability. John Fiske in *Introduction to Communication Studies* (Methuen, 1982; see 3rd edition, Routledge, 2010) says 'the English language is about 50% redundant. This means we can delete about 50% of any utterance and still have a usable language capable of transmitting understandable messages'.

Redundancy is established through frequent use until it becomes a convention – both technical, in terms of correctness, and social, in terms of general acceptability. It is essential if the MEANING of messages is to have wide currency and be 'on wave-length' with the codes and reference tables of the receiver.

The entropic challenges these codes and reference tables with novelty – new expression, new thought, overturning predictability and probability. The art of the avant-garde is entropic; at least in its initial phase, it speaks in a language the general public find difficult to understand, and it is often provocative. Of course the shock of the new passes: yesterday's outrage is today's fashion; yesterday's entropy is today's redundancy.

A scan of the popular arts reveals their reliance on the conventional forms and practices that make up redundancy – the predictable rhymes and metres of pop songs, for example, or the repetitive refrains of folk songs. Fiske writes, 'Redundancy is generally a force for the status quo and against change. Entropy is less comfortable, more stimulating, more shocking perhaps, but harder to communicate effectively'. See PHATIC LANGUAGE; SHANNON AND WEAVER'S MODEL OF COMMUNICATION, 1949.

Referent The actual object, entity in the external world to which a SIGN or linguistic expression refers. The referent of the word 'table' is the object, 'table'.

Referential code See CODES OF NARRATIVE.

Reflexivity Self-monitoring in terms of COGNITIVE practice; but more significantly for the analysis of the individual's self-positioning within a fast-changing society in which NORMS, VALUES and practices are rendered less certain, less distinct. Reflexivity is central to the construction of identity. It operates intuitively and aesthetically as well as cognitively, and mass communication is seen to be an agency in the control or liberation of self-interpretation in relation to the READING of and reaction to media TEXTS. Reflexivity makes critical use of NARRATIVES, personal and collective, through which sense is forged out of experience. See SELF-IDENTITY.

Refutation The employment of counter-arguments, evidence and proof to dispute the arguments of another person. Strictly speaking, to disprove allegations.

Register Term describing the compass of a voice or instrument, the range of sound-tones produced in a particular manner. The soprano and the bass sing in different registers. The word also describes the structures of language used in varying social contexts: its levels of vocabulary, sentence construction, tones and inflexions. Thus the register adopted by an infant school teacher in his/her class will differ from the register selected for the staff room, just as a scientist will adjust his/her register between conversations held with scientific colleagues and with casual acquaintances in the local pub. In printing, register refers to the exact adjustment of position, as of colours in a picture, or letterpress on opposite sides of the page.

Regulation of Investigatory Powers Act (RIPA) (UK), 2000 One of the most far-reaching pieces of government SURVEILLANCE legislation, RIPA extends blanket powers of interception on TELEPHONE and INTERNET traffic not only to the police and security agencies such as MI5, but also to a broad spectrum of government departments as well as local government. In 2002 what had initially been claimed to be a means of tracking online crime was suddenly opened out to be what a UK *Guardian* leader, 'British Liberty RIP' (11 June 2002), called 'a mockery of the right to privacy that the Human Rights Act is supposed to protect'. RIPA was seen to 'have profound civil liberty implications'.

The Act opens up all telephone messages and e-mails to official scrutiny; in addition it empowers employers to monitor the e-mail exchanges of their employees. It obliges Internet service providers (ISPs) to install 'black boxes' which record all server traffic. It makes illegal any ENCRYPTION that might deny access by the authorities. Refusal on the part of individuals or GROUPS to declare keys to encryption is punishable by up to two years' imprisonment. Unwittingly, ISPs become the snouts of government and its agencies.

The 'spy-in-the-wire' has access to who you talk to, when, what you talk about and where you have been talking from. It can accumulate vast amounts of information about you which will be made available to people you have never met,

never heard of, about whom you know nothing. The fact that information about you has been gathered and stored is kept secret from you, and you will not know how that information is to be used or for what purpose.

Sections 21 to 25 of the Act grant the state powers to gather data from Internet traffic where the following might be considered to be at risk: national security, the detecting or preventing of crime, matters of disorder, traffic which may be deemed to be in the interests of the UK's economic well-being, public safety, public health, the levying/collecting of taxes, and for any purposes the Secretary of State specifies, subject to parliamentary approval.

The initial question, widely asked, has been, will RIPA succeed in its stated aim of catching terrorists and criminals? Equal concern has been expressed about the widespread practice of subjecting individuals and families to surveillance by local government. The Conservative-Liberal Democrat coalition government elected in May 2010 announced its intention of requiring local authorities to seek the permission of magistrates to conduct covert electronic or manual surveillance.

RIPA remains a target of human rights groups in the UK such as Big Brother Watch and Spy Blog ('Watching them, watching us'), the Convention on Modern Liberty and the website of campaigning journalist Henry Porter (Henry Porter on Liberty). See USA – PATRIOT ACT, 2001. See also *TOPIC GUIDE* under MEDIA: FREEDOM, CENSORSHIP.

▶ Rosemary Bechlor, *The Convention on Modern Liberty: The British Debate on Fundamental Rights and Freedoms* (Imprint Academic, 2010).

Regulatory favours In an age when multinational corporations have acquired local, national and global voice by investing in media, it comes as no surprise to observe them using that voice to promote corporate interests, to employ those media to pressurize government to grant them favours. Jeremy Tunstall and Michael Parker in *Media Moguls* (Routledge, 1991) use the term *regulatory favours* that governments cede to big media-owning companies in return for a 'good press'. These favours principally constitute the abolition or waiving of media regulations that might hinder expansionist interests. See CONGLOMERATES; GLOBAL MEDIA SYSTEM: THE MAIN PLAYERS; MURDOCH EFFECT; POLITICS OF ACCOMMODATION (IN THE MEDIA); PRIVATIZATION; STRATEGIC BARGAINING. See also *TOPIC GUIDE* under MEDIA: POLITICS & ECONOMICS.

Reinforcement There has been much argument

over the role of the mass media in reinforcing, in underpinning, certain social and political VALUES and structures. Considerable attention has been given to two areas: the media's portrayal of violence, and the role of the mass media in political communications.

There are those who claim that the frequent incidence of violence in the media has contributed to an increase in acts of violence in society. Research evidence, however, gives few clear pointers as to the nature or extent of any media influence. One school of thought rejects the notion that the media directly encourage violent behaviour in all viewers, but argues that the media violence may reinforce already existing tendencies to violence in some viewers.

This position is open to question. As Sonia Livingstone comments in an article, 'On the continuing problem of media effects', published in *Mass Media and Society* (Arnold, 1996), edited by James Curran and Michael Gurevitch, 'It is difficult to know what beliefs people might have espoused but for the media's construction of a normative reality, and difficult to know what role the media plays in the construction of those needs and desires which in turn motivate viewers to engage with the media as they are rather than as they might be.'

Paul H. Lazarsfeld, Bernard Berelson and Hazel Gaudet in a classic study of the effects of political communication by the mass media on voting behaviour, *The People's Choice* (Columbia University Press, 1948), were of the opinion that the media's main effect is to reinforce *existing* political preferences. The notions of *selective perception*, SELECTIVE EXPOSURE and *selective recall* are used to explain how the same output can reinforce the diverse views, values and beliefs of a mass audience. It is suggested that the audiences, rather than being passive receptacles for media output, select from the output those messages which are in accordance with their own prior dispositions, and give attention to these – a point confirmed by Garth J. Jowett and Victoria O'Donnell reviewing research into the effects of persuasion and propaganda in their work, *Propaganda and Persuasion* (Sage, 1999). They state: 'Selectivity in the perception of messages is generally guided by preexisting interests and behaviour patterns of the receivers ... mass communication effects tend to take the form of reinforcement rather than change.'

Whilst in recent years there has been a tendency to adopt a more multiculturalist perspective in many areas of broadcasting, this may result in the inadvertent reinforcement of more subtle negative attitudes. For example, Simon Cottle in *Ethnic Minorities and the Media* (Oxford University Press, 2000), edited by Cottle, concludes from his study of regional TV news programmes in the UK that despite attempts to present a multiculturalist perspective, 'such "multiculturalist" representations ... may actually serve to reinforce culturally sedimented views of ethnic miniorities as "Other" and simultaneously appear to give the lie to ideas of structural disadvantage and continuing inequality'.

Another area of concern is that celebrity culture may endorse or reinforce certain values at the expense of others: the importance of appearance, charisma, fame, wealth, glamorous lifestyles, and self-promotion as opposed to modesty, loyalty, charity and thrift, for example. Celebrity culture permeates and is arguably driven by the media. Celebrities can serve as role models. According to Hamish Pringle in *Celebrity Sells* (John Wiley & Sons Ltd, 2004), 'Very large numbers of people use stars as role models and nowhere is this more evident than in the area of personal appearance.' It is not then surprising that they are frequently used to reinforce messages promoting products used in self-presentation, like cosmetics and clothes. See AUDIENCE: ACTIVE AUDIENCE; EFFECTS OF THE MASS MEDIA; POLITICS OF ACCOMMODATION (IN THE MEDIA); RESONANCE; ROLE MODELS.
▸ P. David Marshall, ed., *Celebrity Culture Reader* (Routledge, 2006).

Reithian Attitudes to BROADCASTING as typified by the first Director General of the BBC, Sir John Reith (1889–1971), who dominated the rise of broadcasting in the UK like a colossus. Dour, high-principled, autocratic, paternalist and a Scottish Presbyterian to boot, Reith was appointed General Manager of the newly formed British Broadcasting Company in December 1922. His philosophy was that broadcasting was a heaven-sent opportunity to educate and enlighten the people in the ways of quality, and that 'giving the people what they wanted' was the way to perdition.

This 'Tsar of Savoy Hill', as the press called him, believed, in the words of the *New Statesman* on Armistice Day 1933, 'in the medicinal effects of education – a cultural dictatorship'. Though George Lansbury MP said of Reith, 'I have always felt that Sir John Reith would have made a very excellent Hitler for this country', Clement Attlee saw advantages: 'He puts up a splendid resistance to vested interests of all kinds.'

Elitist, imperious and sabbatarian, Reith

nevertheless created in the BBC an organization resistant to commercialism, favouring the arts, serious debate and notions of public responsibility. Reith strove for IMPARTIALITY but never achieved *balance*: coverage of Royal activities in the 1920s and 1930s was not in any way matched by coverage of the activities of the Labour movement and the unions and, during the General Strike of 1926, the BBC remained strictly 'neutral': it stayed silent. Reith, the Napoleon of Broadcasting, as Colonel Moore Brabazon called him, resigned as 'DG' (Director General), as his own staff spoke of him, in 1937. See BBC, ORIGINS. See also *TOPIC GUIDES* under MEDIA HISTORY; MEDIA INSTITUTIONS.

Relationship marketing See MARKETING.

Relic gestures Those physical gestures that have outlived their original situation, yet continue to be used to effect even though their derivation is no longer obvious or explicable. Such gestures survive not only from historical past, but also from a human's infantile past – for example the rocking to and fro of disaster victims in the face of intolerable grief.

Remediation; reconfiguration See MEDIATION.

Repertoire of non-verbal behaviour See NON-VERBAL BEHAVIOUR: REPERTOIRE.

Reporters: embedded reporters See EMBEDDED REPORTERS.

Reporters Sans Frontières (Reporters Without Borders) Montpellier-based group of journalists set up in 1987 to defend press freedom worldwide, and campaign on behalf of journalists in trouble. Produces valuable data on the plight of reporters, photographers and filmmakers – those injured, imprisoned or killed in bringing home the news.

Report-talk, rapport-talk This is one way in which men and women's conversational style differs, according to Deborah Tannen in *You Just Don't Understand: Women and Men in Conversation* (Virago Press, 1992). Men, she argues, are confident with public speech or what she calls *report-talk*, whether this be in a formal or an informal situation where several people are in conversation.

In these situations, when the company is mixed, men typically participate more in conversation than women and in part their performance may be a way of establishing status and control. In a more private setting, though, this difference in the participation rate between men and women may change or even reverse. Here *rapport-talk*, with which women, Tannen argues, are more comfortable, is more appropriate. Rapport-talk is used for establishing and reinforcing intimacy. These differences reflect the different GENDERLECTS that Tannen believes men and women use, which in turn reflect one main difference in their use of conversation: men using conversation to establish *status* and control, women to establish *intimacy*. See *TOPIC GUIDE* under GENDER MATTERS.

Representation A core function of media is to 're-present' to AUDIENCES the realities of 'the world out there'. Most of our knowledge of that world is brought to us via the media; and our perception of reality is MEDIATED by newspapers, TV, advertisements, films, etc. The media *image* the world for us. They do this by means of selection and interpretation which operate through GATEKEEPING and according to AGENDAS which are suffused by IDEOLOGY. The media represent to us the past as well as the present, and representations – or interpretations – of the past affect our perceptions of the present. Out of such representations arise issues concerning, for example, the representation of women, of race, asylum seeking, poverty, minorities.

What we as audience know of Africa and Africans, of Serbs and Albanians, of Israelis and Arabs, of Moslems or Sikhs, is what we have experienced through the reports and pictures brought to us by the media. The study of media representation, therefore, is central to cultural, media and communication studies. Because it is impossible to represent the world in all its massive complexity, media representation has to be viewed as a 'version' of reality, in which FRAMING has taken place according to criteria such as NEWS VALUES or pressures to propagandize, sensationalize, binarize (that is, divide 'us' from 'them' – see WEDOM, THEYDOM) or a desire to impose MEANING upon webs of complexity. Representation is essentially about *definition*, and media representation tends to be about promoting certain definitions, and therefore meanings, over others; thus endeavouring to affect the preferences of the public. See DISCOURSE. See also *TOPIC GUIDE* under REPRESENTATION.

Representation, machinery of See MACHINERY OF REPRESENTATION.

Representation of crime on screen See CRIME: TYPES OF CRIME ON SCREEN.

Representative sample See SAMPLING.

Repressive state apparatus See IDEOLOGICAL STATE APPARATUSES.

Repressive use of the media See EMANCIPATORY USE OF THE MEDIA.

Resistance (of audience to media) See DOMINANT, SUBORDINATE, RADICAL; POLYSEMY.

R

259

Resistive reading Occurs when AUDIENCE chooses not to accept without question the PREFERRED READING of media messages. Considerable research has been conducted into the capacity of audiences, and of segments of audiences such as women, to react independently to DOMINANT DISCOURSES: hence the *active-audience* thesis. See AUDIENCE: ACTIVE AUDIENCE; DOMINANT, SUBORDINATE, RADICAL; EMPOWERMENT.

Resonance Occurs when messages match the expectations of the receiver, when they are in alignment with or confirm the experiences, perceptions, values, beliefs or attitudes of the receiver. For example, Garth S. Jowett and Victoria O'Donnell, in *Propaganda and Persuasion* (Sage, 1999), note that propaganda messages are more likely to succeed if they resonate with the audience's existing viewpoints. See EFFECTS OF THE MASS MEDIA; MAINSTREAMING; MEAN WORLD SYNDROME.

Reterritorialization According to James Lull in *Media, Communication and Culture* (Polity Press, 1995), reterritorialization means '... first that the foundations of cultural territory – ways of life, artefacts, symbols and contexts – are all open to new interpretations and understandings', and secondly, 'implies that culture is constantly reconstituted through social interaction, sometimes by creative uses of personal communications technology and the mass media'. Thus *cultural territory* is potentially dynamic and changing, so reshaping is constantly possible.

Rhetoric Traditionally, the theory and practice of eloquence, whether spoken or written; the use of language so as to persuade others. The word is almost always used today as a term of criticism: rhetoric is the style in which bare-faced persuasion – politicking – is used. It is emotive; it belongs to speeches; and while it is very often resounding, it is rarely eloquent because it trades in empty phrases and endless repetitions. It is essentially redundant in that it tells supporters what they already know and antagonists what they know and don't want to hear.

Rhetoric is the stock-in-trade of the press, and of the popular press in particular. Practically every front-page headline is rhetorical in that it is soaked-through with the ideological attitudes of the newspaper, not least the belief in what sells newspapers, what commands attention, what readers want to be told. Indeed it might be said that one of the prime functions the popular press sets itself is to translate actuality into rhetoric: complex issues are translated into the simplifying mode of MYTH, of WEDOM,

THEYDOM, Militant and Moderate, Order and Disorder, Black and White, Management and Unions, Dries and Wets. See NEWS VALUES; OTHER. See also *TOPIC GUIDE* under LANGUAGE/DISCOURSE/NARRATIVE.

Rhetoric of the image See IMAGE, RHETORIC OF.

Rhetoric of numbers Phrase used by Itzhak Roeh and Saul F. Feldman to describe how the press, the popular press in particular, use numbers and amounts for *rhetorical* rather than *factual* purposes. The authors' analysis of the headlines of two Hebrew dailies, one ELITE, one popular, is reported on in 'The rhetoric of numbers in front-page journalism: how numbers contribute to the melodramatic in the popular press', published in *Text* 4/4 (1984). In the UK, broadsheets and tabloids both use numbers, statistics and charts to reinforce news texts; and the rhetoric is extended to pictures: for example printing whole pages of the faces of British military personnel killed in Afghanistan, the aim to bring home varying messages concerning the cost of armed interventions.

Right of reply A long-established practice in continental countries, the right of reply in the UK press has been argued for long, hard and generally unsuccessfully. Such a right would require newspaper editors to publish within a given time the replies of individuals or organizations who allege serious press misrepresentation, or to face a special court and a fine if found to be in error. It is argued that such a right would act as a deterrent to editorial bias and unethical practices. Newspapers do publish apologies, but these are usually for printing factual errors that might land them with libel actions. See CAMPAIGN FOR PRESS AND BROADCASTING FREEDOM; PEOPLE'S COMMUNICATION CHARTER.

Rights and the media See CULTURAL OR CITIZEN RIGHTS AND THE MEDIA.

Riley and Riley's model of mass communication, 1959 John W. Riley Jr and Matilda White Riley in 'Mass communication and the social system', in *Sociology Today: Problems and Prospects* (Basic Books, 1959; Harper Torch Books, vol. 2, 1965), edited by R.K. Merton, L. Broom and L.S. Cottrell Jr, pose a model in which the process of communication is an integral part of the social system. For Riley and Riley, both the Communicator (C) and the Recipient (R) are affected in the message process of sending, receiving, reciprocating, by the three social orders: the *primary group* or groups of which C and R are members; the larger *social structure*, that is the immediate community – social, cultural, industrial – to which they belong; and the *overall social system*. All of these are in dynamic interaction, with messages flowing multi-directionally.

The mass media audience Riley and Riley perceive as being neither impassive nor isolated but 'a composite of recipients who are related to one another, and whose responses are patterned in terms of these relationships'. See TOPIC GUIDE under COMMUNICATION MODELS.

RIPA See REGULATION OF INVESTIGATORY POWERS ACT (RIPA) (UK), 2000.

★Rogers and Dearing's agenda-setting model, 1987 Published in the *Communication Yearbook 11* (Sage, 1987) and examined in *Communication Models for the Study of Mass*

Communication, McQuail and Windähl, eds, (Longman, 2nd edition, 1993), this development by E.M. Rogers and J.W. Dearing of previous AGENDA-SETTING models is a welcome acknowledgment of the competing agendas in the public sphere. In their Yearbook article, 'Agenda-setting, where has it been, where is it going?' the authors see the public agenda as existing separately, though locked between, the policy agenda, of the state, of government, and the media, each subject to influence by the others.

The triad of agendas is itself influenced by a number of contextual factors 'out there', for example spectacular news stories. There are substantial factors that shape one, two or all

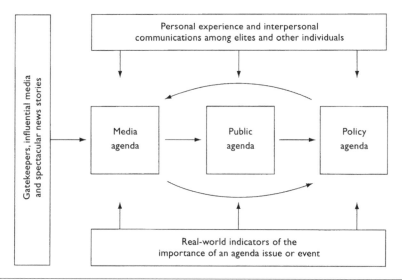

Rogers and Dearing's agenda-setting model, 1987

R

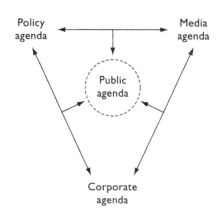

Tripolar model of competing agendas

agendas but which may also temper, or restrict, the effectiveness of those agendas, such as personal experience or what Rogers and Dearing call 'real world indicators' of the importance of an agenda issue. In this sense, reality remains something other than what is constructed in the media, or 'fed to' the public as reality by those who promote the policy agenda.

One problem with the model is its linearity, in that it does not sufficiently indicate the interactive nature of competing agendas. It also presents the public agenda as being in the same league, in terms of power, as the other agendas. Lastly, the model could arguably have a fourth agenda added to it, the *corporate* agenda, in order to reflect the increasingly dominant role in all aspects of policy, public debate and media operation, played by transnational companies on the global stage.

The *Dictionary*'s authors would pose here a modest alternative to Rogers and Dearing, which emphasizes the *interactive* nature of the dominant agendas while shifting the public agenda into no less central a position, but one which is by its nature less defined, inevitably more diffuse and thus more open to influence. See REGULATORY FAVOURS. See also *TOPIC GUIDE* under COMMUNICATION MODELS.

Rokker Radio See RADIO: ROKKER RADIO.

Roles A social role consists of the expected behaviour associated with a particular social position. Thus the social position of a 'journalist' identifies a body of behaviours expected of a journalist, that is the role of the journalist in society. 'Role' is a relational term: people play roles within a context in which other people are also playing roles, and these constitute the 'role set'. Roles within society or a social group carry with them responsibilities, obligations and rights.

Most people play a variety of roles in everyday life; for example a woman may play the roles of daughter, surgeon, sister, niece, mother, aunt and friend. Roles can be seen to constitute what Eric M. Eisenberg, in his article entitled 'Building a mystery: toward a new theory of communication and identity', published in the *Journal of Communication*, September 2001, describes as our 'multiplicity of selves' and they can influence the way in which we choose to communicate in a given situation. We may not always welcome some of the roles that others assign to us but play them anyway in order to remain within the group.

Roles carry with them expectations about how the role occupant should behave. In some cases these expectations arise through everyday interaction between group members. Many roles, however, are well established, such as the role of police officer, and there are widely held expectations about how the roles should be performed. We may have stereotypical images regarding typical role occupants and the behaviour expected of them. Some roles may be specific to a particular social group whilst others, like the role of teacher, may be found almost universally. However, the behaviour expected in these more universal roles may vary across time and cultures.

Behaviour identified with a role is not necessarily rigidly prescribed. Through interaction with others, individuals can change the expectations that determine a particular role. To some extent roles can be negotiated within a social context; within small, informal groups roles are often arrived at through interaction alone. It is therefore possible for an individual to choose a PERSONA through which they will play the role; thus people can to some extent play the same role differently whilst still keeping within the core expectations.

Role expectations can influence our use of LANGUAGE. SLANG might be appropriate when talking with friends in the pub but not when advising customers in a bank. For those who are multi-lingual, moving from one role to another may involve a change of language – for example, English for talking with fellow students but Urdu for talking with grandparents.

This multiplicity of roles tends to generate problems of conflicting demands, known as *role strain*. The individual may often have to adjust his/her communication pattern, non-verbal as well as verbal, to suit each particular role. Role strain occurs when our communication patterns cut across each other; when unexpected encounters take place between people from different role situations or, more seriously, when the role is deeply unnatural to us – an apparent denial of 'true' self.

The concept of role is used not only to describe the position of individuals within a social structure, but also that of groups or organizations. In this sense commentators write of the role or roles of the mass media in society; hence the role of the press as WATCHDOGS, defenders of the public good. Roles played by media in society vary according to who is defining such roles, but regular classifications include definers of reality, a nation's conscience, public entertainers, policers of deviance, defenders of tradition, and guard dogs of HEGEMONY. See EISENBERG'S MODEL OF COMMUNICATION AND IDENTITY,

2001; GROUPS; MOTHER TONGUE; ROLE MODEL; SELF-PRESENTATION.

Role model Albert Bandura, among other theorists, identified that we may under certain conditions model our behaviour on those of others. A role model is a person on whom others model their behaviour in some respect (see for example: 'Influence of models' reinforcement contingencies on the acquisition of imitative responses', *Journal of Personality and Social Psychology*, 1965, 1, 589–595). Role models may be those we know and admire in everyday life; they can also be those we learn about through the media. There are a number of reasons why someone may be a role model.

Erwin P. Bettinghaus and Michael J. Cody in *Persuasive Communication* (Thomson Learning, 1994) refer to a number of studies that have identified factors which tend to result in a role model being influential, for example: the model is seen as similar to the observer; the model is observed to receive mostly positive rewards for given behaviour; the model is viewed as competent, reliable and knowledgeable; the model is seen to behave in a consistent manner and to have high status. One or more of these factors may account for a role model's influence in any given situation. Bandura, though, points out that the potential influence of the role model will also depend on whether we are motivated to obtain the rewards associated with the role model, and whether we believe that such rewards will be achievable for us.

The influence of role models may be found in any situation. The potential of role models to influence behaviour has not been lost on professional persuaders, and a number of studies have shown that the use of role models can be an effective tool in ADVERTISING. Celebrities can serve as role models for consumers, and this is one of the reasons why celebrity endorsement is used as a tactic in the promotion of a wide range of products and services. Hamish Pringle in *Celebrity Sells* (John Wiley & Sons Ltd, 2004) provides an example: 'Very large numbers of people use stars as role models and nowhere is this more evident than in the area of personal appearance.' No wonder, then, that they are frequently used to promote cosmetics, fashion and related products.

Rotary press See CYLINDER PRESS.

Royal Commissions on the media See TOPIC GUIDE under COMMISSIONS, COMMITTEES, LEGISLATION.

Rumour Indirect and unsubstantiated information; *hearsay*; transmitted along informal channels by word of mouth. Rumour has the following characteristic features: it can rarely if ever be traced back to its origin; it can spread (almost) at the speed of light; it will only spread if the rumour has the momentum of credibility (even if this credibility is only the size of a pinch of salt); and it thrives in close-knit communities that have either no regular or formal channels of communication, or channels which are inefficient or not recognized as important.

A process of MEDIATION occurs at most or all points of telling, the original narrative being exaggerated and usually decorated with envy, spite or resentment. Good news rarely travels as quickly as bad news. In organizations, rumour often circulates most strongly in SUB-CULTURES of those people generally well down in the HIERARCHY and who tend to be last in the queue when information is passed through formal channels.

The only antidote to rumour is efficient, full and open, participative communication, with strong lines of horizontal as well as vertical interaction. The impact of rumour is rarely beneficial; in the main, rumour is corrosive of relationships, fuels suspicion and bad feeling. Its favourite habitat is a communication vacuum. One dubious compensation is that the subjects, or 'victims', of rumour are generally the last to hear of it; unless, of course, they started the rumour themselves. See INTERPERSONAL COMMUNICATION; LOONY LEFTISM.

Running story See SPOT NEWS.

Rushdie affair See FATWA.

Rushes In film-making, prints of 'takes' that are made immediately after a day's shooting; these are examined by the film team, led by the director, before the next day's shooting. Produced at a 'rush' from negative, they are also known as 'dailies'.

S

Salience All messages are not given equal attention by the receiver; some messages, or parts of a message, appear more prominent, more *salient*, to the receiver. This predisposition towards certain messages, or parts of a MESSAGE, can be the result of a complex range of factors such as life experience, attitudes, VALUES and interests. There has been considerable research into the role of the media in the formation of salience, particularly in the field of current affairs.

The focus of investigation here is the extent to which media coverage of certain issues leads the AUDIENCE to perceive those issues as being politically significant. See AGENDA-SETTING; ATTRIBUTE DIMENSION; MCCOMBS AND SHAW'S AGENDA-SETTING MODEL OF MEDIA EFFECTS, 1978.

Salon discourse According to Susan Herbst and James R. Beniger in 'The changing infrastructure of public opinion' in *Audiencemaking: How Media Create the Audience* (Sage, 1994), edited by James S. Ettema and D. Charles Whitney, the first use of the term 'public opinion' was made by Jacques Necker, the finance minister to the French King Louis XIV (1638–1715). Necker was referring specifically to the salons of the day, generally if not always presided over by women of high birth and attended by intellectuals, poets, statesmen and philosophers.

Here, among many things, matters of state were freely discussed and later diffused by the writings of those who attended the salons. Herbst and Beniger refer to this as the *elite model* of public opinion infrastructure: 'The public in the model is composed only of the most highly educated and influential members of society, while the bulk of the people are purposely excluded because their opinion is thought to be uninformed, and are in any case irrelevant – most people have no political power.' The authors argue that this model of public opinion held sway until the American and French revolutions.

Salutation display Means by which we demonstrate that we wish someone well, or at the very least do not ostensibly wish them harm: greeting them when we meet and when we part company. Salutation display varies according to such factors as the nature of our relationship with the greeted person, the context of the encounter and the length of prior separation. See GESTURE; SHORTFALL SIGNALS.

Samizdat Russian, meaning 'self-published', a secret publication during the Soviet-Communist era, circulated by hand, usually printed on a duplicator or simply on a typewriter with carbon copies, by dissident writers, at great personal risk of reprisals by the authorities. *The First Circle* (1968) by Russian novelist Alexander Solzhenitsyn (1918–2008) began life in Samizdat. The word *Tamizdat* described work produced by Russians in the West, published there and then smuggled into the Soviet Union. *Dr Zhivago* (1957) by Boris Pasternak (1890–1960) is an example of this. See GLASNOST.

Sampling A statistical method of selecting a group for analysis, from a larger social group known as the *population*; the statistical term for all those persons, events or entities that are relevant to the subject of the enquiry. The aim of sampling is to be able to use what is discovered about the sample group as a basis for inference about the behaviour of the population. The reliability of such inferences depends upon how far the sample is representative of the population. A *representative sample* is constructed in such a way that it contains members of various significant categories and classifications in the same proportion as they appear in the population.

Not all samples are representative, or quota, samples: *random sampling* techniques are also used. A random sample is selected in such a way that every member of the population has an equal chance of being chosen. Such a sample is used when it is felt that the population is not divided into particularly significant categories or classifications. See *TOPIC GUIDE* under RESEARCH METHODS.

Sapir-Whorf linguistic relativity hypothesis Developed by two notable linguists, Edward Sapir (1884–1939) and Benjamin Lee Whorf (1897–1941). Succinctly stated, the hypothesis proposes that ways of thinking and patterns of CULTURE (and also to some extent social structure) are determined by the structure of the language used in a particular culture. An individual's or group's thought and DISCOURSE about life generally can only be expressed in language and is thus constrained by the language structure available.

Satellite transmission There are three main types of satellite: (1) weather and observational satellites; (2) communications satellites; and (3) space probes. Sputnik in 1957 was the first observational satellite; Telstar, in 1962, the first communications satellite. Working off solar-powered batteries, satellites have equipment for monitoring the conditions in and around themselves and sending data back to earth for control purposes. Also, they carry reception equipment for control signals from earth for correction of orbital travel, etc. Satellites orbiting the earth have generally given way to geo-stationary operation, that is satellites stationed some 23,000 miles out in space at a constant altitude and keeping pace with the revolutions of the earth.

Signals from ground stations are beamed to the geo-stationary communications satellites and reflected by them to receiving stations that then relay the signals by cable for recording or transmission, or to receiving 'dishes' or antennae. Most communication satellites receive and transmit simultaneously from a number of earth stations.

TV pictures were first transmitted via satellite on 10 July 1962 when Telstar was launched at Cape Canaveral, USA, and circled the earth every 157.8 minutes, enabling live TV pictures transmitted from Andover, Maine, to be received at Goonhilly Down, Cornwall and in Brittany (11 July). In 1964 the unmanned Syncom relayed pictures of the Olympic Games from Tokyo. The first commercial communications satellite was Early Bird, which marked the beginning of regular TV transmission via satellite (2 May 1965).

The UK franchise for a three-transponder direct-broadcast satellite (DBS) was granted in 1986, with a start date of 1990. After financial and investment doubts which led to early backers such as the BBC withdrawing from DBS plans, the contract for Britain's first two DBS channels was awarded to British Satellite Broadcasting (BSB). Rupert Murdoch's Sky Satellite arrived ahead of BSB, beginning programme transmission in the UK in March 1989.

Between them, the rival companies are estimated to have spent £1.25 billion, yet by October 1990, such were the colossal start-up expenses that British Satellite Broadcasting was forced into a merger with Sky. The 'squarial' dish, created to bring BSB programmes into the home, suddenly became scrap. The founding principle of the free market – that competition is the basic dynamic of success – was itself 'squarialized'. Sky took on the initials of BSB, becoming British Sky Television. Corporate monopoly of satellite transmission joined that of those other 'free enterprise' industries in the UK – rail transport, gas, water and electricity.

Murdoch's ambition to make NEWS CORP a global provider of TV programming was marked in the 1990s with the acquisition of Star Television in Asia. In November 1995 News Corp joined with the Globo Organization of Brazil, Grupo Televisa of Mexico, and Telecommunications Inc. of the US to set up a satellite TV service for Latin American and Caribbean markets with estimated total launch costs of US$ 500 million. See COMMUNICATIONS ACT (UK), 2003; CROSS-MEDIA OWNERSHIP. See also *TOPIC GUIDE* under MEDIA: TECHNOLOGIES.

Scheduling Process by which programmes or types of programme are 'timetabled' in order to attract maximum audiences, and to keep them attracted in the face of competition from rival programmes. The aim of the programme scheduler is to minimize the danger of audiences switching off, or even worse, over. Low-appeal programmes are usually placed against weak opposition, or they are 'hammocked', that is placed between 'bankers', trusting to the INHERITANCE FACTOR. Conversely there is the so-called 'pre-echo' effect where anticipation of a really popular programme can induce viewers to switch on earlier and thus watch a programme with less popular appeal.

Scheduling techniques assume a high degree of passivity on the part of an audience, and might be said seriously to underestimate audience potential for variety and challenge. Competitive scheduling above all reduces the range of choice open to the viewer simply by making risk-taking more difficult. In any case, the ability of viewers to decide their own viewing schedules by video and DVD recording complicates the best intentions of programmers, though *custom* and *habit* continue to serve as vital allies of planning.

Schema (plural, schemata) A schema is basically a framework or pattern, stored in the memory, which preserves and organizes information about some event or concept. The framework may be expanded as new information about the event or concept is acquired. It is argued by several researchers concerned with learning and memory that existing schemata affect our PERCEPTION of new information, and that there is a tendency for us to try and fit new information into our existing frameworks, at least initially.

Schemata themselves can form cross-linkages to provide a wider mental or conceptual map of an area of knowledge or experience. This perspective on the way in which we receive and process information has important implications for the analysis of the way in which we send and receive messages in the communication process.

★**Schramm's models of communication, 1954** Wilbur Schramm built on SHANNON AND WEAVER'S MODEL OF COMMUNICATION, 1949 (The Mathematical Theory of Communication), but was more interested in mass communication than in the technology of communication transmission. In 'How communication works' in Wilbur Schramm, ed., *The Process and Effects of Mass Communication* (University of Illinois Press, 1954) the author poses three models (see figure). Shannon and Weaver's 'Transmitter' and 'Receiver' become 'Encoder' and 'Decoder', and their essentially linear model is restructured in Schramm's second model to demonstrate the overlapping, interactive nature of the communication process and the importance of what the Encoder and Decoder bring with them to the communication situation – their 'Field of Experience'. Where that field of experience overlaps

S

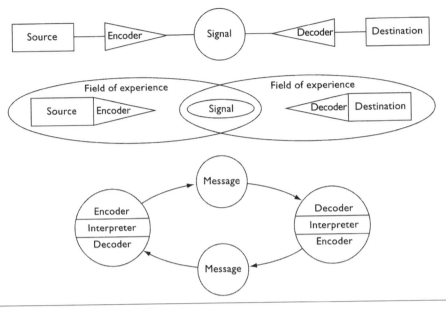

Schramm's models of communication, 1954

is the signal. Schramm's third model emphasizes FEEDBACK, and in doing so points up the circularity of the communication process. See TOPIC GUIDE under COMMUNICATION MODELS.

Scripts These are described by Eric Berne in *What Do You Say After You Say Hello?* (Corgi Books, 1975) as 'a preconscious life plan' by which an individual structures 'longer periods of time – months, years or his whole life'. Scripts are developed in our early years but then have the capacity to influence and shape our transactions with others. A script contains within it an individual's SELF-CONCEPT and his/her general perception of and orientation towards other people and the world. It thus forms a basis for action. Berne identifies a number of possible scripts individuals may have as a result of their early experiences.

One example is the 'You Can't Trust Anybody' script. An individual with this script would obviously be suspicious and distrustful of others and act accordingly. Such a script has obvious implications for communication with others. Berne argues that individuals tend to seek proof that their scripts are valid, by behaving in a way or interpreting behaviour in a manner that will reinforce them. So to a greater or lesser extent, behaviour might be script-driven. Scripts can obviously be limiting but can, of course, be changed.

In *TA Today* (Lifespace, 1987) Ian Stewart and Vann Joines discuss three main types of script: Winning, Losing (or *hamartic*, from the Greek,

meaning basic flaw) and Non-winning (or *banal*) scripts. A 'winner' is an individual who achieves the goals he/she has set for him/herself. It is also implied that these are met 'comfortably, happily and smoothly'.

A loser does not achieve set goals, or does but is unhappy or damaged as a result. The losing script may resemble ancient Greek drama, when the basic flaw seems to lead inexorably to tragic finale. A non-winning or banal script is one focused on playing safe and not taking risks. It may result in small gains and losses but the individual will remain a 'non-winner'. It seems that many people have a mixture of scripts: winning in some aspects of life whilst losing in others.

Berne's ideas have been applied to the development of interpersonal communication skills in a range of fields such as management, therapy and customer relations. See LIFE POSITIONS; TRANSACTIONAL ANALYSIS.

▶ Claude M. Steiner, *Scripts People Live: Transactional Analysis in Life Scripts* (Grove Press, 1990); Graeme Burton and Richard Dimbleby, *Between Ourselves: An Introduction to Interpersonal Communication* (Hodder Arnold, 2006).

Secondary viewing Term describing the circumstances in which TV viewing forms an accompaniment to other activities such as homework and reading.

Segmentation Refers in a specific sense to the constituent nature of TV – chopped up into segments, of NEWS, comedy, drama, commercial, DOCUMENTARY, quiz shows, etc.

John Fiske in 'Moments of television', in Ellen Seiter *et al*, *Remote Control: Television, Audience and Cultural Power* (Routledge, 1989), writes, 'Segmented texts are marked by abrupt transformations from segment to segment that require active, experienced, televisionally literate viewers to negotiate.'

In a wider sense, and in relation to ADVERTISING and the targeting of AUDIENCES for the sale of goods and services (not to mention the marketing of images, ideas, ideologies, political parties, etc.), segmentation relates to current practices dividing consumers into lifestyle categories. Segmentation indicates a recognition that audiences are heterogeneous (characterized by difference) rather than homogeneous (characterized by sameness). Classification of audience into socio-economic groupings has become an industry in its own right. See *TOPIC GUIDE* under ADVERTISING/MARKETING.

Selective exposure Individuals have a tendency to attend to – expose themselves to – messages that are consistent with their existing attitudes and beliefs. Equally they practise *selective perception* – reading messages in accordance with their existing attitudes. Thus they may either ignore or misinterpret those messages, or parts of a message, which conflict with or are dissimilar to held attitudes and expectations. Sometimes also referred to as *selective negligence*. See DISSONANCE; REINFORCEMENT.

Self-actualization See MASLOW'S HIERARCHY OF NEEDS.

Self-concept A person's self-concept is the total view that person has of him/herself. It includes such elements as an individual's view of his/her character, body image, abilities, emotions, qualities and relationships with others. The self-concept is commonly seen as being composed of the self-image and self-esteem. The self-image can be seen as the descriptive part of the self-concept; it is the picture we have of ourselves. Self-esteem on the other hand is the evaluative part; how we feel about ourselves.

The self-image can be further divided into three elements: 'the self as I think I am'; 'the self as I think others see me'; and 'the self I would like to be' (the ideal self-image). Discrepancies between the ideal self-image and 'the self as I think I am' can result in a low level of self-esteem, as our self-esteem is usually based on our perceived successes and failures in life. Other people are clearly very influential in shaping any individual's conception of self, as an individual's self-concept depends in part upon his/her perception of the ideas others have about them. Individuals also attempt to influence the ideas others have, by controlling the impressions they create in self-presentation. The feedback received from self-presentation enables the individual both to evaluate and to shape his/her self-image.

Messages concerning the self abound in the content of INTERPERSONAL COMMUNICATION, whilst INTRAPERSONAL COMMUNICATION also plays a vital role, not only in the generation of ideas about ourselves – some of which we may incorporate into the self which we present to others for feedback – but also in the decoding and evaluating of messages that we receive from others and in deciding whether or how to act on them.

How we see ourselves affects the way we communicate. If, for example, we see ourselves as popular and sociable, we are likely to be confident and outgoing in our communication with others. Excessive concern over self-esteem can lead to self-consciousness. People who are self-conscious are often shy, easily embarrassed and anxious in the presence of other people.

It should be remembered that the self-concept is not fixed, but rather is subject to continuing modification and change; it can alter according to the situations we are in, the people we are with, and over time; it may also be found in mass communication, for example in images of idealized men and women found in advertisements. See ASSERTIVENESS TRAINING; CONFIRMATION/DISCOMFIRMATION; DEVIANCE AMPLIFICATION; IMPRESSION MANAGEMENT; JOHARI WINDOW; LABELLING PROCESS (AND THE MEDIA); LOOKISM; SELF-DISCLOSURE; SELF-FULFILLING PROPHECY; SELF-IDENTITY; SELF-MONITORING; SELF-PRESENTATION.

▶ Brian Morris, *Anthropology of The Self: The Individual in Cultural Perspective* (Pluto 1994).

Self-disclosure Process by which, through statements verbal and non-verbal, we transmit new information about ourselves to others. Self-disclosure is based on honest, open interaction between people. Our decision to disclose information about ourselves is usually related to the development and intimacy of a relationship. Usually when we self-disclose to others, they reciprocate and in this way a deeper understanding and relationship may develop. As Steve Duck notes in *Human Relationships* (Sage, 2007), 'people feel they should reveal personal information about themselves as appropriate to the script for stages' in the development of that relationship.

Of course we have to make careful choices in

the first place about those to whom we will self-disclose, at what rate, to what extent, on what topics and in what situations. Self-disclosure usually requires trust, as it involves an element of risk; if, for example, we self-disclose too much too soon in a relationship, the result may be a rebuff.

Through self-disclosure we not only learn more about others, we also learn more about ourselves, in that others' disclosures can contain views about us. It is also a means by which we can come to terms with the positive and negative aspects of our self-image. See JOHARI WINDOW; SCRIPTS; SELF-CONCEPT; SELF-PRESENTATION.

▶ Kathryn Dindia and Steve Duck, eds, *Communication and Personal Relationships* (John Wiley & Sons, 2000); Sandra Petronio, *Boundaries of Privacy: Dialectics of Disclosure* (State University of New York Press, 2002).

Self-fulfilling prophecy This effect occurs when the act of predicting that certain behaviour will take place helps cause that behaviour to occur and the prediction or prophecy is fulfilled. The expectations people have of an individual's behaviour can, if communicated to the individual, help create a situation in which the individual conforms to the expectations and fulfils the prophecy. There is a clear link between LABELLING and the self-fulfilling prophecy effect in that the act of applying a label can be the first step in ensuring a self-fulfilling prophecy.

The effect may be found particularly in situations where individuals have differing amounts of power, and where one or more individuals are involved in the evaluating of others. Clearly the message contained in interpersonal and mass communication may often carry labels and thus have the potential for triggering self-fulfilling prophecy effects, but it is largely through INTRAPERSONAL COMMUNICATION that an individual decides whether or not to conform to the expectations of others. Further, the self-fulfilling prophecy effect is only one of many influences on our behaviour and it may not be relevant in all cases. See DEVIANCE AMPLIFICATION; LABELLING PROCESS (AND THE MEDIA); SELF-CONCEPT. See also *TOPIC GUIDE* under COMMUNICATION THEORY.

Self-identity Stella Ting-Toomey in *Communication Across Cultures* (Guildford Press, 1999) comments that 'individuals acquire their identities via interaction with others'. Theorists from a number of intellectual traditions have explored the connections between social interaction and the development and maintenance of the SELF-CONCEPT and self-identity. These form part of an ongoing debate concerning the relative importance of structure (societal influences) and agency (an individual's thoughts and actions) in the formation of the self.

Charles H. Cooley in *Human Nature and Social Order* (Shocken, 1902) developed the notion of the 'looking-glass self'. For Cooley, an important influence on the development of the self is the responses that others make to us and to our behaviour. These responses serve as a looking-glass from which we learn to see ourselves as we imagine others see us. This feedback aids us in understanding who we are.

Building on Cooley's work, George H. Mead in *Mind, Self and Society* (University of Chicago Press, 1934) argues that the self is made by a reflexive process involving self-interaction between the 'I' and the 'Me'; the 'I' being the act of experiencing and the 'Me' the socialized part of the self, the object with which the 'I' experiences and interacts. The 'Me' is the view of the self that an observer might have.

Language is seen as a crucial medium by which the individual represents itself to itself. Self-interaction enables the human being to develop the self, to define and interpret his/her world and to organize actions based on such interpretations; in short to be an active social agent. It is through interaction with others, especially role-playing, that the individual learns the ability to see him/herself as others do, an ability which aids awareness and identification of the self, and allows the 'Me' to expand.

In particular, through developing the mechanism of the 'generalized other', the individual acquires the ability to predict how people in general might evaluate him/her in the light of his/her behaviour. For Mead, 'it is this generalized other in his experience which provides him with a self'. Mead's ideas highlight the role that others can play in construction of self-identity.

Erving Goffman in The *Presentation of Self in Everyday Life* (Allen Lane, Penguin Press, 1959) highlights the way in which the self-concept is developed through a process by which the individual presents aspects of the self to others on which he/she then receives feedback. The degree of calculation in acts of SELF-PRESENTATION, though, will usually vary with the situation. Goffman argues that the sustaining of everyday performances is important both to the development and maintenance of the self-concept, and thus also to self-identity. Disturbances in such performances constitute, therefore, a threat: 'Life may not be much of a gamble, but interaction is'. Competent performances require considerable day-to-day control and the appropriate employment of personae. In a similar vein, Eric M. Eisenberg writes of 'the "multiplicity of selves" that each one of us may perform at any given moment' ('Building a mystery: toward a new theory of communication and identity', *Journal of Communication*, 534–52, 2001).

As Kath Woodward comments in *Understanding Identity* (Arnold, 2002), 'identity involves the interrelationship between the personal and the social; between what I feel inside and what is known about me from the outside'. Psychoanalytic theories such as those of Freud and Jung focus more on internal processes and the conflict between inner desires and the demands of others, of society. These theories view much of our behaviour as influenced by forces within the unconscious. Self-knowledge is therefore limited and self-identity partial, provisional and vulnerable to fracture.

For Freud there is an inevitable conflict between what he argued are the three components of an individual's personality: the id, the ego and the superego. The id reacts to basic biological instincts and operates on the Pleasure Principle, in that it encourages behaviour that seeks pleasure and avoids pain.

The ego, according to Richard D. Gross in *Psychology: The Science of Mind and Behaviour* (Hodder Arnold, 2005), can be 'described as the "executive" of the personality, the planning, decision-making, rational and logical part of us'. The ego operates on the Reality Principle. It is concerned with the social consequences of our behaviour and the resulting judgments others would make. Thus it seeks to control influences from the id that would, if acted on, result in social criticism or rejection.

The superego contains our ideas about what is morally right or wrong. It also seeks to control influences from the id, through the ego, if they are likely to result in behaviour of which our own superego would disapprove. The ego may on occasions counsel against behaviour in line with the superego's demands.

Richard Gross comments, 'the ego, the person's conscious self, is caught in the middle of opposing sets of demands, it is the battleground on which three opposing factions (reality, the id and the superego) fight for supremacy'. The id lies in the unconscious part of the mind, whilst parts of the ego and superego are in the conscious and parts in the unconscious mind.

The ego mediates between these factions to obtain a compromise and, according to Freud, is aided by three processes: Dreams, Neurotic

Symptoms and Defence Mechanisms. We are not usually aware of the operation of these processes. The Defence Mechanisms (for example: Repression, Denial, IDENTIFICATION, Sublimation, PROJECTION) in particular can be seen to have consequences for the study of social interaction and for the analysis of responses to mass media messages (see TRANSACTIONAL ANALYSIS).

Another perspective offered by Anthony Giddens in *Modernity and Self-Identity* (Polity Press, 1991) considers the impact of societal influences upon the formation of self-identity. Giddens defines self-identity in the conditions of late modernity as 'the self as reflexively understood by the person in terms of his or her biography'. Whilst self-identity is seen as normally having a degree of continuity, it is 'such continuity as interpreted reflexively by the agent'. Self-identity also involves cognitive awareness of the self: 'To be a "person" is not just to be a reflexive actor, but to have a concept of a person.' Self-identity is an integral element of the SELF-CONCEPT.

Further, Giddens agues that 'a person's identity is not to be found in behaviour, nor – important though it is – in the reactions of others, but in the capacity *to keep a particular narrative going*'; a narrative that enables us to make sense of ourselves. INTRAPERSONAL COMMUNICATION clearly also plays a crucial role in this process as we reflect on our everyday encounters.

Giddens identifies four influences evident in the structure of post-traditional societies which create the plurality of choices that make difficult the struggle of maintaining a coherent self-identity, and which make necessary a PROJECT OF SELF. Identities can only be achieved through choice – 'we have no choice but to choose' – given that much of the tradition which allowed them to be ascribed or indicated has lost its hold.

Individuals inhabit a 'pluralization of life-worlds' in which they have to present a number of different identities as they move from one social sphere to another, often negotiating differing expectations of their behaviour as they do so. What Giddens terms 'methodological doubt' is yet another feature of late modernity; certainty is seen as fragile as truth is seen as contextual and authority and reason provisional. 'Mediated experience' is seen to be at the heart of social life. Through the mass media and travel, a vast range of 'lifeworlds' are presented to audiences, thus increasing the range of options available in the construction of identities.

Further, such identities have to be adjusted

S

to cope with the range of changes that an individual is likely to encounter in such a society; the change to self-identity that usually accompanies a divorce being but one example. Giddens argues that little help is available to individuals in making such choices, although artefacts within consumer CULTURE may promise guidance – self-help manuals, for example. The ability to control SELF-PRESENTATION and in doing this to actively construct and reconstruct bodily appearance is seen by Giddens as essential to maintaining a coherent self-identity.

Don Slater notes in *Consumer Culture & Modernity* (Polity Press, 1997) that another influence on late modernity – 'commercialization' – has resulted in 'a greater fluidity in the use of goods to construct identities and lifestyles'. It has also resulted, arguably, in individuals perceiving themselves, in part, as consumers; a perception which would reinforce the notion that individuals must make choices.

There are, of course, innumerable attempts to appeal to aspects of the self in ADVERTISING and marketing. The danger, warns Giddens, is that 'the project of self becomes translated into one of possession of desired goods and the pursuit of artificially framed styles of life ... The consumption of ever-novel goods becomes a substitute for the genuine development of self'.

Eric M. Eisenberg in 'Building a mystery: toward a new theory of communication and identity', *Journal of Communication* (2001) echoes Giddens's view that awareness of uncertainty, whilst not unique to modern times, presents a significant challenge to the narrative and development of self-identity – especially to the development of the flexible self-identity needed to effectively deal with such uncertainty. He also, among others, argues that for those in the Western world, the self is often viewed as resting in the uniqueness of the individual; whereas in the Eastern world it is more often seen as located within and subject to the collective identity.

In the digital age it is now possible to also construct a second-life identity and virtual relationships. This raises the question of whether the line between online and offline identities can become blurred, and to what extent one can seep into the other. There is certainly some evidence that people can become very engrossed in online identities and relationships. David McNeill writing in the *Independent* ('Virtual killer faces real jail after murder by mouse', 24 October 2008) tells the story of a Japanese woman whose second-life character was 'divorced' by the second-life character of a man she 'married' in an

online game. She was so enraged that she hacked into his computer and 'erased his carefully constructed digital character'. She was arrested on the charge of illegally using his password and ID, not for virtual murder. See EISENBERG'S MODEL OF COMMUNICATION AND IDENTITY, 2001; IMPRESSION MANAGEMENT; MASLOW'S HIERARCHY OF NEEDS; SELF-CONCEPT; SELF-MONITORING; VIRTUAL REALITY; secondlife.com.

Self-image See SELF-CONCEPT.

Self-monitoring This term refers to the degree to which people are sensitive to, and able to respond to, the demands of social situations with regard to their own behaviour. Richard D. Gross in *Psychology: the Science of Mind and Behaviour* (Hodder Arnold, 2006) identifies high and low self-monitors. High self-monitors are motivated to and able to assess the demands of different situations and adjust their SELF-PRESENTATION and general behaviour accordingly.

Low self-monitors on the other hand tend to behave in a similar fashion regardless of the situation, and their behaviour is more likely to be influenced by their own internal states. High self-monitors appear much more able to conceal their own moods, feelings and so on. Evidence suggests that high self-monitors have better social skills; for example, they can interpret nonverbal communication more accurately than low self-monitors.

Self-presentation Term used to describe the way in which we behave and communicate in differing social situations. It carries with it the implication that to some degree, we consciously present ourselves to others in any given situation. The feedback we gain from self-presentation plays a role in shaping and changing our SELF-CONCEPT. Erving Goffman in *The Presentation of Self in Everyday Life* (Anchor, 1959; Penguin, 1971) employs the dramaturgical perspective to analyse social interaction. Goffman writes, 'Life itself is a dramatically enacted thing. All the world is not, of course a stage, but the crucial ways in which it is not are not easy to specify ... In short, we all act better than we know how.'

Goffman puts forward several useful concepts that have become influential in analysing self-presentation. A key concept is that of *persona*. The persona is the character we take on to play a part in a particular social situation. Different situations will usually require us to play different parts and therefore to adopt different personas. So, for example, the persona an individual would adopt when visiting a folk festival with friends might be very different from the persona he/she would adopt in carrying out his/her work role as a High Court judge or an attorney.

The persona is part of our way of dealing with different people and the demands of different social situations. Once chosen for a particular situation, it influences how we communicate in that situation. The ability to choose an appropriate persona for a situation and to communicate accordingly can be seen as an important communication skill, as can the ability to shift from one persona to another as situations demand it. Also, it is likely that the role a person is playing may dictate the kinds of persona it would be appropriate to adopt in any given situation.

Goffman uses the term *performance* to describe the act of self-presentation, and in many cases these performances can be seen as staged. In staging a performance in everyday life we would use props just as actors would on a theatre stage; obvious examples here are dress, cars and furnishings. A well-established pattern of action that may be used as part of a performance is known as a *routine*. An example here would be a characteristic display of temper.

According to Goffman we also perform from behind a *front*, which he defines as 'that part of the individual's performance which regularly functions in a general and fixed fashion to define the situation for those who observe the performance'. Standard parts of the front are the setting, for example one's home, and the personal front – age, dress, sex. See CONFIRMATION/DISCOMFORMATION; IMPRESSION MANAGEMENT; PROJECT OF SELF; SELF-MONITORING. See also TOPIC GUIDE under INTERPERSONAL COMMUNICATION.

Self-regulation Although BROADCASTING in the UK has traditionally been regulated by acts of Parliament and governing charters, the press has been self-regulating. The Press Council was an advisory body, set up by the newspaper industry; its successor, the PRESS COMPLAINTS COMMISSION, which started work on 1 January 1991, has similarly no statutory powers. The question often asked is whether the press, dominated by a handful of media barons, can be left to regulate itself – that is, be judge of its own malpractices.

In the wake of the death of Princess Diana of Wales in 1997, issues of self-regulation were widely discussed, and the UK newspaper industry responded to public concern by agreeing to bide by criteria for respecting PRIVACY and curtailing media intrusion. In any event, the UK Labour government's incorporation into British law of the European Convention on Human Rights (see HUMAN RIGHTS ACT, 2000) made the privacy of the individual a legal right in Britain for the first time.

However, the most recent scandal concerning the conduct of the press broke in July 2011, and focused on alleged phone-hacking activities by the *News of the World* – although a number of other newspapers are also suspected of being involved in such activities. The scandal prompted widespread discussion of the perceived failure of self-regulation under the auspices of the Press Complaints Commission. The Prime Minster, David Cameron, ordered an inquiry into the regulation of the press with a view to introducing more robust procedures. See CALCUTT COMMITTEE ON PRIVACY AND RELATED MATTERS, 1990 AND 1993; PHONE-HACKING. See also TOPIC GUIDE under BROADCASTING.

★**Self-to-Self model of interpersonal communication, 2007** Published at the conclusion of a chapter on models, 'Communication by design' in *Key Themes in Interpersonal Communication* (Open University, 2007) by Anne Hill, James Watson, Danny Rivers and Mark Joyce, this model assembles and connects constructs of, and influences upon, people in communication. The chapter, by James Watson, cites a previously illustrated model posited by Eric M. Eisenberg (see EISENBERG'S MODEL OF COMMUNICATION AND IDENTITY, 2001), where *identity* and *circumstance* are seen in a relationship where the latter constantly influences the nature and activity of the former. In the Self-to-Self model, key factors of self-awareness, self-concept, self-image and self-belief operate in relation to such variables as communicative competence and awareness of other.

This process is varyingly influenced by events and circumstances outside of our interaction with others and those which are part of what we bring to every interaction, such as our education, ethnicity, culture and motivation (see INTERVENING VARIABLES (IVs)). We recognize the vulnerabilities – the uncertainties – concerning our self-identity as we do with that vital contributory factor, confidence. In Note 7 of the chapter in *Key Themes*, the author writes how 'in encounters and interactions communicators use strategies to reduce uncertainty about each other, a key aim being to increase the ability to predict the behaviour of self and other in communicative situations' and to react accordingly.

Selsdon Committee Report on Television (UK), 1935 The task of Lord Selsdon's Committee was 'to consider the development of Television and advise the Post-master-General on the relative merits of several systems and on the

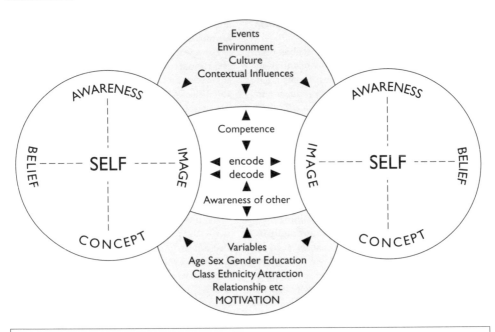

Self-to-Self model of interpersonal communication, 2007

conditions under which any public television should be provided'. The Report recommended that the BBC be made the initiating body, and that the cost of TV broadcasting be borne from the revenue derived from the existing 10 shilling radio licence fee. See *TOPIC GUIDE* under COMMISSIONS, COMMITTEES, LEGISLATION.

Semantic code See CODES OF NARRATIVE.

Semantic differential The analysis of semantic differential is one of three traditional empirical methods of measuring AUDIENCE response to the media, the others being CONTENT ANALYSIS and the investigation of uses and gratifications (see USES AND GRATIFICATIONS THEORY). In exploring semantic – or MEANING – differentials, analysts concentrate on people's attitudes, feelings and emotions towards certain concepts and VALUES as actuated by media performance. The values under scrutiny are presented in preliminary form by words or statements.

These are then selected and expressed as binarily opposed concepts (Offensive-Not Offensive, for example) on a five- or seven-point scale. Binary opposition is the most extreme form of significant difference possible. A sample audience, or selected group, is tested on the scale or scales, and the results averaged. The method was given currency by Charles Osgood in *The Measurement of Meaning* (University of Illinois Press, 1967). See *TOPIC GUIDE* under RESEARCH METHODS.

Semantics A major branch of linguistics in which the MEANING of language is analysed. The study of the origins of the form and meaning of words is Etymology, a branch of Semantics. The crucial point about the study of Semantics is that it is an exploration of change – how the context of usage, historical, social, cultural, etc. – alters the meanings of words and expressions used. When King James II observed that the new St Paul's Cathedral was 'amusing, awful and artificial' he did not intend to be derogatory about Sir Christopher Wren's masterpiece; rather he meant that it was 'pleasing, awe-inspiring, and skilfully achieved'.

The differences are, of course, far from merely evolutionary. What, for example, is the meaning of the word 'equality'? Its definition is modified by the perceptions and VALUES of all those who use it, and the situation in which it is used. As Simeon Potter points out in *Our Language* (Penguin, 1950), 'Men frequently find themselves at cross-purposes with one another because they persist in using words in different senses. Their long arguments emit more heat than light because their conceptions of the point at issue, whether Marxism, democracy, capitalism, the good life, western civilization, culture, art, internationalism, freedom of the individual, equality of opportunity, redistribution of wealth, social security, progress, or what not, are by no means identical. From heedless sloth, or sheer lack of intelligence men do not trouble to clarify their conceptions.' Semantics, therefore, must lie at the heart of any serious study of communication processes. See *TOPIC GUIDE* under LANGUAGE/DISCOURSE/NARRATIVE.

Semiology/semiotics Word derives from the Greek, *semeion*, meaning sign, and semiology is the general science of sign systems and their role in the construction and reconstruction of MEANING. All social life, indeed every facet of social practice, is *mediated* by language conceived as a system of signs and representations, arranged by codes and articulated through various discourses. Sign systems, believes the semiologist, have no fixed meaning. The perception of the sign system rests upon the social context of the participants and the interaction between them.

Semiology examines the SIGN itself, the CODES or systems into which the signs are organized, and the CULTURE within which these codes and signs operate. The primary focus of semiology is upon the TEXT, preferring the term *reader* (even of a painting, photograph or film) to receiver because it implies a greater degree of activity, and that the process of reading is socially and culturally conditioned. The reader helps to create the meaning and significance of the text by bringing to it his/her experience, values and emotional responses.

There is special emphasis on the link between the reading and the IDEOLOGY of the reader. 'Wherever a sign is present,' writes V.N. Volosinov in *Marxism and the Philosophy of Language* (Seminar Press, 1973), 'ideology is present too. Everything ideological possesses a semiotic value'; or as Umberto Eco says, 'Semiology shows us the universe of ideologies arranged in codes and sub-codes within the universe of signs' (in 'Articulations of the cinematic code' in *Cinematics* 1, undated).

The theories of Swiss linguist Ferdinand de Saussure (1857–1913) provided the foundation stone of Semiology. His lectures, *Cours de Linguistique Générale* (1916), were published after his death by two pupils, Charles Bally and Albert Sechehaye. De Saussure set out to demonstrate that speech is not merely a linear sequence like beads on a string, but a system and structure where points on the string relate to other points on the string in various ways (the so-called *syntagmic* structure) and operate in a network of relationships with other possible points which could substitute for it (the *paradigmic* structure).

The American logician and philosopher C.S. Peirce (1834–1914) approached the structure of

language with a wider-angle lens, conceiving semiotics (the term preferred in the US) as being an interdisciplinary science in which sign systems manifested in structures and levels could be analysed from philosophical, psychological and sociological as well as linguistic points of view. Peirce and other philosophers such as Charles Morris and Rudolph Carnap saw the field as divisible into three areas: *semantics*, the study of the links between linguistic expressions and the objects in the world to which they refer or which they describe; *syntactics*, the study of the relation of these expressions to each other; and *pragmatics*, the study of the dependence of the meaning of these expressions on their users (including the social context in which they are used).

The terminology of semiology/semiotics is complex and daunting, but the names Peirce gave to his categories are worth quoting here: the sign he called an *icon* resembles the object it wishes to describe, like a photograph; an *index* establishes a direct link between the sign and its object (smoke is an index of fire); finally, the *symbol* where there is neither connection nor resemblance between sign and object. A symbol communicates only because there is agreement among people that it shall stand for what it does (letters combined into words are symbols).

Semiology has come to apply, as a system of analysis, to every aspect of communication. There is practically nothing that is not a sign capable of meaning, or signification. The work of the French philosopher Roland Barthes (1915–80) has exercised particular influence on our understanding of areas such as music, eating, clothes and dance as well as language. See PARADIGM; MYTH. See also *TOPIC GUIDES* under COMMUNICATION THEORY; LANGUAGE/DISCOURSE/NARRATIVE.

▶ Elliot Gaines, *Media Literacy and Semiotics* (Palgrave Macmillan, 2011).

Semiosic plane See MIMETIC/SEMIOSIC PLANES.

Semiotic power The power, by members of the public – AUDIENCE, consumers – to turn the consumerist signs and symbols which dominate contemporary life to their own uses. The case is put by John Fiske who, while acknowledging the power of ADVERTISING and consumerist PROPAGANDA generally, gives substantial credit to individuals to exercise a 'semiotic power' – resistance – of their own.

Our initial impression of the public flocking, for example, to an enticing new shopping mall might be to see it as a clear indicator of corporate influence at work. However, Fiske argues in his chapter 'Shopping for pleasure' in *Reading the Popular* (Unwin Hyman, 1989) that 'the department store was the first public space legitimately available to women' and the 'fashionable commodities it offers provide a legitimated public identity and a means of participating in the ideology of progress'.

For Fiske 'the meanings of commodities do not lie in themselves as objects, and are not determined by their conditions of production and distribution, but are produced finally by the way they are consumed'. While he readily agrees that resistance from the bottom up in society is difficult and rarely likely to be effective beyond the micro-level of everyday life, this is not a reason to deny its existence. He writes, 'Scholarship that neglects or devalues these practices seems to me to be guilty of a disrespect for the weak that is politically reprehensible'.

Big companies may make style, in clothes or more broadly in lifestyle, but such styles are not followed slavishly. Rather they are appropriated: 'Women, despite the wide variety of social formations to which they belong, all share the experience of subordination under patriarchy and have evolved a variety of tactical responses that enable them to deal with it on a day-to-day level. So, too, other subordinated groups, however defined – by class, race, age, religion, or whatever – have evolved everyday practices that enable them to live within and against the forces that subordinate them'.

Fiske refers to people as forging their own meanings out of the signifiers available to them, exerting semiotic power, and though working only at the micro-level of society 'may well act as a constant erosive force upon the macro, weakening the system from within so that it is more amenable to change at the structural level'. See AGORA; AUDIENCE: ACTIVE AUDIENCE; NETWORKING: SOCIAL NETWORKING.

Sender/receiver In early transmission models of the communication process, a message was seen to be conveyed, simply, from a sender to a receiver. *Transmitter* was also used, while the linguist Roman Jakobson preferred *Addresser* and *Addressee* (see JAKOBSON'S MODEL OF COMMUNICATION, 1958). The terms *author/reader* and *encoder/decoder* recognized both the complexity and the interactive nature of communication, and the role of CODES and encoding in that process. In these cases due weight was given to the TEXT which was encoded and decoded as well as the *context* in which the encoding/decoding took place. Such terms acknowledge the critical nature of the reception of messages

and the diverse ways in which such messages are interpreted. At the same time they reflect the shift of emphasis away from a preoccupation with *sending* to a fuller recognition of the *power* that rests in reception; hence the importance of research into audience uses of media. See DECODE; ENCODE; SEMIOLOGY/SEMIOTICS.

Sensitization The process by which the media can alert the public, and specific social groups, to the fact that certain social actions are taking place, or to the possibility that certain social actions might take place. Stanley Cohen, for example, concludes in 'Sensitization: the case of the Mods and Rockers' in *The Manufacture of News: Deviance, Social Problems and the Mass Media* (Constable, 1973; 3rd edition, 2002), edited by Cohen and Jock Young, that media coverage of the Bank Holiday activities of the Mods and Rockers gangs, at certain southern holiday resorts in the mid-1960s, played a significant role in 'reinforcing and magnifying a predisposition to expect trouble: "Something's going to happen"'.

Cohen argues that once this perception had been established, there was a tendency to interpret new, similar incidents in the same manner so that fairly trivial events, normally overlooked, received media attention. Thus, 'through the process of sensitization, incidents which would not have been defined as unusual or worthy of attention ... acquired a new meaning'. In this particular case sensitization was the first step in a process of media coverage which, Cohen argues, significantly affected the course of real events. See MORAL PANICS AND THE MEDIA.

Sentence meaning, utterance meaning In his two-volume work, *Semantics* (Cambridge University Press, 1977), John Lyons makes a useful distinction in the matter of 'meaning' versus 'use' in our employment of language. Sentence meaning is directly related to the grammatical and lexical (choice of words) meaning of a sentence, while utterance meaning includes all 'secondary' aspects of meaning, particularly those related to the context in which a linguistic exchange takes place. It is this distinction, between sentence and utterance meaning, that allows a person to say one thing and actually mean something else.

Set A state of mental expectancy which is grounded in pre-formed ideas about some future event. The impact of a message is always influenced, to some extent, by the mental set of the receiver. See SCHEMA (PLURAL, SCHEMATA).

Seven characteristics of mass communications See MASS COMMUNICATIONS: SEVEN CHARACTERISTICS.

Sexism Discrimination against people on the grounds of assumed differences in their qualities, behaviours and characteristics resulting from their sex. Such discrimination may be targeted against men as well as women, but generally women are seen as its main victims. Sexism may manifest itself in an individual as a form of prejudice or bigotry, but more fundamentally concern focuses on the degree to which such discrimination is embedded within the structure and language of a society. In this respect the role that the media may play in generating or perpetuating this discrimination has been a theme of considerable recent research. See FEMINISM; GENDER; MALE-AS-NORM; PORNOGRAPHY; STEREOTYPE. See also TOPIC GUIDES under GENDER MATTERS; MEDIA ISSUES & DEBATES.

S4C The Welsh counterpart of CHANNEL 4 (UK) – Saniel Pedwar Cymru. Approximately half the channel's output is in Welsh to serve the 500,000 Welsh-speakers in Wales.

Shadowing See COCKTAIL PARTY PROBLEM.

Shannon and Weaver's model of communication, 1949 Developed by Claude Shannon and Warren Weaver to assist the construction of a mathematical theory of communication which could be applied in a wide variety of information-transfer situations, whether by humans, machines or other systems. It is essentially a linear, process-centred model in which an information source is conveyed by a transmitter (communicator) by means of a signal to a receiver, the activity being subject to a 'noise source' (interference).

Shannon and Weaver were engineers working for the Bell Telephone Laboratories in the US and their objective was to ensure maximum efficiency of the channels of communication, in their case telephone cable and radio wave. However, in *Mathematical Theory of Communication* (University of Illinois Press, 1949), they claim for their theory a much wider application to human communication than solely the technical one.

Within the framework of their model of transmission, the authors identify three levels of problems in the analysis of communication: Level A (technical); Level B (semantic – the meaning as emanating from the Transmitter's mode of address); and Level C (effectiveness in terms of reception or understanding on the part of the Receiver). Shannon and Weaver's model was constructed mainly to tackle Level A problems, and the assumption seems to be that to sort out the technical problems by improving encoding will, almost automatically, lead to improvements at Levels B and C.

Shannon and Weaver stressed the importance of REDUNDANCY in telephonic communication, that is the practice of inserting words, salutations, phrases, expressions not strictly relevant to the central message. Such a practice, conducted by all of us in everyday conversation, serves a vital purpose. As far as exchanges on the telephone are concerned, Shannon and Weaver estimated that as much as 50 per cent of the conversation can be lost, say as a result of crackle on the line, yet the gist of the message would still be understood. See CHANNEL CAPACITY; CYBERNETICS. See also TOPIC GUIDE under COMMUNICATION MODELS.

Shawcross Commission Report on the Press (UK), 1962 The five-member Commission chaired by Lord Shawcross, lawyer and former Labour minister, declared that the real enemy of good-quality newspapers was competition; and competition threatened diversity. 'Within any class of competitive newspapers,' said the Report, 'the economies of large-scale operation provide a natural tendency for a newspaper which already has a large circulation to flourish, and to attract still more readers, whilst a newspaper which has a small circulation is likely to be in difficulties.'

Shawcross offered no radical solution to the problems his Committee had delineated, trusting in the free market, albeit reluctantly: 'There is no acceptable legislative or fiscal way of regulating the competitive and economic forces so as to ensure a sufficient diversity of newspapers.'

The Report put forward an idea for a press amalgamations court which should scrutinize proposed mergers of all daily or Sunday papers with sales over 3 million, and to give the go-ahead only if the court considered such mergers to be of no threat to public interest. In 1965 the Monopolies Commission was created by the Labour government under Harold Wilson, by means of the Monopolies and Mergers Act, which ruled that issues were to be decided by government, not the courts. See TOPIC GUIDE under COMMISSIONS, COMMITTEES, LEGISLATION.

'Shock-jocks' See RADIO: 'SHOCK JOCKS'.

Shortfall signals In interpersonal contact, a shortfall signal is, for example, a smile of greeting that disappears too soon; in other words it fails to carry conviction as a true smile of greeting. In the main, shortfall signals consist of simulated warmth in salutation. The evasive glance, the pulled-away glance, the frozen smile, the smile of mouth without eyes – all of these and many more are INDICATORS of personal unease about the encounter.

The explanation may be because the person you greet is someone you dislike or fear, though the shortfall signal may have as much to do with personal mood, and preoccupation, as anything else. Conversely, there is the so-called *overkill signal*, where the greeting is too friendly, too effusive, the handshake too forcible. The overkill signal may be a simulation of sincere greeting; on the other hand, when people of different cultures or nations meet, one person's shortfall may be another's overkill. See GESTURE; PROXEMICS.

Showbusiness, age of The present age of advancing communications technology has been given many titles – the Age of Information, the Telecommunications Age, the Age of the Global Village. Neil Postman in *Amusing Ourselves to Death* (Methuen, 1986) calls it the Age of Showbusiness, a period in which TV dominates the lives of the community, turning people, in his view, into a population 'amusing ourselves to death'. In the Age of Showbusiness, Postman argues, all DISCOURSES are rewritten in terms of entertainment; substance is translated into IMAGE and the present is emphasized to the detriment of historical perspectives.

Postman's criticism is targeted at the commercial TV of his native America. He believes it 'does everything possible to encourage us to watch continuously. But what we watch is a medium which presents information in a form that renders it simplistic, non-substantive, non-historical and non-contextual; that is to say, information packaged as entertainment'. It is doubtful whether Postman would have been any more sanguine about the effect of today's burgeoning rival to TV ratings, online entertainment and interactivity. See CONSUMER SOVEREIGNTY; EFFECTS OF THE MASS MEDIA; MAINSTREAMING; PILKINGTON COMMITTEE REPORT ON BROADCASTING (UK), 1962; NETWORKING: SOCIAL NETWORKING; PSEUDO-CONTEXT.

Sign In communication studies, a little word that triggers complex explanations. Father of SEMIOLOGY/SEMIOTICS, Swiss linguist Ferdinand de Saussure (1857–1913) regarded language as a 'deposit of signs'; he viewed the sign as a phenomenon comprising an 'acoustic image' and a concept (the thing signified). A word or combination of words in a language refers to, is an indicator of, some externally existing object or idea.

Charles Peirce (1834–1914), the American philosopher and logician, posed a triangular relationship involving the activation of the sign: the object is that which is described by the sign, but the sign only signifies – has MEANING – in

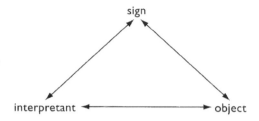

the process of it becoming a mental concept (*interpretant*), or what de Saussure named the *signified*.

The point to emphasize here is that the sign depends for its meaning on the context in which it is communicated. Edmund Leach in *Culture and Communication* (Cambridge University Press, 1976) says that signs do not occur in isolation; 'a sign is always a member of a set of contrasting signs which function within a specific cultural context'. Also, a sign only conveys information when it is combined with other signs and symbols from the same context. 'Signs signal', writes Donis A. Dondis in *Contact: Human Communication and its History* (Thames & Hudson, 1981), edited by Raymond Williams, 'they are specific to a task or circumstance'.

Of course there are not only different kinds or levels of meaning (or signification), there are also many different kinds of sign. Peirce divided signs into three categories: the *icon*, the *index* and the *symbol*. These, like the triangular sign-object-interpretant, are interactive, and they are overlapping. The icon is a resemblance or a representation of the object – a photograph or a map would constitute an iconic sign. An index is a sign connected or associated with its object – an indicator: smoke is an index of fire, for example.

The symbol may have no resemblance whatever to the object or idea. It is arbitrary. It comes about by choice, it exists by convention, rule or assent. It means something beyond itself. As Dondis neatly points out, 'signs can be understood by animals as well as humans; symbols cannot'. They 'are broader in meaning, less concrete'. Raymond Firth, in *Symbols, Public and Private* (Allen & Unwin, 1973), adds a fourth sign type to Peirce's three – *signal*, a sign with an emphasis on 'consequential action', a stimulus requiring some response.

Signs combine to form systems, or codes, from the basic Morse Code or Highway Code to, for example, the complex codes of musical notation. See LANGUE AND PAROLE; JAKOBSON'S MODEL OF COMMUNICATION, 1958; TRIGGERS. See also

TOPIC GUIDE under LANGUAGE/DISCOURSE/ NARRATIVE.

Signal The physical manifestation of a message which allows it to be conveyed. See SHANNON AND WEAVER'S MODEL OF COMMUNICATION, 1949.

Significant others The analysis of the effects of a media message, of its impact, relies on the response not only of the direct respondent, but also of those persons close to, influential upon, the respondent – relatives, friends, work colleagues. These are 'significant others'. In the case of a child watching TV commercials, his/ her response may be conditioned and modified by parents, brothers and sisters, and friends. See INTERVENING VARIABLES (IVs); OPINION LEADER; OTHER.

Significant symbolizers G.H. Mead in *Mind, Self and Society* (University of Chicago Press, 1934) uses this term to indicate how the social organization of a society, human or animal, needs the support of reliable, regular and predictable patterns or signs if it is not to be destroyed by accumulating discrepancy and misinformation. The symbol or symbolizer, whether vocal sound, GESTURE or SIGN, achieves meaningful definition only when it has the 'same effect on the individual making it as on the individual to whom it is addressed'. Thus, according to Mead, a person defines him/herself by 'talking to himself in terms of the community to which he belongs'. Through contact with 'significant' (meaningful) objects of the social world, a person develops a coherent view of him/herself and of his/her relations with others. See INTER-PERSONAL COMMUNICATION; INTRAPERSONAL COMMUNICATION.

Signification One of the most valuable contributions made by Swiss linguist Ferdinand de Saussure (1857–1913) to the study of language was his idea of differentiating between the name, the naming and the MEANING of what has been named. This process enabled the linguist more effectively to examine the *structural* elements of communication. Saussure contrasted the *signifiant* (or signifier) with *signifié* (or that which is signified).

The relationship between these, the physical existence of the sign, and the mental concept it represents, becomes signification which, for Saussure, is the manifestation of external reality or meaning. Signification, it is important to realize, is culture-specific, as is the linguistic form of the signifier in each language. Saussure terms the relationship of signs to others in the sign system, *valeur*, and it is *valeur* that primarily determines meaning. Thus meaning is an active force, subject to constant change, the result of dynamic interaction. See SEMIOLOGY/SEMIOTICS.

Signification spiral Stuart Hall and co-authors in *Policing the Crisis: Mugging, The State and Law & Order* (Macmillan, 1978) use this term for the process by which discrete, local problems and occurrences are linked by the media into a framework of NEWS coverage in such a way as to suggest the existence of a more widespread and serious social problem. They argue that, for example, during the 1970s there emerged a signification spiral in which problems previously presented as atypical or parochial – such as student protests, industrial unrest, and mugging – were presented by the media as part of a wider concern: the breakdown in law and order.

The term has been widely used since. In *Moral Panics* (Routledge, 1998) Kenneth Thompson notes that a signification spiral – 'a way of publicly signifying issues and problems which is intrinsically escalating' – by the media plays a crucial role in the generation of a moral panic. Panics over the breakdown of law and order are perhaps perennial. Another contemporary panic is arguably that focused on the effects of migration and immigration, and links are being made in some areas of the media with issues such as unemployment and social cohesion. See DEMONIZATION; FOLK DEVILS; MORAL ENTREPRENEURS; MORAL PANICS AND THE MEDIA; SENSITIZATION.

Significs Enquiry into questions of meaning, expression and interpretation, and the influence of language upon thought.

Silence In certain circumstances, silence is as effective a means of communication as speech. In *The Dynamics of Human Communication* (McGraw-Hill, 1985), Gail and Michele Myers state: 'Silences ... are not to be equated with the absence of communication. Silences are a natural and fundamental aspect of communication, often ignored because misunderstood.' Silences are used to give meaning to verbal communication but can also communicate a range of information in their own right, such as feelings of anger, a state of mourning or preoccupation with one's own thoughts. There are many kinds of silence and we often need other non-verbal or verbal cues to help us identify what is meant when someone is silent.

Being aware of the range of meanings that silence may convey, and the ability to accurately interpret them and react sensitively to them, is an important communicative skill, as in the abil-

S

ity to fill an embarrassing gap in a conversation. There is a tendency in our culture to perceive silence caused by lapses during a conversation as awkward. Myers and Myers point out that masking behaviours, which include coughing, whistling and sighing, are often employed to cover up such lapses until someone thinks of something to say. The use and acceptability of silence does vary from one culture to another. See APACHE SILENCE; COMMUNICATION, NON-VERBAL (NVC); SILENCE: STRATEGIC SILENCE.

Silence, spiral of See NOELLE-NEUMAN'S SPIRAL OF SILENCE MODEL OF PUBLIC OPINION, 1974.

Sipdis (secret Internet protocol router network distribution) US military electronic database run by the Defence Department in Washington, also serving American embassies worldwide. In 2010 Sipdis proved itself vulnerable to hacking when the contents of ambassadorial reports and exchanges were revealed to public view in vast quantities. See WIKILEAKS.

Sitcom Situation comedy on TV, the comedy growing out of context and recurringly generated or fuelled by amiable antagonism of one kind or another. Where the SOAP OPERA demands a substantial range of characters, the sitcom generally focuses upon narrow circles of acquaintance and relationship, such as families or groups of friends. Rarely does the narrative of one instalment of a sitcom continue from the previous one or continue to the next, again contrasting with the soap whose narrative key is balancing a number of ongoing stories and spinning these along over days and weeks.

Each instalment of a sitcom begins with a situation that is resolved within a single timescale. Characters may be rounded, even complex, but rarely do they, or the situations they are involved in, develop or change. This does not mean that they are sealed against the events of the real world; indeed they often reflect real-world conditions and make use of current issues and trends. For example, the UK sitcom *Men Behaving Badly* explored, amusingly and wittily, the 'gender war' of the 1990s in which men had to adjust to the threat to their traditional dominance by women confident that the future is theirs.

Writers of sitcoms have succeeded in creating diverse themes, from comedy in prison – *Porridge*, to comedy in space – *The Red Dwarf*, to aliens on earth – *Third Rock from the Sun*. The Korean War was the setting for one of the best and most incisive sitcoms, *MASH*, starring Alan Alda, while the zany antics of New York's thirty-somethings in *Friends* proved a worldwide success.

The best sitcoms have a long and recurring screen life: *The Phil Silvers Show* and *Dad's Army* have been introduced and reintroduced to succeeding generations of audience. Notable sitcoms from the UK stable have been *Till Death Us Do Part, Steptoe and Son, The Likely Lads, Rising Damp, The Good Life, Fawlty Towers, Last of the Summer Wine, Birds of a Feather, Father Ted, Goodness Gracious Me* and *The Office*; from the US, a few of many notable sitcoms have been *Bewitched, Rhoda, Taxi, Cheers!, Cybill, Roseanne* and *Frazier*.

Brett Mills in *The Sitcom* (Edinburgh University Press, 2010) talks of the 'comic impetus', a force which 'drives sitcom as an industrial product and as a GENRE'. Over the years it has been characterized by flexibility, hybridity, and is a 'form of programming which foregrounds its comic intent' by its length, domestic settings, character types, shooting style and use of the LAUGH TRACK. 'Promotional material and opening titles for sitcoms', writes Mills, 'signal comic intentions before the narrative of the programme is encountered.'

They tell us what the sitcom is *not*, that is 'not-news, or not-documentary, or not serious, as much as they mark them as comic'. There has been much talk of the 'death of the sitcom' (the UK's Channel 4 broadcast a documentary *Who Killed the Sitcom?* in 2006), but in Mills's view it is 'likely to remain a potent force within television for as long as communities want to come together to enjoy laughter. That is, it's going to be around for some time'.

▶ Gerard Jones, *Honey, I'm Home! Sitcoms: Selling the American Dream* (St Martin's Press, 1992); Nick Lacey, *Narrative and Genre: Key Concepts in Media Studies* (Palgrave Macmilian, 2000); John Byrne and Marcus Powell, *Writing Sitcoms* (A & C Black, 2003); Mary M. Dalton and Laura L. Linder, eds, *The Sitcom Reader: America Viewed and Skewed* (University of New York Press, 2005); Glen Creeber, ed., *The Television Genre Book* (British Film Institute, 2nd edition, 2008).

Site The theoretical or physical space where a struggle over MEANING and the power to reinforce a particular meaning occurs.

Situational proprieties Erving Goffman in *Behaviour in Public Places* (Free Press, 1963) employed this phrase to describe rules of behaviour common to interpersonal and group situations which oblige participants to 'fit in'; to accept the particular normative behaviour suitable for a successful, dissonance-free interaction. Such properties might be to avoid making a scene or causing a disturbance; to refrain from talking too loudly or too assertively; to hold back from attempting to dominate proceedings or, in contrast, to check oneself from withdrawing from what is going on.

S-IV-R model of communication Derives from general theories of learning/communication, where the relationship between stimulus (S) and response (R) is regarded as providing the key to both learning and communication. Actually it is a teaching-orientated model rather than learner-centred, and implies a predominantly one-way traffic of information from teacher to pupil. The IV stands for INTERVENING VARIABLES (IVs), those factors in the communication situation that help, hinder or modify the response to the intended message. These variables are innumerable: NOISE (technical or semantic), lack of motivation or concentration, personal problems and, very importantly, the influence of other people – peer groups, friends, parents, etc. See MEDIATION; OTHER; SIGNIFICANT OTHERS. See also *TOPIC GUIDE* under COMMUNICATION MODELS.

Slander A false or malicious report by spoken word or by SIGN or GESTURE. In law, slander may constitute DEFAMATION – of character or reputation – and may be subject to heavy fines. However, no legal aid is granted in the UK for defamation cases. LIBEL is the written or printed equivalent of slander.

Slang Colloquial language whose words and usages are not generally acceptable within formal modes of expression. The word was not used until about 1756. Prior to that it was called *cant*, and referred to the secret language of the underworld, of thieves and rogues; also termed *argot*. Slang usually begins as in-group language, then moves into popular use. For example, the criminal world's slang nouns for policemen (coppers, rozzers, bluebottles, the fuzz), for magistrates (beaks), for prison (stir time, bird, porridge) and for youth (chaz, gothics) have achieved broad currency.

Rhyming slang, associated with London cockneys, uses slang words that rhyme with the intended word. Thus 'apples and pears' means stairs, 'trouble and strife' means wife. The point of rhyming slang is to conceal the MEANING of the language used from unwanted listeners. See COLLOQUIALISM; DIALECT; JARGON.

SLAPPS Strategic Lawsuits Against Public Participation; a practice originating in the US but spreading globally, in which big corporations put legal frighteners on critics of their activities. Wherever corporate interests – whether in the environment, in foodstuffs, in publicizing information – are deemed at risk, out come the lawsuits, focusing on accusations of DEFAMATION, invasion of PRIVACY and interference with business.

Julian Petley in an article 'SLAPPS and Chills' in *Index on Censorship*, 1 (1999), writes, 'These cases ... are a form of strategic legal intimidation or gamesmanship, designed to frighten, harass and distract actual critics, and to discourage potential ones from even voicing their views in the first place.' Most cases do not reach court, nor are they intended to.

However, for Helen Steel and Dave Morris, distributors of a leaflet entitled 'What's Wrong With McDonald's?' there was to be no escape from LIBEL proceedings. Their trial was the longest in British history and took every penny the defendants possessed (defendants are ineligible for legal aid in defamation cases); they squared up to a company that spends an estimated US$ 2 billion a year on advertising (see John Vidal's *McLibel: Burger Culture on Trial*, Macmillan, 1997).

In June 1997 it was revealed that a TV documentary made by Franny Armstrong, *McLibel: Two Worlds Collide,* had been rejected by both the BBC and Channel 4 because of the risk of libel action. Existing, well-established programmes such as the BBC's *Newsnight, Panorama* and *Watchdog* have stirred up choruses of protest from multinationals such as British Aerospace, Ford, Dixons, Hotpoint and Proctor and Gamble. See CENSORSHIP; McDONALDIZATION. See also *TOPIC GUIDES* under MEDIA: FREEDOM, CENSORSHIP; MEDIA ISSUES & DEBATES.

Sleeper effect Researchers into the responses of audiences to messages have noted how these responses can be delayed and only become manifest some time after exposure. This is the 'sleeper' effect. See EFFECTS OF THE MASS MEDIA.

Slider Many experiments have been conducted to investigate the effect of group pressure upon the individual and the manner in which such pressure manifests itself in the INTERPERSONAL COMMUNICATION of the group. In a typical experiment, one member of the group may take on the role of slider, that is he/she will initially disagree with the majority of the group on a matter but is persuaded to agree with them. The member of the group who takes on the role of *deviant*, however, consistently disagrees with the majority. Of those in the experimental situation, some may be naïve, that is unaware of what is to take place in the experiment, and some members may be *confederates*, that is in league with the experimenters.

Slow-drip Term sometimes used to describe the regular, long-term coverage of certain issues by the media with a view to influencing the formation of opinion; a softening-up process that builds evidence and feelings in preferred directions. See EFFECTS OF THE MASS MEDIA.

Slow motion Has been used varyingly in the cinema to convey dream-like or fantasy situations, to emphasize reactions such as grief or bewilderment, or to concentrate attention upon happenings which in real life would be here and gone before the full visual impact has been made. In contrast, accelerated motion has been generally used for comic effects, especially by the early silent-movie comedians whose own actors' timing was rendered even more remarkable by the speeded-up action.

Reverse motion is another technique by which the cinema defies time: that which can happen can unhappen. In *October* (1927), for instance, Sergei Eisenstein (1898–1948) uses the magic of reverse motion to show a statue of the Tzar, previously smashed to pieces, miraculously restored, thus portraying with impressive symbolism the restoration of the old order.

Lastly, there is stopped motion, using either still photographs or stopping the action of an otherwise moving sequence by repeating the same frame when editing the film. The freezing of action may signal transition from one time-zone to another, or may be used for special emphasis or sometimes to underscore comic effects or impressions. See SHOT.

Smart mobs Term used by Howard Rheingold (2002) to describe protest groups that mobilize support for demonstrations through the use of the mobile phone and the social networks that these give access to. He argues that President Joseph Estrada of the Philippines was the first head of state to be ousted by a 'smart mob' in 2001. Other instances of the effective use of the mobile phone to organize protests include the 1999 demonstration held outside a meeting of the World Trade Organization in Seattle, and the Fuel Protests in Britain in 2000.

The mobile phone facilitates not only the mobilization of support for a protest, but also the progress of a demonstration, for example the effective deployment of 'swarming' strategies in a protest. In *Smart Mobs: The Next Social Revolution* (Basic Books, 2002) Rheingold describes 'swarming' strategies with reference to the 'Battle of Seattle': 'Individual members of each group remained dispersed until mobile communications drew them to converge on a specific location from all directions simultaneously, in coordination with other groups.'

Of course protest groups are not the only example of a smart mob; governments and their military strategists also make use of such technology. Governments can also call upon companies to curtail the use that might be made of mobile phones by protesters. In an article in the *Independent on Sunday* (13 February 2011) entitled 'What are the business ethics of revolution 2.0?', Margaret Pagano notes that during the protests in Tunisia and Egypt which were current at the time, the governments were successful in persuading some mobile operators and Internet service providers to shut down their networks. However, it seems that quite a few protesters managed to find ways round this.

Smartphone What is usually considered to mark the difference between the mobile phone and the smartphone is the latter's capacity to key into the INTERNET, plus the availability of innumerable 'apps' (or applications). The video as well as photographic capacity enables users to join the ranks of citizen journalists (see JOURNALISM: CITIZEN JOURNALISM), be their own feature and short documentary film-maker, participate in social networking (see NETWORKING: SOCIAL NETWORKING), post contributions to YouTube and download music, films, radio and TV. The smartphone allows users to operate across informational, entertainment and social platforms. It has been judged a powerful weapon of communication and record in assisting the MOBILIZATION of popular political protest (see SMART MOBS).

By 2011 smartphones were outselling desktop computers, largely because these handheld devices can do most things that computers can do. The smartphone can translate words and signs, tell you where you are and where your friends are, give you the menu of the restaurant up the road or in Hong Kong or San Francisco, and keep abreast of the latest exchanges on FACEBOOK and TWITTER.

Whether the smartphone actually improves the quality of communication in all ways and at all levels is seriously open to question. It makes it easier, facilitates greater diffusion, is infinitely faster than pen on paper, but it is capable of proving an instrument of distraction especially in face-to-face communication. See APPLE MACINTOSH; GOOGLE; MEDIA ACTIVISM; MICROSOFT WINDOWS; PODCAST; TECHNOLOGY: THE CONSUMERIZATION OF TECHNOLOGY.

SMCR model of communication See BERLO'S SMC MODEL OF COMMUNICATION, 1960.

Smiling professions Namely, the media, and

TV in particular. John Hartley in *The Politics of Pictures: The Creation of the Public in the Age of Popular Media* (Routledge, 1992) writes that smiling 'has become one of the most public virtues of our times, a uniform that must be worn on the lips of those whose social function is to create, sustain, tutor, represent and make images of the public'. Hartley asserts that 'smiling, in fact, is now the "dominant ideology" of the "public domain", the mouthpiece of the politics of pictures'.

Snap-shot Term invented by astronomer Sir John Herschel (1792–1871), writing in 1860 of 'the possibility of taking a photograph as it were a snap shot'. He may well have been referring to Thomas Skaife's Pistolgraph of 1858. See CAMERA; PHOTOGRAPHY, ORIGINS.

Soap opera RADIO or TV domestic drama series; the term emanates from the US, where such programmes were initially sponsored by big soap companies who had the housewife viewer in mind. Of the long-running soap opera in the UK, *Coronation Street*, poet laureate John Betjeman once announced, 'At half-past seven tonight I shall be in paradise'.

Traditionally soaps have been characterized by an immediately identifiable set-up, a stereotypical cast of characters and a distancing from contemporary reality and anxieties. However, the end of the 1980s saw the arrival of soaps exploiting social problems for all they were worth. From the BBC, *EastEnders*, featuring abortion, rape, illegitimacy, murder, robbery, incest and unemployment; from Channel 4, *Brookside*, demonstrating that Merseyside can vie problem for problem with London's East End, featuring rape, stabbings, euthanasia, homosexuality and, of course, unemployment. The BBC's import from Australia, *Neighbours*, proved it could do more than hold its own, with beatings-up, meningitis, divorce *et al*.

In a sense, soaps have become a PARADIGM for television itself. In terms of TEXTS they take up a staggeringly large amount of viewing time and occupy centre-stage in the minds of vast and international audiences. Critical theory has located in soaps rich seams for investigation, especially in an age when the way MEANING is read into texts by AUDIENCE and the ways audiences *use* media have come to dominate critical thinking and much media research.

Generally soaps are less concerned with action than with INTERACTION, primarily between the characters on the broad socio-cultural canvas but also, in a proactive way, between the characters and the viewers (see PARASOCIAL INTERACTION). The gap between one episode of a soap and the next may be used by members of the audience to mull over latest developments, talk about these to members of the family, fellow workers, friends, thus heightening anticipation and enjoyment and making the viewer a more active 'reader' of the text.

Because most soaps distribute interest among numerous characters, no single character is indispensable. Of key importance is the *community* of characters in their situation. As Robert C. Allen writes in 'Reader-orientated criticism' in *Channels of Discourse: Television and Contemporary Criticism* (Methuen, 1987; Routledge, 1990), edited by Allen, 'anything might happen to an individual character, but, in the long run, it will not affect the community of characters as a whole'.

In a *European Journal of Communication* article, June 1998, entitled 'European soap operas: the diversification of the genre', Tamar Liebes and Sonia Livingstone identify three types, or models, of soap opera – the *Dynastic*, the *Community* and the *Dyadic*. The first focuses on one powerful family with a number of satellite outsiders. The American soap *Dynasty* was an example of this model, while the UK soaps *Coronation Street* and *EastEnders* typify the community model. These are characterized by a number of interconnecting and interrelating families 'all living within one geographical neighbourhood and belonging to one community'.

The dyadic model concerns a 'destabilized network of a number of young people, densely interconnected, mostly unigenerational, interchanging couples, with past, present and future romantic ties, continually absorbed in the process of reinventing kinship relations'. The authors cite the American soap *The Young and the Restless* as a prime example of the dyadic model; to this we might add *This Life*, which won something of a cult status in the UK until in 1998 the BBC decided not to commission further episodes.

Community soaps, Liebes and Livingstone say, 'have been produced in the spirit of public broadcasting, indicating certain pedagogic aims' and 'constitute a type of public for debating social issues'. A notable example of a soap which has proved both pedagogic and a source of public debate is the highly popular Spanish drama, *Cuentame Como (Tell Me How It Happened)*, first produced in 2002.

The soap revisits – and retrieves – Spanish history, its characters and situations being cast in the period of Fascist rule under General

S

Franco. An era which, to a modern generation, had seemed a closed book, closed off by official reluctance to examine a past of terror following the Spanish Civil War, had the curtains of forgetfulness drawn back; all at once, the nation focused on its past as never before.

Elizabeth Nash, writing from Madrid, in a news report entitled 'Spain gripped by soap set in dark years of Franco's rule' (UK *Independent*, 9 August 2002), says 'The series has caught the imagination of all generations of Spaniards: those who remember Franco relish the authenticity of every detail; youngsters who never knew him are fascinated by this window on their otherwise silent and invisible history.' See EMPOWERMENT; FEMINISM; GENDER; GENDERED GENRE; GOSSIP NETWORKS; NARRATIVE.

▶ Mary Ellen Brown, *Soap Opera and Women's Talk* (Sage, 1994); Robert C. Allen, *To Be Continued: Soap Operas Around the World* (Routledge, 1995); Ian Ang, *Watching Dallas: Soap Operas and the Melodramatic Imagination* (Methuen, 1985; Routledge paperback, 1996); Charlotte Brunsdon, *Screen Tastes: Soap Opera to Satellite Dish* (Routledge, 1997); Dorothy Hobson, *Soap Opera* (Wiley-Blackwell, 2003); Lesley Henderson, *Social Issues in Television Fiction* (Edinburgh University Press, 2007); Sam Ford, Abigail De Kosnik and C. Lee Harrington, eds, *The Survival of Soap Opera: Transformations for a New Media Era* (University of Mississippi Press, 2010).

Soaps: docu-soaps Popular variant of the fictional soap, presenting documentary series in the fashion of soaps with the same emphasis on characters the audience can readily identify with, real-life situations intercut with parallel situations in the typical manner of soaps. Examples in the UK have been *Airport*, *Driving School* and *Hotel*.

Such programmes have tended to supplant serious, probing documentaries and are largely the result of the intense pressures of competition. Their fascination lies in the actuality of the mini-dramas and their sense of immediacy. Where docu-soaps are different from fictional soaps is in the freedom the 'characters' are given to comment on the mini-dramas that fill their working days.

Social action (mode of media analysis) Stresses the role of the individual as a potent force within a dynamic social system. It sees conflict as central to the process of change, in particular conflict between GROUPS seeking influence, power and status. Social action analysis concentrates on the media as a special group both reflecting and involved in the conflicts that concern social change, or resistance to it.

A pluralist society, of competing ideologies and varying, changing definitions of truth and meaning, is acknowledged by social action analysis, as are the complex influences at work upon media and media audiences and the interaction between them. See FUNCTIONALIST (MODE OF MEDIA ANALYSIS); MARXIST (MODE OF MEDIA ANALYSIS); PLURALISM. See also *TOPIC GUIDE* under RESEARCH METHODS.

Social action broadcasting A broad term describing RADIO and TV programming that sets out not only to analyse current social problems and issues and bring them to public attention, but to encourage people to take action in response to what they have heard or seen. In the UK such programmes range from the BBC's adult literacy series *On the Move* or *Crimewatch UK* to Capital Radio's *Helpline*.

The culinary broadcaster Jamie Oliver exemplified this social action with a Channel 4 series in 2005 set in Kidbrooke School, East London: he went into partnership with the school dinners manager with the aim of encouraging pupils to eat more varied and nutritious food. The series was popular, prompting government action to bring about healthier eating in schools, and gave social action broadcasting added status and impetus.

Social anthropology The study of the evolution of human communities and cultures.

Social class See CLASS.

Social influence theory See IDENTIFICATION.

Socialization The shaping of human behaviour through experience in and knowledge of certain social situations: the process by which individuals are made aware of the EXPECTATIONS others have of their behaviour; by which they acquire the NORMS, MORES, VALUES and beliefs of a social group or society; and by which the CULTURE of a social group or society is transmitted. Socialization continues throughout life as individuals change their ROLES and membership of social GROUPS.

There exist what are commonly known as *agents of socialization*. In modern industrial societies, the family, school and friendship groups are thought to be the most significant agents in shaping the behaviour of the individual. The mass media are also agents of socialization and are considered to be particularly influential in transmitting awareness and expectations concerning a wide range of societal behaviour.

Individuals and societies may undergo radical change; if so, *re-socialization* may occur – the peeling away of learned patterns of behaviour and their replacement with quite different ones.

There is interest as to the media's potential role in this process: its capacity as a disseminator of PROPAGANDA, for example, could be of significance. Additionally, media organizations are themselves social institutions and as such have their own patterns of behaviour, attitudes and beliefs into which their members are socialized. The degree to which the culture of media organizations affects their output is a considerable source of interest. See TOPIC GUIDE under MEDIA: VALUES & IDEOLOGY.

Social lubricators Richard Hoggart in *Speaking to Each Other* (Chatto & Windus, 1970) uses this term to describe those people involved in the research, design and presentation of material aimed at aiding the smooth running of a technologically advanced society: communications experts, public relations officers and advertising executives, for example. See PUBLIC RELATIONS (PR).

Social networking See NETWORKING: SOCIAL NETWORKING.

Socially unattached intelligentsia See IMPARTIALITY.

Social perception See PERCEPTION.

Social system Consists of a collective of people who undertake different types of tasks in order to achieve common goals and solve common problems. The term can be applied to a group of two or more individuals, complex organizations or whole societies. For the members of a social system to cooperate, there must be a shared language and some cultural similarities between them, although within the overall system there may be a variety of sub-cultures and language CODES, as well as other individual differences. All social systems are liable to undergo transition, a process by which the structures and functions are altered. One focus for research has been the role of the communication of innovation in the process of social change. See SOCIALIZATION.

Societally conscious See VALS TYPOLOGY.

Sociolinguistics The study of the way in which an individual's linguistic behaviour might be influenced by the social communities to which he/she belongs. It investigates also the linguistic variations found between groups and their identification through language.

Richard A. Hudson in *Sociolinguistics* (Cambridge University Press, 1996) comments that 'in sociolinguistics ... the social questions are in full focus'. Areas within the field include the study of dialects, codes, registers, Pidgins, Creoles, the relationship between language and thought, and gender differences in the use of language. A number of aspects of contemporary research as well as debates within sociolinguistics are of relevance to the study of interpersonal communication. See TOPIC GUIDES under INTERPERSONAL COMMUNICATION; LANGUAGE/DISCOURSE/NARRATIVE.

Sociology French philosopher Auguste Comte (1798–1857) was the first to use the word. The discipline attempts a scientific and systematic study of society, employing precise and controlled methods of enquiry. It is concerned with social structure; social systems; social action; the various GROUPS, institutions, categories and classes which go to make up a society or social system; the CULTURE and lifestyle of a society and the groups of which it is composed; the processes of socialization by which such cultures are communicated and maintained; and the types and allocation of social roles. Social groups, their inter-relationships and INTERACTION, and their conditioning of individual behaviour could be seen as the building-blocks of the discipline.

▶ Gregory McLennan, *Story of Sociology: A First Companion to Social Theory* (Bloomsbury Academic, 2011).

Sociometrics (and media analysis) Sociometrics is the analysis of small GROUPS, their coherence and the interpersonal relationships and communication within them. This mode of analysis has been extended and applied within media studies to ascertain the nature of the relationships between owners of media organizations and owners of other industrial or commercial concerns and the degree to which they are interlocking. The purpose of such a sociometric map of capitalism is to discover whether or not shared positions in and patterns of social and economic life produce recognized shared interests and a common cluster of beliefs, VALUES and perspectives which feed back into and influence media organizations and their products.

Increasingly, owners of communications concerns are also owners of other businesses, and these contacts are reinforced by overlapping directorships. Board members of top media corporations have been found to hold membership of elite London clubs also favoured by directors of leading financial institutions and some business corporations. Of course evidence of points of contact does not necessarily constitute evidence of shared values, beliefs and perspectives, or deliberate influence of media products. See CONVERGENCE. See also TOPIC GUIDE under RESEARCH METHODS.

Sokal Hoax, or Sokal Scandal New York

S

professor of physics Alan Sokel, outraged by what he saw as the 'gibberish' of postmodernist texts (see POSTMODERNISM) and with tongue firmly in cheek, wrote a paper in 1996 entitled 'Transgressing the boundaries towards a transformative hermeneutics of quantum gravity'. It has been described as 'a carefully crafted parody of postmodern twaddle'. The paper was submitted to the US journal *Social Text* and was accepted and published – not as a hoax, but as the real thing.

Commenting afterwards on his hoax, Sokal acknowledged deliberate half-truths, falsehoods and *non sequeteurs* and confessed that his article contained 'syntactically correct sentences that have no meaning whatever'.

▸ See Alan Sokel and Jean Bricmont, *Intellectual Impostures* (Profile Books, 1998); also published by Picador in the US, with the title *Fashionable Nonsense* (1998).

Sound-bite Term originally derives from RADIO but has come to apply equally to TV; describes a film or tape segment within a NEWS story, in which a reporter talks to a source such as a politician or an eyewitness. With the advent of more sophisticated technology for handling news reports, the use of jump-cutting has added to the complexity and the drama of the sound-bite. The *ellipsis* jump-cut splices two or more segments of the same person speaking in the same setting: these are classified as single sound-bites. The *juxtaposition* jump-cut places together contrasting segments, usually from different settings, in such a way as to make evident the discontinuity. These tend to be treated as separate sound-bites.

Research into the nature and degree of sound-bites in news broadcasting in the US indicates that contemporary news employs far more, and far shorter sound-bites, than in the past. In 'Sound-bite news: television coverage of elections, 1968–1988' in *Journal of Communication*, Spring, 1992, Daniel C. Hallin reports that the average sound-bite has been shrinking, from more than 40 seconds in length in 1968 to less than 10 seconds in the 1980s. The conclusion Hallin draws from this is that the news is much more *mediated* than the TV news of the 1960s and 1970s.

He writes, 'Today's television journalist displays a sharply different attitude towards the words of candidates and other newsmakers. Today, those words, rather than simply being reproduced and transmitted to the audiences, are treated as raw material to be taken apart, combined with other sounds and images, and reintegrated into a new narrative.'

Hallin cites three reasons for the sound-bite revolution, as apposite in the twenty-first century as when he was writing: the technological one already mentioned; the weakening in political consensus and authority following Vietnam and WATERGATE; and the discovery by the TV industry in the States that news was big business – if, that is, presentation was 'punchy' enough to attract and retain audience attention. Ironically, the approach derives from the very people journalists often accuse of manipulating the media – political campaign managers – so-called 'spin doctors' whose techniques of packaging candidates have centred around sound-biting images, one-liners, the use of triumphalist music, etc.

Dan Hallin acknowledges that modern news is far more 'professional', far more varied, slicker than in the past, but he identifies serious worries. 'First and simplest, it is disturbing that the public never has the chance to hear a candidate – or anyone else – speak for more than 20 seconds', especially as showing 'humans speaking is something television does very effectively'. Also the modern pace of exposition raises questions concerning audience comprehension, the ability of viewers to understand what is coming at them at such speed. Not the least concern is that sound-bite journalism emphasizes techniques over substance: the very sin the journalist accuses the spin doctor of committing. See JOURNALISM; NEWS MANAGEMENT. See also *TOPIC GUIDE* under NEWS MEDIA.

▸ David Stayden and Rita Kirk Whillock, eds, *Sound-bite Culture: The Death of Discourse in a Wired World* (Sage, 1999).

Sound broadcasting See RADIO BROADCASTING.

Sound Broadcasting Act (UK), 1972 Gave the go-ahead to COMMERCIAL RADIO in the UK. The name Independent Television Authority (ITA) was changed to Independent Broadcasting Authority (IBA), and the IBA was empowered to create a new group of contractors in up to fifty British cities to run local commercial radio stations and collect advertising revenue in a manner similar to that of the TV programme companies. The first commercial radio stations went on the air in October 1973.

Sound, synchronous See SYNCHRONOUS SOUND.

Source An individual, group or institution that originates a message. In media terms, source is where information starts, and it is an axiom of good reporting that the material supplied by source is reliable and true. Best practice suggests that single sources be checked against other sources. It is also a matter of journalistic principle that in some cases the source of information, especially if it is of a particularly sensitive, or sensational, nature, is kept secret; that the provider of information is assured of anonymity (see DEEP THROAT).

Where the information provided by source is perceived to impugn those in authority, by suggesting corruption or other wrong-doing, reporters may be charged with criminal offences if they refuse to divulge their sources. If they give in to pressure, retreat from the guarantee of *confidentiality*, it is unlikely that they will ever be trusted with sensitive information again; on the other hand, they may end up in jail, as happened to *New York Times* journalist Judith Miller in 2005 after she refused to reveal the source of an enquiry into the leaking of the name of a CIA undercover agent.

The mass media are often criticized for over-reliance on official sources, or failing to question information which has been supplied to them by those in authority. Equally they are seen to pay selective attention to sources, valuing some, ignoring others. At worst, they serve the interests of the powerful by transmitting PROPAGANDA as if it were NEWS. See NEWS VALUES.

Source domination See PRIMARY, SECONDARY DEFINERS.

Spatial behaviour Michael Argyle in *Bodily Communication* (Methuen, 1988) notes that 'proximity, orientation and territorial behaviour' are the main aspects of spatial behaviour. PROXEMICS is the study of the distance people keep between themselves and others within an encounter. This distance can depend upon a number of factors, such as the nature of relationships, culture and the social context. It seems that individuals generally sit or stand closer to those whom they like and those whom they perceive as being similar. However this norm can be deliberately disregarded in order to intimidate or dominate others by standing too close to them. In certain circumstances, in crowds for example, individuals seem able to tolerate much closer proximity to others than is usually preferred.

There appear to be definite norms that mark the appropriate distance people observe between each other in communicative encounters, although these norms vary from one culture to another. According to Edward Hall in *The Hidden Dimension* (Doubleday, 1966), these distances relate to four main zones. The intimate zone is for those with whom we have the closest relationships, typically family and friends; everyday encounters usually take place within the personal zone; in a more formal context, such as that of a workplace meeting, the social zone is more likely to apply, whilst the public zone operates in very formal situations and refers to the distance kept between the key figures and members of an audience or the public. Hall noted that the usual distances kept by middle-class European Americans in each zone were: intimate, 6–18 inches; personal, 18 inches to 4 feet; social, 4–12 feet; and public, over 12 -25 feet.

Desmond Morris in *People Watching* (Vintage, 2002) argues that for Western Europeans, from the outstretched arm to the fingertips is a comfortable distance for an everyday conversation, whereas for those from Eastern Europe the distance is from the outstretched arm to the wrist. For people from the Mediterranean area it is the stretch from the upper arm to the elbow. Stella Ting-Toomey in *Communicating Across Cultures* (Guildford Press, 1999) also comments that in several cultures – Latin American, Caribbean and Arab cultures, for example – people sit or stand closer to one another in everyday conversations than would be the norm among Western Europeans. In culturally diverse societies, however, it could be expected that a range of practice would be found depending on the cultural heritage of the communicators. Such cultural differences have the potential to be a source of NOISE in everyday encounters.

The term PERSONAL SPACE is often used to denote the space within which an individual feels easy and which, if encroached upon, causes anxiety, tension or resistance. Personal space is fluid and mobile, a kind of bubble around the individual. Stanford M. Lyman and Marvin B. Scott in 'Territoriality: a neglected social dimension' in *Social Problems* 15 (1967) refer to personal space as 'the most private and inviolate of territories belonging to an individual'. When our personal space is violated we respond, argues Morris (2002), with a reduction in our social signals: we may, for example, avoid eye contact, and reduce the number of body movements and facial expressions. There are, however, cultural differences in the way in which individuals respond to such incursions. According to William B. Gudykunst and Stella Ting-Toomey in *Culture and Interpersonal Communication* (Sage, 1988), people from individualistic cultures tend to deal with encroachments in an assertive, if not aggressive, manner, whereas people from collectivistic cultures tend to adopt a more passive, withdrawn manner.

TERRITORIALITY, that is the human need to establish, define and defend territory, is also an aspect of spatial behaviour. Three different kinds of territory are noted by Morris (2002): personal, family and tribal. Personal territories include such spaces as an individual's house, car or favourite chair. Individuals often mark what they consider to be their personal territory as a means of defining and defending it. Thus a bag may be left on a favourite chair in the sitting room.

The home and garden are often the key areas of territory for the family, and people may devote significant amounts of time and energy on activities such as gardening and DIY in order to customise and mark it. Non-family members usually enter this territory by invitation only. Morris (2002) notes the way in which the family may extend its notion of family territory. A family trip to the beach usually involves finding a space that can be used throughout the stay; once the spot is secured, several markers may be placed to defend this territory such as windbreaks, towels, beach chairs and a picnic hamper.

In certain situations displays of tribal territory can also be seen. According to Morris (2002), groups, gangs, communities and nations are all capable of generating tribal identities. These identities can be displayed and communicated by various 'territorial signals', such as national flags, logos, styles of dress, football club strips, and the face-painting found among some sports fans.

ORIENTATION, that is the angle at which people sit or stand in relation to one another, is also an aspect of spatial behaviour. Orientation can be used to convey a range of messages about relationships, status, mood, personality and social context. According to M. Cook (1970) in 'Experiments on orientation and proxemics', *Human Relations* 23, if people are in a potentially hostile or competitive situation they usually face each other head on, whereas when in a co-operative relationship or situation, people tend to sit next to or adjacent to each other. Ting-Toomey (1999) notes that there are cultural differences here: for example, people from high-contact cultures tend to prefer a more direct orientation. Orientation can also be employed in interaction regulation: when circulating at a crowded party, for example, we would signal our intention to move on by moving our body round towards new conversational partners (Argyle, 1988). See COMMUNICATION: INTERCULTURAL COMMUNICATION.

▶ Allan & Barbara Pease, *The Definitive Book of Body Language* (Orion, 2004).

Spatial zones See SPATIAL BEHAVIOUR.

Special effects (SFX) The 'real' gorilla in *King Kong* (1933) was just 18 inches high – that is special effects. Simulations of earthquakes, explosions, floods, fires, storms, of the interior of Hell, of war in space or 40 fathoms deep are what SFX wizards specialize in, while in the case of Roland Emmerich's *2012* (2009), audiences are treated to the destruction of the world (or as the director put it, 'you see the whole world going to shit').

Tim Dirks's filmsite.org webpage provides a useful listing of outstanding examples of SFX down the years, noting the particular areas of effects innovation. In his introduction to *Visual Special FX Milestones* Dirks writes, 'The earliest effects were produced within the camera (in-camera effects), such as simple jump-cuts or superimpositions, or were created by using miniatures, back projection, or matte paintings.

'Optical effects came slightly later, using film, light, shadow, lenses and/or chemical processes to produce the film effects. Film titles, fades, dissolves, wipes, blow ups, skip frames, bluescreen, compositing, double exposures, and zooms/pans are examples of various optical effects. Cel animation, scale modelling, claymation, digital compositing, animatronics, use of prosthetic makeup, morphing, and modern computer-generated or computer graphics imagery (CGI) are just some of the more modern techniques that are widely used for creating incredible special or visual effects.'

In fact, 'trick' photography goes back to such photographic pioneers as Oscar Rejlander, who produced allegorical multi-photo compositions (*The Two Ways of Life*, 1857), and Eadweard Muybridge (*The Horse in Motion*, 1878). Among moving picture experimenters were Georges Méliès (*The Vanishing Lady*, 1896, and *La Voyage Dans La Lune*, 1902) and Edward S. Porter (*The Great Train Robbery*, 1903).

Throughout cinema history SFX have proved the stimulus to innovation, the allurement of mass audiences and the generation of profits as well as sky-high costs: James Cameron's *Avatar* (2009) cost an estimated US$ 300 million, but it also made more money than any other film in history.

Landmarks of SFX have been Stanley Kubrick's *2001: A Space Odyssey* (1968), George Lucas's *Star Wars* series (from 1977) and Steven Spielberg's *Close Encounters of the Third Kind* (1977). Computer generated imagery (CGI) soon became the key creator of effects, the first movie to be made entirely by computer being Disney's US$18 million *Tron* (1982), to be followed by

Spielberg's ground-breaking *Jurassic Park* (1993), the Pixar/Disney animation *Toy Story* (1995, and later sequels), Cameron's *Titanic* (1997) and the Wactowski brothers' *The Matrix* (1999).

In 2004 Robert Zemeckis' *The Polar Express* introduced *performance capture*, a system that digitally captures an actor's live performance using computerized cameras. This provides a blueprint for creating virtually all-digital characters. Zemecki took the process further in *Beowolf* (2007).

Special effects pose two problems: by their often amazing achievements, they raise audience expectations, succeeding effects arguably having to be more amazing than the last; and, perhaps more importantly, there is the danger that effects become the main player in the NARRATIVE – a case of style dominating content, as a number of critics pointed out when reviewing *Star Wars: Episode II: Attack of the Clones* (2002).

Speed photography See HIGH-SPEED PHOTOGRAPHY.

Spin: spin doctor See NEWS MANAGEMENT; SOUND-BITE.

Spiral of silence See NOELLE-NEUMANN'S SPIRAL OF SILENCE MODEL OF PUBLIC OPINION, 1974.

Spiral model of communication See DANCE'S HELICAL MODEL OF COMMUNICATION.

Spoiler Device used by one or more newspapers to detract from a rival paper's scoop story; usually by running a different version of the story as told by lesser characters.

Sponsorship There is scarcely any field of the arts, sport, entertainment or media that is not to a greater or lesser extent dependent on sponsorship; and this sponsorship originates for the most part from industry, business and commerce. However, it could be said that sponsorship is as old as the pyramids; indeed the pyramids constitute one of the most impactful examples of state sponsorship. Tombs, yes, but also symbols of the pharaohs' will to dominate the lives of their subjects: the pyramids were a constant reminder to the Egyptians that 'We are here'. Similarly, sponsorship of the arts by monarchs and the church was at base born of a desire to enthrone the sponsor in the minds and memories of the people.

Some powers of monarchy and the church have been inherited by big business, as well as certain duties within the community. A company or corporation will sponsor a major art exhibition designed to give pleasure and illumination to thousands. And those thousands will in turn, so it is hoped, acknowledge the communal benefit made possible by the sponsoring company. Thus culture comes to us through the arch of sponsorship. At the same time the company will benefit by association (see SYNERGY).

To sponsor Mozart or Rembrandt is somehow to be touched by their greatness; their quality rubs off on the sponsor. The danger is for Mozart to be hijacked from the public domain and transformed into yet another device for selling goods – processed, packaged and 'profitized'. Such is the awareness in public bodies of this danger that codes are written to regulate the degree of sponsorship, as well as its nature. See PRODUCT PLACEMENT.

Sponsorship of broadcast programmes (UK) Responsibility for establishing rules concerning the sponsorship of broadcast programmes in the UK, and monitoring its practice, rests with the Office of Communications (Ofcom; see OFCOM: OFFICE OF COMMUNICATIONS (UK)). Sponsorship is dealt with in Section 9 of the Ofcom Broadcasting Code. The BBC does not come under Ofcom regulation in this matter.

The Code states that sponsorship may occur subject to certain conditions: there must be *transparency*, *separation* and *editorial independence*. It must be made clear that while a sponsor may have financed a programme, or materially supported that programme, it has not influenced the programme's content and that the acknowledgment of sponsorship makes clear the difference between itself and the programme. Excluded from any form of sponsorship are news bulletins and newsdesk presentations on radio, and news and current affairs programmes on TV.

Ofcom's position on sponsorship and PRODUCT PLACEMENT has been one of conceding ground on initial safeguards, bearing in mind that its mission has been not only to uphold standards of broadcasting, but also to encourage profitability. After lengthy consultations in 2009–10, Ofcom amended regulations contained in the Communications Act (2003), issuing the Audiovisual Media Services (Product Placement) Regulation which came into force in February 2011.

This allowed sponsorship credits to be broadcast during programmes ('internal credits'), though with limitations on their content. These internal credits would not be permitted in programmes, such as children's programmes, which barred product placement; all sponsorship credits must make clear the relationship between the sponsor and the sponsored content. See www.ofcom.org.uk.

Spot news Term used to describe unexpected or unplanned news events, such as natural disasters, aircrashes, murders or assassinations, often referred to as *breaking* news, and to be distinguished from *diary stories*, which are known well in advance and can be planned-for by the newspaper, RADIO or TV news team – for example news conferences, state visits, elections or budgets. The *running story* is that which is ongoing and may stretch over several days or weeks, such as strikes, wars and famines; all stories that transcend the newsday cycle.

Sputnik First artificial satellite launched into space by the Russians in 1957. See SATELLITE TRANSMISSION.

Spycatcher case A book by former British Secret Service employee Peter Wright, first published in the US in 1987 and banned from publication in the UK, became the centre of the most celebrated case of attempted government censorship in the 1980s. *Spycatcher: The Candid Autobiography of a Senior Intelligence Officer* (Viking/Penguin, 1987) was not dissimilar in its revelations about the activities of MI5 to other books that had been permitted to appear, but Wright, having signed the OFFICIAL SECRETS ACT (UK), was deemed to have breached confidence and arguably set a precedent for other secret agents to 'spill the beans' on security.

The Conservative government was determined not only to prevent publication of *Spycatcher* in the UK, but also to block the intentions of newspapers such as the *Guardian*, the *Observer*, the *Independent* and the *Sunday Times* to publish extracts from Wright's book. At the same time, government law officers pursued the book across the world to the courts in Australia and Hong Kong, stirring publicity and interest that made it a worldwide bestseller. Only the British people were to remain in the dark about Wright's revelations.

The government did not prosecute under the Official Secrets Act but pushed their case on the grounds of *confidentiality*; that members of the Secret Service, having sworn never to divulge information about their work, must in law be held forever to that allegiance. Eventually the Law Lords deliberated on the saga of *Spycatcher* and in October 1988 rejected government demands for a blanket injunction against the publishing in the UK of extracts from Wright's book.

'In a free society', said Lord Goff, one of the five Law Lords, 'there is a continuing public interest that the workings of government should be open to scrutiny and criticism.' The Law Lords attacked the government's conduct of the litigation and its claims that it is for government alone to judge what information must remain confidential. An estimated £3m was spent by the government on court proceedings.

This triumph for free speech was followed by government measures to revise the Official Secrets Act in order to achieve the kind of CENSORSHIP which had been so conspicuously rejected in the Lords' judgment. See TOPIC GUIDES under MEDIA: FREEDOM, CENSORSHIP; MEDIA HISTORY; MEDIA: POLITICS & ECONOMICS.

Stages in audience fragmentation See AUDIENCE: FRAGMENTATION.

Stakeholders A term used in PUBLIC RELATIONS (PR) practice to refer to those who have an interest or stake in, and thus are likely to be affected by, the activities and plans of an organization or individual client. Stakeholders may not always be aware of their potential involvement. Paul Baines, John Egan and Frank Jefkins in *Public Relations: Contemporary Issues and Techniques* (Elsevier Butterworth-Heinemann, 2004) identify four categories of stakeholders, based on their relative levels of power and interest as regards a particular situation.

Firstly there are the 'key players' who have considerable power to affect the activities of a company or industry sector. Secondly, there are stakeholders with low levels of power but a high degree of interest in the situation, and who will look to be kept informed of activities. Then there are those stakeholders with a high level of power but a low degree of interest in activities, but who should still receive a satisfactory amount of information. Fourthly are those stakeholders who have both low levels of power and interest: consequently relatively less effort may be expended to keep them informed.

A key media example of stakeholder influence in practice is broadcasting regulation. OFCOM, the UK regulator of broadcasting, is required to consult stakeholders in its formulation of policy and is subject to pressure from agencies with vested interests in broadcasting and advertising (see PRODUCT PLACEMENT; SPONSORSHIP OF BROADCAST PROGRAMMES (UK)). Thanks in part to stakeholder influence, Ofcom opened the doors of British broadcasting to product placement in February 2011. See JOHNSON AND SCHOLES: STAKEHOLDER MAPPING; PUBLICS.

Stamp Duty A government tax on newspapers in late eighteenth- and nineteenth-century Britain, with the express intention of controlling the numbers of papers and access to them by the general public. With news of the French Revolution (1789) across the water, Stamp Duty was raised to two pence per newspaper copy, with an additional Advertising Tax at three shillings per advertisement. In 1797 Stamp Duty was raised to three-and-a-half pence, and the hiring-out of papers was forbidden. In the year of the Battle of Waterloo, 1815, the Duty went up to four pence and the Advertising Tax was also raised.

These *Taxes on Knowledge*, as they were described, eventually provoked the 'War of the Unstamped' – the struggle of papers unable or unwilling to pay the duties. William Cobbett (1763–1835) dropped news from his *Political Register* so as to evade tax, and concentrated on opinion. Unstamped, and costing two pence, Cobbett's periodical achieved sales of 44,000. 'Here, in these critical years', writes Raymond Williams in *The Long Revolution* (Penguin, 1965), 'a popular press of a new kind was emerging, wholly independent in spirit, and reaching new classes of readers.'

Two of the six Acts of 1819 were directed against the press, and the 1820s and early 1830s featured clashes, fines, imprisonments and heroic defiance. In 1836 Stamp Duty was reduced from four pence to one penny, three years after the Advertisement Tax had been reduced from three shillings and sixpence to one shilling and sixpence per insertion. In 1853 the Advertising Tax was finally abolished; in 1855 the last penny of the Stamp Duty was removed; and in 1860 the duty imposed on paper was abandoned. 'The era of democratic journalism had formally arrived,' writes Joel H. Wiener in *The War of the Unstamped* (Cornell University Press, 1969), 'and the daily newspaper became the cultural staple of the social classes.' See NEWSPAPERS, ORIGINS; PRESS BARONS; UNDERGROUND PRESS. See also *TOPIC GUIDE* under MEDIA HISTORY.

Standards and practice in advertising See ADVERTISING STANDARDS AUTHORITY (ASA).

Status The concept of status derives from the work of the sociologist Max Weber, who argued that status, though linked to CLASS, is a distinct dimension of social stratification. Status is the social evaluation of an individual or group; the degree of prestige or honour accorded to him, her or it by society. Wealth and high income may confer status, but do not necessarily do so. The reasons why individuals or GROUPS may enjoy considerable status within a community or society are complex, subject to change and derive from many sources, such as the degree of power or authority a person or group may have, the perceived social usefulness of the abilities of an individual or group, or the level of education an individual has (see CULTURAL CAPITAL).

Occupation or the ownership of property may bestow status or require attributes such as a high level of education – hence the link between status and class. Status may be *ascribed*, that is based on fixed criteria over which a person may have no control – such as ancestry, ethnic affiliation or sex – or *achieved*, that is gained by endeavour or luck. Status given may not coincide with an individual's perception of his/her status.

Status must normally be endorsed by behaviour, such as the possession of status symbols, accent, manners, and social skills consistent with the status position. Much communicative behaviour is involved in the *display* of status, for example the use of accent and dress. The mass media carry many images of status. Advertisers in particular appeal to status-consciousness as a way of selling a wide range of products and services.

Status quo As things are: the way in which things are done or were done in a period of time under discussion. Within the social-science disciplines the term is often used to mean the prevailing or recent social, economic or political system – the way it works, usually by tradition, and who in the community works it.

There is some controversy within media studies as to whether or not the mass media generally play an important role in reinforcing the status quo by presenting it as the 'natural' or 'real' state of things, and by rarely, in their presentation of aspects of human life, calling it into question. For example, Denis McQuail in *Mass Communication Theory* (Sage, 2010) argues that within critical political-economic theory rests the proposition that 'opposition and alternative voices are marginalized' within the mass media. If this is the case, media output clearly services the maintenance of the status quo. See COMMON SENSE; CONSENSUS; ESTABLISHMENT; IDEOLOGY; POWER ELITE.

Stereophonic sound See GRAMOPHONE.

Stereoscopy The creation of the visual illusion of relief or three dimensions. The stereoscope was invented by Sir Charles Wheatstone (1802–75) in 1838. The process has had many applications. In photography, two separate photographs, taken from minimally different angles and corresponding to the position of two human eyes, are mounted side by side on a card. Viewed through the angled prisms of the stereoscope, they interact to give the appearance of depth or solidity.

In the cinema, experimental processes of stereoscopy were demonstrated as early as the 1930s. The technique was developed as Natural

Vision, or 3D, in the early 1950s, but never caught on – mainly perhaps because members of the audience had to wear special glasses. Only in Russia has a stereoscopic process that does not require the wearing of glasses been developed, yet even there it does not appear to have been widely adopted. However, 3D (with glasses) was brought experimentally to TV screens in the UK by ITV in 1982–83. It took on a new lease of life with the sensational special effects of the movie *Avatar* (2009) directed by James Cameron. Some commentators in 2010 and 2011 predicted that the TV of the future would be 3D. See HOLOGRAPHY.

Stereotype Oversimplified definition of a person or type of person, institution, style or event; to stereotype is to pigeon-hole, to thrust into tight slots of definition which allow of little adjustment or change. Stereotyping is widespread because it is convenient – unions are like this, Jews, Muslims, teenagers, women, gays, asylum-seekers are like this. Stereotyping is often, though not always, the result of or accompaniment to PREJUDICE. It serves the media well because they are in the business of instant recognition and ready cues. It is very rare that we actually know any stereotypes: we only read of them, hear of them or have them 'framed' for us on TV. See HALO EFFECT; LABELLING PROCESS (AND THE MEDIA); SELF-FULFILLING PROPHECY. See also *TOPIC GUIDE* under MEDIA ISSUES & DEBATES.

▶ Michael Pickering, *Stereotyping: The Politics of Representation* (Palgrave Macmillan, 2001).

Stigma According to Erving Goffman in *Stigma: Notes on the Management of Spoiled Identity* (Penguin, 1963), stigma denotes 'undesired differentness' and may result in the individual becoming 'reduced in our minds from a whole and usual person to a tainted, discounted one'. The sources of stigma are varied, but once the information is in the open it has the potential to damage reputations and trigger social rejection. Consequently an individual may feel apprehensive about disclosing information that is perceived to have the potential to confer a stigmatized identity. Goffman comments that the individual concerned is faced with numerous dilemmas: 'To display or not to display, to tell or not to tell, to let on or not to let on, to lie or not to lie; and in each case, to whom, how, when and where,' so there are clearly implications for communicative behaviour. Of course the individual may not always have much choice here, as others may control access to and disclosure of the information. See IMPRESSION MANAGEMENT; JOHARI WINDOW; SELF-DISCLOSURE.

Stopwatch culture See IMMEDIACY.

Storyboard Sequence of sketches or photographs used by the director or the producer of a film to sketch out, scene by scene, and sometimes frame by frame, the film's progression; its sight and sound.

Storyness See NARRATIVE.

Strategic silence See SILENCE: STRATEGIC SILENCE.

Strategy A term sometimes used to describe a communicative act that has been planned to some extent beforehand, which is deliberate and which has a clear purpose. Strategies can become a matter of habit: an example here might be the strategy used by a door-to-door salesperson. There are many different kinds of strategies used in INTERPERSONAL COMMUNICATION, and we learn to use them through experience. Some, like the greetings strategy, are commonly used by many people; some we invent for ourselves to deal with particular situations; and some may be specific to certain groups or circumstances. See TACTICS AND STRATEGIES.

Streaming The process by which data is compressed for transmission over the INTERNET, then recompressed for consumption by the user. The audio or visual content reaches the recipient in a continuous stream, played in real time on arrival, thus avoiding delay caused by downloading. Special software is required to facilitate the process of *un*compression and the directing of data for consumption.

Street view (Google Maps) Massive data bank of images of the urban scene, SURVEILLANCE on a universal scale: countries, regions, cities, towns, villages, streets, houses, shops, people, cars, bicycles; all are on GOOGLE camera. Having your front door online is not compulsory; requests for removal from the database can be registered in an online form, and sophisticated technology blurs human faces and car registration plates. Such 'intrusion' nevertheless prompt ongoing concerns over PRIVACY.

Stringer Name given in the NEWS reporting business for a non-staff reporter.

Structuralism A twentieth-century term of wide definition to describe certain traditions of analysing a range of studies – linguistics, literary criticism, psychoanalysis, social anthropology, Marxist theory and social history. Swiss scholar Ferdinand de Saussure's *Cours de Linguistique Générale* (1916), translated as *Course in General Linguistics* (1954), is probably the initial key work in this movement, later developed and diversified by Claude Lévi-Strauss and Roland Barthes. Structuralism is something of an umbrella term linked with the study of SIGN systems or SEMI-OLOGY/SEMIOTICS.

Structuralists would argue that language has both a natural and a cultural source. The natural source refers to language as a genetic endowment of the human race, and this is framed within a network of meanings derived from the CULTURE of society. Structuralism explores the deep and often unconscious assumptions about social reality that underlie language and its use.

In particular, it examines the way language is employed to construct MEANING from social events. However, assumptions about social reality are themselves also a product of social conditioning. Thus different cultures and sub-cultures, and indeed individuals, may generate different patterns of meaning from the same objective event or situation. See POSTMODERN-ISM. See also *TOPIC GUIDE* under COMMUNICA-TION THEORY.

Style A means by which the individual or group expresses identity (see IDENTIFICATION; SELF-IDENTITY), attitudes and VALUES, about self, about others and about society. Style takes many forms – hair style, dress style, aesthetic style, or a complete pattern of living: lifestyle. Styles may enable the individual to secure a sense of personal identity; to acquire a sense of belonging, of being 'in' with a favoured group; to make a gesture of rebellion (against the conventional style of parents, for example, or the older generation in all shapes and forms); and to achieve STATUS, that is a status awarded him/her by others in the favoured group, and by his/her peers generally.

Defiance of society at large is often cited as a reason why certain styles are adopted. This may or may not be true in all cases, but what is certain is that society often interprets such styles as acts of defiance or rejection, and the arbiters in this process of interpretation (or MEDIATION) are the mass media. Coverage by the media, researchers have found, tends to overdramatize the significance of style, to create STEREOTYPES and summon up exaggerated fears in the community.

In the world of the arts, style is that particular set of characteristics of approach and treatment which gives a work its identity. As with styles in hair or dress, styles are first created, then imitated. In painting, the style of Paul Cézanne (1839–1906) is highly distinctive and instantly recognizable by anyone with a particular interest in art.

However, it took Cézanne many years to develop that style, which was a visible manifestation of everything he believed about visual art; thus style represents the outer part of a whole structure that is made up of personality, experience, learning, theory, belief – and fused, if the style is successful. Those coming after may slavishly imitate the style of the master or, like the Cubists in the case of Cézanne, assimilate the style and then re-create it, thrusting it in new directions. See CULTURE; DRESS; FOLK DEVILS; LABEL LIBEL; LABELLING PROCESS (AND THE MEDIA); SUB-CULTURE; YOUTH CULTURE. See also *TOPIC GUIDE* under REPRESENTATION.

Sub-culture Alternatives to the dominant CULTURE in society, sub-cultures have their own systems of NORMS, VALUES and beliefs and in some cases their own language CODES. Such systems are often expressions of rejection of or resistance to the dominant culture. Members of sub-cultures are frequently those to whom the dominant culture awards low, subordinate and/or dependent STATUS: youth, for example. Each sub-culture represents the reactions of a particular social group to its experience of society.

Some sub-cultures and their members may be labelled *deviant* by others in society. It has been argued that because of the fragmented social nature of modern society, the mass media play an increasingly important role in relaying images of such sub-cultures both to their own members and to members of the dominant culture. Dick Hebdige in *Subculture: The Meaning of Style* (Methuen, 1979, reissued 2002) writes that in doing so, the media tend to accommodate the sub-cultures within the framework of the dominant culture, thus preserving the CONSEN-SUS; a procedure which he calls the 'process of recuperation'.

The postmodern (see POSTMODERNISM) perspective is that the solidarity of sub-culture has given way to a more fluid and fragmented sense of association; an association that might be more transitory, with styles and experiences drawn from a diverse range of influences – including those found in cyberspace. Contemporary groupings, it is argued, are more likely to resemble small tribes than the larger youth sub-cultures of the past. Further, it can be argued that the media, fashion and cultural industries now play a more significant role in shaping and marketing youth culture and associated identities.

As regards style, in Ted Polhemus and UZi PART B, *Hot Bodies, Cool Styles: New Techniques in Self-Adornment* (Thames and Hudson, 2004) Polhemus argues that whilst there are still sub-cultures that express their group membership through style, the emphasis for many young

S

people is now focused on communicating a sense of personal identity, and they adopt a DIY approach to personal appearance as a means of declaring 'I am here'. An individual's style can be assembled using a diverse range of artefacts 'borrowed' from numerous cultures and sub-cultures, past and present. Speaking of Western culture, Polhemus argues, 'What you look like is no longer strictly determined by social situation and culture or even fashion. Free from rules, appearance is now a matter of personal creativity.' Individuals may frequently change their personal style.

▸ David Muggleton and Rupert Weinzierl, eds, *The Post-subcultures Reader* (Berg, 2003).

Subliminal Signals that act below the threshold of conscious reception. Most familiarly we use the word in reference to subliminal ADVERTIS-ING – the trick of flashing up on the screen, or recording on tape, messages so rapid that they are not consciously recorded but which may subsequently affect future attitudes or behaviour.

In the UK, subliminal advertising is illegal and its use in other media is banned by the Institute of Practitioners in Advertising. In the US there is no such control. Many department stores use subliminal seduction to counteract shoplifting. Messages such as 'I am honest, I will not steal' are mixed with background music and continu-ally repeated. One retail chain reported a drop of one-third in thefts in nine months as a result of its subliminal conscience-coaxing.

Computer games escape rules concerning subliminal messages. The UK *Sunday Times* published a major story, 'Children "drugged" by computer games' (8 October 1995), concerning the Time Warner game *Endorfun*. The messages are there, admit the manufacturers, but they are positive, one message being 'I forgive myself completely'. Randeep Ramesh, author of the article, quotes the opinion of Howard Shevrin, Professor of Psychology at the University of Michigan: 'It does not pay to fool around with subliminal messages. The results may not be good if you are the wrong person for the wrong message.' See SLEEPER EFFECT. See also *TOPIC GUIDE* under MEDIA: PROCESSES & PRODUC-TION.

Subtitle Or striptitle, a text near the bottom of the projected image, usually providing a translation of foreign-language dialogue. These days it is possible with foreign-language films screened on TV to generate subtitles electronically so that the words are not actually on the film itself. In some multilingual areas, such as Cairo, where three or more titles in different languages and scripts are required, subtitles are projected onto separate screens at the sides and bottom of the main screen.

Super-injunction A legal block in the UK to the publication of information – the 'super' element being that even the publication of information that a block has taken place is banned. The super-injunction hit the headlines in 2011 when an anonymous TWITTER user posted details of legal injunctions taken out by celebrities in 'kiss-and-tell' stories. According to CNET UK news, Twitter broke all visitor records in May, as 'gossip hungry users flocked to the site'.

In the UK *Sunday Mirror* (15 May) Vincent Moss, defining super-injunctions as 'gagging orders [that] wealthy celebrities use to hide their indiscretions', reported that a survey by the paper found that eight out of ten members of the public believed such injunctions 'are only for the rich'. See DEFAMATION; PRIOR RESTRAINT; PRIVACY.

Supervening social necessity Notion that social or cultural pressures give the impetus to technological development, serving as *accelerators* in the process of change. Brian Winston suggests this feature in 'How are media born?' in *Questioning the Media: A Critical Introduction* (Sage, 1990), edited by John Downing, Ali Mohammadi and Annabelle Sreberny-Mohammadi. He cites the arrival of TV in the US as being accelerated by the 'rise of the home, the dominance of the nuclear family, and the political and economic need to maintain full employment' after the Second World War. Winston argues that 'supervening social necessi-ties are at the interface between society and technology'. They may operate as a result of the needs of corporations, or because of new or rival technologies.

As well as accelerators, social necessities may serve as *brakes* upon technological develop-ments, which 'work to slow the disruptive impact of new technology. I describe the operation of these brakes as the "law" of the suppression of radical potential, using "law" in the standard social science sense to denote a regular and powerful general tendency'. In this case, new technology, though available, is resisted, checked or even suppressed. Says Winston, 'the brakes ensure that a technology's introduction does not disrupt the social or corporate status quo'.

Winston is of the view that while TV had been 'accelerated' after 1945, it had been 'braked' prior to the war: 'Thus in the case of TV, the existence of facsimile systems, the rise of radio ... and the need not to destroy the film industry all acted

to suppress the speed at which the new medium was introduced, to minimize disruption.' Winston returns to, and expands on, his analysis of the development of media technologies in his book *Media Technology and Society: A History from the Telegraph to the Internet* (Routledge, 1998). See TECHNOLOGICAL DETERMINISM. See also *TOPIC GUIDE* under MEDIA: TECHNOLOGIES.
▸ M. Hank Hausler, *Media Facades: History, Technology and Media Content* (AVEdition, 2009).

Surround See EISENBERG'S MODEL OF COMMUNICATION AND IDENTITY, 2001.

Surveillance Keeping watch; used in a media sense, the word indicates the way in which listeners, viewers or readers employ the media with the aim of gleaning information from them: 'TV news provides food for thought' or 'I like to see how big issues are sorted out.' Equally surveillance implies the process of authority and its agencies keeping watch on the public. See USES AND GRATIFICATIONS THEORY.

Surveillance society New technology has vastly increased and speeded up access to personal data by those in authority, or those individuals or organizations involved in financial, administrative or commercial transactions with members of the public. Each time we use a switch card; each time we dial a telephone number, drive past a CCTV camera (or even leave our front door), we offer notification of our activities, our whereabouts, and our lifestyle. David Lyon in *The Electronic Eye: The Rise of Surveillance Society* (University of Minnesota Press, 1994) identifies four domains of surveillance in contemporary life – government administration, policing and security, the workplace and the consumer market place; and for Lyon, a key characteristic of surveillance is that it operates *across* boundaries.

The concept of a surveillance society is not new. The English philosopher, social and legal reformer Jeremy Bentham (1748–1832), in a proposal for the humanitarian treatment of prisoners, suggested the construction of what he called a *Panopticon*. This was a circular building of cells with a central watchtower from which constant surveillance of the prisoners would take place, without their being certain at any given time that they were being directly observed. They would be well aware, of course, of the presence of surveillance and this knowledge would, without coercion, rule their behaviour until, so Bentham theorized, their good behaviour would become self-regulating.

For several commentators the Panopticon has become a metaphor for our own times.

In particular, the French philosopher Michel Foucault (1926–84) has focused on the 'all-seeing' Panopticon (see PANOPTICON GAZE). In *Discipline and Punish* (Penguin, 1977) he likens the Panopticon to the Christian God's infinite knowledge, and to computer monitoring of individuals in advanced capitalism. He argues that surveillance as represented by the contemporary Panopticon creates subjects responsible for their own subjection (see PRIVACY).

We are subject to surveillance not only as citizens but also as AUDIENCE for media. In an article entitled 'Tracking the audience', in *Questioning Media: A Critical Introduction* (Sage, 1990), edited by John Downing, Ali Mohammadi and Annabelle Srebemy-Mohammadi, Oscar Gandy Jr remarks how the fragmentation of audience for media, rendered possible by new technology, has resulted in a desperation among programme-makers that has led to two strategies aimed at survival.

These, Gandy identifies as *rationalization*, that is 'the pursuit of efficiency in the production, distribution, and sale of goods and services', and *surveillance* which 'provides the information necessary for greater control'. Increasingly, says Gandy, 'the surveillance of audiences resembles police surveillance of suspected criminals' and people are less and less aware that their behaviour as audience is being measured.

In *A Report of the Surveillance Society* for the UK Information Commissioner (2006), edited by David Murakami Wood, the team of authors write of 'massive surveillance systems that underpin modern existence'. While acknowledging that surveillance has benefits to society, the proliferation of modes of surveillance is producing 'situations where distinctions of class, race, gender, geography and citizenship are currently being exacerbated and institutionalized'.

A danger identified by the Report is that we 'may become accustomed to being surveilled', our 'activities and movements tracked and also anticipated, without our noticing it, and – especially in the public services – without the ability to opt in or opt out, or to understand fully what happens to our data'.

The Report, freely available as a download, explains in detail a range of devices and developments in surveillance, touching on *social sorting*, *function creep* and *location technology*. The editors warn that 'technologies are at their most important when they become ubiquitous, taken for granted and largely invisible'.

Of course in the age of social networking (see NETWORKING: SOCIAL NETWORKING), surrendering privacy rather than guarding it has become the online fashion. Through FACEBOOK, YOUTUBE and TWITTER, etc. we post details of ourselves for all to read; we risk surveillance (some call it stalking) because it is a two-way process, an opportunity for interactivity, regardless of the dangers of 'consorting with strangers'. See BIOMETRICS; CCTV: CLOSED-CIRCUIT TELEVISION; ECHELON; INTERNET: MONITORING OF CONTENT; REGULATION OF INVESTIGATORY POWERS ACT (RIPA) (UK), 2000; JOURNALISM: PHONE-HACKING; USA – PATRIOT ACT, 2001. See also *TOPIC GUIDES* under MEDIA: FREEDOM, CENSORSHIP; MEDIA ISSUES & DEBATES.

SWOT Analytical approach widely used to scan and evaluate the internal and external environment of an organization. It can also be employed to evaluate specific organizational activities, for example the design of new products, as well as in planning MARKETING and PUBLIC RELATIONS campaigns. The approach taken is to analyse Strengths, Weaknesses, Opportunities and Threats. In *Exploring Public Relations* (Pearson Education, 2009), Ralph Tench and Liz Yeomans provide some examples: *strengths* may include brand loyalty and well-motivated employees, whilst a limited range of products or an ageing customer-base may be identified as *weaknesses*; potential *opportunities* could include new markets and *threats* can include the possibility of political instability affecting operations. They further comment that whilst the organization itself can often determine its strengths and weaknesses, 'opportunities and threats, are generally external to the organization and can be derived from wider environmental analysis ... but are usually related to those factors that have a direct impact on it'. See EPISTLE.

Sykes Committee Report on Broadcasting, 1923 See BBC, ORIGINS.

Symbol Any object, person or EVENT to which a generally agreed, shared MEANING has been given, and which individuals have learned to accept as representing something other than itself: a national flag represents feelings of patriotism and national unity, for example. Symbols are almost always culture-bound. See ICONIC; METAPHOR; MYTH; SEMIOLOGY/SEMIOTICS; SIGN; SIGNIFICATION.

'Symbolic annihilation of women' (by the media) See NORMS.

Symbolic code See CODES OF NARRATIVE.

Symbolic convergence theory Ernest G. Bormann in his article 'Symbolic convergence theory: a communication formulation' in the *Journal of Communication*, Autumn, 1985, writes of 'shared fantasies' which 'provide group members with comprehensible forms for explaining the past and thinking about the future – a basis for communal and group consciousness' (see NARRATIVE PARADIGM).

Bormann posits a three-part structure to the theory: (1) the part which deals with the discovery and arrangement of recurring communicative forms and patterns that indicate the evolution and presence of a shared group consciousness; (2) the part which consists of a description of the dynamic tendencies within communication systems 'that explain why group consensuses arise, continue, decline, and disappear', and the effects such group CONSENSUS has in terms of meanings, motives and communication within the group: the basic communication process is the dynamic of people sharing group fantasies; and (3) that part of the theory which consists of the factors which explain why people share the fantasies they do, and when.

By 'fantasy' Bormann means the creative and imaginative shared interpretation of events 'that fulfil a group psychological or rhetorical need'. What the author terms 'rhetorical fantasies' are the result of '*homo narrans* in collectives sharing narratives that account for their experiences and their hopes and fears'. Such rhetorical fantasies may include 'fanciful and fictitious scripts of imaginary characters, but they often deal with things that have actually happened to members of the group or that are reported in authenticated works of history, in the news media, or in the oral history and folklore of other groups and communities'.

The sharing of fantasies brings a 'convergence of appropriate feelings among participants ... when members of a mass audience share a fantasy they jointly experience the same emotions, develop common heroes and villains, celebrate certain actions as laudable, and interpret some aspect of their common experience in the same way'.

This Bormann names *symbolic convergence*. Whilst the 'rational world paradigm' claims that there is an objective truth which speakers can mirror in their communication, and against which its logic and argument can be tested and evaluated (and therefore regards MYTH and fantasy as untrue, as the recounting of falsehoods), for those giving credence to shared fantasies, 'the stories of myths or fantasy themes are central'.

An underlying assumption of the theory seems to be that fantasies are not only creative but also benign. It would be interesting to apply symbolic convergence theory, the notion of *homo narrans*, to fantasies entertained about racial superiority, where fantasy becomes a nightmare. See TOPIC GUIDE under COMMUNICATION THEORY.

▶ Ernest G. Bormann, *Communicative Theory* (Holt, Rinehart & Winston, 1980); *The Force of Fantasy: Restoring the American Dream* (Illinois University Press, 1985).

Symbolic interactionism Term associated with the ideas of American scholar Herbert Blumer and crystallized in his book *Symbolic Interactionism: Perspective and Method* (University of California Press, 1969; first paperback edition, 1986). Blumer sees 'meaning as arising in a process of interaction between people'. The meaning of an object or a phenomenon for one person 'grows out of the ways in which other persons act towards the person with regard to the thing', that is the thing's *symbolic value*. Symbolic interactionism sees MEANING as a social product, as a creation 'formed in and through the defining activities of people as they interact'. All meanings, emphasizes Blumer, are subject to a constant and recurring 'interpretative process'; and this is a 'formative process in which meanings are used and revised as instruments for the guidance and formation of action'. See SELF-CONCEPT; SELF-IDENTITY; SEMIOLOGY/SEMIOTICS; SEMIOTIC POWER.

Symmetry, strain towards Concept posed by Theodore Newcomb in 'An approach to the study of communicative acts', *Psychological Review*, 63 (1953). The act of communication is characterized, believes Newcomb, by a 'strain towards symmetry', that is towards balance and consistency. See CONGRUENCE THEORY; INTERPERSONAL COMMUNICATION; NEWCOMB'S ABX MODEL OF COMMUNICATION, 1953.

Synchronic linguistics See LINGUISTICS.

Synchronous sound In film, sound effects synchronized with the visual image were first used commercially in 1926, in *Don Juan*, but it was *The Jazz Singer* in November 1927 that caused the sensation among audiences and marked the birth of the 'Talkies'. Warner Brothers had been heading for oblivion in the cutthroat world of the HOLLYWOOD studios when the company adopted a system developed by the Bell Telephones Laboratories which reproduced sound from large discs, matching sound and picture by mechanical linkage. Nothing in the cinema was ever the same again.

The 'Talkies' marked the end of many careers made in the silent era, but created new opportunities for actors from the theatre, writers, musicians, vaudeville and RADIO stars. As a technical possibility, synchronous sound had been inviting interest from movie makers from as early as 1902. In that year Monsieur Gaumont gave an address to the Société Française de la Photographie, on film and employing synchronous sound. Indeed, two years earlier Herr Ruhmer demonstrated what he called 'light telephony' to record sound directly onto the film itself – the first soundtrack.

Following the inventions of the thermionic valve by John Fleming in 1904 and the audion vacuum tube by Lee De Forest in 1907, amplification of sound by comparatively simple electric methods was feasible: the studios were simply not interested, fearing, perhaps, the impact language differences might have on the universal appeal of film as mime, whose only verbal language was easily translatable titling (see reference to *suppression of radical potential* in SUPERVENING SOCIAL NECESSITY).

Though Lee De Forest's Phonofilm of 1923 demonstrated how light waves could synchronize sound and image, and though the Germans had developed the finest early sound system of all, Tri-Ergon, the continuing profitability of the silent movie blinded the studios to two significant facts: the potential of silent film had practically been exhausted; and audiences were becoming bored.

Lights of New York (1928) was the first all-talking picture and within a year thousands of cinemas had been equipped for sound. Warner's VITAPHONE disc was soon replaced by optical sound systems where images and sound were put together on the same film, to make the married print where sound synchronization with the picture could not be lost. As sound recording techniques developed, dialogue, sound effects and music were recorded separately, using a magnetic sound process, and then mixed at a later stage, thus allowing latitude for changes and creative editing.

The introduction of sound did not rescue the cinema from the general economic slump that followed the Wall Street Crash of 1929. During 1931, cinema attendances in the US dropped by 40 per cent and in 1932 the movie business lost between US$ 4 and 5 million. However, it was probably the new dimension of sound in the cinema that enabled the industry to rally so quickly.

The 'Talkies' interacted substantially with RADIO, the one drawing technical and creative ideas as well as talented personnel from the other. By 1937, 90 per cent of US-sponsored

S

national radio programmes in the US were transmitted from Hollywood. See *TOPIC GUIDES* under MEDIA HISTORY; MEDIA TECHNOLOGIES.

Synergy The establishment of relationships between differing areas and/or organizations within the cultural and media industries that allow for greater efficiency in the production and promotion of two or more cultural/media artefacts. An example of synergy is when the launching of a new film is accompanied by the promotion of a wide range of related merchandise. Conglomerates (see CONGLOMERATES: MEDIA CONGLOMERATES) are in an enviable position to take advantage of the benefits of synergies.

Examples of synergic partnerships have multiplied until they have become a NORM, and involve a range of sponsors and beneficiaries; thus McDonald's burgers and fries synergize with Disney movies while Coca-Cola synergizes with Harry Potter books and films. Perhaps the classic synergic relationship is between sport and big business, though the arts and business are not far behind. See PRODUCT PLACEMENT.

Syntactics A branch of SEMIOLOGY/SEMIOTICS; the study of the SIGNS and rules relating to signs, without reference to MEANING.

Syntagm See PARADIGM.

Syntax The combination of words into significant patterns; the grammatical structure in sentences.

T

Tabloid, tabloidese, tabloidization In '"Tabloidization" of news: a comparative analysis of Anglo-American and German press journalism' (*European Journal of Communication*, September 1999) Frank Esser writes that the term 'tabloid' orginally referred to a pharmaceutical trademark for the concentrated form of medicines as pill or tablet: 'This narcotic tabloid effect and the fact that it is easy to swallow have been readily transferred to the media.'

The term, in the UK, is used to refer to the size of a newspaper (in comparison with the *broadsheet* format), but in general 'tabloidese' describes the nature of news content and style. Esser quotes Marvin Kalb, Director of the Shorenstein Centre on the Press, Politics and Public Affairs at Harvard University: tabloidese is characterized by 'a downgrading of hard news and upgrading of sex, scandal and infotainment'. At the micro level, states Esser, tabloidization 'can be seen as a media phenomenon involving the revision of traditional newspaper and other media formats driven by reader preferences and commercial requirements', whilst on the macro level it 'can be seen as a social phenomenon both instigating and symbolizing major changes to the constitution of society'.

Esser's study focuses on the micro level of the tabloidization process, meaning 'a change in the range of topics being covered (more entertainment, less information), in the form of presentation (fewer longer stories, more shorter ones with pictures and illustrations) and a change in the mode of address (more street talk when addressing readers)'. He argues that the nature, evolution and relative predominance of tabloidization varies between America, the UK and Germany; thus it is an 'extremely problematic term' and can 'therefore only be analysed with reference to the respective media cultures and journalistic traditions' of the countries in question.

For example, tabloidization has never taken hold in Germany to the extent that it has in the UK; in part because, as far as sex scandals are concerned, Germany has a strong PRIVACY law that 'also protects public figures'. He cites research evidence showing that extensive coverage of scandals can increase public disillusionment with public life, hence the fears which many commentators have 'that a shift towards sensation, emotion and scandal may have some negative effects on democracy' (see JOURNALISM: PHONE HACKING).

Currently the term *tabloidization* is used to describe what many critics see happening both to the serious, broadsheet newspaper, and to TV NEWS, in the sense that they are 'getting more and more like the tabloids', matching them for populist content and design, and demonstrating the same fascination for covering the lives and antics of celebrities. In other words, the accusation is that while the tabloids – in the UK referred to as the 'red tops' – are already dumbed down, the dumbing-down process is actually what is happening to traditionally serious media. See *TOPIC GUIDE* under LANGUAGE/DISCOURSE/NARRATIVE.

▶ Rodrigo Uribe and Barrie Gunter, 'Research note: the tabloidization of British tabloids', *European Journal of Communication* (September, 2004); Martin Conboy, *Tabloid Britain* (Routledge, 2005); Anita Biressi and Heather Nunn, eds, *The Tabloid Culture Reader* (Open University Press, 2008).

Tactics and strategies These terms are used in a number of contexts within the media, culture and communication field. The term *tactics* refers to the varying activities that can be undertaken within a *strategy*. A strategy refers to the intentional co-ordination of activities; tactics, to achieve a desired, often long-term, goal. Numerous tactics may be employed within a strategic plan: for example, a PUBLIC RELATIONS (PR) practitioner may use tactics such as press conferences, press releases or launch events within a long-term strategy of raising the profile of a client.

Michel de Certeau in *The Practice of Everyday Life* (University of California Press, 1984), when analysing everyday cultural consumption, draws a distinction between the strategies of the powerful controllers of the cultural industries and the tactics of the relatively powerless ordinary consumers in finding their own space for creating MEANING, by adapting to their own use mass-produced cultural artefacts.

Some of these tactics subvert or resist the intentions and intended messages of the powerful. De Certeau's distinction, whilst acknowledging that audiences/consumers may be active in their consumption, does not imply that they have by any means the degree of power over cultural consumption exercised by those who own and control the cultural industries.

A more recent example of the use of such strategic power by those who own or control companies within the media, culture and communications sector can be seen in the use of social media within the protests that occurred in 2011 in areas of the Middle-East. Margareta Pagano in the 13 February 2011 edition of *The Independent on Sunday*, commenting on the-then current protests in Egypt, noted that some mobile operators and Internet service providers bowed to pressure from the Egyptian government and closed down their services for several days, despite their obligations to their customers. However, this government strategy was undermined by a tactical response from those protesters able to use their technical knowledge to circumvent the shutdowns and continue mobilization of support for the protests. See AUDIENCE: ACTIVE AUDIENCE; SEMIOTIC POWER; SMART MOBS.

Tag A key word or phrase used for quick and convenient identification in online postings; a pointer to the nature of the content or theme. Take, for example, a posting on the topic of NEWS VALUES. The following tags might be employed to attract the attention of users/visitors: *amplification, frequency, familiarity, correspondence*, etc.

Tag questions The addition of phrases such as 'Isn't it?' or 'Don't you think?' at the end of a statement as tag questions, according to some linguists, suggests tentativeness on behalf of the speaker, and weakens the impact of what is said. However, there is some debate here. Tag questions can serve a range of functions, some relating to the content of speech, others relating to the facilitation of interaction and the relationships and attitudes of the participants to one another.

When used to facilitate interaction, tag questions do not seem to be associated with tentativeness; indeed, the tendency here is for tags to be associated with powerful speakers. Several studies suggest that women use more tag questions than men when acting as facilitators in an interaction.

Take See SHOT.

Talkies See SYNCHRONOUS SOUND.

Talloires Declaration, 1981 Concerned at the attempts by the United Nations Educational, Scientific and Cultural Organization (UNESCO) seemingly to impose upon world information systems a 'New Order' which would be characterized by far-reaching controls, representatives from news organizations of twenty countries met in the French village of Talloires in May 1981. They issued a Declaration which insisted that journalists sought no special protected status, as was perceived to be UNESCO'S intention, and that they were united in a 'joint declaration to the freest, most accurate and impartial information that is within our professional capacity to produce'. The Declaration asserted that there could be no double standards of freedom for rich and poor countries. See MACBRIDE COMMISSION; MEDIA IMPERIALISM. See also *TOPIC GUIDE* under GLOBAL PERSPECTIVES.

Tamizdat See SAMIZDAT.

Taste In a media sense, the notion of good or bad taste generally relates to decisions about how much and how far; the answers to these questions depend upon AUDIENCE expectations and readiness, and the degree of access and immediacy. A photograph of an execution, reproduced in a newspaper or magazine, is sufficiently controlled by the frame of print and the fact that the event took place in the past, to escape the accusation of bad taste.

However, there were vigorous protests when, on TV news, a Vietcong prisoner had a pistol put to his head, and the trigger pulled. This was bringing, as it were, too much reality into the sitting room. It may have been the truth, ran the argument, but somehow the reproduction and presentation turned reality into theatre, indeed into macabre entertainment. As such it appeared an insult to human dignity, to that of the victim and to that of the audience cast in the role of voyeurs.

T

Taste can also be used to refer to the cultural or aesthetic tastes of an individual or group, and such tastes can be used as signifiers of economic and CULTURAL CAPITAL and used as a means of social distinction. This perspective on taste owes much to the work of Pierre Bourdieu outlined in *Distinction: A Social Critique of the Judgment of Taste* (Harvard University Press, 1984). He argued that an individual's taste was significantly influenced, though not totally determined, by his/her CLASS background, and thus aspects of taste could be read as both a product and a signifier of class affiliation.

Bourdieu uses the term *habitus* to refer to the collection of unconscious dispositions that individuals may have as a result of their location within the class structure; these may then influence tastes, body image and bodily communication: a person might buy an Armani suit but he/she will also need to look at ease wearing it, to carry off the statement it may make about his/her social position.

Bourdieu's view that class significantly influences an individual's tastes has been criticized, in part because some commentators argue that class distinction in modern-day society is less easy to define than in the past, and generally considered of diminishing importance. However, this is not to say that people are unaware of the signs of distinction located in some tastes. See COMMUNICATION, NON-VERBAL (NVC); CONSUMPTION BEHAVIOUR; CULTURE: CONSUMER CULTURE; CULTURE: POPULAR CULTURE; OBJECT LANGUAGE; SELF-IDENTITY.

▶ Mike Featherstone, *Consumer Culture and Postmodernism* (Sage, 1991); Fran Martin, ed., *Interpreting Everyday Culture* (Edward Arnold, 2003); David Bell and Joanne Hollows, eds, *Ordinary Lifestyles: Popular Media, Consumption and Taste* (Open University Press/McGraw-Hill Education, 2005); Jean-Pascal Daloz, *The Sociology of Elite Distinction* (Palgrave Macmillan, 2010).

Taxes on knowledge See STAMP DUTY.

Taxonomic conquistadors Term used by Bill Nicholls in *Blurred Boundaries: Questions of Meaning in Contemporary Culture* (University of Indiana Press, 1994) to describe the agencies, sociological and marketing, that subject humans to classification or SEGMENTATION. Nicholls admits the dangers inherent in placing people into (often stereotypical) slots, but concedes that 'with no categories at all culture itself would disappear'. The use of the term *conquistadors* suggests that such taxonomies – lists of classification – have an enforcing and shaping capacity through powers of persuasion and of inclusion/

exclusion. See AUDIENCE DIFFERENTIATION; AUDIENCE MEASUREMENT; VALS TYPOLOGY.

Technique: Ellul's theory of technique In a number of books written between the 1950s and 1990, Jacques Ellul saw contemporary society as being dominated by technological advances, each aiding the MEDIATING power of mass communication; and together leading to a society in which efficiency and consequently conformity become the key determinants of human affairs. Ellul uses the term 'technique' to suggest the generality of attitudes to, and uses of, machines in everyday life, applying equally to social production as to material production.

His view is a bleak one, seeing efficiency, brought about by the wholesale adoption by those who rule and those who are ruled, as being both authoritarian in tendency and beyond the control of governments: 'Technical advance,' says Ellul in *The Technological Society* (Knopf, 1964), 'gradually invades the state, which in turn is compelled to assume forms favourable to this advance.' Politicians, Ellul sees as 'impotent satellites of the machine, which with all its parts and techniques, apparently functions as well without them'. However, the politicians do not step down. Instead they create an illusion of politics and political leadership.

Ellul anticipates the response that the Information Age has brought about a more involved public in the political process. For him the sheer volume of information works to reinforce the technological society by overwhelming the citizen. In a detailed analysis of Ellul's theory of technique in 'Hegemony, agency, and dialectical tension in Ellul's technological society' in the *Journal of Communication* (Summer 1998), Rick Clifton Moore writes: 'This is not to say that all of the blame for the political illusion must be laid at the feet of the state and the media. Ellul's orientation suggests the complicity of the citizens themselves ... The modern citizen is much too willing to accept the comfortable route of technique, rather than make difficult choices that would require humanness.'

The public, in Ellul's view, is subject to, and in thrall to, the 'spectacle-orientated society' in which everything is 'subordinated to visualization' and 'nothing has meaning out of it'. In today's society, Ellul says, there are many, and powerful, deterrents of human freedom. A key question is whether, in societies where 'covetousness and the desire for power' are human constants across all cultural boundaries, there is sufficient agency among citizens to achieve freedom. See HEGEMONY; IDEOLOGICAL STATE

APPARATUSES; IDEOLOGY; INTERNET; McDON-
ALDIZATION; SEMIOTIC POWER; SURVEILLANCE
SOCIETY; WEB 2.0. See also *TOPIC GUIDE* under
MEDIA: TECHNOLOGIES.

Technological determinism The view that if
something is technically feasible, then it is both
desirable and bound to be realized in practice.
Evidence points to the fact that such determinism is only partly convincing. Much technology
usage is a by-product of technology devised for
other purposes. RADIO became an 'inevitability',
for example, largely because its determinant was
radar, required to fulfil military needs, while
satellites had a long record of military/political
functions before they began to beam sporting
events to the peoples of the world.

Set against notions of technological determinism is a second theory, *symptomatic technology*,
which argues that technology is a by-product
of a social process which itself has been otherwise determined. In *Television: Technology
and Cultural Form* (Fontana, 1974), Raymond
Williams says that basically both theories are
in error because in different ways they have
'abstracted technology from society' instead of
examining the crucial interaction between them.
Of course part of that interaction is the belief
in technological determinism, and the risk of it
becoming a SELF-FULFILLING PROPHECY.

Dwayne Winseck in 'Pursuing the Holy Grail:
information highways and media reconvergence
in Britain and Canada' in the *European Journal
of Communication*, September 1998, argues
that contrary to 'the belief that technological
factors determine how media are organized', the
primary drivers of media evolution 'are machi-
nations between governments and industries,
visions of how markets should evolve, and ideas
about whether communication constitutes
just another commodity or is something more
imbued with cultural consideration and public
service values'. See INTERNET; SUPERVENING
SOCIAL NECESSITY. See also *TOPIC GUIDE* under
MEDIA ISSUES & DEBATES.

**Technology: the consumerization of
technology** A neat definition is offered by
Wikipedia: 'In many ways, consumerization is
the process by which the IT industry is being
transformed from its roots as a business tool
into primarily a social medium. Its consequences
are expected to grow sharply in the future.' The
shift from a base of business and industry to one
of individual use has been driven by popular
demand, which has run neck and neck with
technological development: today's device is
tomorrow's museum piece.

Despite problems of competing formats and
divergent standards, consumption through
economies of scale has turned niche markets into
a global industry fed by an insatiable appetite for
new and better applications (termed *apps*). Such
all-embracing comsumerization raises questions
concerning the interplay between leisure and
work: should companies permit or forbid their
employees from, for example, surfing the Net
during working hours; or should they embrace
the practice as potentially – being essentially a
social medium – of integral value in business
operations? See MOBILIZATION; WEB 2.0. See
also *TOPIC GUIDE* under MEDIA: TECHNOLOGIES.

Telecommunication *Tele* means far off, at a
distance; a telecommunication is communication
by TELEGRAPHY or TELEPHONE, with or without
wires or cables. In telephony and telegraphy,
signals are transmitted as electric impulses along
wires. In RADIO and TV the signals are transmitted through space as modulations of carrier
waves of electromagnetic radiation. See TELE-
TEXT; WIRELESS TELEGRAPHY; WORLD TRADE
ORGANIZATION (WTO) TELECOMMUNICATIONS
AGREEMENT, 1997.

Teledemocracy Term used to describe theories
that telecommunications serve to advance
democracy by the rapid transmission of information across boundaries, the openness of
debate, interactive exchange and participation
in the digital age. Optimistic commentators
see the Internet as a powerful agent of change,
likening it to the AGORA, where citizens are
better informed about what is going on locally,
regionally, nationally and globally, and better
able to take part in democratic action.

It has become increasingly difficult for governments to suppress information or to prevent
citizens from diffusing that information across
the population, and thus easier for popular pressure to grow and shift from online platforms to
the streets. The 30-year absolutist rule of Hosni
Mubarak in Egypt appeared to be toppled in
February 2011 by mass demonstrations which,
at least in part, were inspired by computer-
facilitated information and calls by any teleco-
municative means to assemble and demand an
end to authoritarian rule and progress towards
democracy.

A sober word of caution is offered by Timothy
Garton Ash in a UK *Guardian* article written at
the time of Mubarak's fall, 'Not 1989. Not 1789.
But Egyptians can learn from other revolutions'
(10 February 2011). The author, referring to the
perceived power of communication technologies, says that while they 'matter enormously ...'

T

they 'did not prevent popular protest movements being crushed in Belarus and Iran'. They have a catalytic effect but 'they do not determine the outcome ... we must remind ourselves that these moments are always transient. The hard grind of consolidating liberty is all ahead'.

As for the specific impact of online 'people power', a similar warning was issued by Ron Deibert in 'Blogging dangerously' (*Index on Censorship*, Vol. 39. No. 4, 2010). He writes, 'In no other time during the internet's history has it been as dangerous to publish on the web as it is now ...Whereas once governments were either incapable of, or chose not to, regulate the internet, today they are reasserting themselves dramatically and forcefully' by 'the implementation of new and more rigid laws around slander, libel and copyright'.

Diebert believes it is important to remember that 'cyberspace is owned and operated by the private sector. Decisions taken for market reasons can end up having major consequences, though often without public accountability or transparency'.

Social networking has 'led to a proliferation of voices' but has 'also produced a much deeper exposure of personally incriminating information'. See BLOGOSPHERE; CENSORSHIP; DEMOCRACY AND THE MEDIA; DIGITAL OPTIMISM; EFFECTS OF THE MASS MEDIA; FACEBOOK; INTERNET: DENIAL OF SERVICE; MOBILIZATION; NETWORKING: SOCIAL NETWORKING; TWITTER. See also *TOPIC GUIDE* under MEDIA: POLITICS & ECONOMICS.

Telegenic Looking good on TV – a factor that has had particular significance in the domain of politics, but also applies in many other walks of life, including working on TV, where the telegenic is associated with youth and ageing, especially among women broadcasters. See LOOKISM.

Telegraphy Only after the discovery of the magnetic effect of electric current was telegraphy possible. The first telegraph consisted of a compass needle that was deflected by the magnetic field produced by electric currents which flowed through the circuit whenever the transmitting key was depressed and contact established. The first patent for an electric telegraph was taken out by William Fothergill Cooke and Charles Wheatstone in June 1837, and later in the same year they demonstrated a five-needle telegraph to the directors of the London and Birmingham railway.

A year later the Great Western Railway connected Paddington and West Drayton by telegraph line, which soon gave a considerable boost of publicity to telegraphy: in 1845 a suspected murderer was spotted boarding a London-bound train at Slough; the news was telegraphed to Paddington and the man was arrested on arrival and later found guilty and hanged.

In the US, Samuel Morse's first working telegraph of 1837 depended on the making and breaking of an electric current: an electromagnetically operated stylus recorded the long and short dashes of Morse Code on a moving strip of paper. After much persuasion, the US Congress, in 1843, voted to pay Morse (1791–1872) to build the first telegraph line in America, from Baltimore to Washington. It was in the following year, using the Morse Code on this line, that Morse transmitted his famous message: 'What hath God wrought!'

Development of telegraphy was swift. By 1862 the world's telegraph system covered some 150,000 miles, including 15,000 in the UK. A method of printing the coded telegraph messages had been invented in 1845 and was developed in the US as 'House's Printing Telegraph'. In 1850 a telegraph cable had been laid across the English Channel. In 1858 the Atlantic was spanned by telegraph cable. The duplex telegraphy of Thomas Alva Edison (1847–1931) made it possible to transmit two messages simultaneously over the same line; soon, four- and five-message systems followed, and ultimately the teleprinter. Picture transmission by telegraphy resulted from the development work of English physicist Shelford Bidwell, the first such transmissions taking place in 1881. See TELEX.

'The significance of telegraphy,' writes James W. Carey in *Communication as Culture* (Routledge, 1992) 'is that it led to the selective control and transmission of information. The telegraph operator was able to monopolize knowledge, if only for a few moments, along a route; and this brought a selective advantage in trading and speculation.' It also ushered-in a new language of JOURNALISM, what Ernest Hemingway called 'the lingo of the cable' – terse, precise; as Carey puts it, 'a form of language stripped of the local, the regional, and colloquial ... something closer to a "scientific" language, a language of strict denotation in which the connotative featurers of utterance were under rigid control'.

Telegraphy continues to be widely used by news services, the Stock Exchange telex service, public message services, certain police and fire alarm systems and private-line companies for data transmission. See TELEPHONE; WIRELESS

TELEGRAPHY. See also *TOPIC GUIDE* under MEDIA HISTORY.

▸ Brian Winston, *Media, Technology and Society: A History: From the Telegraph to the Internet* (Routledge, 1998).

Telematics Term referring to the merging of telecommunications and computers, brought about by DIGITIZATION. The 1s and 0s of the computer are converted into tones relayed over telephone lines and then reconverted at the other end of the line by another computer. Thus information can be held centrally, dispatched rapidly, updated easily and networked internationally. This trans-border data flow (TBDF) is enhanced by SATELLITES, the advantage of whose use is that transmission costs do not rise in relation to the distance being covered (as is the case with microwaves and cables); as long, that is, as the communication falls within the 'footprint' of the same satellite.

Telephone In his early years a Scotsman, Alexander Graham Bell (1857–1922), knew Charles Wheatstone (1802–75), co-inventor of TELEGRAPHY, and also Alexander John Ellis, an expert in sound. Ellis showed Bell that the vibration of a tuning fork could be influenced by an electric current. He was able to produce sounds very like those of a human voice. Bell, teaching deaf-mutes in Boston, Massachusetts, experimented on a musical telegraph (1872). He produced artificial 'ear-drums' from sheets of metal and linked these with electric wire.

In 1876 Bell succeeded in passing a vocal message along a wire to an assistant in another room. The first telephone switching system was installed in New Haven, Connecticut, in 1878. However, while claiming credit for 'his' invention, and being acknowledged down the years as the inventor of the telephone, Bell must surrender the accolade to an unknown Italian, Antonio Meucci (1808–89), who demonstrated his 'teletrofono' in New York in 1860. Alas, Meucci's poverty (he could not afford the US$ 250 needed to patent his 'talking telegraph') and his failure to secure financial backing left the way open for Bell – who had shared a laboratory with Meucci and thus had access to his findings – to file a patent and pursue a lucrative deal with Western Union.

A hundred years later, the US telephone system, largely the monopoly of the company Bell founded, was handling an average of over 240 million phone conversations a day and, as Maurice Richards points out in *The World Communicates* (Longman, 1972), the telephone system had 'developed into a communications network infinitely more versatile than could have been envisaged by the pioneers'.

Now telephone lines serve complex computer data systems; documents are transmitted via telephone – a scanning head records the light and shade of the document as it turns on a rotating drum, translating intensity of tone into electrical impulses for transmission over the wire to be retranslated at the receiving end. Telephone lines also carry telex services.

Microwave transmission techniques now allow telephone calls through air, free of wires, poles or underground conduits. Transmitting from point to point, tall towers now beam as many as 1,500 calls on a single carrier wave. The London Post Office Tower has a potential load capacity of 150,000 telephone calls and capacity to transmit 100 TV channels.

Mobile phones (see MOBILIZATION) can be said to be the technological advance that, more swiftly than any other, became a means of communication on a mass scale, to the point where their use began to be seen as a public nuisance. Their increasing sophistication (and the fact that they had become a STYLE accessory) created a new crime – mobile mugging, setting the manufacturers the challenge of making the devices inoperable except by the legitimate owner. Today, in addition to phoning in the traditional way, and text-messaging, users of mobiles can tune into the INTERNET as well as RADIO and TV broadcasts, download music and play computer games.

Belatedly, in the summer of 2002, justice was done to the memory of the Florentine, Antonio Meucci. The US House of Representatives voted in favour of recognizing Meucci as the true father of telecommunications, 113 years after his death. See *TOPIC GUIDES* under MEDIA HISTORY; MEDIA: TECHNOLOGIES.

Telephone tapping See JOURNALISM: PHONE-HACKING; PRIVACY.

Teletext Data in textual or graphic form transmitted via the TV screen; the BROADCASTING version of viewdata, which is telephone-linked. In the UK, the BBC provides its CEEFAX information service; the commercial television equivalent was, until 1993, the Oracle service. In the auction for such services, empowered by the BROADCASTING ACT (UK), 1990, the licence-winner was Teletext UK, a consortium headed by Associated Newspapers and Philips, the electronics company. The name of the new service from 1993 is Teleview.

Television See TELEVISION BROADCASTING. See also *TOPIC GUIDE* under BROADCASTING.

Television Act (UK), 1954 Gave birth to commercial television in the UK; the Act set up the Independent Television Authority (later to be named the Independent Broadcasting Authority with the advent of COMMERCIAL RADIO). A rigorous set of controlling rules was imposed on the Authority, requiring 'that nothing is included in the programmes which offends against good taste or decency or is likely to encourage or incite to crime or to lead to disorder or to be offensive to public feelings or which contains any offensive representation of or reference to a living person'.

Required were a proper balance in subject-matter, a high general standard of quality and due 'accuracy and impartiality' in the presentation of any news given in programmes, in whatever form. There were also to be 'proper proportions' in terms of British productions and performance in order to safeguard against the dumping of American material.

Of vital significance in the Act were the elaborate precautions that were made to prevent advertisers gaining control of programme content. The governing body of ITV as set up by the Act was similar in size and function to that of the BBC, with seven to ten governors each serving for five years and dismissible at the behest of the Postmaster-General. Like the BBC, the ITA was to have a limited period of existence, followed by parliamentary review and renewal. See SOUND BROADCASTING ACT (UK), 1972.

Television broadcasting Technical developments in the UK, the Soviet Union and the US combined to make TV a feasibility by 1931, when a research group was set up in Britain under Isaac Shoenberg (1880–1963), who had had considerable experience in radio transmission technology in the Soviet Union. He furthered the evolution of a practical system of TV broadcasting based on a camera tube known as the Emitrion and an improved cathode-ray tube for the receiver. Shoenberg elected to develop a system of electronic scanning which proved far superior to the mechanical scanning method pioneered by Scotsman John Logie Baird (1889–1946), who had first demonstrated his system publicly in 1926.

The BBC was authorized by government to adopt Shoenberg's standards (405 lines) for the world's first high-definition service, which was launched in 1936; a system that proved sufficiently successful to continue in the UK until 1962, when the European continental 625-line system was introduced. In the US, TV was slower to develop. It was not until 30 April 1939, at the opening of the New York World's Fair, that a public demonstration was made by the National Broadcasting Company (NBC).

The BBC's nascent TV service closed down during the Second World War (1939–45), which also hampered TV development in America, though by 1949 there were a million receivers in the US and by 1951, 10 million. In the UK, TV transmission resumed in June 1946. Swiftly TV became, in terms of reach, diversity and popularity of content, the most influential and most powerful form of mass communication. The arrival of colour, transmission by cable and satellite, the possibilities of VIDEO recording and eventually DIGITIZATION confirmed and carried forward the Age of Information while at the same time turning it into the Age of the Image.

While TV has displaced, and sometimes marginalized, other forms of communication, it has also proved their willing customer, borrowing and adapting forms from print, RADIO and cinema, in turn proving for them a constant source of material: how, for example, would popular newspapers survive without 'stories' from TV dramas such as SOAPS? TV fact and fiction have become so much a part of the culture of the modern age that they have become its benchmarks and its reality.

What's real is what is on TV; who appears on TV is deemed real. If an event does not appear on TV it is argued (at a metaphysical level) that the EVENT has really not taken place. Because of the nature of the medium, TV accentuates the image over the word, the dramatic over the analytical, and critics such as Neil Postman, in *Amusing Ourselves to Death* (Methuen, 1986), claim that TV transforms all things into pure entertainment.

TV delivers audiences to advertisers; in turn advertisers use TV to reinforce the dominance of the image, in their case the image arising from imperatives of consumerism. TV news is seen to be a window on the world, a view attracting critical attention from media analyists, who see in its underlying intentions frameworks essentially Western in orientation, highly selective and thus offering a skewed vision of the world.

TV is where partnerships are forged, between sport and business, fashion, food, health and property and business. It is the venue of lifestyle, the route to celebrity, and for these and many other reasons it is a battleground between those who are ambitious to control it, the axis of the ongoing struggle being the tussle between public and private ownership. The study of the effects, influence, impact and power of the media largely centres on TV and the questions prompting answers are legion: does TV and its blizzard of images confuse rather than clarify? Does it distract rather than aid attention? Does it fulfil the fears of those who (subscribing to the notion of a so-termed three-minute culture) rob viewers of the ability to concentrate for more than a few moments at a time? Does its constant plethora of images of violence desensitize audiences to examples of violence in the real world? Will the onward march of online rivals for the attention of people to TV fragment audiences, with implications for culture and community?

Most important of all, in an age of multimedia provision, what future lies in store for PUBLIC SERVICE BROADCASTING (PSB)? See: CATCH-UP TV; DAB: DIGITAL AUDIO BROADCASTING; DEMOTIC TURN; DISPLACEMENT EFFECT; FACE-BOOK; MEDIAPOLIS; MOBILIZATION; NETWORK-ING: SOCIAL NETWORKING; PODCAST; WEB 2.0; YOUTUBE.

▸ Anthony Smith, ed., and Richard Patterson, associate ed., *Television: An International History* (Oxford University Press, 1998); Asa Briggs and Peter Burke, *A Social History of the Media: From Gutenberg to the Internet* (Polity, 2002); John Fiske, *Reading Television* (Routledge, 2004); Toby Miller, *Television Studies* (Routledge, 2009); John Fiske, *Television Culture* (Routledge, 2011); Michael Kackman *et al, Flow TV: Television in the Age of Media Convergence* (Routledge, 2011).

Television: catch-up TV The majority of broadcasting services in the UK, Europe and the US provide a catch-up TV service enabling viewers to retrieve programmes that have been missed, usually in the last seven days. For the most part INTERNET-based, catch-up facilities generally only allow viewers to watch content created by the specific broadcaster. BBC TV and RADIO shows, for example, can be tuned into free of charge via the BBC's iPlayer on Windows, Mac or Linux; content from ITV shows via the ITV Player; from Channel 4 via 4 on Demand; from Channel Five via Demand Five; and from Sky programmes via the Sky Player.

Catch-up is also available on the TV set using Digitial TV Services: BT Vision offers BBC, ITV, 40D and Demand 5 via the TV Replay service. Other services such as Virgin Media, Sky, TalkTalk TV, Top Up TV and Fetch TV offer selective access. Currently no catch-up is offered via Freeview.

Television drama In an interview printed in *The New Priesthood: British Television Today* (Allen Lane, 1970), edited by Joan Bakewell and Nicholas Garnham, TV playwright Dennis Potter (1935–95) said of TV, 'It's the biggest platform in the world's history and writers who don't want to kick and elbow their way on to it must be disowning something in themselves.' While the PILKINGTON COMMITTEE REPORT ON BROADCASTING (UK), 1962 found that the chief 'crime' of TV was triviality, much of TV drama (from the very first drama production on experimental TV, the BBC's *The Man with a Flower in his Mouth* by Luigi Pirandello on 14 July 1930) has been a striking exception to that judgment.

In fact, few might argue with the claim that TV's most substantial achievement has been to encourage generations of quality dramatists working specially for the medium, and a canon of plays and drama series, from the BBC and commercial TV companies, and, particularly in the US, the cable company HBO (Home Box Office), to rival anything produced in the live theatre during the same post-Second World War period.

In the early days of TV drama, plays were stage-bound, or more accurately, studio-bound, both in concept and execution, taking for their model the theatre rather than the cinema; but the ideas of young directors making their mark during the 1960s, excited by the possibilities of filming on location, prevailed. Nell Dunn's *Up the Junction* (BBC, 1965) marked the first occasion when virtually the whole story was told on film. The camera was seen to be as important as the pen; indeed the camera in many ways became the pen. The social and sometimes political themes favoured by many writers and directors took the cameras more and more out of the studio and into 'real life', and many plays looked like, and had the impact of, documentary.

Produced by Tony Garnett, written by Jeremy Sandford and directed by Ken Loach, *Cathy Come Home* (BBC, 1966) detailed the decline into tragedy of a homeless family in affluent Britain. The sense of reality was almost unbearable: the camera was often hand-held, the scenes staged so realistically that the audience was tempted to forget it was watching something constructed, not something happening before their very eyes.

The intimacy, the close scrutiny of humans under stress at which film and TV can excel, has rarely been used to more disturbing effect than with John Hopkins' quartet of plays *Talking to a Stranger* (BBC, 1966), described as the first authentic masterpiece of television. The immediacy of the medium was stunningly demonstrated in Colin Welland's epic *Leeds United!* (BBC, 1974) about Leeds clothing workers who struck spontaneously in 1970 for an extra ten pence an hour: the camera became part of the

T

ongoing action to such an extent that it was impossible to detect what had been scripted and what was happening for real.

Much of this kind of drama obviously grew from the opportunities of the moment, and from improvisation, a method used most notably by Mike Leigh (*Hard Labour*, 1973; *Abigail's Party*, 1977), who works with actors for long periods before filming, encouraging them to become the characters and eventually invent or improvise their speech and actions. TV drama produced a host of talent, writers and film-makers never afraid to deal with challenging subjects, ever-ready to push the boundaries of their chosen genre.

In the UK these included Peter Watkins (*The War Game*, 1965), Tony Parker (*No Man's Land*, 1972), Alan Plater (*Land of Green Ginger*, 1973), Alan Bennett *(Sunset Across the Bay*, 1975), Alan Bleasdale (*Boys From the Blackstuff*, 1982), Don Shaw (*The Falklands Factor*, 1983), Troy Kennedy Martin (*Edge of Darkness*, 1985) and Stephen Potter (*The Singing Detective*, 1986). It is difficult to compare the quality of much of the drama output of the 1960s and early 70s and that of today, because so little was recorded and, where it was, productions were often wiped.

The one-off play eventually hit the buffers of economic necessity. In a 1982 publication for the IBA, *Television and Radio*, David Cunliffe, then Head of Drama at Yorkshire TV, wrote: 'The inescapable fact is that over the last few years the television single play has spiralled in production costs and plummeted in popularity.' Having moved from the studio to location, plays had become 'nearly Hollywood-size movies'. Cunliffe cited dramas such as Stephen Potter's LWT series, *Rain on the Roof, Blade on the Feather* and *Cream in My Coffee* as works that, despite their quality as drama, appealed to 'relatively small sections of viewers'.

There was to be no dearth of drama series, which have more over-time impact and are more saleable commodities on the international programme market. Drama on both sides of the Atlantic proved broad-ranging, from the portrayal of the lives of the elite (ITV's *Brides-head Revisited*, 1981; CBS's *Dallas*, 1978–1991; ABC's *Dynasty*, 1981–89) to those at the bottom of the heap (BBC's *Boys From the Blackstuff*, 1982), from crime series (ITV's *The Sweeney*, 1975–78; NBC's *Hill Street Blues*, 1981–87) to spy series (BBC's *Tinker, Taylor, Soldier, Spy*, 1979), from the lives on the street (ITV's *Coronation Street* from 1960; the BBC's *Eastenders*, from 1985) to the stately homes of England (the BBC's

Pride and Prejudice, 1995; ITV's *Downton Abbey*, 2010–11).

Crime has dominated the drama airwaves, HBO's *The Sopranos* (1999–2007) being judged by a panel of UK *Guardian* journalists in 2010 as the best TV drama series of all time. Also in their Top 50 came ITV's *Prime Suspect* (1991–96) with a woman in the traditionally 'male' lead (DCI Jane Tennyson).

Hospitals have proved popular locations for TV drama (BBC's *Casualty* from 1996; *Holby City* from 1999), as have schools (BBC's *Grange Hill*, 1978–2008). The world of the supernatural has been well-served (CBS's *The Twilight Zone*, 1959–64; Fox's *The X Files*, 1993–2002; WB/UPN's *Buffy the Vampire Slayer*, 1997–2003), though the doyen of all has to be the BBC's *Dr. Who*, the longest-running TV drama of its kind. First screened on 23 November 1963, *Dr. Who* commanded the early-evening airwaves until 1983. It was relaunched in 2005 and has, at the time of writing, chalked up eleven doctors.

Matching crime has been literary adaptation. ITV's *Brideshead Revisited* was based on the novel by Evelyn Waugh, since when class and costume have proved staple escapist fare. See WEB OR ONLINE DRAMA.

▶ John Tulloch, *Television Drama: Agency, Audience and Myth* (Routledge, 1990); David Paget, *No Other Way to Tell It: Dramadoc/Docudrama on Television* (Manchester University Press, 1998).

Television news: inherent limitations In analysing the degree of 'informedness' between viewers of TV news and readers of newspapers, two American researchers found that TV makes for less effective *retention* than the printed page. John P. Robinson and Dennis K. Davis in 'Television news and the informed public: An information-processing approach', *Journal of Communication* (Summer 1990), found that in none of their studies 'do viewers of TV news programmes emerge as more informed than newspaper readers'.

They identify seven inherent limitations of TV as an information medium: (1) a TV newscast has fewer words and ideas per news story than appear in a front-page story in a quality news-paper; (2) attention to a newscast is distracted and fragmented compared to attention when reading; (3) TV newscasts provide little of the repetition of information, or redundancy, neces-sary for comprehension; (4) TV viewers cannot 'turn back' to, or review, information they do not understand or that they need to know to under-stand subsequent information; (5) print news stories are more clearly delineated, with headlines, columns, etc; (6) TV news programmes fail to coordinate pictures and text; and (7) TV has more limited opportunity to review and develop an entire story.

It is the authors' view that 'while TV has the power to evoke empathy and interest, time and other constraints prevent this power from being exercised'. Clearly a number of these limitations has been circumvented by developments in media technology (the availability of news online, on mobile and on iPad) and as a result of the growth in the number and variety of news services, not the least the arrival of 24-hour TV news. These factors do not necessarily undermine Robinson and Davis's theory, but they do raise questions about the current practice of newspaper reading in the age of the INTERNET. See *TOPIC GUIDE* under NEWS MEDIA.

▶ Steven Barnett, *The Rise and Fall of Television Journalism: Just Wires and Lights in a Box?* (Bloomsbury Academic, 2011).

'Television without frontiers' See EUROPEAN COMMUNITY AND MEDIA: TELEVISION WITHOUT FRONTIERS.

Telstar Communications satellite launched on 10 July 1962; transmitted the first live TV pictures between the US and Europe. See SATELLITE TRANSMISSION.

Ten commandments for media consumers In 'Ethics for media users' published in the *European Journal of Communication* (December 1995), Cees J. Hamelink discusses the role the viewer, reader and listener should adopt in relation to the 'quest for freedom, quality and responsibility in media performance', arguing that the consumer must not only be aware of the nature of media messages, but also be proactive in responding to them. The ten 'commandments' Hamelink suggests in order to assist the consumer with moral choices concerning the media are: Thou shalt – (1) be an alert and discriminating media consumer; (2) actively fight all forms of censorship; (3) not unduly interfere with editorial independence; (4) guard against racism and sexist stereotyping in the media; (5) seek alternative sources of information; (6) demand a pluralist supply of information; (7) protect thine own privacy; 8) be a reliable source of information; (9) not participate in chequebook journalism; and (10) demand accountability from media producers.

The author, however, cautions against over-reliance on such a code of user response, for moral issues and dilemmas ought to be addressed according to situation and context, a point well made when we take a global view of the 'commandments'. A pre-existing code must not be imposed on a situation; rather, the situation must be examined in the light of evolving and changing approaches to moral dilemmas. See MEDIAPOLIS. *See also TOPIC GUIDES* under MEDIA ISSUES & DEBATES; MEDIA: VALUES & IDEOLOGY.

Tenth art See VIDEO GAMES.

Terrestrial broadcasting That which is transmitted from the ground and not via SATELLITE.

Territoriality See SPATIAL BEHAVIOUR.

Terrorism: anti-terrorism legislation (UK) Following the destruction of New York's World Trade Centre's twin towers on 11 September 2001, the UK government hastened to tighten the Terrorism Act of 2000 with the 125-clause Anti-Terrorism, Crime and Security Act of 2001, parts of which directly affect media communication. The Act allows for the arrest and internment for up to six months of suspected terrorists. It permits confidential information about an individual held by any government agency to be disclosed to the intelligence services and the police – for any criminal investigation, not just for investigations of alleged terrorist offences. Detention without charge was brought in for foreign nationals suspected of being terrorists or considered to be planning terrorist attacks.

Clause 93 makes it a punishable offence for anyone to refuse a police request to remove a disguise, such as a mask, or face paint. Following the terrorist bombs on the London Underground in July 2005, the Prevention of Terrorism Act (2005) introduced control orders for suspects, based on suspicion not proof, and prohibited the 'glorification' of terrorism. The Counter-Terrorism Act (2008) amended the definition of terrorism by inserting a racial clause.

In March 2010 a committee of MPs chaired by Labour MP Andrew Dismore urged that all anti-terrorist legislation be reviewed, prompting the response from government that the threat of terrorism 'remains real and serious'. With the election to power of the Conservative-Liberal Democrat coalition government in May 2010, a decision was taken to abandon the previous government's plans to introduce identity cards (IDs) for the British population, as much on the grounds of cost as removing a broadly held view that IDs were a curtailment of liberty and would have little impact on the war on terrorism. See REGULATION OF INVESTIGATORY POWERS ACT (RIPA) (UK), 2000; USA – PATRIOT ACT, 2001.

Terrorism as communication The main aim of terrorist activity in liberal democracies is publicity. The existence of a free press, and TV and

T

radio companies independent of government authority within societies which subscribe to the sanctity of the individual's right to life, provides fertile ground for headline-seeking by acts of terror such as hijacks, abductions, assassinations and bombings.

Publicity for terrorism, and the means to plan, organize and manage it, was given global momentum with the development of the INTERNET (see MOBILIZATION). The *experience* of modern-day terrorism can be instant. Within minutes of 9/11 – the most devastating act of terrorism in history, the destruction of New York's Twin Towers on 11 September 2001 – the world was witness to the vulnerability of the most powerful nation on earth.

Suddenly in countries suffering the carnage of terrorism, security takes precedence over citizen rights. The terrorist draws satisfaction from seeing states (often egged on by the media) rush to curtail rights (such as free speech) and liberties (such as freedom of movement and assembly) which may have taken centuries to establish. Even the most well-set communities, confident of their values and ways of life, can be destablized by terrorism. In a democracy, the ultimate danger is that the state will answer terrorism with terror: in such a situation, the role of the media (as watchdog or guard dog) becomes immensely important.

Further, as happened in the case of the US, not only were the rights and liberties of American citizens reined in by legislation (see USA – PATRIOT ACT, 2001), the country also converted the (ungrounded) suspicion that Iraq was behind the 9/11 atrocity into military invasion, aided and abetted by Britain, which incurred its own version of 9/11 in July 2005. See *TOPIC GUIDES* under MEDIA ISSUES & DEBATES; MEDIA: POWER, EFFECTS, INFLUENCE.

Text According to Tim O'Sullivan, John Hartley, Danny Saunders and John Fiske in *Key Concepts in Communication* (Methuen, 1983), text refers to '... a signifying structure composed of signs and codes which is essential to communication.' This structure can take a variety of forms: film, speech, writing, painting, records, for example. O'Sullivan *et al* argue that the word text usually '... refers to a message that has a physical existence of its own, independent of its sender and receiver and thus composed of representational codes.'

Text is the focal point of study in SEMIOL-OGY/SEMIOTICS. Texts are not normally seen as being unproblematic but as capable of being interpreted in a variety of ways, depending on the socio-cultural background and experience

of the reader. The central concern of semiology is to discover the ways in which given texts can generate a range of meanings.

Occupying the special attention of analysts in recent years is the relationship between texts, the way they interconnect, interweave and interact upon one another. *Intertextuality* oper-ates essentially in the perception and experience of AUDIENCE. A TV movie tells the story of a serial killer; TV news reports carnage caused by a madman loose with an axe; newspaper billboards report the latest gang stabbing; and an art historian claims that the Mona Lisa was actually a man. What does the individual make of all this; how does one text influence another in the mind's eye; and what part is played by the response of other individuals?

In a basic sense, intertextuality works at the level of simple publicity and promotion. A film may be writ large in our consciousness, but perhaps not only because of the power of the individual text: there will have been trailers, publicity material, interviews with the stars on TV; there will have been conversation about it.

The power of intertextuality is to blur the boundaries between individual texts, sometimes to morph them. For example, which is the text in a promotional DVD – the chart-busting song of the rock group, their live TV performance at Glastonbury, or memories audiences cherish of earlier gigs, earlier recordings, juxtaposed with those of predecessors and rivals? Roland Barthes, the French media philosopher, was of the view that culture is a web of intertextuality and that texts tend to refer essentially to one another rather than anchor their referral in reality. See CODES; DECODER; ENCODER; MESSAGE; NARRA-TIVE. See also *TOPIC GUIDE* under LANGUAGE/DISCOURSE/NARRATIVE; TEXTUAL ANALYSIS.

Text: integrity of the text With the coming of the INTERNET, two major issues concern the producers of texts – books, articles, scripts, photographs, music, etc.: the questions of *integrity* of the text, and of *paternity*. Copyright laws have until now protected the work of an author. While a book can be quoted from, it cannot be reprinted, reproduced in any way or altered without due permission. The Net, as yet an open space for the communication of items of all kinds, uncontrolled by traditional regulation and so far evasive of what controls, legal and techni-cal, might be applied, has threatened to rob texts of integrity and to ignore their paternity (that is, the right of the author, composer, artist or performer to command 'ownership' of the text).

In short, networking is open to the abuse

of SOURCE; indeed texts often soar through CYBERSPACE with little or no acknowledgement of source. Released from the tie of ownership, possibly doctored in whole or in part for whatever reason, are texts reliable any more? Does authorship continue to have any meaning?

The *moral rights* of paternity and integrity are enshrined in the Berne Convention. They are central to the UK's Copyright Designs and Patents Act (1988). The right of paternity is the right to be identified as the author of a copyright work, and that includes adaptations, film rights, etc. The major exception in the Berne Convention is authorship of the 'news of the day'. The UK Copyright Act also excludes from protection all work made for the reporting of current events, and this includes articles in newspapers and journals.

A major legal curtailment of the 'free' use (and sometimes abuse) of texts online was passed into law in 2010, in the form of the DIGITAL ECONOMY ACT (UK); a measure deemed by many to be in its turn an abuse of freedom by permitting SURVEILLANCE methods not altogether different from stalking. See TOPIC GUIDE under MEDIA ISSUES & DEBATES.

Texts See OPEN, CLOSED TEXTS.

Text: tertiary text The primary TEXT is that which is produced and transmitted –the painting, the poem, the poster, the film, what Roland Barthes terms the 'work'; the secondary text is that which members of an AUDIENCE receive, what is *perceived* as the text. The tertiary text results when the first two texts are translated into conversation between members of the audience, their families and friends. John Fiske uses the term in *Television Culture* (Methuen, 1987) to denote the many uses media messages can be put to – interpretative, analytical, affirmative or rejective.

The existence of the tertiary text indicates that audience has within its capacity the potential to be independent of the PREFERRED READING residing in the primary text or work (see AUDIENCE: ACTIVE AUDIENCE; EMPOWERMENT; RESPONSE CODES).

A more general use of the terms primary and secondary is current. The primary text is that which is produced; the secondary text, arising out of the first, may take many forms – publicity, trailers, critiques, interviews with the author or director, documentaries, translations into other creative forms (a novel into a movie or a TV series).

Secondary texts at least begin as dependants upon the primary text; they are its satellites. However, these may become more and more

divorced from connection with the original until, arguably, they become primary texts in their own right. Where texts interact, interconnect and are interdependent we have what is termed *intertextuality*.

Theatre censorship See LORD CHAMBERLAIN.

Theories and concepts of communication See TOPIC GUIDES under AUDIENCES/CONSUMPTION & RECEPTION OF MEDIA; COMMUNICATION THEORY; COMMUNICATION MODELS; LANGUAGE/DISCOURSE/NARRATIVE; MEDIA: POWER, EFFECTS, INFLUENCE; MEDIA: VALUES & IDEOLOGY; REPRESENTATION.

38 Degrees See ONLINE CAMPAIGNING.

Three-dimensional (3D) For the early days of three-dimensional technology, see STEREOSCOPY. We associate 3D with the cinema and television, and specifically with the 1950s onwards. The aim of creating for audience an experience that springs, three-dimensionally, from the screen to add to the thrill and wonder of cinema has had surges and recessions caused by technical problems, expense brought about by the need to either convert cinemas to 3D or, in the case of IMAX cinemas, to purpose-build them, and the volatility of audience interest. Not the least of 3D's problems has been the need for audiences to wear special tinted-lens glasses, and reports that prolonged use of these to view the pyrotechnics of 3D has health hazards.

The *anaglyph* method of 3D projection employed two projection systems angled towards the screen. The *polarized* method projects images at right-angles to each other. The *active-shutter* method exposes each eye to alternating images; in this case the 3D glasses, linked to hardware, open and close the shutters over the eyes, enabling each eye to see the correct image. *Autostereoscopy*, still largely at a stage of experiment and development, avoids the use of glasses altogether.

Synchronization of images proved a major headache, less so once a single-strip format was introduced, giving 3D cinema popular momentum from the 1970s. The IMAX company, projecting on 70mm film, carried the flag of 3D during the 1980s. Polaroid glasses were introduced in 1986, but the biggest boost to 3D came with the introduction of computer animation, digital projection and digital video capture (see SPECIAL EFFECTS).

James Cameron's filmless *Ghosts of the Abyss* (2003) anticipated his highly innovative 3D feature *Avatar* (2009), which illustrated the wonders of modern cinema technology but also exemplified a longstanding criticism of 3D cinema, the dominance of effects over content: if what is told on screen does not shock, startle or amaze audiences in some way, then that content does not properly serve the nature of the medium.

A glance at the 3D industry, at its many innovatory companies dedicated to bringing to the TV screen the wonders of cinema 3D, indicates that the quandary of effects/content is a challenge to be met and overcome. There is a proliferation of systems with competing brand names such as Dolby 3D, RealD, TD Vision Systems, XPAND 3D as well as IMAX. Competing manufacturers of 3D television are Mtsubishi, Panasonic, Philips, Sony and Toshiba, all chasing the possibilities of autostereoscopic (glasses-free) screening that has presented serious problems concerning focus, field of vision and judder.

In 2008 the Japanese cable channel BS11 began broadcasting regular 3D programmes, while in the US Cablevision launched a subscriber 3D channel in 2010. 3D TV programme projection came online in Australia, France, Russia and South Korea. In the UK, Channel 4 ran a short season of 3D films in 2009. British Sky Broadcasting (BskyB) was the first station to screen a football match in 3D, Manchester United versus Arsenal on 30 January 2010 to public houses across the country.

In the US, 3net, a joint venture of major media organizations (Discovery Communication, IMAX, Sony) was launched on DIRECT TV in February 2011. Faith in the continuing viability of 3D can be gauged by ambitious announcements of future productions, including Star Wars projects and *Avatar 2*.

At the World Mobile Congress in Barcelona in February 2011, LG's 4.3 inch touchscreen, glasses-free Optimus 3D mobile phone was demonstrated to delegates. On sale shortly afterwards from Carphone Warehouse, Network 3, Orange, T-Mobile and Vodaphone, it not only provides the usual batch of apps, but also allows users to view and film in 3D, play back through 3D TV and supplement visits to YouTube 3D with video games.

Third-person effect Where we judge the impact/influence of the media to be stronger on others than ourselves; and this effect is countenanced largely when the media message is negative or when persuasion by the MESSAGE is perceived to be less than desirable. In other words, *we* might not be affected, but others, usually differentiated from us by cultural or social difference, are more likely to be.

▶ Xigen Li, 'Third-person effect, optimistic bias

and sufficiency resource in Internet use', *Journal of Communication* (September, 2008); Ye Sun, Zhongdang Pan and Lijiang Shen, 'Understanding the third-person perception: evidence from a meta-analysis', *Journal of Communication* (June, 2008).

Tie-signs Any action – GESTURE or posture – that indicates the existence of a personal relationship is termed a tie-sign: linked arms, held hands, body closeness (or proximity), comfortable silence between two people, instinctive reciprocal movements. *Symbolic* tie-signs are wedding rings, lovers' tree engravings, etc. See COMMUNICATION, NON-VERBAL (NVC); PROXEMICS.

Time-lapse photography See HIGH-SPEED PHOTOGRAPHY.

Time-shift viewing Made possible by the introduction of the video or DVD recorder. By recording TV programmes, viewers are released from the schedules of the broadcasting companies to watch programmes of their choice whenever and as often as desired.

Tor An INTERNET routing network enabling users to conceal their identity and protect them from traffic analysis. First created by the US Naval Research Lab, it is currently produced by the Tor Project, a United States NGO. Tor blocks attempts by governments, police and all agencies of SURVEILLANCE to 'spy' on what is being transmitted by whom and to whom. It defends users against the scrutiny by authority and commerce of patterns of exchange; that is, it serves to resist unwanted or unknown intruders tracking the data trails of users. See CRYPTOGRAPHY; DATA FOOTPRINT.

Touch Commonly used to communicate intimacy and friendship, for example in displaying affection, giving reassurance and comfort and offering congratulations. Touch can be employed to reinforce attempts to persuade others during interpersonal encounters; on occasion it can also be employed to express aggression and dominance. The rituals of interaction found within ceremonies may also involve touch. Touching is commonly used, across many cultures, in rituals of greeting and farewell. Those of higher social standing often initiate touch. STATUS and ROLES are inextricably involved in touch-permission or touch-prohibition: a nurse may touch a patient, but it is unusual for the patient to touch the nurse, where it constitutes a trespass.

There can be significant cross-cultural differences in the rules for the degree and display of touch, and these can lead to embarrassment and misunderstanding within social encounters between people from different cultural

backgrounds. A number of researchers have identified high-, moderate- and low-contact cultures. Stella Ting-Toomey in *Communication Across Cultures* (Guildford Press, 1999) provides some examples: high-contact cultures are to be found in Russia, France and Italy, whilst moderate-contact cultures are located in Northern Europe, Australia and the US and low-contact cultures in Japan and China. Those from high-contact cultures tend to make frequent use of touch in conversations – behaviour that might prove disconcerting to those from low-contact cultures. An example of a cultural difference in the rules for the display of touch is that in Latin American countries it is more common for males to fully embrace one another in public than it is in Britain. See COMMUNICATION, NON-VERBAL (NVC); EYE CONTACT; GESTURE; INTER-PERSONAL COMMUNICATION; NON-VERBAL BEHAVIOUR; REPERTOIRE; SPATIAL BEHAVIOUR.
▸ Michael Argyle, *Bodily Communication* (Methuen, 1988); Desmond Morris *People Watching* (Vintage, 2002); Allan and Barbara Pease, *The Definitve Book of Body Langauge* (Orion, 2004).

Tracks In film-making, tracks are the portable 'railway lines' along which the camera, mounted on a DOLLY, moves. The term is also used to identify separate sound reels accompanying a film. These are harmonized into one at the dubbing (see DUB, DUBBING) stage of film production.

Traffic data Information about a message sent electronically – by whom, to whom and when (excluding contents of the message itself). Refers to e-mails, websites and TELEPHONE calls. Phone bills include all traffic data, time, destination and length of call. In the case of mobiles, the data includes the base station used.

Transactional analysis Originally an approach to psychotherapy introduced by Eric Berne, transactional analysis is now more widely used as a technique for improving INTERPERSONAL COMMUNICATION and social skills. In essence it aims to increase the individual's awareness of the intent behind both his/her own and others' communication, and to expose and eliminate, or deal with, subterfuge and dishonesty.

The details of the framework are fairly complex and readers are referred to the works recommended below for an introduction to this area. Basically, however, transactional analysis investigates any act of interpersonal communication by considering what are called the 'ego states' of the communicators.

The hypothesis is that we are all able to function out of three 'ego states' that Berne identified as the Parent, the Adult and the Child. The states are produced by a playback of recorded data of events in the past involving real people, real times, places and decisions and real feelings. Everyone is seen as carrying these voices inside them. We interact out of these 'ego states'.

The Parent is much influenced by the pronouncements of and examples set by our own parents and other authority figures, early in our life. It is concerned with our responsibility towards ourselves and others. It can be critical and set standards but it can also be protective and caring. The Adult within us is the part of us that rationally analyses reality.

The Adult collects information and thinks it through in order to solve problems, reach conclusions and judgements, and make decisions. The Adult develops throughout life and can arbitrate between the Parent and the Child. The Child is one of our most powerful states; it contains our feelings and carries our ability to play and act creatively. It can be spontaneous and risk-taking. It can also be rebellious or alternatively compliant and servile.

A *transaction* is a two-person interaction in which an ego state of one person stimulates an ego state of another. Transactions are analysed by assessing out of which 'ego state' people are speaking. We can distinguish these states in ourselves and others by such non-verbal cues as tone of voice or facial expression, as well as by the verbal content of the transactions. One of the chief values of transactional analysis is that it has the capacity to help clarify communication problems.

Other concepts commonly employed in TA are *games*, LIFE POSITIONS and SCRIPTS. Eric Berne in *Games People Play* (Penguin, 1964) describes a game as 'an ongoing series of complementary ulterior transactions progressing to a well-defined, predictable outcome'. Games are recurring sets of transactions, identifiable by their hidden motivations and the promise of psychological payoffs or gains for the game players.

The victim of the game is called a *mark*, and it is the known weakness of the mark, known as the *gimmick*,which allows the game player to hook his/her victim and achieve his/her desired *payoff*. Every game, Berne believes, whether played consciously or unconsciously, is essentially dishonest, generally taking the form of a defensive strategy in communication as far as the manipulator is concerned. Examples of such games played in everyday life, identified by Berne, are 'If it weren't for you' and 'See what you made me do'.
▸ Thomas A. Harris, *I'm OK, You're OK* (Harper &

Row, 1969); Eric Berne, *What Do You Say After You Say Hello?* (Corgi Books, 1975); Ian Stewart and Vann Joines, *TA Today* (Lifespace, 1987); Claude M. Steiner, *Scripts People Live: Transactional Analysis in Life Scripts* (Grove Press, 1990); Amy and Thomas Harris, *Staying OK* (Arrow Books, 1995); Abe Wagner, *The Transactional Manager* (The Industrial Society, 1996); Graeme Burton and Richard Dimbleby, *Between Ourselves: An Introduction to Interpersonal Communication* (Hodder Arnold, 2006).

Transculturation The movement of cultural forms across geographical boundaries and periods of time resulting in cross-cultural interaction that may give rise to new cultural forms. See HYBRIDIZATION.

Transmission model of mass communication See ATTENTION MODEL OF MASS COMMUNICATION.

Trigger events See AGENDA-SETTING.

Truth, visualization of See VISIONS OF ORDER.

TV: catch-up TV See TELEVISION.

TV: independent producers See TELEVISION: INDEPENDENT PRODUCERS.

Twitter A social networking (see NETWORKING: SOCIAL NETWORKING) and microblogging service, launched in the US in 2006. The 'tweet' is a message restricted to 140 characters. You can post tweets and follow them. Celebrity tweeters (called Twitterati) can prompt thousands if not millions of subscribers. Encapsulating a message in 140 characters or fewer can be said to encourage succinctness. On the downside, triviality prevails, with side-orders such as narcissistic self-promotion on the one hand and highly contentious declarations on the other.

Twitter has varyingly been described as 'diabolically addictive', a 'shout in the darkness hoping someone is listening', twitterers being in a constant process of 'self-affirmation'. Searching the dictionary for an appropriate word to describe the essence of Twitter-to-be, founder Jack Dorsey 'came across the word "twitter", and it was just perfect', the term describing 'a short burst of inconsequential information'; or what the San Antonio market research firm Pear Analytics in 2009 termed 'pointless babble'.

Two-step flow model of communication See ONE-STEP, TWO-STEP, MULTI-STEP FLOW MODELS OF COMMUNICATION.

Typewriter A patent for an 'Artificial Machine or Method for Impressing or Transcribing of Letters Singly or Progressively one after another, as in Writing, whereby all Writing Whatever may be Engrossed in Paper or Parchment so Neat and Exact as not to be distinguished from

Print' was taken out in the UK as early as 1714, but the first practical typewriter working faster than handwriting was probably that of American Christopher Latham Sholes (1868) who, after several improvements to his machine, signed up with E. Remington & Sons, gunsmiths of New York. The first Remington machines were marketed in 1874.

1878 saw the introduction of the shift-key typewriter, followed by machines that for the first time allowed the typist to actually see what he/she was typing (1883). That jack-of-all-trades among inventors, Thomas Alva Edison (1847–1931), produced an electrically operated machine containing a printing wheel, in 1872, though it was many years before a commercially viable electric machine was produced (by James Smathes in 1920).

IBM introduced the famous 'golf-ball' electric typewriter in 1961, allowing for different type faces and type sizes to be used with the same machine. Today electronic typewriters (and even manual machines) continue to be manufactured and sold despite being to all intents and purposes displaced by the computer. See *TOPIC GUIDE* under MEDIA HISTORY; MEDIA: TECHNOLOGIES.

U

U-certificate See CERTIFICATION OF FILMS.

UK Gold Launched on 1 November 1992, UK Gold is a satellite channel run jointly by BBC Enterprises and Thames Television based on their combined programme libraries.

Ullswater Committee Report on Broadcasting, 1936 This government-appointed committee under the chairmanship of Viscount Ullswater was given the task of making recommendations on the future of the BBC once its first charter expired on 31 December 1936. The Report praised the BBC for its impartiality and catholicity, but chided it for the heaviness of its Sunday entertainment. The Charter of the BBC was renewed following the Report for another ten years; the number of governors was increased from five to seven and the ban on advertisements was to continue, though sponsorship was to be permitted in the case of TV (a right the BBC only seldom exploited).

Like reports before and after it, Ullswater made clear the very serious public responsibility of BROADCASTING: 'The influence of broadcasting upon the mind and speech of the nation' made it an 'urgent necessity in the national interest that the broadcasting service should at all times be conducted in the best possible manner and to the best possible advantage of the people.' Two other matters elicited concern. The first related to criticisms of the monolithic nature of the BBC (under the rigorous direction of Lord Reith – see REITHIAN) and the Committee recommended more internal decentralization of control, especially towards the national regions.

The second concern, published in a Reservation written by Clement Attlee (1883–1967), future Labour Prime Minister, called into question the BBC's 'impartiality' at the time of the General Strike (1926): 'I think,' wrote Attlee, 'that even in war-time the BBC must be allowed to broadcast opinions other than those of the Government.' See PUBLIC SERVICE BROADCASTING (PSB). See also *TOPIC GUIDE* under COMMISSIONS, COMMITTEES, LEGISLATION.

Ultra-violet/fluorescent photography Used in the examination of forged or altered documents, identifying certain chemical compounds, and in the examination of bacterial colonies. See HOLOGRAPHY; INFRA-RED PHOTOGRAPHY.

Underground press Or radical, alternative or SAMIZDAT; those newspapers that are committedly anti-establishment, opposing in part or entirely the political and cultural conventions of the time; often publishing information or views seen as threatening by those in authority, and likely to incur CENSORSHIP.

In the UK the so-called 'pauper press' of the nineteenth century, finding its readership in the increasingly literate working class, was subject to harshly repressive measures by government. Editors such as William Cobbett, Henry Hetherington, William Sherwin, Richard Carlile and James Watson courted arrest and imprisonment and the shutting-down of their presses as a routine professional hazard. Wooler's *Black Dwarf* stirred the government to wrath with its criticism of the authorities in their handling of the Peterloo Massacre (1819). Wooler escaped libel action on the plea that he could not be said to have written articles which he set up in type without the interventions of a pen.

Cobbett's *Weekly Political Register* had a substantial circulation despite the crippling STAMP DUTY that forced him to charge one shilling and a halfpenny per copy. Carlile's *Republican* was both republican and atheist; the Chartist *Oracle of Reason* incurred blasphemy prosecutions, while Bradlaugh's *National Reformer* declared itself 'Published in Defiance of Her Majesty's Government'.

As long as radical newspapers could fight off the need to win ADVERTISING, they could survive, despite prosecutions, relying on circulation alone. Edited by people close to the working class, they reflected the chief perspectives of the vanguard of the working-class movement and directed themselves to its increased politicization.

What beat the radicals of the nineteenth century was competition by papers more dedicated to entertainment and sensationalism; papers expanding through the power of advertisements and sensitive to the values and requirements of the advertisers. The radicals found themselves faced with a challenge: remain true to principles and thus risk being trapped in a ghetto of reduced readership, or attempt to marry principles with popularization.

Radicalism retreated during the twentieth century but never surrendered. However, the costs of publishing and the reliance upon advertising proved increasingly formidable barriers to underground, radical or alternative newspapers and periodicals in the post-Second World War period (from 1945). In the 1960s there was a brief renaissance of protest: periodicals such as *Oz*, *IT*, *Frendz* and *Ink* in one way or another got up the nose of Authority, the *Oz* Schoolkids Issue earning for itself the longest-ever obscenity trial (see OZ TRIAL).

Distribution proved yet another hazard for the small radical press. In the UK this has been practically a duopoly of W.H. Smith and Menzies, whose hesitancy over providing the radical press with distribution outlets has been rather more to do with a view that radicals are just not good business rather than for ideological reasons.

With the advent of the INTERNET dissenting voices found new platforms for comment and debate, further threatening the viability of newspapers, especially the local press (already challenged by free papers and the burgeoning growth of local council newsletters). See BLOGGING; INDY MEDIA; JOURNALISM: CITIZEN JOURNALISM; MOBILIZATION; PODCASTING. See also *TOPIC GUIDE* under MEDIA HISTORY.

▶ Patricia Hollis, *The Pauper Press* (Oxford University Press, 1970); Stanley Harrison, *Poor Men's Guardians: A Survey of the Struggles for a Democratic Newspaper Press, 1763–1973* (Lawrence & Wishart, 1974); Stephen Koss, *The Rise and Fall of the Political Press in Britain* (Collins 1990); Elisabeth Eisenstein, *The Printing Press as an Agent of Change* (Cambridge University Press, 1999); Chris Atton, *Alternative Media* (Sage, 2001); Jeremy Black, *The English Press 1621–1861* (Sutton, 2001); John D.H. Downing (with Tamara Vallareal Ford, Geneve Gil and Laura Stern), *Radical Media: Rebellious Communication and Social Movements* (Sage, 2001); Kevin Williams, *Get Me a Murder*

U

a Day! A History of Mass Communication in Britain (2nd edition, Bloomsbury Academic, 2009).

Unitary, pluralist, core-periphery, breakup models of audience fragmentation See AUDIENCE: FRAGMENTATION OF.

Universality Principle that public services such as education, health and justice must be available to all within a society; applies equally to the notion of PUBLIC SERVICE BROADCASTING (PSB).

USA – Patriot Act, 2001 Surveillance measure that became law within a month of the terrorist attacks on New York and the Pentagon, 11 September 2001. Under its full title – Strengthening America by Providing Appropriate Tools Required to Intercept and Obstruct Terrorism – the Patriot Act, all 342 pages of it, provides the US government and its agencies with a formidable armoury of new powers to rein-in civil liberties. Basically, security agencies are granted extended powers to intercept wire, oral and electronic communications relating to terrorism; to share criminal investigation information; to seize voice-mail messages pursuant to warrants; to use DNA identification of terrorists and other violent offenders; to demand disclosure of educational records; and to confiscate the assets of organizations suspected of planning or carrying out terrorism.

Uses and gratifications theory View that mass media audiences make active use of what the media have to offer, arising from a complex set of needs which the media in one form or another gratify. Broadly similar uses have been categorized by researchers based on questionnaires or interviews. An example is the *compensatory use* of the media – to make up for lack of education, perhaps, lack of STATUS or social success. Where the media have a *supplementing use*, the AUDIENCE may be applying what they see, hear and read in social situations as subject-matter for interpersonal exchange.

In 'The television audience: a revised perspective' in Dennis McQuail, ed., *Sociology of the Mass Media* (Penguin, 1972), McQuail, Jay G. Blumler and J.R. Brown define four major categories of need which the media serve to gratify. (1) *Diversion* (escape from constraints of routine; escape from the burdens of problems; emotional release). (2) *Personal relationships* (companionship; social utility). (3) *Personal identity* (personal reference; reality exploration; value reinforcement). (4) *Surveillance* (need for information in our complex world – 'Television news helps me to make up my mind about things').

Blumler and Elihu Katz, in the book of which they are editors, *The Uses of Mass Communication* (Sage, 1974), emphasize the social origin of the needs that the media purport to gratify. Thus where a social situation causes tension and conflict, the media may provide easement, or where the social situation gives rise to questions about VALUES, the media provide affirmation and REINFORCEMENT.

Uses and gratifications theory has been subjected to criticism by a number of commentators. In *The Export of Meaning: Cross-Cultural Readings of Dallas* (Polity Press, 1993), Tamar Liebes and Elihu Katz state, 'The idea that readers, listeners, and viewers can bend the mass media to serve their own needs had gone so far [with gratificationists] that almost any text – or indeed no text at all – was found to serve functions such as social learning, reinforcing identity, lubricating interaction, providing escape etc. But it gradually became clear that these functions were too unspecified.' In other words, theorizing about use has to be linked to the TEXTS that are judged to fulfil audience needs.

The INTERNET has opened up new and exciting avenues for uses and gratifications research, and the four main categories suggested decades ago by McQuail, Blumer and Brown continue to serve, at least as a useful starting point of enquiry into the many reasons users surf the Net. See COGNITIVE (AND AFFECTIVE); FACEBOOK; IDENTIFICATION; MASLOW'S HIERARCHY OF NEEDS; MOBILIZATION; NETWORKING: SOCIAL NETWORKING. See also *TOPIC GUIDE* under COMMUNICATION THEORY.

Utterance meaning See SENTENCE MEANING, UTTERANCE MEANING.

V

VALS typology Arnold Mitchell's *Nine American Lifestyles: Who We Are And Where We're Going* (Macmillan, 1983) describes a landmark in the documentation of human needs – a massive research project funded and carried out in America in 1980 by SRI International. The principle on which the research was based, and which Mitchell's influential book articulates, is that humans demonstrate their needs in their lifestyle, and that both needs and lifestyle fluctuate according to circumstance and 'drive'. VALS stands for Values and Lifestyle.

The VALS approach, and its typology of categories of lifestyle, pigeon-holes people on an all-embracing scale. It has given a significant boost to marketing trends that have increasingly been preoccupied with *segmenting* people into consumer categories. VALS links the pursuit of lifestyle with personal growth: 'With this growth comes change, so that new goals emerge, and in support of these new goals come new beliefs, new dreams, and a new constellation of values,' writes Mitchell.

Though the main focus of research – ongoing rather than a one-off exercise – was upon the population of the United States, what Mitchell terms 'side spurs' of research explored VALS in five European countries – France, Sweden, Italy, West Germany and Britain. The VALS typology to a considerable degree reflects Abraham Maslow's notion of a hierarchy of needs (see MASLOW'S HIERARCHY OF NEEDS) and gives support to his categorization.

The VALS typology has been updated since the 1980s and is currently owned by Strategic Business Insights. There are now eight segments that reflect the psychological and demographic profiles of consumers. The segments are arranged across two dimensions according to the *resources* (education, income, health, energy and consumerism) and *primary motivations* (ideals, achievement needs and drive for self-expression) of consumers. At the top are the *Innovators* – successful people with high self-esteem. They are likely to be change leaders and active consumers particularly of premium and niche products or services. *Survivors* are at the bottom and their reduced circumstances mean that they focus on meeting the more basic needs of safety and security, on value for money, on trusted brands and on getting by.

Ideals are the primary motivators for both *Thinkers* and *Believers*, but of the two, *Thinkers* have more resources and therefore more choices. *Thinkers* are financially comfortable, educated and well-informed. They tend to support the STATUS QUO but are also open to new ideas. They are fairly conservative consumers who look for both quality and good value. *Believers* are conservative and traditional in outlook and thus have considerable respect for traditional institutions and beliefs. Their lives focus on family and community. They are classed as predictable consumers favouring familiar and established brands.

For both *Achievers* and *Strivers* the need for achievement is a primary motivator, but *Achievers* have more resources than *Strivers*. Achievers have a goal-oriented lifestyle and are fairly conventional and conservative. They are active, image-conscious consumers who like to demonstrate their success through their choice of products and services. *Strivers* have yet to achieve their goals. They see financial success as important, like to have a good time and to keep up with the latest trends. They seek approval from others and try to demonstrate success through their purchases, particularly of the kinds of consumer goods associated with those who are more successful.

Self-expression is a primary motivator for both *Experiencers* and *Makers*, but *Experiencers* have more resources. *Experiencers* are younger, more impulsive, seek variety and are inclined towards novel and even risky experiences, but move on quickly from one trend to another. They are enthusiastic consumers, particularly in the fashion and leisure markets. *Makers* are more traditional, wary of new ideas and large organizations, and value self-sufficiency and individual rights. *Makers* find self-expression through practical activities centred on homemaking, such as DIY, and are mostly interested in practical, value-for-money products and services. See *TOPIC GUIDE* under ADVERTISING/MARKETING.

See www.strategicbusinessinsights.com.

Values Each society, social group or individual has certain ideas, beliefs, ways of behaving, upon which is placed a value. A collection of these values, the criteria for judgement of one often acting as REINFORCEMENT for others, may amount to a *system* of values. Such a system, if it is not to cause DISSONANCE in a person, has either to be generally consistent or perceived as generally consistent.

Values are not merely systems of personal belief; they represent shared attitudes within social GROUPS and society at large, of approval and disapproval, of judgments favourable and unfavourable towards other individuals, ideas, objects (such as the value placed on property), social action and events. Like NORMS, values vary from one social group or society to another; and they change over time and in different circumstances.

An individual's perception and interpretation of reality will be influenced by the values of the social groups or society to which he/she belongs. The pervasiveness of such values ensures that they are enmeshed in all aspects of communication processes. The images and codes which are the stock-in-trade of the mass media are shaped by value systems and in turn can be used to support certain values. Senders of communication messages, the mass media being no exception, also need to consider the values of receivers if they wish to avoid causing NOISE. Success in persuasion, for example, often rests on a skilful

V

appeal to the values of the target audience. See CULTURE; IDEOLOGY; MYTH; NEWS VALUES; VALS TYPOLOGY.

Vamp Early word for sex-star in the movies. In 1914 producer William Fox (1879–1952) created a star by going to the farthest extreme away from screen-idol Mary Pickford, symbol of purity and innocence, and imposing a parody of sensuality and eroticism on Theda Bara in the film adaptation of the Kipling poem, *A Fool There Was*. The word 'vamp' was used in the publicity for the film, whose financial success helped Fox set up his own studio, among the most important of the 1920s.

V-discs In 1943, during the Second World War (1939–45), record companies and musicians agreed to waive fees and contractual rights to a series of very high-quality musical offerings to the US forces. Such recordings, many of them by giants of the jazz world such as Benny Goodman, Louis Armstrong and Duke Ellington, are now prized by collectors.

Verbal devices in speech-making Max Atkinson in his illuminating study of the speech-making techniques of politicians and other well-known contemporary orators, *Our Masters' Voices: The Language and Body Language of Politics* (Methuen, 1984), analyses various forms of what the Shorter Oxford English Dictionary terms *claptraps* – linguistic or non-verbal devices to catch applause. Particularly successful, says the author, is the list of three, which stimulates audience response, reinforces that stimulus and then pushes it to the climax. Antithesis is also an effective claptrap ('I come to bury Caesar, not to praise him'). Atkinson cautions the would-be orator that these devices require skill, timing and judgment to be effective, and that claptrap 'always involves the use of more than one technique at a time'. See *TOPIC GUIDE* under LANGUAGE/DISCOURSE/NARRATIVE.

Video Wikipedia defines video as 'the technology of electronically capturing, recording, processing, storing, transmitting, and reconstructing a sequence of still images representing scenes in motion'. Cassette tape video dominated the late 1970s and 1980s until overtaken by the DVD (see DIGITAL VIDEO DISC).

For audiences, video recording equipment made TIME-SHIFT VIEWING possible, while video cameras made film-making a viable proposition for all (see YOUTUBE). Video recording on tape or on disc has benefited every aspect of public communication, though conflict over formats has occurred in highly competitive markets, and an intruder into free expression has been

government legislation (see VIDEO RECORDINGS ACTS, 1984, 2010). See AUDIENCE: FRAGMENTATION OF. See also *TOPIC GUIDE* under MEDIA: TECHNOLOGIES.

▶ Sean Cubbitt, *Timeshift: On Video Culture* (Comedia/Routledge, 1992).

Video/DVD games Like so many examples of popular CULTURE, the video/DVD game has incurred condemnation for being anti-social, a threat to the minds and mentality (not to mention the eyesight) of the young, who are seen to be the main players, and loaded with harmful features. However, games have also achieved cultural status and have been claimed by some critics as amounting to an important art form, while 'cult status' is awarded to some of the protagonists of such games.

A key trend in marketing has been the cross-pollination between films and games and the opportunity games-players have to read the 'the novel of the game'. With the convergence of digital technologies, games feature on the menus of palmtop computers and mobile phones (from 2011 in 3D), though manufacturers have become sensitive to the use of the word 'games', preferring to market their products as multimedia entertainment centres.

Video nasties A market that developed in the 1980s of specially-made-for-video films of a singularly nasty, brutal and sexist nature. Court action in the UK in 1982 against several of these films led to their enforced withdrawal from circulation, but, to the considerable disgust of Mary Whitehouse and the National Viewers' and Listeners' Association – among many others – there was no order made for their destruction. However, the Conservative government brought in rigorous controls of video nasties with the Video Recordings Act, 1984 (see next entry).

In 1994 there was dramatically renewed interest in the possible effects of video nasties on behaviour following the Jamie Bulger case, in which two 11-year-old boys were convicted of murdering the small boy they had abducted. The judge in the trial, Mr Justice Morland, conjectured that the boys may have been influenced by seeing *Child's Play 3*, whose plot paralleled, to a degree, the real actions of the killers.

Though this connection was dismissed by many in the TV and film industry, there was support from child psychologists, in particular from Elizabeth Newson, Professor of Development Psychology at the University of Nottingham, who spoke of the need for special concern when children – or indeed, adults – are repeatedly exposed to images of cruelty in the context of entertainment. See MORAL PANICS AND THE MEDIA.

Video Recordings Acts (UK), 1984, 2010
Passed through Parliament in the UK with all-Party support, MP Graham Bright's measure, the first VRA (1984), was designed to restrict the access of young persons to VIDEO NASTIES, many of which eluded the usual vetting process of the BRITISH BOARD OF FILM CENSORS.

The Act established by statute an Authority (initially the BBFC) whose purpose was to classify video cassettes as suitable for home viewing and to censor those deemed unsuitable. Fines of up to £20,000 were liable for dealers and distributors breaking the law. All video works were to be submitted for scrutiny, classification and certification unless they were educational or concerned with sport, religion or music.

However, if such videos 'to any extent' were deemed to portray 'human sexual activity' or 'mutilation, torture or other acts of gross violence' or to show 'human genital organs', they too had to be submitted to the censors.

It came to light in 2009 that the Act was invalid, being in breach of European Union law. By this time over seventy films were on the Director of Prosecution's list of banned videos. Dozens of prosecutions had to be dropped: good news for free expression? Not exactly. Without delay, the UK government revoked VRA 1984 and re-enacted it in identical form as VRA 2010. The Department of Culture, Media and Sport announced that previous prosecutions would stand. See CENSORSHIP; MORAL PANICS AND THE MEDIA; YOUTUBE.

Viewers: light, medium and heavy Research into the amount and nature of TV viewing discriminates between the light viewer, generally classified as watching TV for two hours or fewer a day; the medium viewer, watching for between two and three hours a day; and the heavy viewer, watching for four hours or more a day. In the analysis of viewer response, special attention has been paid to the differences of attitude to issues and controversies that can be detected between light and heavy viewers, and thus the influence TV programmes may have on attitude formation and attitude change. See CULTIVATION; MAINSTREAMING; MEAN WORLD SYNDROME; RESONANCE.

Violence and the media See VIOLENCE ON TV: THE DEFENCE. See also *TOPIC GUIDES* under AUDIENCES/CONSUMPTION & RECEPTION OF MEDIA; MEDIA: FREEDOM, CENSORSHIP; MEDIA ISSUES & DEBATES; MEDIA: POWER, EFFECTS, INFLUENCE; REPRESENTATION.

▸ Barrie Gunter and Jackie Harrison, *Violence on Television. An Analysis of Amount, Nature, Location and Origin of Violence in British Programmes* (Routledge, 1998); Karen Boyle, *Media and Violence* (Sage, 2005).

Violence on TV: the defence The portrayal of violence on screen, whether in the cinema or on TV, has long attracted controversy and is an ongoing ISSUE of our time. The dominant tendency among commentators is to deplore it, its nature, its extent and its amount. Simulated violence is seen to prompt some members of the AUDIENCE to re-enact that violence in real life; and violence is judged to desensitize viewers to the real thing.

Taking issue with these perspectives is Jib Fowles. In *The Case for Television Violence* (Sage, 1999), Fowles argues that contrary to the notion that screen violence breeds real violence, it is more likely to inhibit or reduce it: 'Television violence is good for people.' Recognizing in human beings an in-built violent impulse, Fowles says that society requires 'outlets' for this impulse. Violence is ever-present and has to be managed: 'In isolation, television violence may seem reproachable and occupy the foreground with a menacing intensity, but with a longer perspective it can seem comparatively like an improvement – a purer distillation of the age-old processes for containing and redirecting violence.'

We have to remember, says Fowles, 'that television violence is symbolic only ... Nobody actually suffers for our pleasure.' For the author, 'the assault on television violence is absolutely unwarranted'. It is 'simply the most recent and least damaging venue for the routinized working out of innate aggressiveness and fear'. The fuss over TV violence Fowles describes as a variant on the moral panic (see MORAL PANICS AND THE MEDIA), which is usually accompanied by the fervour and 'extreme righteousness of the condemners as they lash out at conjured or magnified transgressions'; and the response 'is always out of proportion to whatever instigates it' (see THIRD-PERSON EFFECT). Fowles concludes: 'Perhaps, to give television violence its due, we need first to respect ourselves more fully, to have greater regard for the complex, semiviolent creatures that we are.'

As in addressing all theories, a cautionary note is perhaps required here, for cases occur from time to time in which the enactment of real violence echoes and sometimes directly simulates screen violence. The UK *Observer* (9 June 2002) reported under a headline, 'Murder linked

V

to horror trilogy' that French authorities were blaming the savage stabbing in Saint-Sebastien-sur-Loire by a teenager of a girl he had invited for a walk on the youth's seeming obsession with *Scream* movies.

Two similar murders, by teenagers, had alerted the authorities to the possible influence the films exerted on impressionable young people. An *Observer* listing of what seemed to be copy-cat offences between 1999 and 2002 indicated that it was not only teenagers working out fantasies of violence on real-world victims, but older men too, or in the case of a murder in Massachussetts in 2000, a woman and two men wearing *Scream* masks.

In his *Observer* report, Paul Webster quoted psychiatrists worried 'about the inability of some young people to distinguish between reality and fiction'. Dave Grossman, American expert on the psychology and physiology of killing, would plainly challenge Jib Fowles's assertions. His belief, reported by Webster, was that 'repetition, desensitization and escalation reduced the normal human unwillingness to kill'.

Virtual reality Simulation of the real by technological means, using multi-media inputs – head-mounted display, data gloves, three-dimensional audio system and magnetic position tracker (to name the basics); what has been termed a 'technological cluster'. Generally, the simulation of the real exists in that 'window of realities', the TV monitor.

In a paper entitled 'The ultimate display' for the Proceedings of the IFIPS Congress 2, published as early as 1965, Ivan Sutherland defined the VR dream: 'The screen is a window through which one sees a virtual world. The challenge is to make that world look real, act real, sound real and feel real.'

Virtual reality technology is three-dimensional (see 3D) and interactive. It is extensively used in engineering and architectural design, in medicine and telecommunications. It is potentially a vital component in reconstructing the past. At the first Virtual Reality Heritage conference in Bath, UK, November 1995, IBM's Brian Collins described the VR reconstruction of a church that no longer exists, the Frauenkirche in Dresden, fifty years after its destruction by bombing. Using the few drawings and plans and colour photographs taken by the Nazis, VR technology provided a detailed reconstruction enabling the original to be rebuilt.

A more general application of the term 'virtual reality' centres on the worlds 'out there' as brought to users of the computer, the INTERNET

and the myriad experiences available online. It has become a matter of widespread concern that so many users seem to prefer life as it can be realized online. Mark Slouka in *War of the Worlds: Cyberspace and the High-Tech Assault on Reality* (Basic Books, 1995; Abacus, 1996) talks of a 'culture of simulation' that blurs 'fiction and reality'; and this in his view risks creating in the public a fear 'of unmediated reality', especially considering our willingness to buy in to the virtual, that 'we're buying in to a fake'. It follows that reality itself 'is beginning to lose its authority'. See CYBERSPACE. See also TOPIC GUIDE under MEDIA ISSUES & DEBATES.

Virtuous circle Term used by researchers into how media use links with active participation in politics, and vice-versa: users who take an interest in news reporting on politics are likely to complete the 'virtuous circle' by being more likely to take some part in political activity. Recent research indicates that the most likely direction is from interest to activity.

Visibility See GLOBAL SCRUTINY; PRIVACY.

Visions of order A notion long associated with the role and function of the journalist is that of 'bringer-of-light', of enlightenment. The French writer Jacques Derrida in *Writing and Difference* (Routledge & Kegan Paul, 1978) posed the 'heliological metaphor', describing the journalist as a human version of the heliograph, recorder and transmitter of light, of revelation to AUDIENCE. The process is one of *envisioning* – offering a vision of the world: light for others to see by. In *The Politics of Pictures: The Creation of the Public in the Age of Popular Media* (Routledge, 1992) John Hartley takes up this theme in a chapter entitled 'Heliography: journalism, and the visualization of truth'. What journalism brings to light, what it renders visible are, Hartley argues, 'distant visions of order'. It is not so much the actual truth that is brought to light as the *vision* of truth as visualized in terms of order.

▶ Richard V. Ericson, Patricia M. Baraneh and Janet B.L. Chan, *Representing Order: Crime, Law And Justice in the News Media* (Open University, 1991).

Vitaphone Trade name of the first successful synchronous movie sound, introduced in 1926 by Warner Brothers. On 6 August at the Warner Theatre in New York, John Barrymore starred in *Don Juan*, to the accompaniment of a Vitaphone 16-inch 33⅓ rpm disc recording of voice and music. Curiously *Don Juan* caused less audience excitement than the Vitaphone shorts that accompanied it, such as the New York Philharmonic playing Wagner's Tannhauser Overture. The real sensation of the 'Talkies' was

Warners' next picture, *The Jazz Singer* (1927) starring Al Jolson. There were, in fact, only 281 words spoken in the film, all of them ad-libbed by Jolson. See SYNCHRONOUS SOUND. See *TOPIC GUIDE* under MEDIA HISTORY.

Vlog Video blog (see BLOGGING; YOUTUBE).

Vocal cues All the oral aspects of speech except the words themselves: pitch – the highness or lowness of voice; rate – rapidity of expression; volume; quality – the pleasantness or unpleasantness of voice tone or delivery; and enunciation – pronunciation and articulation. See PARALANGUAGE.

Voiceover In film and TV film production, a framing device in which a commentator offers explanation of what the AUDIENCE is seeing on screen. In feature films, voiceover is often that of the chief character in a story, though the DOCU-MENTARY approach of an unidentified narrator is also common. Voiceover plays a significant role in shaping the MEANING of a film TEXT. It signals the way in which audience is expected to read what is seen and heard. In this sense, voiceover closes down a text to a prescribed meaning, allowing the viewer little room for interpretation. See NARRATIVE; OPEN, CLOSED TEXTS.

Vox popping Collecting the opinions of large numbers of the general public (*vox populi* is Latin for 'voice of the people') in order to gauge public reaction to a current issue or topic.

W

War of the Worlds Title of the American CBS network radio adaptation by Howard Koch, produced and narrated by Orson Welles (1938), of H.G. Wells's famous story. Conveying the immediacy of a combat report from a war correspondent, the production actually convinced many listeners that an interplanetary war had broken out. However, reports to the effect that Orson Welles's radio 'hype' had caused panic in the streets have taken on the magic of legend, and become somewhat exaggerated in the telling. See IDENTIFICATION; PARA-SOCIAL INTERACTION.

War: four stages of war reporting According to Phillip Knightley in a UK *Guardian* article 'The disinformation campaign' (4 October 2001), Western media coverage of military conflicts is highly predictable, passing through four stages: (1) the event is described as a crisis; (2) the enemy leader is DEMONIZED; (3) the enemy as a whole is demonized; while stage (4) focuses on atrocities.

Knightley writes, 'Comparing the leader with Hitler is a good start because of the instant images that Hitler's name provokes' (see HISTORICAL ALLUSION): 'The crudest approach is to suggest that the leader is insane' and those who publicly question any of this 'can expect an even stronger burst of abuse'.

The simplest way of demonizing a whole people, says Knightley, is the atrocity story: 'Take the Kuwaiti babies story. Its origin goes back to the first world war when British propaganda accused the Germans of tossing Belgian babies into the air and catching them on their bayonets. Dusted off and updated for the Gulf War [1991] this version had Iraqi soldiers bursting into a modern Kuwaiti hospital, finding the premature babies ward and then tossing the babies out of incubators so that the incubators could be sent back to Iraq.'

This story, as well as others, was a fabrication, but it had served its propagandist function. See NEWS MANAGEMENT IN TIMES OF WAR. See also *TOPIC GUIDE* under NEWS MEDIA.

▶ Phillip Knightley, *The First Casualty: The War Correspondent as Hero and Myth-Maker from the Crimea to Kosovo* (Prion paperback, revised edition, 2000; John Hopkins paperback, 2004; first published 1975 by Harcourt Brace Jovanovich, entitled *The First Casualty: From the Crimea to Vietnam: The War Correspondent as Hero-Propagandist and Myth Maker*).

War of the Unstamped See STAMP DUTY; UNDERGROUND PRESS.

Watchdogs The media pride themselves on their role as watchdogs of injustice, abuse and corruption; champions of public interest. The watchdog barks on behalf of the people, in their defence against the powerful, whether these are in government, business, industry or any walk of life where the interests of the public can be affected. The role of the watchdog may be seen as key to media functions, and a guiding principle.

Research tends to point to the media being rather less than wholly effective in this capacity; generally to follow rather than initiate the investigation of abuse; indeed to be guilty of *omission* as much as commission (see GUARD DOG METAPHOR).

True 'watchdoggery' can only come about through genuine media independence – from ADVERTISING and sales revenue, from the influence of capital or institutional control. Fulfilling the role of watchdog becomes problematic when that role is seen to trespass upon the vested interests of those who own and control the watchdogs in question.

W

An arms manufacturing company with a portfolio that includes newspapers, radio and TV stations is unlikely to smile benignly on these media if, in the interests of the public, they wish to challenge arms manufacture and export. The result, usually, is not overt CENSORSHIP, but *self-censorship*. With the trend in recent years of CONVERGENCE of ownership, the risks of self-censorship, of failing to fulfil the role of public watchdog, have inevitably increased.

It is for this reason, among others, that media commentators express concern about convergences of media ownership worldwide, fearing that watchdogs will be 'seen off' by guard dogs. See CONGLOMERATES; DEMOCRACY AND THE MEDIA; HEGEMONY; JOURNALISM: CITIZEN JOURNALISM; NEWS VALUES; WATERGATE.

Watergate Scene of one of history's most famous break-ins, and source of one of modern history's most dramatic scandals that eventually led to the resignation of the US President. The apartment block called Watergate in Washington DC was the 1972 election campaign headquarters of the National Committee of the Democratic Party. It was broken into in June by agents of the rival Republican Party's Committee to Re-elect President Richard Nixon. They were caught in the act as they were removing electronic bugging devices.

The ensuing cover-up was penetrated and revealed by two reporters on the *Washington Post*, Bob Woodward and Carl Bernstein, fed with significant information by a mysterious DEEP THROAT within government and close to the President. A Senate investigation committee pushed fearlessly against presidential closed doors. Eventually the Supreme Court forced the White House to give access to tape recordings made, at Nixon's command, over a long period in the President's office. The tapes proved Nixon's complicity in the Watergate Affair.

He was the first President of the US to resign; if he had not resigned, he would have been impeached by Congress. His successor, President Ford, extended a blanket pardon to Nixon, but not to his associates, several of whom ended up in jail (and most of whom wrote successful books on their experiences). Watergate is varyingly cited as a supreme example of investigative journalism, a classic case study of official corruption and an alarming illustration of the paranoia that sometimes comes with power and authority. However, it is perhaps most importantly a breathtaking glimpse of the nature of open government and the potential of the democratic process. See SPYCATCHER CASE; WIKILEAKS.

Web or online drama The INTERNET has proved fertile ground for made-for-the-web drama, usually in serial form, each episode (or webisode) of a few minutes' duration. Online drama was made possible with the arrival of broadband, and was soon being tuned into, via computer or mobile phone, by hundreds of thousands and occasionally millions of fans. The first advertisement-supported web drama, indeed the first web soap, is considered to be ad-executive Scott Zakarin's *The Spot* (1995), a drama based on movie clips and photos of the day-to-day activities of the characters.

Viewers were encouraged to e-mail writers and cast with advice for storylines. Another early web drama from the US was *Homicide: Second Shift* which was tied into the TV series *Homicide: Life on the Street*. Started in 1997, it ran into financial difficulties soon afterwards. In 1999 *Muscle Beach* took to the airwaves in eight-minute weekly instalments. This combined drama with a fitness programme.

Audiences soon began to top the million mark with often short-lived web dramas – *Red v Blue*, *Soup of the Day*, *Sam Has 7 Friends* and *Lonelygirl 15* which, during its 26-month run, attracted 100 million views and stretched over 500 episodes. *Kate Modern* (2007) picked up on this success, while *Roommates* attracted the sponsorship of the Ford Motor Company. By 2008 the corporate media giants had become interested in web drama. From NBC came *Gemini Division* and from Warner Brothers, *Sorority for Ever*.

In the same year the International Academy of Web Television was founded, initiating in 2009 a range of annual awards – the Streamy Awards. A UK contribution to the oeuvre, *Toyboize*, broadcast on YouTube was nominated for a Bafta Award in 2009 in the Interactive Creative Contribution Category. The drama was acquired by the UKTV network and was broadcast on the Dave TV channel from March 2009. Other UK notables have been *Kirill*, *The Gap Year* and *Cell*, all from the Endemol company.

Web drama has prospered – at least in terms of viewer popularity – in Ireland, where Radio Television Eire (RTE) launched Storyland, a competition for web dramas which progressed or bit the dust according to viewer preferences. The winner of the first ever Storyland award was *Hardy Bucks* (2009). *Zombie Bashers* was the 2010 winner.

Web radio See COMMUNITY RADIO.

Web 2.0 A term that has been contested but which has proved useful in describing a significant watershed in the development of INTERNET

...ι and the growth of the NETWORK . First use of the term is considered to ...by Dale Dougherty, Vice-President of the O'Reilly Media corporation in 2004, during a team discussion ahead of an international conference of web operators and participants, a think-tank gathered to point the way ahead for global networking.

Tim O'Reilly, the driving-force behind the notion of Web 2.0, published an influential paper in 2005, 'What is Web 2.0: design, patterns and business models for the new generation of software?' This included reference to key features of Web 2.0, such as participation, with the emphasis on the Net user as contributor. O'Reilly's prime focus was the multiplication of Net uses driven by the possibilities of new technology in the context of the incursion of powerful corporate and government players, this raising far-reaching issues concerning the public and private domain.

Inventor of the World Wide Web, Sir Tim Berners Lee, sees the factors that characterize Web 2.0 as simply an extension of the original ideas and direction of the Web. However, 2005 and the name Web 2.0 mark a lift-off in the ways users interact with each other, typical of those ways being BLOGGING – user-generated content (UGC), interactivity, syndication, multi-media sharing, data transmitted and received on an epical scale, and openness as never experienced previously in the world of communications.

Paul Anderson in a paper for JISC Technology and Standards Watch, 'What is Web 2.0? Ideas, technologies and implications for education' (2007), sees a crucial element of Web 2.0 as harnessing 'the power of the crowd'. In his conclusion he writes that collective power will become 'more important as the Web facilitates new communities and groups. A corollary to this is that online identity and privacy will become a source of tension'. Further, 'the growth in user or self-generated content, the rise of the amateur and a culture of DIY will challenge conventional thinking on who exactly does things, who has knowledge, what it means to have élites, status and hierarchy'.

New technology, Anderson stresses, has in the age of Web 2.0, 'lowered the barrier to entry' in Net communication: 'Collaboration, contribution and community are the order of the day, and there is a sense in which some think that a new "social fabric" is being constructed before our eyes'. See NETWORK NEUTRALITY; NETWORKING: SOCIAL NETWORKING.

Web: World Wide Web (www) Formulated in 1992 by Tim Berners-Lee at the European Nuclear Research Centre as a computer network capable of delivering information more swiftly and comprehensively than any previous delivery system. Darin Barney in *Prometheus Wired: The Hope for Democracy in the Age of Network Technology* (University of Chicago Press, 2002) writes, 'Information on the Web is organized as a massive, searchable database of "pages" existing, not in just a single computer somewhere, but in all the computers linked to the network via servers.' Thus the Web is a network that 'is itself a giant expanding database' capable of linking documents, etc. to any number of other Web documents, brought about by *hypertexting*.

The Web, Barney points out, 'accentuates the capacity of networks to enmesh with one another and become networks of networks in an exponentially increasing matrix of connectivity'. See CYBERSPACE; INTERNET. See also *TOPIC GUIDES* under DIGITAL AGE COMMUNICATION; MEDIA TECHNOLOGIES.

▶ David Gaunlett and Ross Horsley, eds, *Web Studies* (Arnold, 2004).

Wedom, Theydom Version of 'Them-and-Us'. John Hartley uses the term in *The Politics of Pictures: The Creation of the Public in the Age of Popular Media* (Routledge, 1992) to describe the *binary* nature of popular journalism. Hartley sees the practices of popular journalism as being determinedly *adversarial* in nature, defining the world in terms of opposites – private and public, reality and illusion, allies and enemies. He speaks of a tradition of 'foe creation' which is related to notions of order, and the upholding of it.

What the press does, he argues, is operate a 'process of photographic negativization, where the image of order is actually recorded as its own negative, in stories of disorder'. In *Visualizing Deviance: A Study of News Organizations* (Open University Press, 1989), Richard Ericson, Patricia Baraneh and Janet Chan had come to the same conclusion: 'In sum,' they argue, 'journalists are central agents in the reproduction of order'.

★**Wesley and MacLean's model of communication, 1957** In their article 'A conceptual model for communications research' in *Journalism Quarterly*, 34, B.H. Wesley and M.S. MacLean develop NEWCOMB'S ABX MODEL OF COMMUNICATION, 1953 with the aim of encapsulating the overall mass communication process. To Newcomb's A (communicator) B (communicator) X (any event or object in the environment of A, B which is the subject of communication), Wesley and MacLean add a fourth element, C. This represents the editorial communicating

W

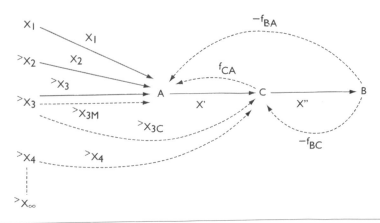

Wesley and MacLean's model of communication, 1957

functions – the process of deciding what and how to communicate.

Newcomb's model represented chiefly interpersonal communication; it was a triangular formation, with A, B and X interacting equilaterally. Wesley and MacLean indicate that the mass media process crucially shifts the balance, bringing A (in this case the would-be communicator) and C (the mass communication organization and its agents who control the channel) closer together. C is both channel and mediator of A's transmission of X to B (now classifiable as audience), and B's contact with X is more remote than in the Newcomb model, if it exists at all save through the combined 'processing' of AC. FEEDBACK is represented by f.

It can be seen from the model that X need not go through to B via A and C but can go via C alone. The role of C as intermediary has a dual character, purposive when the process involves conveying a message through C from an 'advocate', a politician for example, and non-purposive when it is a matter of conveying the unplanned events of the world to an audience.

The main thrust of the model appears to be emphasizing the *dependency* of B upon A and C. What is missing from the model, and what later thinking about mass media processes insists upon, are the numerous message sources and influences that work upon B other than AC, and counter-balance the influence of AC – family, friends, members of peer groups, workmates, colleagues, or wider influences such as school, church, trade unions, etc. An interesting analytical variant would be to 'splice' C into two parts, one traditional mass communication, the other, the INTERNET. See INTERVENING VARIABLES (IVS); NETWORKING: SOCIAL NETWORKING; SIGNIFICANT OTHERS. See also TOPIC GUIDE under COMMUNICATION MODELS.

Western Hollywood's most popularly successful transformation of the past into MYTH, with the enshrining of heroic VALUES: self-help, individualism, the legitimization of violence in the name of timeless (though rarely analysed) notions of Law and Order, and of human rights equated with access to and possession of the earth. The Western has held a firm grip on the imagination of every generation of film-goer since 1903, when Edwin S. Porter's *The Great Train Robbery* set the GENRE off at a brisk gallop.

Much of the fascination in studying the genre of the Western lies in relating its ideological shifts to cultural and political changes taking place in America. Several commentators see the Western as a metaphor for American VALUES, or 'Americanness': configurations of the lone hero, the community threatened by lawlessness, the appeal of the frontier and the sense of old values and lifestyles being overtaken by the urban and the corporate, continue to prompt serious research and analysis. Writing in *Westerns: Aspects of Movie Genre* (Secker & Warburg, 1973), Philip French says of the Western that it is it is among the most didactic of film genres; as he memorably puts it, 'For every Showdown at Wichita there's a little teach-in in Dodge City.'

Westernization of Media Studies See MEDIA STUDIES: THE INTERNATIONALIZATION OF MEDIA STUDIES.

★**Westerstähl and Johansson's model of news factors in foreign news, 1994** A useful complement to GALTUNG AND RUGE'S MODEL OF SELECTIVE GATEKEEPING, 1965 and the ROGERS AND DEARING'S AGENDA-SETTING MODEL, 1987, this model is featured in an article, 'Foreign

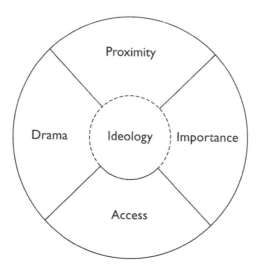

Westerstähl and Johansson's model of news factors in foreign news, 1994

news: news values and ideologies' by Jorgen Westerstähl and Folke Johansson, published in the European *Journal of Communication*, March 1994. Just as the environment or context is the centre and axis from which communicative action springs in the ANDERSCH, STAATS AND BOSTROM'S MODEL OF COMMUNICATION, 1969, IDEOLOGY is the central 'generator' of news coverage according to Westerstähl and Johansson.

The prevailing ideology of national interest works through four primary criteria for news selection: *proximity, importance, drama* and *access*. The first refers to perceived closeness to 'us' varyingly in terms of geography, culture, politics, the economy and language. While the US is distant geographically from the UK, it is nevertheless important – an ELITE nation. The Netherlands, in contrast, while being geographically close, is less 'important'. Events occurring in the US are therefore more likely to be reported than events in The Netherlands, unless those events have a direct relevance to the UK.

We recognize the NEWS VALUES as identified by Galtung and Ruge here – ethnocentrism and elitism in particular. The notion of *drama* is obvious enough but *access* is a welcome criterion: where reporting is possible, where reporters have access, there is greater likelihood that foreign events will be covered. The nature of that access is also critical. There was massive coverage of the Gulf Wars of 1991 and 2003, but access to the kind of information reporters wanted if a full picture of events was to be transmitted

was severely curtailed by *news management* on the part of the military authorities and by ideological pressures requiring the activities of the 'home team' to be presented in the best light (See EMBEDDED REPORTERS; NEWS MANAGEMENT IN TIMES OF WAR).

Westerstähl and Johansson use their model to illustrate how coverage might run counter to traditional news values. They cite the case of the West's interest in Poland during strikes and protests mounted by the Polish trade union Solidarity in the 1980s. The events were dramatic, yet Poland was neither near nor 'important'. The key to this special attention was, in the view of the authors, ideology. Solidarity's actions threatened the chief ideological rival to capitalism – communism.

If performed in the West, Solidarity's actions would have incurred critical media attention: strikes are bad for business. However, such strike action taking place in an Iron Curtain country, and in the context of the Cold War, led to Solidarity's trade unionists being cast as heroes fighting for freedom against Soviet socialist totalitarianism.

'In our view,' write Westerstähl and Johansson, 'ideologies are the main source of deviation in news reporting from a standard based on more or less objectified news values.' See DISCOURSE OF POWER. See also *TOPIC GUIDE* under COMMUNICATION MODELS.

Westminster view Opinion that the media in the UK take their cue from and align their perspectives to the standpoint of the activities

W

of parliament. This produces the simplistic equation – politics equals parliament, and can result in a less-than-adequate coverage of political events which take place away from Westminster; this has been referred to as the 'airless and incestuous "Westminster bubble"'. See POLITICS OF ACCOMMODATION (IN THE MEDIA).

▶ Mike Wayne, Julian Petley, Craig Murray and Lesley Henderson, *Television News, Politics and Young People: Generation Disconnected?* (Palgrave Macmillan, 2010).

Whistleblowing Whistleblowers are most usually individuals within an organization – industrial, commercial, governmental, etc. – who can no longer keep silent about practices in that organization; perhaps because they perceive them as unsafe, corrupt, dishonest or misleading. Almost invariably whistleblowers act out of conscience. Their need for security is outweighed by a higher-order need, to square behaviour with a sense of VALUES (see MASLOW'S HIERARCHY OF NEEDS): they must speak out against the perceived abuse, even though their 'going public', by leaking information to the media, may result in dismissal.

In the UK a degree of protection is offered to whistleblowers in the Public Interest Disclosure Act of 1999. Substantial compensation may be granted to whistleblowers who have suffered victimization, or dismissal, as a result of their raising concerns about financial malpractices, breaches of contract, or cover-ups generally.

▶ Kathryn Bolkovac with Cari Lynn, *The Whistleblower: Sex Trafficking, Military Contracts and one Woman's Fight for Justice* (Palgrave Macmillan, 2011).

★White's gatekeeper model, 1950 The existence of 'gate areas' along channels of communication was identified by Kurt Lewin in 'Channels of group life' in *Human Relations*, 1 (1947). At such points, decisions are made to select out information passing through the gate areas. Lewin's particular study was concerned with decisions about household food purchases, but he drew a comparison with the flow of news

in mass communication. David M. White in an article entitled 'The "Gatekeepers": a case study in the selection of news', in *Journalism Quarterly*, 27 (1950), applied Lewin's idea in a study of the telegraph wire editor of an American non-metropolitan newspaper, whom he called Mr Gate.

Today the model is only acceptable as a starting point for analysis of the GATEKEEPING process; indeed it is a handy exercise for the student to build on the model by adding important factors which White does not include, such as the organizational elements of the mass communication process that constrain and direct it. The model also indicates only a single gate and a single gatekeeper, where in practice news passes through many gatekeepers, official and unofficial, direct and indirect. White's model should be studied in relation to MCNELLY'S MODEL OF NEWS FLOW, 1959 and GALTUNG AND RUGE'S MODEL OF SELECTIVE GATEKEEPING, 1965. See also *TOPIC GUIDE* under COMMUNICATION MODELS.

Wi-fi See INTERNET: WIRELESS INTERNET.

Wikileaks A non-profit-making website created in 2007 by Australian Julian Assange and dedicated to leaking information to the public which has been withheld from it by governments, organizations and institutions. The website's mission statement says, 'We believe that transparency in government activities leads to reduced corruption, better government and stronger democracies. All governments can benefit from increased scrutiny by the world community, as well as their own people.' That scrutiny requires information, much of it highly embarrassing to the authorities that have tried to conceal or suppress it.

Though starved of funding and with only a small team of full- and part-time staff, Wikileaks has commanded global headline news, for example by making public the operating procedures at the Guantanamo Bay US military camp. This stirred a reaction from the US authorities which prompted Assange to comment, 'They want me dead!'

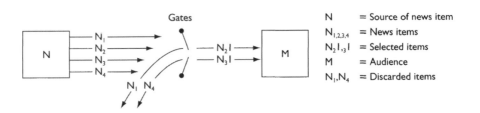

White's gatekeeper model, 1950

Wikileaks was also responsible for posting dramatic video footage of a US helicopter attack on unarmed civilians in Baghdad, July 2007. The website's issue of an 18-minute film entitled *Collateral Murder* attracted worldwide attention, as did the 'War Logs', 400,000 field reports detailing the practice by coalition forces in Iraq of turning over prisoners to teams of Iraqi torturers, notably the so-called Wolf Brigade, under the control of the Iraqi Ministry of the Interior.

If the leaks already listed were not enough, Wikileaks soon broke the bank in November 2010 with the airing of 251,287 secret dispatches from more than 250 US embassies, described in one paper as 'an unprecedented picture of secret diplomacy by the planet's sole superpower'. The cables made transparent what hitherto had been going on behind locked doors. Referred to as the US Embassy Cables, they revealed often dramatically frank comments concerning foreign statesmen and politicians, royalty and public figures. Regarded as the biggest security breach in diplomatic history, the 'outed' cables caused high dudgeon in the States from the American President downwards, the White House condemning the leaks as an attack not only on the US but also the international community.

In December a request from Sweden for the extradition of Lasange on the grounds that he had been reported for sexual assault led to him being taken into custody in Britain and denied bail, even though ample surety had been offered by friends and well-wishers. Concurrently, companies such as eBay, Pay-Pal and AMAZON either froze Wikileaks assets or refused to do business with the organization. This prompted 'Operation Payback', described as a cyberwar, where supporters of Lasange and Wikileaks targeted the refusants online in a number of damaging ways.

Further sensational and embarrassing revelations concerning the treatment by US authorities of prisoners at Guantanamo Bay became public knowledge through the pages of the *New York Times* and the UK *Guardian* (their information obtained from Wikileaks) in the spring of 2011, one story claiming that an an Al-Qaeda 'assassin' had actually worked for the British MI6. See ISLANDIC MODERN MEDIA INITIATIVE; SIPDIS.

▸ David Leigh and Luke Harding, *WikiLeaks: Inside Julian Assange's War on Secrecy* (Guardian Books, 2011).

Wiki, Wikipedia The brainchild of Jimmy Wales, and started up in January 2001, the Wiki is a website everyone can contribute to and edit; the Wikipedia is what thousands of contributors worldwide have assembled. Wiki had become so popular by 2005 that 400 delegates attended the first Wikimania Foundation conference in Frankfurt, Germany. 'What we are doing,' Wales told Sean Dodson of the UK *Guardian* ('Worldwide Wikimania', 11 August 2005) is building a world in which every person on the planet is given free access to the sum of human knowledge.' By the time of the conference, the Wikipedia contained over a million-and-a-half entries in 200 different languages, all contributed by 'wikipedians'.

'Never has such an anarchic idea produced such a democratic outcome as the Wiki,' writes Iranian blogger journalist Hossain Derakhshan in a posting on the *OpenDemocracy* website (3 August, 2005). Entries are made by specialist volunteers, but its pages are open to contributions from members of the public, for the use of the public: pose it, write it, alter it or any other entry: 'It's as if for every single change in an entry, a referendum is taking place.'

Subject to constant addition, rewriting, alteration, Wikipedia has incurred criticism concerning accuracy and reliability; by the nature of such a vast, open and free compendium of the world's knowledge, this is inevitable. Used along with other sources, Wikipedia is nevertheless an invaluable fount of instantly summonable information.

Windows See MICROSOFT WINDOWS.

Wireless network See INTERNET: WIRELESS INTERNET.

Wireless telegraphy In the 1870s, James Clark Maxwell (1831–79), first Professor of Experimental Physics at the University of Cambridge, argued that wireless telegraphy would be possible by employing electro-magnetic waves. In 1885, Welsh electrical engineer Sir William Preece (1834–1913) sent currents between two insulated squares of wire a quarter of a mile apart. Two years later Heinrich Rudolf Hertz (1857–94), German physicist, proved the existence of radio waves and in 1894 English physicist Sir Oliver Lodge demonstrated how messages could be transmitted and received without wires.

Similar pioneer work had been conducted by Italian Guglielmo Marconi (1874–1937), who arrived in England to further his ideas. Supported by Preece – then Engineer-in-Chief of the Post Office – Marconi filed an application for a wireless patent (1896) and was soon sending long-distance messages by Morse Code, first across the Bristol Channel and then the English Channel. His telegraph was used to save a ship in distress in the North Sea and it was rapidly

W

accepted that radio equipment was essential on board all ships. The British Admiralty paid Marconi £20,000 a year for the use of his system in the Royal Navy.

By 1901, wireless messages were being transmitted from Cornwall to Newfoundland, tapped out in Morse. A year later R.A. Fissenden of the University of Pittsburg transmitted the sound of a human voice over a distance of a mile. Further progress was made possible by the invention of the thermionic valve or electron tube, by English electrical engineer John Ambrose Fleming (1904). This device served to change the minute alternating current of a radio signal into a direct current, capable of actuating a TELEPHONE receiver or the needle of a meter. American physicist Lee De Forest improved the valve by making amplification possible. In 1910 De Forest fitted what he named a 'radio-phone' on the roof of the Metropolitan Opera House in New York, enabling listeners to hear the voices of the singers 100 miles away.

The First World War (1914–18) accelerated developments in radio, where it received baptism as a weapon of PROPAGANDA, by the Germans. The future possibilities for radio were encapsulated by American engineer David Sarnoff when in 1916, he declared, 'I have in mind a plan of development which would make a radio a "household utility" like the piano or electricity. The idea is to bring music into the house by wireless.' See RADIO BROADCASTING. See also *TOPIC GUIDES* under BROADCASTING; MEDIA HISTORY; MEDIA: TECHNOLOGIES.

Wireless Telegraphy Act (UK), 1904 The result of a meeting of the major international powers held in Berlin in 1903 to prepare an international plan for the regulation of wireless telegraphy at sea. The UK government required legislation in order to sign the ensuing agreements that enforced uniform rules of working. The Act established universal wireless licensing in Britain, shore and sea, granted by the Postmaster-General with the consent of the Admiralty and Army Council and the Board of Trade.

Workers in communications and media So diverse is the labour market for the communications industry that the vast aggregate size of labour in communications worldwide is often overlooked in study and research. Yet whether it is journalists, broadcasters, telecommunication engineers, operatives in the knowledge and publishing industries or workers in New Media that are being focused on, similar pressures and challenges are being encountered in the age of GLOBALIZATION. A key trend is CONVERGENCE.

Media companies expand in reach but also seek to economize on labour. In-house work, if its costs threaten profit-growth, is replaced by outsourcing (to low-wage economies),whether or not that harms efficiency or standards or puts people out of work.

Worker rights and protection that may have been established within nation states risk being ignored or actively resisted by employers working across international boundaries. The hazards are numerous: workers find themselves at the mercy of 'take it or leave it' new contracts demanding more for less, impacting on job security in contexts where traditional union protection can no longer be guaranteed.

As never before the dynamics of information capitalism shape labour globally, undermining worker power and control. In response, organizations representing the interests of communication and media workers are reconstituting themselves as global operators by converging in alliance with like-minded institutions – the aim, worker protection and worker MOBILIZATION.

For example, the International Federation of Journalists (IFJ) represents over half a million journalists worldwide and comprises more than 160 member unions in over a hundred countries. The recently established Union Network International (UNI) serves workers in electronic communication and has proved itself effective in pressurizing global companies on its members' behalf.

Such alliances work for the maintenance and extension of worker rights. These prominently include defence of women workers, who are particularly vulnerable in harsh global climates. A product of the global activity of labour organizations is the Global Framework Agreement (GLA), still in its infancy, where a communications company operating worldwide agrees standards of employment that apply to all workers in its employ, ensuring minimum labour standards, health and safety and training opportunities.

Vincent Mosco and David O. Lavin conclude their chapter, 'The labouring of international communication' in *Internationalizing Media Studies* (Routledge, 2009), edited by Daya Kishan Thussu, 'rather than asking again and again "what will be the next new thing?" it may be time to ask a more important question: will communication workers of the world unite?'.

World Trade Organization (WTO) Telecommunications Agreement, 1997 Signed by sixty-eight countries, this agreement to abolish national and regional barriers to free trade in telecommunication services was, as the WTO believed, 'an important step towards fully competitive markets'. This radical move towards DEREGULATION was widely challenged by critics who argued that more freedom actually meant more American dominance; and that fully competitive markets were likely to reward the strong and punish the weak.

Edward Herman and Robert McChesney write, in *The Global Media: The New Missionaries of Corporate Capitalism* (Continuum, 1997), 'It may be worth noting that the United States is home of ten of the sixteen largest telecommunications firms in the world, and these are the firms that are the major beneficiaries of free trade'. The authors believe that while this and other liberalizing measures in global markets have 'improved services for business and the affluent in the developing world, the principle of universal access has been compromised, if not abandoned'. Also, such measures have 'led to numerous episodes of large-scale graft and corruption'.

The liberalization (meaning PRIVATIZATION) of telecommunications has encouraged mergers, partnerships and joint ventures among the decreasing number of giant players, leading to what the UK *Financial Times* (2 April 1996) termed 'a handful of giants, straddling the world market'. See GLOBAL MEDIA SYSTEM: THE MAIN PLAYERS; NETWORK NEUTRALITY. See also *TOPIC GUIDES* under GLOBAL PERSPECTIVES; MEDIA ISSUES & DEBATES.

X

X-certificate See CERTIFICATION OF FILMS.

Xerography Reprographic process using a photo-electric surface that converts light into an electronic charge. Documents can be reproduced in black and white and in colour to a very high standard, and reduced in size or enlarged. The electrostatic image of a document attracts charged ink powder, which in turn is attracted to charged paper. A visible image is formed and fixed permanently by heating.

Xenophobia Fear of foreigners; from the Greek, *xeno* – strange, foreign, guest, and *phobos*, fear. The media's role in cultivating xenophobic tendencies in the public has a long, and often tragic, history. The speed at which such tendencies can be provoked and manipulated is a vital area of media research. See DEMONIZATION; EFFECTS OF THE MASS MEDIA; FOLK DEVILS; MORAL PANICS AND THE MEDIA; RADIO DEATH; STEREOTYPE; WEDOM, THEYDOM.

Y

Yahoo! Or in its early days, 'Jerry's Guide to the World Wide Web', renamed after 'rude, unsophisticated, uncouth' and pretty despicable characters in Jonathan Swift's *Gulliver's Travels* (1776), on the grounds that it was an eye-catching title. The global INTERNET service was the creation of Jerry Yang and David Filo, Stanford University graduate students. Its headquarters are in Sunnyvale, California.

One of the most visited sites (3–4 billion hits a day), Yahoo! provides a wide range of online services, its development characterized by diversification, acquisition and alliances while at the same time fighting off bids to buy it out (such as Microsoft's failed takeover bid, 2008). It was incorporated in 1995 and was soon absorbing other enterprises that would contribute to Yahoo's growth: in 1997 Rocketmail became Yahoo!Mail, ClassicGames became Yahoo!Games. A marketing alliance with GOOGLE followed. In 2005 Yahoo! acquired the photo-sharing service, Flickr. Then came Yahoo!Maps (setting the competition nerves jangling with GOOGLE) and social media sites (My Web, Yahoo!Personal, Delicious and Yahoo!Buzz).

As with other online providers, Yahoo! has incurred widespread criticism and not inconsiderable litigation. The organization's global ambitions, in particular its business in China, have been the target of accusations that collusion took place with the Chinese government, namely concerning Yahoo!'s identification of Chinese dissidents using the Yahoo! platform to communicate their opinions.

Following the jailing of journalist and dissident Shi Tao for ten years in 2005, the British and Irish National Union of Journalists (NUJ) called for a boycott of Yahoo!'s products and services as a result of the organization's activities in China. A ten-year sentence awaited another 'outed' dissident, Wang Xiaoning. In 2007 Wang's wife Yu Ling, supported by the World Organization for Human Rights USA, sued Yahoo! in a San Francisco court.

Speaking for the human rights organization, Morton Sklar stated that 'Yahoo! had reason to know that they provided China with the identification information that these individuals would be arrested'. The issue proceeded as far as the US House Foreign Affairs Committee, Yahoo! being criticized for failing to provide full information, this being described as 'at best inexcusable negligence' and at worst 'deceptive'.

XYZ

A further questionable connection with China was the revelation that Yahoo! held a 40 per cent share in Alibaba, a company trading in crocodile products. In its defence, the organization argued that 40 per cent ownership of the company precluded it from exerting control over Alibaba's trade in China.

Yamousoukrou declaration Issued by African leaders in 1985, the declaration states that 'one of the main keys to solving Africa's development problems lies in mastering the national management of information in all its forms'. The text of the declaration that appeared in an International Bureau of Information report (1986) argued that information management and control are 'not only a positive force for regional and continental integration but also an essential condition for the survival of Africa within the community of nations in the twenty-first century'. See CORE NATIONS, PERIPHERAL NATIONS; DEVELOP-MENT NEWS; INFORMATION GAPS; McBRIDE COMMISSION; MEDIA IMPERIALISM.

★**Yaros' 'PICK' model for multimedia news, 2009** 'PICK' stands for three linked processes: Personalization, Involvement and Contiguity; the fourth, 'Kick-out', indicates that P, I and C have not worked. The model posed by Ronald A. Yaros relates to news reception in the multi-media world of the INTERNET; its theoretical intention 'to maximize interest in and understanding of complex news by non-expert citizens'.

In 'Producing citizen journalism or producing journalism for citizens: a new multimedia model to enhance understanding of complex news' published in *Journalism and Citizenship: New Agendas in Communication* (Routledge, 2009), edited by Zizi Papacharissi, Yaros notes the 'overwhelming complexity in news' which 'appears to be growing exponentially'. He raises the question, 'why and how should citizens with limited expertise engage in complex news issues on a medium that offers so many other choices'?

Yaros' model 'attempts to answer with the hypothesis that more citizens might better understand complex news if the content was presented with more personalization, involvement and coherent multimedia structures'. The process the author sees as an interactive one between professionals and news-consuming citizens.

The elements of the model work together; and where they don't enhance interest and understanding it is because kick-outs have occurred, that is consumer switch-off or switch-over. Kick-outs might be technical difficulties, information seen to be outdated, confusing, irrelevant, too

much, too little; or quite simply the existence and persistence of advertisements distracting from news content (see NOISE).

Yaros defines personalization as 'the degree to which content is tailored for an individual for consumption', web research indicating that user responses are usually more positive the more personalized the content and presentation: the more users can personalize their choice, the more they become their own information GATEKEEPERS.

The author sees Involvement as made up of two elements, *interest* and *interactivity*. Web browsing is largely swift and cursory; a user might spend only fractions of a second with a text before moving on. This will depend on what Yaros terms 'individual interest': something users bring with them to new texts, knowledge and interest which 'develops over time'. 'Situational interest' on the other hand comes about as a result of an encounter with text, pictures, sound or video communication. User engagement will depend on a number of factors, including well-written and easily comprehended text with helpful and attractive aids such as pictures, graphs, animations, colour and attractive page design.

The PICK model defines interactivity as 'the degree to which content assists citizens to input choices, responses or content ... any ability for citizen journalists to serve as the source of content – through blogs, forums, uploaded video, etc. – represents more meaningful interactivity because the model focuses on the user'.

Contiguity 'is the extent to which the combinations of hypertext, photos, animation, slides, links, blogs, video and audio relate to each other to maximize coherence of the single message while preventing cognitive overload'. Quite simply, do all the elements of a page 'relate to each other to form one coherent message'? For example, the closer pictures are to the text they illustrate, the more effective their contiguity, the greater will be user understanding; equally, 'contiguity within the *structures* of text and hypertext is important'.

The Kick-out element of the PICK model 'addresses those elements that threaten engagement'. Yaros states, 'if news is not personalized enough for the user's experience, prior knowledge or interest, or is not interactive enough for citizen involvement or is not contiguous enough to quickly form a coherent message, the content itself will likely "kick out" citizen engagement'.

Yaros argues that in a world of 'overwhelming content' and characterized by a media environment that is 'increasingly fragmented',

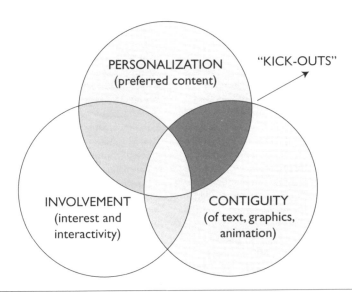

Yaros' 'PICK' model for multimedia news, 2009

multimedia journalism will have to accept that traditional ways to structure the news text 'are now only a subset of all the important variables to be considered when producing multimedia news'.

At the macro-level of the website and the micro-level of the news story, the operation of the components of the PICK model will 'be paramount if the audience member is to be retained'. Yaros puts the case that 'concepts in the PICK model will be the determining factors that separate mediocre content with content that will be truly worth the time for the audience to engage'.

Yellow journalism Phrase used in the US to describe newspapers involved in the internecine (dog-eat-dog) warfare of the popular metropolitan press empires of the late nineteenth century; a battle which has continued to the present day with mass-circulation tabloids competing for readership with all sorts of exploitative offers, lurid revelations and blockbuster bingo.

Yellow Kid Newspaper cartoon character, the possession of whose widely popular image – and the use of that image – was fought over by New York's press barons, Joseph Pulitzer (1847–1911) and William Randolph Hearst (1863–1951). The pictorial image was fast dominating the pages of newspapers at the beginning of the twentieth century, proving a circulation-booster and a marketing device. Pulitzer's *New York World* first featured Richard B. Outcault's cartoon, *Shantytown* (renamed *Hogan's Alley*). Hearst 'raided' the *World's* Sunday edition, buying-in the entire production team of the paper for his own, newly purchased *Journal*. The gap-toothed Kid in his yellow smock, whose grin was recognized throughout the city on billboards and sandwich boards, joined the *Journal* as cartoon and promotional image. Soon Hearst was organizing the Yellow Fellow Transcontinental Bicycle Relay followed by a bike carnival in New York's Central Park.

In response, Pulitzer hired Richard Buks to continue the original cartoon strip, and in 1895 two Yellow Kids were in competition. 'For contemporaries,' writes Andrew Wernick in *Promotional Culture: Advertising, Ideology and Symbolic Expression* (Sage, 1991), 'the Kid's colour became emblematic of the effects of intensified consumerization on the whole character of the popular press'.

Visual appeal had become central to the process of promotion. When Hearst followed Pulitzer in issuing a full-colour Sunday supplement, the *Journal* announced its own 'eight pages of irridescent polychromous effulgence that makes the rainbow look like a lead pipe'. It is perhaps more than a coincidence that the most popular TV comic strip, *The Simpsons*, continued with the effulgence of yellow. See TOPIC GUIDE under MEDIA HISTORY.

Youth culture Since the Second World War (1939–45), considerable attention has been paid to the cultures and sub-cultures of young people – to their symbols, SIGNS, philosophies, MORES, NORMS, language, and music. Music is an essential part of all youth cultures and sub-cultures, a mode of self-identification (see SELF-IDENTITY),

XYZ

and different GROUPS favour different musical styles and use music in different ways.

Youth cultures and sub-cultures differ not only over time but can also vary between CLASS, sex and racial groups. Whilst they manifest significant differences, there are some links between them and individuals may move from one to another. They adopt and adapt aspects of each other's cultural style and those of past youth cultures and sub-cultures. The more dramatic sub-cultures have attracted attention from the media and academics. Their often spectacular modes of expression offer contrast and challenge to society, usually communicated by STYLE – the hairstyle of the Punks, for example.

The media have been a notable mediator of society's reaction to such challenges, and this role has been a focus of media research. Essentially, youth culture is seen as deviant, or potentially deviant; and since a function of media is to patrol the boundaries between the norm and the deviant, particular interest is expressed in youth culture, often leading to DEMONIZATION and a tendency to work up concern that threatens the social order. See FOLK DEVILS; MORAL PANICS AND THE MEDIA; SENSITIZATION.

YouTube An audio-visual network platform launched in February 2005 to which millions post their videos. Its slogan is 'Broadcast Yourself' and it has been described as a 'speakers' corner'. It limits submissions by individuals to 15 minutes. Part of the GOOGLE empire since 2006, YouTube is easy to use, observes no criteria for selection, is anarchic in the sense that there are no classifications of order, and is virtually impossible to regulate, monitor or censor. It renders copyright protection of content extremely problematic.

In 'Alternative modes of civil engagement' in the book she also edited, *Journalism and Citizenship: New Agendas in Communication* (Routledge, 2009), Zizi Papacharissi writes that the 'main draw is that YouTube user generated content serves a variety of purposes, ranging from catching a politician in a lie to impromptu karaoke, with no restrictions'.

'Where BLOGGING provides the pulpit,' Papacharissi writes, 'YouTube provides the irreverence, humour, and unpredictability necessary for rejuvenating political conversation trapped in conventional formulas' and serves as a potent vehicle for citizen journalism (see JOURNALISM: CITIZEN JOURNALISM). She states that 'YouTube content completes the media and news sphere that the monitorial citizen scans while surveying the political environment, by adding various and diverse takes on political reality'.

It provides 'an opportunity for expression different from conventional mobilization, opinion expression, or protest'. This explains why YouTube suffers frequent blocking in many countries, a practice that will spread as the range of languages becomes increasingly *internationalized*, and content and language *localized*, that is tailored to both international and local consumption. See FACEBOOK; MYSPACE.

▶ Jean Burgess and Joshua Green, *YouTube: Online Video and Participatory Culture* (Polity Press, 2009); Michael Strangelove, *Watching YouTube: Extraordinary Videos by Ordinary People* (University of Toronto Press, 2010).

Z

Zapping, zipping The practice of TV channel-switching, especially when the commercials come on, is referred to as 'zapping'; made worryingly easy – as far as the advertisers are concerned – with the arrival of remote control. In France, an anti-zapping strategy designed to keep viewers glued to the commercials was introduced in the late 1980s: individual numbers placed in the corner of the screen offer viewers bingo-style competition. A full line of numbers wins a cash prize. 'Zipping' is fast-forwarding through recorded programmes, again most generally to escape the commercials.

Zinoviev letter, 1924 Probably forged by Russian émigrés and used as a 'Red scare' tactic by the UK *Daily Mail* to put the frighteners on the electorate immediately before the 1924 election. Labour lost the election and the Zinoviev letter probably made some difference, if not a substantial one. It was a 1,200-word document marked *Very Secret*, bearing the address of the 3rd Communist International, the organization in Moscow responsible for international communist tactics.

The letter was addressed to the Central Committee of the British Communist Party and its tenor was the need to stir the British proletariat to revolutionary action against their capitalist masters. Among other recommendations, the letter urged the formation of cells in the armed forces – the 'future directors of the British Red Army'.

The impact of the forged letter was due to its timing. It was 'intercepted' by the Conservative *Daily Mail* just a few days before the election of October 1924 and published four days before Polling Day. The *Mail* used a seven-deck (or lines) headline, topping the deck with 'Civil War Plot By Socialists' Masters'. With the exception of the *Daily Herald*, the entire British press swallowed and regurgitated the story. *The Times* discovered 'Another Red Plot in Germany' and on voting day the *Daily Express* warned, in red ink, 'Do Not Vote Red Today'. Labour lost fifty seats but gained more than a million votes.

Eventually (but always too late) the truth will out; and in February 1999 Gill Bennett, Chief Historian at the UK Foreign Office, produced a 126-page report, commissioned by the-then Foreign Secretary Robin Cook, pointing a sure finger of accusation at Desmond Morton, an MI6 officer and friend of Winston Churchill, as the official who supplied the *Mail* with its sensational disclosure. Also named is Major Joseph Ball, an MI5 officer who joined the Conservative Central Office in 1926. Bennett reported that the forged letter was 'probably leaked from SIS [the Secret Intelligence Service, alias MI6] by somebody to the Conservative Party Central Office'. See DISINFORMATION; FREEDOM OF INFORMATION. See also *TOPIC GUIDES* under MEDIA: FREEDOM, CENSORSHIP; MEDIA: POWER, EFFECTS, INFLUENCE.

Zircon affair In 1986 in the UK, *New Statesman* journalist Duncan Campbell made a series of six TV programmes for the BBC entitled *Secret Society*. The first of these was about a Ministry of Defence project – Zircon – to put a spy satellite into space, at an estimated cost of £5m. On 15 January 1987, Alisdair Milne, the BBC's soon-to-be-dismissed Director-General, banned the Zircon programme on grounds of national security, a decision the *Observer* made public on 18 January.

The most notorious aspect of the Zircon affair was the police raids. Special Branch descended upon the *New Statesman* offices – upon Campbell's home as well as the homes of two other *Statesman* journalists; and finally there was a raid on the Glasgow offices of BBC Scotland, where all six of the *Secret Society* films were seized. Two days before, Milne had been sacked as the BBC's Director-General.

The irony of the case is that Zircon was not really a closely guarded state secret; indeed the position of the proposed satellite was filed by the Ministry of Defence at the International Communications Union, an institution of which the former USSR was a member. Eventually the Zircon programme was transmitted by the BBC in September 1988, by which time the Zircon project had been cancelled. See *TOPIC GUIDES* under MEDIA: FREEDOM, CENSORSHIP; MEDIA:

POLITICS & ECONOMICS; MEDIA: POWER, EFFECTS, INFLUENCE.

Zoetrope Or 'wheel of life'. Early nineteenth-century 'toy' in which pictures inside a spinning drum, viewed from the outside through slits, appear to be in motion. Invented in 1834 by Englishman W.G. Horner, the zoetrope simply but effectively demonstrated the phenomenon of PERSISTENCE OF VISION, the realization of which opened the way for the birth of cinema.

Zones In *The Hidden Dimension: Man's Use of Space in Public and Private* (Bodley Head, 1966), Edward T. Hall identifies four distinct zones, or territorial spaces, in which most men and women operate. These are *intimate* distance; *personal* distance; *social* distance; and *public* distance, each with its close and far phases. See PROXEMICS.

Zoopraxography Pioneer photographer Eadweard Muybridge (1830–1904) was not the inventor of cine-film, but he made the first photographic moving pictures, a process he called Zoopraxography, fifteen years before Lumière's first films. Muybridge described his Zoopraxiscope as being 'the first apparatus ever used, or constructed, for synthetically demonstrating movements analytically photographed from life'.

In 1878 he set up an experiment at Palo Alto, California, to ascertain by photography whether all four hooves of a galloping horse were ever simultaneously clear of the ground (they are). Twenty-four cameras were aligned along the running track, each triggered off by the horse as it galloped past.

The Zoopraxiscope consisted of a spinning glass disc bearing the photographs in sequence of movement. The disc, when attached to a central shaft, revolved in front of the condensing lens of a projecting lantern parallel to and close to another disc fixed to a tubular shaft that encircled the other, and round which it rotated in the opposite direction.

By 1885 Muybridge had produced an encyclopaedia of motion: men and women, clothed and unclothed, performed simple actions such as running, drinking cups of tea or shoeing horses; and a massive and varied study of animals and birds in movement. His carefully catalogued work was published in 1887. See *TOPIC GUIDE* under MEDIA HISTORY.

XYZ

A chronology of media events

This Chronology is drawn from many sources, but our best thanks go to Patrick Robertson whose *The New Shell Book of Firsts* (Headline, 1994), a remarkable piece of historical detective work, has been immensely helpful. *UK* is used in a generalized sense as a composite reference to England, Britain and the United Kingdom.

AD 105 Paper produced from pulp; invention attributed to Ts'ai Lun, China.

AD 704 First printed book, the *Dharani Sutra*, created in Korea from woodblocks on a scroll, and discovered in the foundations of the Pulguk Sa pagoda in Kyongju, South Korea, October 1966.

1174 First evidence of woodblock printing in Europe, by Benedictine monks at Engelberg, Switzerland, used to print capital letters in illuminated manuscripts.

1234 *Compendium of Rites and Rituals*, first book printed using movable type comprising 50 chapters, 28 copies of which were published in Korea. The type was made using a sand-moulding technique developed in 1102 for casting coins.

1451 *Donatis Latin Grammar*, two leaves of a 27-line publication, the first evidence of the use of movable type in Europe, possibly the same type as that used by John of Gutenberg in his 42-line Bible believed to have been printed at Mainz between 1451 and 1454, 48 copies of which survive, 36 printed on paper, 12 on vellum.

1454 Gutenberg prints the first calendar.

1461 Albrecht Pfister of Bamberg publishes the first books in the vernacular: Ulrich Boner's *Edelstein* and Johann von Tepl's *Ackermann aus Böhmen*.

1474 In Bruges, the Englishman William Caxton publishes *The Recuyell of the Histories of Troye*, a translation from original French text. Caxton moved to London where he printed in 1477 *The Dictes and Sayengis of the Philosophres*, a work of 74 leaves 'drawn out of frensche into our Englisshe tonge' by Anthony Earl Rivers.

1475 Jodocus Pflanzmann of Augsburg prints the first illustrated Bible.

1484 Caxton prints *Morte D'Arthur*.

1494 John Tate of Stevenage is the first to manufacture paper in England. Tate produced the first-known watermark in the UK – a star and circle.

1513 Nicolo Machiavelli's *The Prince* published.

1517 Martin Luther nails his 95 Theses, protesting against the sale of indulgences, on the church door at Wittenberg. The printing and distribution of his works ignites the Reformation, and the division of Europe between Roman Catholic and Protestant faiths.

1526 William Tyndale's translation of the New Testament into English is published by Peter Schoeffer in Worms, Germany.

1527 Leipzig: printer Hanz Hergot executed for twice publishing *On the New Direction of Christian Life*, a pamphlet advocating common ownership of land and goods.

1536 Myles Coverdale's complete translation of the Bible into English published, probably in Cologne. This was printed in London by James Nicholson the following year.

1559 Roman Catholic church promulgates the Index Librorum Prohibitorum, a list of prohibited books; and in 1571 the Index Expurgatoris, of books permitted after censorship.

1588 Dr Timothy Bright introduces the first recorded system of shorthand. His system appeared under the title *Characterie; the art of short, swift, and secret writing*.

1608 The civil authorities of Norwich open the first municipal public library, chiefly for 'the use of preachers'. In 1656 Chetham's Library in Manchester became the first to employ a librarian. Chetham's was open to all. As late as 1849 it remained the only substantial collection of books fully accessible to the public. Manchester also took the lead with the lending of books. In 1852 the Manchester Free Library instituted a lending system, issuing over 70,000 books in its first year. This followed the Public Libraries Act of 1850.

1611 Issue in the UK of the Authorized Version

of the Bible (called the King James Version), the composite work of 46 translators and revisers.

1619 State of Weimar becomes the first to introduce compulsory education for all between the ages of 6 and 13. In the UK similar legislation had to wait until 1870.

1621 First *Corantos* published in London, followed in same year by first Proclamation against Corantos.

1637 Star Chamber Decree regulating printing, followed in 1643 with Ordinance for regulating printing, and in 1649 the first Printing Act.

1642 The *Mayflower* arrives in America from Plymouth, England, with a printing press on board.

1644 Publication of John Milton's *Areopagitica* presenting the case for the freedom of the press.

1649 UK: Charles I beheaded. During the period in power of the Lord Protector, Oliver Cromwell, and until the restoration of the monarchy in 1660, under Charles II, England becomes a hotbed of radical, chiefly religious, publications. John Lilburne issues *England's New Chaines Discovered.*

1650 At Leipzig, the first daily newspaper, the *Einkommenden Zeitungen*, is published by Timotheus Ritzsch. In the UK the *Perfect Diurnall* was published daily, except Sunday, between February and March 1660, though British readers had to wait till 1702 for the first successful daily, the *Daily Courant.*

1651 Publication of Thomas Hobbes' *Leviathan.*

1657 First classified advertisement in a UK paper printed in Thomas Newcombe's *Publick Advertiser*, the first English paper devoted entirely to advertising.

1660–1 Parliament prohibits publication of its proceedings.

1680 Royal Proclamation suppressing all newsbooks except those under licence from the authorities.

1693 In UK, the *City Mercury* is the first giveaway newspaper.

• London bookseller John Dunton issues the first women's magazine, the *Ladies' Mercury.*

1695 Parliament does not renew the Licensing Act.

1701 First provincial newspaper in the UK, the *Norwich Post*, a weekly, with an approximate circulation of 400–500 copies.

1702 First daily newspaper in Britain, the *Daily Courant*, is published in London.

1704 John Campbell publishes *Boston Newsletter*, the first newspaper in the US not to be a one-issue failure.

1709 English Copyright Act, the first enactment

to secure the rights of authors and publishers by offering legal protection against 'pirating' of texts. A similar act was passed in France in 1793 and in the Grand Duchy of Saxe-Weimar in 1839 (the first to employ the 30-year term of protection after an author's death). The principle of international reciprocity of rights was established in the Berne Convention of 1886.

1712 In Britain, first 'Taxes on Knowledge' introduced – duties on newspapers and advertising and excise duty on paper.

1720s Benjamin Franklin begins successful publishing career with *Pennsylvania Gazette.*

1725 Stamp Act in Britain applies 1712 regulations to all newspapers, whatever their size or format.

1739 Scotsman William Ged devises method of preserving pages of type for future reprints, using a mould made from plaster of Paris from which metal plates were made. In fear of their livelihoods, Scottish printers wrecked the invention; 60 years later it was revived by Firmin Didot who reversed the process by creating the metal plate from sunken surfaces. Eventually stereotyping, as the process came to be known, was made a commercial proposition by amateur inventor Lord Stanhope, in 1805, at the Clarendon Press, Oxford.

• In 1829 the plaster and metal plates gave way to papier mâché, reducing time, weight and bulk – innovations happening at virtually the same time in Italy, France and England. Stanhope also improved the printing press by replacing the wooden press with an iron structure and by increasing the bed of the machine in order to produce one-pull larger-scale sheets.

1741 First magazines, in US, Andrew Bradford's *American Magazine*, followed by Benjamin Franklin's *General Magazine.*

1757 UK: increases in taxes on newspapers; increased again in 1776, 1780, 1789 (the year of the French Revolution), 1797 and 1815.

1764 London: prosecution of firebrand editor/journalist John Wilkes for seditious libel published in the *North Briton.*

1770s Thomas Paine in America. His *Common Sense* (1776), arguing powerfully for the separation of the States from English rule, will prove an immensely influential bestseller.

1771 Press permitted to report the proceedings of the House of Commons, followed by those of the House of Lords (in 1775).

• The *Morning Post* published in London.

1776 Publication of Adam Smith's *An Inquiry into the Nature and Causes of the Wealth of Nations.*

• Publication of Tom Paine's *Common Sense: Addressed to the Inhabitants of America*, a summons to the people of America to rise up in battle and overthrow British rule. As one English historian believed: 'It would be difficult to name any human composition which had an effect at once so instant, so extended, and so lasting.' 120,000 copies *of Common Sense* were sold within three months of publication.

1780 UK: first Sunday newspaper published – the *British Gazette and Sunday Monitor*.

1785 Founding of *The Times* newspaper followed by the *Observer* in 1791.
• Paris: fortnightly *Le Cabinet des Modes* is published, the first fashion magazine.

1787 First recorded advertising agency formed in London by William Tayler, who for a handling fee booked advertisements in the provincial press.

1788 UK: publication of first daily evening newspaper – *Star and Evening Advertiser*.

1789 Revolution in France: the Declaration of the Rights of Man and Citizens is promulgated 27 July; the key to this being the notion of popular sovereignty. The principles of the Revolution were to be an inspiration to radicalism in Britain and a guiding light of the Radical press.
• In turn events in France provoked the authorities in Britain to take repressive measures against the Radicals and the causes they advocated.

1790 Orator and conservative theorist Edmund Burke publishes *Reflections on the Revolution in France* condemning the uprising of the common people.

1791 Tom Paine's *The Rights of Man* Part 1 published, a stirringly eloquent riposte to Burke's *Reflections*.
• English philosopher Jeremy Bentham designs a 'panopticon', (the all-seeing one) for the central inspection of convicts; an idea given new life in the twentieth century in an age of electronic surveillance.
• First Amendment to the American Bill of Rights guarantees the freedom of the press.

1792 First Libel Act becomes law in Britain.
• Part 2 of Tom Paine's *Rights of Man* published. Also Mary Wollstonecraft's *Vindication of the Rights of Women*, demanding equal educational opportunities for women.

1793 John Bell, Yorkshire-born founder of the *Oracle or Bell's New World* becomes the first-ever foreign correspondent, reporting to his own paper the fighting between the British and French in the Low Countries. He chose to march with the French rather than with the forces of the Duke of York. He reported on the British victories at Le Cateau-Cambrésis, Villiers-en-Cauche and Troixelle as well as the defeat at Tournay.

His example was emulated by *The Times* in 1808 when Henry Crabb Robinson was commissioned to cover the Peninsular War.

1798 France, at the Essonne mill: Nicolas Robert introduces the first paper manufacturing machine; the first in England established at Frogmore, Hertfordshire, in 1805 by brothers Henry and Sealy Fourdriner, and at St Neots, Huntingdonshire, by John Gamble. Paper output increased tenfold.
• Prime Minister William Pitt increases the tax on British newspapers from 1½ pence to 2½ pence and bans the import into the UK of foreign newspapers.

1800 Bavarian Alois Senefelder takes out English patent for lithographic process, printing from the surface of a specially prepared stone. Photography is incorporated into the printed page, using lithography, from 1840.

1802 Founding of the *Weekly Political Register* by William Cobbett, one of the outstanding journalist/editors of the nineteenth century. Paper survives until 1835.

1805 Lord Stanhope's improved stereotyping machine set up at Oxford's Clarendon Press.

1811 Thomas Bensley makes first use in the UK of the Frederick Koenig steam-driven press to print in London 3000 sheets of the *Annual Register*.

1814 *The Times* installs the Koenig press, the most significant technological advance in printing since the age of Gutenberg. The steam-driven press made mass production of newspapers a reality and, in the company of other inventions in paper manufacture and stereotyping, ushered in the first age of mass communication. The initial run was 1100 sheets per hour. The first book to be printed on the power press in the UK was Johann Blumenbach's *Physiology*, in 1817.

1821 In Britain, the Six Acts passed, including two targeting the radical press.
• *Manchester Guardian* founded.

1822 Invention of the camera by Frenchman Joseph Nièpce who produced the first photograph (1826). Also in 1822, William Church's letter-founding machine makes for reductions in production costs. Hand-assembly could cast between 3,000 and 7,000 letters a day, Church's machine between 12,000 and 20,000.
• *Sunday Times* founded.

1826 Leipzig publisher F.A. Brockhaus applies Koenig's steam press to the printing of books.
• First permanently fixed photograph created by Nicéphore Nièpce. This was taken from an upper storey at Nièpce's home at Gras, Chalon-sur-Saône.

1829 Four-cylinder steam press, invented by

Augustus Applegarth and Edward Cowper for *The Times*, speeds the delivery of print, allowing 4,000 sheets per hour. The same inventors follow this up in 1848 with the rotary press, which printed 8,000 sheets per hour.

1830s UK: the 'War of the Unstamped' waged by the radical, unstamped press against the Taxes on Knowledge.

1831–5 Publication of Henry Hetherington's *Poor Man's Guardian*, one of the outstanding radical papers of the nineteenth century.

1832 W.E. Weber and K.F. Gauss construct the needle telegraph in Grottingen.

• The *Penny Magazine* of London becomes the first mass-circulation paper selling over 100,000 copies.

1833 Advertising Duty reduced, followed in 1836 with the reduction of Stamp Duty and Excise Duty on paper. It was not until 1853 that Advertising Duty was abolished. 1855 saw the abolition of Stamp Duty and 1861 Paper Duties.

• US: *New York Sun*, concentrating on stories of sex and violence, published by Benjamin Day. This was followed in 1835 by the *New York Herald*, published by John Gordon Bennett, with specific pages dedicated to sport and finance.

1835 Henry Fox-Talbot, British pioneer in the development of photography, publishes a description in the February edition of the *Literary Gazette* of the positive–negative process, which would enable the reproduction of photographs in any number.

• Fox-Talbot's work coincided with that of the Frenchman Louis Daguerre, who was the first to commercially exploit photography. The Daguerrotype used only the one-off positive, but it advanced exposure time from eight hours to only 15 to 30 minutes. The French government acquired the rights from Daguerre and Isidor Nièpce, heir of Nicéphore Nièpce (died 1833) who had gone into business with Daguerre. Thus the process became public property for all to use. Daguerre's own cameras were on sale before the end of the year.

1836 US: Samuel Morse builds his first telegraph.

1838 *The Times of India* founded.

• Publication of the radical *Northern Star* (until 1852).

1839 In Paris, Alphonse Giroux manufactures for sale the first Daguerrotype camera.

1842 *Illustrated London News* is founded.

• Samuel Morse lays first submarine telegraph cable, New York Harbour.

1843 Giuseppe Mazzini obtains patent for a composing machine, though the idea had originated as early as 1682 with Johann Joachim

Becher, a political economist.

• Though some 1500 patents had by 1900 been registered in the US for composing machines those invented by Robert Hattersley and Charles Kastenbein dominated. With each, the chief problem was the need to justify the lines by hand, a problem resolved by Linotype and Monotype machines, and the punch-cutting machine of Linn Boyd Benton of Milwaukee in 1885.

• A Saxon weaver, Friedrich Gottleb Keller, produces paper from wood pulp, another innovation suggested much earlier but not developed or taken up.

• The first public telegraph service is introduced following the completion of the Great Western Railway telegraph line from Paddington to Slough. William Cooke who had patented the system transferred the licence, for an annual fee, to Thomas Home and the first paid telegrams were sent by Cooke's double-needle electromagnetic telegraph along a 20-mile wire. Eventually the Electric Telegraph Company took up the licence and pioneered nationwide telegraphy. By 1847 two systems, north and south, were in operation, linking major towns and cities. Unification of the regions took place in November.

• Foundation of the *News of the World*, the *Economist* and, in Newcastle, the *Miners' Journal*.

1844 Transmission of the first press telegram, from a Congress reporter in Washington DC to the editor of the *Baltimore Patriot*, by Morse telegraph. In the UK the first press telegraph was sent in the same year, from Windsor Castle to *The Times* via the Slough-Paddington telegraph, announcing the birth of Prince Alfred to Queen Victoria.

• William Fox-Talbot's *The Pencil of Nature* is the first book in the UK to be published with photographs. This was issued by Longman in six parts.

• Society of Women Journalists founded in London.

1846 London: *Daily News* founded, with Charles Dickens (briefly) as editor.

1847–8 Karl Marx and Frederick Engels produce *The Communist Manifesto*. Having settled in the UK Marx produced his monumental work, *Das Kapital* (*Capital*) in 1859.

• Paris: the photographic journal *Le Daguerrotype* published.

1848 In Havana, Cuba, Italian Antonio Meucci creates instrument with which he communicates between apartment floors with his invalid wife. However, it is 1860 before there is a public demonstration of the telephone, by Johann Philipp Reis of Germany, using a violin-case for a resonator, a hollowed-out beer-barrel bung for a mouthpiece and a stretched sausage skin for a diaphragm. In 1861 Reis demonstrated an improved version to the Frankfurt Physical Society, transmitting verses and songs – albeit with very poor clarity – over a 300-foot line.

• The editor of the UK *Morning Chronicle* employs Eliza Lyn Linton to write features and reviews. She later became the paper's Paris correspondent. On her return to the UK she became Fleet Street's first-ever full-time woman journalist. She became known for her antipathy to women's suffrage.

1850 UK: Public Libraries Act.

• Philadelphia: Frederick Langenheim patents first photographic slides.

1852 J.W. Brett lays first submarine telegraph cable between Dover and Calais.

• UK: House of Commons Press Gallery opens.

• Surgeon John MacCosh is first British war photographer; 47 studies survive of his photo-coverage of the Second Burma War.

1853 Liverpool: the *Northern Daily Times* becomes England's first daily provincial paper.

1854 Paris: *Le Figaro* founded.

1855 Englishman Alexander Parkes invents celluloid.

• Foundation of the *Daily Telegraph*.

• In UK, newspaper tax abolished.

1858 First transatlantic telegram sent by John Cash, American name-tape manufacturer, from London to his New York representative. At £1 a word, it read: 'Go to Chicago.'

1860 Antonio Meucci demonstrates, in New York, his 'telefono' but has insufficient funds to patent his invention. Only in 2002 was he acknowledged, by the US House of Representatives, as the true originator of the telephone (rather than Alexander Graham Bell who had access to Meucci's materials and had shared a laboratory with him). However, it was Bell who patented a version of Meucci's device in 1876.

1865 Father Giovanni Caselli developed the first fax machine between 1857 and 1864. It was introduced for public service over the Paris-Lyons telegraph line in May 1865. However, the first office fax did not become commercially available until the Xerox LDX was demonstrated in the company's showroom in New York, May 1964. The Japanese firm Sharp introduced the first colour fax in 1984.

1866 Mahloon Loomis of Washington DC, having described a system of radio signalling in a paper of July 1866, succeeds in October in broadcasting messages over a 14-mile distance. He was granted the world's first wireless patent in 1872. Lack of funds in a period of recession prevented Loomis

developing radio commercially before his death in 1886. In the UK David Edward Hughes proved a significant pioneer into the phenomenon of radio waves, but he met with little encouragement. It was left to Heinrich Hertz, the German electrical scientist, to convince the scientific community of the existence and significance of radio waves, thus making possible the development of radio telegraphy and broadcasting.

1867 Invention of the typewriter by American Christopher Sholes.

1868 London, Press Association founded.

• New York: *Staats Zeitung* first newspaper to be printed on wood-pulp paper.

1870 UK: Education Act inaugurates systematic primary school education for all.

1870–1 Jessie White Mario becomes world's first woman war correspondent, covering the Franco-Prussian War for several US and British papers.

1872 Issue of first illustrated daily newspaper, the *New York Daily Graphic*.

1873 The *New York Daily Graphic* is first to publish a half-tone photograph, 2 December – an illustration of the city's Steinway Hall appeared on the back page.

1874 American writer Mark Twain becomes the first author to possess a typewriter – made by Remington. By 1890 in the US there were 30 manufacturers producing typewriters. In the UK none were on sale until 1889, from the Maskelyne British Typewriter & Manufacturing Company.

• In the same year George C. Blickensderfer's Connecticut company produced the first portable, the Blick. The introduction of the typewriter into business created new employment opportunities for women.

1876 Scotsman Alexander Graham Bell successfully initiates telephonic communication. Bell, of Edinburgh, patented the telephone on 9 March, and on 10 March, in Boston, US, the first truly coherent transmission took place – a message from Bell to his assistant, Thomas Watson: 'Come here, Watson, I want you.' The speaking telephone was demonstrated by Bell at the Centennial Exhibition, Philadelphia, 25 June. In July of the following year the first telephone line between two separate buildings was laid, in London, between the Queen's Theatre and Canterbury Hall. In the same year the first telephone exchange was created on behalf of the New England Telephone Company by Isaac D. Smith.

1877 Thomas Alva Edison of America patents the Phonograph, the first sound-recording system. The prototype being completed by Edison's mechanic, John Kruesi at West Orange, New

Jersey, on 6 December, Edison proceeded to make history by reciting into the recording apparatus, 'Mary had a little lamb'. The Edison Speaking Phonograph Company began production in April 1879. The tin-foil cylinder provided so short a duration that public interest in the Phonograph declined.

• The wax-cylinder Graphaphone developed by Chichester Bell and Charles Sumner Tainter was patented in 1886, to be countered by Edison, his interest in recording renewed, with the Improved Phonograph. Edison Laboratories were the first to record music by an accredited musician, the boy pianist Josef Hofman, in 1888. There was no means of duplicating wax discs before 1892.

1878 The microphone, demonstrated in London by Professor David Edward Hughes.

1880 The Radiophone, devised by Charles Sumner Tainter and Alexander Graham Bell, successfully transmits speech between the top of Franklin School, Washington DC, and Bell's laboratory on 14th Street.

• Telephony without wires had been the invention of A.C. Brown of the Eastern Telegraph Company two years earlier. Reginald Fessenden produced the first conventional system of radio telephony capable of transmitting speech across distances regardless of obstacles between transmitter and receiver. He demonstrated his system for the first time, over a distance of a mile, 23 December 1900. His words were addressed to his assistant, 'Is it snowing where you are, Mr Thiessen?'

• In UK *Titbits* founded, followed in 1888 by *Answers* – two immensely popular weeklies.

1883 In US, Joseph Pulitzer starts up the *New York World*.

1884 Lewis Waterman in the US creates the first fountain pen.

1885 Louis Aimé Augustin Le Prince, French-born but living in the US, projects the first moving pictures – on to a wall at the Institute for the Deaf, New York, applying in November 1996 for an American patent for an 'Apparatus for producing Animated Pictures'. This was granted in January 1888 but reference to cameras and projectors was disallowed because of Dumont's British patent of 1861 (though this involved an arrangement of glass plates to form the facets of a prismatic drum and had nothing to do with the reproduction of moving images on a screen).

• On the point of going into commercial production in 1890, Le Prince boarded a train in Dijon, bound for Paris where it was his intention to demonstrate his invention to the secretary of the Paris Opera. He – and his apparatus – disappeared; a mystery that remains unsolved.

1886 *New York Herald Tribune* installs the first Linotype machine, the invention of Ottmar Margenthaler.

• Paris: *Le Petit Journal* becomes first paper to reach 1 million circulation.

1887 German Emile Berliner working in the US applies for a patent for the first gramophone or disc-recorder player. He demonstrated his invention at the Franklin Institute in Philadelphia in the following year. The hand-cranked gramophone was initially produced as a toy by Kammerer & Rheinhardt, Germany, using a five-inch vulcanized rubber disc at an approximate speed of 70rpm. Electrically operated machines were marketed by the United States Gramophone Company in Washington in 1894, using seven-inch records.

• First overseas edition of a newspaper – *New York Herald* in Paris.

• The Berliner Gramophone Company of Philadelphia produced the first shellac records in 1897. This company was also the first to create a recording studio and record shop. Double-sided discs were first manufactured in 1904 by the International Talking Machine Company, Germany, under the imprint Odeon Records.

• San Francisco: William Randoph Hearst takes command of his father's paper, the *Examiner*, initiating a career as press baron to out-rival and out-live all his contemporaries. In 1895 he bought the *New York Journal*, which became the star and exemplar of Yellow Journalism.

• Also in 1887, monotype printing invented in the US by Tolbert Lanston. Commercially established by 1897, the Monotype had the advantage over Linotype in that it cast each letter separately instead of in a compact line, thus making it easier to correct the text.

1888 George Eastman of Rochester, New York, produced the first snapshot camera – the Kodak – for use by the general public. This used pre-loaded paper-roll film. It took 100 circular pictures 2.5 inches in diameter. Mass produced by the Eastman Company, Kodak No. 1 proved an immediate success in the US and worldwide.

• In the same year John Carbutt of Philadelphia introduced celluoid film. This was made from celluloid sheets one-hundredth of an inch thick, and obtained from the Celluloid Manufacturing Company. However, the first celluloid roll film to be manufactured commercially was another Eastman coup. The Eastman Dry Plate Company produced roll film for its Kodak cameras, beginning in August 1889. The first colour roll film came much later, and was invented by Robert

Krayn in Germany in 1910. Amateurs had a longer wait – until Kodrachrome produced three-colour roll film in 1936.

• UK: *Financial Times* founded.

1889 UK's first Official Secrets Act.

• Kansas City undertaker Almon B. Stowger patents the first automatic telephone exchange. The first exchange was opened at La Porte, Indiana, in November 1892. Dial telephones were introduced in 1896.

1890 Alfred Harmsworth, later Lord Northcliffe, publishes the first comic, the eight-page *Comic Cuts*, edited by Houghton Townley. Nearly 120,000 copies of the first edition were sold and this rose to 300,000 within a month. In October 1890 a rival to *Comic Cuts*, *Funny Cuts* appeared with the first-ever front-page strip cartoon.

• Telephoto lens invented by New Zealand geologist Alexander McKay.

• London evening *Star* prints the first front-page newspaper headline, 16 July. This read: 'Many Happy Returns of the Day – Wedding of Professor Stuart MP'.

1891 Peep-show projector, the Kinetoscope, developed by William Dickson at the instigation of his employer, Thomas Alva Edison, has first public showing in Edison's workshops in West Orange, New Jersey, to 147 representatives of the National Federation of Women's Clubs.

• The first commercial showing took place at Holland Bros' Kinetoscope Parlor, Broadway, in April 1894. The films were produced by the Edison Co., which was thus the first-ever film production company. In the same year Greek showman George Trajedis installed six kinetoscopes in a converted Old Bond Street store in London, October, charging 2 pence per film.

1893 UK: first issue of the *Sketch*.

1894 The first commercially viable radio communication was the work of the Italian Guglielmo Marconi of Bologna. Experiments conducted in 1894 and 1895 led Marconi to offer his invention to the Italian Ministry of Posts and Telegraphs. Failing to elicit interest, the inventor moved to England where customs officials broke open his equipment, suspecting him of being an anarchist. Undaunted, Marconi settled in London and in 1896 applied for a patent for a method by which 'electrical actions or manifestations are transmitted through air, earth or water by means of electrical oscillations of high frequency'.

• The first public demonstration of Marconi's wireless took place on 12 December 1896. In the following year the Marconi Wireless Telegraph & Signal Company was formed.

1895 Brothers Auguste and Louis Lumière project the first-ever film on to a screen – *Workers Leaving the Lumière Factory*, 22 March, to members of the Société d'Encouragement a L'Industrie Nationale, at 44 rue de Rennes, Paris. On 28 December the Lumières entertained a paying audience at the Grand Café on the Boulevard des Capuchines: cinema was born.

• William Randolph Hearst buys up the *New York Journal* having built up the *San Francisco Examiner*, given to him by his father, with sensational stories of gangsters and Hollywood sex scandals.

1896 First permanent cinema, the 400-seater Vitascope Hall, opened in New Orleans, 26 June, by William T. Rock. Admission was 10 cents, plus another 10 to view the Edison Vitascope projector. The 5,000-seater Gaumont-Palace, formerly the Hippodrome Theatre, opened in Paris in 1910. The largest cinema ever built was the Roxy Theater in New York, with 6,200 seats. In Berlin 300 cinemas were opened during 1908. In the UK by 1912 there were 4,000 cinemas.

• J.H. Rigg of Leeds manufactures the first motorized cinema projector. An electrically powered model was demonstrated at the Royal Aquarium, London, 6 April.

• UK *Daily Mail* founded by Alfred Harmsworth, later Lord Northcliffe.

1897 First wide-screen film on 70mm stock introduced by Enoch J. Rector of the Veriscope Co., New York.

1898 The Telegraphone, the first magnetic recorder, is patented by Danish engineer Valdemar Poulsen employed by the Copenhagen Telephone Company. Demonstrated in public for the first time at the Paris Exposition of 1900, the Telegraphone used magnetized piano wire running between spools at 7 feet per second.

• Commercial production began in America in 1903. An improved model was used by Lee de Forest for experiments in talking film. The use of metal tape instead of wire came in 1929 with the Blattnerphone, again used in film production, at Elstree Studios.

• The use of plastic tape originated in Berlin with the Magnetophon produced by the firm AEG. This proved the archetype for all recorder developments from that time.

1900 Film: sound on disc demonstrated to a paying audience at the Paris Exposition. The first sound-on-film process was patented by French-born Eugene Lauste of Brixton in 1906. His first successful experiment in recording and reproducing speech on film came in 1910. He was ready to exploit his system commercially, only to be interrupted by the outbreak of war in 1914. He crossed the Atlantic with his idea but met with the same lack of interest as America itself entered the war.

1901 Marconi transmits messages by wireless telegraph from Cornwall to Newfoundland.

1902 Canadian-born Reginald Fessenden of the US introduces the first radio-telephone; makes the first transmission of speech by wireless.

• UK: Arthur Pearson founds the *Daily Express*.

• Alfred Harmsworth founds the *Daily Mirror*.

1906 Fessenden makes the first radio broadcast, using the 420-foot-high radio mast of the National Electric Signalling Company's radio station at Brant Rock, Massachusetts. On 24 December the programme began with Fessenden playing Gounod's 'O, Holy Night' on the violin, followed by him singing and reciting from St Luke's Gospel. The first gramophone record to be broadcast came next, a recording of Handel's 'Largo'. The transmission ended with Fessenden wishing his listeners a happy Christmas. The audience for the broadcast turned out to be ships' operators within a five-mile radius. Fessenden's second broadcast, on New Year's Eve, in better atmospheric conditions, was received as far away as the West Indies.

• In the UK the first radio broadcast came in the following year – from the radio room of HMS *Andromeda*. It was initiated by Lieutenant Quentin Crauford RN and transmitted to other ships at Chatham. News of the broadcast was not made known, for the Admiralty saw the possibilities of radio in military use, in particular as aiding communication between submarines and shore and other vessels.

1907 First regular experimental broadcasts conducted by Lee De Forest's Radio Telephone Company from the Parker Building, New York. Two years later De Forest introduced his mother-in-law Harriet Stanton Black to listeners. She gave the world's first broadcast talk; her theme was women's suffrage.

• Lord Northcliffe purchases *The Times*.

• In UK foundation of National Union of Journalists (NUJ).

• First patent, in London, Berlin and St Petersburg of all-electric television cathode-ray tube receiver, by Russian Boris Rozing. On 9 May 1911 Rozing succeeded in transmitting by wireless over distance 'a distinct image ... consisting of four luminous bands'.

1909 In US, National Board of Censorship of Motion Pictures established.

1911 UK Copyright Act requires copies of all British publications to be supplied to the British Museum and to five other copyright libraries.

• First Hollywood studio, the Nestor Studio, opened on Sunset Boulevard by David Horsley.

1912 Foundation, initially as the *Herald*, of the *Daily Herald*.

1913 The British Board of Film Censors, formed in 1912 by the Kinematograph Manufacturers' Association, begins operation.

1914 Price of *The Times* reduced to one penny.

• First full-length feature film in colour, *The World, the Flesh and the Devil*, shown to the trade in February, and opened at the Holborn Empire in April. Kinemacolor was a two-colour system. Gaumont Chronochrome (1914) produced three colours, but three-colour processing was costly and slow in development.

• Technicolor successfully produced, in 1932, the Disney cartoon *Flowers and Trees*; while the first feature-length film in Technicolor was Rouben Mamoulian's *Becky Sharp*, released in 1935.

1914–18 First World War.

1915 UK: *Daily Express* bought by Max Aitken, Lord Beaverbrook, for £17,500.

1916 Film, *The Battle of the Somme* – first-ever war documentary.

• Clydeside workers are supported in their refusal to make munitions by the Labour paper *Forward*. It is suppressed.

1918 UK: first Film Society, the Stoll Picture Theatre Club, opens with a presentation by Baroness Orczy of *The Laughing Cavalier*.

1919 UK: Arthur Mee founds the *Children's Newspaper*.

1920 The Marconi Company begins radio transmission from its Chelmsford works on 19 January. On 15 June Dame Nellie Melba gives a 30-minute recital, from Chelmsford, sponsored by Lord Northcliffe. Her fee was £1,000. In November transmissions from Chelmsford were suspended on the grounds that they interfered with radio communication to aircraft and ships. Broadcasts resumed from Marconi's Station 2MT at Writtle, February 1922. 2MT was the first regular broadcasting station in the UK.

1922 Marconi's new station 2LO broadcasts from Marconi House in the Strand, London. Along with three other radio stations, 2LO was merged into what was to become the British Broadcasting Company Ltd., created in December 1922, licensed to broadcast from January 1923.

1923 First programme of sound-on-film production at Berlin's Alhambra cinema using the Tri-Ergon process developed by Joseph Engl, Joseph Massolle and Hans Voght. In the US Lee De Forest's Phonofilm process is demonstrated to the first paying audience, at the Rialto Theater in New York.

1924 UK: Sykes Committee Report on Broadcasting, followed in 1925 with the setting up of the Crawford Committee from which emerged the prime principles governing public service broadcasting in the UK until the coming of commercial TV – monopoly, funding by licence, administration by an independent public corporation. These remain the guiding principles of public service broadcasting.

• Publication in the *Daily Mail* of the notorious Zinoviev Letter, a fake, now considered to have emanated from the UK's own secret service, MI6.

• Felix the Cat becomes the first film character to be merchandized. Licences issued on behalf of Felix's creator Pat Sullivan for Felix to 'feature' on packaging and later as a soft toy.

1925 Using a mechanical scanner for transmitting and receiving, Scotsman John Logie Baird (with others) creates the first television pictures on 30 October. Baird transmitted an image with gradations of light and shade using a primitive amalgam of parts, including an empty biscuit-box for the lamphouse. For test purposes a dummy's head was used, to be replaced shortly afterwards by 15-year-old office boy William Taynton, who consented to be the first star of TV for the fee of half a crown.

• Baird demonstrated his invention to the press on 7 January 1926, and gave a public demonstration on 27 January for members of the Royal Institution. Baird's mechanical system was soon to be overtaken by electronic TV transmission, first developed in Los Angeles by Philo T. Farnsworth in July 1929, though a more practical system developed by Russian-born Vladimir Zworykin of Westinghouse showed the way ahead. All modern TV systems derive from Zworykin's Kinescope and the Ionoscope, the camera tube he developed in 1933.

• Lionel Guest and H.O. Merriman of London apply their electrical recording process to record the burial service of the Unknown Warrior at Westminster Abbey, proving that it was possible to substitute a microphone for the studio horn, thus location recording was born. The process was not pursued commercially, but location recording was set in progress in both the US and the UK in the same year. The all-electric record player, with loudspeaker amplification instead of the usual horn, was the Brunswick Panatrope, made by the Brunswick Company of Iowa. This year also saw the introduction of the automatic record-changer, built by 20-year-old Eric Waterworth of Hobart, Tasmania.

• First issue of the *New Yorker*.

• BBC broadcast first full-length play for radio,

Reginald Berkeley's *The White Chateau*, 11 November.

1927 Royal Charter establishes the non-commercial British Broadcasting Corporation, licensed to broadcast from 1 January. The BBC grew to be the largest public service broadcasting organization in the world.

• *The Jazz Singer*, using the Vitaphone synchronized disc system, opens at the Warner Theater on Broadway, 6 October. Directed by Alan Crosland and starring Al Jolson, the film is generally acknowledged to have inaugurated the age of sound cinema and marked the death knell of silent movies. There are only two talking sequences in the film and 281 words spoken, but the reception the film received on both sides of the Atlantic was phenomenal.

• *The Lights of New York*, also from Warner Bros, was the first all-talking feature film. It was premiered at New York's Strand Theater, 6 July 1928. Fox Movietone's *In Old Arizona*, a Western directed by Raoul Walsh, screened in December 1928 in Los Angeles, was the first all-talking sound-on-film feature. The first all-talking colour film was Warner Bros' *On With the Show*, screened at New York's Wintergardens, 1929.

1928 On 9 February John Logie Baird makes the first international TV transmission, sending 30-line images of his own face from London by land-line to the transmitting station G2KZ at Coulsdon, Surrey, and then across the Atlantic to a receiving set manned by his assistant, Ben Clapp, at Hartsdale, New York State. On 3 July Baird became the first to transmit television in colour. Employing a Nikow scanning-disc with red, blue and green filters he screened red and blue scarves, a lighted cigarette and red roses. Baird was to be the first to demonstrate high-definition colour – at the Dominion Theatre, London, on 4 February 1938.

• Walt Disney release *Steam Boat Willie*, the first animated film using synchronous sound.

1929 Radar invented, by Scotsman Robert Watson-Watt.

• UK: first issue of the Communist *Daily Worker*.

1931 Experiments in electronic high-definition TV transmission are carried out by an EMI research team at Hayes, Middlesex, under the direction of Russian-born Isaac Shoenberg. The EMI system was demonstrated to the BBC in the following year – a film of the Changing of the Guard at Buckingham Palace, viewed on a 130-line cathode ray receiver with a five-inch square screen.

• RCA Victor launches the 33⅓rpm long-playing record. The first recording was of Beethoven's

Fifth Symphony. However, the radiograms required to play the long-player were expensive in a time of acute recession and the venture was not a success. The LP did not come into its own until 1948 when Columbia issued microgroove records developed by Peter Goldmark – vinylite discs with a playing time of 23 minutes per side, and 224–300 grooves to the inch.

1932 Stereophonic cinema sound patented by French film-makers Abel Gance and André Debrie. Gance's eight-hour silent 1927 epic *Napoléon Bonaparte* was re-edited with added dialogue and sound-effects, and screened at the Paramount Cinema, Paris, in 1935. Warner Bros' *House of Wax* (1953) was the first feature film with complete stereo sound.

• The first stereophonic disc recordings are made by Arthur Keller of the Bell Telephone Laboratories. Made on wax masters at 78rpm, they were not produced commercially but were demonstrated at the Chicago World's Fair, 1933. The first stereo discs to be manufactured for sale were produced by Emory Cork of Stamford, US, in 1957.

1933 Chief of the German Navy's Signals Research Department, Dr Rudoph Kühnold produces the first working radar system. Radar in the UK was the brainchild of Robert Watson-Watt, superintendent of the radio research laboratory at Ditton Park. Experiments with radar in February 1935 led to the establishment of a number of air-defence radar stations which were to prove critical in the Second World War (1939–45).

1934 The Emitron electronic camera is an advance on the system developed by Shoenberg in 1931. In the following year Shoenberg inaugurated the 405-line system and on 1 November 1936 the EMI–Marconi system became standard as the BBC television service began operation from Alexander Palace.

1935 Berlin: first television mobile unit comes into operation, employed at the opening of the Berlin TV station of the Reichs Rundfunk, 22 March. The first mobile units in the UK, designed by T.C. Macnamara, were used in the BBC's first major outside broadcast, of the Coronation, May 1937.

1936 First full-length animated film, *Snow White and the Seven Dwarfs* from the Disney Studios.

1938 Russian hypnotist, sculptor and journalist Lazlo Biró constructed a prototype ball-point pen with quick-drying ink. Having acquired British rights, Biró began manufacture in a disused RAF hangar in 1944. In 1953 Baron Bic, in France, introduced the first 'throwaway' ball-point. In the UK priced at 1 shilling, sales during 1959 totalled 53 million.

1939–45 Second World War.

1939 US: William C. Huebner introduces photo-setting of type.

• Premiere of *Gone with the Wind*.

1940 UK: statutory newsprint rationing introduced; ended 1956.

1941 Release of Orson Welles' film masterpiece *Citizen Kane*, based on the life and lifestyle of American media baron William Randoph Hearst.

• USSR: Tamara Lobova becomes first woman to shoot a feature film, *Suvarov*, released in January.

• John Logie Baird demonstrates 3D television in colour, a 500-line system, 18 December, at Sydenham.

• The Communist *Daily Worker* is suppressed in the UK.

1944 Automatic digital computer, by American Howard Aiken, is followed in the next year by the electronic computer invented in the US by J. Presper Eckert and John W. Mauchly.

1945 BBC launches the Light Programme, now Radio 2; and the following year, the Third Programme, now Radio 3.

1946 The Southwestern Bell Telephone Company of St Louis, US, offers the first commercial car phone service.

1947 Polaroid camera introduced by Edwin Land, US.

• Soviet Union: first 3D colour feature film, *Robinson Crusoe*, directed by A.N. Andreyevsky. Special spectacles were not required.

• US: Private Commission on Freedom of the Press, founded by publisher Henry Luce and chaired by the chancellor of the University of Chicago, Robert Hutchens, to 'examine areas and circumstances under which the press of the United States is succeeding or failing; to discover where freedom of expression is or is not limited, whether by government censorship, pressure from readers or advertisers or the unwisdom of its proprietors or the timidity of its management'. The Commission report broached, formally for the first time, the concept of *social responsibility* and listed criteria for its fulfilment.

1947–9 First UK Royal Commission on the Press – the Ross Commission.

1948 The Universal Declaration of Human Rights is adopted by the United Nations Assembly in Paris, 10 December.

• NBC of America screens first TV Western series, *Hopalong Cassidy*, starring Bill Boyd.

1948 Bell Telephone Company scientists John Bardeen, Walter Brattain and William Shockley introduce the first transistor.

1949 Xerography invented by Chester Carlson,

US, the same year as Peter Goldmark of the US introduces the first long-playing record.

• CBS launches first TV thriller series, *Suspense*.

1950 Yoshiro Nakamats of the Imperial University, Tokyo, develops the floppy disc.

1952 First video recorder demonstration conducted in the US by John Mullin and Wayne Johnson at the Bing Crosby Enterprise laboratories in Beverly Hills, California, 11 November. A colour video was demonstrated by the same company in September of the following year. Neither was developed commercially. Ampex was the first to go into production, its initial production model being acquired by CBS.

• In the UK the BBC's VERA came into operation in April 1958 with a recording of *Panorama*. Sony brought out a transistorized video recorder in 1961, while the first domestic video recorder, also from Sony, was launched in the US in July 1965. It was not until 1972 that Sony launched, in Japan, its first video cassette recorder.

• In Europe Philips introduced the first domestic video cassette recorder in 1974. The VHS format was introduced in 1976 by JVC of Japan; and in the same year JVC produced the first camcorders for amateur use.

1953 Inauguration of the British Press Council.

• BBC demonstrates colour TV. An outside broadcast of the Coronation procession was relayed by closed circuit at Great Ormond Street Hospital for Sick Children.

• The first movie in Cinemascope, 20th Century Fox's *The Robe*, is premiered at Grauman's Chinese Theater, Hollywood, and in the same month, September, *This is Cinerama* opened in New York.

1954 In the UK in July, the Television Bill is given royal assent, creating the Independent Television Authority. Commercial TV began broadcasting in Britain in September 1955.

• Eurovision is inaugurated on 6 June when TV services in eight European countries linked together with a 4,000-mile chain of relays. The first programme to be screened was the Festival of Flowers from Montreux, Switzerland.

1955–6 First daily TV soap broadcast in Britain – *Sixpenny Corner*, running for 15 minutes daily. It failed even though it was transferred by ITV to an evening slot.

1959 The *Manchester Guardian* becomes the *Guardian*.

1960 Bell Telephone's Touch-Tone telephone is successfully tested and becomes commercially available in 1963.

• ITVs *Coronation Street* opens its record-breaking run.

• The American Telephone & Telegraph Company makes the first transatlantic satellite transmission on 11 July, from Andover, Maine, to Goonhilly Downs, Cornwall, via Telstar.

• America launches first communications satellite, Echo 1.

• UK: death of the *News Chronicle*; first issue of the *Sunday Telegraph*.

1962 UK: Pilkington Committee Report on Broadcasting and the Shawcross Commission Report on the Press.

• First nights on UK TV for *Z Cars*, *Steptoe and Son* and the satirical series *That Was The Week That Was*. In the following year, *Dr Who* and *World in Action*.

1963 Founding of International Publishing Corporation (IPC); following year, IPC launches the *Sun*, replacing the *Daily Herald*.

• UK: BBC ends its ban on the mention of religion, politics, royalty or sex in comedy programmes.

• University of Michigan scientists Emmett Leith and Juris Upatnicks develop the first hologram.

1964 BBC launches new channel, BBC2, in April.

• UK starters: *Match of the Day* and *Crossroads*.

• *Radio Caroline*, the first British pirate radio station goes on air.

1965 Via the Early Bird satellite on 2 May 300 million viewers in nine countries sample the first transatlantic programme relay; 15 days later America's NBC was first with a colour transatlantic satellite programme transmission.

• Influential drama-documentary, *Cathy Come Home*, about Britain's homeless is broadcast by the BBC.

• Smoking advertisements are banned from UK television.

1966 Lord Thomson buys *The Times*.

• China: Chairman Mao launches the Cultural Revolution against 'reactionary bourgeois ideas in the sphere of academic work, education, art and theatre and publishing'.

1967 First colour TV broadcast in the UK, BBC2, 1 July.

• Marine Broadcasting Offences Act UK is passed and outlaws pirate radio stations.

• BBC Radio 1 is launched, 30 September.

• The Postmaster-General, Edward Short MP, opens BBC Radio Leicester, the first local radio station in the UK.

1968 In UK first broadcast of comedy series *Dad's Army*.

1969 First commercially produced microprocessor developed by Edward Hoff of the Intel Corporation of California.

• Australian Rupert Murdoch buys the *Sun* and

the *News of the World*.

• Denmark: film censorship is abolished.

• UK: York University launches first university radio station.

1972 US: first pre-recorded video tapes offered for hire by Sears, Roebuck. Pre-recorded tapes were not available in the UK until 1979, supplied initially by Intervision who acquired 200 film titles from United Artists for £250,000. By the end of the year they had franchised some 150 outlets. Such was the immediate competition that Intervision soon went under despite the increase in the sales of VCRs and rental outlets.

• The UK *Sunday Times* is banned on 17 November from publishing a series of articles on Thalidomide, a drug taken by expectant mothers and causing horrific deformities in babies.

• Cable TV transmission starts in UK.

1973 London Broadcasting (LBC) is the first commercial radio station in mainland UK, on air 8 October.

1974 UK: BBC inaugurates Ceefax, the UK's first teletext service.

1975 Angela Rippon becomes first regular female newsreader on British terrestrial television (BBC). ITN's News at Ten waited until 1978 before employing Anna Ford to front the news.

1977 UK: Annan Commission Report on Broadcasting and the McGregor Commission Report on the Press.

1978 UK: first series of the comprehensive school-set series *Grange Hill*.

• First video cassette recorder introduced in the UK.

• Japan: the Sony Walkman is launched.

• 1979 UK: Williams Committee Report on Obscenity and Film Censorship.

• First digital recording, by Decca, of a New Year's Day concert in Vienna; recorded live by the Vienna Philharmonic Orchestra and issued in April.

1980 The compact disc (CD), developed by Philips over several years, is demonstrated at the Salzburg Festival in April. By agreement with Philips, the Japanese firm Sony launched the first CD in 1982. With a playing time of 75 minutes, the CD used a grooveless miniature 12cm disc using a laser beam to read digitally encoded information.

• MacBride Commission Report for UNESCO.

• UK: ITV documentary *Death of a Princess* causes offence to the government of Saudi Arabia; millions of pounds in trade orders are lost as a result. The British government apologizes to the Saudis, 22 April.

1981 UK: Australian media baron Rupert

Murdoch acquires the British newspapers, *The Times* and *Sunday Times*, having been exempted from a monopolies enquiry by the Conservative government, led by Margaret Thatcher.

• The microprocessor makes possible the introduction by the IBM company of the first personal computer.

1982 UK: Hunt Committee on Cable Expansion and Broadcasting Policy.

• UK: Channel 4 television begins transmission.

1983 Breakfast TV starts on the BBC; the CD player, the pocket TV and the first cordless telephone are introduced to the UK.

1984 UK: first satellite TV channel – Rupert Murdoch's Sky – begins transmission, 16 January.

• Civil servant Clive Ponting is acquitted by a jury of breaking the Official Secrets Act. His relevation to the press of details concerning the British sinking of the Argentine battleship *The Belgrano* were justified in court as being in the public interest. Later the Act was redrafted to exclude public interest as a defence.

• Robert Maxwell takes over the *Daily Mirror* group.

• Apple launch the Macintosh personal computer.

1985 Rupert Murdoch buys American film company 20th Century Fox.

• Panasonic of Japan introduces to the UK the first VHS camcorder in January, and in May Sony launches the digital video-recorder.

• British Board of Film Censors issues age classification for videos, following the passing of the Video Recordings Act (1984).

1986 Eddy Shah's *Today* newspaper, published in the UK, is the first to use on-the-run colour. Launched on 4 March the 44-page paper carried 16 pages in colour.

• Australian TV soap *Neighbours* is introduced to UK on BBC.

• USSR: Michail Gorbachev announces new policy of Glasnost, 'openness'.

• Wapping, London: thousands of print workers picket Murdoch's new premises, protesting about computerization and the loss of jobs.

• Czechoslovakia: the Jazz Union is closed down for urging the freedom of the arts.

1987 Sydney, Australia, September: British government is rebuffed in its courtroom appeal against the decision to permit the publication of *Spycatcher*.

1988 The first transatlantic optical fibre cable is laid, costing £220 million, between the US and UK/France, able to carry simultaneously 40,000 telephone calls.

1989 The Iron Curtain that divided eastern European nations – Poland, Hungary, Czechoslovakia and East Germany etc. – from the West, is drawn aside. The trades union Solidarity is permitted to contest elections in Poland; in Hungary border troops tear down the barbed-wire frontier with Austria. Most significantly, the Berlin Wall is dismantled. However, in June, freedom protests in Beijing are crushed in Tiananmen Square. The rest of the world watches events on TV.

• In Iran, the Ayatollah Khomeini condemns as blasphemous the novel *The Satanic Verses* by British writer Salman Rushdie and issues a fatwa, or edict, calling on all Muslims to strike down the offender. Despite worldwide protests, the death sentence remained active until September 1998 when the government of Iran distanced itself from, without rescinding, the Khomeini edict.

• Tim Berners-Lee, British inventor of the World Wide Web, first scrawls the following on a blackboard: w.w.w.

1990 UK: Broadcasting Act separates control of commercial television (ITC, Independent Television Commission) and radio (the Radio Authority).

• The *Northern Echo* edited in Darlington becomes the first UK newspaper on CD-ROM.

• The first tapeless answering machine, the ADAM (All-Digital Answering Machine), storing messages on a silicon chip, launched in the US by PhoneMate.

• Iraq: Farzad Barzoft, journalist on the UK *Observer*, is executed in Baghdad after 'confessing' to spying.

• UK: Calcutt Committee reports on its deliberations concerning 'a wide public aversion to newspaper intrusion', and recommends 'reform by self-regulation' and a Code of Practice. The Press Complaints Commission emerged from Calcutt recommendations.

1991 Robert Maxwell, British media tycoon, dies in a drowning accident.

1992 Los Angeles: street riots after screening of police beating up a black motorist, Rodney King.

• UK: first land-based national commercial radio station – Classic FM – launched 7 September.

• Canada: government Bill C-128 bans the depiction of under-18s engaging in any form of 'explicit sexual activity', including kissing.

1993 UK: carried via London Interconnect cable network, the first black TV service – Identity TV – begins, 13 July, with estimated audience of 150,000, and on 1 September BSkyB launches first women's TV channel.

• Transmitting from coaches driving round London, the BBC begins first experiments in DAB (Digital Audio Broadcasting).

1994 BBC converts generalist service, Radio 5, which featured programmes for young listeners, to Radio 5 Live dedicated to sports, news and chat.

1998 UK: Sky TV launches digital television service, 1 October.

1999 A jury in Oregon, US, fines anti-abortionist campaigners for publishing on their Internet website a 'wanted' list of abortion doctors, their clinics and addresses, seeing it as a thinly veiled death threat.

• During the war for Kosovo, NATO bombers target TV stations in Serbia's capital, Belgrade.

• UK: Greg Dyke is appointed new director-general of the BBC in succession to Sir John Birt.

2000 UK: Regulation of Investigatory Powers Act (RIPA), extending official surveillance to Internet communication.

• US: merger of the world's biggest media giant, Time Warner, with AOL (America On Line).

• Launch of Women's Enews, Internet news service.

• Ukraine: campaigning journalist Georgi Gongadze abducted, murdered and beheaded, allegedly with the connivance of government authorities.

• Google becomes the world's biggest search engine.

2001 11 September: TV viewers across the world witness the terrorist destruction of the twin towers of New York's World Trade Center.

• Italy: Silvio Berlusconi, media magnate, becomes Italy's Prime Minister for the second time.

2002 Labour government issues Communications Bill proposing the loosening of broadcasting regulations and abandoning rules concerning cross-media ownership. With modifications, becomes Act of Parliament, 2003.

• ITV Digital services go bust, but a consortium led by the BBC steps in to offer over 20 digital channels (freeview). New digital services from the BBC: CBBC (for children, aged 6–13), Cheebies (for under 6s) BBC Four (art, history, current affairs), BBC Three (drama, entertainment, music). At the same time, BBC radio goes digital (BBC Digital, Asian Network, 6Music, 1Xtra, Five Live Sports Extra and BBC7 (comedy, drama and children's programmes).

• China: analysts estimate that the state employs 30,000 people to monitor and control information.

• Gulf Cooperation Council, meeting in Oman, warns satellite TV station al-Jazeera to make

programmes 'more respectful'.
• Poland: Church-run Radio Maryja is shut down on the orders of the Catholic primate, Cardinal Josef Glemp.
• US: Iranian film-maker Abbas Kiarostami is denied a visa permitting him to enter the country at the invitation of the New York Film Festival to lecture at Harvard University.
• UK: David Shayler, former MI5 officer, is jailed for six months for breaking the Official Secrets Act by leaking documents concerning alleged malpractice in the UK secret service.
• Announcement of plans for a £2.6b merger between Granada (seven ITV licences) and Carlton Communications (five ITV licenses), subject to approval by the UK office of Fair Trading. The merger leaves only three independent UK franchises – Grampian, Scottish and Ulster TV.
• Report on human rights in 50 countries by the Electronic Privacy Information Center and Privacy International declares that post-11 September 2001 'many new anti-terrorist laws adopted by national governments ... threaten political freedom'.

2003 Federal Communications Commission (USA) initiates major shift towards loosening regulations concerning the delivery of TV and radio news, considering that many in-place rules are 'antiquated'; that is, standing in the way of further media mergers.
• Global publics find their voice in protesting against war in Iraq, but million-strong marches do not prevent US and UK forces going into battle despite the failure to obtain a United Nations mandate for military action.
• Natalie Maines, lead singer of the Dixie Chicks tells fans in London that the prospect of the invasion of Iraq makes her ashamed to be from the same state as President Bush. Radio stations part of the conglomerate Clear Channel Communications (which had offered financial sponsorship and on-air promotion for pro-war 'Rallies for America') pull the Dixie Chicks from their playlists. Clear Channel suspends two DJs in Colorado Springs for defying the ban. Cumulus Media, owning 262 radio stations, bans the Country Chicks from all of its country stations.
• UK: Merger between independent television broadcasters Carlton and Granada.
• 29 December in the UK the responsibilities of the Broadcasting Standards Commission (BSC), the Independent Television Commission (ITC), the Office of Telecommunications (Oftel), the Radio Authority and the Radiocommunications Agency pass to the new regulatory body, the Office of Communications (Ofcom).

• During 2003, 42 journalists were killed worldwide, 766 arrested, 1,460 physically attacked or threatened and 501 media censored, according to Reporters Without Borders (Reporters Sans Frontières).

2004 Hutton Report, UK, examines the circumstances surrounding the alleged suicide of government weapons expert Dr David Kelly who was the source of an early morning BBC radio report by Andrew Gilligan suggesting government claims that Iraq possessed weapons of mass destruction had been exaggerated. The Report, exonerating the government of any blame in the 'outing' of Kelly, resulted in the resignation of the Chairman of the BBC, Gavyn Davies, the Director General, Greg Dyke, and Gilligan.
• Rupert Murdoch's BskyB wins contract, in face of competition from Independent Television News (ITN), to supply news to UK's Channel Five.
• Butler Report subjects government claims concerning weapons of mass destruction (WMD), and the performance of the security services in monitoring the true situation in Iraq, to highly critical scrutiny. However, finds no one intentionally to blame for claims which proved unfounded.
• Phillis Review of Government Communications.
• Facebook website is launched.
• By now Blogging has become a mainstream online activity.
• Russia: journalist Anna Politkovskaya is poisoned on her way to cover the school massacre in Beslan; later, she is murdered in the stairwell of her block of flats.
• UK: Piers Morgan, editor of the tabloid newspaper *Daily Mirror*, resigns following the publication of pictures – later declared fake – purporting to show British soldiers ill-treating Iraqi civilians.
• US: The Disney company blocks distribution of Michael Moore's documentary, *Fahrenheit 9/11* exposing links between the American President George W. Bush and prominent Saudi-Arabian families, including that of Osama bin Laden.
• 14th Press Freedom Day. Reporters Without Borders (Reporters Sans Frontières) announce that ten journalists and media assistant were killed between January amd May, 431 journalists arrested worldwide, 366 physically attacked o threatened and 178 media censored. In 22 coun tries, 133 journalists are imprisoned, including 'cyber-dissidents', 61 in China.
• Birmingham, UK: the depiction of a rape sce in a Sikh temple sparks a riot outside the (

Repertory Theatre in protest at Gunpreet Kaur Bhatti's play, *Behzti* (Dishonour). Despite the play being written by a Sikh (or perhaps in a way because it was written by one of the faith) the action against the play – 400 protestors battling with riot police – leads to its closure.

• Launch in the UK of Spinwatch, a collaborative venture between practising investigative journalists and academics with the aim of countering government and corporate 'spin'.

2005 Freedom of Information Act (UK) comes in to force.

• Somalia: BBC correspondent Kate Peyton is fatally wounded on her way to interview the speaker of the country's transitional parliament. According to Reporters Without Borders 38 of the 636 journalists killed since 1992 have been women. In the same month, journalist Raeda Mohammed Wageh Wassan was found dead in Mosul, northern Iraq, after being kidnapped by masked men.

• In the run-up to the UK General Election in May, the Association of Gypsy Women releases a statement protesting at laws that 'are being used to target Gypsies and Travellers', with the open encouragement of the popular press. 'We categorically reject the terrifying image of Gypsies that is being promoted by the *Daily Mail*, *Sun* and *Daily Express*. We call on the British Press Council to intervene'.

• UK: 3rd reading of bill to ban incitement to religious hatred passes through the House of Commons.

• *New York Times* journalist Judith Miller imprisoned for refusing to declare a source; spends 85 days behind bars for breach of a law forbidding the revealing of the names of secret service (CIA) agents.

• al-Jazeera journalist Taysir Alouni is jailed for seven years by a Spanish court after being found guilty of collaboration with the terrorist group, al-Qaeda.

• Rania-al-Baz, a TV announcer with Saudi-Arabian TV, in order to publicize domestic violence in her country, publishes pictures of her disfigured face after being beaten up by er husband. To avoid reprisals, she escapes to ance.

K: Channel Four television launches new 't entertainment' channel, More4.

kfurt, Germany: first international Wiki-conference (see entry, WIKI, WIKIPEDIA).

dents at the University of Lancaster are y the University authorities with aggra-ass after protesting against a 'corpo-ng' event in University's George Fox

building; press comments link the action with the New Labour government's anti-terrorism bill passing through Parliament.

• The same unease concerning terrorism and legislation aimed at stifling it, is highlighted during the annual Labour Party conference in Brighton in October: an elderly party member, Walter Wolfgang, once a refugee from Hitler's Germany, was forcibly ejected from the conference hall for shouting 'Rubbish!' during a speech by the foreign secretary Jack Straw justifying the Iraq war. Mr Wolfgang, 57 years a party member, was held by the police under the Prevention of Terrorism Act and later released; the event forcing apologies from Labour ministers and causing a press furore.

• The BBC announces plans to open a new World Service broadcasting channel directed to the Arab region, and in competition with the 24-hour Arabic news channel, al-Jazeera.

• China: 400 million viewers – the largest TV audience in history – tune in to see 21-year-old Li Yuchun, without make-up, with spiky hair, singing songs aggressively, including songs written for men, win the Mongolian Cow Sour Yogurt Supergirl Concert award. Within days the shopping malls of Shanghai were heaving with Li Yuchun mugs, keyrings and T-shirts. A concert sponsored by the Better Posture Equipment Company in the city's largest, 39,000-seater stadium, was sold out in hours.

• Percentage of UK households with digital TV has grown from 15.5% in 2000 to 61.9% in 2005.

• Turkey: best-selling author Orhan Pamuk faces trial for 'denigrating the Turkish identity' for speaking out concerning the Armenian genocide of 1915, when almost a million Armenians were killed in the Ottoman Empire.

• British playwright, poet, actor, scriptwriter and political protester Harold Pinter (b. 1930), author of *The Birthday Party*, *The Caretaker*, *The Dumb Waiter* and *The Homecoming*, is awarded the Nobel Prize for Literature.

• Following harassment by the authorities in Uzbekistan, the BBC closes its World Service operation.

• YouTube, an audio-visual network platform, is launched.

• US search engine Google resists request by American Department of Justice to provide a list of every website address operating through Google for June and July 2005; but then announces net link with China, offering a service available to 110 million online users. This agreement is subject to Google's willingness to operate as a filter – a censor – of information exchange.

In short, Google subscribes to the Great Firewall of China, restricting access to many Western websites and blocking words such as 'freedom' and names such as 'Tiananmen Square'.

• In a US Congress House international relations committee meeting Yahoo! Cisco Systems, Microsoft and Google are accused of collusion with a repressive regime (China).

• Following publication in Danish and Norwegian newspapers of cartoons satirizing the prophet Mohammed, widespread Muslim protests occur across the arab world, the Danish and Norwegian embassses in Damascus being burnt to the ground. Crowds of protestors also burn Danish flags in several other countries. Violent demonstrations take place in Lebanon and Afghanistan. In Jordan, two newspaper editors who published the cartoons are charged with offences.

• UK House of Commons votes to reinstate the 'glorification of terrorism' clause in new anti-terrorism legislation; this shortly following on from parliament's assent to New Labour plans to introduce ID cards for British citizens.

• Mexican goverement admits that it staged a kidnap and rescue operation as proof that it is winning the war on organized crime.

• Australia: Dateline, current affairs programme of the Special Broadcasting Service, publishes images, previously unseen by the public, of abuse of Iraqi prisoners by American military personnel at the Abu Ghraib jail.

• al-Jazeera, the Arab news station, begins news service in English. British broadcaster Sir David Frost is contracted to front a one-hour daily programme.

• UK: Government White Paper announces that the BBC licence will be extended to 2016. The govenors will be replaced by a trust with sovereign control of the corporation, leaving responsibility for the day to day running of the BBC to an executive board. The White Paper urges that entertainment be placed at the heart of the corporation's broadcasting mission.

• Twitter is launched.

• Reuters merges with the Thomson Organisation in an £8.7 billion deal.

• Iran: Launch of English-speaking TV channel, Press TV; with British journalist Yvonne Ridley employed to host live political show, The Agenda.

• July: Rupert Murdoch's News International acquires *Wall Street Journal*. December, Murdoch makes over his newspaper empire to his son James; including control of Sky Italia and the Star TV Network in Asia.

• Media mogul Silvio Berlusconi again becomes Italy's Prime Minister.

• The BBC launches a new Arabic TV channel (BBC Arabic TV), estimated to cost £25m a year.

• The Martha Gellhorn Prize for Journalism is won by 24 year old Palestinian Mohammed Omer. On his return from the London prize-giving he was arrested by Shin Bet, Israel's security organization, emerging after 12 hours' detention in need of hospital treatment.

• After a nine-year legal battle, the European Court of Human Rights rules that UK government phone-tapping practices violate citizens' right to privacy.

• Indian Space Research Organization launches record 10 satellites in one flight.

• *Times of India* group acquire British Virgin Radio, renaming it Absolute Radio.

• The BBC refuses to transmit the Disasters Emergency Committee Gaza Appeal in case it would be seen to be 'unbalanced' in terms of its professed neutrality.

• Former KGB agent Alexander Lebedev becomes owner of the UK London *Evening Standard* which shortly becomes a free sheet.

• PolitiFact.com, online news and comment service of the *St. Petersburg Times*, Florida, becomes the first website to be awarded the prestigious Pulitzer prize for journalism.

2010 March. For £1 Lebedev purchases the titles of the UK *Independent, Independent on Sunday*. In October, the *Independent* launches a new daily, entitled 'i', a condensed version of the Indie for readers in a rush.

• April. The Apple Company of the US launches the i-Pad, described by Apple's chief executive, Steve Jobs, as 'our most advanced technology in a magical and revolutionary device and at an unbelievable price'.

• America On Line (AOL) sells off Bebo, the social networking platform, for a fraction of the $850m it paid for it in 2008.

• December. *Coronation Street* (UK ITV), the world's longest-running TV soap opera, celebrates its 50th anniversary, while BBC Radio's *The Archers* reaches 60.

• Kuwait shuts the offices of the news network al-Jazeera and removes its accreditation for having broadcast news of an opposition member of the country's National Assembly, and its use of film footage of police beating oppositio' members and supporters gathered to discus government crackdowns on public freedom.

• UK: The Video Recordings Act of 1984, havi been found to be in breach of European Union I in 2009, is reeneacted in one parliamentary da'

2011 Popular uprisings in a number of north African and Middle Eastern countries are seen to have been aided by Internet and mobile communication.

• US: Jill Abramson becomes the first female editor of the *New York Times* in the paper's 160-year history.

• UK: Engulfed in a phone-hacking scandal, the 168-year-old *News of the World*, part of Rupert Murdoch's News International (UK wing of News Corp), is shut down, its final issue appearing on Sunday 10 July. The UK government sets up a public inquiry chaired by Lord Justice Leveson to investigate hacking and regulation of the media. Rupert Murdoch, his son James, chairman of News International, and the organization's chief executive (until her resignation) Rebekah Brooks, are summoned for questioning by House of Commons select committees. Their connections with the Murdoch press made public, the Commissioner of the London Metropolitan police, Sir Paul Stephenson, and his deputy John Yates resign.

• Italy: November. Financial crisis in Eurozone brings to an end the premiership of media mogul Silvio Berlusconi, the country's longest-serving Prime Minister.

programmes 'more respectful'.

• Poland: Church-run Radio Maryja is shut down on the orders of the Catholic primate, Cardinal Josef Glemp.

• US: Iranian film-maker Abbas Kiarostami is denied a visa permitting him to enter the country at the invitation of the New York Film Festival to lecture at Harvard University.

• UK: David Shayler, former M15 officer, is jailed for six months for breaking the Official Secrets Act by leaking documents concerning alleged malpractice in the UK secret service.

• Announcement of plans for a £2.6b merger between Granada (seven ITV licences) and Carlton Communications (five ITV licenses), subject to approval by the UK office of Fair Trading. The merger leaves only three independent UK franchises – Grampian, Scottish and Ulster TV.

• Report on human rights in 50 countries by the Electronic Privacy Information Center and Privacy International declares that post-11 September 2001 'many new anti-terrorist laws adopted by national governments … threaten political freedom'.

2003 Federal Communications Commission (USA) initiates major shift towards loosening regulations concerning the delivery of TV and radio news, considering that many in-place rules are 'antiquated'; that is, standing in the way of further media mergers.

• Global publics find their voice in protesting against war in Iraq, but million-strong marches do not prevent US and UK forces going into battle despite the failure to obtain a United Nations mandate for military action.

• Natalie Maines, lead singer of the Dixie Chicks tells fans in London that the prospect of the invasion of Iraq makes her ashamed to be from the same state as President Bush. Radio stations part of the conglomerate Clear Channel Communications (which had offered financial sponsorship and on-air promotion for pro-war 'Rallies for America') pull the Dixie Chicks from their playlists. Clear Channel suspends two DJs in Colorado Springs for defying the ban. Cumulus Media, owning 262 radio stations, bans the Country Chicks from all of its country stations.

• UK: Merger between independent television broadcasters Carlton and Granada.

• 29 December in the UK the responsibilities of the Broadcasting Standards Commission (BSC), the Independent Television Commission (ITC), the Office of Telecommunications (Oftel), the Radio Authority and the Radiocommunications Agency pass to the new regulatory body, the Office of Communications (Ofcom).

• During 2003, 42 journalists were killed worldwide, 766 arrested, 1,460 physically attacked or threatened and 501 media censored, according to Reporters Without Borders (Reporters Sans Frontières).

2004 Hutton Report, UK, examines the circumstances surrounding the alleged suicide of government weapons expert Dr David Kelly who was the source of an early morning BBC radio report by Andrew Gilligan suggesting government claims that Iraq possessed weapons of mass destruction had been exaggerated. The Report, exonerating the government of any blame in the 'outing' of Kelly, resulted in the resignation of the Chairman of the BBC, Gavyn Davies, the Director General, Greg Dyke, and Gilligan.

• Rupert Murdoch's BskyB wins contract, in face of competition from Independent Television News (ITN), to supply news to UK's Channel Five.

• Butler Report subjects government claims concerning weapons of mass destruction (WMD), and the performance of the security services in monitoring the true situation in Iraq, to highly critical scrutiny. However, finds no one intentionally to blame for claims which proved unfounded.

• Phillis Review of Government Communications.

• Facebook website is launched.

• By now Blogging has become a mainstream online activity.

• Russia: journalist Anna Politkovskaya is poisoned on her way to cover the school massacre in Beslan; later, she is murdered in the stairwell of her block of flats.

• UK: Piers Morgan, editor of the tabloid newspaper *Daily Mirror*, resigns following the publication of pictures – later declared fake – purporting to show British soldiers ill-treating Iraqi civilians.

• US: The Disney company blocks distribution of Michael Moore's documentary, *Fahrenheit 9/11* exposing links between the American President George W. Bush and prominent Saudi-Arabian families, including that of Osama bin Laden.

• 14th Press Freedom Day. Reporters Without Borders (Reporters Sans Frontières) announce that ten journalists and media assistant were killed between January amd May, 431 journalists arrested worldwide, 366 physically attacked or threatened and 178 media censored. In 22 countries, 133 journalists are imprisoned, including 73 'cyber-dissidents', 61 in China.

• Birmingham, UK: the depiction of a rape scene in a Sikh temple sparks a riot outside the city

Repertory Theatre in protest at Gunpreet Kaur Bhatti's play, *Behzti* (Dishonour). Despite the play being written by a Sikh (or perhaps in a way because it was written by one of the faith) the action against the play – 400 protestors battling with riot police – leads to its closure.

• Launch in the UK of Spinwatch, a collaborative venture between practising investigative journalists and academics with the aim of countering government and corporate 'spin'.

2005 Freedom of Information Act (UK) comes in to force.

• Somalia: BBC correspondent Kate Peyton is fatally wounded on her way to interview the speaker of the country's transitional parliament. According to Reporters Without Borders 38 of the 636 journalists killed since 1992 have been women. In the same month, journalist Raeda Mohammed Wageh Wassan was found dead in Mosul, northern Iraq, after being kidnapped by masked men.

• In the run-up to the UK General Election in May, the Association of Gypsy Women releases a statement protesting at laws that 'are being used to target Gypsies and Travellers', with the open encouragement of the popular press. 'We categorically reject the terrifying image of Gypsies that is being promoted by the *Daily Mail*, *Sun* and *Daily Express*. We call on the British Press Council to intervene'.

• UK: 3rd reading of bill to ban incitement to religious hatred passes through the House of Commons.

• *New York Times* journalist Judith Miller imprisoned for refusing to declare a source; spends 85 days behind bars for breach of a law forbidding the revealing of the names of secret service (CIA) agents.

• al-Jazeera journalist Taysir Alouni is jailed for seven years by a Spanish court after being found guilty of collaboration with the terrorist group, al-Qaeda.

• Rania-al-Baz, a TV announcer with Saudi-Arabian TV, in order to publicize domestic violence in her country, publishes pictures of her disfigured face after being beaten up by her husband. To avoid reprisals, she escapes to France.

• UK: Channel Four television launches new 'adult entertainment' channel, More4.

• Frankfurt, Germany: first international Wikimania conference (see entry, WIKI, WIKIPEDIA).

• Six students at the University of Lancaster are charged by the University authorities with aggravated trespass after protesting against a 'corporate venturing' event in University's George Fox building; press comments link the action with the New Labour government's anti-terrorism bill passing through Parliament.

• The same unease concerning terrorism and legislation aimed at stifling it, is highlighted during the annual Labour Party conference in Brighton in October: an elderly party member, Walter Wolfgang, once a refugee from Hitler's Germany, was forcibly ejected from the conference hall for shouting 'Rubbish!' during a speech by the foreign secretary Jack Straw justifying the Iraq war. Mr Wolfgang, 57 years a party member, was held by the police under the Prevention of Terrorism Act and later released; the event forcing apologies from Labour ministers and causing a press furore.

• The BBC announces plans to open a new World Service broadcasting channel directed to the Arab region, and in competition with the 24-hour Arabic news channel, al-Jazeera.

• China: 400 million viewers – the largest TV audience in history – tune in to see 21-year-old Li Yuchun, without make-up, with spiky hair, singing songs aggressively, including songs written for men, win the Mongolian Cow Sour Yogurt Supergirl Concert award. Within days the shopping malls of Shanghai were heaving with Li Yuchun mugs, keyrings and T-shirts. A concert sponsored by the Better Posture Equipment Company in the city's largest, 39,000-seater stadium, was sold out in hours.

• Percentage of UK households with digital TV has grown from 15.5% in 2000 to 61.9% in 2005.

• Turkey: best-selling author Orhan Pamuk faces trial for 'denigrating the Turkish identity' for speaking out concerning the Armenian genocide of 1915, when almost a million Armenians were killed in the Ottoman Empire.

• British playwright, poet, actor, scriptwriter and political protester Harold Pinter (b. 1930), author of *The Birthday Party*, *The Caretaker*, *The Dumb Waiter* and *The Homecoming*, is awarded the Nobel Prize for Literature.

• Following harassment by the authorities in Uzbekistan, the BBC closes its World Service operation.

• YouTube, an audio-visual network platform, is launched.

• US search engine Google resists request by American Department of Justice to provide a list of every website address operating through Google for June and July 2005; but then announces net link with China, offering a service available to 110 million online users. This agreement is subject to Google's willingness to operate as a filter – a censor – of information exchange.

In short, Google subscribes to the Great Firewall of China, restricting access to many Western websites and blocking words such as 'freedom' and names such as 'Tiananmen Square'.

• In a US Congress House international relations committee meeting Yahoo! Cisco Systems, Microsoft and Google are accused of collusion with a repressive regime (China).

• Following publication in Danish and Norwegian newspapers of cartoons satirizing the prophet Mohammed, widespread Muslim protests occur across the arab world, the Danish and Norwegian embassses in Damascus being burnt to the ground. Crowds of protestors also burn Danish flags in several other countries. Violent demonstrations take place in Lebanon and Afghanistan. In Jordan, two newspaper editors who published the cartoons are charged with offences.

• UK House of Commons votes to reinstate the 'glorification of terrorism' clause in new anti-terrorism legislation; this shortly following on from parliament's assent to New Labour plans to introduce ID cards for British citizens.

• Mexican goverement admits that it staged a kidnap and rescue operation as proof that it is winning the war on organized crime.

• Australia: Dateline, current affairs programme of the Special Broadcasting Service, publishes images, previously unseen by the public, of abuse of Iraqi prisoners by American military personnel at the Abu Ghraib jail.

• al-Jazeera, the Arab news station, begins news service in English. British broadcaster Sir David Frost is contracted to front a one-hour daily programme.

• UK: Government White Paper announces that the BBC licence will be extended to 2016. The govenors will be replaced by a trust with sovereign control of the corporation, leaving responsibility for the day to day running of the BBC to an executive board. The White Paper urges that entertainment be placed at the heart of the corporation's broadcasting mission.

• Twitter is launched.

• Reuters merges with the Thomson Organisation in an £8.7 billion deal.

• Iran: Launch of English-speaking TV channel, Press TV; with British journalist Yvonne Ridley employed to host live political show, The Agenda.

• July: Rupert Murdoch's News International acquires *Wall Street Journal*. December, Murdoch makes over his newspaper empire to his son James; including control of Sky Italia and the Star TV Network in Asia.

• Media mogul Silvio Berlusconi again becomes Italy's Prime Minister.

• The BBC launches a new Arabic TV channel (BBC Arabic TV), estimated to cost £25m a year.

• The Martha Gellhorn Prize for Journalism is won by 24 year old Palestinian Mohammed Omer. On his return from the London prize-giving he was arrested by Shin Bet, Israel's security organization, emerging after 12 hours' detention in need of hospital treatment.

• After a nine-year legal battle, the European Court of Human Rights rules that UK government phone-tapping practices violate citizens' right to privacy.

• Indian Space Research Organization launches record 10 satellites in one flight.

• *Times of India* group acquire British Virgin Radio, renaming it Absolute Radio.

• The BBC refuses to transmit the Disasters Emergency Committee Gaza Appeal in case it would be seen to be 'unbalanced' in terms of its professed neutrality.

• Former KGB agent Alexander Lebedev becomes owner of the UK London *Evening Standard* which shortly becomes a free sheet.

• PolitiFact.com, online news and comment service of the *St. Petersburg Times*, Florida, becomes the first website to be awarded the prestigious Pulitzer prize for journalism.

2010 March. For £1 Lebedev purchases the titles of the UK *Independent, Independent on Sunday*. In October, the *Independent* launches a new daily, entitled 'i', a condensed version of the Indie for readers in a rush.

• April. The Apple Company of the US launches the i-Pad, described by Apple's chief executive, Steve Jobs, as 'our most advanced technology in a magical and revolutionary device and at an unbelievable price'.

• America On Line (AOL) sells off Bebo, the social networking platform, for a fraction of the $850m it paid for it in 2008.

• December. *Coronation Street* (UK ITV), the world's longest-running TV soap opera, celebrates its 50th anniversary, while BBC Radio's *The Archers* reaches 60.

• Kuwait shuts the offices of the news network al-Jazeera and removes its accreditation for having broadcast news of an opposition member of the country's National Assembly, and its use of film footage of police beating opposition members and supporters gathered to discuss government crackdowns on public freedom.

• UK: The Video Recordings Act of 1984, having been found to be in breach of European Union Law in 2009, is reenacted in one parliamentary day.

2011 Popular uprisings in a number of north African and Middle Eastern countries are seen to have been aided by Internet and mobile communication.

• US: Jill Abramson becomes the first female editor of the *New York Times* in the paper's 160-year history.

• UK: Engulfed in a phone-hacking scandal, the 168-year-old *News of the World*, part of Rupert Murdoch's News International (UK wing of News Corp), is shut down, its final issue appearing on Sunday 10 July. The UK government sets up a public inquiry chaired by Lord Justice Leveson to investigate hacking and regulation of the media. Rupert Murdoch, his son James, chairman of News International, and the organization's chief executive (until her resignation) Rebekah Brooks, are summoned for questioning by House of Commons select committees. Their connections with the Murdoch press made public, the Commissioner of the London Metropolitan police, Sir Paul Stephenson, and his deputy John Yates resign.

• Italy: November. Financial crisis in Eurozone brings to an end the premiership of media mogul Silvio Berlusconi, the country's longest-serving Prime Minister.